A TWO-EDGED SWORD

CARLETON LIBRARY SERIES

The Carleton Library Series publishes books about Canadian economics, geography, history, politics, public policy, society and culture, and related topics, in the form of leading new scholarship and reprints of classics in these fields. The series is funded by Carleton University, published by McGill-Queen's University Press, and is under the guidance of the Carleton Library Series Editorial Board, which consists of faculty members of Carleton University. Suggestions and proposals for manuscripts and new editions of classic works are welcome and may be directed to the Carleton Library Series Editorial Board c/o the Library, Carleton University, Ottawa K1S 5B6, at cls@carleton.ca, or on the web at www.carleton.ca/cls.

CLS board members: John Clarke, Sheryl Hamilton, Jennifer Henderson, Laura Macdonald, Paul Litt, Stanley Winer, Barry Wright

191 *A Wampum Denied*
Procter's War of 1812
Sandy Antal

192 *The Blacks in Canada:*
A History (Second edition)
Robin Winks

193 *A Disciplined Intelligence*
Critical Inquiry and Canadian
Thought in the Victorian Era
A.B. McKillop

194 *Land, Power, and Economics on the Frontier of Upper Canada*
John Clarke

195 *The Children of Aataentsic*
A History of the Huron
People to 1660
Bruce G. Trigger

196 *Silent Surrender*
The Multinational
Corporation in Canada
Kari Levitt

197 *Cree Narrative*
Expressing the Personal Meanings
of Events
Richard J. Preston

198 *The Dream of Nation*
A Social and Intellectual
History of Quebec
Susan Mann

199 *A Great Duty*
Canadian Responses to
Modern Life and Mass
Culture, 1939–1967
L.B. Kuffert

200 *The Politics of Development*
Forests, Mines, and Hydro-Electric
Power in Ontario, 1849–1941
H.V. Nelles

201 *Watching Quebec*
Selected Essays
Ramsay Cook

202 *Land of the Midnight Sun*
A History of the Yukon
Ken S. Coates and
William R. Morrison

203 *The Canadian Quandary*
(New edition)
Harry Johnson

204 *Canada and the Cost
of World War II*
The International Operation of the
Department of Finance, 1939–1947
Robert B. Bryce
Edited by Mathew Bellamy

205 *Lament for a Nation*
(40th Anniversary edition)
George Grant

206 *Confederation Debates in the
Province of Canada, 1865*
(New edition)
P.B. Waite

207 *The History of Canadian Business, 1867–1914*
R.T. Naylor

208 *Lord Durham's Report*
(New edition)
Based on the Abridgement
by Gerald M. Craig

209 *The Fighting Newfoundlander*
A History of the Royal Newfoundland Regiment
G.W.L. Nicholson

210 *Staples and Beyond*
Selected Writings of Mel Watkins
Edited by Hugh Grant
and David Wolfe

211 *The Making of the Nations and Cultures of the New World*
An Essay in Comparative History
Gérard Bouchard

212 *The Quest of the Folk*
Antimodernism and Cultural Selection in Twentieth-Century Nova Scotia
Ian McKay

213 *Health Insurance and Canadian Public Policy*
The Seven Decisions That Created the Canadian Health Insurance System and Their Outcomes
Malcolm G. Taylor

214 *Inventing Canada*
Early Victorian Science and the Idea of a Transcontinental Nation
Suzanne Zeller

215 *Documents on the Confederation of British North America*
G.P. Browne

216 *The Irish in Ontario*
A Study in Rural History
Donald Harman Akenson

217 *The Canadian Economy in the Great Depression*
(Third edition)
A.E. Safarian

218 *The Ordinary People of Essex*
Environment, Culture, and Economy on the Frontier of Upper Canada
John Clarke

219 *So Vast and Various*
Interpreting Canada's Regions in the Nineteenth and Twentieth Centuries
Edited by John Warkentin

220 *Industrial Organization in Canada*
Empirical Evidence and Policy Challenges
Edited by Zhiqi Chen
and Marc Duhamel

221 *Surveyors of Empire*
Samuel Holland, J.F.W. Des Barres, and the Making of
The Atlantic Neptune
Stephen J. Hornsby

222 *Peopling the North American City*
Montreal, 1840–1900
Sherry Olson and Patricia Thornton

223 *Interregional Migration and Public Policy in Canada*
An Empirical Study
Kathleen M. Day
and Stanley L. Winer

224 *How Schools Worked*
Public Education in English Canada, 1900–1940
R.D. Gidney and W.P.J. Millar

225 *A Two-Edged Sword*
The Navy as an Instrument of Canadian Foreign Policy
Nicholas Tracy

A TWO-EDGED SWORD

THE NAVY AS AN INSTRUMENT OF CANADIAN FOREIGN POLICY

NICHOLAS TRACY

Carleton Library Series 225
MCGILL-QUEEN'S UNIVERSITY PRESS
Montreal & Kingston • London • Ithaca

© McGill-Queen's University Press 2012

ISBN 978-0-7735-4051-4 (cloth)
ISBN 978-0-7735-4052-1 (paper)

Legal deposit fourth quarter 2012
Bibliothèque nationale du Québec

Printed in Canada on acid-free paper.

This book has been published with the help of a grant from the Canadian Federation for the Humanities and Social Sciences, through the Aid to Scholarly Publications Program, using funds provided by the Social Sciences and Humanities Research Council of Canada.

McGill-Queen's University Press acknowledges the support of the Canada Council for the Arts for our publishing program. We also acknowledge the financial support of the Government of Canada through the Canada Book Fund for our publishing activities.

Library and Archives Canada Cataloguing in Publication

Tracy, Nicholas, 1944–
A two-edged sword : the Navy as an instrument of Canadian foreign policy / Nicholas Tracy.

(Carleton library series ; 225)
Includes bibliographical references and index.
ISBN 978-0-7735-4051-4 (bound)
ISBN 978-0-7735-4052-1 (pbk)

1. Canada–Foreign relations–20th century. 2. Canada. Royal Canadian Navy–History. 3. Canada–History, Naval. 4. Canada–Military relations. I. Title. II. Series: Carleton library series ; 225

FC242.T73 2012   327.71009'04   C2012-904693-0

This book was designed and typeset by studio oneonone in Sabon 10.3/13.5

Navigation everywhere contends with the same monster;
the sea is one and the same Hydra.
Victor Hugo, *Toilers of the Sea*

For the first time, I have seen Pearson look really frightened.
He looked almost terrified. Quite evidently he had at last come
to see what the decision was. Quite all right to be in on all
these things; when it comes to actually have one's country involved
in war, there were limits to what we might be able to do, and the
commitments that it was wise to make. I think if anything he was
relieved at the govt.'s attitude which really was quite the opposite
of what his memo to St L[aurent] had proposed earlier in the day
as to the policy of [External Affairs].
Diary of William Lyon Mackenzie King, 30 June 1948,
at the time of the Berlin Blockade Crisis

Canada has no particular tradition of strategic calculation. Such
tradition as we possess seems to be that strategy is a suitable diversion
for retired generals who need not be taken very seriously.
Robert J. Sutherland, director of operational research,
Department of National Defence, 1962

What still stands in the way of a strictly objective, intellectually
unfettered approach to Canadian security concerns is the ragtag
and bobtail of tradition, the deadweight of old ideas, and perhaps
an inbred inferiority complex which, in matters of defence, has made
and still makes Canadians defer to the opinions of others rather
than form their own.
John Gellner, York University and editor of
Canadian Defence Quarterly, 1977

Always keep a-hold of nurse, for fear of finding something worse.
Hilaire Belloc, "Jim," *Cautionary Tales for Children*

CONTENTS

Illustrations / xi
Preface and Acknowledgments / xiii
Abbreviations and Acronyms / xv

Introduction / 3
1 A National Navy in an Imperial Context: The Beginning / 18
2 A National Navy in an Imperial Context: Between the Wars / 38
3 Lessons of the Second World War / 64
4 The Navy and the New Imperium / 92
5 The Cold War: Suez, the Cuban Crisis, and the End of the "Golden Age" / 126
6 The Cold War: Détente, Rust-out, and Renewal / 156
7 The Cold War: Endgame / 179
8 Sanctions Enforcement: Iraq / 198
9 Sanctions Enforcement: Yugoslavia and Haiti / 220
10 Constabulary Action and International Leverage: The "Turbot War" / 243
11 Continental Defence and Global Policing / 254
12 The Navy and the Arctic / 287
Conclusion: The Past Is Prologue / 299
Appendix 1: Pro-active Sanctions / 319
Appendix 2: Milestones in Canadian Naval History / 327

Notes / 339
Bibliography / 407
Index / 457

ILLUSTRATIONS

HMCS *Niobe*, ca. 1914. / 27
HMCS *Aurora*. / 45
HMC Ships *Aurora* (foreground) and *Patriot* and *Patrician* in Esquimalt Harbour, circa 1921. / 45
HMCS *Patriot*. / 50
Plan and elevation of HMCS *Skeena* (D 59). / 52–3
HMCS *Peterborough* (K 342). / 66
HMCS *Chebogue* (K 317). / 75
HMCS *Huron* (G 24/216). / 83
HMCS *Micmac* (R 10/214). / 85
HMS *Nabob* (D 77). / 87
HMCS *Ontario* (C 53). / 111
HMCS *Fort Erie*, (K 670). / 111
HMCS *Magnificent* (CVL 21). / 112
HMCS *Labrador* (AW 50). / 114
HMCS *Sioux* (R 64/225). / 116
HMCS *Sioux* (DD 225). / 121
HMCS *Bonaventure* (CVL 22). / 133
A *Sea King* helicopter. / 135
HMCS *Protecteur* (AOR 509). / 149
HMCS *Bras D'Or* (FHE 400). / 159
CP 140 *Aurora*. / 171
Canadian Patrol Frigates under construction at Saint John Shipbuilding, ca 1991. / 172
HMCS *Halifax* (FFH 330). / 173
HMCS *Onondaga* (S 73). / 184–5
Refuelling HMCS *Skeena* (DDH 207) at sea from HMCS *Preserver* (AOR 510). / 193

HMCS *Huron* (DDH/G 281). / 205
HMCS *Fraser* (DDH 233). / 231
Lt (N) MacKinnon examines a Somalian patient, 1 Jan. 1993. / 255
HMCS *Victoria* (SSK 876). / 258
HMCS *Victoria* (SSK 876), Combat Control Room. / 259
HMCS *Victoria* (SSK 876), Search Periscope. / 259
Naval Boarding Party from HMCS *Montréal* (FFH 336). / 267
CCGS *Henry Larson* and HMCS *Goose Bay* (MM 707), anchored at Pond Inlet, Nunavut, while participating in Operation Nanook. / 295

PREFACE AND ACKNOWLEDGMENTS

It is the objective of this book to describe the manner in which the Royal Canadian Navy has supported Canadian foreign policy in the hundred years since it was formed. It is important to plot the course that took Canada through the shoals and tide rips, with back-bearings on the important navigational marks. The burden of this study is to record the largely successful means by which the Canadian Navy has participated in the independence of Canadian policy, but not to gloss over the difficulties experienced, the political problems of relationships with powerful allies, and the ethical defects of policy.

There has been more continuity than discontinuity, but following the end of the Cold War in 1989 there has been a distinct change in the operational means by which the Canadian Navy has pursued its strategic purposes. In some quarters in Ottawa there is a prevailing concern that the Canadian Navy is so focused on its institutional success that it strays from its responsibility for Canadian national interests. In a work of this size, administrative and operational history can only be sketched in. The focus is on the interface between the Canadian Navy and Canada's international relationships. In his great study *On War* written following the Napoleonic war, Carl von Clausewitz expressed the truth that "war is not merely an act of policy but a true political instrument, a continuation of political intercourse, carried on with other means ... The political object is the goal, war is the means of reaching it, and means can never be considered in isolation from their purpose ... War should never be thought of as something autonomous but always as an instrument of policy."[1] This truth is even more central to the study of military and naval roles in circumstances short of war. The book's sub-title is a deliberate echo of Admiral Sir Herbert Richmond's posthumously published 1953 book, *The Navy as an Instrument of Policy*, in which Richmond demonstrated the strategic utility of the Royal Navy in the early eighteenth century. The implications of the main title will be developed in the following pages.

The use of the word "navy" in the present work is somewhat ambiguous because of the important role played in the naval defence of Canada by the Royal Canadian Air Force. It is generally employed because it conveniently expresses the institutions that have military roles in the management of Canada's responsibilities at sea, and certainly includes the Maritime Air Group, whose commander is deputy chief of naval staff. It will also become apparent that study of the strategic role of the Canadian navy unavoidably provides support for the Paul Hellyer doctrine that defence policy is a national policy that cannot treat the role of individual services in complete isolation. The Canadian navy is, and always has been, a part of the Canadian Armed Forces. Nevertheless, its structures, equipment, and training are all identifiable, and very expensive. Study of the strategic role of Canada's naval forces is important for the development of rational national policies.

The completion of a book such as this, written over the course of four decades, has benefitted from the help and criticism of many people, and it is impossible to mention them all by name.[2] I particularly want to thank Dr Alec Douglas, sometime director of the Directorate of History, and Dr Kenneth Calder, formerly assistant deputy minister policy, both of the Department of National Defence; Dr Richard H. Gimblett, Navy Command historian; Professor John Hattendorf, director, Center for Advanced Research, U.S. Naval War College; Captain Peter Hore, RN Ret., in whose London flat the decision was made to complete this work; Captain David Hudock, CF, formerly director of naval strategy, DND; Janet Lacroix, National Defence Image Library; Dr George Lindsey, sometime chief of operational research, DND; Dr Robert McRae, ambassador to NATO; John Neilson, Government Documents librarian and Teri Noel, Document Delivery librarian, at the Harriet Irving Library, University of New Brunswick; Dr Roger Sarty, professor of history, Wilfrid Laurier University; Don Sinclair, director general International Security Bureau, Department of Foreign Affairs; Captain Joe Sipos, CF, director of naval strategy, DND, in 2011, and Commander Steve Thompson, CF; and Dr Geoffrey Till, dean of academic studies at the UK Joint Services Command and Staff College. Thanks are also in order for the permission given by Mélanie Mckinnon, Crown Copyright officer, to use the Department of National Defence photographs.[3]

ABBREVIATIONS AND ACRONYMS

1st Lord   First Lord of the Admiralty
AAA   Anti-Aircraft Artillery
AAW   Anti-Air Warfare
Add. MS   Additional Manuscript
ADM   Admiralty Papers
AIMP   Aurora Incremental Modernization Project
AIP   Air Independent Propulsion
AOR   Auxiliary Oiler Replenishment Ship
ASLEP   Aurora Structural Life Extension Project
ASPPR   Arctic Shipping Pollution Prevention Regulations
ASROC   Anti-Submarine Rocket
ASW   Anti-Submarine Warfare
BL   British Library
Can.   Canada
CANCOM   Canadians in Command
CANCOMLANT   Commanding Officer Canadian Atlantic Region, NATO
CANLANT   Canadian Atlantic Region, NATO
CANUS   Canada/U.S.
CAST   Canadian Air Sea Transportable Brigade
CBC   Canadian Broadcasting Corporation
CDS   Chief of Defence Staff
CF   Canadian Forces
CFB   Canadian Forces Base
CFDS   Canada First Defence Strategy
CFMETR   Canadian Forces Maritime Experimental Test Range
CHOP   Change of/in Operational Control/Command
CIA   Central Intelligence Agency, USA

CID   Committee of Imperial Defence
CIWS   Close-in Weapon System
C-in-C   Commander-in-Chief
Cmd   Command Papers
CO   Colonial Office Papers
Commons   House of Commons
COMSUBLANT   Commanding Officer, Atlantic Submarines, USN
CTF 150   Combined Task Force 150
CTF 151   Combined Task Force 151
CTG 217   Commander North Anti Submarine Defence Force Atlantic
CUSRPG   Canada-US Regional Planning Group
DATAR   Digital Automated Tracking and Resolving
DEA   Department of External Affairs
DDE   Destroyer Escort
DDG   Guided Missile armed Destroyer
DDH   Helicopter-equipped Destroyer
DFAIT   Department of Foreign Affairs and International Trade
DFO   Department of Fisheries and Oceans Canada
DHH   Directorate of History and Heritage, Department of National Defence
DND   Department of National Defence
DP   Admiralty Director of Plans
DTSD   Admiralty Director of Training and Staff Duties
FELEX   Frigate Life Extension
FRY   Federal Republic of Yugoslavia
GB   Great Britain
GG   Governor General
GIUK   Greenland/Iceland/United Kingdom
GOC   Government of Canada
GP   General Purpose
HCM   *Halifax* Class Modernization
HF/DF   High Frequency/Direction Finding
HQ   Headquarters
ICCS   International Commission of Control and Supervision
IFOR   Multinational Peace Implementation Force
IGME   UN Inter-agency Group for Child Mortality Estimation
INCSEA   Incidents at Sea Agreement, 1972
INF   Intermediate-Range Nuclear Forces
INTERFET   International Force East Timor

ITAR   International Traffic in Arms Regulations
KLA   Kosovo Liberation Army
LAC   Library and Archives Canada
LHD   Landing Helicopter Dock
LOFAR Low Frequency Analysis and Recording (later known as SOSUS)
LRPA   Long-Range Patrol Aircraft
M   Minister of
MAD   Magnetic Anomaly Detector
MC   Military Committee
MCC   Military Cooperation Committee
MCDV   Maritime Coast Defence Vessel
MIF   Multinational Interception Force
MIO   Maritime Interdiction Operations
MSD   Minister of State for Defence
NARA   National Archives and Records Administration, College Park, Maryland, USA
NATO   North Atlantic Treaty Organization
NA/UK National Archives of the United Kingdom, Kew, London, UK
NAVFOR Naval Force Somalia – European Union – Operation *Atalanta*
NDHQ   National Defence Headquarters
NEF   Newfoundland Escort Force
NTDS   Naval Tactical Data System
NORAD North American Air Defence Agreement
NSF   National Security File, USA
NSHQ   Naval Services Headquarters
OPEC   Organization of the Petroleum Exporting Countries
OSP   Operational Surveillance Patrol
PD   An Admiralty Registry Number
PJBD   Permanent Joint Board on Defense
PM   Prime Minister
PMO   Prime Minister's Office
PRO   Public Record Office, National Archives, London
PUSS   Permanent Under-Secretary of State
RAN   Royal Australian Navy
RCAF   Royal Canadian Air Force
RCMP   Royal Canadian Mounted Police
RCN   Royal Canadian Navy

RCNVR   Royal Canadian Navy Volunteer Reserve
RN   Royal Navy (UK)
RNR   Royal Navy Reserve
RNVR   Royal Navy Volunteer Reserve
RyaN   Raketno-Yadernoe Napadenie, meaning Nuclear Missile Attack
SACEUR   Supreme Allied Commander, Europe
SACLANT   Supreme Allied Commander, Atlantic
SCEAND   Standing Committee on External Affairs and National Defence
SCNDVA   Standing Committee on National Defence and Veterans Affairs
SFOR   Stabilization Force
SLAMEX   Sea-Launched Attack Missile Exercise
SNMG1   Standing NATO Maritime Group 1
SOSUS   Sound Surveillance System
SOUP   Submarine Operational Update Program
SS   Secretary of State
SSBN   Ballistic Missile Submarine
SSK   Hunter-Killer non-nuclear Submarine
SSN   Nuclear-Powered Submarine
STANAVFORLANT   NATO's Standing Naval Force Atlantic
STANAVFORMED   NATO's Standing Naval Force Mediterranean
TRUMP   Tribal Class Update and Modernization Program
UHF   Ultra-High Frequency
UK   United Kingdom
UN   United Nations
UNEF   United Nations Emergency Force
UNICEF   United Nations International Children's Emergency Fund
UNMOVIC   UN Monitoring, Verification and Inspection Commission
UNPD   United Nations Population Division
UNPROFOR   United Nations Protection Force
UNSC   United Nations Security Council
UNSCOM   United Nations Special Commission
UNSCVR   United Nations Security Council Verbatim Report
USA   United States
USAF   Unites States Air Force
USN   United States Navy
USNAVCENT   United States Naval Forces, Central Command
USS   Under-Secretary of State
V.Adm.   Vice-Admiral
VDS   Variable Depth Sonar

WEU   Western European Union
WMD   Weapons of Mass Destruction
WWII Second World War

A TWO-EDGED SWORD

INTRODUCTION

In a recent pamphlet intended to inform Canadians about their navy, it was pointed out that Canada has the longest coastline of any nation in the world, with an exclusive economic zone approaching 8 million km^2 and the world's second-largest continental shelf area. Seven million Canadians live in coastal areas, and 11,000 companies operate in the ocean sector, employing 145,000 Canadians and generating $19 billion of economic output. Of Canada's $977 billion gross domestic product, over 40% is accounted for by exports. Of the country's exports to the United States, 20% go by sea; and in trade with other countries, 97% of Canadian exports and 70% of Canadian imports move across ocean routes. Canada's ocean fisheries generate over $4 billion of export income annually, and 50% of Canada's frontier oil reserves are estimated to lie in Canada's offshore.[1]

Statistics of this nature were also employed by the Liberal politician George Brown in a speech in 1865 supporting confederation of the British North American colonies.[2] Such numbers, however, tell little about the means by which the navy can be employed to protect Canadian interests. In some contexts the Canadian navy is an appropriate tool, or perhaps the only appropriate tool. A review of Canadian naval history over the century of its existence shows that Ken Booth was mistaken when in 1977 he wrote, "it is only the greatest navies which have important foreign policy implications."[3] Nevertheless, the strategic options of naval force are relatively limited, and the strength of sea power can also be its weakness.

It is particularly important to understand the politico-military and economic mechanisms by which navies may develop their force. An understanding of the mechanism of power is needed both at the micro level at which ships at sea conduct their business, and at the macro level at which nations in alliance interact. Hew Strachan has recently written an article for *Survival*, the journal of the International Institute for Strategic Studies, in which he notes that during the Cold War concepts of operational art came to be based exclusively on tactics because of the preoccupation of strategists with nuclear forces, but that it is important to rediscover the relationship between grand strategy and operational strategy.[4]

Much can be learned from general study of naval history. In the *Naval Review* nearly twenty years ago Matthew Allen dismissed the idea that the conduct of naval strategy could be "based on enduring timeless principles," but added that "the work of previous eras [should be afforded respect] as part of our intellectual heritage." The naval scholarship of the nineteenth and twentieth centuries should not be "revered as a source of omniscient authority which can be quoted to provide weight to shallow strategic argument," but, he added, "the rejection of enduring naval principles is not a rejection of abstract or rigorous theoretical thinking about the immediate strategic issues. Nor is it a rejection of the value of history. Good history shows how leaders, from their own historical perspective and set of values, tackled the issues of their day. This may illuminate contemporary issues through a judicious enumeration of the differences as well as the similarities with the past."[5]

The fundamental historical motives for state investment in naval forces have been power projection across the sea, and defence against such foreign aggression. Navies have been most employed to support land forces, as seaward extensions of coastal defences, as means for lateral communication to respond to invasion, and to carry the war overseas to the enemy. In 1911 Sir Julian Corbett, the great British apologist of sea power and unofficial Admiralty historian, in his *Some Principles of Naval Strategy*, wrote: "Since men live upon the land and not upon the sea, great issues between nations at war have always been decided – except in the rarest cases – either by what your army can do against your enemy's territory and national life or else by the fear of what the fleet makes it possible for your army to do."[6] Certainly this priority can be seen in Canadian history. Conjunct operations at Louisbourg and Quebec, supported by blockade and battle in European waters, put an end to French control of Canada during the Seven Years' War, and vigorous naval action deterred French efforts to recover their loss in the following decades.[7] During the American Revolutionary War and the War of 1812 (and later in the dangerous years following the American Civil War), the Royal Navy kept open the communications to British

North America, and deterred invasion by its capacity to act against the towns and trade of the American coast. Following the Treaty of Ghent concluding peace with the United States in 1814, the Royal Navy gave substance to the "Doctrine" first expressed by President Monroe in 1823 that included Canada in its sweeping assertion that the Americas should never again be an adventure playground for European conquerors.

The capacity of navies to influence events ashore is not entirely restricted to their direct support of armies. Since the sixteenth century it has been recognized that wars are waged with economic resources that in some instances are vulnerable to action at sea. In 1581 the Venetian ambassador to France, Lorenzo Priuli, wrote that the strategy for a naval state should be to seize the wealth of the enemy – as the English had done in 1568 when they seized ships transporting the pay chests for the Spanish army in Flanders: "this is the true way to humble the pride of Spain by plucking their pen feathers."[8]

Economic warfare in the age of sail was all about the bottom line. Because of technical constraints on station-keeping under sail, no amount of naval or privateer effort could prevent enemy merchant cargoes from being shipped, or a large part of them from reaching their destinations, but the seizure of even a small proportion of the enemy merchant fleet could force its merchants to sell at a loss, or price their goods out of the market. The objective of what is known as mercantilist trade war was to use naval action to maximize the belligerent's own commercial profits – profits that could be funneled into the national treasury through taxation and used to fund the navy, and also to subsidize allied military forces.[9] British trade control, enforced by sea power, supplied the economic muscle that in the Seven Years' War financed the war on the continent, and which defeated the Napoleonic empire half a century later.

Steam power and nineteenth-century economic globalization at the time of the American Civil War led to a new emphasis on the injury that trade control could inflict on an enemy. The blockade of the central powers in the First World War became the great practical example of economic warfare conducted so as to deny the enemy access to trade, and the concept of punitive economic sanctions derived from naval blockade was embodied in the Covenant of the League of Nations when it was established as part of the 1919 peace treaty. It remains a tool of the United Nations. Article 41 of the United Nations Charter authorizes the Security Council to effect a "complete or partial interruption of economic relations and of rail, sea, air, postal, telegraphic, radio, and other means of communication, and the severance of diplomatic relations," and Article 42 extends the action to "demonstrations, blockade, and other operations by air, sea, or land forces of Members of the United Nations." The enforcement of economic sanctions has been a prominent role of the Canadian navy since the end of the Cold War.

But the extent to which the naval blockade of the Confederate States in the Civil War, or of the central powers in the First World War, contributed to their defeat is open to continuing debate. In his great study, *England in the Seven Years' War*, Corbett noted that "we are inclined to forget how impotent [sea power] is of itself to decide a war against great Continental states, how tedious is the pressure of naval action unless it be nicely coordinated with military and diplomatic pressure."[10] Admiral Sir John Jellicoe, hero of the battle of Jutland and then British First Sea Lord, firmly told Vice-Admiral Sir David Beatty as early as February 1917 that Germany would not be defeated by the blockade: "We may cause them a great deal of suffering and discomfort by the blockade, but we shall not win the war by it. The war will not be won until the enemy's armed forces are defeated – certainly on land and probably on sea."[11] Admiral Sir Herbert Richmond was a strong apologist of sea power, but in 1934 he wrote: "it is important to recognize that sea power possesses the strength which it demonstrated in the Napoleonic Wars and the recent war only when it is allied to land power. Single-handed sea power can do little against any great power."[12]

Economic warfare continues to be as much about defending and promoting trade in wartime as it is with denying supply to an enemy. It was the need to defend shipping worldwide, including the then still substantial Canadian shipping industry, that the Admiralty chiefly recognized in a 1921 memorandum as a legitimate call upon dominion naval resources: "The primary role of Dominion Navies may be defined as to assist in the control of imperial communications in distant seas and the protection of their own coastal trade."[13] During the Second World War Britain did not deliberately employ armed force to channel trade homeward, but the official historian of Britain's economic war, W.N. Medlicott, notes that a key advantage of the blockade of Germany was its diversion of resources to Britain's own war production.[14]

The importance of trade defence is limited only by the extent to which great industrial powers like Germany have been able to achieve a functional autarchy. But mercantilist trade manipulation and belligerent blockade have proved to be far more problematic. As long ago as the sixteenth century Sir Francis Bacon expressed the mantra of sea power:

"This much is certain, that he that commands the sea is at great liberty, and may take as much and as little of the war as he will."[15] Naval forces are mobile and relatively self-sufficient. They can carry out their tasks with the minimum of incursion into national sovereignty. And, because they traditionally have a lower public profile, naval forces provide governments with an instrument they can employ flexibly and over protracted periods. But Bacon's words do not adequately represent the danger posed to belligerents by resort to trade warfare.

Three centuries of experience have shown that the naval strategy of trade control has a particularly high potential for lateral escalation. Conflict with neutral countries was the inevitable consequence of Lord Chancellor Hardwicke's famous "Rule of War of 1756," which established the principle that neutral shipping lost its immunity by serving enemy commercial interests. In his *England in the Seven Years' War*, Corbett wrote: "The prolonged exercise of belligerent rights" over mercantile shipping "even of the most undoubted kind, produces an interference with trade that becomes more and more oppressive."[16] Canadian history was very much affected by this reality, and by the seizure of French fishing stations in Île Royale (Cape Breton Island), which intensified the naval challenge by limiting French access to the Grand Banks fishery, where manpower for both the French and British navies were trained in seamanship. The danger that the Netherlands and Denmark might join France to prevent Britain from acquiring a permanent ascendancy at sea was only narrowly averted by modification of British privateer law, but it proved impossible to deflect Bourbon Spain from allying with Bourbon France, and declaring war on Britain in 1762 and again in 1779. Prime Minister William Pitt, "in his vision of England as sole mistress of the sea," wrote Corbett, "fell into an error as enticing and as fatal as that which brought the Grand Monarque [Louis XIV] and Napoleon to their ruin. Magnificent as was his strategy, it broke the golden rule."[17]

In 1772 the statesman and philosopher Edmund Burke described the situation following the succession of Canada to the British crown as "an armed peace. We have peace and no peace, war and no war. We are in a state to which the ingenuity of our ministry has yet found no apt name."[18] When in 1778, Louis XVI's minister Charles Gravier, chevalier de Vergennes, seized the opportunity presented by the American Revolution to undermine British power in the new world, Spain refused to participate in a war of colonial liberation, but a year later joined in one intended to reduce British sea power. As is well known, British forces as a result lost control of the thirteen American colonies, and fell back on Nova Scotia and Quebec.

The risk of lateral escalation has been especially great when naval forces have been employed to conduct a *guerre de course* on the high seas. This mode of naval warfare has been characterized as the strategy of the weaker power, but it is only true to say that it is a strategy a weaker naval power might attempt. *Guerre de course* was the operational mode predominantly employed by maritime nations at war during the age of sail. Indeed, the raiding of neutral shipping by privateers and naval cruisers was what led to the Spanish and later the American declarations against Britain, and to conflict with the Baltic states. That experience persuaded the powers to outlaw privateering – and naval action against neutral shipping – by an international convention known as the Declaration of Paris in 1856. In defending Britain's agreement to this fundamental change to the historic British understanding of the laws of naval warfare, the Earl of Clarendon told the House of Lords that a refusal to sign would have turned every maritime power against Britain; "and most properly so – because we should have been maintaining a law which was contrary to the public opinion of the world, which was hostile to commerce, and as unfavourable as possible to a mitigation of the evils of war."[19] The United States was the only great power not to sign – a refusal that it came to regret on the outbreak of the Civil War. Confederate raiders then forced American shipowners to abandon their participation in Atlantic commerce, leading to the great expansion of the mercantile fleets of Nova Scotia, New Brunswick, and East Canada (Quebec). The diplomatic spat between Britain and the United States that followed the British failure to prevent the Confederate cruiser *Alabama* being built in a British harbour precipitated the Confederation of Canada, and set in motion the political process that ultimately led to the creation of the Canadian Navy.

Corbett published *England in the Seven Years' War* in 1907, the same year as the Second Hague Conference was convened to address the laws of war, and the rights and obligations of neutrals during naval war. The Admiralty opposed a proposal made at the Hague to establish an international prize court, out of concern that it could reduce Britain's freedom to impose trade control in wartime. But Sir Eyre Crowe, the senior clerk of the British foreign office, echoed Corbett's warning that it was natural that "the power of a State supreme at sea should inspire universal jealousy and fear, and be ever exposed to the danger of being overthrown by a general combination of the world."[20] That danger became very real during the First World War when British cruisers diverted American merchant shipping from trade with the central powers. Anglo-American diplomatic conflict over belligerent rights was to continue into the 1930s, and be an important consideration in Canada's interwar defence planning.

Despite the national commitment to the Declaration of Paris, following the American Civil War the *jeune école* of the French navy advocated the use of torpedo boats for a terror *guerre de course* in the event of war with Britain, and the German navy resorted to a U-boat *guerre de course* against Britain in 1915, 1917–18, and in the Second World War, with no regard to the restrictions agreed to at the Hague Conference. The consequences for Germany were profound, especially as President Woodrow Wilson was attempting in the spring of 1917 to mediate peace on the basis of the "Freedom of the Seas." The lethality of the operational means vastly multiplied the consequences of interference with trade. The unrestricted U-boat operations were instrumental in bringing the United States into both wars as a belligerent. It is significant that during the Vietnam war the Soviet Union refrained from any action against American supply ships crossing the Pacific, and that the United States also avoided acting against those of the Soviet Union on the high seas, preferring to close Haiphong harbour by clearly reported mining operations. When international shipping came into danger during the Iran-Iraq war, there was an immediate naval reaction by the international community. Although the threat of Somali pirates in the present century is of far less concern to the international community, it has led to a massive international deployment of naval forces.

With the formation of the United Nations at the end of the Second World War, the old restraints imposed by the rights of neutrals were eliminated by the universality of Security Council resolutions. Throughout the Cold War, however, the United Nations was unable to order economic sanctions, except when the Soviet Union was boycotting the Security Council at the beginning of the Korean war, and when the Soviets agreed to their being ordered to support decolonization of Rhodesia.

The escalatory tendency of all forms of belligerent control of trade, including blockade and economic sanctions, results in part from their serious ethical implications – ones that the United Nations has not yet fully reconciled. Nicholas Rodger's review of the politics of sea power in the sixteenth to eighteenth centuries brought out the extent to which in England sea power was considered to be inherently more virtuous than land force, because sea power was seen as the achievement of a free people who made a profit from defending their country and their religion.[21] That trope was gradually supplanted in the later eighteenth century, but there is still a conviction among advocates of sea power that it is somehow a lighter burden on the state, and a lesser moral burden. This notion is alive and flourishing in the Canadian navy to this date, but the part taken by the Canadian navy in sanctions enforcement against Iraq, Yugoslavia, and Haiti in the 1990s makes it essential that the limitations and consequences of the exercise of lethal naval force be fully understood in Ottawa. Historical experience shows that even if the operational methods by which trade control is enforced are not in themselves inherently lethal, the consequences may well be.

As long ago as 1920, when reviewing in an Admiralty Staff history of the wartime economic blockade of the central powers between 1914 and 1919, Lieutenant Commander W.E. Arnold-Forster cautioned against the temptation to use the economic weapon without regard for its consequences for civil society:

> For there is a peculiar danger attaching to the use of this particular weapon, a danger which has not yet been sufficiently realized. It has now been found by experience that blockade is an instrument which can be wielded without any uncomfortable exertion, and can to a large extent be created, by men sitting in offices far from any visible sign of the consequences of its use. Men thus fighting with their pens in London come naturally to thinking that pens are cleaner weapons than bayonets, besides being much more convenient for the amateur. No danger, no mess, merely a Government ukase.
>
> And that is just what makes blockade so dangerous a weapon in bureaucratic hands; it is so infernally convenient.
>
> It would be a good thing if everyone who may have to use this weapon in future, whether at sea or ashore, would devote some serious study to the real nature of its consequences.[22]

One of the requirements of Aquinian "Just War" theory is that acts of war can be justified only if they are effective. If punitive sanctions are ineffective, or their results are disproportionate to the degree of suffering experienced by the general public, they must be viewed as in violation of the law of armed combat.

In a seminal study of "gunboat diplomacy" published in 1971, Sir James Cable created a taxonomy of the mechanisms by which naval force may be applied to national objectives. His focus was on circumstances short of war, but the same concepts are no less applicable to all military action. Cable labelled the direct application of force "Definitive Force," and gave the name "Purposeful Force" to military action that persuades a foreign government to change its policy. "In its purposeful application force does not itself do anything: it induces someone else to take a decision which would not otherwise have been taken."[23] Canadian naval commitments during the two world wars can largely be considered as falling into the former category. To employ a metaphor from medicine, one could describe the naval operations to defeat the U-boats in two world wars, and later to keep track of Soviet ballistic missile submarines – the "boomers" – as topical applications of force. The naval and military dimension of Canada's relationship with the United States, on the other hand, amounts to an exercise of purposeful force, in the form that Edward Luttwak has characterized as "supportive suasion."[24] But labels can be Procrustean. In the pursuit of supportive suasion vis-à-vis the United States since the end of the Cold War, the Canadian navy has increasingly been employed in partnership with the United States in measures of definitive and purposeful force vis-à-vis third countries and non-state actors in efforts to meet threats to international peace. That partnership occurs almost always in the context of multilateral forces, but it is a special relationship nonetheless. At times, such efforts may appear to be primarily intended for what Cable refers to as "Expressive Force," when their purpose is to signal the extent of Canadian commitment or to underscore Canadian interests. Only Cable's final category, "Catalytic Force" dispatched to deal with a mounting but undetermined threat, has little application to the navy of a middle power.

During the United Nations police action to protect South Korea, a rigorous blockade was imposed on North Korea, with Canadian destroyers forming part of the blockade force. Blockade can be viewed as an act of definitive force if it seeks to enhance the belligerent's capacity to make war, or to reduce that of an enemy, but it can also be regarded as purposive force if it serves to intimidate an enemy. Trade controls, when manifested as economic sanctions, usually seek to obtain their objective through a purposive mechanism, but they may also have definitive purposes, and consequences that may inflict disproportionate collateral injury.

The British naval scholar Eric Grove says that when he and Commander Mike Codner, RN, were engaged in writing the Royal Navy's *The Fundamentals of British Maritime Doctrine*, they decided not to employ Cable's taxonomy, preferring to categorize actions of naval force in support of diplomacy as "Presence" operations, "Symbolic Use" of naval forces, "Coercion," and "Preventive, Precautionary and Preemptive Naval Diplomacy." All such labels are useful in focusing understanding. "Symbolic Use" may be a more effective term than Cable's "Expressive Force." But Cable's division of "Coercion" into "Definitive" and "Purposive" is an important one.[25]

Sir Francis Bacon's words not only fail to express the problem of lateral escalation; they also obscure the extent to which the flexibility of sea power is as much a source of weakness as of strength. At a conference at the Centre for Foreign Policy Studies, Dalhousie University, in 2004, Captain (N) Kelly Williams, then director of maritime strategy in the Canadian Navy, nailed his colours to the mast: "I must state right at the outset that it is our belief that regardless of the focus of operations, whether international or domestic … the best way to achieve the required results [is] through the preservation of expeditionary, balanced combat-capable and globally deployable maritime forces."[26] The terms "expeditionary" and "maritime," Grove tells us, are code for sea-deployable naval and military forces.[27] But their very flexibility affects the capacity of naval expeditionary forces to support allies or apply pressure on hostile governments. Rear Admiral Bob Davidson, CF, acknowledged this, writing in 2008:

> Naval deployments also allow a degree of flexibility both in applying national power and in withdrawing it. The exit strategy is always easier with maritime forces, though to be fair, this is at the expense of lasting effect that can be delivered on the ground. It is in this latter area that land-based forces will always deliver more effect. Over the horizon threats affect governments and produce military and economic effects but they rarely influence the behaviour of ordinary people, unlike the soldier on the street corner who serves as a visible deterrent. Nevertheless, the naval capability that Canada can deliver can still represent a significant national commitment that is rapidly deployable, self-sustaining and versatile in application.[28]

❖ ❖ ❖

Matthew Allen, in dismissing the idea that the conduct of naval strategy could be "based on enduring timeless principles," asserted that "the use of sea power needs to be anchored in contemporary realities." Geographic characteristics, both physical and political, as well as political history, are of fundamental importance, he said, and give each nation's defence history unique characteristics. This national defence experience is "part of our intellectual heritage" as much as is the more general study of defence history.[29]

In September 1963 the chief of operational research, Dr Robert J. Sutherland, wrote in a confidential report: "It would be highly advantageous to discover a strategic rationale which would impart to Canada's defence programs a wholly Canadian character. Unfortunately, such a rationale does not exist and one cannot be invented."[30] A month later, when testifying before the House of Commons Special Committee on Defence, John Gellner asserted that Canada had "so far, not developed a national defence policy."[31] At a conference held at Dalhousie University thirty years later, in June 1993, Jan Breemer commented that the United States Navy was the only Western navy that had "articulated a vision of its purpose after the Cold War."[32] Only the boldest would dispute Gellner's observation that Canadian forces had gone to war "in accordance with foreign patterns, plans, and strategic and tactical concepts," but Breemer's choice of words was the more accurate. The substance of Canada's national defence policy can be traced through the words and actions of the Canadian government since Confederation, and before, but its actions speak louder than its words.

Seemingly spurred into action, the year following Breemer's comment the Canadian Navy published *The Naval Vision: Charting the Course for Canada's Maritime Forces into the 21st Century*, which Aaron Jackson says was intended to influence the Defence Policy Review instituted by the newly elected administration of Jean Chrétien.[33] When the Department of National Defence subsequently published a *White Paper on Defence* explaining the commitments of Canadian defence forces, the requirement for direct defence of Canadian territory was quickly disposed of: "Canada should never find itself in a position where, as a consequence of past decisions, the defence of our national territory has become the responsibility of others." Foremost amongst those others, of course, is the United States. And the White Paper was almost as terse in its assurance that Canadian defence was inevitably a product of healthy Canadian-American relations. "First, Canada-US defence cooperation continues to serve this country's fundamental interests extremely well.

Second, the Government wants the Canadian Forces to maintain the ability to work closely with their US counterparts in a variety of situations. Third, even if the Government decided to reduce significantly the level of defence cooperation with the United States, Canada would still be obliged to rely on the US for help in protecting its territory and approaches – and this assistance would then come on strictly American terms, unmitigated by the influence Canada enjoys as a result of its defence partnership with the United States and with our other NATO allies."[34]

The White Paper's public focus on the importance of the American relationship inevitably understated the problem of ensuring that the ties to U.S. policy had positive implications for Canada. The greatest theme in Canadian defence history has been the problem of developing appropriate command and control relationships with powerful partners, first the imperial mother country Britain and, since the Second World War, the United States. Writing in 1965 before his appointment as secretary of state, Henry Kissinger observed that "in an alliance of sovereign states, a country's influence requires that its effort be considered essential and that its partners do not take it for granted. In determining an ally's real – as opposed to his formal – role, one can do worse than inquire what its choices are in case of disagreement."[35] It is Canada's diminishing capacity to make choices to disengage in the wake of the 2001 "9/11" terrorist attack on the World Trade Center that worries Michael Byers: "At issue here is not Canada's legal sovereignty, but its practical sovereignty – its ability freely to make choices at the international level."[36]

In June 2001 the Department of National Defence published *Leadmark*, a document on the strategic roles of the Canadian Navy, and followed it up in the aftermath of 9/11 with *Securing Canada's Ocean Frontiers: Charting the Course from Leadmark*. "The model developed in *Leadmark* to illustrate 21st century naval roles and functions provides for all the naval responses demanded by the government's new security policies. It is based upon internationally recognized scholarly theory that conceives 'use of the sea' as the unity underlying a trinity of *roles* – military (Defend), diplomatic (Support) and constabulary (Secure) – which inter-relate across the spectrum of conflict, with the diplomatic and constabulary roles drawing their relevance from a solid military foundation."[37] The navy, it noted, has taken the responsibility for a "coordinated whole-of-government" response to maritime incidents, while the Department of Foreign Affairs is the lead in direction of naval action in support of diplomacy. Perhaps, however, the essential coherence of diplomatic, constabulary, and military considerations was not adequately emphasized: rarely can the navy carry out its work without a strategic plan that involves an understanding of the socio/political mechanisms by which naval action may be employed to satisfy national goals.

Writing in 2002, Sean Maloney listed the characteristics of Canada's strategic tradition:

> *Forward Security*: This is the deployment of Canadian military forces overseas to ensure that violent international activity is kept as far away from North America as possible and that Canadian interests overseas are protected.
> *Coalition Warfare*: Canada has a comparatively small population and its industrial base is maximized for civilian purposes. Canada cannot generate large standing armed forces like its allies can.
> *Operational Influence*: The ability to determine what deployed Canadian forces can and cannot do within the coalition and prevent their misuse by larger coalition members.
> *Saliency*: Canada must have effective forces allocated to the coalition which have unique capabilities or employment which makes up for the lack of numbers and permits operational influence in the coalition command structures.

The first two of these characteristics, "Forward Security" and "Coalition Warfare," are fundamentally reactions to the limitations of Canada's means of managing its defence relationship with the United States, while pursuit of "Operational Influence" and "Saliency" are consistent with Kissinger's dictum.[38]

The strategic imperatives are inextricably mixed with the institutional ambitions of the world's navies. To defeat moves in Congress in the 1940s to amalgamate the services, the U.S. Navy sought to demonstrate that it could participate effectively in the complexities of nuclear deterrence against the Soviet Union. Some U.S. naval officers even argued that carrier aircraft were the best means of delivering theatre atomic weapons, as part of a Single Integrated Operational Plan that pre-selected targets for the strategy of "Massive Retaliation." Even before the Soviet Union tested its first hydrogen bomb in 1953, however, it began to be realized that the value of naval forces lay primarily in their ability to parry successive attacks of which none could warrant resort to nuclear Armageddon. As Chief of Naval Operations from 1955 to 1961, Admiral Arleigh

Burke USN deployed fleet ballistic missile submarines, the SSBN force, and the doctrine of discretionary targeting, which was called "finite deterrence." When the Soviet Navy developed its own seaborne deterrent forces, the U.S. Navy and the navies of other North Atlantic Treaty nations were committed to "strategic anti-submarine operations" to guard against surprise attack. Strategic anti-submarine warfare (ASW) had the potential to justify the continued maintenance of large-deck aircraft carriers needed to carry the war to the enemy, thereby keeping Soviet submarine forces away from Atlantic trade and out of range for shore bombardment. In the early 1980s the U.S. Navy began to formulate a new "Maritime Strategy," which combined attack by carriers and submarines on Soviet nuclear forces with classical amphibious assault on the flanks of the central battlefront. The same capabilities also strengthened American influence in areas outside the European central front.

Following the end of the Cold War, the need to manage the nuclear deterrent diminished, but the collapse of the Soviet Union opened an era of conflict as former client states sought to establish their positions in the world schema. In 1992 the U.S. Navy promulgated a new strategy paper, *From the Sea*, which focused attention on support of operations ashore; in the circumstances prevailing with the virtual immobilization of the Soviet navy, it was possible to contemplate expeditionary operations without its being necessary to deal with a contested command of the sea. "Maneuver from the sea, the tactical equivalent of maneuver warfare on land," it concluded, "provides a potential warfighting tool to the Joint Task Force Commander – a tool that is literally the key to success in many likely contingency scenarios."[39] Two years later a second paper, *Forward ... from the Sea*, fleshed out the operational concept for expeditionary operations. In a foreword, Admiral Jay L. Johnson, U.S. Chief of Naval Operations in 1997, wrote: "We conduct forward naval operations both to ensure unimpeded use of the seas and to project American influence and power into the littoral areas of the world."[40]

Matthew Allen commented at the time: "The speed with which the US Navy has articulated a new strategy is impressive. This may reflect the range and depth of strategic thinking at its disposal." But he also noted: "The emphasis on joint operations is recognised to need a new culture. A Naval Doctrine Command has been set up, surely recognition that the old cold war skills cannot simply be transferred to the new environment. All this would suggest that a claim that maritime strategy is based on enduring naval principles is an empty proposition for hard-pressed naval leaders trying to defend their shrinking budgets."[41]

The Canadian navy also harnessed the prevailing strategic perceptions to its institutional ambitions, piggy-backing first on those of the Royal Navy, and later on those of the U.S. Navy, and exploiting the strategic and political concerns of the Canadian government. The extent to which this process serves the interests of Canadians is an open question. There is a coherence between blue-water and coastal roles because of the significance of the former in great-power relations, because the two tasks mutually support the maintenance of national naval forces of a reasonably critical mass, and because the technical requirements of collective naval defence are similar to those of coastal control in northern waters. But it must always be asked whether the bottom line serves the interests of Canadians, or only those of the navy.

It is most important to ask that question with respect to purposive force, and particularly with the use of economic sanctions to manipulate the world order. Purposeful, systemic, strategies are inherently problematic. The linkages between military inputs and economic and political outputs, like all extended linkages, encounter significant friction that may frustrate the objective, or even create so much heat as to be counter-productive.

✦✦✦

The following pages explore the ways in which the Canadian government has employed its naval forces to manage its relationship with its powerful friends, Britain and the United States, and participated in naval actions that supported Canada, her allies, and the international community. The labour will be to define the continuities and discontinuities in Canadian naval strategy, its strengths and its perils, and perhaps to use the historical record to suggest ways forward, while avoiding the trap of forecast.[42] Generations of scholars have studied the institutional history of the Canadian navy, while others have studied its operational history. Even more scholarship has been devoted to study of Canadian foreign policy and defence policy. The general study of naval history continues in libraries and archives around the world. Here the intent will be to draw upon those studies and at the same time narrow the perspective, to assess the historic and continuing utility of Canadian sea power.

1

A NATIONAL NAVY IN AN IMPERIAL CONTEXT: THE BEGINNING

The Royal Navy had made it possible for what is now Canada to remain British when the lower thirteen American colonies violently severed their connections with the crown. It helped them resist the hostile embrace of the United States in 1812 and again at the time of the American Civil War, and made it possible for political development in Canada to take a different form than south of the border. But local means had to be found to meet local needs and to deal with sudden threats, and Canada's dependence on imperial forces was an irritant in Canada's relationship with the United States.[1]

A Provincial Marine had been formed in the eighteenth century for control of the Great Lakes, but it was abandoned in 1813 when Royal Navy officers and men were able to take over Canadian defence against the American invaders. When Upper and Lower Canada were united in 1840, provision had been made in the Militia Act for a naval militia, and "Naval Brigades" were formed throughout the lakes in 1861 at the time of the *Trent* Affair, when it looked as though actions of the Union navy during the American Civil War might lead to war between the Empire and the United States. The depredations of the Confederate cruiser *Alabama* between 1862 and 1864 again threatened war between the Empire and the United States, but also greatly stimulated the growth of the mercantile marine in the Canadian provinces. When Fenian raiders invaded in 1866, the naval brigades saw action, using shipping taken up from trade and supported by Royal Navy gunboats in the St Lawrence. In 1868 a naval brigade was formed at Halifax following an attempted Fenian invasion of New Brunswick that was thwarted by a Royal Navy Squadron. The Royal Navy continued to supply offshore defence against existential threats following Confederation, but the aggressive pursuit of the "*Alabama* claims" by the victorious American Union government underlined the importance of minimizing potentially dangerous confrontation between the Empire and the United States, and made it difficult for the Royal Navy to discharge its constabulary commitment in Canadian waters.

The Maritime provinces had formed a Fisheries Protection Service in 1852, and a Department of Marine and Fisheries was formed by the Canadian government in 1867.[2] A Marine Police force was also created, using six chartered schooners which in 1870 boarded over four hundred American fishermen, but it was disbanded after Prime Minister John A. Macdonald conceded, in the 1871 Treaty of Washington, American access to the Canadian fishery.[3] In 1880 the Canadian government requested that Britain supply a ship to be employed as a fisheries protection cruiser, and for training. The Admiralty made available, initially as a loan and then as an outright gift, a recently decommissioned sail and steam corvette, HMS *Charybdis*. After repair and maintenance in England, she was brought across to Saint John in 1881. But she was found to be unsuitable for her role, as she required too large a crew and was a clumsy vessel whether under sail or steam. She was decommissioned from government service the following year, and the *Charybdis* embarrassment discouraged further development of the Fisheries Protection Service for a decade.[4]

Events far away from Canada were to accelerate Canadian naval development. From the time of the Russian war scare of 1878, there had begun to be discussion of ways in which constituent parts of the British Empire could contribute directly to its naval defence. Reluctant to divert any resources for that purpose, Macdonald testified before the Imperial Defence Commission of 1879 (the Carnarvon Commission), that "war with the United States was 'in the highest degree improbable,' and that, in any event the country was indefensible against a full-scale invasion from the south."[5] But Canada could not in fact distance itself from American and European military developments. In 1890 U.S. Admiral Alfred Thayer Mahan published his seminal book, *The Influence of Sea Power upon History, 1660–1783*, asserting his conviction that naval wars are determined by major fleet actions with capital ships, and in the same year the U.S. Naval Act provided for the construction of three 10,000-ton battleships, USS *Indiana*, *Massachusetts*, and *Oregon*, armed with four 13-inch and eight 8-inch rifled guns in large turrets, low freeboard, and with the heaviest armour in any contemporary navy. In 1900 the U.S. Navy ranked sixth in the world and two years later it would rank fourth.[6]

The expansion of the American fleet was a problem for Canada because it coincided with, and stimulated, the development of the Imperial German Navy, perhaps to replace the "Pax Britannica" by a "Pax Germanica." In 1897 Kaiser William II commissioned Grand Admiral Alfred von Tirpitz to construct a High Seas Fleet of forty-one battleships, and twenty large and forty smaller cruisers, to be ready in twenty years' time.[7] Tirpitz's declared strategic objective was to create a "risk fleet" that Britain could only defeat with losses to its own battle fleet that would inevitably leave it vulnerable to a coalition of France and Russia. Canadians had such close family and business ties with the imperial mother country that any threat to its security was of immediate consequence to Canadians.[8] That reality aside, German destruction of Britain's navy would have posed a very real danger to Canada's worldwide maritime trade and left Canada vulnerable to American ambition.

When Canada went to war in 1914, imperial sentiment was the political driving force, but the strategic purpose was to sustain the naval power of Britain, upon which Canadian autonomy and prosperity depended.[9] In October 1910 during a political campaign speech in Montreal, Prime Minister Sir Wilfrid Laurier defended in those terms his decision to form a Canadian navy, and anticipated his support for Canada's participation in the war: "s'il y avait une guerre dans laquelle la suprématie navale de l'Empire serait mise en péril ... je crois que nous devions aider l'Angleterre de toutes nos forces."[10]

The perspective of more strident imperialists, such as Clive Phillipps-Wolley of Victoria, BC, vice-president of the Canadian Navy League, which had been founded in Toronto in 1895, saw support for the Royal Navy as important in enabling the British Empire to continue its God-given mission to spread Christianity throughout the world. "I believe," he wrote in 1911, "that the British Empire is the Life's Work of the British race; the express image of the British ideal; the monument to the mighty dead of our own kin; the great trust of the men of our own day; the hope of humanity in the future; the very best thing that we have been able to devise in over a thousand years of work for the betterment of man, to insure [sic] a fair field for the development of the individual and perfect fair play for rich and poor, weak and strong alike." The rhetoric was certainly overblown, but in its context, with the world teetering on the brink of a disaster triggered by Kaiser Wilhelm and his anti-democratic ministry, there was at least as much grounds for it as there would later be for the rhetoric used by President Ronald Reagan and President George W. Bush to rally American support for containment of the Soviet "evil empire" and the Iraq-Iran-North Korean "axis of evil."[11]

The Navy League initially preferred that Canadians contribute to the Royal Navy, but Laurier recognized the value of an independent Canadian navy as a means to manage the relationship with the United States. Unlike the naval efforts early in the century, which served a straightforward defensive purpose, the naval force that was eventually created in 1910 addressed the continental problem more by virtue of its national character than its military potential. It was to serve its continental purpose by participating in the solution to a trans-Atlantic one, serving as a symbol of Canadian autonomy.

The Monroe Doctrine and the American fleet contributed to Canada's immunity to the threat of direct German power projection, or that by any other naval power, but Canadians did not consider dependence on the United States for their defence a comfortable option. The 1895 Venezuela boundary dispute, in which British interests had been opposed by the United States, had raised the spectre in Ontario of the United States invading Canada to punish Britain, and had forced Laurier to consider the need for local naval defence on the lakes. At the 1897 Colonial Conference Laurier, echoing Macdonald, asserted that any differences with the United States were "family troubles which mean nothing very serious," and he reportedly told General Douglas Cochrane, Earl of Dundonald, arriving in Canada in 1902 to take charge of the militia, that Canada was quite comfortable relying upon the Monroe Doctrine for her defence.[12] But the reality was somewhat different. The U.S. Navy demonstrated its new power in the Spanish-American war, at the battle of Santiago de Cuba on 3 July 1898, when the Spaniards lost 160 men killed and 1,800 captured, while the Americans lost only one man killed and another wounded. The spoils of war included the American acquisition of the Philippines and Guam, the establishment of naval bases on Puerto Rico, Cuba, Guam, and at Subic Bay, in the Philippines, and the annexation of independent Hawaii. Vancouver wondered whether it might be the next to experience American naval power. In 1902 President Theodore Roosevelt made it clear that Canadian interests in the outcome of the Alaska boundary dispute were hostage to British good behaviour in the Venezuela debt crisis, and the 1903 Alaska boundary arbitration largely ignored Canadian claims. The following year Roosevelt issued a "corollary" to the Monroe Doctrine, proclaiming that the United States, as a "civilized nation," would serve as the "international police power" in the Americas.[13]

The practical expression of Canada's national concern was its gradual devolution of the Fisheries Protection service into a proto-naval force. The Admiralty had a strong preference that the self-governing colonies and dominions contribute sums of money to support the imperial fleet, and the Australasian colonies did agree to do so in 1887, in return for the stationing of a Royal Navy squadron in the antipodes. The Canadian government, however, resisted pressure to do the same. Between 1891 and 1904 eight cruisers were acquired for the Canadian Fisheries Protection Service, partly by taking over former naval sloops and gunboats. In a memorandum prepared for the 1902 Colonial Conference, the Earl of Selborne, First Lord of the Admiralty, noted that Newfoundland had voted funds to establish a drill ship for the use of the Royal Naval Reserve – indeed, the Newfoundland naval reservists saw action in the Venezuela dispute as part of an Anglo-German fleet firing on coastal forts to enforce a "pacific" blockade – and Selborne informed the conference that Laurier had advised him that: "His Majesty's Government of the Dominion of Canada are contemplating the establishment of a local Naval force in the waters of Canada."[14] The 200-foot-long *Canada* was ordered in 1904 for east coast service from Vickers Barrow in England, and, although a civilian ship, she was armed with a ram and quick-firing guns. The 175-foot *Vigilant* was ordered from the Ontario firm of Polson's for service on the Great Lakes.[15] The Honourable J. Raymond Préfontaine, minister of marine and fisheries, prepared legislation for the transformation of the Fisheries Service by the re-establishment of a naval militia, into which the existing crews of the Fisheries vessels, who were then only employed seasonally, would be transferred on three-year contracts.[16] The November 1905 annual report of the Department of Marine and Fisheries emphasized the naval training and evolutions undertaken by its "unmistakable warships," which were described "as the nucleus of Canada's Navy."[17]

That perception was a little less clear in London, where the growing threat from Germany was seen to diminish the ability of British forces to protect Canada. In November 1903 the Admiralty director of naval intelligence, Captain Prince Louis of Battenberg, acknowledged in a memorandum to the Committee of Imperial Defence (CID) that: "if war should break out with the United States at a time when relations between this country and an European Power were uncertain, the Admiralty propose to abandon the sea command in the Western Atlantic to the American fleet." The naval dockyard at Halifax, along with those at Bermuda, Jamaica, and St Lucia, would be "at the mercy, sooner or later, for a time at least, of the forces of the United States, if hostile." The following year the Admiralty began to concentrate naval forces in home waters to meet the German challenge. There was discussion in 1905 of replacing all the Canadian Fisheries vessels with Royal Naval sloops, to be concentrated at Montreal ready to pass through the Lachine locks and provide an effective defence of Lake Ontario, but Battenberg, and his successor as director of naval intelligence, Rear Admiral Sir Charles Langdale Ottley, advised against, as being too obviously threatening to the United States. "The view of the Admiralty," expressed a month later to the Committee of Imperial Defence, "is that Canada must primarily rely upon her own resources for defence against invasion by the United States." It could not, the memorandum continued, "be seriously maintained that Canada, contributing as she does nothing towards the maintenance of the British navy, can have any moral or material claim to such additional naval effort on our part for her sole benefit."[18] This perception, however, did lead to a change of heart at the Admiralty about colonial navies. At the 1907 Colonial Conference Lord Tweedsmouth, the First Lord, admitted: "You cannot take the small craft such as torpedo boats and submarines across the ocean, and for warships to arrive in South Africa or in Australia or in New Zealand or in Canada, and find ready to their hand well-trained men in good vessels of this kind, would be an enormous advantage to them ... There is, I think, the further advantage in these small flotillas, that they will be an admirable means of coast defence."[19]

The plan to reform the naval militia was never formally tabled, probably on account of Préfontaine's death in December 1905, and because of the expense undertaken by Canada when Laurier agreed that the dockyards at Halifax and Esquimalt, their defences, and the coastal radio stations, be taken over by the Canadian government and maintained for the use of the Royal Navy to a standard based on the historic threat from the United States. Militia estimates had to be increased by nearly 40 percent to meet the new garrison expenses.[20] But the men drafted into CGS *Canada* for a West Indies training cruise were described as "naval militia recruits," and at the 1907 Colonial Conference the new minister of marine and isheries, Louis-Philippe Brodeur, made the point that the $3 million that had been spent since 1895 on the Fisheries Protection Service was a very real contribution to the cost of the naval defence of the Empire.[21] Apart from fisheries protection, the maintenance of aids to marine transport, its anti-smuggling patrols, and its proto-naval training, the Fisheries Protection Service was tasked with the establishment of Canadian sovereignty in the arctic following the transfer in 1880 of the arctic territories to Canada. The Alaska boundary settlement, which reflected the lack of Canadian settlement or military occupation, persuaded Laurier that the arctic archipelago was in danger of being lost to the Americans. A ship was chartered, *Neptune*, and over the summer of 1903–04 was employed establishing North-West Mounted Police posts in the eastern arctic. Captain Joseph-Elzéar Bernier made voyages in 1906–07, 1908–09, and 1910–11, penetrating as far as Melville Island in a Canadian fisheries protection cruiser, *Arctic,* leaving a plaque there on 1 July 1909 stating the Canadian claim.[22]

The world cruise of the U.S. Navy's "Great White Fleet" in 1907 heightened concern about the undefended nature of the Canadian Pacific coast. Laurier's deputy minister of labour, William Lyon Mackenzie King, the future prime minister, noted in his diary that he was opposed to Roosevelt's suggestion that the fleet should visit Vancouver. He did not think it "desirable that we should encourage a sentiment of dependence on the United States or to strengthen the annexationist feeling in the west ... if there was to be any fleet in our waters we would prefer to have the British fleet." The situation, he added, "reveals to me ... the necessity of our doing something in the way of having a navy of our own." In 1908 Laurier appointed the Royal Navy captain, Charles E. Kingsmill, who had been born in Guelph, Ontario, in 1855, director of the Marine Service.

The 1908 German Navy Law accelerated battleship construction, and public pressure in Britain forced the government to increase its planned order for four *Dreadnought* battleships to eight. Catching the public mood, on 29 March 1909 the Canadian House of Commons passed a resolution approving "any necessary expenditure designed to promote the speedy organization of a Canadian Naval Service in co-operation with, and in close relation to, the Imperial Navy, along the lines suggested by the Admiralty at the last Imperial Conference, and in full sympathy with the view that the naval supremacy of Britain is essential to the security of commerce, the safety of the Empire, and the peace of the world." But in May the governor general, Earl Grey, reported: "[Laurier] will not admit that there is any necessity for taking immediate action. He repeats that Canada will be ready to shed her last drop of blood and to spend her last dollar to maintain the naval supremacy of the Crown; but he will not do anything to prevent that supremacy from being challenged." His assertion was that Canadian investment in transcontinental railways and canals was important to the economic strength of the empire, and should not be threatened by expenditure on defence.[23]

The Admiralty, under the leadership of Reginald McKenna, took a great step forward from its 1907 acceptance of the value of colonial navies of small ships, and indicated at the 1909 Imperial Conference on Defence that it wished the dominions to create balanced forces based on a battle cruiser and cruisers that could deal with any threat from Japan. After the Japanese naval victory at Tsushima in 1905, Britain had withdrawn its armoured ships from the Pacific, leaving Australia and New Zealand feeling exposed.[24] Canada did not equally share that alarm, although there was concern about Japanese immigration into British Columbia. But a fleet unit structured around a single battle cruiser, which the Admiralty thought should be based in the Pacific, would not serve Canadian needs because of the difficulty of moving ships from the Pacific to the Atlantic prior to the construction of the Panama Canal. Rejecting the Admiralty's advice, Laurier's Naval Service Act the following year authorized the construction of a Canadian fleet of cruisers and destroyers.[25] In 1912 Winston Churchill, who had succeeded McKenna as first lord of the admiralty, would again propose that the dominions form fleet units, which should be united into an Imperial Squadron – but he wanted it based at Gibraltar, where it would have contributed to the security of the English Channel more than to the local concerns of the Pacific dominions.

The United States loomed far larger in Canadian calculations than did Japan. The House of Commons resolution of 29 March 1909 was a ministerial response to one placed on the Commons order paper by a Conservative former minister of marine and fisheries, George E. Foster, which declared that Canada ought "no longer delay in assuming her proper share of the responsibility and financial burden incident to the suitable protection of her exposed coastline and great seaports." Foster made it clear that Canadian relations with the United States were central to his line of thought: "Mr Speaker, the Monroe Doctrine and the United States of America might guarantee our safety from foreign invasion, but ... the price we would have to pay would be continual demand, continual concession until at last absorption finished the craven course."[26] The negotiations Laurier was conducting with the American government for the establishment of free trade in primary products – "reciprocity" – between Canada and the United States made all the more important the establishment of an independent Canadian navy to define Canada's autonomous status within the empire. The decision emanating from the 1909 Imperial Conference that the step should be taken beyond devolution of the Fisheries Protection Service to the formal creation of a navy, which would take over the naval functions of the FPS, was consistent with the need to enhance the symbol of Canadian autonomy.[27]

Richard Gimblett, the Canadian Navy Command historian, stresses that the decision in March 1909 to embark upon a Canadian naval service had not been precipitous, but rather was "the logical conclusion of many years of slow and careful progress preparing the nation to look to the protection of her maritime sovereignty by her own means."[28] The motive for the Naval Service Act of May 1910 was more to strengthen Ottawa's capacity to control Canada's coastal waters and to define Canada's relationship with the United States, than it was to contribute to the war fleet of the Empire. The cross-currents of Canadian politics ensured that the growth of the Royal Canadian Navy was slow, but a Royal Naval College of Canada was established at Halifax, and naval training was begun with two serviceable cruisers acquired from the Royal Navy, the thirteen-year-old HMCS *Niobe* with sixteen 6-inch guns, stationed at Halifax, and the smaller nineteen-year-old HMCS *Rainbow* with two 6-inch guns, stationed at Esquimalt.[29]

✦✦✦

As a means to strengthening the independence of Canadian policy, however, the establishment of a navy was a two-edged weapon. Although the need to avoid conflict at sea with the United States was a fundamental reason for the formation of the Canadian navy, the Canadian fleet was not capable of acting in isolation; nor was it expected to. The cruisers of the Royal Navy's North American squadron, which in turn operated under the protection of the Atlantic fleet, were important in ensuring that the Canadian naval and civilian forces could carry out their constabulary tasks. The chain of the deterrents to war between the United States and the British Empire stretched from the vessels of the Marine Police, and the Fisheries Protection Service, to the central forces of the empire. When the Canadian navy was formed and took over the naval responsibilities of the Department of Marine and Fisheries, it became a part of that chain. It was freer to act in Canadian waters by virtue of its purely national character, but it was a very limited force and depended upon its relationship with the Royal Navy. Its value, both domestically

HMCS *Niobe*, ca. 1914. A *Diadem* class protected cruiser built in 1897, she was given to Canada in 1910 and became the first commissioned warship in the Royal Canadian Navy. She was damaged in the 1917 Halifax explosion and was scrapped in the 1920s. DND CN-6732

and internationally, was a product of its character as an auxiliary squadron of the imperial fleet. The difficulty lay in the ambiguous character of the Royal Navy as simultaneously the guarantor of the Pax Britannica, which made it possible for the empire to live in peace, and the instrument of British foreign policy. The dominions had the right not to participate in the military operations of the Empire, but could not easily distance themselves from its foreign policy. Whatever their wishes might be, the dominions could only opt out of the common foreign policy of the empire if foreign countries chose to overlook the juridical unity of the empire under the crown.[30] For Canada, it was primarily the attitude of the United States that would determine its capacity to adopt a quasi-neutrality. When introducing his Naval Service Bill in January 1910 Laurier explained Canada's paradoxical situation to parliament: "If England is at war we are at war and liable to attack. I do not say that we shall always be attacked, neither do I say that we would take part in all the wars of England. That is a matter that must be determined by circumstances, upon which the Canadian parliament will have to pronounce and will have to decide in its own best judgment."[31]

The liability of Canada to circumstances not originating in Canada was matched by the vulnerability of the empire to the consequences of actions by Canada or the other dominions. Logically, the dominions could not be accorded a right to carry out independent military action outside their own territorial seas. In 1908 it was pointed out in the report of the Interdepartmental Conference on the Status of Dominion Ships of War that, since "under international law there is only one executive authority in the British Empire capable of being recognized by foreign States, Colonial ships of war cannot operate independently of the Royal Navy."[32] A memorandum prepared by the Admiralty in 1910 for the Committee of Imperial Defence noted that the problem of arranging for peace-time control was more difficult politically than the task of making arrangements for wartime co-operation, but that it must be borne in mind that "wars arise out of acts done in times of peace … It must be recognized that international difficulties of a very grave nature may arise, owing to the fact that a mobile armed force has been established, over whose action the Central Government would have no control, though the ultimate responsibility would rest with them."[33]

No less difficult to reconcile with local autonomy was the strategic requirement for instant collective action at the outset of war. The constitutional problem created by the formation of dominion navies was made acute by the work of naval historians such as the American Admiral Mahan and the British scholar Sir Julian Corbett, who proclaimed the transcendent importance of naval power in world history, and the strategic necessity of centralized control. Naval defence, it was believed, had to be conceived as a worldwide problem, necessitating unity of control and freedom of movement to ensure that overwhelming force could be brought to bear at the decisive battle that it was supposed would determine the outcome of the war.

At the 1897 Colonial Conference the first lord of the Admiralty, George Goschen, said that the Admiralty welcomed the limited financial support received from the colonies because it produced "certain ties which we value." However, he continued: "From the strategical point of view, we should be glad that the Admiralty should have a free hand."[34] Five years later, at the 1902 Colonial Conference, the assembled prime ministers were given a memorandum on "Sea-Power and the Principles Involved," in which they were told that "the immense importance of the principle of concentration and the facility with which ships and squadrons can be moved from one part of the world to another ... points to the necessity of a single navy, under one control, by which alone concerted action between the several parts can be assured." The prominence given to forward operations in naval strategic thinking emphasized the need for central control: "the traditional role of the Royal Navy is not to act on the defensive, but to prepare to attack the force which threatens – in other words to assume the offensive."[35] When at the Imperial Conference on Defence in the summer of 1909 the Admiralty declared an interest in the dominions' constructing fleet units based on battle cruisers, it was a significant policy shift, but even then the *Ottawa Citizen* was not convinced that Canada should risk dividing the Empire's naval potential: the fate of the British "dreadnought fleet ... will decide the fate of the colonies. If that fleet met with disaster, any trifling squadron, or warlike revenue cutters, or cheap warships, would be only so much more loot for the conquerors."[36] The Admiralty director of naval intelligence, Rear Admiral Alexander Bethell, sent Churchill a memorandum on 1 November 1911 cautioning: "the theory of the sea being all one has its limitations as far as the necessity for defending outlying possessions is concerned and does not hold good unless you can get at your enemy to destroy him in the decisive waters," but Churchill nonetheless quietly abandoned the plan to send capital ships to the Pacific.[37]

The struggle to develop acceptable compromises that would make possible collective defence of freely associated autonomous governments was without precedent, and its relative success established norms for later defence alliances. The focus on operational efficiency conflicted – and inevitably always will conflict – with the political requirements of a system of collective defence. Recent Canadian history provided no reason to accept the diminution of Canadian independence. Canada's relationship with successive imperial mother countries has been as much concerned with minimizing their capacity to determine Canadian policies and actions as it has been with securing their protection. In defending to Parliament his initial decision to support Laurier's formation of an independent navy for Canada, the Conservative leader, Robert Borden, said that the arguments for the strategic value of a unified Imperial navy were strong, but that "from a constitutional and political standpoint" he was opposed: "In the first place I do not believe it would endure. In the second place it would be a source of friction ... It would conduce, if anything could conduce, to severing the present connection between Canada and the Empire."[38] A nationalist perspective was expressed by Honoré Gervais, Liberal member for the Montreal riding of Saint-Jacques: "While helping England, I prefer to see Canada doing so as a British dominion, realizing thoroughly her present status, than to see Canada rendering such service as a so-called member of an empire, composed of one state and a great number of conquered but statuteless provinces having no representatives in the imperial parliament ... By the passing of this Bill, Canada is promoting herself to a higher place in the eyes of the world." He also recognized the defensive importance of a Canadian navy: "Should we have no navy, what Wolfe was able to do, one Von der Goltz or one Henri de Hohenzollern may try to repeat."[39]

Laurier wanted to equip the new Canadian Navy with a unique flag, a naval White Ensign with a green maple leaf in the centre, but in the end, for practical, political, and strategic reasons, decisions about a flag and a name for the new service served to emphasize the participation of Canada's navy in the collective naval defence of the Empire. The Committee of Imperial Defence in 1911 determined that "The British, Canadian, and Australian fleets" should be considered to be "sister members of the King's Navy, hoisting the white ensign at the stern and the distinctive flag of each nation on the jack staff." This was agreed to, and the Canadian government requested that the new service be named the Royal Canadian Navy, "with a view to promote [its] dignity and importance."[40]

The infant Canadian navy depended heavily upon the Royal Navy for professional support, and help was generously given, despite the feeling that Canadians were tending to take a free ride. In 1903 Lord Minto, the governor general, had warned that if naval training ships were established in Canada there was too much probability that their officers and men, like those of the Fisheries Service, would be "appointed almost entirely for their political qualifications, the patronage for each vessel belonging to the member of Parliament representing the district from which it is manned."[41] The development of a purely professional promotion system was to be a work in progress for decades, but the training problem was solved by the adoption of common standards for the Royal Navy and the Dominions navies, and by the adoption of a common code of naval discipline.[42] The 1910 Naval Service Act extended the British Naval Discipline Act of 1866 to the Canadian navy, and RCN discipline continued to be linked with RN discipline until a new Canadian Naval Service Act was passed in 1944 and implemented after the end of the Second World War.[43]

As early as 1915 it was recognized that any attempt simply to replicate the Royal Navy in Canada would likely cause difficulties. An anonymous officer writing on "The Future of the Royal Canadian Navy" in the Royal Navy journal, *Naval Review*, commented that "owing to the undoubtedly higher average of intelligence existing amongst those men most likely to join the Royal Canadian Navy over those that join the Royal Navy, the officers and petty officer instructors from the Royal Navy should be most carefully chosen, the officers for their known zeal and interest in their profession, and the petty officers for their tact and ability in handling and instructing all sorts of men."[44] When Admiral Sir John Jellicoe advised on the development of independent dominion navies in 1919, on the other hand, he cautioned that, "From the very nature of things it is more difficult to keep a small navy at a high pitch of efficiency than a large fleet," and advised the Canadian government that it was of the "great importance that the Royal Canadian Navy and the Royal Navy should hold themselves in the very closest relationship."[45] Small navies might not be able to attract the right sort of men if they could not offer reasonable chance of promotion. Recruitment and retention of suitable Canadian naval officers was recognized to be difficult.

✦✦✦

The compromise solution to the problem presented by the need to reconcile constitutional autonomy with centralized strategic control, common naval discipline, and the juridical unity of the empire was for the dominions to accept the operational authority of the British Admiralty and its commanders-in-chief when proceeding outside their own areas of national responsibility. For Canada these were defined in very wide terms, as north of N30° and west of E40° in the Atlantic and east of 180° in the Pacific. The same principle applied when Royal Navy ships were attached to the Canadian Atlantic and Pacific stations or to the Australian station, within which areas the dominion governments were held to represent the interests of the entire Empire – although Canadian naval commanders, even if senior to the commanders of British ships entering the area, were not "to interfere with the execution of any orders which the junior might have received from his own government." To ensure wartime operational efficiency, Laurier's naval bill adopted the same formula as had the Australians, permitting the government to transfer control to the Admiralty. It did not, however, arrange for automatic transfer upon the outbreak of hostilities. Scholarly opinion is that the very comprehensiveness of the authority accorded to the dominions over naval command served to cement an effective concept of Imperial unity.[46]

Canadians were not very happy with this arrangement, but could not agree on a better one. Canadian ultra-nationalists objected that the Liberals were in fact creating a rod for their own backs, whatever their intentions. Frederick Debartzch Monk, Conservative member of Parliament for Jacques Cartier and later minister of public works in 1911–12, condemned the idea of "a navy which will be Canadian when it has to be paid for, in order to be Imperial when it is required for use."[47] Henri Bourassa, who had left the Liberal Party at the time of the South African war and was now the leader of the Nationalist Party, objected that if Canada constructed a navy of value to the empire it would be impossible for Canadians to resist the request for military assistance even if they disagreed with Britain's policy at the time. On that platform the Nationalists defeated the Liberals in Quebec, and the argument has resonated in Canada's strategic debate over the rest of the twentieth century, and into the twenty-first.[48]

Logically, the solution to the problem of operational and strategic control of the naval forces of the empire could have been solved by the development of effective means of collectively formulating the common foreign policy for the wider political entity, which was then the empire.[49] During the first quarter of the century a great deal of effort was put into the attempt, but in the end the problem defeated the wisdom of the age.[50] Politicians with more parochial concerns prevailed in the dominions and Great Britain alike. While Kim Richard Nossal believes that Canadians have always seen their "realm" as extending into a broader transnational context, the idea of Imperial Federalism "always foundered on the rocks of the contradictions implicit in the imperial arrangement."[51] Laurier rejected the idea of centralized institutions that might be responsive to Canadian attitudes but which would certainly make it harder to opt out, should Imperial policy prove inconvenient. He preferred, if pressed, to establish a Canadian navy but to avoid formal obligations to participate in Imperial defence.

Borden was more comfortable with imperial institutions, and collective defence, and more impressed by Canada's vulnerability should the Royal Navy suffer defeat. His initial support for the formation of a Canadian navy was short-lived, and his change of heart contributed to Laurier's defeat. He succeeded Laurier as prime minister in October 1911, and on 16 May 1912 he told the secretary of state for the colonies,

Lewis Harcourt, that he was considering acquiring two full fleet units for the Canadian navy, but Churchill induced him instead to put on the Canadian budget a commitment to build three of the latest design of oil-fired battleships, "the largest and strongest ships of war which science can build or money supply," for service in the Royal Navy. Although the Anglo-Australian naval agreement had been terminated and the Royal Australian Navy formally established on 11 July 1911, Australia, New Zealand and the Federated Malay States were each paying for the construction of a capital ship for service in or with the Royal Navy. Introducing the Naval Aid Bill in the House of Commons on 5 December 1912, Borden stated his belief that in the developing crisis there was no alternative to the established and proven organization of the Royal Navy. "In my humble opinion," he told parliament, "nothing of an efficient character could be built up in this country within a quarter or perhaps half a century. Even then it would be but a poor and weak substitute for that splendid organization which the Empire already possesses." He held open the possibility that the super-dreadnoughts might eventually be taken into the Canadian navy, but his emphasis was on collective control of a common resource. Speaking in the House of Commons, Borden noted the "problem of combining co-operation with autonomy," but stated that when in Britain to discuss naval issues he had "ventured on many public occasions to propound the principle that the great dominions, sharing in the defence of the Empire upon the high seas, must necessarily be entitled to share also in the responsibility for and in the control of foreign policy ... It is satisfactory to know," he added, "that to-day not only His Majesty's ministers but also the leaders of the opposite political party in Great Britain have explicitly accepted this principle." He believed there was agreement that a Canadian representative should become a permanent member of the Committee of Imperial Defence.[52]

There were, however, many daggers in the back of the idea that Imperial defence and foreign policy should be developed collectively. London was inconsistent about its willingness to share control. At the 1902 Colonial Conference, Colonial Secretary Joseph Chamberlain had ventured "to refer to an expression in an eloquent speech of [his] right honourable friend, the Premier of the Dominion of Canada [Sir Wilfrid Laurier] ... 'If you want our aid, call us to your councils.' Gentlemen, we do want your aid. We do require your assistance in the administration of the vast Empire which is yours as well as ours. The weary Titan staggers under the too vast orb of its fate." At the 1911 Imperial Conference the

British foreign secretary, Sir Edward Grey, told the assembled dominion leaders: "The creation of separate fleets has made it essential that the Foreign Policy of the Empire should be a common policy. If it is to be a common policy, it is obviously one on which the Dominions must be taken into consultation." However, Herbert Asquith, Britain's prime minister, declared the collective formation of foreign policy to be impossible, and it is doubtful that Borden was correct in suggesting there had been a change of heart in London.[53]

A memorandum sent to the Admiralty in 1914 by Lionel Curtis, founder of the *Round Table Review*, noted that the Canadian constitutional objective was to obtain control of foreign policy, either by separation from the Empire or by establishing a more "Imperial" foreign policy separate from British control, in effect reducing the United Kingdom to the status of a dominion.[54] This observation reflected Curtis's own conviction, born from his work in "Milner's Kindergarten," the group working to establish the Union of South Africa under the British high commissioner for Africa, Viscount Alfred Milner, but his assessment of Canadian objectives was broadly correct. On the threshold of war, however, this was not to be. The transfer of discussion of foreign and defence policy from the Imperial Conference, in which the dominions controlled the agenda, to the CID, which was controlled by the British prime minister, might even be viewed as a diminution of dominion influence over policy. Dominion premiers were invited to attend for briefings and discussion, which they found useful, but they could not use the CID as a forum for discovering common ground with the other dominions in matters of high policy.[55]

Borden's Naval Aid Bill was debated in the Commons for thirty-six days, with closure enforced for the first time, and finally defeated in the Senate because Canadian nationalism and the Liberal party were stronger forces than the idea of imperial federalism.[56] There may also have been economic reasons. In 1909 Borden had supported the proposal to invest in naval forces with an appeal to economic self-interest: "In this connection may we not hope that there shall be given a stimulus and encouragement to the shipbuilding industry of Canada which has long been lacking. To-day should be Nova Scotia's opportunity." The lukewarm reception Churchill gave to the idea of offsetting some of Canada's expenses by ordering small craft built in Canada may have been an important factor in his abandonment of the project in the face of parliamentary opposition.[57]

A compromise solution to the Canadian dilemma was suggested in a *Naval Review* article in 1913 attributed to Lieutenant William Scott Chalmers, who was to be assistant navigating officer of HMS *Lion* at the battle of Jutland and later the biographer of admirals Beatty and Ramsay. He pointed to the value of combining Canadian support for the Royal Navy and the separate development of the Royal Canadian Navy.

> Canada should firstly contribute to the main fighting fleet of the Empire by monetary contributions and by the supply of a certain number of officers. Secondly, she should provide herself with a small local navy, manned by Canadians, consisting of submarines and torpedo craft to defend her coastal waters, and a few small cruisers to protect her ends of the trade routes.
>
> This arrangement appears to be the best compromise between the conflicting claims of concentration of power, centralised direction, and the legitimate aspirations of the Canadian people. The latter factor most to be reckoned with, for the federation of the Empire will not be brought about by strategical doctrine alone; less tangible but none the less vital forces must also be considered.[58]

Borden did not repeal the Canadian Naval Service Act, and Canada's naval strategy over the succeeding century was in fact to combine the local and the wider perspectives.

❖❖❖

Colonel C.P. Stacey, director of the Historical Section of the General Staff from 1945 to 1959 and professor of history at the University of Toronto until 1975, viewed Borden's naval policy as "a national disaster ... His policy destroyed the unity of Parliament on the fundamental question of national defence; it produced the bitterest of controversies but no ships." The Australians – with British help, he pointed out – developed between 1909 and 1914 an effective small fleet that contributed to naval defence in the war.[59] Nevertheless, the admittedly small-scale operations of the Canadian navy in the First World War did set a pattern for the future. On the outbreak of war in August 1914 HMCS *Rainbow*, commanded by Commander Walter Hose, was immediately sent to sea from Esquimalt with a scratch crew, to defend trade and to provide protection for two British sloops that were at sea. It was fortunate that she failed in her efforts to meet cruisers *Leipzig* and *Nürnberg* of the German East Asiatic squadron operating off the American coast. Four Canadian midshipmen trained at the Royal Naval College of Canada were killed when the German force sank the better equipped but still obsolete cruiser HMS *Good Hope* during the subsequent battle of Coronel. The Canadian fleet on the west coast was added to by the purchase of two submarines from their builder in Seattle, CC1 and CC2, both of which were to be commanded by retired Royal Navy submarine officers living in Canada and manned by volunteers from the recently formed Royal Canadian Navy Volunteer Reserve. The two British sloops had avoided contact with the German cruisers, and were laid up so that their crews could be sent to Halifax to bring HMCS *Niobe* forward for service. With a further draft of 106 ratings of the Royal Naval reserve from Newfoundland, *Niobe* undertook patrols in defence of trade. By the summer of 1915, however, she had to be decommissioned as no longer fit for seagoing service. The RCN refused a British offer of another cruiser, as it preferred to put its efforts into developing a fleet of small craft. A seasonal base for patrolling the Gulf of St Lawrence and the south coast of Newfoundland was established at Sydney, Nova Scotia, away from the main British squadron commanders at Halifax and Bermuda.[60]

In May 1917 *Rainbow* was decommissioned so that her crew could be transferred to Halifax to help man the flotilla, the need for which had become manifest when the Imperial German Navy's U-53 attacked trade off the American coast in October 1916. German U-cruisers returned to Canadian waters in 1917 and 1918. The flotilla initially consisted of converted vessels, with over a hundred trawlers entering service late in 1917 and early 1918, most of which had been originally ordered for the Royal Navy from Canadian yards. The two Canadian submarines were also transferred to Halifax late in 1917 en route to Europe, but were condemned there as unfit to cross the Atlantic. They were the first British Empire warships to transit the new Panama canal, and remained in Halifax where they were employed to train the flotilla.[61] In 1919 they were replaced by two old British submarines, CH14 and CH15. A Royal Canadian Naval Air Service was established in 1918, with flying stations at Dartmouth and North Sydney, but was unready for operations before the end of the war, when it was disbanded. Following the transfer of British and Canadian sailors to Halifax, defence of the west coast was accepted as a responsibility by the Imperial Japanese Navy.

In addition to providing some of the crew for *Niobe*, the Newfoundland division of the Royal Naval Reserve served onboard British merchant cruisers in the 10th Cruiser Squadron north of Scotland, enforcing the blockade of Germany, on trawlers and minesweepers in British waters, onboard defensively armed merchant ships, and in Canadian-built trawlers that had seen service in the Mediterranean. They also manned a Q-ship guarding the Grand Banks fishery, provided local defence and communications at St John's, and ultimately helped man the Royal Canadian Navy flotilla.[62]

During the war Borden was frustrated by London's refusal to consult him, or even fully brief him, on the employment of Canadian forces. The Committee of Imperial Defence was suspended for the duration, and no information was passed through the High Commissions.[63] In 1915 Colonial Secretary Andrew Bonar Law rejected as impracticable Borden's wish to "have some share of the control in a war," and with the formation of the autocratic administration of David Lloyd George in December 1916 the attempt of the new colonial secretary, Walter Long, to establish a weekly telegram to dominion leaders was frustrated by his own lack of access to the War Cabinet on a regular basis.[64] Lloyd George did form an Imperial War Cabinet in 1917, and briefed the dominion leaders, but the commitment of the Canadian Army to the Passchendaele battle in the autumn of 1917, with the unobtainable and probably pointless objective of capturing German submarine bases in Flanders, was not even mentioned.[65] This experience, resonating as it did with the strategic debate of the previous decade, was to have implications for the Canadian navy following the end of the war.

2

A NATIONAL NAVY IN AN IMPERIAL CONTEXT: BETWEEN THE WARS

The Canadian navy barely survived the postwar decades. The disasters of the First World War disenchanted many Canadians with the affairs of Europe. Canadian politics and policy in the postwar period tended strongly toward isolationism, and there were those who would have been content to leave defence to the Monroe Doctrine.[1] The collective naval defence of the Empire evoked little enthusiasm in a nation more concerned about American attitudes. Britons suffered even worse losses than Canada in the First World War, and the effects on British politics were parallel to those that occurred in Canada, but Canadian nationalism and the Atlantic ocean gave a unique character to the Canadian fear of being cannon fodder under the orders of British generals.

The Imperial War Cabinet was to be more effective when reassembled in 1918 and 1919 to discuss peace terms, but Robert Borden's frustrations in dealing with London led him to use the occasion to promote Canadian sovereign control of foreign and defence policy. He insisted that Canada sign the Versailles peace treaty in its own right, and have a seat in the League of Nations, but he also attempted to limit the commitment to collective security expected of nations such as Canada that were geographically removed from scenes of conflict.[2] Of particular concern were the strains in the Anglo-American relationship caused by the blockade of the central powers during the war, which inevitably had interfered with neutral traders. The Foreign Office had controlled interceptions to minimize protests by American business interests, and American acting secretary of state, Robert Lansing, assisted the process by suggesting that shipping laded for any neutral port that became an *entrepôt* for the enemy might be seized.[3] Nevertheless, the U.S. Navy planning section in London had prepared a paper in 1917 in which it warned: "Four great powers have arisen in the world to compete with Great Britain for commercial supremacy ... Each one in succession has been defeated by Great Britain and her fugitive allies. A fifth commercial power, the greatest one yet, is now arising to compete for at least commercial equality. Already the signs of jealousy are visible." The paper was sent in 1918 to Admiral Benson who was U.S. Chief of Naval Operations and naval representative at the Paris Peace Conference in 1919, at which the United States sought to establish a concept of the "Freedom of the Seas" that would make commercial blockade illegal.[4] This Lloyd George successfully resisted, but his resistance only strengthened the determination of the American government to ensure that the British fleet could never again blockade American trade, as it had a hundred years before in defence of Canada. The Anglo-Japanese alliance was seen as threatening the United States with a two-front war. Perhaps it was fortunate the German fleet scuttled itself when interned at Scapa Flow so that it could not be seized by Britain as war reparations. All the same, the threat loomed of an Anglo-American naval arms race, with serious implications for Canada.

Following the conclusion of peace, all the naval powers were invited by President Warren G. Harding to a naval armaments conference in Washington between 12 November 1921 and 6 February 1922, at which naval parity between Britain and the United States was agreed to, and Japan reluctantly agreed not to build a fleet exceeding 60 percent of their numbers. But the agreement did not end the conflict. The navies of the three great powers all regarded the settlement as prejudicial to their national interests, and to their institutional interests. Agreement had only been possible for battleships and aircraft carriers, but not for the cruisers that could be used to defend trade, or to blockade it. Out of concession to the United States, the Anglo-Japanese alliance was not renewed. A Canadian naval committee, composed of Admiral Sir Charles Kingsmill, Captain Walter Hose, and Georges Desbarats, deputy minister of marine and fisheries, had concluded in an occasional paper that the alliance "may be looked upon more in the light of an encumbrance, as it is a potential means of embroiling us with the United States," and then somewhat illogically that "Japan is the enemy." But while non-renewal of the alliance was probably an unavoidable concession to American pressure, and was urged at the conference by Borden and Arthur Meighen, who succeeded him as Canada's prime minister, letting the alliance lapse only accelerated the pace toward the outbreak of war in the Pacific.[5]

Borden and Meighen participated in the Washington Naval Conference as part of the British empire delegation, but the Round Table movement was a casualty of the war. The Liberal prime minister who ousted Meighen at the end of 1921, William Lyon Mackenzie King, based his political success on a nationalism that had the potential to bridge the differences between francophone Quebec and the anglophone provinces. He was comfortable with the idea of the empire as a family of sovereign nations, and was instinctively British in his outlook, but he distrusted Britain's Tory leadership, and placed great importance on Canada's relationship with the United States. Norman Hillmer writes that for Mackenzie King "independence was a requirement if Canadians were not to become, as they had in 1914, the cat's-paw of British imperialism."[6] At the time of the 1922 Chanak crisis, when Lloyd George wanted dominion assistance to oppose Kemal Atatürk's rebellion against British occupation forces, Mackenzie King refused. C.P. Stacey acknowledges that he was right to resist a "plot" designed to return Lloyd George to power, but adds that "the tragedy of Chanak is that it tended to confirm Mackenzie King's suspicions of English Tories and their centralizing practices."[7]

The structure of imperial naval defence in the postwar period mirrored the trend toward autonomy in foreign policy, and in Canada reflected the priority that had to be given to relations with the United States. The war made it evident even to naval planners in London, but only after a struggle, that, at least in peacetime, operational inefficiencies had to be tolerated in order to obtain the more vital requirement of public political support. Admiral Sir John Jellicoe, when in Ottawa in 1919 to advise on Canada's future naval development, gave the impression to Mackenzie King, a year before the latter became Canada's prime minister, that "even in the offices of the Admiralty they had rejected the idea of a centralized navy."[8] A 1919 Admiralty memorandum on "Imperial Naval Defence" observed that "discussion as to the best form of co-operation is, in fact, somewhat academic because the statements of Dominion statesmen make it clear that future co-operation from Canada and New Zealand will eventually follow the Australian model. Quite irrespectively, then, of the advantages of this system, the Admiralty will be required to assist in the development of these navies, and to find a place for them in a comprehensive system of Imperial defence."[9]

For the 1921 Imperial Conference, the Admiralty prepared a paper on the development and coordination of independent naval forces, but made it clear it did not consider the development of dominion navies "the ideal policy, which would be a unified navy under a single command."[10] Two years later, however, Captain Dudley Pound, Admiralty director of plans – and from 1939 to 1943 First Sea Lord – drew the necessary conclusion when he prepared a paper to outline the progression of Admiralty policy vis à vis the dominions and to detail the means which had been established for coordinating the naval policies of the Empire. "Wars," he wrote, "are no longer waged by Navies and Armies alone, but by nations in arms. The success or failure of any measure of defence rests ultimately on the sanction of the people ... It is for this reason that public interest is placed first in the list of requirements to be fulfilled."[11] At the 1923 Imperial Conference, Mackenzie King whipped himself into a fury when Captain Pound's memorandum was provided by the colonial secretary, the Duke of Devonshire. "I was quite incensed," he wrote in his diary, "to see Admiralty proposed to issue a plan to the several dominions. An outrageous interference with the autonomy & self government of the dominions. They will break up the Empire yet. It is no longer Downing St. It is now the Admiralty."[12] He made it clear to his Commonwealth colleagues when he spoke on Canada's foreign policy on 8 October that "self-government means the right of each part of the Empire to control its own affairs, whether those affairs are domestic or foreign, or both." But his later statement on defence to the conference was more measured: "We in the dominions have most in mind ... co-operation rather than centralisation in these matters of defence. The original point of view of the Admiralty was that the more centralised in every particular [the] matter of defence could be, the more effective and better the outcome. I think we might admit at once that, from the point of view of strategy, efficiency and economy, the Admiralty were perhaps right, speaking of the defence of the empire as a whole. On the other hand, there is always the difference between the political point of view and the technical point of view, and the political point of view, inasmuch as it lies at the basis of all the rest, cannot receive too full consideration."[13]

In 1927 the Australian naval representative in London responded to the Admiralty's final efforts at centralization in similar terms: "The 'single Navy' theory has much to commend it if we are considering preparation of a definite, and immediate, war problem ... The Dominions are not ... It is a theory that leaves the Dominion taxpayer cold ... And, speaking generally no political [sic] is concerned with a question that does not interest the voter. Certainly he that controls the Exchequer would not be."[14] The British idea in 1929 that the Canadian high commissioner should represent Canada from time to time on the Committee of Imperial Defence was rejected.[15] When in 1937 Colonel Maurice Pope, who later served on Mackenzie King's staff, prepared a "Memorandum on a Canadian Organization for the Higher Direction of National Defence," he echoed Pound in his introductory observation that "War, including defensive war, is an instrument of national policy; National policy is a responsibility of government; Government, in Canada, must obtain the consent if not the support of the majority of the people."[16]

Mackenzie King had supported his assertion in favour of an independent Canadian foreign policy at the 1923 Imperial Conference by stressing the influence the United States had on Canadian opinions: "for 3,000 miles we lie side by side with a great foreign country which is yet of English speech, and with which our people have constant and unending business and social intercourse." He used negotiations with the United States over the Rush-Bagot naval arms limitation treaty neutralizing the Great Lakes dating back to 1817, and the Halibut treaty of 1923, to establish a practical separation of Canada from the United Kingdom. Nominal independence in foreign policy was confirmed when the 1926 Imperial Conference declared the Dominions to be fully autonomous, and Mackenzie King used the 1927 naval disarmament talks at Geneva to obtain from the United States a grudging recognition of Canadian independence.[17] John Erskine Read, in his 1967 article "Problems of an External Affairs Legal Adviser, 1928–1946," states that governmental guidelines required officers to promote the creation of a sovereign Canadian state.[18]

The under-secretary of state for external affairs from 1925 to 1942, O.D. Skelton, had a strong anti-British bias and was determined to keep Canada from automatic involvement in policies made in London, even if they were made collectively and were consistent with League of Nations objectives.[19] In January 1926 Skelton savagely warned: "not a country on the Continent of Europe would lift its little finger to help if the United States were to attack," and added that the United States in his experience was "a neighbour that any free country in the continent of Europe or elsewhere would thank its stars to have."[20]

But it was not possible to ignore the military potential of the United States. The Canadian Army director of military operations and intelligence, Lieutenant Colonel James "Buster" Sutherland Brown, completed a plan in April 1921 to meet a threatened American invasion of Canada by pre-emptive raids into the United States to buy enough time for

British forces to arrive. An American "War Plan Red" was formulated in the mid-1920s, and approved by the secretaries of war and the navy in May 1930, for a potential war against the British Empire, with provision for multiple invasions of Canada, including a gas attack on the naval dockyard in Halifax and a landing at St Margaret's Bay. Christopher Bell writes that "from the historian's perspective" War Plan Red is important "as a window into the strategic mind of the US navy. The same is true," he continues, "of British plans for a naval war with the United States ... An examination of British and US naval strategies ... highlights the competitive, often antagonistic side of Anglo-American relations during the 1920s and the level of mutual mistrust that existed: it is too often forgotten that naval rivalry, war debts, and arguments over belligerent versus neutral rights placed considerable strain on Anglo-American friendship during this period."[21]

The threat of American invasion was never a dominant consideration in Canada at this time, but the need to manage the relationship with the United States was taken seriously and was recognized to have defence implications. Mackenzie King took imperial co-operation as seriously as he did Canadian sovereignty. At the 1923 Imperial Conference he had added: "If a great and clear call of duty comes, Canada will respond, whether or not the United States responds, as she did in 1914."[22] The Canadian government endorsed the resolution of the conference that the security of the territory and trade of all the dominions was the responsibility of all parts of the empire, a formula taken from the Covenant of the League of Nations and which found echoes after the Second World War in the North Atlantic Treaty Organization. Commitments were made that the dockyards at Halifax and Esquimalt would be available for the Royal Navy in the event of Britain's going to war, regardless of Canadian policies at the time, and Canada undertook to store equipment in Canada for wartime conversion of British Columbia–based liners into armed merchant cruisers.[23] An important method of ensuring that a policy of co-operation would be effective was a 1924 agreement that dominion naval officers would be seconded to serve on the Royal Navy Staff, and British officers would serve on the staffs of the Canadian and Australian navies.[24]

✦✦✦

The limitations of the Imperial defence compromise were reflected in the scale and nature of Canada's investment in naval forces in the interwar period. The suggestion that the Admiralty send Admiral Jellicoe to advise on Canadian naval policy had first been made shortly before the outbreak of war in 1914. After the armistice, he set out on a tour of the dominions and India, making his last stop in Canada.[25] Kingsmill's advice to Laurier in 1909 had been for the Canadian navy to develop at a very modest pace, and a decade later, when a series of study papers was prepared by the Canadian Naval Committee, that attitude continued to be expressed. Jellicoe returned to the idea of the Canadian navy being built around a fleet unit led by a battle cruiser, but Kingsmill was unmoved. Jellicoe's most modest proposal for a Canadian fleet consisting of three light cruisers, a flotilla leader, twelve torpedo craft, and eight submarines with a parent ship, although similar to that of Kingsmill's Naval Committee, was further scaled back to a cruiser and two destroyers, HMC ships *Aurora*, *Patrician* and *Patriot*, two submarines (CH14 and CH15), and four trawlers, costing $4 million per year.[26] Jellicoe advised that "any naval unit, to be complete, must, in the future, possess its proper complement of aircraft for the different purposes required. The co-operation of aircraft with naval forces will be of great and increasing value, and aerial operations will influence naval tactics and strategy."[27] But the Royal Canadian Naval Air Service was abolished.[28] The reduced Jellicoe establishment was implemented in 1920 by the Borden administration, but only after pressure in the Union caucus nearly led to the Canadian navy's being abolished altogether.[29]

The local panic caused by the operations of U-cruisers off the Canadian coast in 1917–18 had made it clear that the Admiralty's staff appreciations were not infallible, or consistent, and demonstrated the value of the Canadian navy's making its own threat analyses.[30] In October 1917 the Canadian navy had resisted the idea that the Royal Navy commander-in-chief take over the Halifax Intelligence Centre because in practice that would have kept the Canadians dependent for intelligence. Co-operation in intelligence was essential for the small Canadian navy, however, and in 1921, at its suggestion, the Admiralty established in Ottawa the intelligence centre for North America north of Bermuda. This ensured that the Canadian navy would have access to the information it needed for strategic planning.[31]

At the 1923 Imperial Conference, and again in 1926, it was agreed that there was a common responsibility to maintain "adequate provision for safeguarding the maritime communications of the several parts of the Empire and the routes and waterways along and through which their armed forces and trade pass." The Admiralty repeatedly urged the

HMCS *Aurora*. An *Arethusa* class light cruiser, she was commissioned in the Royal Navy in 1914 and transferred to the Royal Canadian Navy in 1920, but decommissioned the following year. DND CN-6411

HMC Ships *Aurora* (foreground) and *Patriot* and *Patrician* in Esquimalt Harbour, circa 1921.

dominions to make the task of protecting oceanic shipping their guiding principle. Consistent with their imperial experience, Canada's sailors always recognized the essential coherence of blue-water and coastal sea-control, acknowledging that the "the sea is one," and that local defence is a product of worldwide power balances. Strategy is an art of the possible, however, and political requirements do have to be met. The Imperial conferences also agreed that the "primary responsibility of each portion of the empire is for its own local defence," and the Canadian government limited its efforts to meeting that part of the undertaking.[32] Despite the Admiralty's advice that they were inappropriate, the Canadian fleet was built around its destroyers, which had the potential to keep hostile cruisers away from Canada's coasts, although the limited range of interwar destroyers was a distinct disadvantage.[33] The continued Canadian dependence on British shipyards for warships, even though initially they were gifts from the British government, had a chilling effect on naval development.

The focus on local defence was motivated by the need to provide effective naval support for the Halifax harbour defences and by the 1917–18 experience that suggested the Royal Navy might not be able to meet an emergency in Canadian waters. It also accommodated anti-imperial attitudes in Quebec, and was important in fulfilling the navy's part in managing the relationship with the United States.[34] Lieutenant Chalmers, in his 1913 *Naval Review* article, had contrasted Australia's obvious need for a fleet due to her proximity "to a rising naval power and the isolation of her position point" with Canada's good fortune "in being next door to a powerful country whose interests in the Pacific Ocean are identical with her own." Accordingly, he had favoured an Atlantic orientation for Canadian naval effort. Two years later, however, the anonymous but clearly well-informed contributor to the *Naval Review*, writing about "The Future of the Royal Canadian Navy," suggested that: "owing to the presence of the Royal Navy in the Atlantic, and its absence in any force in the Pacific it will be advisable to make the safety of the coast of British Columbia the first consideration."[35] After the termination of the Anglo-Japanese alliance, the need to ensure that the United States was confident about Canada's ability to prevent Japanese use of its Pacific coastal waters became increasingly important as Japan's relationship with the United States deteriorated.

✦✦✦

The 1920 establishment did not last long. In 1922 Mackenzie King, using as an excuse the Washington Conference, which did not in fact place any limitations on cruiser and destroyer numbers, cut the Navy budget to $1.5 million.[36] The Naval Committee had to reduce the navy to an all but shore-bound reserve force, retaining only the two destroyers for training purposes. Mackenzie King, in his diary entry for 22 April 1922, wrote that George Perry Graham, whom he had appointed to both the Naval Service and the Militia portfolios, now proposed "doing away with the submarines & cruiser & Naval College & starting a volunteer Naval Reserve, training men part of the year, & utilizing for patrol purposes etc., getting rid of fighting force. It may occasion some comment, & will certainly create disappointment in Eng[land] but will be strongly supported in H of C ... No need for Navy at present. [Jacques] Bureau & I had great laugh over Graham's job in demobilizing these various forces."[37] When the Royal Canadian Air Force (RCAF) was formed in 1924, Graham's portfolio was extended, and he was sworn in as minister of national defence. A Defence Council was created by adding naval and air members to the existing Militia Council, and later, in 1927, a Joint Staff Committee was established. In 1926 James Ralston succeeded Graham as minister of national defence.

The explanation given to the Admiralty for the fleet reductions was that "overhead charges would have been out of all proportion to the defence value obtained." That produced a tart comment from their Lordships: "The Admiralty cannot help feeling that this bears out the view ... that the ideal form of Dominion co-operation lies in a unified navy with [a] quota of men and ships supplied by the Dominions and India."[38] In 1922 the United Kingdom government spent seventeen times as much per capita on naval defence as did Canada, and Australia spent five and half times as much as Canada.[39] The most useful Canadian contribution to collective naval defence was the maintenance of Halifax and Esquimalt for Imperial naval forces, and the build-up of fuel supplies.[40] Repeated requests that fuel reserves be brought up to 100 percent, however, were not met. As late as 1937 the Naval Intelligence and Plans Division in Ottawa expressed the belief that "Canada's war requirements of fuel could be met without laying down reserve stocks in peace."[41]

Kingsmill, who had been promoted a full admiral in 1917 and knighted in 1918, went on leave in July 1920 and finally resigned at the end of December 1921.[42] Hose, replacing Kingsmill as director of naval services and promoted rear admiral, implemented the drastic budget cut by reducing the Canadian navy to little more than a reserve force, hoping to keep alive in inland Canada some awareness of naval concerns by establishing reserve training units across the country. The Australian rear admiral James Goldrick, commander Australian Defence College, characterizes the decision as "a stroke of genius [which] not only raised awareness of the navy in a continentally minded country, but also provided the basis for the extraordinary expansion of 1939–45." The establishment of reserve divisions across the country "also meant that the government's ability to cut the very limited funds made available to the RCN was limited by the likely reaction from local communities."[43] But the necessity of closing the Royal Naval College of Canada, sending Canadians to Britain for their officer training, opened a gap between their experience and that of their fellow countrymen.[44]

Arthur Meighen's minister of the naval service, C.C. Ballantyne, had suggested establishing a common officer list for the Empire, so that dominion officers, once they became too senior to find work in their small fleets, could look for advancement in the Royal Navy.[45] This would have maintained the image of a separate Canadian navy and helped ensure that it maintained professional standards, but it would not have ensured the strategic unity wanted by the Admiralty. Their Lordships rejected the idea out of concern that the new junior officers created for the dominion fleets would clog prospects for promotion within the Royal Navy. Arrangements for cross-training, however, continued.[46] During the 1920s and '30s Canadian officers spent two years out of every six in the Royal Navy and at any time an average of 10 percent of the Canadian navy's ratings and warrant officers were on course or sea duty with the Royal Navy.[47] The presence of British staff officers on the Canadian Naval Staff, and the provision for Canadian naval officers and those of the other dominions, to fill staff positions at the Admiralty, ensured a unity of technical control.[48] The names of dominions officers appeared on the Navy List in a separate listing for each dominion fleet, with a note indicating who had been lent to the Royal Navy. So long as the Empire maintained at least a facade of a common foreign policy the problem of divided loyalties was accommodated, but the Royal Navy perspective of Canada's naval officers was not always consistent with the general trend of Canadian constitutional history.

At the 1926 Imperial Conference, Mackenzie King pointed to the training achievement that made it possible to man the Canadian navy with the assistance of only forty Royal Naval personnel. All the same, the total active service was only five hundred. "I cannot say when that 'active and determined support of public opinion' which is so properly stated in the Committee of Imperial Defence memorandum on Empire Naval Policy and Co-operation of 1923 as being essential for the effective maintenance of naval forces will make it possible to advance to a further phase, but the question is receiving consideration."[49] A year later, following Ralston's appointment as minister of national defence, the Admiralty was approached about lending Canada two newer destroyers to replace *Patriot* and *Patrician*, which were nearing the end of their useful life, a request that led to a somewhat acid debate about the propriety of facilitating penny-pinching policies in Canada. It came as an agreeable surprise when Mackenzie King telegraphed that it had been decided to order the construction of new destroyers. With the loan, the new construction increased the Canadian fleet to four destroyers. The defence budget in 1926/27 totalled at $12.9 million and was to rise to $21.7 million for 1930/31, but then fell dramatically during the depression years to $13.3 million.[50]

✦ ✦ ✦

Mackenzie King's pacifist and humanitarian perspective in the wake of the disasters of the First World War is shown in his diary entry made while enjoying a voyage from Prince Rupert to Comox in HMCS *Patrician* in October 1924. "We started out about 2 a.m. I looked thro' the port hole of my cabin, saw the moonlight on the water & shores not far distant – a unique experience, on the Pacific Ocean in a Man-of-War – sleeping in the captain's cabin while he was on the bridge – Who says fact is not stranger than fiction." After daybreak and a tour of the ship, including the pressurized boiler room, he added: "What heroism is in common man – the men who are unknown & unnoticed, not seeking decoration or even recognition! We were also shewn the operation of the big gun & torpedo firing. I could not help thinking how perfected is this science of killing [compared] with efforts to save & conserve life, – the contrast of two ideals, the militarist & the industrial, this warship & the Edmonton elevator."[51] All the same, pacifist attitudes did not blind Mackenzie King to the importance of the navy in isolating Canada from great-power conflict. He did not welcome the possibility that the disarmament conference at Geneva in 1927 might prevent the acquisition for the Canadian navy of replacements for the worn out *Patrician* and *Patriot*. Commodore Hose, now chief of naval staff, was sent to Geneva as an advisor to the Canadian delegation, with the objective of ensuring that British concessions to the United States on the number of destroyers allowed the British Commonwealth did not affect the Canadian navy.

The collapse of the negotiations at Geneva, when the British and American sailors could not agree on limitations for cruisers, put an end to any danger the conference would affect Canadian naval procurement. HMC destroyers *Champlain* and *Vancouver* were commissioned at the beginning of March 1928. But the failed conference also heightened concern in Ottawa about Anglo-American relations and led the now formally independent Canada to take careful steps to avoid being caught between the manoeuvring giants. Austin Chamberlain, the British foreign secretary, told a sub-committee of the Committee of Imperial Defence in October 1927 that "the present difference on this subject [Belligerent Rights at

HMCS *Patriot*. A *Thornycroft* M class destroyer launched in 1916, she served in the Royal Navy and was recommissioned in the Royal Canadian Navy in 1920. After the decommissioning of *Aurora* and *Patrician*, she remained the only ship in active service until 1928 when she was paid off. In 1921 she was employed in assisting Alexander Graham Bell in his experiments with hydrofoils in Bras d'Or Lake. DND CN-6732

Sea] between the United States and ourselves is the only matter which makes war between our two nations conceivable."⁵² Because of concern in Ottawa about the naval dispute, a British request to permit the operational basing of Royal Navy cruisers at Esquimalt in the event of an Anglo-Japanese War was shelved until 1929, agreement then being made conditional on Canada having itself declared war.⁵³

By the end of the 1920s, however, the tensions between Britain and the United States began to ease. After his election as head of state in November 1928, President Herbert Hoover wrote in his memoirs: "elimination of friction with Great Britain must be one of the foundation stones of our foreign policies ... The most dangerous of these frictions was of course competitive naval building." In London, Prime Minister Ramsay MacDonald took a personal interest in Anglo-American relations.⁵⁴ In a May 1929 issue of the *Naval Review* devoted to belligerent rights, and dominated by the determination of its editor, Admiral Sir Herbert Richmond, to preserved Britain's freedom to impose naval blockade, Admiral of the Fleet Sir Arthur D. Fanshawe struck a note of reality: "Our position *now* appears to me to be *totally* different to that before the war. The United States are our equals upon the sea, and surely therefore in the event of war it would be impossible for us to impose a blockade in sheer defiance, so surely the whole question of the Freedom of the Seas is taken out of our hands ... The whole matter of our security points, to my mind, to [the need for] a full and complete agreement with the United States."⁵⁵ An American historian, James P. Baxter III, advised the *Naval Review* that agreement on belligerent rights was a hopeless quest, and that Britain and the United States should concentrate their efforts on naval arms reduction to render moot conflict in matters of law.⁵⁶

The *rapprochement* between Britain and the United States was welcomed in Canada, although Mackenzie King evidently suspected that Canadian interests would not be high on the agenda. When in October 1929 MacDonald visited Ottawa en route to meet President Hoover, Mackenzie King noted in his diary that his Cabinet "made it plain that any *agreement* re Halifax & Esquimalt not being a menace to US w[oul]d have to be on a reciprocal basis – US making same statement."⁵⁷ Hoover and MacDonald agreed that civilians should control a new effort at naval arms limitation that would be mounted in London in 1930. The outcome of the London Conference disappointed both navies, and infuriated the Japanese. As John Ferris writes, MacDonald was gambling that if Britain took the lead in naval disarmament it could bring about

179/31 AX

H.M.C.S. 'SKEENA'
PROFILE & UPPER DECK, AS FITTED
SCALE ⅜=1FOOT

1092

Plan and elevation of HMCS *Skeena* (D 59), *River* class destroyer ordered built by John I. Thornycroft & Co. for the Royal Canadian Navy in 1928. *Skeena* and her sister ship *Saguenay* were the first ships built and paid for by Canada. National War Museum, George Metcalf Archival Collection, CWM 20030289-001 a general reduction of armaments. Unfortunately, his gamble had the opposite effect: "Stability reigned during the 1920s largely because 'liberal' and status quo powers ... dominated the seas. The London Conference crippled armed liberalism at sea," by simultaneously alienating Japan, increasing the relative naval power of Japan, Germany, and Italy, and bringing about the collapse of the British naval armament industry. Those consequences were very serious, but set against them, the London Conference at which Canada was represented by Ralston was important in forging links between the democracies that were to be vital a decade later.[58]

In this changing atmosphere, Canadian naval strategy might also have begun to change. The election in August 1930 of a Conservative administration under Prime Minister R.B. Bennett might have accelerated the adoption of a more Imperial defence policy, which would have been a British Commonwealth defence policy following the proclamation of the Statute of Westminster in 1931.[59] In January 1932 the British commander of the America and West Indies squadron, Vice-Admiral Sir Vernon H.S. Haggard, requested the dispatch of the Canadian destroyers *Skeena*, which had been built in Britain for Canada and commissioned into the RCN in June 1931, and *Vancouver* to protect Britons and British property in El Salvador threatened by a peasants' revolt. They responded immediately, with the subsequent concurrence of Hose and Bennett. Bennett was careful to touch base with Washington, and the American Navy hurried a superior squadron to El Salvador to assert their primacy. This episode might have been the beginning of a more prominent role for the Canadian navy in Commonwealth gunboat diplomacy, but the great depression was the dominating consideration, and Bennett all but abolished the Navy in 1933, for a second time. The Canadian chief of the general staff, Major-General Andy McNaughton, used the El Salvador events as ammunition for restricting the budget of the Canadian navy, which he characterized as being large enough "to provoke trouble, but too weak to meet it."[60] It may only have survived because any decisive return to dependence on the Royal Navy suggested an obligation to hand over to the mother country the two new destroyers, *Skeena* and *Saguenay*, and because the navy was needed to enforce Canadian neutrality in the event of the United States going to war with Japan.[61]

The need for a Canadian navy to manage Canadian-American relations increased with President Hoover's defeat in the November 1932 American election. When in 1934 it appeared in Washington that Britain might again be willing to cut a deal with Japan over naval armament,

President Franklin D. Roosevelt warned that "Anglo-American cooperation is of more vital importance to the British Empire than to us and that in case of trouble with Japan, Canada as a practical matter would in fact become our hostage."[62] In the opinion of Galen Perras, this threat adds to the evidence that Roosevelt was already "tentatively exploring the possibility of forming a hemispheric defence system." Leaked testimony by senior U.S. Army officers to a Congressional hearing on proposed air stations embarrassed the White House with alarmist opinions that Canada might be used as a staging point for British air raids on the United States. General Frank Maxwell Andrews went so far as to suggest that the United States needed to be able to deploy air power against Canada. All this was ammunition for General McNaughton, and even for Skelton, which brought Bennett to approve another $3 million for the RCAF budget to pay for two maritime patrol squadrons and a few torpedo bombers. In 1935 Bennett showed some interest in replacing the loaned destroyers, *Champlain* and *Vancouver*, with two younger ones, but the initiative collapsed when it was discovered that the British Treasury was unwilling to authorize the transfer as a gift.[63]

Mackenzie King returned to power in October 1935, and at a July 1936 meeting at Quebec, Roosevelt continued – not too subtly – to drop hints that the United States was ready to intervene should Japan invade British Columbia waters. This was not lost on Colonel Harry D.G. Crerar when two months later he signed off on the Joint Staff Committee's "Appreciation of the Defence Problems Confronting Canada." He warned that in the event of a Japanese incursion "American public opinion will demand what would amount to the military occupation of British Columbia by US forces."[64] Defence plan No. 2, approved by the government in 1936, focused attention on the defence of the West Coast. "While air forces can provide much that is required in the nature of reconnaissance of the coast," wrote Commodore Percy Nelles, who had succeeded Hose as chief of naval staff at the beginning of 1934, "naval vessels are essential to make use of their information. No belligerent would consider air forces alone as capable of providing the measure of supervision that international law requires of a neutral."[65] Mackenzie King visited Roosevelt again in February 1937, at which time the need for Canada to develop her defences on the west coast was discussed in "a nice way."

Concern about American attitudes was central to Mackenzie King's acceptance of the necessity for rearmament, and also firmed up Canadian policy with respect to collective imperial defence. In Colonel Pope's

March 1937 "Memorandum on ... the Higher Direction of National Defence," he noted that "even such a local problem as ... the maintenance of our neutrality in [the] event of war between the United States and Japan must be of Imperial as well as Canadian concern, because of the fact that failure on our part might involve the Empire in war."[66] Mackenzie King, visiting Neville Chamberlain in May after the latter's appointment as Britain's prime minister, urged the necessity of bridging the gap between Britain and the United States.

Roosevelt heated the story by making a visit to Victoria, BC, on 30 September 1937, but had to be careful out of concern for the negative reaction among the American public to any sort of defence "alliance" with a British country. When on 12 December Japanese forces attacked and sank the U.S. gunboat *Panay* in the Yangtze river, Roosevelt accepted a British invitation to begin staff talks in London, with Captain Royal E. Ingersoll, USN arriving there at the end of December. But this did not mean that American isolationism had been overcome. It was decided that it would be easier for Canadian officers to visit Washington unrecognized than for Americans to come to Ottawa. When Nelles and Major-General E.C. Ashton did so they were astonished by an offer by General Malin Craig, chief of staff of the U.S. Army, to take over the defence of British Columbia. It was a relief to the Canadians to find that Admiral Daniel Leahy, U.S. Chief of Naval Operations, was more interested in discussing a possible naval campaign against Japan and that he regarded British Columbia waters to be of minor significance. On their return to Ottawa Nelles and Ashton advised Mackenzie King to avoid extensive contact with the Americans, as it would only lead to commitments. A Joint Staff plan released in January 1938, concerned about "possible action by the United States actually to occupy Canadian territory or territorial waters with sea, land or air forces," warned: "Unless the United States is confident that Canada's arrangements to protect her neutrality are such as to make it impossible for the Japanese to make use of Canadian territorial waters and air in ways useful to the prosecution of the Japanese plans, there is danger that they maybe impelled to take such action." To forestall this danger, it was understood to be "important openly to institute all measures indicative of the national will to maintain neutrality, immediately on the outbreak of war." The task would require "the destroyer sub-division on the East Coast be transferred for duty on the West Coast," along with five minesweepers, four of which were still under construction, and an auxiliary flotilla.[67]

It is generally regarded that the Rubicon moment in Canadian-American defence relations occurred in August 1938. In a speech at Queen's University in Kingston, Ontario, Roosevelt declared that the United States would not "stand idly by if domination of Canadian soil is threatened by any other empire," and Mackenzie King responded two days later with an undertaking to prevent the United States being threatened from Canadian territory. At the time, however, this embrace was not without reservations on both sides. On a trip to the Caribbean with Skelton in October 1938 following Neville Chamberlain's Munich capitulation, Mackenzie King noted in his diary: "I do not like to be dependent on the US; change of leaders there might lead to a vassalage so far as our Dominion was concerned. There was more real freedom in the British Commonwealth of Nations, and a richer inheritance. This I truly believe. We have all the freedom we want, and are strengthened by being part of a great whole, with kindred aims, ideals and institutions."[68] The most immediate consequence of the growing American interest in Canadian defence was to increase Mackenzie King's willingness to develop Canada's ability to support Britain, even to the extent of beginning to prepare for the dispatch of a four-division expeditionary force overseas.

❖ ❖ ❖

The El Salvador episode was virtually unique for the infant Royal Canadian Navy. In light of the part the Canadian navy was to play in the 1990s enforcing United Nations sanctions, Canada's disavowal of sanctions against Italy at the time of the 1935 Ethiopian (Abyssinian) crisis is significant. The Italian sanctions were not being enforced by naval forces, because of American hostility to naval interference with trade and British concern that naval enforcement would unduly expose her to Italian resentment, but the episode is important to the story of naval strategy.

Canada's commitment to the League was limited to the original idea that it should defuse international conflict simply by arbitration, and if necessary by naming and shaming transgressors. When it was discovered that something more was required, Mackenzie King was not the one to provide it. In 1924 Senator Raoul Dandurand, in a famous address to the League of Nations, had asserted that Canadians "lived in a fireproof house, far from inflammable materials."[69] Eleven years later, the newly re-elected Mackenzie King repudiated the motion made by Canada's representative at the League, Dr Walter A. Riddell, that the economic sanctions imposed on Italy should be made effective by the inclusion of oil in the list of prohibited trade. The "Canadian Amendment" had been greeted by widespread approval, but Italy responded with a threat that "oil sanctions mean war." Mackenzie King's avoidance of commitment contributed significantly to the failure of the League to call Mussolini's bluff.[70]

In his diary, Mackenzie King remarked in September 1936 that he really believed this was the strongest argument against sanctions: "I doubt if they will restrain an aggressor but they may lead to a war which might [not] be localized, becoming a world conflict." Having dined with the British foreign minister, Anthony Eden, he also concluded that "both [Howard] Ferguson [high commissioner in London until 1935] and Riddell were seeking to meet the wishes of the British Government in forcing along sanctions, oil sanctions included." Nineteen months later, when reading a warning telegram from London that German ambitions in Czechoslovakia could lead to war, Mackenzie King expressed the hope that some secret deal had been made with Hitler, and sadly noted his belief that "the League has been the sinister influence in the whole affair. I have felt more real concern since reading these despatches than I have at any time, thus far, and have felt oppressed by the reading of them today."[71]

It was to Lester Pearson, a junior External Affairs officer who two decades later was to put Canada so prominently on the world stage, that the task of extricating Canada from the Ethiopian commitment was given. Peter Gellman writes: "Politics is an art often guided by a wish to avoid the repetition of past mistakes. The Ethiopian débâcle became such an error for Pearson." At the time, Pearson concluded that the League was a flawed structure that tended to globalize local conflicts without adequate means to address them, but he recognized in a memorandum that "Canada cannot occupy her rightful place in international society so long as security is dependent on American benevolence. If we are to escape from permanent inferiority our security must be found in an organization to which we ourselves contribute and in which we have a voice in control."[72]

✦ ✦ ✦

The 1935 Ethiopian (Abyssinian) crisis had called attention to the limitations of the Royal Navy's capabilities. A Naval Service of Canada study paper in August 1936 observed that "in case of emergency in European or Far Eastern waters we must expect and be prepared for a concentration of British naval forces near the seat of the trouble, leaving the trade routes for the time relatively undefended." The official RCN history, however, believes that increased appropriations "had less to do with the Abyssinian crisis than with an improving Canadian economy," and that "naval planning had more to do with the relationship between the United States and Japan than with events in Africa."[73] In August 1936 the minister of national defence, Ian Mackenzie, called at the Admiralty and indicated that the Canadian government wanted a six-destroyer navy, and were interested in minesweepers.[74] The British were willing to transfer two ships of the same class as *Skeena* and *Saguenay*, at a favourable price. The additional ships, which were named *Fraser* and *St Laurent*, would meet the need for four destroyers to patrol British Columbian coastal waters. The defence budget for 1935/36 was $16.2 million of the deflated post-depression currency, a sum not very different in purchasing power from the 1930 budget. Opposition to rearmament was strong in Quebec, but the navy was more easily justified as a necessary local defence and could be pushed ahead. Mackenzie King wanted to double the defence budget for 1939/40 from $35 million to $70 million, but the Cabinet would not agree to more than $60 million.[75]

By the outbreak of war in 1939 the six destroyers were in the Canadian fleet, with a seventh, which would have been a destroyer leader with accommodation for an afloat tactical staff, about to be transferred from the Royal Navy.[76] Admiral Lancelot Holland RN, who was later killed when commanding HMS *Hood* and HMS *Prince of Wales* in action with the German battleship *Bismarck*, assured Mackenzie King in December 1939 that "Canada had been wise in the purchases she had made. She had got the right kind of ships (destroyers) for the purpose of our coasts, and got the best value for her money."[77] The Royal Canadian Air Force established Eastern Air Command to support the naval defence of the east coast. In strategic terms this was a development of Canada's naval potential, even if organizationally the naval air units were not part of the navy. Mackenzie King, however, rejected a plan by Vickers Shipbuilding for a co-operative sloop and destroyer construction project at Montreal. Nelles urged that educational orders be placed at

Canadian yards so that they could develop the necessary specialist skills, but Mackenzie King refused.[78]

This small force provided a nucleus of training and experience that was to make possible the vast expansion of the Royal Canadian Navy in 1939. The embryo navy, however, had had virtually no impact on international events during the 1920s and 1930s, save in the negative sense that its weakness had to be considered by British statesmen when confronting threats from Italy, Germany, and Japan. The 100 percent increase in Canada's naval budget in 1936 did something to reawaken interest in the Canadian navy at the Admiralty, but could not affect to any important extent the correlation of strategic forces. Nor could Canada's destroyer fleet do much to deal with the level of threat posed by German armoured surface ships, battle cruisers, and pocket battleships armed with 11-inch guns. When his policy was attacked in the Commons Committee of Supply, Ian Mackenzie was only able to reply that he was implementing the advice he had received from the chief of naval staff. His performance was so weak that on 19 September 1939 Mackenzie King replaced him with Norman Rogers.[79]

✦ ✦ ✦

Clearly the compromise between constitutional and strategic considerations was imperfect, yet it had an inherent political strength and realism. It enabled the empire and the British Commonwealth to survive two world wars. Later, following the Second World War, it provided a model for the development of the multi-lateral North Atlantic Treaty Organization for collective defence.[80] Norman Hillmer writes that "the Anglo-Canadian 'alliance' was not based on specific commitments to defined ends; it held its vitality through shared allegiances, shared ideals, customs, and institutions, a shared sense of community in a British world."[81] From the perspective of internationalism, the virtue of the British system was that it was structurally strong enough that the Empire and Commonwealth could coalesce into an effective force for legitimate defensive purposes but would unlikely act together for more aggressive ends. And for Canada, the loose nature of the structure of collective Imperial naval defence was important as facilitating the management of Canadian-American relations.

The weakness of the compromise was that the Commonwealth found it difficult to mobilize coherent strength for the purpose of deterrence.

This was to be a significant problem, with respect both to Britain's confrontation with Germany and to the antipodean dominions' concerns about Japan. As the Imperial chiefs of staff put it in October 1930, "the extent of co-operation by the Dominion forces, even where it is assumed that the latter would be co-operating, cannot be gauged, and the Dominion forces have to be regarded largely as an extra asset not to be taken into account."[82] With the rise of the Nazi party in Germany, the Canadian policy of limited commitment and limited effort became a positive danger to Canadian interests.

The visit to Canada in 1936 by Sir Maurice Hankey, secretary to the British Cabinet and to the Committee of Imperial Defence, convinced him that the Canadian government could be depended upon. Nevertheless, at the 1937 Imperial Conference Mackenzie King resolutely defeated British efforts to prepare a common military response to the aggressors. The Canadian government was motivated for the first time to pursue a common foreign policy, but the policy sought was one of appeasement. Writing in 1937 when he was still national secretary of the Canadian Institute of International Affairs and a year before he joined the Department of External Affairs, Escott Reid said: "[the] main purpose of this 'back seat' policy is to give Canada as much freedom of action as possible in the event of war by trying to ensure that Canada does not in advance, by her actions at Geneva or elsewhere, become involved in a 'moral' obligation to send armed forces overseas to participate in war or in the application of other forms of force. She might well become involved in a 'moral' obligation if her representatives at Geneva, London, or elsewhere were responsible for initiating a policy, which, when adopted by other nations, led to war."[83] Even in 1938–39, the Admiralty did not know how much it could count on from Canada. In May 1938 Hankey wrote to Sir Edward Harding, the permanent under-secretary of state for dominion affairs: "It would be clearly disastrous if we laid our plans on the assumption that we could count upon Canada, and then when the day comes we found that we had been building on false premises."[84]

Hankey advised against even talking about what to do if the dominions chose to keep out of a war; the prospect was too awful, and thinking about it too demoralizing. Harding warned Sir Francis Floud, the British high commissioner in Ottawa: "it is regarded as most important that no indication should be given to the Canadian government that the possibility of their standing aside in an emergency is being seriously considered here." Floud replied that Mackenzie King was determined "to keep his eye on what he considers to be the main objective, *viz* the preservation of Canada's unity, which he believed required his refusing any commitment to Imperial defence until, in the event of war, the matter could be decided in 'Parliament as the interpreter of the people's wishes.'" This was "unsatisfactory," but there was nothing to be done about it. He added, however, that Mackenzie King was sympathetic to the policy of the British government. "All I myself really fear," Floud continued, "is a period of hesitancy, and I am afraid that we cannot necessarily count on Canada being in with us from the very beginning."[85]

Concern about political attitudes in the dominions was a factor in Britain's weak policy in the Munich crisis. However, the Canadian government did its best to support the needs of collective defence during the crisis. There was some confusion at Canadian Naval Service Headquarters because the warning telegram sent by the Admiralty had not been preceded by one from the dominions secretary, but informally the Canadian navy moved quickly to carry out the Admiralty's prepared plans.[86] Shortly after the dénouement, Mackenzie King dined with the governor of Bermuda, Lieutenant General Reginald Heldyard, and the Royal Navy commander-in-chief of the American and West Indies station. Vice-Admiral Sir Sidney Meyrick reported that Mackenzie King "fully agreed" that the Canadian navy should have pre-arranged war stations, and that they could not protect Canadian interests by staying in harbour.[87] Admiralty thinking about Canada's reliability was transformed by the crisis, but the Dominions Office continued to be concerned.[88]

German occupation of the rump of Czechoslovakia in March 1939 finally put an end to Britain's attempt to appease the Nazi appetite and also firmed up Roosevelt's efforts to find ways of providing practical support for the democracies. Despite opposition even among White House aids, the president arranged for the staff talks with Britain to continue, and obtained British agreement to American use of British island bases stretching from Trinidad to Bermuda for American warships patrolling the Atlantic seaboard. Mackenzie King was more guarded about American use of Halifax, and he admitted in his diary to "feeling an almost profound disgust" when he heard Roosevelt's neutralist broadcast following the British and French declaration of war against Germany. But Roosevelt did obtain from the Pan-American Union an agreement to the formal establishment of a neutrality zone up to a thousand miles wide along the Atlantic seaboard, incorporating the

Canadian seaboard despite the fact that Canada was not a neutral in the war, and succeeded in amending American neutrality legislation so that arms could be sold to the democracies An American opinion poll in January 1940 indicated that nearly three-quarters of Americans favoured defending Canada.[89] Circumstances were forcing Canada closer to the United States, but Mackenzie King's cautious attitude expressed during his 1938 Caribbean cruise with Skelton was not lightly cast aside.

3

LESSONS OF THE SECOND WORLD WAR

The Second World War made it evident to many in Ottawa that the compromise between autonomy and strategic effectiveness would have to be recast, with greater emphasis on the latter part of the equation. The Canadian government had not in fact gained much ability to stand aside from British foreign policy, and had forfeited any ability to influence it. In a reprise of imperial relations in the opening years of the First World War, when Britain made its defence commitment to Poland on 31 March 1939, the dominions were not consulted. The new dominions secretary, Sir Thomas Inskip, explained, in terms Escott Reid would have understood, that London believed that dominion leaders "would not have wished that the United Kingdom should invite them to share responsibility for the decision." In May 1939 O.D. Skelton, the under-secretary of state for external affairs, noted caustically: "The first casualty of this war has been Canada's claim to control over her own destiny. If war comes to Poland and we take part, that war comes as a consequence of commitments made by the Government of Great Britain, about which we are not in one iota consulted, and about which we were not given the slightest inkling of information in advance." Skelton's complaint, however, was shallow. Canadian independence was less threatened by British attitudes than by the strategic realities of an interdependent world.

Jack Granatstein writes that Mackenzie King's careful public statements, and careful diplomacy, were part of an effort to steer British foreign policy away from conflict, and to bring Britain and the United States together, and "his actions, particularly between 1937 and 1939, indicate his sure grasp of the public mood and his recognition that public opinion cannot be wished into existence simply because one course of action or another is 'right.'"[1] His capacity to control the accelerating events in Europe was exceedingly limited, but in September 1939 the House of Commons was free to decide what should be Canada's response to Britain's declaration of war on Germany, and responded with a unity which, although it might have been even more valuable at the time of Munich, was nonetheless of very great significance for the outcome of the war. In presenting his case for a declaration of war in September 1939, Mackenzie King made clear his belief that Canada could not realistically hope to isolate herself from events in Europe. If Hitler were "able to crush the peoples of Europe," he asked, "what is going to become of the doctrine of isolation of this North American continent? If Britain goes down, if France goes down, the whole business of isolation will prove to have been a mere myth."[2] Lester Pearson, then a junior officer in the High Commission in London, thought the vote in parliament had been clear from the time of King George VI and Queen Elizabeth's visit to Canada in May and June: "all this talk of Canadian isolation and neutrality is academic eye-wash."[3] A week before the declaration of war, the Canadian navy had been ordered to combat readiness.

❖ ❖ ❖

The exponential growth of the Canadian navy during the war was a remarkable achievement. During hostilities 70 frigates, 123 corvettes, 336 minesweepers and other light craft were built in Canada, and Canadian yards completed for service 19 escort aircraft carriers. Shipyards had to be converted to naval construction, designs had to be acquired from Britain, and production lines started. This represented a fifty-fold increase in strength, two and a half times that undertaken by the Royal Navy and the U.S. Navy. It called for the full-time attention of a minister, and when Norman Rogers was killed in an air crash, Mackenzie King divided the Defence portfolio. He persuaded the premier of Nova Scotia, Angus L. Macdonald, to come to Ottawa as minister of national defence for Naval Services, where he was sworn in on 12 July 1940.

Canadian industry was not geared to complex production, and in the beginning technical liaison with the British defence industry was poor.[4] A British Admiralty Technical Mission was established in Ottawa in July 1940 to facilitate the transfer of technical information and the management of procurement. To fill the gap before the ships could be ready for service, yachts were purchased in the United States, smuggled across the border and converted into escorts. Heavily gunned "Tribal" class destroyers were also built for Canada in Britain, and others in Canada.

HMCS *Peterborough* (K 342), *Flower* class corvette built at Kingston Shipbuilding Co. 1942–44. After decommissioning in 1945, she was sold to the Dominican Republic in 1947 and served as *Gerardo Jansen* until 1972. DND CN-3621

The latter took so long to complete that the war was over before they could enter service, but as they had been put into the navy budget partly to ensure its institutional survival in the lean years that would follow the war, their completion was important in the shadow world of defence politics.[5] The fleet almost immediately outgrew pre-war training establishments, and officers and men had to be sent to sea with little more than basic training. By the end of the war in 1945 the navy numbered nearly 100,000 men and women and 365 ships, and at its peak in late 1943 RCAF Eastern Air Command had eleven squadrons in its maritime role, four in maritime strike roles and seven in anti-submarine, as well as six fighter squadrons and one army co-operation training squadron.[6]

On 19 October 1940 Mackenzie King reviewed the fleet at Halifax as the guest of Commodore George C. Jones and was most impressed: "The day began with a review of the naval forces and witnessing morning services of the sailors, a sight that was truly inspiring when one realized these were all members of our own Canadian navy. Over a couple of thousand on parade, some seven thousand in all about Halifax. Took the salute." He also inspected HMC destroyers *Restigouche* and *Assiniboine*. He was quite humbled by the experience, writing that he "did not feel at all at ease in this particular job, because of the presence of reporters and the feeling of the actions of the men themselves, daily sacrifices as told in the life they lead at sea and what they are called upon to endure in battle. It is all so much greater than anything one can do oneself that words seemed out of place." He also had mixed feelings about Commodore Jones: "a very pleasant fellow, but [someone] I can see might be exceedingly disagreeable. Much more of a disciplinarian than is really necessary. During the day I saw several evidences of his quick temper which discloses anything but a fine nature." Two weeks later he attended a memorial service in Ottawa for the sailors who had drowned in *Margaree*, which had sunk following a collision while escorting a convoy. "One feels Canada growing into a nation with the navy coming to take the part it is. It was the first really important service associated with those who have lost their lives in the Canadian Navy at a time of war. Such has a historic significance. I confess I feel very deeply for those brave men and for those who have been bereaved." After listening to Macdonald's first speech in the House of Commons as navy minister, Mackenzie King added: "The foundations of a great navy are being laid. Liberal policy of Ralston's day fully vindicated."[7] Did he ever reconsider the wisdom of his decision in 1922 to reduce the navy to a two-destroyer training squadron?

Strategic direction of the allied war effort was controlled at the outset by the British and French, and later by the British, Americans, and Russians. Mackenzie King made little effort to obtain a voice. His refusal before the war to develop the institutions that might have ensured a voice for Canada in strategic planning left him ill-equipped.[8] Pearson wrote in his diary at the end of April 1940: "there are people in Ottawa who would prefer to be left in ignorance and without influence rather than agree to the setting up of some Imperial machinery which might, in their suspicious minds, start a centralizing development which would continue after the war."[9] Mackenzie King complained about the lack of consultation, but was more concerned about appearances than substance, and found that it was better to avoid situations that emphasized his inability. His complaints tended to be confined to his diary and his Cabinet. Until the last year of the war, his active participation in wartime grand strategy was limited to his insistence on putting local Canadian defence needs high on the order of Canada's own priorities, at least in part for domestic political reasons, while providing firm support for Britain's defence. Only after victory in Europe was assured, and Britain began to prepare to recover her imperial position in Asia, did he make decisions that, through curtailing Canadian commitments, had strategic importance.

When Winston Churchill visited him in Ottawa in January 1931, Mackenzie King had noted in his diary: "It tires me tho' to talk with these young men whose ideal is 'power' – material power – labour a commodity etc etc and [against] prohibition – against peace propaganda – all for powerful navy to hold what we have etc etc. [Norman] Rogers [then minister of labour] is infinitely finer and higher type."[10] In June 1939, with the world teetering on the edge of war, he had pumped King George VI for his views on Churchill, and had noted in his diary that he thought him "one of the most dangerous men I have ever known."[11] On the outbreak of war, however, Churchill had been appointed first lord of the Admiralty, and in May 1940 he succeeded Chamberlain as prime minister following the German assault on France. By then Mackenzie King had already revised his opinion. After hearing Churchill speak on the radio he "became increasingly impressed with his speech, the effectiveness of the language, and the imagery and its moral tone, particularly its interpretation of the significance of the war and its appeal to the moral sense of mankind."[12] It became clear to him that Churchill was an essential force. He had sent Churchill a congratulatory telegram, and was generally content to let him provide strategic direction.

Had he sought to give any direction to the strategic planning of Britain and the United States, Churchill and Roosevelt would have quickly disabused him. Britain needed no guidance from Canada in defending itself, and the United States viewed Canada as a subordinate state. The dominions were allowed no part in the Anglo-American military staff conversations in Washington early in 1941, although the talks were supposedly intended to "determine the best methods by which the armed forces of the United States and the British Commonwealth, with its allies, could defeat Germany and its allies." Britain's representatives were careful to refer to themselves as the United Kingdom delegation, but the Americans simply referred to them as "British."

The ground lost in the 1920s Mackenzie King would not make up in the context of the war. He rejected the British idea of a conference of Commonwealth prime ministers in the summer of 1940, and again in 1941. Robert Borden's prolonged visits to Britain in 1917 and 1918 had had negative political consequences for his administration, and Mackenzie King was careful not to repeat that mistake. He believed it was better to make effective use of telegraph communications for near continuous consultation between governments. But while the use of this means of communication was a major development from the frustrated efforts of Lloyd George's colonial secretary Walter Long to establish such a routine in the First War, and although the correspondence between governments was voluminous, the British record on keeping the dominions informed of critical developments was patchy. A notable gap in the personal communications made by Churchill to dominion prime ministers was his failure to advise them of the Anglo-American decision to invade North Africa, in which operation Canadian naval forces were to be employed.

Colonel C.P. Stacey viewed the impossibility of Canada taking a leading part in collective strategic planning in wartime as unavoidable, despite the vital nature of Canada's military and financial contribution. "The directing authority of a coalition will normally be some sort of committee; and the larger the committee, and the more numerous the interests it has to reconcile within itself, the less effective its leadership is likely to be. It would be poor economy to seek to safeguard national sovereignty at the cost of a sacrifice of military efficiency which may lead to national sovereignty being extinguished totally and permanently by the enemy." For that reason, Churchill firmly rejected the creation of an Imperial War Cabinet: "Some people [think] the way to win the war is to make sure that every Power contributing armed forces and every branch of these armed forces is represented on all the councils … and that everybody is fully consulted before anything is done." But that, he told Parliament on 17 January 1942, "is, in fact, the most sure way to lose a war." As Mackenzie King was not a military man and had no experience directing military campaigns, he would in any case have had little to contribute to allied planning. No one in his Cabinet had any training in the higher direction of war.[13] What Mackenzie King did have to offer was a realistic assessment, as he had noted in his diary after the German assault on France, "that the real place to defend our land is from across the seas." He was amused by the extent to which even Skelton had come to that opinion: the worst possible outcome of the Battle of France would be German insistence on peace terms "so strong that she will come to have the command of the seas as well as the complete domination of Europe."[14] Unfortunately the great powers could not be trusted to act only in the common good, and might not even be aware of the implications of their actions. "In these circumstances," wrote Stacey, "the position of a 'middle power' is bound to be uncomfortable, and its policy is almost certain to be a succession of compromises."

When Churchill suggested that Mackenzie King should be permitted to join the top level "Quadrant" Conference held at Quebec in the summer of 1943, Roosevelt objected. Undisturbed, Mackenzie King noted in his diary: "Churchill and Roosevelt being at Québec, and myself acting as host, will be quite sufficient to make clear that all three are in conference together and will not only satisfy but please the Canadian feeling, and really be helpful to me personally."[15] By the words "make clear" he really meant "appear."

❖ ❖ ❖

Ottawa was more interested, and successful, in establishing its authority over operational control, motivated by a concern to ensure that Canadian forces were used intelligently so as to avoid high casualty rates and futile engagements. At the beginning of hostilities in 1939, operational control of the Canadian fleet was not transferred to the Admiralty as it had been in the First World War. Mackenzie King asked the chief of naval staff, Commodore Nelles, if it would be adequate for the RCN to "co-operate" with the Royal Navy. Nelles pointed out that the RN was providing two eight-inch gun cruisers to protect the east coast from German surface raiders, and needed Canadian destroyers to hunt submarines in the Caribbean: "The case in point is that four destroyers cannot defend our East Coast and focal areas. The Commander-in-Chief has therefore stationed two eight inch cruisers to add to our efforts." Nelles believed that the only realistic course was for the Canadian navy in the Atlantic to be placed under the command of the Royal Navy commander in chief West Indies and North America: "It is most desirable," he wrote to Minister of National Defence Ian Mackenzie, "that we have one Officer and Staff only directing naval operations at sea on the America and West Indies Station. To have more than one person and staff directing operations will cause confusion, delays and will not produce the efficient effort necessary."[16] Mackenzie King would only go so far as to amend the order in council to read "co-operate to the fullest extent with Royal Naval Forces."[17] That proved, on the whole, to be a workable rubric as Canadian commanders had all been trained in the Royal Navy and recognized the need for a coherent chain of command.

Canadian naval officers assumed an increasing role in the direction of naval operations in the western Atlantic, managing the needs of naval intelligence, organizing the dispatch of convoys to Britain, and undertaking local defence. But more was soon to be required. In May and June 1940 the German army overran France, and London requested that Canada send all available assistance for the defence of England. The First

Canadian Division had already sailed to England in December and would provide the core of landward defence following the French collapse, and the evacuation of the British army from the French Channel ports, leaving all their heavy equipment behind. Mackenzie King's Cabinet War Committee authorized the dispatch of four destroyers, all that were ready for overseas service, and ten corvettes.[18]

Having arrived in time to assist in the evacuation of the British and part of the French army, these destroyers were then assigned to antisubmarine and trade defence training in preparation for convoy defence in the Western Approaches to Britain. When Churchill negotiated with Roosevelt the exchange of British bases in the West Indies and Bermuda and at Argentia in Newfoundland for fifty old American destroyers, Canada undertook to man six of them, and to take over and man ten corvettes being built for Britain in Canada. With great difficulty the overage destroyers built for more southerly waters, and the still incomplete corvettes, were hurried across the Atlantic where, after further dockyard work that included fitting the main gun armament in the corvettes, entered service in the western approaches to Britain. Commodore Leonard W. Murray, who had been appointed senior officer Halifax force in June 1940, hauled down his pennant, and crossed to Britain to take charge of Canadian naval forces serving there.[19]

These were heavy commitments, and more was to be asked for when the effectiveness of local convoy west of England led in April and May 1941 to the Germans' sending their U-boats west of Iceland. A Newfoundland Escort Force (NEF) was established, based at St John's, Newfoundland. Despite the fact that Newfoundland was under British administration, Canada was asked to take a major part in providing escorts for convoys between Newfoundland and a meeting point southwest of Iceland. Mackenzie King welcomed the arrangement that returned Canadian ships nearer home, where their presence would reduce the political implications of the American naval presence at Argentia.

Mackenzie King also welcomed the return of the destroyers to the western Atlantic because he was concerned about German surface raiders. This was a realistic concern. Canada had already had some experience of the potential of these ships when on 5 November 1940 the British merchant cruiser HMS *Jervis Bay* engaged the German pocket battleship *Admiral Scheer* in defence of a convoy, and was sunk. *Jervis Bay* had been refitted for war service at Saint John, New Brunswick, and had Canadians serving onboard. The NEF, however, was not intended to provide protection against surface raiders, and Canada's destroyers only had limited abilities to engage one if they did come into contact. Nelles's advice on 26 February 1941 had been that "at no time would Canada have been in a position to deal with a pocket battleship, even had we retained all our naval forces [in Canadian waters]." Commander Kenneth Hansen regards this admission as an indictment of the interwar policy of building a navy around destroyers, but the context for Nelles's force planning had been the effective integration of the Royal navies of Britain and Canada to meet a general threat. A fleet unit built around a battle cruiser or heavy cruisers had never been a political possibility.[20]

Mackenzie King welcomed the return of Canadian ships to the western Atlantic, but he was less pleased by the initiative shown by the naval minister, Angus Macdonald, and the Navy Board in wishing to take "the whole command of the Battle of the Atlantic on this side." He protested that such a possibility was "far beyond its capacity," and that neither Britain nor the United States would agree. Having found that the Americans actively urged the measure, however, he gave his consent at the Cabinet War Committee meeting on 24 June. It served national interests for the Canadian navy to be established in Newfoundland, and the Canadian government undertook to oversee the construction of the base at St John's, and pay the cost of its administration and maintenance.[21] The eighteen Canadian warships that by then were serving in British waters were transferred to the NEF along with ten new corvettes, and by December 1941 the number of Canadian ships operating out of St John's had reached seventy.

The NEF was a Royal Navy formation, but Murray, a Canadian, was put in command and in December promoted to Rear Admiral. Many of the staff positions at St John's were filled by Canadians. The Admiralty directed the Commander in Chief Western Approaches, located at Liverpool in England, to communicate directly with Murray. This ensured the effective use of U-boat intelligence and management of escort resources, but to ensure that the British would not drain Canadian coastal waters of warships, the Canadian escort groups at St John's were assigned to a Canadian Newfoundland Command separate from the Canadian Atlantic Coast Command.[22]

The British were unhappy with this fragmentation of command in the western Atlantic, but before they were able to persuade Canada to relinquish local control the United States began its tardy transformation from a benevolent but skeptical neutral into an ally. In August 1941 Churchill and Roosevelt met at Argentia and agreed that the U.S. Navy would undertake to escort convoys to Iceland. This should have increased the resources available, but the British needed to redeploy more escorts to meet a growing U-boat threat on the Gibraltar run. Communication between the Admiralty and the U.S. Atlantic fleet commander, the anglophobic Admiral Ernest J. King, were difficult; the Americans were reluctant at first to communicate at all with the Canadian Naval Services Headquarters. They refused to put any of their ships under the command of foreign officers, and the price of their participation was that the NEF was placed under the command of the U.S. Atlantic Fleet, Task Force 4, later renamed 24, with Western Approaches Command providing guidance. Command was assumed by Rear Admiral A. LeR. Bristol Jr, USN, with instructions to leave to Canadian authorities the question of what ships were available, and only to assert "coordinating supervision of the operations of Canadian escort units." Colonel Stacey observed that "the quiet acceptance" by the Canadian Cabinet of the formal transfer of the largest part of the Canadian navy to American command was "noteworthy."[23]

Without consulting the British, Mackenzie King asked the Canadian navy to assume responsibility for the escort of the slow convoys from Sydney, Nova Scotia, while the U.S. Navy provided escort for the fast convoys from Halifax. Misunderstanding about the number of Canadian ships that could be continuously available for service was never cleared up, and the Canadians found themselves undertaking the most difficult of the escort operations with inadequate forces, under the command of an American admiral with no practical experience of trade defence.[24]

When the Japanese attacked the U.S. Pacific Fleet at Pearl Harbor in December 1941, Germany declared war against the United States, and Admiral Karl Dönitz, commanding German submarines, ordered U-boats to the American seaboard, where they found shipping virtually undefended. The U.S. Navy was reluctant to tie up resources in coastal convoys and a heavy toll was taken of ships that had been escorted across the Atlantic and then sailed independently along the American coast. The U-boats were also sent into action close to the Canadian coast, but because the Canadian navy ran coastal convoys, often escorted only by a single ship, they suffered half the rate of sinkings. To meet the crisis off the U.S. seaboard and in the Pacific, the Americans withdrew most of their ships from the battle in the western Atlantic, and diverted destroyers to escorting troop convoys to Britain.[25] These circumstances made the chain of command that placed the bulk of the Canadian navy under the orders of the U.S. Atlantic Fleet even less defensible.

✦✦✦

This reality, and Canada's cautious defence policy during the interwar years, had nearly disastrous technical consequences. Like the Royal Navy, the Royal Canadian Navy had paid little attention to anti-submarine warfare in the interwar period. The corvettes ordered in 1939, intended for coastal escort but pressed into service as ocean escorts, lacked gyro compasses and high frequency radio direction finders and were fitted with an obsolescent sonar; and when radar was retrofitted, it was a primitive model that could not provide all-round surveillance and was badly affected by wave clutter. When German U-boats were fitted with radar detectors, they were able to detect the metric transmissions from these early sets, but not those from the more effective centimetric sets that were brought more rapidly into service by the Royal Navy. Because of these and other equipment shortcomings, Canadian escort groups lacked the tactical intelligence necessary for planning defensive action against U-boat attacks. When in December 1941 seven Canadian corvettes from the Newfoundland Escort Force crossed the Atlantic, the Royal Navy found them so defective that they were given two months' structural work and fitting in British yards before being sent for work-ups at the Tobermory anti-submarine school. The Canadian navy did not receive the first of the twin-engined frigates that succeeded the corvettes until the summer of 1943.[26]

The fall of France and the subsequent German acquisition of the western French harbours had shattered the basis of the Royal Navy's threat assessment. Had the Canadians not undertaken to supply the numbers required without waiting to perfect equipment and training, it might not have been possible to run escorted convoys right across the Atlantic. Had the U.S. Navy in 1941 released more destroyers for escort work, the crisis might have been avoided. As it was, in the winter of 1942–43 the shortage of worked-up escorts, and the limitations on their equipment, made worse by the failure of overworked staff officers at St John's to provide effective after-action analysis, resulted in near collapse. In October 1942 seventeen Canadian corvettes were detached to the Mediterranean to escort the transports for Operation *Torch*, in which British and American forces occupied North Africa. Mackenzie King was impressed: "It is an amazing thing for Canada having a navy, some of whose ships are fighting in the Mediterranean."[27] To do so, however, traffic in the Gulf of St Lawrence had to be suspended because there were no resources for dealing with U-boat attacks, and the five corvettes

HMCS *Chebogue* (K 317), a *River* class frigate. DND E-3045

serving on the Pacific coast had to be withdrawn. Any reserve that might have been available to reinforce escorts in the North Atlantic, or make possible more effective training, was lost. The Canadian fleet was reduced to the necessity of sending on operations ships fresh from dockyard, without work-ups, and turning ships around without adequate rest – a sacrifice that enabled the British and American navies to run more realistic maintenance, training, and rest cycles, despite their heavy commitment to *Torch*.[28] A more experienced and self-confident Canadian navy might have avoided the trap.

To naval commanders on both sides of the Atlantic seeking to assess the situation, the scale of the attack was not always clear. When in September 1942 a third of convoy ON 127 was destroyed by U-boats, and the Canadian escort group was found seriously at fault, it was believed it had been attacked by six U-boats, whereas it is now known that it had faced no fewer than thirteen. The criticism may have been unfair, but it cannot be denied that there was a serious problem. In the second half of 1942, the four Canadian escort groups working in the mid-Atlantic amounted to 35 percent of allied forces, but suffered 80 percent of the merchant-ship losses.

"When operations around transatlantic convoys heated up again in the summer of 1942," Marc Milner has observed, "senior RN staff officers complained about the failure of Murray's escorts to adhere to the tenets of the Western Approaches convoy instructions, which admonished escorts to concentrate on defending the convoy first. The idea of

Canadians charging madly about the ocean looking for trouble while their convoys suffered became the dominant theme in postwar British accounts of the Battle of the Atlantic." Murray, Milner adds, "was absolutely correct about NEF laying the foundations of the RCN's reputation in the war. Unfortunately, it was not a good one, and the British pointed directly to Murray and his staff in St John's as the cause."[29]

A U.S. Navy escort commander, Captain H.C. Fitz, reported in October 1942 after a visit to Western Approaches Command Headquarters, that "British naval officers as a class think the Canadians very ineffective. In all the time I was there I did not hear one single word in their favor. When I pointed out the expansion in their Navy and that they had always seemed to be giving their best efforts and were quite keen, they usually said that one of their main objections was that they would not take advice or would not benefit from British experience." In December 1942, shortly after his appointment to Western Approaches Command, Admiral Sir Max Horton complained to the Admiralty that "Canadian escorts were insufficiently trained in the use of their equipment and the handling of their ships both in individual and group tactics."

Churchill himself weighed in on the matter, urging Mackenzie King on 17 December 1942 to agree to an Admiralty proposal that Canadian escort groups be transferred to the shorter Gibraltar run so that they could take advantage "of using the unique training facilities available" in Britain. Macdonald and Nelles expressed their indignation, but Acting-Captain Harry G. DeWolf was placed in charge of managing the issue. At a conference in Washington he bluntly told the British and American officers that the Allied demand for escorts had created the crisis – because the Canadians were "convinced that any ship is better than none," he said, "we have kept [ships] at sea against our better judgment." Nevertheless, he recommended accepting the British proposal.[30]

Canadians tended to put more of the blame on poor equipment and tactical doctrine than on the training problem, and complained that the British were not sending their best destroyers to work in the western Atlantic. The disastrous outcome of the battle for ONS 154 at the end of December, however, forced Naval Services Headquarters (NSHQ) to recognize the need for drastic measures. A badly equipped, and poorly led, Canadian escort group that had been routed outside effective air cover encountered a strong patrol line of U-boats and lost fourteen merchant ships. The official naval history comments that "with the benefit of a longer perspective and access to records from both sides, it can be seen that the efficiency of the escorts was only one factor in a complex equation. Evasive routing; weather; the availability of air cover; the number of U-boats that could actually reach a given convoy; how many that could then concentrate; which groups were defending the slower convoys as they plodded across the air gap; whether individual groups had more than one destroyer to prosecute HF/DF bearings; the size of the convoy relative to the number of escorts; whether the parent navy had a margin of fresh resources when required; tactical leadership; the state of training and equipment of both escorts and submarines; and, finally, luck, were all relevant." Nevertheless, the history also recognized the "tragedy of epic proportions" around ONS 154 as "probably the worst defeat in our navy's history."[31]

For national and political reasons, Mackenzie King insisted that the deployment to the Gibraltar run should only be a temporary measure. He telegraphed London: "It has been our policy to build up Canadian escort forces for the specific purpose of protecting North Atlantic trade convoys in addition to our coastal communications. Public interest in the Canadian Navy is centered on the part it has taken in this task, which is without question one of the highest and enduring priority upon which the outcome of the war depends. We are satisfied that the Canadian Navy can serve no higher purpose than to continue to share this task, which we have come to look upon as a natural responsibility for Canada and one which geographically and strategically we are well placed to undertake."[32] The political significance of employing Canadian naval forces in operations based on Canadian and Newfoundland harbours, and close to Canadian shores where Canadians were witnesses to the ravages of German U-boats, was unspoken – but all-important.

The redeployment lasted only six to ten weeks, and by March–April 1943 the Canadian navy was back in the North Atlantic. During that period, the disasters that the Royal Navy had itself suffered put the Canadian situation more in perspective. In December British cryptography re-established its ability to read German U-boat traffic, which it had lost in February. The combined effects of improved signals intelligence, the redeployment of RN destroyers to the Atlantic from the arctic convoys to Russia that had been suspended, Ottawa's request for a few experienced senior RN officers to command two destroyers entering service stripped down for anti-submarine operations, the formation of five support groups with two British and one American escort carrier to reinforce convoys under attack, the commitment of very long range Liberator aircraft to convoy defence, and reorganization of allied command structure, rapidly mastered the threat from U-boat wolf-packs.

❖ ❖ ❖

At the same time as Ottawa indicated its acceptance of the British offer, it had made its case for Canada taking full control of all escort operations in the Western Atlantic. Captain Horatio Nelson Lay, director of the Operations Division of NSHQ and a nephew of the prime minister, drafted a memorandum stressing the value of Canada's seeking full command authority. On a Canadian initiative an Atlantic Convoy Conference was held in March 1943, at which it was decided that the Canadian navy should assume operational control of escort forces in the Western Atlantic. For the first time RCAF Eastern Air Command was placed under the naval commander, and the two Canadian Atlantic commands, Newfoundland Escort Force and Atlantic Coastal Command, were amalgamated. Murray was appointed commander-in-chief, Canadian North-West Atlantic, and thus became the only Canadian in either world war to command a theatre of operations.

The time was right. Churchill had formed an Anti-U-boat Warfare Committee that had recommended unified command, and U.S. Admiral King came to regard simplification of command structure in the North Atlantic as necessary. He was skeptical about Murray's ability to assume command, but Murray reminded the Americans that they had learned about convoy escort from Canadians, who could safely be left to get on with the job. Once Mackenzie King was convinced that Ottawa could manage the needs of naval intelligence, he gave his consent. The upshot was that the two Royal Navies established the closest possible degree of co-operation, even to the extent that NSHQ became a recipient of decrypts of U-boat signals upon which it could act without waiting for recommendations from Western Approaches Command.[33] In the longer history of the Canadian navy, this command reorganization was to be of very great importance. Unfortunately for Murray, his arrival in Halifax coincided with a German U-boat incursion into the Gulf of St Lawrence, which could only be met by closing it to shipping, with powerful political consequences in Ottawa.

❖ ❖ ❖

Although the Canadian escort groups had returned to service in the North Atlantic, they continued to be poorly equipped, partly on account of difficulties in completing the new frigates under construction in inexperienced St Lawrence shipyards. Retrofitting the new anti-submarine mortar, "Hedgehog," in Canadian corvettes proved to be very difficult because their structures had not been altered from the 1939 short foredeck design, their sonar was antiquated, and their wiring would need to be replaced. The repair facilities on Canada's east coast were so inadequate that only a few ships could be proceeded with at a time. The slow progress in modernization was important because, once the early need for quantities of escorts had been met, advances in German submarine design were elevating the importance of quality in allied anti-submarine forces.

"A small and vocal fringe element of seagoing RCNVR officers" at St John's and Londonderry, where Canadian escorts waited for return convoys, were convinced that their complaints about inadequate and outdated equipment were not being responded to at NDHQ, despite private visits by Royal Canadian Navy Volunteer Reserve (RCNVR) officers to the navy minister. The fact that Macdonald was willing to meet with the reserve officers is indicative of how politicized Ottawa's administration continued to be. He had been sensitized to the possible implications of weakness in the administration of the Navy because of an earlier episode involving an RCNVR commander, Andrew Dyas MacLean, who had been commander of the elitist York reserve division before the war and was well connected to the political opposition. MacLean had attempted to bully his superiors both in the Royal Navy, which sent him back to Canada, and in the Canadian navy, and was eventually hustled into resigning in October 1942. But he had continued to pressure Macdonald. In the first week of February 1943 he had published in *Boating Magazine*, of which he was editor, a highly charged article on the supposed prejudice against reserve officers. Macdonald weathered the political storm this caused, but in Richard Mayne's opinion the experience had weakened his trust in the naval leadership.[34]

Out of concern that reserve officer grumbling could trigger another political storm, Lieutenant Commander William Strange, assistant director of naval information at NSHQ, was sent on a fact-finding mission in July 1943 from Newfoundland to Londonderry onboard a Royal Navy ship commanded by Commander Peter Gretton, RN. Responding to Strange's prompting, the latter described the predicament of Canadian escort commanders, and later introduced Strange to Commodore G.W.G. Simpson, RN, Commodore (Destroyers) at Western Approaches command. Simpson and other British and Canadian naval officers insisted on briefing Strange despite his being outside the chain of command, and Strange later conveyed his story to John J. Connolly,

Macdonald's executive assistant. Connolly then made a voyage of his own, to St John's, Londonderry, and London. He confirmed Strange's account, and a Canadian Technical Liaison Group was set up in the United Kingdom to facilitate the modernization of the Canadian fleet.[35]

Fearing that he might be held politically accountable for the equipment problem, Macdonald on 14 January 1944 dismissed Nelles, by then a vice-admiral, as chief of naval staff. This was an injustice. The measures necessary to meet the equipment problem had already been taken. According to Richard Mayne, Nelles fell victim to the preferential consideration that Canadian politicians still allowed the socially connected, to the weakness of the navy minister, and to the ambition of Nelles's successor, Rear Admiral Jones. "Nelles's integrity sealed his fate. It guaranteed that he would be offered as a sacrificial lamb to protect Macdonald's reputation."[36] Nelles's dismissal was softened by the creation of a commission for him as senior Canadian flag officer (overseas) with responsibility for the Canadian navy's growing participation in the war in the eastern Atlantic. Jones was a much tougher man, who ensured that the means employed to bring Nelles down would not be employed against himself.

The problems that the Canadian escort groups faced certainly were not limited to the slow delivery of state-of-the-art equipment, or even to the pace of operations preventing proper training. Doug McLean characterizes the effort in the latter half of the war to apply eclectically very different British and American anti-submarine doctrines as forcing "the RCN overnight into adolescence." As the official Canadian naval history puts it, RCN escort commanders were put "in the unfortunate position of having to please two masters ... who wanted to fight the same battle differently." The British, because of their total dependence on the Atlantic lifeline, never abandoned their guiding principle that convoy operations must emphasize the safe and timely arrival of cargoes, while the Americans retained the superficially more aggressive focus on the destruction of U-boats. When in 1944 the RCN had to deal with attacks in the shallow and thermally complex waters of the Gulf of St Lawrence made by U-boats equipped with schnorkel tubes that permitted the use of diesel engines while submerged, it had to find a way of making effective use of sometimes contradictory advice, and without training arrangements that were in any way adequate. "The absorption of innovations introduced by allies became a matter of selective choice and subsequent adaptation, an infinitely greater challenge than simple imitation."[37]

✦ ✦ ✦

The turning point in the Battle of the Atlantic was in early May 1943 when the British escort of convoy ONS 5 commanded by Peter Gretton, and its air support, destroyed five U-boats of an attacking force of forty, twenty-eight of which had made sighting reports, badly damaged four others, and engaged a further four, for a loss of thirteen merchant ships. It became evident that the U-boat commanders were becoming less confident and were holding back from aggressive attack.[38] The Canadians also had their successes. Gimblett writes that in the pursuit and destruction of U-774 in March 1944 "over a period of thirty hours, and a distance of eighty miles," the RCN showed that it had come of age. U-774 endured twenty-three depth-charge attacks by two Canadian destroyers, a frigate, two corvettes and an RN destroyer, before being forced to the surface, and destroyed. "A sustained operation of this duration against an invisible enemy reflects teamwork of the highest order. Command and control, suggesting the unifying will of an individual, are not sufficient. It requires the co-operation and coordination of a 'band of brothers.' Effective detection devices would have guaranteed an early kill; unlimited weapons would have permitted saturation assault. Neither was available in those circumstances. Only co-ordination between hunters, and maintenance of pressure, could have permitted multiple attacks and continuous tracking to a kill. It was experience and dedication, aided by devices and weapons that achieved the result."[39]

In retrospect it can be seen that the German concept of the "tonnage war" was too ambitious. By setting as their operational goal the destruction of allied shipping wherever it could be most easy accomplished, the Germans had in effect enabled the British to use general cargo as cover for military logistics, sacrificing the needs of the general public to those of the military. As early as September 1942 Dönitz's naval staff had suggested that it might be impossible to sink the entire output of allied shipbuilding yards, and that the U-boats should change their strategy to a "supply war" against particular high-value cargoes. Probably the most valuable strategy would have been the classic one of attack on troop ships. The German navy, however, was ill-equipped for that purpose and Dönitz never abandoned his faith in the tonnage war.[40]

In the last two years of the war, the Germans continued the U-boat campaign at a reduced level, as a defensive measure that reduced the rate of allied tonnage growth, and hence effected tonnage limitations upon Anglo-American operations. The threat of attack required the allies to continue to use convoy which, in all respects except those of defence, is inefficient use of tonnage. Defence of convoy continued to tie up Allied warships and aircraft that might otherwise have been a greater threat to German interests, and required the continued construction of defensive types of warships using materials that might otherwise have been available for offensive purposes. Hitler made clear his policy of containment in a statement to Dönitz on 31 May 1943: "There can be no talk of a let-up in submarine warfare. The Atlantic is my first line of defence in the West, and even if I have to fight a defensive battle, that is preferable to waiting to defend myself on the coasts of Europe. The enemy forces tied up by our submarine warfare are tremendous, even though the actual losses inflicted by us are no longer great. I cannot afford to release these forces by discontinuing submarine warfare."[41] New German technologies, such as the homing torpedo, and the schnorkel, helped to keep the battle going.

The development at the end of the war of type XXI and XXIII U-boats with greatly increased underwater endurance and mobility has led to the conclusion that the German navy might well have won the U-boat war technologically had allied bombers not disrupted German bases and building yards, and allied armies ultimately occupied them. However, it may also be said that the German navy lost the U-boat war operationally, in part because the Royal Navy campaign in Norwegian waters prevented the withdrawal of crews from older U-boats for training on the new types, with many of the experienced crews being killed.

Because of the threat to Germany posed by the Red Army, the German navy had no choice but to continue a losing campaign in the hope of reducing the flow of American and British supplies to Murmansk. From the allied point of view, apart from the direct importance of supporting the Soviet land offensive, this was an effective use of the classic naval strategy to prevent an enemy maintaining a "fleet in being" safely in harbour. The commander-in-chief Western Approaches, Admiral Sir Max Horton, stated a belief in May 1944 that the arctic "represent[ed] the only prolific area remaining where heavy losses can still be inflicted on both enemy U-boats and long-range aircraft, and this consideration should in no way become secondary in importance to securing the safe and timely arrival of the convoy."[42] This opinion was not fully shared at the Admiralty or in the British Home Fleet, and the battles around the arctic convoys were to be some of the fiercest in the war, fought under difficult conditions. Nevertheless, there was a synergy between the need to maintain capital ships in the Home Fleet, and destroyers and aircraft carriers to support them, with the requirements for defeating the U-boats and the Luftwaffe's torpedo bombers. Canada's British-built *Tribal* class destroyers serving with the Home Fleet based at Scapa Flow played an important part in that campaign, and a supporting role in sinking the German battle cruiser *Scharnhorst*.[43]

Although the escort of convoys across the Atlantic continued until the end of the war, the U-boats were no longer able to mount wolf-pack attacks. Allied escorts were contained in the Atlantic by making sporadic attacks, while the focus of U-boat operations was redirected close to the English coast. These measures did fulfill the purpose of tying up allied resources, but did not stop the transport of cargoes to England. Canadian ships participated in these actions, and in the naval part of the amphibious assault of allied armies on the French coast, operation *Neptune*. More Canadian warships took part in operation *Neptune* than did American, with some ten thousand Canadian sailors. Canadian coastal forces and minesweepers helped the Royal Navy clear paths to the beaches, Canadian corvettes hunted submarines, and Canadian destroyers engaged German destroyers and bombarded gun emplacements. At the same time the Canadian navy took over the entire burden of escorting convoys across the Atlantic.[44]

✦ ✦ ✦

HMCS *Huron* (G 24/216). A wartime *Tribal* class destroyer built by Vickers-Armstrong on the Tyne in England, she served in the Royal Canadian Navy from 1943 to 1963. Her battle honours were won in the Arctic, 1943–45; the English Channel, 1944; Normandy, 1944; and Korea, 1951–53. DND A-1116

Apart from fighting the U-boats in the Caribbean, on both sides of the Atlantic, and then in convoys that had to be escorted for the entire Atlantic crossing, the Canadian navy saw service in South American, African, Mediterranean, and Pacific waters. Soon after the outbreak of the war in 1939 the three Canadian National Railways liners, *Prince David*, *Prince Henry*, and *Prince Robert*, had been converted into merchant cruisers using the guns and equipment stored for the Royal Navy, and in November 1941 the *Prince Robert* escorted, and partly transported, the Canadian brigade destined to fight and die in Hong Kong. On its return voyage it touched at Pearl Harbor three days before the Japanese attack. A mixed collection of ships, corvettes, and converted yachts strove to keep watch along the extended British Columbia coastline to prevent Japanese infiltration. A fishermen's reserve was created to extend the capacity of the navy on the west coast.[45] *Prince David* and *Prince Henry* were later converted to landing ships infantry (medium) and employed both in the Normandy operations and in the Mediterranean, while *Prince Robert* was converted to an anti-aircraft escort. At the time that the life and death battle was being fought in the mid-Atlantic, little could be spared for the Pacific. But even before the defeat of Germany in 1945, the Canadian navy began to develop plans to participate in the final defeat of Japan.

✦ ✦ ✦

While striving with all their might to defeat the U-boat menace and to carry the war to the enemy, Canadian naval officers had also sought to ensure that the force they created would have the structure and ships that would ensure its institutional survival in the postwar world. This aim naturally reflected their own ambitions, but they also firmly believed that Canada needed its navy and needed it to be effective on the high seas, and in partnership with allies. Bill Glover has characterized their thinking as being more imperial than national.[46] The acquisition of heavily gunned *Tribal* class destroyers, the first to be ready for service being built in Britain, was followed by the Canadian navy developing the two *Prince* ships as a small but independent amphibious warfare capability. There was initially no idea that the latter would survive into the peace, but the naval officers were most eager to extend their fleet with cruisers, and possibly even aircraft carriers, despite Mackenzie King's resistance.

The expansion of the war into the Pacific was their justification for accepting responsibility for larger ships, and Britain's shortage of man-

HMCS *Micmac* (R 10/214), a Canadian-built *Tribal* class destroyer completed by Halifax Shipyard in November 1945, having taken nearly twice as long to build as those constructed in Britain and Australia. DND A-1593

power was the opportunity. There was no potential for Canadian coastal forces, or Canadian geography, being important in the campaign against Japan. Only the possession of capital ships capable of independent, or semi-independent operations in the western Pacific would give Canada any credit among the great powers. In July 1943 Lieutenant-Commander George Frederick Todd prepared a paper for NSHQ Plans Division in which he urged the "vital" importance "for the maintenance of Canadian prestige that the Canadian Navy takes a direct and important part in the war against Japan." He also foresaw the need to protect the British Columbia coast in the event of a war with the Soviet Union. Nelles arranged for the first sea lord, Admiral Dudley Pound, to prime Churchill to ask at the 1943 Quadrant Conference at Quebec for Canadian help manning cruisers, and Mackenzie King, although he sensed that he was being manoeuvred, agreed. He drew the line at the formation of a Canadian fleet air arm, unless it could be paid for by reductions in other areas of the navy budget. In the hope of finding a way around, Nelles agreed to provide the crew for an RN escort carrier, without waiting for Cabinet approval.

It had become clear by the middle years of the war that air support was vital to convoy defence against submarines. In his diary Mackenzie King complained about the "war ministers" forcing the pace for their services. "Certainly," he added, "none have had consideration for the taxpayer." On 23 February 1943 the then vice-chief of naval staff, Rear Admiral Jones, ordered the director of operations division, Captain Horatio Nelson Lay, and the director of plans division, Acting-Captain DeWolf, to report on the British and American models for a Canadian fleet air arm. Lay in particular was a strong advocate of the formation of a Canadian support group including an escort carrier. However, the two Canadian manned escort carriers, HMS *Nabob* and *Puncher*, served mainly in the Home Fleet, taking part in the arctic convoys, and air attacks on the German battleship *Tirpitz*.[47] *Nabob* was torpedoed on her return from operation *Goodwood III* against *Tirpitz* on 24 August 1944, and damaged so greatly as to be withdrawn from service.

When in November 1943 the head of the British naval delegation in Washington, Admiral Sir Percy Noble, confirmed Mackenzie King's suspicion that the drive for acquisition of capital ships had come from NSHQ without his authorization, he established an Advisory Committee on Post-Hostilities Planning, chaired by the deputy minister of external affairs, Norman Robertson, and firmly controlled by the civil service. Nelles continued to work for naval expansion from his position heading the Canadian Naval Mission Overseas, and then as naval member on the Canadian Joint Staff Mission in London that Mackenzie King created in January of 1944. Before meeting with Churchill and the British chiefs of staff at the "Octagon" conference at Quebec in September 1944, Mackenzie King summoned the service chiefs to a meeting of Cabinet at which he made clear his concern about the drift toward a return to an imperial defence concept. In the words of the official history, "King's views ... did make perfect sense to those who opposed, failed to understand, or gave little support to the concept of a blue water navy – or those who felt that such a navy would be operating in British, not Canadian, interests." He eventually felt that Macdonald had made a good case for the acquisition of aircraft carriers for the Pacific war, but was not blind to the hidden agenda. In his diary for 9 and 11 October 1944 he wrote: "What I dislike about the defence dept. and the naval dept. and Macdonald's attitude as Minister is that they have never been frank with the War Committee and the Cabinet in making the situation perfectly clear. They have tried to build up a complete fleet unit by acquiring different classes of ships, allegedly for escort duty, etc. whereas

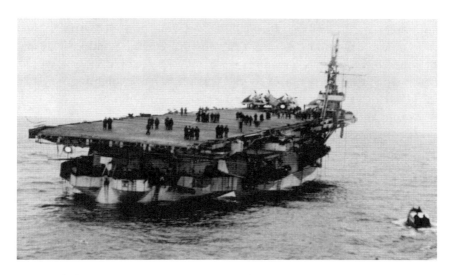

HMS *Nabob* (D 77), American-built by Seattle-Tacoma Shipbuilding. This *Bogue* class escort aircraft carrier was commissioned in the Royal Navy September 1943 but manned by a Royal Canadian Navy crew. Seen here after being torpedoed off North Cape, 28 August 1944, following a raid on the German battleship *Tirpitz*, she was brought safely into port but then decommissioned and scrapped. From the album of Lt (RCN) L.B. Jenson. DND CN-3619

what they have really been after is a powerful war fleet obtaining the carriers in a surreptitious rather than in an open way ... While I feel that the Department has not been straightforward in dealing with the Cabinet in the way it has gone about securing these ships as a gift from England, the real object being to make a fleet unit for post-war purposes rather than for the war, I nevertheless see the wisdom of making effective whatever we do." Nelles was brought home and was told he would be retired from naval service.[48] Macdonald lasted another year but resigned when Mackenzie King called an election for June 1945, and was replaced by Douglas Abbott.[49]

Earlier, at a War Committee meeting in Quebec on 13 September following an Octagon meeting with Churchill and Roosevelt, Mackenzie King had made it clear that the Canadian navy would not be employed in the Indian Ocean area, to the dismay of the Royal Navy planners who had been counting on employing *Prince David* and *Prince Henry* in the campaign to drive the Japanese out of Rangoon. "I held very strongly to the view that no government in Canada once the European war was over would send its men to India, Burma and Singapore to fight with any forces and hope to get through a general election successfully. That to permit this would be to raise at a general election, a nation-wide cry of Imperial wars versus Canada as a nation ... Our people, I know, would never agree to paying our taxes for Canadian troops fighting whether in the air or at sea or on land for the protection of India, the recovery of Burma and Singapore."[50]

The final humiliation for the proponents of Canadian sea power was Mackenzie King's insistence that no one should be ordered to participate in naval operations in the western Pacific who had not expressly indicated his willingness. As a result HMCS *Uganda*, serving with the British Pacific Fleet, had to be sent home prior to the defeat of Japan. Thirty-seven thousand sailors did sign the agreement, and would have manned a fleet of two cruisers, two light fleet carriers, the anti-aircraft cruiser *Prince Robert*, nineteen destroyers, and smaller craft, but the war was over before many of them were ready to proceed to sea. The *Prince Robert*, however, was in Hong Kong in time for the surrender of the Japanese garrison and to bring home the survivors of the Canadian brigade.[51]

✦ ✦ ✦

The Second World War established the Royal Canadian Navy as a national institution. The threat posed by German surface raiders and submarines effected its transformation from a controversial commitment many believed only served British Imperial interests into an accepted part of Canada's own defence. The battle of the St Lawrence brought home to Quebec the need for a navy. The war also made it abundantly clear to Canadians that the naval defence of Canada could not be improvised on the outbreak of hostilities, nor be limited to coastal forces. Even the prime minister, intent as he was on domestic political questions, seemed at times to recognize that the sea was indivisible; that naval defence for a small country had to be a collective effort.

The wartime naval leadership made great strides in transforming the Royal Canadian Navy. Doug McLean's summation is that the RCN had entered the war almost completely dependent on the Royal Navy and later became dependent on the U.S. Navy, "but ended it well on the road to modest self-sufficiency. What is perhaps surprising is not that there was room for improvement, but that so much was accomplished."[52] The establishment of a Directorate of Plans at NSHQ during the leadership of Rear Admiral Jones was an important step in transforming a fleet into a fully capable navy. In Gimblett's words, Jones "paired a batch of brilliant young RCNVRs (in their ranks were several Rhodes scholars) with more senior regular officers who could provide a leavening of practical experience, and he specifically gave them a free reign from their Admiralty counterparts to explore innovative concepts for the future needs of a growing service. Increasingly through the Post-Hostilities Planning Committee they came into contact with the mandarins at the Department of External Affairs and in the Privy Council (the list included Lester Pearson and Hume Wrong). This next generation of Canadian political leaders recognized the limitations of the pre-war policy of isolationism, and their international activism provided naval commanders the firm political endorsement that Canada required a postwar military force with global reach, which in those days only a navy with a balanced fleet structure of carriers and cruisers could provide."[53]

It can be argued that some at least of the problems of the Royal Canadian Navy during the war stemmed from an unwise insistence on premature Canadianization. James Goldrick notes that, unlike their Australian counterparts, Canadian wartime naval leaders lacked warm and close personal relationships with British naval leaders. The lack of personal relationship may account, at least in part, for the difficulties the Canadian navy experienced in keeping pace with technical developments. The insistence on putting Canadians in all senior command positions put an impossible strain on the greatly inadequate personnel resources trained in the minuscule pre-war navy. Unlike the Royal Australian Navy, which required all its officers to qualify for promotion through Royal Navy peer review, Canada's naval leadership came from a very small pool of men who had survived fifty years of intense competition for far too few command positions. Jellicoe's 1920 advice that it was difficult to keep a small fleet efficient had been sound, especially in a country where the political connections of the yachting fraternity-cum-RCNVR officers could be used to bypass naval discipline. When Jones was appointed chief of naval staff, he made matters worse by forcing into retirement the former Royal Navy officers who had been living in Canada at the outbreak of the war and had offered their services in Ottawa.[54]

Not everyone shared equally the goal of having a navy that was an intimate part of Canadian society, "warts and all." Murray was more imperially minded than was Jones, who benefitted from the cabal of the Upper Canadian elite. Mackenzie King did not share the belief that the Canadian navy was a vital aspect of Canadian nationalism, although he did swell with pride when he thought about it. Nevertheless, he did employ it as an instrument of policy. The passivity he had shown at the August 1943 Quadrant Quebec Conference, when he had been willing to let Churchill and Roosevelt map out the grand strategy of the allies, should not be taken as a full definition of his interests and capacity. Admittedly, his objectives could be characterized in negative terms. In 1939 he valued the navy because it contributed to the war effort without necessarily committing the country to the scale of involvement in European battlefields that had led to such a death toll in the First World War. His intervention in 1944 to limit the scale of Canada's naval commitment to the Pacific war and to block its participation in British concerns in the Indian ocean constituted an intervention in the strategic concept of the allied powers. It was consistent with the historic concern of Frederick Monk and Henri Bourassa that Canadian forces should not become instruments of British imperialism.

In taking the line that he did about the Canadian navy, army, and air force participating in the reconquest, or liberation, of South East Asia, Mackenzie King was not only projecting Canadian values and interests but was also indicating the limitation of his understanding of strategic realities. His denial of the British request for the *Prince* ships to participate in the amphibious force intended to liberate Rangoon might be considered a refusal to take part in an imperial reconquest, but it was also a refusal to participate in the reconstruction of the line of naval communications upon which Australia and New Zealand had based their security. That strategy originated in the nineteenth century for cruiser deployment and in the interwar years developed into a plan for battle-fleet response to possible Japanese aggression. The "30 days to Singapore" plan was supposed to have seen the dispatch of the main fleet to Singapore via the Suez canal, but had been frustrated by Axis naval and air forces in the Mediterranean region and by the German fleet in Norwegian waters. Consequently it had been superseded by the attachment of the antipodean dominions to the American theatre of operations. There is no evidence that the Canadian prime minister took any of this into consideration.[55]

Few, however, would question that Mackenzie King had been right about the probable Canadian political reaction were Canadians to be killed in the liberation of Burma and Singapore, and few would dispute that national politics are an important consideration in strategic planning. "Also," as Mackenzie King had noted in his diary in January 1944, "we may be sure we will get little credit for anything we do, either on the part of the US or Great Britain."[56] Following the end of the war there were to be more than a few occasions when Canadian leadership would attempt to channel international action by a degree of disengagement – and at least one when that policy would have been preferred to that which actually transpired.

The war had indeed shown that the navy was, in Monk's words, "Canadian when it has to be paid for, in order to be Imperial when it is required for use."[57] It was indeed a two-edged weapon that was difficult to wield, and not without dangers to the possessor. But it had also served Canada well by helping defeat the Nazi horde. The lessons learned, but not fully assimilated until it became clear that the surrender of Germany and Japan had not put an end to the dangers in Europe and Asia, were that to meet wartime needs more was required than a vestigial and largely reserve peacetime force, and that deterrence of war required constant engagement in the problems of world security.

4

THE NAVY AND THE NEW IMPERIUM

American intervention in the European war, which first took the form of naval effort in the Atlantic, was of fundamental importance to the defeat of National-Socialist Germany; and ongoing American engagement in the strategic problems of the postwar world was a central objective of Canadian policy. Nevertheless, the transformation of the United States into the strategic pillar of democratic society posed difficulties for Canada, and it was recognized that the Canadian navy continued to have a role in addressing this problem. Only in the late 1940s and early 1950s, after careful negotiations and a steep learning curve, was a balance achieved which provided for Canadian autonomy and security through Canada's participation in the bilateral defence relationship with the United States and participation in collective security at the United Nations and in what became the North Atlantic Treaty Organization (NATO). During that first decade of the postwar world, Canada remained a central figure in the Commonwealth.

In July 1940, within days of the defeat of France, a "Committee of Twenty," which included noted Canadian intellectuals, journalists, and future leaders Brooke Claxton, Jack Pickersgill, Frank R. Scott, Edgar J. Tarr, Bruce Hutchinson, Hugh L. Keenleyside, and Arthur R.M. Lower, met at the Château Laurier in Ottawa to discuss the war situation. Although only a few had official positions in government, their opinions were well informed and would have been heard in government. They came to a stark realization: "Above all we are confronted with a startling new possibility: war on our own shores. This we have never seriously contemplated, and for it our defence strategy is woefully unprepared. When Canada's first line of defence was the Maginot Line, her second was the English channel, and the Atlantic coast was an unlikely third line. Now the Atlantic is the second line, and the first line on the channel is threatened as never before." To meet the crisis the group urged closer co-operation with the United States, and recommended that Canada take the lead in formulating measures of continental defence, to minimize the risk of losing her national identity: "Geography makes Canada an integral part of any North American defence system. Co-operation with Washington is going to be either voluntary on Canada's part, or else compulsory; in any event it is inevitable." Although the defence of Britain was central to Canadian strategy, a second line of defence was "of paramount importance ... to maintain our independence *vis-à-vis* the United States, since the United States is now determined to see that the whole continent is effectively defended." The report urged the necessity of developing forces for home defence "capable of operating under the special conditions of this country," and a "new board of strategy" because "the traditional task of our general staff has been to provide a force to co-operate with British forces overseas."

The new circumstances required a new emphasis on the Canadian navy: "Continental defence requires heavy sea power, and as Canada cannot provide this herself the United States will have to bear the main burden of naval defence. Nevertheless, a stronger naval policy for Canada is desirable as a necessary part of coastal defence. Since, however, Canada cannot bear a large part in the provision of naval armament, the provision of more localized defence – coastal troops, aircraft, small naval craft and coastal bases – could well come within the Canadian share. Canada should provide, in Nova Scotia or Newfoundland, naval bases large enough to accommodate British or United States naval forces." On 14 June Mackenzie King had warned the Cabinet War Committee that "consideration would have to be given, at once, to the possibility of having to provide bases in Canada for the British Fleet, if the military situation in Europe continued to deteriorate." The Committee of Twenty, however, warned that any attempt to fight on against the Nazis following a British defeat, perhaps by the transfer of the British government and fleet to Canada, would be impossible unless the Americans became belligerents.[1]

A growing public sentiment for a formal Canadian-American military alliance found some echoes in External Affairs, and the career foreign service officer Hugh Keenleyside advised Mackenzie King that if such were ever to become a reality Roosevelt would "expect, if necessary demand, Canadian assistance in the defence of this continent and this hemisphere." The diplomatic exchanges led to a meeting between Mackenzie King and the president in August 1940 at Ogdensburg, New

York. There Roosevelt proposed and Mackenzie King agreed to establish a Permanent Joint Board on Defence (PJBD) to facilitate co-operation between Canada and the United States in defence matters. It was, and remains, a consultative body reporting directly to the prime minister and the president. Amerophiles such as O.D. Skelton warmly welcomed its creation. Robert Alexander MacKay, External Affairs member of the PJBD from January 1951 to October 1955, remarked to David Beatty twenty years later that the Ogdensburg Agreement "was not an equal partnership, but it was remarkably free, due to the United States' restraint in declining to use its great military strength as a support for diplomacy vis-à-vis Canada."[2] But it was a significant move for a prime minister who had refused Canadian representation on the Committee of Imperial Defence, and Mackenzie King was to stoutly resist American efforts to transform it into a formal alliance. When the question of American bases was brought up again, he was careful to assert Canadian interests in Newfoundland and to indicate that American use of facilities in Nova Scotia would not extend to permanent ownership. When he informed the House of Commons about his agreement with Roosevelt, he asserted that the effect would be that Canada could safely deploy its resources to the defence of Britain. In November 1940, when the crisis of the Battle of Britain was over and Britain's survival appeared more certain, Mackenzie King remarked in the Cabinet War Committee: "the new responsibility undertaken by Canada for the joint defence of North America made it all the more necessary to develop the Royal Canadian Navy so that we could bear our share of the burden."[3]

This warning was to be reiterated throughout the war. Appendix Two of the first document produced by the Anglo-American Staff "conversation" in early 1941, known as ABC-1 and the basis for Anglo-American co-operation following the American entry into the war, indicated that the United States would assume strategic direction of forces in the Pacific and the western Atlantic, with the exception of "the waters and territories in which Canada assumes responsibility for the strategic direction of military forces, as may be defined in United States–Canada joint agreements." ABC-22, drawn up later in 1941, recognized that the United States would accept principal responsibility for the defence of North America, but also recognized a need for Canada "to avoid undue subordination" and to be able to respond on its own to any attack by forces below the level of a hostile battle squadron. Admiral Ernest King's determination to control all naval operations in the western Atlantic made it difficult to avoid such subordination. He was furious when in

July 1942 Rear Admiral Nelles set up a conference to rationalize escort of tanker traffic to the Caribbean, which led ultimately to the dispatch of convoys directly from New York to England, thereby reducing the strain on escort forces. "Any meetings concerning their [i.e., the U.S.'s] sphere of strategic control," the prime minister demanded of the Canadian liaison staff, "must be held in Washington not Canada!"[4] The appointment of Rear Admiral Murray in the spring of 1943 as commander-in-chief, Canadian Northwest Atlantic, was a major accomplishment that countered the general trend of Canadian-American defence relations.

In April 1944 General Maurice Pope advised: "to the Americans the defence of the United States is continental defence, which includes us, and nothing that I can think of will ever drive that idea out of their heads." He cautioned, therefore, that "what we have to fear is more a lack of confidence in the United States as to our security, rather than enemy action.'"[5] In the summer of 1944, in a paper prepared for the naval director of plans, Lieutenant-Commander Todd returned to the theme, warning that, as the U.S. Navy was acting under orders to provide support for Canada, only significant Canadian participation could keep that support from becoming oppressive. Consistent with the strategic policy of the 1920s, it argued that Canada must not put itself in the position of depending on American forces for local defence. It was also important that Canada not become so dependent on American good will that she could not choose to provide active support for the Commonwealth without American concurrence. If the Canadian navy were to be an effective instrument of an independent Canadian foreign policy, Todd argued, its primary operational foci would have to be coastal control and the protection of overseas communications.[6]

In January 1945 the Advisory Committee on Post-Hostilities Planning warned: "the United States may be expected to take an active interest in Canadian defence preparations in the future. Moreover, that interest may be expressed with an absence of the tact and restraint customarily employed by the United Kingdom in putting forward defence proposals."[7] And that was before the first use of atomic weapons in August transformed the requirements for continental defence. On 10 August Mackenzie King wrote in his diary that the week had "been the most important ... in the history of the world excepting alone that of the birth and death of Christ. The change that will be wrought through the discovery of the atomic bomb is so beyond conception that it is next to impossible for the human mind to begin to grasp what it may lead to."[8]

Although Ottawa's wartime efforts to obtain proper recognition as an independent ally in Washington were largely frustrated, that was more of an irritant than a matter of supreme national importance. Canadian war objectives differed from those of the United States only in the degree to which they were focused on the European theatre. From 1942 the new under-secretary of external affairs, Norman Robertson, and his deputy, Hume Wrong, laboured to establish what became known as the "functionalist" principle, which would accord to nations making major contributions to international efforts a proportionate voice in their direction. The new dimension was that the Canadian government was prepared to accept the responsibilities implied by its representation. But a leadership role in the formation of grand strategy was not one of Ottawa's goals.[9] If it had been, the scale of Canada's commitment of troops to the European theatre would in any case have been too small to justify an access to the Combined Chiefs of Staff that was denied to all the smaller allies, including the Free French.

✦ ✦ ✦

Roosevelt's death on 12 April 1945, and his succession by Harry S. Truman, who had been his vice-president, put an end to Mackenzie King's confidence in American intentions. There was apprehension that the United States might wish to retain permanent possession of the defence installations it had constructed in Canada during the war, and the interest the United States was showing in the arctic was a matter for concern. At the time of the German invasion of Denmark in 1940 the Danish ambassador to the United States, Henrik Kauffmann, had signed an agreement permitting American military basing on Greenland, leading to the establishment by the U.S. Army Air Force of bases at Narsarsuaq, Sondrestrom Fjord, and Thule in 1941. The development of long-range bombers capable of delivering nuclear weapons transformed the Canadian north into a defensive glasis for fortress America. In March 1946 the U.S. Navy carried out "Operation Frostbite" in the Davis Strait, testing cold weather air operations with the fleet carrier USS *Midway*. "The long range policy of the Americans," Mackenzie King said to Cabinet in May 1946, was "to absorb Canada. They seek to get this hemisphere as complete a one as possible."[10] In January 1947 the minister of external affairs, Louis St Laurent, warned a University of Toronto audience: "the relationship between a great and powerful nation and its smaller neighbour, at best, is far from simple. It calls for constant and imaginative attention on both sides."[11]

Paradoxically, the need to meet the threat posed by the Soviet Union also served to address Canadian concern about American intentions. Canada had been an early and consistent supporter of the formation of the United Nations Organization, first envisaged when Churchill met Roosevelt at Argentia in 1941, but in the postwar years the Soviet Union rendered it all but powerless by its use of the veto. To compensate for the weakness of the UN, Article 51, the provision in its charter that permitted states the right of self-defence, was used to create a multi-lateral alliance of the western-European democracies with Canada and the United States.[12] In December 1946 Pearson, who was at the time undersecretary at External Affairs, had made it clear to American defence officials that Canada's "global strategy would be to fight a future war away from North America."[13] While it is always good to keep war as far away as possible, the Department of External Affairs also had a particular reason. In a memorandum of August 1947 Pearson's second, Escott Reid, expressed his fear that war on any scale would lead to the "Free World" developing into "an American empire." He bluntly declared: "in the event of war we shall have no freedom of action in any matter which the United States Government considers essential ... In peacetime our freedom of action will be limited but it will not be non-existent."[14] The best hope was to help create a strategic environment that would permit the United States to draw its defensive perimeter well beyond Canadian territory. In the words of Hume Wrong, Canadian ambassador in Washington from 1946 to 1953, "if the North Atlantic is bridged by a new defensive alliance, the problems of North American defence would become a small part of the larger plan, the purpose of which would be the means of defeating the larger enemy."[15] In his memoirs Pearson wrote that "for Canada, there was always security in numbers. We did not want to be alone with our close friend and neighbour."[16] The Communist takeover in Czechoslovakia at the end of February 1948 galvanized the United States, Britain, and Canada into action.

Reid wrote in the mid-1960s that for Canadians in general the leading role played by Britain in the creation of a defensive alliance to meet the Soviet threat was important. "The British Labour government, not the Truman administration, launched the tripartite discussions which resulted in the North Atlantic treaty ... A British, not a United States, appreciation of the dangers of the international situation in March 1948 provided the background against which the Canadian government decided to participate in those discussions."[17] David Haglund and Stéphane Roussel write that Reid's conception of a trans-Atlantic alliance was based on traditional thinking about the need for international balance of power, but that he applied it to Canada's relationship with the United States and, because of Britain's postwar weakness, substituted the traditional British make-weight with a "European" one. "And this was his most important contribution, he situated the counterweight far more in international institutions than in individual states."[18] The timing was perfect, as the British initiative provided a way of deflecting a suggestion by the American under-secretary of state, Robert Lovett, that the possibility of a bilateral defence agreement be pursued in step with tentative discussion about free trade (which Mackenzie King eventually abandoned as politically unacceptable).[19]

Following months of Soviet resistance to plans to reconstruct a democratic and viable German state, the Soviet administration on June 24 declared a blockade of all land communications to Berlin from the western occupation zones. On 25 June the western powers began an airlift of supplies into Berlin with a flight of Royal Air Force transports, but Mackenzie King held back, and the Royal Canadian Air Force was not ordered to take part. Reid recalled that during the war Mackenzie King "had urged the creation of an effective collective security system but as soon as the war was over he began to retreat to his pre-war isolationism." There was great uncertainty "in that final sad year of his prime ministership when it was clear he was lingering on the stage too long."[20] Mackenzie King wrote in his diary that he was "surprised beyond words" when Brooke Claxton, whom he had made minister of national defence on 10 December 1946, cautioned that, as Canada was not one of the occupation powers in Germany, Canadian participation could trigger war.[21] Despite his surprise, however, he was unwilling to commit Canada to action: "I think the Cabinet saw for the first time that I had been wise in the fight that I had been making right along against getting too quickly and easily and unnecessarily drawn into situations in all parts of the world." His reaction to a press leak in London indicating that the Commonwealth had been asked to assist was to regard it as a British plot to put public pressure on Ottawa, equating the Berlin crisis with the 1922 Chanak crisis.[22]

It was St Laurent who, regardless of his isolationist Quebec political constituency, took the lead in ensuring that Canada was a founding member of NATO. On 29 April 1948 he had reminded parliament: "the western European democracies are not beggars asking for our charity. They are allies whose assistance we need in order to be able successfully to defend ourselves and our beliefs. Canada and the United States need the assistance of the western European democracies just as they need ours."²³ When he came to the head of the administration in November 1948 following the retirement of Mackenzie King, he acted resolutely to make the alliance one with real commitments.²⁴ Article 5 of the Treaty of Washington, signed on 4 April 1949, employed the formula adopted by the League of Nations and by the Imperial Conference. The signatories agreed "that an armed attack against one or more of them in Europe or North America shall be considered an attack against them all and consequently ... that, if such an armed attack occurs, each of them ... will assist the Party or Parties so attacked by taking forthwith, individually and in concert with the other Parties, such action as it deems necessary, including the use of armed force."

Through its Article 4, the treaty addressed the right of the North Atlantic Council to consider threats to the political or economic independence of any member occasioned by events anywhere in the world, including actions taken by other members, but it was to be Article 5, which served well in keeping the peace in Europe for over half a century, that was to be formally invoked for the first time in 2001 to meet a security threat to the United States.

Canada's policy toward NATO was at once an attempt to avoid the dangers of non-commitment, and a continuation of the effort to preserve Canada's freedom of choice. As with any compromise, the outcome could not be entirely satisfactory. The concept of functionality that External Affairs had forged found a practical application in the North Atlantic Council where Canadian Ambassadors to NATO could influence NATO planning in proportion to the commitment of Canadian forces. When NATO formed a "Standing Group" to provide continuity for the Military Committee of NATO Chiefs of Staff, which met bi-annually, Pearson, who had moved into politics and on 10 September 1948 became minister of external affairs in the final months of the Mackenzie King administration, and Claxton, who retained the Defence portfolio, succeeded in establishing the principle that member governments would have to be invited to participate in discussions by the Standing Group when plans were being developed for the employment of its forces or territory. This arrangement addressed to some extent the fear of Canadian forces being used in dangerous ways. On the other hand, Canada did not lobby for a permanent seat on the Standing Group out of concern that if Canadians were singled out for participation in the central control of NATO planning it would be impossible for Canada to retain its freedom of decision.²⁵

Apart from the civilian North Atlantic Council, the organization of NATO was to represent military rather than civilian values, and was to do little to give the Canadian military leverage in matters of continental defence. When NATO established a Canada-United States Regional Planning Group (CUSRPG) along with planning groups for western Europe, the north Atlantic, and northern and southern Europe, the American military objected to the NATO structure replacing the Canadian-U.S. Military Coordinating Committee (MCC), which had been established in 1946 by the PJBD to undertake bilateral military planning for the defence of North America at a less senior level. External Affairs believed that it should, but the Canadian chief of the general staff, General Charles Foulkes, was willing to accommodate the American objection to European interference in North American defence. The CUSRPG was not stood down when NATO developed more formal command structures in 1952 to replace the other regional planning groups.[26] When a NATO supreme allied commander, Atlantic (SACLANT) was appointed in January 1952, the position was given to the American admiral commanding the U.S. Atlantic fleet in Norfolk, Virginia. Winston Churchill's impassioned plea to President Truman and U.S. secretary of state, Dean Acheson, that "for centuries England has held the seas against every tyrant," got no support from Pearson, who told Churchill the Canadian navy supported the appointment of a supreme commander for technical reasons, and in the interest of standardization. SACLANT'S authority over the Canadian navy came by virtue of his NATO position, and the commander of Canadian naval forces in the Atlantic was made the NATO commander for the "Canadian North-west Atlantic."[27] All the same, for servicemen who respect the chain of command, the fact that SACLANT was an American admiral had psychological importance. CUSRPG managed liaison between Canadian and American forces engaged in Continental defence and those operating in the Atlantic under SACLANT.[28]

✦ ✦ ✦

The concern for autonomy felt in External Affairs and by Prime Minister Mackenzie King was not shared by the navy. After more than five years of struggle to overcome the limitations of pre-war policies, the Canadian navy closed ranks against comprehensive demobilization, and in the struggle for institutional survival its leaders welcomed the development of the closest possible relationship with the United States Navy.

The process had begun before the formation of NATO. General Pope had expressed his view that "the defence relationship between the US and Canada in the post-war period should just be that intimate technical relationship that we enjoy at present."[29] Vice-Admiral Jones had developed Anglophobia during the war as a result of his perception that the Royal Navy was placing unreasonable burdens on the Canadian navy, and his successor as chief of naval staff, Rear Admiral Howard Emerson ("Rastus") Reid, had been characterized by Nelles as anti-British following a dispute arising out of the presence of a British battle squadron in Halifax in 1940. He may have nursed his antipathy from before the war.[30] If, as Marc Milner states, the navy suppressed for thirty years public awareness of its failure against the U-boats in late 1942 and the criticism it received as a result from the Royal Navy, there would have been strong psychological reasons for nursing an Anglophobe bias.[31] Reid had stoutly defended the independence of the Canadian navy from American control at a meeting of the Permanent Joint Board in April 1941, but in the circumstances of postwar retrenchment, he was as ready as Jones was to court the risk of domination by an American chain of command, especially because it was consistent with the shared perception of the military threat posed by the Soviet Union.

The MCC revised the wartime Canada-United States Defence Plan, which, over the years, became the Canada-U.S. Basic Security Plan providing for the coordinated use of both countries' sea, land, and air forces in the event of hostilities.[32] The thirty-fifth recommendation of the PJBD in 1946 was that both countries should be committed to the "adoption, as far as practicable, of common designs and standards in arms, equipment, organization, [and that common] methods of training and new developments ... be encouraged, due recognition being given by each country to the special circumstances prevailing therein."[33] This was too much for Mackenzie King, who had rediscovered a keen awareness of the value of Commonwealth defence links. The Cabinet deferred approval of the PJBD recommendation until January 1947, at which time it accepted a redrafted version that would not suggest that participation in joint planning and co-operative effort would automatically commit Canada to military operations, or that Canada would surrender any degree of control over military activity taking place on Canadian territory.

The revised policy statement established five principles for Canadian-American military co-operation:

- Interchange of select individuals to increase the familiarity of each country's defence establishment with that of the other country;
- General co-operation and exchange of observers in connection with exercises and with the development and tests of material of common interest;
- Encouragement of common designs and standards in arms, equipment, organization, methods of training and new developments, etc.;
- Mutual and reciprocal availability of military, naval and air facilities in each country, applied as may be agreed in specific instances. Reciprocally each country will continue to provide with a minimum of formality for the transit through its territory and its territorial waters of military aircraft and public vessels of the other country;
- As an underlying principle all co-operative arrangements will be without impairment of the control of either county over all activities in its territory.[34]

In January 1947 Claxton wrote a note to Mackenzie King discussing the basis for postwar naval planning: "Our navy's primary purpose is to train personnel rather than to have ready a task force and the training should be definitely designed to equip men to fight in northern waters." Claxton also recognized the need to keep up with the development of defence technology.[35] This reversion to the pre-war concept of a small training squadron, however, did not long survive the realities of the growing international tension and the institutional ambitions of the navy. On 12 February 1947 Washington and Ottawa simultaneously announced the intention to continue joint co-operation for continental defence, and in August 1947 Captain Horatio Nelson Lay, as director of naval plans, wrote: "In view of the vital importance of the defence of the North American war making ability in a future war, RCN planning will in future be largely based on the Naval forces now envisaged in the Basic Security Plan. This will make desirable the complete standardization of the RCN and USN by the time that the Basic Security Plan must be ready for immediate implementation."[36] To a degree the requirement for more effective control had already been addressed when Mackenzie King appointed Claxton minister of national defence, at the same time eliminating the separate ministers for navy, air, and militia. "They should be made to reach joint agreements," he wrote in his diary, which "could never be done under different Ministers. Each would feel it necessary to defend his own particular department."[37]

Peter Haydon and Paul Mitchell have described how the U.S. Joint War Plans Committee drafted a concept plan for collaborative continental defence, which it called *Matchpoint*.[38] Emphasis was placed on air defence, anti-submarine and surface defence naval forces, base defences, and an effective command structure for quick response. Canadian input to the process of fleshing out the collaborative continental defence plan was more politicized than the American system, which left military planning to the military. By "making the process correspond to the American system, the way was technically clear to complete the planning. As an additional planning requirement, though, there was a need to come to terms with the cost of implementation, particularly in the near-term, and this was to be the means of exercising political control." In early 1948 *Matchpoint* was approved as the Basic Security Plan. It contained two naval appendices, for "Mobile Striking Forces," and "Sea Lines of Communication." Initially the latter envisaged Canadian and American co-operation in the defence of Atlantic shipping, but it was revised in March 1949 into a plan for "Protection of Coastal Sea Lines of Communication," and the problem of Atlantic communications was widened to include British forces.

James Goldrick writes that late in the Second World War when it had become evident to Canadian, and to British and Australian, naval officers that the U.S. Navy had established a commanding technical lead, it was inevitable that they should begin to direct their attention toward participation in American fleets, and to develop personal ties with American naval leaders.[39] This may be an overstatement. Norman Friedman shows that in the immediate postwar period the Royal Navy was a leader in the development of data management systems for anti-submarine and anti-air warfare, and the Royal Navy was to lead in the modernization of aircraft carriers with angled flight decks and mirror landing aids.[40] However, the scale of U.S. Navy effort in the Pacific had put it into a class of its own, based on American industrial strength.[41] In the immediate postwar years, as a result of the staggering cost to Britain of the two world wars, there was little alternative to the economic reorientation of Canada toward the United States, and a corresponding dependence of western Europe on American aid.[42] For Canadian sailors it was also a reality that the shared commitment to continental defence began to forge personal links with the U.S. Navy.

The personnel exchanges between the Canadian and U.S. navies recommended by the Permanent Joint Board on Defence began gradually to be implemented. To a limited degree the exchanges were extended to other fleets following the formation of NATO, and the Visiting Forces Act enacted by individual members of NATO served the same purpose as did the common code of naval discipline within the Empire.⁴³ While these exchanges are essential for naval training, they do have a potential for involving Canada in international incidents over which the Canadian government has little or no control. It is a stated Canadian policy that officers seconded to allied forces shall not be employed in combat units if those forces become involved in active service, except when that service is on behalf of the United Nations.⁴⁴ But this principle is not consistently implemented, and it became a political issue in early 2003 when the United States invaded Iraq without the sanction of the United Nations.

✦ ✦ ✦

Despite the growing relationship with the U.S. Navy, the Canadian navy did not lightly shed its Royal Navy heritage or its imperial perspective. The service culture of the Royal Canadian Navy in the postwar years was framed by British and American relationships. A new and distinctively national culture was to develop in time, but the transnational values were never to be lost, and the quasi-colonial, or post-colonial, cast of mind, swinging between the Empire and the American Eagle, had implications for Canada's place in the world order.

Wartime experience had borne out Admiral Jellicoe's warning about the difficulty of sustaining the quality of a small naval force, and the development of increasingly technical naval forces exacerbated the problem. In meeting the need for the navy to maintain a critical mass, reliance continued to be placed on the existing relationship with the Royal Navy. Following his appointment as chief of naval staff in September 1947, Rear Admiral Harold T.W. Grant went so far as to order officers not to wear the Canada flashes on their uniforms that had been introduced late in the war for those serving overseas.⁴⁵ They were soon restored to the Canadian fleet, however, and Wilfred Lund writes that Grant's "hard-driving Nova Scotian Presbyterian character" was "misconstrued as that of a hidebound British traditionalist."⁴⁶ Partnership with both the U.S. Navy and the Royal Navy did not keep him from seeking to enhance the independent status of the Royal Canadian Navy, at least when a nationalist argument served institutional purposes.⁴⁷

Incidents in the navy in 1947 and 1949, which might have been described as mutiny had there not been a mandatory death sentence for that naval crime, suggested that dependence upon Royal Navy training and tradition to provide officers with the mental conditioning required for combat could conflict with Canadian social conditions.⁴⁸ In October

1949 Rear Admiral "Rollo" Mainguy signed off on a report produced by a commission he chaired on the discipline problem that called attention to the breakdown of the divisional system and personnel management. One of its conclusions was that the Royal Navy culture of senior Canadian officers failed to prepare them for leadership in a fleet in which the largest number of sailors had served in the Voluntary Reserve during the war and had a more democratic attitude to command relationships.[49] A conclusion of the Mainguy Report was "the need to 'Canadianize' our navy."[50]

Officer training had been recommenced in Canada in 1942, at HMCS *Royal Roads*, Esquimalt, where training of RCNVR had begun two years earlier. But the cadet program had been set up to replicate the Royal Navy training system as much as possible without any recognition that the Royal Navy was itself grappling with the consequences of a deeply flawed training system. That summer Angus Macdonald, minister of national defence for naval services, had sent his assistant John Connolly to investigate complaints about relations between permanent force and reservists. Amongst those whom Connolly contacted was Louis Audette, an old friend from his law firm who commanded a corvette, HMCS *Amherst*. Audette had expressed his opinion that the regular force suffered from its entirely service-oriented and rote-based education.[51] In 1947 the Air Force began sending cadets to Royal Roads, which became the Canadian Services College Royal Roads, and in 1948 it became a tri-service college offering university-level education. The navy, however, continued to question the value of academic education, and cadets in the executive branch were hurried off to sea after two years in the classroom. In the longer term the navy was to be brought to accept Audette's valuation of a broad education in humanities and social sciences, but less fortunately it accepted the Mainguy report's bias toward Canadianization.

The paradox, as Nicholas Rodger has pointed out, is that the Royal Navy had similarly made extensive use of its RNVR officers to provide wartime leadership for its escort forces. These had only begun their naval service after receiving a full course of civilian education, and possibly years of employment in civilian occupations. As was to happen in Canada, these reserve officers suffered a cultural divide from their regular force brother officers, but ultimately proved to be what the postwar Royal Navy required to lead it through the Cold War.[52]

Goldrick's analysis of the question of the relationship between the Canadian, Australian, and British Royal navies shows that they were complex and context-specific, and at their best highly creative, but tending toward a concept of the brotherhood of the sea that extended to the U.S. Navy. This relationship could tend to conspiracy against civilian leadership, as occurred around the British gifts of cruisers and carriers to the Canadian navy toward the end of the Second World War. But Goldrick suggests that to identify the gulf as lying between the British acculturation of Canadian naval officers and the growing national insularity of the general Canadian population is to discount the extent to which the intellectual leadership of Canada sustained strong British connections late into the twentieth century, and to some extent to this day. For instance, all the civilian officers in the Directorate of Strategic Analysis, Operations Research, DND, in the early 1970s had earned PhD degrees from British universities before returning to Canada to seek employment.

To the extent that there was Canadianization of the navy, it may have been too precipitous. Bill Glover has pointed to the fact that only five lieutenants and one lieutenant commander from the pre-war RCN who remained in the navy following demobilization failed to reach the rank of commodore. Goldrick writes that "promotion on this scale made nonsense of any attempts at quality control."

Probably more important than the effect of Royal Navy culture – for better or for worse – upon the postwar Canadian navy was the stress on personnel caused by the difficulty of retaining hostilities-only sailors in an underfunded service. In 1946 the Naval Board had agreed that the fleet should be reduced to 10,000 men and women, but the rush of sailors to civilian jobs was such that only 6,600 were retained. Severe cuts to the seagoing fleet were unavoidable, and only the carrier was manned to its full peace establishment. Even keeping the ships in service required cutting into shoreside training and rest periods. To remedy the problem it was necessary to address issues of pay scale, accommodation, food, and clothing. The "mutinies" had been triggered by the work burden placed on under-strength crews. Richard Gimblett points out that the 1949 events were not the anomaly they were represented to be, either in the Canadian or in the British navy. From at least 1936 there had been incidents in the Canadian fleet when the seamen locked themselves into their mess decks in order to call attention to difficulties, or to unsatisfactory or incompetent officers.[53] The Mainguy Report ascribed more importance to service conditions than it did to service culture, but little could be done until the political atmosphere was changed by the outbreak of the Korean war.[54]

❖ ❖ ❖

In light of the growing demands of continental defence, and the continuing necessity of sustaining the strategic relationship with Great Britain through NATO, the Canadian navy had to accept that its dream of a balanced fleet could not be fully realized. It was recognized that defence of shipping remained a central commitment, and Shawn Cafferky shows that the idea of national fleet specialization was a result of consultations of the Permanent Joint Board on Defence.[55] In October 1949, at the first meeting of NATO's North Atlantic Regional Planning Group, Canada's naval representative, Vice-Admiral Grant, requested membership on Sub-Group B, "Atlantic Ocean Lines of Communication," and indicated that Canada wished to concentrate on the "organization, control and protection of convoys."[56] Because of budgetary restraints, and because the fast rate of technical development left the political leadership gasping, this perspective was to remain the central focus of the Canadian navy throughout the Cold War.

The concern in the late 1940s had been that the Soviet navy had captured German type XXI submarines with extended underwater speed and endurance, and would be able to mount an assault on shipping with up to 300 submarines – although the Soviets would probably have been able to send to sea no more than 60 submarines divided between their Northern, Baltic, Black Sea, and Pacific fleets. Between 1949 and 1958 the Soviet navy only launched 16 *Zulu* class submarines, which were the true clones of the German Type XXI. Although 236 *Whiskey* class boats were commissioned, they were less capable and were intended for defensive coastal operations.[57] To counter this threat, the U.S. Navy exploited another German development, LOFAR, "Low Frequency Analysis and Recording," a large passive acoustic display mounted on the sea bottom to form a deep-water very-long-range Anti-submarine Acoustic Surveillance System, known as CAESAR or SOSUS ("Sound Surveillance System"). Later LOFAR was also mounted on "Hunter-Killer" submarines that would be employed as mobile extensions of SOSUS. By use of signal intelligence, SOSUS was cued onto Soviet submarines leaving their bases, and in turn would be used to vector very-long-range maritime patrol aircraft equipped with sonobuoys and magnetic anomaly detectors (MADS) to localize and prosecute hostile submarines. After an initial test in the Bahamas in 1951, SOSUS was ordered deployed on the Atlantic coast in 1952 and on the Pacific in 1954, becoming operational by 30 June 1956.[58]

To meet the Soviet submarine threat, the Navy Board of Canada ordered the first of seven steam-turbine powered *St Laurent* class destroyer escorts in the 1949/50 budget; she was laid down in November 1950, and commissioned in October 1955. Lund attributes this decision, and the increase of the naval manpower target to 9,047, to the effect of the Soviet blockade of Berlin.[59] Michael Hennessy writes: "in almost every quarter, the *St Laurent* class anti-submarine frigates [sic] displayed significant innovations in design and construction. Canada's small fleet dictated a critical selection of fighting equipment and electrics not found in foreign designed vessels. Designed for the nuclear-biological environment, the central sections of the ship could be sealed-off to form an air-tight citadel. The hull was designed so that no matter what damage and flooding occurred the vessel could not capsize. The powerplant and drive train involved re-tooling private industry and the development of special facilities for production and testing."[60] Canada was a leader in the development of digital tactical control systems. DATAR was at first a Canadian Defence Research Board project, but the costs were considered too high, and the work was taken over by Ferranti, which demonstrated it in 1950 by establishing a data link from Toronto to Ottawa. British and American officers were impressed, but the U.S. Navy preferred to develop its own Naval Tactical Data System (NTDS).[61]

The Second World War had transformed Canada's shipbuilding industry, making possible the construction of destroyers in Canada, encouraging the adoption of North American sources of supply and equipment, and making apparent the importance of supporting the viability of naval yards in peacetime. Rear Admiral Frank Houghton, the vice-chief of naval staff, played a key role in the program. Haydon has characterized him as "a pro-USN, but not necessarily anti-RN, Admiral" and comments that "the idiosyncrasies of the Admirals and their key staff officers is a factor that has to be taken into account in analyzing the evolution of the post-war Canadian Navy."[62] Concentration on destroyer-size vessels enabled the Canadian navy to reduce its dependence on foreign yards. All six of Canada's major shipyards, including a few that did not really have the capacity for major warship construction, were employed in building the Cold War destroyer escorts, the *St Laurent* class and their successors. The political desirability of spreading the money to as many parliamentary constituencies as possible encouraged this dispersion of effort, but the cost was high, especially as the inexperienced yards had to be paid on a cost-plus basis because they did not have the expertise to offer a fixed-price contract. Once the destroyer escort series were complete, with all the necessary modifications to increase their ability to deal with nuclear-powered submarines, the design and procurement staffs were dispersed.[53]

The process of fleet modernization was accelerated following the outbreak of the Korean War. Canadian expenditure on defence increased from $30 million a month in June 1950 to $150 million in June 1952, an annual rate for defence spending of $1.97 billion – 45 percent of the federal budget.[64] Robert Bothwell remarks that "such allocations reflected a revolution in the business of government and a startling change in priorities. Defence and foreign policy, at least as measured by the amount of money spent, moved to the top of the government's agenda."[65] During the first postwar decade Canadian economic muscle was an effective driver of foreign policy, giving Canada a degree of influence that was to melt away once Germany and Japan began to recover their places in the world order. But Lund suggests that the Canadian navy, with Vice-Admiral Rollo Mainguy as chief of naval staff, was erring on the side of accepting too great responsibilities, as it had during the desperate days of 1940; Korean war expansion amounted to an increase of 300 percent in the Canadian fleet, compared to the 20 percent increase being undertaking in the Royal Navy.[66]

Hennessy writes: "the scale of the total rearmament effort was staggering. Plans were generated on the premise that Canada should prepare its forces for war, rather than for deterring war. Basic plans for wartime mobilization prepared in 1949 called for peak production to be achieved by 1952, though later modified to mid-1954, by which time Canadian industry was to be geared to producing war-goods at a rate some 32.2 percent greater than the rate achieved in 1944 ... Fundamentals insisted upon were redundancy and self-sufficiency of supply. Essentially that meant Canadian production of all major components, and where that proved impossible, reliance on North American supply. For the shipbuilding industry this entailed being geared-up to produce possibly 100 frigates within three years."[67]

Despite the fact that the Canadian destroyers sent to Korea were frequently employed in coastal gunnery operations, the modernizations replaced heavy gun armament with more effective anti-submarine weapons and sensors. The first of two ex-British 6-inch gun cruisers, HMCS *Uganda*, had been taken into the Canadian fleet in October 1944, but neither *Uganda*, later renamed *Quebec*, nor *Ontario* were to be deployed across the Pacific during the Korean war, and with considerable regret they were both disposed of by 1958. Conversion of war-built *River* class frigates was begun, giving them *Squid* anti-submarine mortars. The first of the class to be refitted, HMCS *Prestonian*, was recommissioned on 28 August 1953. In the period June 1952 to October 1954 a further series of seven destroyer escorts were laid down, with HMCS *Restigouche* being commissioned in June 1958. The launching of the world's first nuclear-powered submarine, USS *Nautilus*, which was commissioned 30 September 1954, served as a warning that the future naval threat could take the form of submarines with virtually unlimited submerged range at speeds that would eventually exceed those of surface craft.

Having overcome the RCAF's conviction that it should control all military aircraft, carrier aviation was retained as part of the anti-submarine commitment. The first Canadian light fleet carrier, HMCS *Warrior*, had entered service in January 1946, and was to be replaced in 1948 by HMCS *Magnificent* and in 1957 by HMCS *Bonaventure*, which was finally paid off in 1970. In response to USS *Midway*'s activity in the Davis Strait, *Magnificent* visited the Hudson Bay port of Churchill with two destroyers soon after commissioning, possibly largely to justify the retention of carrier air by suggesting its importance in the defence of Canadian sovereignty in the arctic. Indeed, Claxton had used that argument in January 1947 to support the acquisition of *Magnificent*.[68] But the focus on ASW was to be reflected in the *Bonaventure*'s standard air complement of twelve ASW CS2F *Tracker* aircraft, which entered service in May 1957, and only eight air defence F2H *Banshee* fighters without any airborne early warning.[69]

The RCAF also built on its wartime experience in maritime operations, and in 1953 a formal agreement was signed by the RCN and RCAF to ensure effective co-ordination of their efforts. A study group formed to determine the optimum balance between sea and air forces noted: "[it is] inevitable that a further stage of their studies will embrace the question of control of Maritime Warfare."[70] In 1952 the design was drawn for a new, specialized, four-engined maritime patrol aircraft, the CP107 *Argus*, which began to enter service in the RCAF in 1957.

In 1952 and 1953 NATO ran exercises *Mainbrace* and *Mariner*, which focused attention on naval reinforcement of the northern flank of a European battlefield. Canada's ambassador to NATO Council, Arnold Heeney, told Pearson that HMC ships *Magnificent* and *Quebec*, the RCN's commitment to the 170-ship fleet deployed for *Mainbrace*, gave "a good account of themselves." Isabel Campbell comments that the navy's decision to send its "light fleet carrier and a training cruiser showed political shrewdness, reinforcing the notion that these large warships

HMCS *Ontario* (C 53). A *Minotaur* class light cruiser built at Harland & Wolff in Belfast for the Royal Navy, she was transferred to the Royal Canadian Navy in July 1944 and completed for service in May 1945 when she joined the British Pacific fleet, too late to see action in the war. She is seen here on a spring training cruise, 24 February 1958, and was decommissioned in 1960. DND E-44527

HMCS *Fort Erie* (K 670), *River* class frigate, 1944–45, then put into reserve until converted to a *Prestonian* frigate, recommissioned with pennant 312 in 1956, and paid off in 1965. The author served as a cadet on this ship in the summer of 1964. DND CN-3516

HMCS *Magnificent* (CVL 21). A *Majestic* class light aircraft carrier, built for the Royal Navy by Harland & Wolff, she was transferred following the war and served in the Royal Canadian Navy between 1946 and 1956. She is seen in this picture nearing the Azores en route to Suez, stripped of her armament and loaded with army vehicles for the first UN Peacekeeping Mission, 2 January 1957. DND MAG-7560

directly supported the land battle in Europe and, importantly, helped to deter Soviet attack in Central Europe, *regardless* of the actual exercise deployment and analysis which remained cloaked in secrecy. What mattered at the political level was public relations and impact on European politics – not tactical performance or actual capabilities."[71]

Mackenzie King had discouraged military establishments in the arctic as possibly counter-productive, being too isolated to defend but possibly useful to an enemy. At a meeting of the joint staff and chiefs of staff in March 1948, it had been agreed that it would be impossible to provide garrisons for bases in the north, and that attention should be given to having available "mobile counter-attack forces" consisting of two airborne brigade groups or regimental combat teams, based in the Fairbanks-Anchorage area, and at Winnipeg.[72] Circumstances, however, made some Canadian naval presence in the arctic a necessity. Construction of the Pine Tree radar line using Canadian and American resources was begun during the Korean war, and in January 1954 the first experimental station that ultimately became the Distant Early Warning line was built by the Americans on Herschell Island. The full line of seventy-eight stations stretching along the 70th parallel from Alaska to Greenland was paid for by the United States, and the original terms gave the USAF control of large areas of Canada. Between 1949 and 1954 the only important vessels working in the Canadian arctic were two American icebreakers, conducting scientific research, but possibly intent on transiting the Northwest Passage to establish a precedent.

The Canadian government recognized that it could not let the Americans establish a claim through what would amount to effective occupation. The Canadian navy needed to contribute to the scientific work in order to support Canadian sovereignty claims. It is significant that the first ship ordered for the Canadian navy after the conclusion of the war should have been intended for arctic service, its one and only icebreaker, HMCS *Labrador*, which was commissioned in 1954. That first summer she became the first large ship to transit the Northwest Passage, and the first warship. For three years she supported scientific work in the arctic, but she was transferred to the Canadian Coast Guard three years after entering naval service. The Royal Canadian Air Force collaborated with the United States Air Force in mapping the arctic archipelago, and the Canadian Army Signals Corps operated arctic radio stations.

It was becoming apparent, however, that the scale of Canadian defence spending could not be sustained without serious implications for economic development. It was not only Ottawa that balked at the strain. Churchill asked the British chiefs of staff to examine the options for a less expensive defence of Europe, and a beginning was made to the introduction of tactical nuclear weapons to defeat an assault by the Red Army.

The threat posed by the Soviet test of a thermonuclear bomb on 12 August 1953 downgraded the importance NATO gave to mobilization potential. Only the forces available at the outset of war would be significant in the outcome of battlefield manoeuvring. In a speech on 12 January 1954, President Dwight Eisenhower's secretary of state, John Foster Dulles, described a "New Look" strategy of "Massive Retaliation," which put the emphasis on nuclear retaliation to deter attack: "Local defense will always be important. But [it] must be reinforced by the further deterrent of massive retaliatory power. A potential aggressor must know that he cannot always prescribe battle conditions that suit him ... The way to deter aggression is for the free communities to

HMCS *Labrador* (AW 50). A *Wind* class icebreaker, she was the first ship ordered built for the Royal Canadian Navy following the war. Built by Marine Industries at Sorel, she was equipped as a floating laboratory, completed a transit of the Northwest Passage, and worked on the construction of the Distant Early Warning line. Seen here alongside a cathedral iceberg, 15 July 1957, she was transferred to the Canadian Coast Guard in November 1957. DND LAB 2240

be willing and able to respond vigorously at places and with means of our own choosing."[73] In mid-1955 NATO strategy was defined by MC48, which envisaged a relatively short war of nuclear forces followed by a longer period of war termination. It was recognized that atomic weapons employed against mercantile port facilities could be the greatest threat to resupply of Europe.[74]

❖ ❖ ❖

The first occasion following the Second World War when a Canadian warship was deployed operationally in support of a Canadian foreign policy objective was in March 1949, when HMCS *Crescent* was ordered to join a Commonwealth naval force stationed at Shanghai to protect foreign nationals during the Chinese Communist defeat of the Nationalist government. Although the addition of a Canadian ship was of little importance to the outcome of the operation, Prime Minister St Laurent and External Affairs minister Pearson were interested in showing that Canada would be taking an active part in the management of international crises.[75] In Sir James Cable's taxonomy, the *Crescent* deployment was certainly an act of expressive force, and may also be considered purposive force to the extent that it was conceived of as a means of adjusting Canada's political stature in London and Washington.

The new activism was confirmed a few months later when the Canadian Navy took part in the Korean war, but it was a participation the Canadian government accepted only reluctantly. For Canada it was the wrong war and it was a war in which the Canadian government would incur obligations without any influence. Due to the absence of the Soviet ambassador, Jacob Malik, who was boycotting the United Nations over the issue of Chinese representation, President Truman was able to use the United Nations to legitimize and fast track the military response of fifteen nations, including Canada. Resort to the Security Council did an end run around the right of the Senate to approve any declaration of war, and also facilitated Canadian participation. In the Commons debate on 30 June, Prime Minister St Laurent assured the Members of the House that "any participation by Canada in carrying out the foregoing resolution ... would be our part in collective police action under the control and authority of the United Nations.' The leader of the Opposition, George Drew, supported Canadian action, warning that the United Nations itself was in danger should it fail to resist aggression. "Our prestige and the prestige of every member nation are committed by these events. On the outcome of this issue in Korea depends the future effectiveness of the United Nations."[76] But Bothwell notes that "nothing Truman did transferred any serious decision making from Washington to UN headquarters in New York. For the duration, US decisions would also be those of the UN, rather than vice versa."[77]

On 5 July three Canadian destroyers were ordered from Esquimalt – *Cayuga*, *Athabaskan*, and *Sioux*. They took up duties escorting U.S., Royal Navy, and Australian aircraft carriers, guarding fishing fleets, and bombarding enemy gun positions and rail communications. Michael Whitby has written that the Canadian navy viewed the Korean war as an opportunity to demonstrate to the Canadian leadership its utility in the post–Second World War period: the deployment of the destroyers "would be seen as meaningful, it would be relatively casualty-free given the small size of the North Korean Navy, and since it would take the destroyers some time to reach Korea the government would be seen to be taking action while still having time to finalize Canada's precise role ... The Korean War helped to turn things around, demonstrating that the navy had a valuable role to play in the post-war world, one at which it could excel." The Canadian carrier was not sent to serve in Korea on the grounds that it was committed to NATO, but a total of eight Canadian ships were rotated through the Korean theatre in the course of the next five years, placing a heavy strain on a fleet that then contained eleven destroyers, of which only nine were in commission.

The dispatch of naval forces to serve the needs of External Affairs without straining postwar economic recovery or Canadian unity was consistent with Sir Francis Bacon's observation noted above and made more than three hundred years earlier, that "he that commands the sea

HMCS *Sioux* (R 64/225). A *V* class destroyer originally built for the Royal Navy and commissioned as HMS *Vixen*, she was transferred to the Royal Canadian Navy in 1944. Having served with the British Home Fleet in the Arctic, and at the Normandy landings, she was modernized in 1950 and is seen here bombarding the North Korean coast in 1951. DND

is at great liberty, and may take as much and as little of the war as he will."[78] Naval forces, however, were not enough to defeat the North Korean invasion. An American State Department official reportedly referred to *Cayuga*, *Athabaskan*, and *Sioux* as the "three tokens." The Canadian government agreed to send transport aircraft and ultimately, after a Cabinet meeting on the train carrying Mackenzie King's body for burial, ground forces. Quite literally, a Special Service Brigade was authorized over his dead body. Pearson would have preferred the creation of a United Nations army, but during the course of the conflict over 21,000 Canadian soldiers fought as part of the 1st (Commonwealth) Division. It was a matter of some concern in Ottawa that Secretary General Trygve Lie had addressed his appeal for forces to the press before contacting governments, a proceeding too reminiscent of imperial London. When a truce was reached and North Korean soldiers withdrew behind the 38th parallel, the last Canadian unit to leave the theatre was *Sioux*, on her third tour to Korea.[79]

✦ ✦ ✦

The deployment of Canadian destroyers to Korea was a measure of expressive force and, together with the land and air deployments, contributed to the collective definitive purpose. But it was to become evident that these deployments had little purposive power vis-à-vis Canada's allies. Peter Gellman writes that Ottawa's commitment to collective security, the United Nations, and American leadership, all took a beating during the war. Chinese warnings that the Americans should not destroy the North Korean government were strongly represented to the American government by Pearson, but were ignored. When General Douglas MacArthur's pursuit of the North Korean army toward the Chinese border led to Chinese intervention on 25 October 1950, and when Truman told the press that the United States might use atomic weapons, Pearson warned the American ambassador, Stanley Woodward, that "if the fighting in Korea spread to China, [the Canadian] Government might have to reconsider its position with respect to the commitment of troops in the Far East." Dean Acheson recalls that Pearson needed to be reassured "that alarm over the safety of our troops would not drive [the United States] to some ill-considered use of atomic weapons," and wished the country would "end [its] conflict with the Chinese in order to resume active participation in security for Europe."[80] When the panic subsided, however, it was discovered that Washington, London, and Ottawa were in general agreement. The British prime minister, Clement Attlee, had hurried to Washington, but was reassured that the United States had no intention of using the atomic bomb on China. He was able to report that reassurance to the Canadian Cabinet when he visited Ottawa on 9 December, and also that the United States agreed with the British and Canadian position that it would be "fatal to pour the resources of the democratic nations into a war with China which would leave the Soviet Union free to act in Europe."[81]

Frustrated by the deadlock in the Security Council that followed the return of the Soviet ambassador, the United States on 3 November 1950 had sponsored a "Uniting for Peace" resolution in the General Assembly, Resolution 377, which made it possible for a majority of nations to take action for collective security when the permanent members of the Security Council disagreed.[82] Pearson used his position as president of the General Assembly in 1952 to seek a cease fire, employing the Uniting for Peace provision. Pearson's peace diplomacy, however, was formative of a strong tendency for Washington to seek to marginalize the United Nations when it could not use it to its own advantage. "It was clear even in the hour of creation," writes John Holmes, whose career as a Canadian diplomat included the role of chargé d'affaires *ad interim* to the Soviet Union, acting permanent delegate to the United Nations, and from 1953 to 1960 assistant under-secretary of state for external affairs, "that although Americans talked the language of international democracy and equality and thought they meant it, there was a prevalent assumption, especially in congress, that the US will must not be thwarted by any system. This was not seen in the US as a major problem because of the easy assumption that right-thinking people would recognize US aims as their own."[83] After his victory in the November 1952 election, Dwight Eisenhower did use diplomatic channels to threaten China with nuclear war if it did not agree to a truce.

The experience of the Korean war seems to have made Pearson ambivalent about collective security, and strengthened his concern about American leadership. On 31 March 1951 he made a speech to the Canadian Bar Association in which he spelled out a new and more limited commitment to "selective collective security," and on 10 April he made a speech in Toronto to the Empire and Canada clubs which came with a warning: "the days of relatively easy and automatic political relations with our neighbour are, I think, over ... Our preoccupation is no longer whether the United States will discharge her international responsibilities, but how she will do it and how the rest of us will be involved."[84]

President Truman dismissed MacArthur the following day, and eventually negotiated a truce, but there is no evidence that Pearson's initiative precipitated Truman's decision. It may only have served to embarrass his colleagues and irritate the Americans. In Gellman's opinion, Pearson "reduced the Canadian commitment to collective security to a form of rhetorical pretence." That may be an excessive reaction to Pearson's assessment that the democracies could only survive if they chose their battles carefully and made their decisions on the basis of balance of power calculations that might or might not reflect collective security. Pearson was not alone in fearing that the Korean conflict was intended to divert military resources away from the central front of NATO defence in Europe.[85]

What the Korean war had demonstrated was that Washington valued Canadians as supporters but not as advisors, and that even if advice from Ottawa proved to be well founded it had little positive effect on the self-absorbed policy-formulation process in Washington. Henry Kissinger's dictum quoted in the introduction, that "in an alliance of sovereign states, a country's influence requires that its effort be considered essential and that its partners do not take it for granted," places the bar for purposive force well above the limited Canadian naval, air, and military contribution to United Nations forces off Korea.[86] Under pressure from the United States, the Canadian mission in Nanking, which had provided warning of the likely consequence of MacArthur's military advance toward the Chinese frontier, was withdrawn and Canada did not extend recognition to the People's Republic of China until 1970. In November 1952 Acheson travelled to Ottawa and advised the Canadian Cabinet to be realistic and positive about its minor role in the new American imperium. In terms of Canada's fundamental interest in keeping the United States engaged in the defence of Europe, however, Canada's military effort was not without value.

✦ ✦ ✦

While the Korean operations were relatively high-profile measures of naval support for Canadian foreign policy, the development of CANUS (Canada/U.S.) concepts and the commitment of Canadian forces to the NATO alliance were the most important ways in which Canadian investment in military forces served Canadian foreign policy interests. Canadian specialization in anti-submarine forces was consistent with the strategic objective of protecting Canadian interests in Canada's coastal waters, but it also served larger defence issues, including the fundamental concern of promoting the continued partnership of the United States with Europe. Dr Robert Sutherland, director of operational research, Department of National Defence, would write in 1963: "there is a specific Canadian national interest in asserting a Canadian naval presence in adjacent ocean areas and especially the Gulf of St Lawrence and its approaches. This objective is compatible with concentration upon the ASW [Anti-Submarine Warfare] role since the most important potential threat in these waters is the Soviet submarine. The fact that it has been possible for Canada, without doing violence to her national interests, to concentrate her efforts upon the ASW role must be regarded as an important national advantage. It is this fact which has enabled Canada to maintain efficient and modern maritime forces notwithstanding our comparatively limited defence budget."[87]

Anti-submarine forces are topically appropriate to the task of monitoring activity off-shore, and make possible national control in coastal waters. Surveillance is the *sine qua non* of coastal control, and control of the water column is the most technically difficult aspect of the task. The situation was unchanged from the 1930s to the extent that Canada needed to be able to meet the most likely local naval threat with its own resources so as to obviate American assumption of control. This requirement is especially significant to the management of offshore resources because at sea, where international law does not preclude the passage of foreign warships, effective occupation is an elastic concept. The limits of Canadian jurisdiction must be reasonably clearly defined by naval forces implementing national policy: as the American poet Robert Frost put it, "Good fences make good neighbors." Showing the flag off Canada's coasts continued to be an important part of the navy's job.

The mechanism by which the blue-water fleet protected local Canadian interests went beyond co-tasking. The NATO and CANUS blue-water roles also served local Canadian requirements by participating in the defence requirements of Canada's friends. Suasion, if needed, could be leveraged by withdrawing from alliance to local commitments. Only naval forces designed to address problems of collective defence, and also capable of carrying out constabulary tasks, could secure that double purpose, while minimizing infra-alliance conflict by keeping the suasion ambiguous. Specialization in strategic anti-submarine surveillance and prosecution, and defence of shipping, ensured that in that area of Alliance activity Canadian forces were as nearly indispensable as could be contrived, but were also appropriate for national sovereignty enforcement.

HMCS *Sioux* (DD 225), firing anti-submarine squid bombs during exercises with HMS *Cossack* out of Chinhae, South Korea, 23 March 1955. DND SO-539

The Cold War strengthened the capacity of the Canadian government to exert this sort of influence by creating an apparently urgent need for Canadian assistance, but at the same time generally progressing at slow enough a pace that Canadian statesmen were less constrained by the iminence of crisis to accept the leadership of the great powers than they had been during the world wars.

Indispensability in one aspect of defence might also serve to generate influence in other aspects. At the end of the day, however, the leverage given the Canadian government by *quid pro quo* military negotiation is little enough. David Bercuson has argued that a factor in the decline of Canadian defence spending from 1952 was the discovery that it generated little direct influence in allied capitals. However much was spent, it was always too little. "For Canada, NATO membership always had an important symbolic meaning, but being a key player – really making a difference militarily – was too costly for too little return."[88]

That marginal disappointment should not obscure the principal point. The main advantage to Canada of effective support of NATO's maritime communications was the success of the NATO nations' efforts to deter a Soviet conquest of Europe, thereby making possible the continued strategic linkage of Europe and North America. The value of Canadian specialization in sea control lay chiefly in its specific effect on the strategic environment. Selection of that role directly reinforced the ability of western European states to resist Soviet control as well as the ability of the United States to extend its defensive perimeter to Europe. The commitment of the Canadian carrier to service in the Eastern Atlantic added to the optics of Canadian participation in European defence.

In Ottawa there was concern that Washington's New Look strategic policy amounted to a lurch back to isolationism, with obvious implications for Canadian independence, a regression which might, it was feared, lead to irresponsible unilateralism. In February 1954 Dana Wilgress, who had succeeded Heeney as Canadian ambassador to NATO, predicted: "Canada must inevitably be part of the fortress 'America'; and it is not difficult to foresee that a greater part of our military effort than hitherto will have to be devoted to the integrated defence system of the American continent."[89] This prospect was anathema to External Affairs. Lester Pearson argued in a radio address that nuclear weapons were such a game changer that they should never be employed without extensive consultation. When that was ignored, he warned the Washington Press Club in March 1954: "an important factor in determining the attitude of Canadians to things American is the feeling that our destiny, so soon after we achieved national independence from colonial status, may be decided, not by ourselves, but across our border 'by means and at places *not* of our choosing.'" It is essential, he continued, "that we work together in any new defence planning and policy ... if the great coalition which we have formed for peace is not to be replaced by an entrenched continentalism which, I can assure you, makes no great appeal to your northern neighbour as the best way to prevent war or defeat aggression, and which is not likely to provide a solid basis for good United States-Canadian relations."[90] In a briefing note three weeks later to Prime Minister St Laurent, Pearson was more explicit: "The new strategy may result, therefore, in greater rigidity, rather than greater flexibility, of policy. If it becomes a question of the atomic bomb and all-out war, or nothing, it may be, too often, nothing." He warned that the United States could be heading toward a maritime strategy, abandoning most of western Europe as it was not providing adequately for its own defence.[91]

Pearson's concern was shared in London. The advice given the Canadian Navy Board in November 1954 by the British First Sea Lord,

Admiral of the Fleet Sir Rhoderick Robert McGrigor, was that the Americans "placed too much emphasis upon atomic bombardment from the air and by guided missiles from submarines to the exclusion of progressing plans to keep shipping lanes open and fight a submarine threat."[92] Haydon suggests that the succession of British naval visitors "could be interpreted as an attempt to keep Canada out of the American camp and to support British efforts for a share in NATO maritime influence," but Sean Malone attributes McGrigor's advice to the concern that the United States might be retreating from a commitment to European defence into a continentalist fortress America.[93] Both interpretations are likely correct, and McGrigor's caution also anticipated a general recognition that the threat of nuclear Armageddon was a blunt instrument, and one unsuited to meeting the danger from incremental aggression.

✦ ✦ ✦

The continued relevance of tactical ASW in the context of NATO's MC48 strategy directive was to be hotly debated for the next twenty years. Writing of this period in 1967, Jon McLin notes the disconnect between the continuing emphasis of the Canadian navy, and NATO navies in general, on preparing to fight a conventional war at sea, and NATO's adoption of a nuclear strategy that relegated the conventional forces in Europe to a trip-wire that would trigger massive nuclear retaliation: "No compelling justification was given of the strategy upon which the antisubmarine capability was based; no effective answer was given, either, to those [such as General Charles Foulkes, from 1951 chairman of the chiefs of staff] who questioned whether the particular collection of ships and aircraft assembled by the early 1960's for conducting ASW operations represented a well-considered policy."[94] But McLin's criticism did not adequately represent the extent to which Canadian naval effort was being redirected to provide effective warning of an attack by Soviet submarine-delivered nuclear ordinance, regardless of the concern felt in Ottawa and London about the American tendency toward a fortress strategy.

In the late 1940s both the Soviet and the American navies had begun work on developing the wartime German V-1 flying bomb into nuclear land-attack cruise missiles that could be launched from surfaced submarines. The American *Regulus I* became operational in 1954, but was taken out of service in 1958 in order to concentrate on the development of ballistic missiles that could be launched while submerged. The first Soviet submarine armed with ballistic missiles was a converted *Zulu* class that successfully launched a missile in September 1955. The first American nuclear submarine armed with ballistic missiles, USS *George Washington*, was to sail on its first patrol on 15 November 1960, three days after the commissioning of the first Soviet *Hotel* class nuclear submarine armed with strategic ballistic missiles.[95]

Malone writes that between 1954 and 1957 "Canadian maritime forces evolved from a SLOC protection force into a more specialized ASW force focused on a damage-limitation strategy. The new emphasis in 1954 on continental defence, which was in the main threat based, provided a starting point for this change. The shift from a projected to a real threat from enemy missile launching submarines prompted a corresponding shift not only in how Canadian maritime forces would be employed but also in how they were equipped. This evolution was continual and, by 1962, Canadian maritime forces were in a position to carry out the damage-limitation task effectively."[96] To help meet the threat the U.S. Navy agreed to give the Canadian navy direct access to SOSUS, and a CANUS processing station was established at Shelburne, Nova Scotia, 1 April 1955. The Canadian navy and air force established subcommittees to study the implications of nuclear-powered submarines and nuclear weapons. They reported to the Chiefs of Staff Committee on 26 October 1955, warning of the threat posed by Soviet ballistic missile submarines in the western Atlantic where they would be able to attack a third of the USAF Strategic Air Command bases.[97] Haydon writes that when on 16 November 1955 the Deputy Minister's Screening Committee examined the navy's intended procurement it reacted sharply to the scale of expenditure and lack of coherent planning.[98] The next day the vice-chief of naval staff minuted that "government policy is to give priority to those projects which will lessen the chance of NATO losing the war in the first 30 days."[99]

While much of Canadian defence effort had to be redeployed in the later 1950s to continental defence, the glacis of Fortress America extended well beyond Canada to the east and west, and there was to be no return to the isolationism of pre-war America. The growing importance of strategic ASW to defend the nuclear deterrent added to the symbiosis between alliance tasks and local defence, on the Pacific as well as the Atlantic.

Recognition in Washington of Canada's naval effort, however, was not an unalloyed blessing, as Canada's freedom of action was necessarily constrained. This was to become starkly apparent during the 1962 Cuban Missile crisis. Experience had shown that little attention was paid to Canadian concerns in the context of general war, and that lesson was to be emphasized by the nearest approach the world has come to nuclear war. Despite its technical focus on NATO and continental defence anti-submarine warfare, in broader strategic terms the Canadian navy had been employed from the outbreak of the Korean war in 1950 to reduce Canada's vulnerability to policies made in Washington by contributing to international stability in support of the United Nations. When the limitations of that strategy became as evident as were the limitations of Ottawa's ability to influence allied policies during the Cuban crisis, Ottawa would revert to a strategy of defence through token armament. The fourteen years following Dulles's formulation of the New Look strategy were to be traumatic ones for Canadian foreign policy. The Suez crisis in 1956 effectively ended the capacity of the Commonwealth to serve as a system of collective defence, and following the Cuban Missile crisis the Canadian government was to have increasing difficulty in devising a strategy for employing Canadian forces to promote Canadian interests.

5

THE COLD WAR:
SUEZ, THE CUBAN CRISIS, AND THE END
OF THE "GOLDEN AGE"

Suez was a crisis in Anglo-Canadian affairs comparable to the 1922 Chanak crisis, and all the more so because it was first and foremost a crisis in Anglo-American relations. Britain remained Canada's most important European partner, and Britain continued to be the centre of a web of Commonwealth defence relationships.[1] Egyptian president Gamel Abdel Nasser's nationalization of the Suez Canal Company on 26 July 1956 was a fundamental threat to Commonwealth security. The matter was taken to the United Nations, where on 13 October the Security Council passed Resolution 118 calling for the operation of the canal to be "isolated from the politics of any country." Pearson strongly urged London to work out a solution on this basis, but Sir Anthony Eden, the British prime minister, was not willing to trust to the UN process.[2] Eden's pre-war experience of trying to make the League of Nations an adequate instrument for peace enforcement, to the failure of which Canada's isolationist policy at the time contributed, led him to believe that the safety of Britain and the Commonwealth could not be left in the hands of the United Nations. The British and French governments secretly agreed to back up an Israeli invasion of Suez, and, unwisely, they were careful that advance warning of the intended action should not reach Washington.

The Canadian government found itself in the familiar position of having to decide whether to support a British *fait accompli*. After the British began to bomb targets in Egypt in preparation for a landing, Eden asked St Laurent for support. Infuriated, St Laurent tasked Eden with imperilling the United Nations, the unity of the Commonwealth, and Anglo-American friendship. Three weeks after the Anglo-French invasion, St Laurent declared in the House of Commons that the "the era when the supermen of Europe could govern the whole world has and is coming pretty close to an end."[3] The Eisenhower administration forced a cease-fire on Britain and France, first by sponsoring a resolution in the Security Council demanding one, which the British and French governments vetoed, and then by denying Britain access to the International Monetary Fund and threatening to sell U.S. holdings of the pound Stirling, which led to a precipitous fall in its value. The United States then appealed to the United Nations General Assembly under the terms of Uniting for Peace. Pearson had flown to New York, and after consultation with the American ambassador to the United Nations, Henry Cabot Lodge, he exploited a comment made by Eden, that the Anglo-French invasion was a police action to separate the combatants, to secure a vote in the General Assembly to establish a United Nations emergency force (UNEF) to monitor a peaceful resolution of the Suez crisis. Writing a decade later, Pearson said he was "impelled" by the following considerations: "extreme concern that the conflict might get out of control and spread beyond the Suez area; extreme concern that the United Kingdom and France, Canada's two Mother Countries, had become isolated from other Members of the Atlantic Alliance, particularly the United States; extreme concern that the armed intervention of the UK in the Israel-Egypt conflict would break up the Commonwealth." Pearson also seized on the opportunity to enhance the reputation of collective security.[4] British diplomats at the United Nations, appalled by Eden's folly, were eager to grasp Pearson's initiative as a way out of the disaster.

The Canadian government had agreed only reluctantly to supply truce observer officers when they were needed by the United Nations in Kashmir, Palestine, and Vietnam, but now the Canadian people proudly accepted the role of peacekeepers. President Nasser refused to have Canadian infantry because Pearson had been diplomatic in his characterization of the Anglo-French adventure, but grudgingly accepted Canadian service and transport troops, aircraft, and an armoured reconnaissance squadron because no one else offered them. To provide transport for the Canadian contingent to this force, the decommissioning carrier HMCS *Magnificent* was stripped of her weapons and employed as a troop ship.

Canada's role in creating and participating in the Suez peacekeeping mission had the important purposive result of defusing the Anglo-American crisis. Jack Granatstein wrote from the perspective of 1974 that "for a few critical weeks, discourse between London-Paris and Washington ceased, and Canada seized the opportunity to become the channel of communication between the old world and the new. The linch-pin, the bridge, the interpreter – all the hoary clichés suddenly came true."[5]

The definitive effect was certainly less satisfactory. In the wake of the Suez crisis, any illusions that the historic British ties could offset Canadian dependence on the United States had to be abandoned. In May 1957 Ralph Campney, the minister of national defence, commented to the Cabinet: "The impression which some [in Britain] would wish to convey was that the UK remained an independent world power but this was no longer economically or physically possible."[6]

The aftershocks from the Suez crisis included the political defeat of the Liberal administration, which had already been discredited by its use of closure during the parliamentary "pipeline" debate. St Laurent's "supermen of Europe" remark was bitterly resented by the Conservative press, and the Conservative leader, John Diefenbaker, harvested that resentment at the 10 June 1957 general election. The armed forces continued to vote for the Liberal party, but the St Laurent government was defeated. In a 1992 essay, Granatstein noted that "most accounts agree that Canada's UNEF role cut little ice with the electors, more of them seeming to turn against the Liberals for their 'betrayal' of Britain than voting for them for Pearson's UN role."[7]

Diefenbaker soon discovered, however, that he could not take Canada back along the older paths. Britain needed to come to terms with the European Common Market. Diefenbaker warned the September 1962 Commonwealth Prime Ministers' Conference that Canadians had "spent a hundred years resisting the magnetic pull of the United States ... Now this will put us in danger of being sucked into their orbit." But with Britain's international influence rapidly waning, Canada was indeed drawn ever more firmly into the American gravitational field.[8] Just how far was to become clearly apparent the following month when American surveillance planes identified Soviet intermediate range ballistic missile launchers nearing completion at San Cristóbal in western Cuba.[9]

Apart from wrapping himself in the Imperial flag, Diefenbaker had campaigned on a platform of northern development. On his arrival in the prime minister's office, he became alarmed at the extent of American military control in the arctic, and resolved, he said, to "put an end to that." His minister of northern affairs in 1957, Alvin Hamilton, flew into the excluded zone and forced the American commandant of one of the radar stations to hoist a Canadian flag.[10] In 1960 the U.S. Navy established SOSUS sensors in Hudson Bay, with signal processing at the American base at Argentia; and Donat Pharand, professor emeritus, Faculty of Law, University of Ottawa, reports that USS *Skate* transited the Northwest Passage in 1960 and USS *Seadragon* in 1962. "It is the author's understanding," Pharand adds, "that both transits were made pursuant to Canada/U.S. defense arrangements. In the case of the USS *Seadragon*, there even was a Canadian representative aboard in the person of Commander O.C.S. Robertson.[11] In other words, those transits were effected with Canada's consent and cooperation."[12]

John Holmes's judgment was that "the U.S. military in fact regarded the North as a diversion. The Canadian front was ... usually seen in Washington as a minor element in more important matters, including their own inter-service rivalries." Nor were Diefenbaker's histrionics representative of official Ottawa's attitude. "Whether or not our fears of the Soviet Union were justified, Canada saw itself in a new air age as open at the top. Conscious of having much larger territorial responsibilities than we could afford to cope with on our own, we wanted help from our powerful neighbour."[13] As an indication of the degree of comfort in Ottawa about the relationship with the United States, Canadian naval visits to the arctic were suspended.[14]

Nevertheless, Diefenbaker's concern was not entirely wide of the mark. The U.S. Joint Chiefs of Staff were determined that continental defence should be independent of the multilateral NATO alliance which Americans, and most Europeans, regarded as exclusively for the defence of Europe. The establishment of an integrated air defence command structure was announced on 1 August 1957 shortly after the Diefenbaker administration was sworn into office, and only later did Diefenbaker take up with President Eisenhower the question of consultation before defensive measures were taken. The NATO defence system acknowledged the right of member states to determine whether their own forces should be engaged in collective action. When the formal exchange of notes on North American Air Defence Agreement (NORAD) was made in May 1958, Norman Robertson, recently appointed as Canada's ambassador to the United States, noted in his letter to Secretary of State John Foster Dulles that the establishment of an integrated air defence headquarters was consistent with the practice of NATO, adding: "The Canada-United States region is an integral part of the NATO area." But the Pentagon was determined to retain enough independence to be able to respond to a surprise attack without waiting for political direction, and the agreed text added only that "defence co-operation between them can be worked out on a mutually satisfactory basis only if such consultation is regularly and consistently undertaken."[15] The secretary general of NATO, General Paul-Henri Spaak, later told a Canadian press conference that the North American Air Defence Command should not be regarded as a NATO command.[16] Robertson had continued, noting that there would be the "fullest possible consultation between the two Governments on all matters affecting the joint defence of North America," but that expectation was very different from a commitment to consult prior to putting defences on alert.

Strategically it was illogical to separate continental defence from NATO. Canada's principal rationale for exposing itself to attack by participating in continental defence arrangements was to enhance deterrence by ensuring the survival of the American nuclear arsenal, primarily with the objective of making the nuclear guarantee of Europe more credible. The participation of NORAD and the Canadian navy in North American sea control in support of the American deterrent forces was central to the defence of Europe. Juridically, the separation of NORAD from NATO was also incoherent. It was only through NATO that Canada and the United States were formally allied. The operational arrangements for continental defence were technical realizations of the alliance relationship Canada and the United States shared through NATO, and these only differed from other alliance arrangements because they were not part of the military organization of NATO. In 1966 France was to establish a similar relationship with its NATO allies when it withdrew from NATO's military organization. Holmes was right when he wrote that NORAD "is not, as often assumed, a Canada-US military alliance, but rather a consequence of the alliance."[17]

As they were understood in the United States, the Canada-United States continental defence arrangements conflicted with Ottawa's longest-held political objective and made Canada automatically an accomplice to American foreign policy. That there appeared to be no other way of fulfilling Mackenzie King's 1938 commitment to prevent hostile attack on the United States across Canadian territory and at the same time support the capacity of nuclear deterrence to defend western Europe was not very comforting. The NORAD Agreement, while it did commit the Americans to consultation with Canada, did not in fact provide for the intervention of the Canadian political leadership before air defence arrangements were put into effect. This the Cuban crisis was to make starkly clear, but in fact Ottawa's attitude to defence partnership had begun to change several years earlier.

✦ ✦ ✦

The pace with which nuclear technology was transforming military planning left little time for patient reconciliation of national, CANUS, and NATO interests. The capacity of the *St Laurent* destroyer-escort was tested against USS *Nautilus* in 1956, and it was demonstrated that what was considered to be the most advanced anti-submarine ship in the world was no match for a nuclear-powered submarine capable of indefinite speed of 23.3 knots, and able to eliminate propellor cavitation noise by going deep.[18] The need for effective teamwork, and infrastructure support, was crucial.

An RCN Naval Warfare Study Group concluded that any diesel-electric Soviet submarine approaching the coast of North America would have to snort two hundred miles offshore to recharge its batteries before closing to attack shipping or launch missiles. In 1957 the Canadian navy established with the air force a "Concept of Maritime Operations" that increased emphasis on sea control in the western Atlantic. An "Inner Combat Zone" was established from two hundred miles offshore to the limits of effective SOSUS detection, within which the air force maritime patrol aircraft would provide quick prosecution of contacts and the navy would respond with surface ships. The navy would extend strategic ASW surveillance into an "Outer Combat Zone" of a further hundred miles, extended in 1958 to three hundred miles. Canadian naval planning called for all shipping to disperse into smaller Canadian harbours during the first phase of a nuclear war. *November* class nuclear attack submarines entered service in the Soviet navy in March 1959, and that same year a joint headquarters was belatedly established under the commander of Maritime Forces to control both the navy's ships and the aircraft of RCAF Maritime Command.[19]

As early as 1957 SACLANT concluded that nuclear depth charges would be necessary to deal with nuclear submarines, and the Chiefs of Staff Sea/Air Warfare Committee concluded that "the lack of nuclear weapons will make Canadian forces less effective."[20] The Canadian navy never acquired nuclear weapons, but was to be affected by the fallout from the controversy that followed upon Canada signing on to NATO's new strategic concept, MC14/2, calling for deployment of tactical nuclear weapons by forces in Europe to establish a clear linkage between the defence of the German frontier and American strategic nuclear forces.[21] David Bercuson writes that, in the pursuit of affordable defence of Europe, "no country pursued the nuclear option more vigorously than Canada."[22] The Canadian government procured five weapon systems intended for nuclear warheads – but the Diefenbaker administration failed to complete the arrangements for them to be provided by the United States under two-key control. There was some suggestion that the Cabinet wanted to obtain unlimited control of the weapons, but there never was any prospect of Washington agreeing to that. In 1908 and 1910 London had reluctantly agreed to the formation of Australian and Canadian navies, despite the concern expressed by the Committee of Imperial Defence that "wars arise out of acts done in times of peace."[23] But there was no prospect whatsoever of Canada obtaining sovereign control of American nuclear weapons, because the American Imperium had a different character than had the British Empire in its time, and because nuclear weapons had so immeasurably raised the stakes.

The speed and detection problems of dealing with a nuclear-powered submarine that came within range in order to attack a convoy were multiplied when the task was to intercept a missile-armed submarine approaching a firing position within range of American air and missile bases. The Soviet P-5 *Pyatyorka* cruise missile with a range of 500 nm and either a conventional of nuclear warhead entered service in 1959 mounted on converted *Whiskey* submarines, and posed a threat to coastal American targets, especially strategic air command bomber bases. The *Hotel* class of strategic ballistic missile-armed submarine (SSBN) entered service in the Soviet navy late in 1960. The more capable *Yankee* class Soviet SSBN would begin its first combat patrol in the Atlantic in June 1969. It was calculated that a 27-knot *St Laurent* destroyer on its patrol station could take one hour and fifty minutes to reach a datum point provided by SOSUS, and an 18-knot *Prestonian* frigate could take two hours and fifteen minutes. A more advanced *Mackenzie* class destroyer escort was designed but its projected cost was prohibitive.

The decision not to transfer the CANUS Basic Security Plan to NATO presented Ottawa with technical, as well as political, difficulties. As Peter Haydon and Paul Mitchell put it: "from a Canadian perspective, activation of NATO plans required a shift from strategic ASW to the reinforcement of Europe and the projection of power against the USSR. Canada's problem was that its naval and maritime air forces were co-tasked to bilateral ASW operations and NATO reinforcement. The Americans did not have this problem because they had sufficient force to undertake both tasks at the same time."

Further complicating the need to meet both tactical and strategic ASW requirements was the operational plan to conduct aggressive forward operations into the Norwegian Sea in the event of war, to contain Soviet

Suez, the Cuban Crisis, and the End of the "Golden Age"

HMCS *Bonaventure* (CVL 22), a *Majestic* class light aircraft carrier, built for the Royal Navy by Harland & Wolff, and purchased for the Royal Canadian Navy in 1952 when she was converted for jet aircraft operations with an angled flight deck and steam catapults. She was Canada's last aircraft carrier and saw service during the Cuban missile crisis. Extensively refitted 1966–68, she was sold for scrap without being recommissioned. Photographed 6 November 1959. DND BN-3043

attack and missile submarines far from Atlantic convoys and out of missile range from the American coast. The USN's Commander Barrier Forces Atlantic was established at the American base at Argentia, Newfoundland, in the mid-1950s, tasked with interdiction of exiting Soviet submarines in the Greenland-Iceland-United Kingdom (GIUK) gap, and the Skagerrak. To accommodate SACLANT's continuing focus on barrier operations in the Iceland Faroes gap and the Skagerrak a new SACLANT command, Commander North Anti-Submarine Defence Force Atlantic, or STG 217, was created. The RCN hunter-killer force based on *Bonaventure* was one of the five groups tasked by the United States, Britain, the Netherlands, and Canada to barrier operations in the eastern Atlantic.[24] In 1960 it was agreed that the Canadian carrier with its escorts would be under CTG 217.1, the Canadian sub-command, and would operate out of Halifax in a CANUS role until D-day plus sixteen days, when it would escort a NATO convoy across the Atlantic and then operate out of Milford Haven or Brest.[25]

In addressing the problem posed by nuclear submarines, the Canadian navy made a quantum leap in ASW technology. The marriage of heavy helicopters and destroyers was a Canadian success story with roots stretching back to the middle of the Second World War when it had become evident that air support was a vital ingredient of convoy defence. In late 1958 the *Annual Review* of the North Atlantic Council urged Canada to bring forward its experimental program. Diefenbaker's first minister of national defence, General George R. Pearkes, was receptive, and on 14 January 1959 the Naval Board agreed to order the conversion of the *St Laurent* destroyer-escorts and the last two of the *Repeat Restigouche* class, which became known as the *Annapolis* class. The "Missile Gap" panic created to support the institutional ambitions of the U.S. Air Force in 1958 and used to support John F. Kennedy's election as American president spread to Canada and led to the navy deciding to convert all twenty of the existing or projected destroyer escorts to support manned helicopter operations, but the Treasury Board refused to be stampeded, and the conversion program was limited to the nine ships. When the *St Laurent*s began to return to service in October 1963 they had been transformed from destroyer escorts (DDE) into destroyers/helicopter (DDH) incorporating accommodation for a heavy *Sea King* helicopter equipped with dipping sonar and armed with anti-submarine torpedos, using a "beartrap" haul-down device to make all-weather operations possible. Variable-depth sonar was mounted on their sterns to increase active sonar ranges to 21,000 yards. HMC ships *Annapolis* and *Nipigon* entered service in 1964 with helicopter deck and hangar.

Much was accomplished. Michael Whitby writes that in the forty-three months that Vice-Admiral Harry DeWolf was chief of naval staff, from January 1956, "twenty-one new or significantly modernized ships were commissioned – including the modern, angled-deck aircraft carrier HMCS *Bonaventure* and thirteen new destroyer escorts derived from the successful *St Laurent* class. Such totals were unprecedented in the navy's peacetime history. And that was not all. The navy also took delivery of a hundred *Trackers*, a state-of-the-art carrier-borne ASW patrol aircraft; sent its first jet-powered, *Sidewinder*-armed, all-weather [*Banshee*] fighters to sea; and won approval for a submarine force, operational support ships and a maritime helicopter."[26] There were more than sixty warships in commission in the Royal Canadian Navy in 1961.

Michael Hennessy writes that "if a collective biography of the Naval Board through this period were to be prepared, it would demonstrate that almost every member had considerable sea combat experience, rang-

A *Sea King* helicopter lifts off the flight deck of HMCS *Saguenay* (DDH 206), a *St Laurent* class destroyer, during a cruise on Lake Ontario, 22 July 1979. *Saguenay* had been built at Halifax Shipyards 1951–56 as a destroyer escort (DDE) but was converted and reclassified in May 1965. DND 456 10C79-157

ing from small ship ASW operations to large fleet unit bombardment missions and even carrier operations. Most had withstood the test of war and many experienced their war far from Canadian home waters ... Those shared experiences influenced greatly their desire to remain technologically advanced and prepared to operate across the great global seas that admit no artificial boundary."[27] They could readily grasp the importance that the Royal and U.S. navies were increasingly giving to forward operations into the Norwegian Sea, in order to forestall the prospect of having to defeat Soviet submarines while providing close escort for shipping. That was an operational strategy that could only be pursued by a navy equipped to fight in a high air-threat environment. An air defence study of January 1961 recommended ship-based anti-aircraft missiles following the arming of Soviet *Badger* long-range aircraft with *Komet* anti-ship missiles.

Between 1956 and 1961, however, expenditure on the Canadian navy fell by 38 percent. The extent to which this drop was a consequence of the controversy over command and control in air defence, or a fall-out from debates over nuclear weapons procurement, has not been established. DeWolf recognized the political realities, and in April 1958 ordered the Repeat Restigouche destroyers, which became known as the *Mackenzie* class, rather than more capable ships that would have cost considerably more.[28] His sense of reality ensured that *Magnificent* was not retained as a helicopter carrier. DeWolf did attempt to get the support of the Chiefs of Staff Committee for Canadian participation in the hugely expensive U.S. Naval Tactical Data System for management of naval ASW, but was defeated in that. According to Julie Ferguson's study of the Canadian submarine service, DeWolf was initially enthusiastic about following the American and British lead with the development of a Canadian nuclear-powered submarine force, stating in an interview in May 1958, "Nuclear Submarines will ... make up half of Canada's fleet." Cabinet agreed on 22 March 1960 to increase the defence budget from $1.5 billion to $2 billion by the 1964/65 fiscal year. But enthusiasm waned, American support disappeared, and DeWolf was replaced on 31 July 1960 by Vice-Admiral H.S. Rayner.[29]

In April 1961 an Ad Hoc Committee on Naval Objectives was formed with the new vice-chief of naval staff, Rear Admiral Jeffrey V. Brock, as chairman, to assess whether "existing activities and future plans" were adequate. When at the end of July 1961 the Brock report was brought forward, it warned against the temptation to economize on conventional forces, as the ability to use nuclear weapons to destroy an enemy had "no positive value whatever to a nation whose opponent can do the same thing." Particular concern was expressed for an effective naval presence in the arctic.

An ambitious building program was sent to the Naval Board for approval, including the simultaneous acquisition of eight general purpose frigates, twelve conventional and nuclear powered submarines, twelve low-end replacements for the *Prestonian* frigates, conceived as ships of a similar size but configured to carry helicopters, two arctic patrol vessels and two additional tankers. Classified as auxiliary oiler replenishment ships (AOR), the first, HMCS *Provider,* had been laid down in May 1961. She was equipped to provide technical support for the *Sea King* helicopters on the destroyers, and was capable of handling three in her hangar and on her flight deck. The tankers were needed as force multipliers, making it possible for the Canadian destroyers to remain on station for extended periods. The missile armament would be needed if Canadian naval formations were to be employed in the Eastern Atlantic after September 1962 when the *Banshee* fighters reached the end of their service life onboard HMCS *Bonaventure*.[30] Hennessy writes that, "although the Brock Report is given to diverse interpretations, the acceptance of the Report by the entire Naval Board demonstrated a shared belief that, unlike most other NATO navies, the RCN should not (or politically could not) restructure around carrier task groups or strike forces." In another study he had noted that "through circuitous means" the naval staff had earlier obtained from SACLANT a recommendation for just such a fleet mix, a tactic reminiscent of the recommendation obtained from the Admiralty at the 1943 Quadrant Conference at Quebec that the Canadian navy should acquire cruisers.[31]

The Brock plan, however, had no hope of being implemented and, as Haydon says, it was not widely circulated. He characterizes it as politically naive and unrealistic at a time when the navy was struggling with budgetary and manpower crises. Vice-Admiral Rayner devised a more acceptable plan for a fleet of six American *Barbel* class diesel-electric submarines, eight general purpose frigates armed with *Tartar* air defence missiles and intended to have some capacity to support operations ashore, and six "heliporter" frigates. The general purpose frigates were ordered in the last days of the Diefenbaker administration, apparently more for their potential to support UN operations than for their capacity to replace *Bonaventure*'s commitment to eastern Atlantic barrier operations, or possibly only for political reasons.[32] The plan for heliporter frigates was dropped.

The greater naval commitment to continental defence implicit in the strategy of massive retaliation did not generate any political heat at the time, but the commitments for air defence had a higher public profile, and both were to come into the limelight at the time of the Cuban Missile crisis.

✦ ✦ ✦

The prologue to the Cuban Missile crisis had been staged in Europe the previous year when First Secretary Nikita Khrushchev attempted to put an end to the three-power occupation of West Berlin, and settled for the construction of a wall to stop the flow of refugees from the east. Khrushchev's Cuban adventure reflected his recognition after the Berlin episode that the Soviets' best hope of extending communist regimes lay in decolonizing the Third World. Ottawa and London had been unwilling to risk nuclear war on behalf of German citizens at a time when memories of the second war against German militarism were still fresh, but the reality was that neither could disconnect from the Cold War.[33]

It appears that Khrushchev ordered the deployment of missiles on Cuba as a result of Kennedy's Missile Gap rhetoric and the failed Bay of Pigs invasion of Cuba by opponents of President Fidel Castro's regime, which suggested the Americans might be tempted to a make a preemptive nuclear attack on the Soviet Union. The situation was complicated by Khrushchev's attempt, against Castro's advice, to introduce the missiles secretly. Castro had apparently urged that Cuba, as a sovereign state, had every right to openly accept nuclear defences.[34] The reality for Cuba, however, as it is for Canada, is that the United States will not let legal niceties affect its security.

President Kennedy ordered the U.S. Navy to blockade Cuba, euphemistically calling it a "quarantine," as a minimum display of expressive force intended to persuade the Soviet Union to withdrew the strategic missiles before their emplacements were completed.[35] British prime minister Harold MacMillan stated he predominant view when he told the British House of Commons that the American action was "designed to meet a situation which is without precedent" by means which were "studiously moderate."[36] Evidence that became available following the collapse of the Soviet Union shows that the quarantine served as a catalyst that exploited Khrushchev's fear that a U.S. invasion of Cuba was imminent, and that nuclear war might become unavoidable. The aggressive pursuit of Soviet submarines in the Atlantic, in which operation the Canadian navy played its part, was an important counterpoint to the less threatening surface interdiction of merchant ships. And American commitments never to invade Cuba, and to withdraw U.S. missiles from Turkey, were fundamental to the outcome. On 28 October Khrushchev announced that the Soviet missiles on Cuba would be withdrawn.[37]

Diefenbaker refused to be stampeded into a state of apprehended war, and the precautionary alert requested by President Kennedy was eventually ordered on his own authority by the minister of national defence who had succeeded Pearkes in October 1960, Douglas Harkness. The Canadian government withheld assent to the blockade, which resonated too closely with the American economic sanctions against Cuba that had been instituted in 1960, and which the Canadian government considered to be an inappropriate interference in another nation's internal affairs, but Ottawa saw that the objective of the quarantine was met by inspecting ships and aircraft in Canadian ports before granting clearances for Cuba.[38] Canadian naval and air forces carried out extensive anti-submarine operations in conjunction with the U.S. Navy initially on the authority of Rear Admiral Kenneth L. Dyer, RCN, flag officer Atlantic Coast. Dyer, as Richard Mayne writes, "was not prepared to take any chances in the nuclear age, and the scope of the Canadian Navy's actions captures the seriousness of the crisis: ships and aircraft were dispersed with wartime payloads and provisions; secondary headquarters and bases were prepared; vessels in maintenance were rushed to sea; and *Bonaventure* and its escorts were ordered home from a NATO exercise in the eastern Atlantic ... It appeared that there were at least two Soviet submarines in the 160-kilometer-deep Canadian patrol area straddling across the Atlantic from Cape Race to a point roughly 599 kilometers to the west of the Azores, and either RCN or RCAF forces detected both of them." The Canadian navy assumed control of anti-submarine operations throughout the North Atlantic, while the U.S. Navy was engaged in operations around Cuba. Soviet submarines were harassed with signal charges, and pursued until they were forced to the surface.[39] Eventually Diefenbaker bowed to the pressure of circumstances and authorized the necessary military measures, recognizing that the Canadian government had no power to formulate an independent policy.

Because Admiral Dyer's active participation in the naval quarantine highlighted the inadequacy of Diefenbaker's leadership, it was seen as a conflict in civil-military relations. The extent to which military leaders should be free to act in times of crisis is an enduring problem, and not just for Canada. Indeed, the fact that Canadian commanders receive their authority from the "Crown," however that abstraction is defined, not the prime minister, supports some degree of independence to carry out their duties when attack is apprehended. A degree of independence can certainly be justified by looking at such precedents as the defence of Norway in 1940 against German invaders, when defences held only where local commanders acted on their own authority. But civilians ultimately control the structure and budget of Canada's armed forces, and the resonance produced by the Cuban crisis was to have profound effects. In all this there was some parallel to the manner in which the Canadian navy had acted in the Munich crisis. In both crises the Canadian military responded positively to the requirements of collective defence despite irregularities in political protocol. The outcome in 1962, however, was less fortunate. The domestic politico-military crisis, and Canadian-American misunderstanding, was to be a major formative force on Canadian defence policy for the next decade and a half.

At the height of the crisis Diefenbaker had suggested that the United States ask the United Nations to organize an on-site inspection of the supposed missile sites on Cuba by the eight non-aligned members of the disarmament committee, and went on to make his suggestion public. This infuriated Washington: all its other allies, even including French president Charles de Gaulle, had accepted President Kennedy's word on the matter. Perhaps it was not such a crazy idea, however, especially in the light of the misuse of evidence in the "Missile Gap" crisis that brought Kennedy to power.[40]

Knowlton Nash reports that Diefenbaker later wrote indignantly that "we were not a satellite state at the beck and call of an imperial master." Howard Green, his external affairs minister, was reported as warning: "If we go along with the Americans now, we'll be their vassals forever." When later an opinion poll found that 79.3 percent of Canadians approved of Kennedy's handling of the Cuban Missile crisis, Diefenbaker reportedly "became so incensed he lost his reason completely."[41] Almost all contemporary opinion, and later scholarly opinion, criticizes Diefenbaker's resistance to Kennedy's – "that young whippersnapper's" – request for support during the crisis. Apart from exasperation with Diefenbaker's procrastination, only one fact justifies that opinion: the scale and immediacy of the nuclear danger. That fact is overwhelming, but Diefenbaker's suggestion could have been as useful in finding a final quiet resolution to the crisis as eventually was to be Kennedy's undertaking not to invade Cuba and to stand down the U.S. *Jupiter* missiles in Turkey.

U.S. national security advisor McGeorge Bundy's characterization of Canadian foreign policy as being the result of an "inferiority complex with respect to the US" is consistent with Holmes's summation that American leaders blandly assumed "right-thinking people would recognize US aims as their own." In 1967 Escott Reid wrote that Washington politicians "weren't very anxious to learn the complex and subtle art of how the leader of an alliance conducts its relations with the other members of the alliance. They hankered after unilateral declarations, unilateral decision-making, unilateral actions. If they were out of step with all their allies, they were apt to believe that it was their allies who were out of step with them ... My [Reid's] impression ... is that this strain of thinking has, from the beginning, been particularly strong in Washington, and that its existence has helped to make the operation of the North Atlantic Alliance even more difficult than it otherwise would have been."[42]

Unfortunately, Khrushchev's undertaking to withdraw the Soviet missiles from Cuba was not really the end of the story. Khrushchev stopped the naval building program undertaken by Admiral Nikolai G. Kuznetsov because he could not see any probability of its being able in the future to match American, and NATO, naval power. However, the Politburo, led by Leonid Brezhnev, forced Khrushchev into retirement in October 1964, and undertook a hugely expensive armament program. In a decade the Soviet land-based strategic missile force was increased from fewer than a hundred to more than 1,500, with qualitative improvement of the weapons. American pressure put an end to a Soviet attempt in 1970 to establish an operational base for ballistic missile submarines in Cuba. In 1972 and 1974 *Golf II* conventionally powered SSM submarines armed with three short-range missiles tipped with a 1 or 1.2 mt nuclear warhead did visit Cuban ports, but these demonstrations were relatively minor in a world that was becoming increasingly dangerous. Under the command of Admiral of the Fleet of the Soviet Union Sergey Georgiyevich Gorshkov, a massive SSBN force was built, along with an SSN and surface fleet primarily for anti-submarine and anti-aircraft carrier defence of the Soviet Union. By the late 1970s the Soviet fleet rivalled the power of NATO fleets.[43]

❖ ❖ ❖

Despite the approval Canadians felt for Kennedy's handling of it, the Cuban crisis had demonstrated to Liberals and Conservatives alike that Canada's contribution to allied military forces counted for little in the management of world order. In the wake of the Suez debacle there could be no return to an effective Commonwealth defence structure, although Britain did maintain something of its world defence commitment until the end of Sir Harold MacMillan's term of office in 1968.[44] Diefenbaker could and did crash the party at the Nassau Conference in December 1962 when MacMillan and Kennedy made the historic agreement that ensured there would continue to be a British nuclear deterrent, and that it would be linked to the American one, but Diefenbaker had to content himself with his picture appearing in Canadian newspapers, along with his gloss on the outcome of the conference, in which he suggested that Canada's commitment to accept nuclear warheads for its air defence forces and strike aircraft in Europe was being reconsidered.[45]

The increasing involvement of the United States in a major war in Vietnam, and the pressure that Washington put on the Canadian government to provide a token military contribution to that campaign, added to the reasons for reassessing Canada's military strategy. The part Rear Admiral Dyer had played during the Cuban Missile crisis had raised questions about the adequacy of Canadian civilian control; the danger first expressed by Henri Bourassa that a Canadian navy operating on the high seas might entangle Canada in international commitments not envisaged by the Cabinet, appeared all too realistic. And the controversy over Canadian acquisition of nuclear weapons was stoked by press leaks from Canadian and American air force officers. As late as 3 January 1963 Canada was viewed by General Louis Norstad, retiring supreme allied commander Europe, on a farewell visit to Ottawa, as "one of the two, perhaps three, countries who have done their best in meeting their commitments in every sense," but he was also brought by the Southam columnist Charles Lynch to admit that Canada had made commitments to NATO about nuclear forces that had not been fulfilled. This statement was then confirmed to the assembled reporters by Air Marshal Frank Miller, RCAF.[46] The political repercussions from the Cuban crisis and the nuclear controversy not only drove Diefenbaker from power, but also undermined the management of the Canadian navy, and in the end led to the abolition altogether of the Royal Canadian Navy through unification of the Canadian services. In keeping with his election promise, Pearson completed the acquisition of nuclear weapons for the Canadian forces in Europe and for North American air defence.[47] This decision led Pierre Trudeau, who would succeed Pearson as prime minister, to characterize him as an "unfrocked prince of peace." Arrangements were made to store anti-submarine nuclear depth charges at the American bases at Brunswick, Maine, and Argentia, Newfoundland, for possible use by Canadian naval forces.[48] The unwanted weapons having been agreed upon, their elimination remained a Canadian objective for the next two decades, being finally realized in 1984.[49]

In a speech to the Scarborough Liberal Association on 12 January 1963 shortly before the election, Pearson indicated that a future Liberal government would seek to recast the Canadian armed forces "to be able to intervene wherever and whenever required for United Nations, NATO or Canadian territorial operation," to which end "the three armed services should be fully integrated." In what may be taken as a muted declaration of independence from collective defence policies, in April 1963 Pearson, having by then been sworn in as prime minister, ordered the sailing of the destroyer *Saskatchewan* to Port au Prince, Haiti, as part of an international force monitoring the insurrection against Papa Doc Duvalier. The carrier *Bonaventure* was warned to stand by to provide support if necessary. *Saskatchewan*, which had been diverted from a transit between Esquimalt to Halifax, remained off the port for a week ready to evacuate Canadian citizens should that be necessary.[50]

The Department of National Defence was more conservative in its views, but its defence of the existing commitment to NATO's ASW forces was consistent with Pearson's focus on war-avoidance and internationalism. The chief of operational research, Dr Sutherland, had been asked to review the navy's procurement plans, and in May released, as Haydon has observed, "the kind of paper the Navy should have written themselves long before." Sutherland noted:

> In terms of the larger political objectives of the NATO alliance anti-submarine defence of North Atlantic sea communications is probably, in the long run, of greater importance than is generally recognized. It also appears probable that the significance of such defence is rather different than has been generally appreciated ... It is very probable that strong ASW forces are part of the price of an emerging detente in Central Europe. It is also probable that such forces play a vital role in widening the limited agenda of feasible measures of arms control and disarmament. ASW should probably be thought of primarily in terms of buying an option. This option is, in essence, the ability to pursue less dangerous strategic policies and a more constructive diplomacy. It follows that NATO in general and Canada in particular would not be justified in reducing their ASW capabilities. It also follows that the primary emphasis upon the ASW role by Canadian maritime forces continues to be sound.

In the context of that strategic assessment, Sutherland supported the design concept for the general purpose frigate because of the growing need for defence of shipping even in the western Atlantic from aerial attack by long-range Soviet bombers armed with stand-off weapons. He also anticipated "within the next decade" that Soviet attack submarines would be armed with cruise or ballistic missiles for attack against surface targets.[51]

A few months later, Sutherland dismissed the chimera of a uniquely Canadian defence focus in the introduction to the report of an Ad Hoc Committee on Defence Policy that Minister of National Defence Paul Hellyer commissioned; "With comparatively minor exception, the purpose of Canadian defence programs and activities is to support an alliance policy. In terms of Canadian national interests, the rationale of Canadian defence is to maintain influence with our allies. The immediate purpose of Canadian defence is to serve as an effective support of Canada's intra-alliance diplomacy ... The primary purpose of Canada's defence programs is to enable her to participate in a system of alliances ... There is, perhaps, no other nation which is so much dependent upon the art and science of alliancemanship." He concluded with the well-known sentences noted above in the Introduction: "It would be highly advantageous to discover a strategic rationale which would impart to Canada's defence programs a wholly Canadian character. Unfortunately, such a rationale does not exist and one cannot be invented." Canada could not dispense with its NATO alliance, and had to accept that, in the circumstances of a Soviet threat to the frontier of a divided Germany, seaborne forces did not constitute an adequate indication of Canadian commitment.[52]

Sutherland's conclusions were received in the context of the questions surrounding the assassination of President Kennedy on 22 November 1963, followed by the naval engagement in the Gulf of Tonkin on 2 August 1964 between a U.S. Navy destroyer and four torpedo boats of the navy of the Democratic Republic of Vietnam, and another unsubstantiated action on August 4. The naval engagement or engagements were used to justify Congress authorizing President Lyndon B. Johnson to "to take all necessary steps, including the use of armed force," to assist South Vietnamese forces. In a 1962 academic article Robert Sutherland had commented: "it is not necessarily true that in a bed which contains fifteen other nations Canada is less likely to get raped ... It is not necessarily in Canada's interest to involve NATO in the entire agenda of Canadian-American relations."[53] But the Cuban crisis and the growing conflict in Vietnam hardly encouraged the Canadian government to accept American leadership unreservedly, and called into question the ability of Canadian military effort to generate influence.

Pearson's interest in employing the Canadian forces for purposes outside NATO plans for general war was reflected in the White Paper on Defence that Hellyer drafted and published in March 1964. Hellyer had expressed his perspective as long ago as 1961: "When each side has the potential to destroy the other's homeland, the threat of massive retaliation ceases to be taken seriously and becomes a mere bluff ... While this double-edged sword hangs over the world it is far more likely that one side would attempt probing actions with conventional forces ... By building up tactical mobile forces we would be making our best military contribution to the maintenance of peace."[54] Within days of the release of the White Paper the Canadian navy transported soldiers to Cyprus as part of the UN observer force, a commitment that helped to prevent the outbreak of war between two NATO countries, Greece and Turkey, and may have led to President Johnson signing the Canadian-American Autopact, allowing for continental free-trade in automobiles and parts. Some thirty thousand Canadians were to serve in the United Nations force in Cyprus over a period of nearly thirty years.

The Pearson-Sutherland dialectic was a genine, and important, debate about strategic options, and Pearson as prime minister had, at least in theory, the last word. When in January 1965 President Johnson asked Pearson for military support in Vietnam, he was rebuffed on the grounds that "Canada could not consider participating in any military or paramilitary fashion, nor in any way that would conflict with her responsibilities as a member of the International Control Commission." Pearson told the Cabinet that Canadian protests in Washington would be ineffectual, but he nevertheless took his message to Temple University in Philadelphia on 2 April, suggesting a pause in American bombing.[55] This led to a confrontation with President Johnson, and was not repeated. Writing in 1971, John Holmes noted that Canada's refusal to participate in the Vietnam war had a distinct effect on Canadian attitudes to its defence partnership; no longer did Canadians view it as inevitable that they would be a partner in any war that was waged by the United States. "For Canadians the disconcerting realization that we could differ in our choice of enemies raises fundamental questions about joint defence."[56] Although Washington was disappointed that the Canadians were not willing to take a part in the Vietnam war, a State Department paper dated April 1967 noted that "the only absolutely essential [defence] requirement we would have to levy on the Canadians would be use of their air space. Everything beyond this would appear to be a bonus."[57]

In 1967 Jon McLin suggested that the absence of any Canadian participation in the discussion relating to the American idea that NATO should establish a multilateral nuclear force, employing *Polaris* missiles deployed on mixed-manned surface ships to serve the deterrence needs of the smaller nations, is an indication of the extent to which Canada was already drawing away from its total commitment to collective defence.[58] Given that General Charles de Gaulle was determined to develop an independent *force de frappe* for France, and that the British priority was to maintain their privileged nuclear relationship with Washington, the project was doomed in any case. Apart from the United States, only the Germans were genuinely interested. A positive spin, however, can be put on the story. James Solomon's perspective is that the five years of negotiations, and the eventual abandonment of the concept, demonstrated the collegiality of the NATO process. The allies could disagree about Vietnam and about a multilateral force, but remain a dynamic partnership that was to outlast the Soviet Union.[59]

✦ ✦ ✦

Uncertainty about alliance relations, and uncertainty about the technology and strategy needed to meet the threat from ballistic missile submarines, affected naval procurement. Cost considerations, and concern that not too much money should be spent on what could prove to be outdated equipment, led Hellyer to reduce the submarine order in April 1963 to three British *Oberon* class submarines, the first of which had already been laid down for the Royal Navy at Chatham in England in September 1962.[60] The need for a submarine for training purposes on the West Coast to replace a borrowed American submarine, *Grilse*, was not to be met until 1968 when an American *Tench* class submarine was purchased from surplus stock, and christened HMCS *Rainbow*. In October 1963 the general purpose frigates were cancelled. Hennessy characterizes these frigates as "neither well thought-out, nor well-planned," and Norman Friedman writes that the U.S. Navy "thought the GP frigate program, with Tartar, was grossly overambitious for its size (and we didn't know about the 200 troops)."[61] The design team that had produced the *St Laurent* class had long since been broken up, and the Navy Board lacked the technical expertise to ensure that the design for the GP frigates was effective, and affordable. Their projected cost had risen from $275 million to $450–500 million, and the government was not prepared to throw money at a problem that was not fully understood, at the same time as it was moving to establish universal government medical insurance, which came into force in 1968. All the same, the design of the GP frigate, with accommodation for 200 ground force personnel, had gone some way toward addressing Pearson's interest in diverting some of Canada's commitment to NATO to an amphibious, tri-service, force suitable for UN operations. *Ojibwa*, the first of the three *Oberon* class submarines, was commissioned in September 1965, but following the commissioning of HMCS *Annapolis*, the last of the destroyer escorts, in December 1964, no new surface combatant was to be commissioned until July 1972.

Trials of the operational marriage of *Sea King* helicopters with the destroyer escorts beginning in May 1963 were discouraging as they revealed the limitations of the system against nuclear ballistic missile submarines. During the NATO SLAMEX exercise run in September 1964 less than six months later, ten of the fourteen "red force" submarines succeeded in reaching launch positions off the American coast. The *Restigouche* class destroyer-escorts were not equipped with helicopter hangars and deck, and when four of them were refitted between 1968 and 1972 they were given instead ASROC anti-submarine rocket-thrown torpedo systems. All subsequent classes of Canadian major surface combatants, however, have been fitted for flight operations.[62]

In 1966 Pearson would send two destroyers, *St Laurent* and *Gatineau*, to represent Canada at the independence celebrations in the Bahamas, the only warships sent by any nation for the purpose. As well as being an expression of good will, the ships had the potential for providing practical support should the Castro regime in Cuba seek to destabilize the new country. In May 1967 HMCS *Provider*, which had been commissioned in September 1963, and two destroyers were ordered to stand by in the eastern Mediterranean when the indications suggested that the Canadian contingent in the United Nations Emergency Force in Gaza might be in danger. They were indeed, but at the insistence of President Nasser they were air-lifted home prior to the Israeli assault that became the Six-Day war.[63] The humiliation clearly showed the limitations of peacekeeping operations and of the capacity of Canada to influence American policy even when Canadian forces were involved. As Robert Bothwell says, "when the United States government signaled Israel that it had no objections to an attack, it acted without telling – much less consulting – *any* of its allies."[64]

In the light of budgetary constraint, and an uncertain technical horizon, there was no practicable alternative to maximizing the utility of the existing DDE and DDH fleet. The auxiliary oiler replenishment (AOR) ships HMCS *Protecteur* and *Preserver* joined *Provider* in August 1969 and August 1970. These force multipliers gave the Canadian navy considerable punch in the low-air-threat environment of the western Atlantic and eastern Pacific, which was to be seen as increasingly important in the 1980s when there came to be concern that the Soviets would seek to disarm the Americans by shortening the warning of attack through firing missiles at short range with reduced trajectories. With the decommissioning of *Bonaventure* in July 1970, the AORs were to replace her as technical support for the *Sea King* helicopters on the destroyers. Friedman writes that the U.S. Navy was at the time also decommissioning escort carriers because improvements in SOSUS made it possible to rely on maritime patrol ASW aircraft.[65] However, as Sutherland had anticipated, the introduction into service in the Soviet navy of submarine-launched tactical cruise missiles – the SS-N-7 deployed from 1968 on the *Charlie* and the single ship *Papa* class SSNs – was to create a serious air threat in the western Atlantic that the Canadian navy could not adequately counter. Without either a carrier or destroyers armed with air-defence missiles, the Canadian navy was dependent upon allied air support when out of the operational range of Canadian air force interceptor aircraft.

✦ ✦ ✦

Budgetary restraint was to be the least contentious aspect of Hellyer's sweeping transformation of the Canadian forces – steam-rolling service advice and tradition in order to integrate leadership, and then to unify the Canadian Army, the Royal Canadian Navy, and the Royal Canadian Air Force into a single service, called the Canadian Armed Forces. Reading Hellyer's memoirs, *Damn the Torpedoes*, it becomes evident that he believed himself to be what is known in management theory as a "Rational Actor" and unsympathetic to the "Organizational Process Model," which seeks choices based on standard patterns of behaviour. Writing in 1991, Haydon concluded that "in implementing the necessary changes" to defence organization, "Hellyer cut too deeply into the military fabric with the result that many of the better parts of his reorganization were masked by the more contentious aspects of the program. In hindsight, it was probably too much change in too short a period of time. As a result, the military were almost emasculated. Although the shift to integrated control of the military

Jackstay transfer at sea between HMCS *Protecteur* (AOR 509), an Auxiliary Oiler Replenishment ship built at Saint John Shipbuilding, 1966–69, and a DDH, February 1985. *Protecteur* was equipped to supply fuel and solid stores, maintain helicopters, and provide medical services. She served in the Persian Gulf in operations *Desert Storm* and *Friction*, at Somalia in 1992, and in Operation *Toucan* at East Timor in 1999. DND IHC85-036

was a great success ... unification of the three services did not achieve the anticipated results."⁶⁶

Hellyer was convinced that the division of the Canadian Armed Forces into three distinct services was inefficient not only in such issues as procurement and supply but also in strategic planning: "Each service was preparing for a different kind of war." The Chiefs of Staff Committee was not an adequate means of bridging the differences.

Instead of spending the time agreeing on the probabilities of different kinds of war and then adjusting their plans and priorities accordingly for different kinds of weapons systems, the committee was little more than a back-scratching club ... Senior officers in each service were painfully aware that they were team leaders who dare not "let the side down." This could be particularly subversive when senior officers were choosing the right weapons mix for a particular job ... especially if some of the systems were the preserve of one service, while others 'belonged' to one of its rivals ... It only required a few weeks as minister to convince me that a single service was the only satisfactory solution ... I decided that the first step should include abolition of the three "chiefs" positions and the substitution of a single Chief of Defence Staff to whom all three services would report. A consequential change was the elimination of the Naval Board, the General Staff, and the Air Staff in favour of one unified defence staff.[67] Hellyer was supported in this opinion by General Charles Foulkes, now retired as chairman of the Chiefs of Staff Committee, and indeed Foulkes's opinion was an echo of one expressed twenty years earlier by an exasperated Mackenzie King. "The truth is," he had confided to his diary in October 1942, "the three Defence services work into each other's hand and each is allowing the other to get all that it possibly can regardless of whether it is justified or not."[68]

For a brief period between 1924 and 1927 following the establishment of a single minister of national defence, the Canadian government had experimented with a unified service command, under Major-General Sir James MacBrien as chief of staff "with overall authority over the Navy and the military elements of the Air Service." This early effort was defeated by Commodore Walter Hose, and deputy minister G.J. Desbarats, but Colonel Maurice Pope's 1937 memorandum had emphasized that "from the standpoint of the Government, the problem of national defence has always been fundamentally a single one, incapable of complete division in terms of the fighting Services."[69] In the interest of efficiency and centralized planning, the process of integrating Canada's three military services had begun again in 1946 when the minister of national defence resumed direct authority over all three services and a Chiefs of Staff Committee was established to coordinate the services and develop defence policy. The integration process was continued in the 1950 National Defence Act, and in 1953 a formal agreement was signed between the navy and the air force to co-ordinate maritime operations. In 1960 the Glassco Commission into government expenditure recommended further integration, and in 1961 General Foulkes had written a staff paper, "The Case for One Service," which may have in some way provided a basis for Pearson's January 1963 speech.

Foulkes noted: "the Canadian effort to support the deterrent in the North Atlantic ... is the largest and most expensive of all the defence undertakings ... There is an urgent need for a complete scientific and operational reassessment of this question and a strenuous effort made to work out with our NATO partners a single and comprehensive solution to ensure that more adequate results are attained commensurate with the effort being expended in this maritime field."[70] This was less an argument for a single service than a plea for a coherent strategy, but the difficulty of achieving that unity of direction while leadership was fragmented and competitive was quite evident. Robert Caldwell has shown that when a tri-service Mobile Force Planning Group reported in November 1963 on a possible transformation of Canadian forces none of the service chiefs were enthusiastic. Vice-Admiral Rayner in particular questioned the ability of the Canadian navy to meet its strategic ASW commitments to NATO and SACLANT if it also had to support a mobile expeditionary force.

Hellyer came also to the conclusion that the naval leadership were living in a world far removed from Canadian social democracy. He was disgusted by his experience on a visit to the fleet as the guest of Rear Admiral Brock, who had succeeded in 1962 to flag-officer Atlantic Coast. Hellyer found it remarkable that his suitcase was unpacked for him, and was convinced that such "old world hospitality was only made possible by treating ordinary seamen as lackeys ... Such practices seemed an abuse of indentured labour reminiscent of the dark ages ... By the time I returned to Ottawa I knew I had my work cut out for me. The navy was going to need a lot of modernization to make it contemporary."[71] It seems likely that something in Admiral Brock's personality rang alarm bells for Hellyer. In June 1947 a seamen's protest onboard HMCS *Ontario* had led to the reassignment of Brock, who was then her executive officer, to another ship.[72]

With the approval of Cabinet, Hellyer brought forward in the 1964 *White Paper on Defence* the concept of a single unified force with a single chief of the defence staff. Command integration was begun in 1964, and unification followed in 1968, when the Royal Canadian Navy was abolished and its resources transferred to Maritime Command of the Canadian Armed Forces.[73] Despite lobbying by Earl Mountbatten, allegedly with the support of the Queen, and by the Royal Canadian Legion, the navy lost its White Ensign on 15 February 1965 and adopted the new Canadian Maple Leaf flag as an ensign. The new head of the navy, the commander Maritime Command, was located in Halifax, far from the centre of defence planning in Ottawa, although Richard Gimblett observes that the naval staff was recreated in all but name in Halifax under the direction of the chief of maritime doctrine and operations.[74]

All maritime air operations – those that had been conducted by the fleet air arm and those conducted by the Royal Canadian Air Force – were combined within Maritime Command. The three services were stripped of their British-style uniforms, and issued uniforms uncomfortably similar to those of the United States Air Force.

The literature agrees that Hellyer was neither respectful of service advice nor interested in professional dialogue. He drove several of his senior officers, including Chief of Naval Staff Vice-Admiral Rayner, into early retirement, and fired Rear Admiral William Landymore, in order to push through unification.[75] Rear Admiral Robert Timbrell, who was commander of Maritime Command from October 1971 until October 1973, has commented that "outside of Canada the support for unification came from the U.S. Secretary of Defence, Robert McNamara, who had many meetings with Paul Hellyer, whereas in the United Kingdom the message from the Chief of Defence Staff was exactly the opposite."[76] Hellyer did have some support for his policy amongst the navy's lower deck and from some more senior officers, and over forty years later few would recommend a return to the system of three entirely distinct services. But because of opposition within NATO to any fundamental change to the roles the Canadian forces were playing in the alliance, the original Foulkes-Pearson-Hellyer objective described in the 1964 White Paper of facilitating the development of more strategic flexibility and coherence for the Canadian forces was dropped from the 1966 "Address on the Canadian Forces Reorganization Act" that Hellyer tabled in the Commons at the time of second reading of Bill C-243.

Writing in 1998, Douglas Bland notes: "this change in the rationale for the unification of the armed forces seriously undermined his support in the defence establishment (such as it was) because unification had little to commend it if the services were to continue in separate and distinct missions." And commenting on the still strong "phantom feeling of old loyalties," he notes that "ironically, these influences may be strongest at a time when the virtues of the single service as envisioned by Hellyer might be most apparent" a decade after the end of the Cold War, and with the services increasingly acting as "joint" forces.[77]

Hellyer's assault on service culture may have been intended to make the integrated leadership effective, but it was not something a military man who knows the importance of symbolism in a fighting service would have undertaken. The conditioning of officers and men for war depends greatly on historic models and symbols, which cannot be fabricated as easily as weapons. During the battle for Crete in May 1941 Admiral

Andrew Cunningham categorically rejected a suggestion that the Royal Navy had taken enough losses in support of the army with the now famous reply that "it takes the navy three years to build a ship, but three hundred to build a tradition."[78] Service traditions are vital to military effectiveness, and the symbols and uniforms are the outward and visible signs of an inner commitment. The destruction of naval symbols also undermined the brotherhood of the sea that supported a professional bond with other navies. As Rear Admiral Landymore put it to the Standing Committee on Defence 12 May 1967, "generally navies are very close to one another and their way of doing things and their manner of presenting themselves and their identity." The self-respect and sense of unit identity of the military is a precious commodity. No one who expects the military to risk their lives under orders should lightly humiliate them. Hellyer sought advice from his commanders, but had a deaf ear for anything not expressed in scientific terms. The political storm raised by unification probably, and rightly, cost Hellyer his chance of succeeding Pearson as prime minister.

As opposition defence critic he had been concerned at the time of the Cuban crisis with Admiral Dyer's assumption of authority. In Brand's analysis: "the gathering demand for a chief of the defence staff ... came not from any perceived failure of military operations or because of any requirement for the unified command of the Canadian armed forces in the field. Rather, the establishment of the office of the chief of the defence staff was another political attempt to correct weaknesses in the administration of defence policy."[79] Hellyer's radical transformation of the Canadian services was a reaction as much to the tendency of the military to impose policies on the government that were consistent with those of Canada's allies as it was to the difficulty of adjudicating between rival services. But it is an open question whether his policy really supported national and civilian objectives. Although his intentions were nationalist, the effect of losing the White Ensign and the traditional uniforms was to emphasize the refocus of defence consciousness on the United States. In his memoirs he dismissed contemptuously the suggestion that unification might lead to the military asserting power over the civilian government, but historically civil rule has been assured by keeping the military divided. Happily Canada will always avoid the "man on horseback" seizing control, but unification of the services and their Americanization was not a formula for ensuring the independence of Canadian policy in alliance with the United States. This was to become evident at the time of the American invasion of Iraq in 2003.[80]

Unification did accelerate a very contentious development that was essential if the Canadian navy was to grow as a national institution – accommodation in the navy for francophones. Effecting this development was a priority of Hellyer's ultimate choice of chief of defence staff, General Jean-Victor Allard. Impetus for the change came from the growth in Quebec of an independence movement that fed on General de Gaulle's anti-American manoeuvres which led in 1967 to his fiery "Vive le Québec Libre" shout to a Montreal crowd. The first ship to be designated for the experiment was HMCS *Ottawa*, in 1968. Twenty years later the requirements of Canadian politics and social change would further complicate the problem of critical mass by the need to create reasonable working conditions onboard ship for women.[81]

✦ ✦ ✦

The fourteen years that began with Dulles's "New Look" speech on 12 January 1954, which downgraded the importance of naval control of the Atlantic, followed by the Suez crisis and the Cuban Missile crisis, had fundamentally changed the place of Canada in the world and the place of the Canadian navy in supporting Canadian interests. Not only had the value to Canada of Britain as a moderator of American power been reduced but Canada's direct ability to influence American policy had been demonstrated to be small. Concern about the independence of civilian control suggested by the action taken by Admiral Dyer during the Cuban crisis, contributing as it did to the Hellyer unification of the services, and the weakness shown in naval procurement, could be seen as symptomatic of a growing sense that the navy was no longer a tool of central importance in Canadian foreign policy. Sutherland's 1963 defence of the strategic importance of ASW not only as a suitable role for the Canadian navy but also as an essential precondition for war avoidance and arms control did indeed justify the heavy investment Canada had made in its navy, but the next decade was to see it under continued pressure until that argument was accepted by the prime minister who succeeded Pearson in 1968, Pierre Trudeau.

In 1967 NATO established a permanent training formation, the Standing Naval Force Atlantic, or STANAVFORLANT. Tony German writes that the enthusiastic participation of the Canadian navy/Maritime Command in STANAVFORLANT was of great importance in maintaining its professional capacity following unification and during the years of "rust out" in the 1970s. It also served to establish professional relationships with officers in allied navies, most of which were European.[82] Typically a destroyer from the Atlantic fleet would be committed to a year's service with STANAVFORLANT. Canada's military role in Europe was also extended in 1967 when it was agreed to earmark forces for reinforcement of Denmark or Norway, the Canadian Air-Sea Transportable Brigade (CAST). However, the army found it difficult to train for warfare in two quite different terrains, and an exercise conducted the following year showed just how unrealistic it was to plan for the movement by sea of heavy equipment to Norway at a time when anti-submarine forces would be engaged in moving traffic across the Atlantic, and when strike forces would be fighting in the Norwegian Sea.[83]

6

THE COLD WAR:
DÉTENTE, RUST-OUT, AND RENEWAL

In December 1967 Belgium's foreign minister, Pierre Harmel, completed for NATO a report recommending a policy of détente with the Soviet Union. The sub-report on "East-West Relations Détente and a European Settlement" stated: "the second purpose of the Allies is, without jeopardizing our freedom or weakening our security, to develop plans and methods for eliminating the present unnatural barriers between Eastern and Western Europe (which are not of our choosing) including the division of Germany."[1] Détente showed real possibilities in January 1968 when the liberalizing Slovak Alexander Dubček came to power in Czechoslovakia. The so-called Prague Spring was crushed, however, on 21 August when the Soviet Union and hard-line Warsaw Pact allies invaded Czechoslovakia. A hawkish perspective is supplied by Robert M. Gates, director of the Central Intelligence Agency under President George Bush Sr, and secretary of defence in both the George W. Bush and the Barack Obama administrations. He writes that "from 1969 to the end of 1974, American policy towards the Soviet Union and US–Soviet relations generally were characterized by smoke and mirrors – obscuring the reality of continued competition and enmity, as well as détente's limits and failures, magnifying its modest successes, a time of secret deals and public obfuscation (and deception), all reflecting more accurately than they imagined the personalities of its principal architects."[2]

The Soviet house-cleaning of its Czech satellite did not deter Pierre Elliott Trudeau, who was chosen to head the Liberal Party and became prime minister in April 1968, two months after Paul Hellyer's unification bill became law and four months before the invasion of Czechoslovakia. The most consistent characteristic of Trudeau's defence policy over the next fifteen years was a commitment to détente, which became the driver of Canadian defence policy. According to a member of the

American delegation to NATO, despite Canada's taking in thousands of Czech and Slovakia refugees, Canadian officials "consistently put a lower estimate than most of the Soviet threat to Western Europe."

Following his election by the party and his victory in the June 1968 general election, Trudeau spent a weekend in March 1969 discussing Canada's defence objectives with his cabinet.[3] On 3 and 12 April he made public speeches in which he declared the need for a defence policy that was a product of foreign policy, rather than a foreign policy which was the unavoidable product of defence commitments. He firmly rejected a neutralist policy for Canada, but questioned whether spending as much money as Canada did on military forces was the best way of defending the country; perhaps developmental assistance would be more cost-effective: "It's in our national interest to reduce the tensions in the world, tensions which spring from the two-thirds of the world's population who go to bed hungry every night, the two-thirds of the world's population who are poor whereas the other third is rich, and the tensions which spring from this great ideological struggle between the East and the West." He openly questioned whether Canada's "defence policy was more to impress our friends than frighten our enemies."[4] It was a rhetorical question, but it did signal a change.[5] Writing in 1971, John Holmes observed that "the obsession with independence as the principal theme of foreign and defence policy" would come to appear "heedless" in the context of a serious threat to human security.[6] Trudeau, however, believed that it was the nuclear arms race that was the threat.

Trudeau's global priorities had an early, and strong, impact on the Canadian navy. A warning had been given by the State Department at a meeting of the Joint Board on Defence in June 1967 that "any wavering" on the renewal of the NORAD agreement was "likely to affect [the] core of the US-Canadian defense relationship," and it may be supposed that any wavering on the Canadian navy's participation in continental defence would have been looked on with disfavour in Washington.[7] NORAD was in fact renewed, and there is no doubt the Canadian navy ensured the job was done at sea to the best of its ability, but the inevitable consequence of the widening disconnect between national purpose as defined at the senior level of government and the transnational perspective of Canadian Armed Forces officers could be measured in the falling defence budgets and stalled procurement.

The trend had begun under Pearson. The proportion of the federal budget spent on defence fell from 22.3% in 1962/63, the last year of Diefenbaker's administration, to 16.1% in 1967/78, the last year of Pearson's administration, and to 12.9% in 1970/71. In the late 1960s and 1970s Canada's relative military contribution to international security, measured quantitatively, fell to the point where, within the NATO Alliance, only Luxembourg and Iceland were behind Canada in the proportion of their gross domestic product (GDP) spent on defence. Revenue was increasingly diverted to social programs, and the Canadian border was opened to American draft dodgers. The proportion of the navy budget devoted to the navy's capital spending fell to 10%, and the proportion devoted to pay and maintenance rose to twice that of the U.S. Navy, in part because of pay raises to match the civilian sector.[8] Despite the increase in service pay, naval personnel strength fell from an establishment of 14,390 in 1968 to 8,781 in 1981. In 1969 Trudeau ordered the carrier *Bonaventure* scrapped, despite the fact that it had just completed a major refit.[9] The highly innovative 65+ knot hydrofoil anti-submarine vessel *Bras d'Or* entered trials, but the navy budget was so tight it was not possible to complete the program, and work on the prototype was stopped in 1971.[10] In 1972 Trudeau "civilianized" command of the forces by folding the Canadian Forces Headquarters into the civilian Department of National Defence.[11] Four state-of-the-art 4,200-ton destroyers (DDH-280) capable of carrying and operating two heavy anti-submarine helicopters and armed with *Sea Sparrow* point defence missiles were delivered in 1972–73, but no new classes of major warship were ordered to follow them until 1983. The destroyer force had fallen to nineteen units by 1974 and aged steadily until in the 1980s it became difficult to keep them operational. It was generally agreed that the eighteen CP-140 *Aurora* long-range patrol aircraft (LRPA) ordered in 1977 to replace the aging *Argus* were first rate, but their numbers were very few to patrol 59,000 coastline miles. The Japanese, with less than 10% of that coastline, had 130 maritime patrol aircraft.

Giving testimony in February 1983 to the Senate subcommittee studying Canada's maritime defences, Rear Admiral Michael Martin painted a dismal picture: "In the Atlantic, four of the destroyers ... could probably do a reasonably effective job; but do not be misled. These ships are at least a generation behind in their capability. The other helicopter-destroyers are so old that all they are really providing is a command and control centre and a deck from which a ... helicopter can operate. In the Pacific, the situation is even worse. The four improved *Restigouche* class destroyers will have some ability to survive, and I put it that way intentionally. However, the *Mackenzie* class will not only be in danger but a liability to the Commander."

The Cold War: Détente, Rust-Out, and Renewal 159

HMCS *Bras D'Or* (FHE 400) experimental hydrofoil, commissioned into the Canadian Armed Forces from 1968 to 1971. Intended for rapid response to data from fixed acoustic sensors, she was never armed, and was put on permanent display at the Maritime Museum in Quebec. She established a speed record of 73 knots. Photographed 18 February 1970, DND REC70-367

The Senate subcommittee summed up the situation: "it has taken eighteen years to reach the current level of incapacity. On 15 January 1965, there were forty-five major warships, frigate-size and above, in commission and ten minesweepers. By December 1967, the number of major warships had dropped to thirty-nine. By 1971, there were only twenty-five, and the only aircraft-carrier had been paid off. In 1975, the number rose to twenty-six, including the three operational support ships. It has remained constant since then – but there are no longer any mine-countermeasure vessels. No new major vessels have been commissioned since 1972. The fleet is aging. All this has taken place during a period when ... Canada's current most likely foe, the USSR, has not only almost totally replaced its fleet but has also significantly increased its capabilities."[12]

Although rejecting a neutralist policy, Trudeau relegated to third place Canadian support of NATO, after "surveillance of Canadian territory and coastlines" and "the defence of North America in cooperation with the United States." In his public statements he supported the need for the strategic linkage with Europe, but the decisions which his administration made about defence structure and equipment were on a scale consistent with the historic views of Henri Bourassa. It had required the threatened resignation of Léo Cadieux, minister of national defence, and possibly that of Mitchell Sharp, minister of external affairs, prior to a Cabinet meeting 26 March 1969 to block Trudeau's wish to take Canadian forces out of Europe altogether, and Cadieux had to accept their reduction. Believing it would reduce the danger of accidental and catastrophic nuclear war, Trudeau ordered Canadian forces in Europe to bring to an end their role in tactical nuclear delivery.[13] Paradoxically, Trudeau's reduction of the Canadian garrisons in Europe, and the scrapping of *Bonaventure*, served only to strengthen the dependence of European defence upon the nuclear deterrence that he regarded as unconvincing.

It was consistent with Trudeau's perspective that there was some revival of interest in the naval defence of the Canadian arctic during his administrations. The matter of immediate concern was an American challenge to Canadian claims to sovereign control over the largely icebound water of the Northwest Passage through the arctic archipelago. The U.S. Navy rejected the claims of all archipelagic states and made no exception for Canada. Dean Rusk, secretary of state from 1961 to 1969, later said to Knowlton Nash that "the US took too theoretical a position on the North, and the Northwest Passage is by no stretch of the imagination an international waterway." But the official position taken by the State Department after Rusk's retirement was that the Northwest Passage, despite its heavy ice coverage, is an international strait: "We cannot accept the assertion of a Canadian claim that the arctic waters are internal waters of Canada ... Such acceptance would jeopardize the freedom of navigation essential for United States naval activities worldwide."[14]

The Canadian position was supported by the reality that there was no significant commercial use of the strait, but in 1969–70 the specially strengthened U.S. tanker SS *Manhattan* transited the passage with the assistance of a Canadian icebreaker. Journalists made much of the fact that it did not fly a Canadian courtesy flag – which would have acknowledged that it was navigating Canadian waters.

In response to the *Manhattan* voyage and the intense pressure it created in the House of Commons, in 1970 the Canadian government enacted the Arctic Waters Pollution Prevention Act, claiming Canadian regulatory control over shipping within a hundred-mile zone, and declared that it would not accept a challenge to the law at the International Court. Holmes has described this as "one of our noteworthy successes ... It was well disciplined action. We were able to do so because we were in situ, because we avoided direct confrontation and produced a new idea, a functional concept of pollution control zones for which coastal states would be responsible. It was a compromise but one which gave us what we needed without unnecessary defiance."[15] Canada also extended its territorial sea from the historic three-mile limit to twelve miles, in line with an international trend but also serving to create "gates" of territorial sea across the Northwest Passage at Barrow Strait and Prince of Wales Strait.[16] The 1971 *Defence White Paper* indicated there might be an increase in surveillance in the arctic, and noted the establishment of the northern region headquarters at Yellowknife. A series of naval "Norploy" exercises were run involving the auxiliary oiler replenishment (AOR) ships HMCS *Preserver* and *Protecteur*, supported by destroyers, and the air force undertook extensive surveillance flights with *Argus* long-range maritime patrol aircraft.

In a interview with Douglas Bland in 1992, General Jacques Dextraze, who was chief of defence staff from 1972 to 1977, scathingly commented that no one was fooled by Canadians "beating our chests about the need to defend Canada, and flying a few aircraft in the north for a look-see every once in a while." Admiral Robert Falls, who succeeded General Dextraze to 1980, also spoke scornfully about Trudeau's commitment to arctic defence: "we conducted superficial acts. We flew aircraft in the north on monthly patrols ... they never made a contact ... we flew in complete darkness, figuratively and literally, most of the time. We sent ships up into the north and damaged their hulls, they weren't made for that type of action. It was a complete waste of time, but it satisfied the politicians."[17]

At the same time as the government rediscovered the importance of the arctic, it also increased the constabulary tasks that had to be fulfilled by civilian Canadian maritime forces in temperate waters, backed up by the navy. The sea area that had to be monitored increased progressively from 1970 to 1977 when Canada adopted a two hundred-mile economic zone offshore. The navy had to provide support for the Department of Fisheries in monitoring 300–400 fishing vessels, half of which were Soviet and provided support for Soviet naval vessels operating on the Grand Banks. In 1976 the navy undertook 480 days of constabulary surveillance in the Atlantic and 135 in the Pacific, with 6,230 hours of air patrol by the air force in the Atlantic and 2,100 in the Pacific.

Trudeau apparently discounted the importance of the navy's alliance roles as indirect means of supporting local defence, but the more subtle explanation is that he was in effect, if not necessarily in intention, putting the alliance on notice that Canadian support was conditional on its active pursuit of détente. Experience had shown that exemplary contribution to NATO forces generated little or no influence. It was logical, therefore, to try other means of bringing his voice to the attention of allies and opponents alike. The "rust-out" of the navy during Trudeau's early years should be considered not simply as drift but also as a policy option. It could be seen as a concomitant to the ostentatious refocusing of Canadian defensive effort on constabulary tasks, including arctic surveillance.

This would be a logical implication of the observation in the six-pamphlet *Foreign Policy for Canadians* published under Trudeau's immediate direction that "what Canada can hope to accomplish in the world must be viewed not only in the light of Canadian aspirations, needs and wants but in terms of what is, from time to time, attainable."[18] Trudeau was an internationalist, but, in Costas Melakopides's words, a pragmatic one. Canada's ability to use the leverage supplied by its military capabilities to further détente was limited, but something might be possible by a degree of disengagement, while continuing deployment of Canadian forces in United Nations peacekeeping missions. In 1971 over six hundred members of the Canadian forces were serving in UN operations, Canada being the only member of the UN to have participated in every one. The Canadian Armed Forces developed a high level of expertise in the field, and an international reputation.[19]

It might have been consistent with Trudeau's internationalist perspective for him to have continued the Pearson-Hellyer concept of a balanced tri-service force that could provide stronger support for the United Nations, but he did not pursue that goal. Indeed, there was a partial reversal of Hellyer's unification on 2 September 1975, with the creation of Air Command uniting Air Defence Command, Air Transport Command, and the Maritime Air Group of Maritime Command. The Maritime Air Group commander was tasked with the provision of aircraft and crew, their maintenance and training, to the commander, Maritime Command, and was given a "double hat" as deputy chief of naval staff. This has proved to be a workable arrangement, but for the navy it is an imperfect compromise that suggests Trudeau's rust-out of the navy was as much visceral as strategic.[20]

Conspicuously absent from the *Foreign Policy* review was any consideration of Canadian-American relations. Because of Trudeau's attitudes to alliance defence commitments and his active pursuit of détente, relations with Washington fell during the early Trudeau years almost to the depths of the Diefenbaker years. In 1970, nearly twenty years after Canadian diplomats were forced to leave Nanking and two years before President Richard Nixon's own visit to Beijing in February 1972, Trudeau extended Canadian recognition to the People's Republic of China. Nixon was furious at being upstaged. Robert Gates writes that the Nixon administration's adoption of détente was a result of concern that the NATO allies would cut their own deals with the Soviet Union, and that the latter was forced to adopt at least the appearance of détente because of the threat implicit in Nixon's *approchement* to China.[21] In May 1971 during a visit to the Soviet Union, Trudeau went so far as to comment that "the overpowering presence of the United States of America" caused "a growing consciousness amongst Canadians of the danger to our national identity from a cultural, economic and perhaps even military point of view."[22] The transnational perspective of the Canadian forces, which had not been diminished by unification, did indeed conflict with their Canadian identity, but Nixon's administration was not amused by Trudeau's choice of audience for his observations. The White House was irritated almost to the point of ordering economic retaliation.[23] The *New York Times*, however, thought that if Trudeau's visit to Russia, and the protocol signed there, made "the United States less inclined to take Canada for granted and more sensitive to Canadian concerns for protecting the Arctic and avoiding American domination, it [would] be all to the good."[24]

When visiting Ottawa in April 1972, Nixon was invited to address Parliament, and spoke forthrightly, but moderately: "In focusing on our peaceful borders and our peaceful history," there has been a tendency "to gloss over the fact that there are real problems between us ... It is time for Canadians and American to move beyond the sentimental rhetoric of the past. It is time for us to recognize that we have very separate identities; that we have significant differences; and that nobody's interests are furthered when these realities are obscured ... We must realize that we are friends, not because there have been no problems between us, but because we have trusted one another enough to be candid about our problems and because our candour has nourished our co-operations." In speaking about NATO and Canada's role in its councils, he acknowledged that it had begun "as a way of pooling military resources. Today, it is a way of pooling our intellectual and our diplomatic resources as well ... And let us remember too, these truths that we have found together, that variety can mean vitality, that diversity can be a force for progress, and that our ultimate destiny is indivisible."[25] In 1979 Henry Kissinger wrote that Canada's "somewhat aloof position combined with the high quality of its leadership" gave it "an influence out of proportion to its military contribution ... It conducted a global foreign policy; it participated in international peacekeeping efforts; it made a constructive contribution to the dialogue between developed and developing nations. At the same time Canada had its own special relationship with the United States ... Convinced of the necessity of cooperation, impelled by domestic imperatives toward confrontation, Canadian leaders had a narrow margin for maneuver that they utilized with extraordinary skill." Bothwell says that Trudeau was captivated by Kissinger's perspective on international relations.[26]

When, a few months after Nixon's visit, Washington asked Canada to participate again in the ICC in Viet Nam, this time named the International Control Commission and Supervision (ICCS), Trudeau did so only with great reluctance. The circumstances were particularly difficult because the Nixon administration had commenced a heavy bombing campaign against Hanoi and Haiphong as part of the process of negotiating peace. Canadian protests, both by the public and by the government, led to Nixon ordering American diplomats to shun Canadian diplomats. Nevertheless, Canadians did participate in the ICCS for a limited period, despite knowing that it was futile. Trudeau's relationship with Nixon's successor, Gerald Ford, was easier, and he was in broad agreement with the foreign policy of Jimmy Carter, who held office from 1977 to 1981, but he had little in common with Carter's Republican successor, Ronald Reagan.[27]

The late 1970s and early 1980s were a very dangerous time. Soviet leadership was geriatric, and in the West there was a determination, led by Reagan, Britain's prime minister, Margaret Thatcher, and Germany's chancellor, Helmut Kohl, to confront force with superior force. In 1977 Trudeau launched a campaign at the United Nations against the structural terror of mutual nuclear deterrence, but he was unsuccessful in bringing about a comprehensive test ban on nuclear weapons.[28] The

Soviet deployment of SS-20 intermediate range road-mobile nuclear missiles into Warsaw Pact countries beginning in 1978 was seen in the West as a serious destabilizing factor, and was responded to in 1979 with a decision to station ground-launch and air-launch theatre ballistic and cruise missiles in Europe and the United States. Soviet forces invaded Afghanistan in December 1979, and the Americans responded by equipping Islamist Mujahideen Resistance fighters. Consistent with the Harmel report, however, NATO also confirmed its decision that it should conduct a two-front response to the crisis with equal emphasis on confidence building.

In a development that would be important for Canada a decade later, NATO abandoned the geographic restrictions on the scope of the alliance that had originally been important to both the Canadian and American governments. In the wake of the Soviet invasion of Afghanistan the North Atlantic Council agreed in May 1980 that: "the stability of regions outside NATO boundaries, particularly in the South West Asia area, and the secure supply of essential commodities from this area are of crucial importance. Therefore, the current situation has serious implications for the security of member countries. The altered strategic situation in South West Asia warrants full solidarity and the strengthening of Allied cohesion as a response to the new challenges. Ministers recognised that maintenance of the special relationships of Allies with the regional countries are in the interests of the West as well as of the countries of the region."[29] General Alexander Haig, supreme allied commander Europe (SACEUR), went even further, telling the American House Armed Services Committee that "the entire globe is now NATO's concern."[30] American forces in Europe were reconfigured to serve national purposes, while NATO provided political cover and back-up. Contingency plans were drawn up in June 1981 by SACLANT for the use of NATO naval forces in the Indian Ocean, and the American commander-in-chief, U.S. Naval Forces in Europe, was relocated from London to Naples closer to the American contribution to NATO's "Rapid Deployment Force," the 1st Battalion, 509th Airborne Infantry Combat Team.

The build-up of weapons on standing alert dominated events. Negotiations toward an Intermediate-Range Nuclear Forces (INF) reduction treaty began in September 1981, but in December the Soviet Navy commissioned the first of its *Typhoon* ballistic missile submarines, the largest in the world. After delays, their twenty tubes were loaded in 1984 with missiles capable of launching ten independently targeted warheads to a range of 4,480 nautical miles.[31]

✦ ✦ ✦

For several years the Department of National Defence struggled to change Trudeau's perception, and eventually was successful. An element in Trudeau's changing attitude to the navy appears to have been reconsideration of the implications of strategic ASW. His concern, expressed as early as his 12 April 1969 speech, that strategic ASW could accidentally trigger nuclear war, was possibly a result of a misperception fostered by the American administration's exaggeration when seeking funds for anti-ballistic missile defences. The acoustic system employed to identify and localize submarines, as Ron Purver has pointed out, did not possess the degree of reliability to make it possible to achieve complete effectiveness. Because a single SSBN possesses the fire power to destroy any nation, the logic of nuclear deterrence would require that all of a hostile force be targeted simultaneously.[32] An early effort to correct the perception was undertaken by Dr George Lindsey, who in 1969 wrote for the Defence Research Analysis Establishment a study entitled *Canadian Maritime Strategy: Should the Emphasis be Changed*, in which he detailed the limitations of the navy's capacity in ASW.[33]

Having dismissed the idea that strategic ASW could push the Soviets to use their SSBN assets rather than lose them, the department returned to the argument made by Dr Sutherland in 1963 that an ability to track, and occasionally localize, hostile submarines was an important support for arms control agreements. The report of the 1971 Management Review Group led to the establishment of a Directorate of Strategic Analysis under the chief of operational research and analysis, and a Directorate of Strategic Policy Planning under the chief of policy planning. These functions had previously been undertaken by the Defence Research Board, which had been established at the end of the war to continue in peacetime the defence analysis that had been undertaken by the National Research Council. As the new chief of operational research, Lindsey wrote in 1972 a defence of routine naval surveillance of submarine movements as a stabilizing factor: "knowledge that they [the Soviet SSBNs] have remained far from the coast in a normal pattern confirms that the situation is normal, making for stability, while knowledge that they have increased in numbers or closed in to short range does permit the taking of non-provocative counter-measures to reduce vulnerability. The most dangerous state is that of ignorance, the most likely basis for unnecessary escalation."[34] The navy began to recover its direction when the Atlanticists won their case in the Defence Structure Review of 1974–75.[35]

Writing in 1976, Colin S. Gray disparaged strategic ASW. "If any Canadian official attempts to defend the LRPA program in terms of strategic ASW, he is either woefully ill-informed as to technical detail or he is not telling the truth."[36] Four years earlier, however, he had acknowledged that there was value in the Canadian navy's "'hour-by-hour' total portrait of Soviet (*et al*) maritime deployment." "By keeping a close watch on the movement of Soviet submarines from the Arctic into the North Atlantic and from the Baltic into the North Sea, it is hoped that strategic warning would be provided of an intended attack." He also recognized that it was only by participation in alliance intelligence operations that Ottawa could obtain the ability to analyze for itself the strategic picture, and if appropriate, seek to influence allied policy. "To be seriously in ASW, as Canada still undoubtedly is, does guarantee a flow of strategic intelligence concerning both world-wide military/commercial maritime developments, and activities being pursued that are of particular relevance to Canada."[37]

In 1977 John Gellner also questioned the utility of strategic ASW: "Since the first strike in a nuclear war would be sure to be in the nature of a surprise attack, and since the craft carrying the submarine-launched ballistic missiles (SLBMs) would be cruising in international waters prior to the launching of their weapons, there never was any chance of preventing the launch." He did, however, accept that strategic ASW was the only means of "keeping tabs in peacetime on the movements of ballistic missile-carrying submarines in the hope of being able to draw from their deployment valid conclusions as to the other side's intentions." Gellner was no more convinced of the practicability of tactical ASW following the equipment of attack submarines with tactical missiles: "Close escort of convoys would obviously be of little use now. What could be of use would be the clearing of a wide transit corridor on either side and well ahead and behind the convoy, a corridor wider than the maximum range of the great majority of attack weapons. There are those who believe that it can be done, while others think that it cannot."[38]

A major component of NATO's planning to confront Soviet Attack and Ballistic Missile submarines was offensive battle fleet operations into the Norwegian Sea. These would suppress Soviet forces in their bases, pose a threat of incursion into the Soviet heartland from the north, and by so doing, draw Soviet surface and submarine forces into an attrition battle. The Soviet navy had its own very active strategic ASW programs, which called for active defence of their own SSBNs and prosecution of American, British, and French ships by surface ships, submarines, and bombardment by ballistic missiles, with reconnaissance satellites and long-range aircraft.[39] The extent to which Trudeau was aware of this battle plan has not been revealed. It would have reinforced his conviction that lines of communication had to be kept open with the Soviet leadership, and it would not have encouraged him to commit resources to Canadian naval forces that could be drawn into such a battle. But Norman Friedman writes that when Admiral Elmo Zumwalt became U.S. Chief of Naval Operations in 1970, he suppressed talk about naval forward operations. His apparent reluctance to go after the Russians in their home waters alarmed critics in the U.S. Navy, who felt it would be suicidal to surrender the initiative, but the priority being given to defence of shipping in the mid-1970s could have been a part of the reason for Trudeau's acceptance of the Atlanticist strategy.[40] The Senate subcommittee's 1983 report on "Canada's Maritime Defence" was still recommending that "Canada's anti-submarine warfare tasks be confined to those of a tactical nature – defence against anti-shipping submarines – and only such strategic surveillance missions as can be carried out with the same equipment."[41] Practically speaking, however, the navy had already made its point.

Economic considerations played a part in Trudeau's conversion. He became interested in establishing a "contractual link" with the European Community, and the newly elected German chancellor, Helmut Schmidt, made it clear his support would come at a price, as a *quid pro quo* for continued Canadian contribution to the defence of Europe.[42] From the German perspective, Canada's abandonment of its role in the triad of linkages between conventional, tactical nuclear, and strategic defence increased the exposure of her allies to political pressure, and substantially reduced her importance as an ally. The continued Canadian military commitment was most valued because Canada had never been an occupying power, a fact that strengthened the political commitment of the Benelux countries to the alliance.[43] Trudeau's minister of national defence in 1975, James Richardson, assured NATO that Canadian forces in Europe would not be further reduced, and the chief of defence staff, General Dextraze, was able to persuade Trudeau to order German-built *Leopard* tanks for it.[44] The army brigade in Germany was brought up to full strength by prepositioning equipment for 1,100 reinforcements to be airlifted from Canada in the event of a crisis. As a means of enhancing Canadian trade prospects in Europe, however, the retention of Canadian land and air forces in Germany was a matter of too little, too late. The proportion of gross national product that Canada spent on defence, 2.1% in 1970, and down to 1.8% in 1973, rose in 1974 to 2.1% and again in 1975 to 2.2%. It then dropped sharply back to 1.8%, comparing unfavourably with the 1978 figures for West Germany of 4.1%, Britain's 4.7% and the United States's 5%.

But Trudeau's gradual, and incomplete, conversion was not simply a matter of economic interest. He had come to recognize that international political realities made it necessary to follow the twin-track of the Harmel report; that détente had to be pursued in tandem with appropriate means of containing possible Soviet adventures. Paul Buteux writes that the redeployment of Canada's reduced forces to southern Germany, and the gradual rebuilding of the conventional commitment that occurred from the mid-1970s onward, was in large part an effort to overcome the politically isolated position in which Canada had been placed. Richardson told the Standing Committee on External Affairs and National Defence on 23 March 1976 that "our central objective ... is for Canada to play its part with our NATO partners in achieving international stability."[45] Richardson's successor as minister, Barnett Danson, considered eliminating Canada's commitment to reinforce Norway, but on a visit there reconsidered when he was persuaded of the importance of Norwegian airfields and fiords in the defence of the North Atlantic against a Soviet naval campaign.[46] "After the dust had settled from the 1969 review," Buteux continues, Canadian governments "were prepared to maintain forces in Germany as the price of the ticket to the diplomatic table." The Atlantic Council was recognized as being a forum Canada did not want to be without: "NATO acted as an 'influence multiplier,' even in circumstances where Canada had little of substance to place on the negotiating table." When in February 1984 Trudeau outlined to Parliament his reasons for the independent peace initiative he undertook he remarked that "An alliance which fails to defend democracy in its councils will surely fail in its defence of democracy in the field. NATO summit meetings have a particular importance." The new tanks and force augmentation in Germany was recognized to be a necessary prerequisite for obtaining German support at Brussels for Trudeau's peace initiatives.[47] In 1986 Canada's Ambassador to NATO, John Halstead, would write that "North America is where Canadian security will be at risk if the US nuclear deterrent fails ... Europe is still the place where the global East-West balance is at stake."[48]

During the Defence Structure Review there had been indications that the Americans might favour a Canadian withdrawal from Germany and a concentration on naval control of the Atlantic. The decision to retain, and re-equip, the forces in Germany did not eliminate that American interest in Canada's naval effort, and the Canadian government was also subjected to considerable pressure by Joseph Luns, secretary general of NATO, and by British Admiral of the Fleet, Sir Peter Hill-Norton, chairman of the NATO Military Committee, with respect to the re-equipment of the Canadian air force and navy for maritime sea control.[49]

The naval commitment to constabulary tasks provided the Canadian navy with political cover, possibly even at Cabinet level, but did not represent the real priority of the navy. Rob Byers pointed out at the time that, in meeting the need in 1977 for offshore surveillance, CP-140 *Aurora* were ordered for the Maritime Air Group, when a more limited aircraft would have sufficed for constabulary work. The decision to make the purchase provides a date for Trudeau's acceptance that there was symbiosis between nationalist and Atlanticist policies, and that it was not constructive to give NATO a cold shoulder. On 13 January 1977 Danson expressed this view in a speech to the Conference of Defence Associations in Ottawa: "sovereignty, North American defence and NATO are almost inseparable. We can't have a free North America without a free Western Europe, and Western Europe cannot be free without a free North America. NATO is a key element." A month later the new chief of defence staff, Vice-Admiral Falls, made the same point during a speech at the Canada Club: "As you know the government's first priority is the protection of Canadian sovereignty ... I cannot, personally, conceive of any view of sovereignty that did not, at the same time, assume a free and viable community of North Atlantic nations."[50]

That same year, authorization was given for the Patrol Frigate program, although the first batch of six were not ordered until 1983, in the last year of Trudeau's leadership of the government. Technical developments in ASW had made it essential that individual ships be equipped to operate on their own, hundreds of miles from their consorts, deploying towed passive sonar arrays. This made it necessary to provide them with strong air defences, and to equip them with fully capable command and control displays with satellite UHF communications, as well as the helicopter landing pads and hangars. They were also armed with *Harpoon* surface-to-surface missiles to enhance their ability to survive as isolated ships in a hostile environment. In effect the ships the naval staff in Halifax developed were the direct decendants of the cancelled general purpose frigates, although without the capacity to provide fire support for landed forces.[51]

The Cold War: Détente, Rust-Out, and Renewal

CP 140 *Aurora* near Stanley Park, Vancouver, BC, 9 September 1992.
DND CXC89-266

Two years after the frigates were authorized, in February 1979, approval was given for a major overhaul of the three *Oberon/Ojibwa* class diesel-electric submarines stationed at Halifax to equip them for participation in sea control operations, the Submarine Operational Update Program, or SOUP. Provided with a Singer-Librascope Mk 1 digital fire-control system, new passive range-finding sonar, improvement to the attack periscope and communications, new batteries to increase their submerged endurance, and wire-guided mark-48 torpedoes, the first of these vessels to be refitted was ready for service in 1983.[52]

Although Trudeau was careful about military commitments to allies, he was prepared to use strong measures when circumstances appeared to call for it, as during the Front de la Libération du Quebec crisis in October 1970.[53] When in 1973 he agreed to supply Canadian Forces personnel for the revived International Commission of Control and Supervision (ICCS) in South Vietnam, HMC destroyer escorts *Terra Nova* and *Kootenay* were deployed to provide for the possibility of a quick sealift evacuation of Canadian citizens. Rob Byers believed the Canadian commitment of forces to the UN peacekeeping force in Cyprus, which was strengthened and reorganized in July and August 1974 following the attempted Cypriot coup and the Turkish invasion, was a milestone in Trudeau's return to Pearsonian ideas of collective defence. In the ongoing conflict between successive American administrations and the Communist regime in Cuba, his sympathies were divided, and in 1979, when it appeared possible that there might be a right wing reaction to the election of the democrat socialist prime minister of Jamaica, Michael Manley, he ordered the Canadian navy to prepare a task force to intervene should that become necessary. In 1980 he agreed to a request by NATO to hold HMCS *Fraser* at Portsmouth over Christmas so that if necessary STANAVFORLANT could be used in the Skagerrak north of Denmark to indicate international concern should the Soviet Union intervene to support the Polish government's confrontation of the Solidarity movement.[54]

Canadian Patrol Frigates under construction at Saint John Shipbuilding, ca. 1991. 2381-20

Opposite: Aerial view of the HMCS *Halifax* (FFH 330), lead ship of the Canadian Patrol Frigates. Built at Saint John Shipbuilding, 1987–92. Photographed prior to commissioning, 11 July 1991. DND HSC91-681-5

The Cold War: Détente, Rust-Out, and Renewal

On 10 February 1982, despite terrific public opposition, the Canadian government signed an agreement to permit testing of American cruise missiles over northern Canadian terrain that resembled the conditions the air-launched missiles would have to navigate in arctic Russia. And even before the *Oberon* submarines were fully refurbished, they began to undertake operational surveillance patrols (OSP) that might be conceived as at least consistent with the developing, and aggressive, U.S. Navy "Maritime Strategy." Joseph T. Jockel and Joel J. Sokolsky have recently reminded us that when defending the decision to permit the missile tests Trudeau was outspoken in his assertion of Canada's obligation to support its allies.[55]

During the 1980s the U.S. Navy had begun to develop a concept of operations that was intended to minimize the effectiveness of Soviet missile-firing submarines. Broadly, it could be characterized as the old strategy of forward action against the Soviet Arctic bases, although the

impetus came from Admiral Thomas Hayward commanding the Pacific fleet between August 1976 and May 1978.[56] In 1979 Admiral Hayward came to Washington as chief of naval operations, and established a study group at the U.S. Naval War College to rethink naval strategy. With the election of President Reagan in 1980 his aggressive approach to strategy became acceptable. In March 1984 Admiral James D. Watkins, who succeeded Hayward in 1982, told the United States Senate Subcommittee on Sea Power and Force Projection: "Our feeling is that an aggressive defense, if you will, characterized by forward movement, early deployment of forces, aggressiveness on the part of our ships, is the greatest deterrent that we can have. And the Soviets really understand that. We can get their attention with that concept."[57]

President Reagan's secretary of the navy, John Lehman, tied strategic and tactical ASW together when he wrote in 1982: "I cannot conceive of a NATO war in which we would not be putting not one but several carrier battle-groups into the Norwegian Sea at some point. What we must seek to do is to seek out and destroy the Soviet capacity to interdict our uses of the sea ... We have to go north of the GIUK gap with sufficient power to defeat the threat." Steven Miller, of the Center for International Studies, Massachusetts Institute of Technology, concluded in a 1986 paper that the Reagan administration's counter-force nuclear strategy would be directed as much at SSBNs as at the land bases systems. "Consequently, the United States has an incentive to monitor Soviet SSBNs in peacetime, to position itself for the conduct of strategic ASW in the midst of conventional war and to carry out strategic ASW missions in the event of nuclear war."[58]

American apologists for the Maritime Strategy did not attach great importance to the danger of weapons being launched to avoid their destruction by anti-submarine warfare. Admiral Watkins dismissed the danger: "Some argue that such steps will lead to immediate escalation, but escalation solely as a result of actions at sea seems improbable given the Soviet land orientation. Escalation in response to maritime pressure serves no useful purpose for the Soviets since their reserve forces would be degraded and the United States retaliatory posture would be enhanced. Neither we nor the Soviets can rule out the possibility that escalation will occur, but aggressive use of maritime power can make escalation a less attractive option to the Soviets with the passing of every day."[59] David Rosenburg, diplomatic and military historian, wrote in 1996 that improved understanding of Soviet defence doctrine made the Maritime Strategy possible. It abandoned the assumption that global war would inevitably and quickly become a decisive and disastrous nuclear conflict.[60] Norman Friedman, in a 2001 review of the Maritime Strategy, takes the glass-half-full position, arguing that so long as the United States retained powerful naval forces, the Soviets could only defeat it by a suicidal nuclear offensive and that, so long as the United States remained undefeated and a naval power, no Soviet victory in Europe would be secure.[61]

This was not the sort of risk taking with which one might have expected Trudeau to agree, but in fact the first Canadian submarine to undertake an operational surveillance patrol, HMCS *Okanagan*, departed Halifax for the purpose on 30 June 1983 during Trudeau's last year in power. The Soviet Navy's *Yankee* class SSBN "boomers" needed to approach the North American coast to be within firing range for their SS-N-6 (2,400 to 3,000 km range) missiles, and usually three *Yankees* occupied positions on the Atlantic coast, one in the Canadian sector, and one on the Pacific coast. Four *Delta* II class SSBNs had 9,100 km range SS-N-8 (2) weapons that permitted them to patrol in the Labrador Sea, or indeed, anywhere in the Canadian arctic archipelago.[62] *Okanagan* had not yet received her SOUP conversion, but was given a mission fix of a narrow sideband sonar analyser to help with discriminating the noise made by a Soviet submarine. The short time allotted for the operation, nineteen days, forced *Okanagan* to operate at too high a speed for successful detection, but it did provide her crew with some experience. The second OSP, by the SOUP-converted HMCS *Ojibwa*, run between 14 November and 6 December, carried out electronic intelligence surveillance on Russian long-range "Bear" patrol aircraft, and may have detected an SSN and an SSBN. Other commitments, conversion schedules and work-ups prevented the running of any OSPs in 1984, so that by the time the Canadian submarines were fully equipped and trained for the purpose Trudeau had retired, and Mikhail Gorbachev, rather than the geriatric leadership that preceded him, was in charge in the Soviet Union.[63]

✦ ✦ ✦

The cruise missile tests, the new procurement for the Canadian navy, and its more aggressive employment, were measures of purposive force that needed effective diplomacy to realize their purpose. Trudeau was never content to leave the serious diplomacy to others, and in his last years in office he took his diplomacy back to the world stage. He was subjected to terrific pressure from Washington, due as much to his left-leaning

National Energy Program, as to his open dialogue with Communist nations.⁶⁴ What was impressive is that, although Trudeau bowed to the pressure and recognized the need to match force with force, he continued to pursue détente when others seem to have abandoned hope.

The American Strategic Defence Initiative "Star Wars" space-based missile defence project, announced on 23 March 1983 by President Reagan, frightened Soviet leadership because American defence technology was so far beyond their own capabilities.⁶⁵ Practical warning of the nervousness of the Soviet leadership came in September 1983 when a Soviet fighter aircraft shot down in the Sea of Japan a Korean airliner, KAL-007, which had strayed into Soviet air space. The public American response ignored the warning from the Central Intelligence Agency (CIA) that the Soviets had possibly mistaken the airliner for an American RC-135 surveillance plane that had earlier been in the area. The Incidents at Sea Agreement (INCSEA), drawn up in 1972 between the U.S. and Soviet navies to prevent collisions and harassment, had to be invoked to stop Soviet forces interfering with salvage operations.⁶⁶ This tragedy was followed on 23 October by the destruction of two barracks in Beirut used by United Nations peacekeepers, with the loss of 299 American and French lives, and two days later by the American invasion of the Commonwealth country of Grenada to evict a Marxist government.

In November the NATO exercise *Able Archer* led the Soviets to put their forces on full alert against a nuclear attack and prepare for a possible pre-emptive strike. Gates later reviewed the episode and concluded: "Information about the peculiar and remarkably skewed frame of mind of the Soviet leaders during those times that has emerged since the collapse of the Soviet Union makes me think there is a good chance – with all of the other events in 1983 – that they really felt a NATO attack was at least possible and that they took a number of measures to enhance their military readiness short of mobilization."⁶⁷ Other collisions occurred between American and Soviet warships off the South Carolina coast, in the Arabian sea, in the Black Sea in February 1984, and again in the Sea of Japan in March.

The first American ground-launch cruise missile arrived in Britain on 14 November 1983, on 16 and 22 November, Italy and Germany voted to accept U.S. missiles, and on 23 November the first U.S. *Pershing II* theatre ballistic missile arrived in Germany. Also in November 1983, the Soviets withdrew from the negotiations toward a Intermediate-Range Nuclear Forces reduction treaty, and these were not resumed until March 1986. First Secretary Leonid Brezhnev had already instituted an intelligence operation, named Operation *RyaN* (Raketno-Yadernoe Napadenie), with agents looking for evidence of a NATO plan to launch a surprise attack.[68]

During this period religious and scientific leaders were meeting under the auspices of the Vatican, and in November 1984 released their apocalyptic warning that "the immediate and long-term consequences of a nuclear exchange could bring such vast destruction upon the peoples of the world as to constitute an unprecedented, planet-wide catastrophe ... Much of the world would be threatened by crop failures, unparalleled famine, mass starvation, and widespread uncontrollable epidemics."[69]

It was in that climate that Trudeau in effect dedicated the rest of his political life to reviving détente. On 15 June 1981, in his first foreign policy intervention in the House of Commons following his re-election, he had warned about the endemic crisis and returned to his preoccupation with the economic roots of conflict. "Madam Speaker, it is obvious to all of us that our world has become unpredictable and unstable ... Violence and disorder have become banal. Injustice no longer causes indignation ... While the superpowers have grown stronger, they often seem to have lost control over events."[70] Writing soon afterward, Harald von Riekhoff and John Sigler said that Trudeau's experience in May 1983 at the Williamsburg summit confirmed his skepticism that the United States was sincere about negotiating a settlement on arms control with the Soviets. A meeting with the scientific community discussing the consequences of nuclear war reaffirmed his fears. In a speech at Guelph University in October 1983 he spoke of how deeply he was "troubled by an intellectual climate of acrimony and uncertainty; by the parlous state of East-West relations; by a superpower relationship which is dangerously confrontational; and by a widening gap between military strategy and political purpose ... Our central purpose must be to create a stable environment of increased security for both East and West. We must aim at suppressing those nearly instinctive fears, frustrations or ambitions which have so often been the reason for resorting to the use of force."[71]

Earlier that year, in what turned out to be Trudeau's greatest contribution to détente, he invited Gorbachev, then the Soviet minister of agriculture, to visit Canada. Gorbachev was impressed by the signs of Canadian affluence, especially on Canadian farms, and by the candour of his grilling by a House of Commons committee.

At the end of 1983 Trudeau set out on a world leader's tour, hoping to revive détente. How useful it was is not clear; Gates did not even mention it in his memoirs. Possibly Trudeau's effort would have been more obviously productive had not Brezhnev's successor, Yuri Andropov, been dying at the time of his initiative. Canada's military power, even after Trudeau abandoned rust-out as a means to his ends, was hardly enough to support intervention in the super-power confrontation, but Michael Pearson, Gregor Mackinnon, and Christopher Sapardanis show that Trudeau's objective was as much expressive as purposeful. It was intended to stimulate an international resolve to address the issues, and they believe it had some value in those terms.[72] Trudeau did not himself overstate his achievement, but in speaking about it in the House of Commons on his return, 9 February 1984, he was positive: "Let it be said of Canada and of Canadians that we saw the crisis; that we did act; that we took risks; that we were loyal to our friends and open with our adversaries; that we lived up to our ideals; and that we have done what we could to lift the shadow of war." Brian Mulroney, the leader of the Opposition, in his reply said: "my Party and I have consistently wished him, as Prime Minister of Canada, well in all of his initiatives. The maintenance of peace is critical to every hope we have for Canada and to every dream we have for Canadians."[73] Two years later, after his retirement from politics on 10 June 1984 and Gorbachev's election as general secretary of the Communist Party of the Soviet Union, Trudeau was invited to visit Moscow. There he was asked about Reagan.[74] In November 1984 Trudeau was awarded the Albert Einstein Peace Prize, in March 1986 the INF negotiations were recommenced, and on 11 October Reagan and Gorbachev agreed at Reykjavík to the destruction of all theatre nuclear weapons in Europe.

7

THE COLD WAR: ENDGAME

After a brief interim administration under John Turner, there was a general election in which the Liberals were swept from power. The Progressive Conservative leader, Brian Mulroney, was sworn in as prime minister on 17 September 1984. Robert Bothwell concludes his study of Canadian foreign policy in the four decades following the Second World War with the comment that "after 1984, Canadian governments faced out, but very largely in one direction, south, and had a different agenda from those that went before."[1] The most important outcome of the Mulroney years was to be the free trade treaty with the United States and ultimately Mexico, that came into force 1 January 1994. It was a leap of faith that was to be as much of a milestone in Canada's defence strategy as the Suez crisis had been.[2] At the beginning of his administration, however, Mulroney pursued traditional Canadian strategies, which he sought to carry out more rationally and by means of dramatic initiatives. These included strengthening Canada's defence position in Europe, but was most notable for a serious effort to strengthen Canada's position in the arctic, and to move the Canadian navy into the big league. Symbolic of the return to older strategies was the Mulroney administration's decision in 1986 to permit the naval and air "environments" of the Canadian Armed Forces to recover something like their traditional uniform, with all naval ranks using the warrant officer style rig.

Writing in 1983, Ken Booth discussed the effect of the "psycho-legal" boundaries at sea that had been established when the Convention on the Law of the Sea legitimized extensive national economic zones. He warned that their existence, whatever their formal legal limitations, created a vocabulary for gunboat diplomacy. Warships could not cross such lines without creating political ripples.[3] Such has certainly been the case with the claims of archipelagic states, including those Canada maintains to control the waters of the arctic archipelago. In 1979 President Carter had authorized a series of "Freedom of Navigation" operations, deliberate incursions into seas claimed by countries around the world. With the swearing in of President Reagan in January 1981 these operations had acquired a more aggressive character. This led in 1982 to the Soviets passing a Law of the State Border, and in 1983 issuing navigation rules, to deny any right of innocent passage for warships through Soviet territorial waters. During this period there were many episodes in which American warships were harassed by Soviet forces, sometime leading to collisions.[4]

In the circumstances, American pressure on Canada was of a very mild order. In May 1985 the U.S. State Department indicated to External Affairs that the U.S. icebreaker CGS *Polar Sea* would transit the Northwest Passage so as to avoid the expense and time involved in going via Panama from Greenland to Alaska. In response, the Canadian government gave the U.S. Coast Guard "permission" to make the transit, and then on 10 September strengthened its claim to the waters of the arctic archipelago, declaring them to be internal waters of Canada by drawing straight baselines around the periphery of the islands.

Mulroney gave the arctic a prominent place in his national and political strategy. His first minister of national defence, Robert Coates, proved to be a loose cannon, but after he was forced to retire following indiscretions in Germany, Deputy Prime Minister Erik Nielsen undertook a NATO-wide tour to scout reaction to the idea of moving the Canadian commitment from Germany to enhance that to Norway, employing a Canadian Forces base to be established in Scotland. The idea of relocating to sub-arctic Norway resonated with the focus the Mulroney administration put on the Canadian arctic, but was firmly rejected by alliance leaders, apart from the Norwegians, and was not liked by the Canadian Army.[5] In March 1985 Mulroney signed an agreement with President Reagan for the modernization of old, and tube electronics–based, Distant Early Warning Line with a new North Warning System. Canada agreed to pay 40 percent of the cost of the new equipment and take over both ownership and operation of the Canadian part of the system. The voyage of the *Manhattan* in 1969 had stimulated a plan to construct a heavy icebreaker, that was eventually decided should be built to meet Polar 8 standards. Polar standards are set by the Arctic Shipping Pollution Prevention Regulations (ASPPR) made under the Arctic Waters

Pollution Prevention Act. A *Polar 8* class vessel would be licensed to operate year round everywhere in the arctic archipelago except the far northwest, where it would be limited to seasonal operation. No decision was made on proceeding with the project, however, until 1985. Then, stimulated in part by the need to provide contracts for the Canadian shipbuilding industry, the Mulroney Cabinet announced an intention to proceed, with a budget of $700 million.[6] The most dramatic and controversial proposal, however, involved the navy.

On 5 May 1986 three American submarines met at the north pole, and in December that same year, following publication of the report of the Special Joint Committee of the Senate and the House of Commons on Canada's International Relations, a question was asked in the House of Commons about whether one or more of them had been routed through Canadian waters and whether the permission of the Canadian government had been sought and received. The secretary of state for external affairs, Joe Clark, would only answer that the Canadian government had "a variety of ways of knowing of the presence in our waters of submarines from the United States or other countries ... there are provisions in place that allow us to know the information and to assert and protect our sovereignty, and those provisions are respected."[7] Presumably the same "provisions" were the justification for Vice-Admiral Nigel D. Brodeur, deputy chief of the defence staff, to tell the House of Commons Standing Committee on National Defence in December 1986 that "we do not have evidence that Soviet submarines are entering into the Canadian Arctic."[8] However, a year earlier, the assistant deputy minister for policy of the Department of National Defence, John Anderson, had acknowledged to the Standing Committee on External Affairs and National Defence that: "we are quite possibly entering a period when use of Arctic waters in particular, in terms of a threat to North America, by Soviet submarines may be something we are going to have to pay a lot more attention to ... I think it is fairly clear that [if] that were seen as a serious emerging threat, the interests of Canada and the United States in doing something about it would be common."[9]

The Soviet Navy had a major interest in the Arctic Ocean, as the navy of the Russian Republic continues to do. Only in the Arctic Ocean was the Soviet Navy reasonably sure of being able to keep its ballistic missile submarines (SSBNS) secure. All maritime activity was closely monitored within naval "bastions" in the Barents and Kara seas close to the Kola Peninsula directly across the permanent polar ice cap from Canadian territory, and in the Sea of Okhotsk, within which surface forces, submarines, and aircraft were deployed to defend the SSBN "boomers." The *Delta III* and *IV* and *Typhoon* classes could launch their missiles (SS-N-18s and SS-N-20s) against both North American and European targets from the Canadian arctic archipelago and the Davis Strait. The Bering Strait and the Norwegian Sea were the principal access routes to the Atlantic or Pacific from the Arctic ocean for the older classes of missile-firing submarines and the attack submarines with missions against naval targets, but the Bering Strait is too shallow, and too easily controlled by hostile forces, for it to be employed by the Soviet Union for operational deployments. Navigational difficulties in the Canadian arctic archipelago greatly reduce the attraction of that route. However, the formidable naval forces of NATO at the southern end of the Norwegian Sea, across the Greenland/Iceland/United Kingdom (GIUK) gap, meant that the Soviet Navy could only expect to be able to use that route in a crisis to deploy its *Yankee* SSBNs, the last of which was not finally taken out of service until January 1995, if its submarines were deployed *en masse* to confuse acoustic sensors, and if surface forces were employed to degrade the effectiveness of NATO and American forces. Depending on how the Soviet Union rated its chances in a naval battle against the NATO anti-submarine barrier, the Canadian route could appear more attractive.[10] In a 1984 article Harriet Critchley wrote: "the NATO monitoring and defensive zone [in the Norwegian Sea] is much like a waterborne Maginot Line: it is static, in the sense of being designed for one area of ocean, and it is vulnerable to a flanking manoeuvre. Submarines can avoid the zone by proceeding from the Arctic Ocean through one or more of the deeper channels in the Canadian Arctic archipelago to Baffin Bay, Davis Strait, and then the Labrador Sea."[11]

It was believed at the time that the development of submarine-launched cruise missiles would give the Soviet Navy another reason for operating in the seas close to Canada's arctic littoral. When on 10 February 1983 the Trudeau administration authorized the testing of American cruise missiles in the arctic, an underlying purpose was to develop the ability to intercept Soviet cruise missiles launched from the Beaufort Sea.[12] In an appearance before the Standing Committee on External Affairs and National Defence in November 1985, Rear Admiral Fred W. Crickard, CF, testified that the weapon (the SS-NX-21) would probably have a range of 3,000 kilometres, a speed of 0.7 mach, and a yield of 200 kilotons and would be launchable through standard torpedo tubes.[13] The flight range limitations for Soviet sea-launched cruise missiles suggested that the preferred launch positions would be off the Atlantic and Pacific coasts of the United States, but the dangers there would also be great.

The possibility that the Soviet navy intended to make use of the arctic archipelagic channels created an operational requirement for American naval deployments into the Arctic ocean to obtain strategic warning of possible attack. The Northwest Passage and associated channels may also have figured in the planning to take the war to the enemy. The Maritime Strategy, with its plan to act aggressively to contain Soviet nuclear forces to prevent their being used as bargaining assets following a nuclear exchange, was conceived on a large scale and involved naval movement into the Norwegian sea and northwest Pacific, but it may also have included naval use of the Northwest Passage. The Bering Strait and the Norwegian sea supply the most direct routes to the polar basin, but the Northwest Passage is shorter than the Panama canal route for United States submarines being deployed from the Atlantic to Siberian waters, and the Bering Strait is as insecure for American forces as it is for those of the Soviet Union.[14]

In 1987, following Nielson's replacement as minister by Perrin Beatty and the appointment of General Paul Manson as chief of defence staff, a White Paper on defence was produced, *Challenge and Commitment*, which left unchanged the operational commitments of the Canadian forces, but attempted to increase resources. Canada's traditional Atlanticist strategy, with its nationalist implications, was stoutly defended. Should the European defence partnership collapse, it warned, "the context in which this nation seeks its destiny would be diminished in every respect and the most profound concerns about Canada's future as an independent nation would arise." To implement this policy it announced that the navy would build and maintain a fleet of up to twelve nuclear attack submarines. "Given the vast distances in the three ocean areas in which Canada requires maritime forces and the SSN's unlimited endurance and flexibility, the Government has decided to acquire a fleet of nuclear-powered submarines to enhance the overall effectiveness of the Canadian navy." Reportedly, the acquisition process had begun 28 August 1985 when Nielsen, who represented the arctic riding of Yukon, requested that the nuclear option be investigated.[15] Jason Delaney comments that it was the "Government of Canada, not the navy" that made the announcement.[16]

Canadian submarines were already engaged in the task of monitoring Soviet SSBNs operating in sub-arctic waters. The first Operational

HMCS *Onondaga* (S 73), an *Oberon* class submarine built at Chatham Dockyard, England, 1964–65, where the author saw her under construction for the Royal Canadian Navy in an eighteenth-century building shed. She is seen here in Bassin Louise, Quebec, 8 July 1985. Decommissioned in 2000, she has become a museum ship at Rimouski, Quebec. DND IMC85-320

Surveillance Patrol (OSP) in 1985, in March, made dramatic contact with a Soviet *Victor III* class SSN and a *Delta* class SSBN south of Greenland. Vectored for three days by a series of *Aurora* maritime patrol aircraft toward the *Victor III*, on March 19 the modernized HMCS *Ojibwa* instead detected the *Delta*. It passed within 800 yards of *Ojibwa* while turning to "clear its baffles," which it needed to do periodically as the cavitation from its own propellers prevented it detecting anything directly astern.

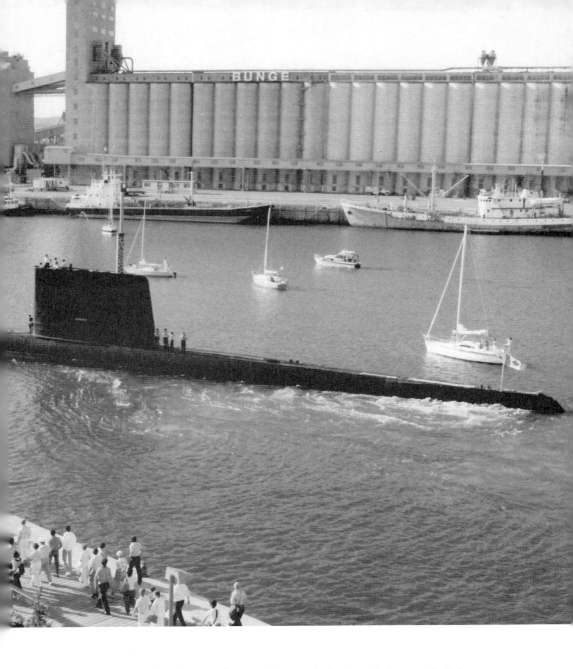

Ojibwa trailed it for nearly two days as it followed the north Atlantic ridge to minimize its signature. Late on March 20, when the *Delta* was again making a 360° turn, what was probably the *Victor III* submarine was suddenly detected. The new contact illuminated *Ojibwa* with active sonar. Having been counter-detected, *Ojibwa* then broke off its pursuit to avoid any risk of collision, accidental or deliberate, and returned to Halifax.

The Commander US Submarine Fleet Atlantic (COMSUBLANT) in Norfolk, Virginia, characterized the intelligence operation as "most impressive and productive," and Michael Whitby comments that it had demonstrated to the Americans "that we could look after our own backyard ... If the *Victor* had in fact detected *Ojibwa*, and perhaps classified it as an O-boat, then the patrol demonstrated to the Soviets as well as to our allies that we were indeed capable of monitoring submarine activity in our waters." It was at least as important to obtain acoustic data and operational reports on the SSN attack submarines as it was on SSBNs. In November 1985 Rear Admiral Crickard was to remind the joint Senate and Commons Committee on External Affairs and National Defence that "the potentially hostile attack [Soviet] submarine operating off the North American coast is ... inherently destabilizing when its mission is to detect or trail the United states ballistic missile-firing submarines ... unless a pattern of such operations is built up by constant and reliable surveillance."[17] Apparently, however, *Ojibwa*'s patrol had been a little more aggressive than Ottawa felt was appropriate. In the subsequent operational patrol in November, *Onondaga* was ordered to attempt to detect transiting Soviet submarines, and to trail them, but "only as far as necessary to record sufficient acoustic data for subsequent analysis."[18]

Had the Canadian submarines been equipped with towed sonar arrays, which they did not receive until the late 1980s, detection of hostile submarines would have been more probable, and the targets could have been trailed at safer distances. The vectoring by *Aurora* aircraft was essential, but lacking satellite communications, contact was not always possible. There was not to be another contact with a Soviet SSBN until late in 1986.

The Canadian nuclear submarines would have discouraged Soviet use of the Canadian arctic archipelagic channels by their military potential, and discouraged unauthorized American, British or French use by virtue of the mechanism by which NATO prevents "Blue on Blue" encounters that at best are a waste of scarce assets, and at worst could lead to "friendly fire" incidents. Submarine Operating Authorities, SUBOPAUTHS, are issued to allies indicating the general location of submarine transit and patrol boxes, and a Notice of Intention may be issued for considerably larger patrol areas. Generally, navies avoid sending their own submarines into the designated areas for safety reasons.[19] They would be particularly careful about dispatching a submarine into the territorial or internal waters of a state possessing capable submarines, or even effective ASW forces. The exception to national control is that navies, and commercial shipping, are permitted to transit international straits through territorial waters, but not through internal waters, and Article 20 of the United Nations Convention on the Law of the Sea requires submarines to transit internal waters on the surface. In effect, if the Northwest Passage is held to be part of Canada's internal waters, as it is by Canada, then foreign warships would not have a right of innocent passage, and the Canadian navy would not even need to issue a Notice of Intent to conduct submarine patrols in the area, although it would use a SUBOPAUTH report to indicate, or suggest, that a submarine was in transit through the Davis Strait to a patrol area in the internal waters of the Northwest Passage.

Admiral Watkins, referring directly to control of the 150 diesel-electric submarines of the NATO allies, described to the U.S. Senate subcommittee how the U.S. Navy acts "as the water manager for the allies in submarine operations ... We know where each of our submarines is located. We control them to avoid mutual interference. We have communications links established. We have intelligence exchanges established. We know what their contingency plans are for wartime. They know ours. The missions are clearly defined, and there is no doubt in my mind that they are going to be very effective at the choke points of the world, which happen to be the exact same choke points that we would identify were we to have our own diesels and have to go it alone."[20] Senator Edward Kennedy asked whether there were ever conflicts between the strategic purposes of the NATO countries concerned and those of the United States. Admiral Watkins replied that even in the case of France there was no evidence of conflict "at the military to military level where those forces will be in wartime."

When Joe Clark declined to tell the House of Commons whether American submarines passed through Canadian waters, he said he did so to prevent "Canada identifying travel patterns of submarines of friendly countries in our waters."[21] It is unclear, however, whether the Canadian navy itself knew. The submarine services of the world's navies are the most secretive of all military forces because their only real security lies in keeping their location imperfectly known. Bilateral "provisions," in Clark's words, are made on a "need to know" basis. Submarines of the United States Navy entering the CANLANT area did not report to the NATO commander at Halifax, CANCOMLANT. NATO is too disparate a group for knowledge of submarine operations to be made generally available. In the event of war, the Commander U.S. Submarine Fleet Atlantic (COMSUBLANT) in Norfolk, Virginia, was designated as NATO Commander, Submarine Allied Command Atlantic, commanding all NATO attack submarines in the Atlantic. From 1976 a Canadian Naval officer had served on the staff of COMSUBLANT.[22]

The creation of Canadian nuclear submarine force would have opened bilateral lines of communication to a greater extent. Speaking at Harvard university in March 1988, Rear Admiral John Anderson, who was in charge of the nuclear submarine acquisition program, insisted it was "ludicrous to suppose that allied submarines will be sent out into ocean areas to listen for other allies' submarines. It doesn't happen now, and Canada's acquisition of nuclear propulsion won't change things. Waterspace management will provide a safe and efficient way of managing our sub-surface northern affairs."[23] But that assertion did not dispose of the matter. As Clark explained to the Standing Committee on National Defence on 18 April 1988, "one of the advantages of our having them ... is that possessing the capacity yourself makes it more likely that others who have that capacity will let you know what they are doing because if they do not know where you are they may run some risks to very expensive apparatus of their own."[24]

Academic and parliamentary discussion about the value of creating a NATO Arctic or Northern Command were doomed to failure, and in any case would not have addressed the problem. The concept was a reversion to the policy objective of the Diefenbaker administration to obtain recognition that Canada's participation in North American air defence was in the context of Canada's founding membership in NATO. The idea of an Arctic Command was even more justified from Canada's perspective because of the possible use of the arctic archipelagic channels by British and French nuclear submarine forces, including ballistic missile submarines. Juridically the idea had merit, but it was unacceptable to the United States. Perhaps it was only put forward to put pressure on the American administration. Rear Admiral Crickard recommended that an arctic submarine surveillance system should be under national control but "integrated with existing US ocean-wide surveillance networks."[25] Reserving these assets to a national command would not preclude effective co-operation with the allies. Time-sensitive information might be reserved to national authority without preventing effective joint development of strategic plans or, indeed, preventing Canadian participation in crisis management.

Exploitation of force level constraints and water management issues was not the only mechanism by which nuclear submarines could have contributed to Canadian sovereign control in the arctic. The decision to invest in nuclear-powered submarines, rather than in other means of monitoring submarine activity, made most sense if the objective of the Canadian government were to participate more fully in the aggressive strategic ASW of the Maritime Strategy. Perrin Beatty told reporters that if Canada "were simply interested in surveillance, submarines would be a bad investment ... They will enhance sovereignty, but that's not why we're buying them. Its for security."[25]

The alternative of mounting fixed acoustic monitors at the chokepoints, with helicopters to prosecute targets, has theoretical advantages. Experimental, historic time, sensors were indeed installed at choke points in the archipelagic channels.[27] However expensive a fixed barrier would have been, it would have been cheaper than a fleet of nuclear submarines. But submarines have an advantage in that they are a mobile system which can be deployed as needed in the arctic or in the Atlantic and are a system which has some chance of survival in a hostile air environment such as was the Norwegian sea in the 1980s. Critchley's Maginot Line metaphor does not adequately represent the mobility of naval forces, although the SOSUS system and air support were more static. The Canadian submarine force was already part of the allied effort in the Norwegian Sea. Its principal patrol areas were in the western Atlantic and eastern Pacific, but on occasion Canadian submarines were exchanged with Royal Navy submarines so that they could familiarize themselves with conditions in the Norwegian sea.

The applicability of an investment in military technology to more than one military problem is cost-effective, and especially so if the secondary purpose is one of fundamental concern to allies. Canada's ability to contribute to solving an alliance problem would provide leverage that would discourage allies from challenging Canadian interests in other areas, and if there were a latent potential for redeployment of the forces from alliance to national objectives that leverage would be reinforced. These advantages would have been inherent in the possession of a fleet of nuclear attack submarines which could serve Canadian objectives in the arctic archipelago directly, and indirectly by serving alliance needs in the Atlantic or Pacific. The leverage implicit in their possession by Canada could also be applied to other national interests, not least including Canadian perspectives on the Maritime Strategy itself. The Canadian navy was already participating in that task.

But the strategy was not without peril. There was a disparity between the importance of the role the Canadian navy would be playing in the alliance, and its ability to develop its own strategic plan.

Perhaps for that reason, the U.S. Department of Defense announced in the summer of 1987 that it would not permit Britain to transfer to Canada nuclear technology that had come to Britain as a result of the 1958 US–UK Mutual Defence Agreement, and the 1962 Nassau agreement. Technical exchange at the time had included the engineering plans for the reactor in Britain's first nuclear submarine, *Dreadnought*. If British engineering were denied, the next option was France, although Canadian submariners had no experience with French engineering. Mulroney persuaded President Reagan in April 1988 to override the Defense Department. The Americans also came under pressure from the British. But reportedly the U.S. Navy continued to resist the Canadian plan.[28]

What impact Canadian consideration of a nuclear submarine program had on American arctic policy is not established. In Christopher Kirkey's account it is not mentioned, and all the credit for the eventual compromise is given to Mulroney's close relationship with President Reagan, and the creativity of the State Department and External Affairs. During his April 1987 visit to Ottawa, Reagan told the House of Commons that he and Mulroney had had "a full discussion of the Arctic waters issue, and ... agreed to inject new impetus to the discussions already under way. We are determined to find a solution based on mutual respect for sovereignty and our common security and other interests."[29] In January 1988 Canada and the United States concluded an agreement on "Arctic Cooperation" that included an undertaking that U.S. icebreakers would not navigate the Canadian archipelagic waters without the consent of the Government of Canada. The carefully crafted wording enabled the United States to retain some semblance of its legal position because it specifically referred to the icebreakers conducting research during their transits, which the Law of the Sea convention had established as within national jurisdiction. It was also made clear that the restraint on icebreaker traffic did not extended to the movement of American submarines, and the fourth clause made it clear that "nothing in this agreement of cooperative endeavour between Arctic neighbours and friends nor any practice thereunder affects the respective positions of the Governments of the United States and of Canada on the Law of the Sea in this or other maritime areas or their respective positions regarding third parties."[30] All the same, it is generally understood that the U.S. Navy accepted the political restraint on its movements in the Canadian arctic.

The Cabinet, satisfied with this compromise, cancelled the discussion of the nuclear submarine scheduled for 11 May 1988, and the item did not appear in the 1989 budget. The project was well beyond Canada's means. It would have required an increase in defence spending to 4 percent of gross domestic product. Meanwhile, the smoke, and perhaps also the mirrors, had led to the cancellation of the last two batches of patrol frigates. In an article in the *Canadian Defence Quarterly* in February 1990, the Supreme Allied Commander, Atlantic, Admiral Frank B. Kelso, II, USN, wrote that "the message to the Canadian Forces and to me, as SACLANT, is clear: do the job the best you can with the resources at hand."[31]

Douglas Bland has commented on the similarity of the 1987 White Paper and the 1961 "Brock Report." "As Brock recommended, a naval policy – especially one aimed at controlling Arctic waterways – must include Arctic bases and air, surface and subsurface patrols – and these are all important elements of the 1987 policy statement ... Versatility – the hedge against a changeable future – is a second repeated objective in *Challenge and Commitment*." His conclusion was that "Canadian maritime defence planners return to a very similar set of objectives and roles for the Canadian Navy whenever they are given an unrestricted opportunity to do so." Also similar were the fates of the two white papers when they encountered budgetary realities.[32]

Perhaps it is unfortunate that the nuclear submarine concept had been conceived on a hubristic scale. A modest acquisition of two or three submarines, dependent on British or French infrastructure support, would have been more within Canadian budgetary reality. It would have given the navy experience in SSN operations, in the arctic and in temperate waters, and could have generated valuable strategic leverage within the alliance structure. As events transpired, the navy soon lost interest in the arctic. The last *Norploy* exercise took place in 1989 when the research vessel HMCS *Quest* and diving tender HMCS *Cormorant* cruised along the eastern coast of Baffin Island, and the arctic surveillance flights were downgraded in 1990 from twenty-four per year to two.[33]

The Canadian navy's interest in submarines, however, continued. In the mid-1980s the navy had begun examining the possibility of employing air-independent propulsion (AIP) in a proposed replacement for its *Oberon/Ojibwa* class submarines, which might have made use of Stirling cycle engines powered by a slow-poke reactor. This work was set aside when the Mulroney administration decided to investigate the construction of nuclear-propelled submarines, but in 1994, five years after their cancellation, the navy restored its project to examine means to employ non-nuclear submarines in the arctic. The research project ran until 1998 and included the construction of a 50KW Exploratory Development Model fuel cell power plant. Subsequently, a follow-on project was mounted in co-operation with Sweden, Norway, and Denmark, employing Ballard Technologies Inc. of Vancouver to develop an Advanced Submarine AIP System. In late 2000, however, Ballard announced its withdrawal from the project, and in early 2001 it was abandoned by all the participants.

The nuclear submarine project having been shelved, and the frigate program reduced, the most enduring heritage from Mulroney's naval policy may be characterized as retrograde, alleviated by tokens such as the new/old uniforms. When in 1988 the military coup that ousted President Leslie-François Manigat reduced Haiti to chaotic conditions, the navy was ordered to be ready to evacuate Canadian citizens should disturbances ashore escalate. The fleet AOR, HMCS *Preserver*, and two destroyers, *Athabaskan* and *Skeena*, were ordered to stand-by offshore.[34] The chaotic result persuaded Chief of Defence Staff General John de Chastelain to launch an investigation that led to another step backward from unification. The stipulated frame of reference was the continuation of a unified service managed by National Defence Headquarters (NDHQ) under the existing system of shared civilian/military control, but as there was no obvious way of making that structure an effective headquarters for the conduct of war, it was agreed at a meeting on 4 October that the authority of the "environmental commanders" would be enhanced. They were given authority over the more junior officers of each service employed at NDHQ.[35] In 1991 the Naval Board of Canada recommenced meetings, not as an executive board but as a forum for senior officers to develop their policies.[36] The admiral commanding Maritime Command recovered direct access to the minister, and a seat at the Defence Council and Defence Management Committee, but his headquarters remained over a thousand miles away in Halifax until 1997.[37]

✦ ✦ ✦

The manner in which, and the extent to which, the Canadian government could employ the Canadian navy to express Canadian foreign policy since the 1940s had been limited by the practice of attaching

Refuelling HMCS *Skeena* (DDH 207) at sea from HMCS *Preserver* (AOR 510), sister ship to *Protecteur*, 1 January 1988. DND IHC88-1-2 (and -3)

Canadian units to American and NATO formations. The fact of their attachment, and the extent to which they helped to meet the strategic goal of international stability, both served Canadian interests, but it would be difficult to point to occasions in which bilateral or NATO formations were employed specifically to carry out operations identified by the Canadian government as of national concern. This limitation was acceptable, because Canada identified multilateral and international co-operation above almost all other objectives. The system had begun to change in 1980 when NATO Atlantic command began to look at the Standing Naval Force Atlantic (STANAVFORLANT) with an eye to transforming it into an operational rather than simply a training formation. A Canadian, Rear Admiral Dan Mainguy, was put in charge of the project, and by 1982 NATO was beginning to employ national task groups as the nucleus for operational forces. A concomitant was that greater importance began to be attached to NATO nations reorganizing their forces along tactical rather than administrative models. The Canadian navy accepted the NATO task of escorting the logistics train for the Strike Fleet Atlantic.

Peter Haydon tells us that in 1984 the commander of SACLANT, Admiral Wesley MacDonald, briefed Canadian parliamentarians on the "new" task group concept, which was in fact little different from Reginald McKenna's 1909 "Fleet Unit" concept and Admiral Jellicoe's 1920 force proposal to the Canadian government. The Canadian navy was more than happy to work toward the goal of national task groups, of which it was hoped the navy would be able to maintain three, or even four, each led by a DDH-280 destroyer. The enduring concern that participation in collective military action could lead to Canadian forces becoming little more than colonial levies controlled by an ally led to the adoption in the 1980s of a CANCOM policy of deliberately seeking command positions within allied formations, and the task group concept implied that the Canadian navy would typically be deployed, not just as single ships, but as a balanced force capable of making a difference – and of determining tactics, if not strategy.

When the Canadian navy first adopted the task group concept it did not possess the assets that would have made possible stand-alone formations that would not need to be stiffened by units from other national navies. It took a decade before that could be realized, when the 280-class destroyers were converted to guided missile destroyers (DDG) capable of providing area air defence and advanced command and control, and when the new patrol frigates entered service in the fleet. The TRUMP conversion of HMCS *Iroquois* took place between 1989 and 1992, and HMCS *Halifax*, the first of the patrol frigates, was commissioned at the end of June in 1992. When, due to the projected cost of the nuclear submarine project, only twelve of the initially planned twenty-four frigates were built, the navy was only able to maintain two task groups on active service.[38]

The 1987 White Paper was criticised by Frank Langdon and Douglas Ross because its Atlanticist focus did not adequately recognize the need for an enhanced Canadian naval presence in the Pacific. "The build-up of the Soviet Pacific fleet in the past decade from a predominantly coastal defence force to a potentially powerful bluewater striking force has raised considerable suspicion throughout the north Pacific ... Ottawa's only option in the event of war in the Pacific would be a resort to the American security crutch – a state of affairs that suggests some rather pointed questions about Canada's functional sovereignty in the area."[39] They were concerned about the safety of trans-Pacific and British Columbia coastwise trade, and about the probability that Soviet submarine and surface units would be taking an interest in the American *Trident* missile submarines forces based in Puget sound, Washington.

This strategic assessment was supported by regional political interest, and implicitly downgraded the importance attached to sustaining the strategic linkage with Europe. But a plan put forward in 1989 to divide the navy more or less equally between the Atlantic and Pacific was not realistic even in terms of supporting constabulary action. The sea area to be patrolled in the Atlantic is several times as large as that in the Pacific. A 1994 publication of the Conference of Defence Associations suggested that a naval task group of one destroyer, three frigates, an operational support ship, and up to eight helicopters, with long-range maritime patrol aircraft and perhaps a submarine in support, could maintain continuous surveillance over some 192,000 km² for a month.[40] That is about half the area of Canada's western seaboard, and one tenth of that on the east. The 1989 plan was revised in 1994. The Atlantic and Pacific squadrons were formed around the rebuilt and reconfigured (TRUMPed) DDG-280 destroyers, with seven patrol frigates on the Atlantic and five on the Pacific coast, supported by an AOR in the Pacific and two in the Atlantic and by a new class of ten Maritime Coast Defence Vessels (MCDVs) intended for minesweeping, coastal surveillance, and reserve training. This new class were divided equally between the Pacific and Atlantic squadrons. Thirteen of the air force's Maritime Air Group *Aurora* long-range maritime patrol aircraft were based at Greenwood in Nova Scotia and five at Comox in British Columbia.[41]

❖ ❖ ❖

It can be argued that Mulroney's contemplated submarine purchase potentially repeated Sir Robert Borden's mistake of thinking Canadian contribution to imperial defence would generate a commensurate ability to direct collective action in a crisis. In January 1985 the British Labour Party spokesman on foreign affairs, Denis Healey, warned that "the danger today is not that the Americans will retire into post-war normalcy, but that they will opt for a policy of global unilateralism under which they intervene all over the world without trying to win the consent of their allies or of the countries in which they operate."[42] "The Europeans recognize," wrote William M. Arkin in 1986 in the *Bulletin of the Atomic Scientists*, "that Washington is impatient about consulting allies who are 'unwilling' to defend their own interests and offers them only a limited role in military cooperation, with no say in overall US political, diplomatic, or economic strategy."[43] Certainly American foreign policy during the 1980s can be characterized as unilateralism run riot, with instances such as the Iran-Contra scandal in 1985 and the air strike on Libya in April 1986 showing a disregard for international law, and even national U.S. law. When in 1987 the U.S. Navy was drawn into the Iran-Iraq war in defence of Persian Gulf shipping, Washington did urge NATO member states to dispatch their own naval forces for the same purpose. International naval intervention in the Iran-Iraq war, however, was never a NATO operation. Under American leadership it could be characterized as a precursor of the later American concept of "a coalition of the willing."[44]

What influence Canada might have been able to exert over the U.S. Navy's Maritime Strategy can only be a matter for conjecture, but Canada's response to the Kuwait crisis of 1990 suggests that Mulroney would have had little to offer, and that the Canadian navy would have been reluctant to buck the transnational chain of command. The acquisition of nuclear submarines might have proven, again, to be enough to get Canada into trouble but not enough to deal with it. Their value as *quid pro quo* bargaining leverage might have been worth something, but that is only conjecture.

In any case, the abandonment of the program proved to be timely. The last Canadian submarine operational surveillance patrol was in 1987 because Gorbachev scaled back Soviet navy SSBN operations off North America.[45] In February 1988 there was a major "Incident at Sea" when two Soviet warships deliberately collided with two American warships exercising the right of innocent passage off the Crimean coast, and a succession of close encounters by aircraft continued into April, but then the provocations at sea stopped.[46] The Berlin Wall came down in November 1989, and in December President George Bush Sr met Gorbachev in Malta. Together they declared an end to the Cold War. In 1990 Germany was reunited, and it was announced in June 1991 that the Canadian garrisons there would be brought home.

Paradoxically, the evaporation of the existential threat of nuclear war did not restore Canadian foreign and defence policy to the happy innocence of the time before war and cold war forged the binary but disproportionate defence partnership with the United States. Rather, the opposite occurred. Kim Nossal commented in a 1992 review of Canadian foreign and defence policies that the decisions to reduce the Canadian military presence in Europe, and then eliminate it, amounted to an acceptance that Canada no longer needed to seek counterweights in Europe for the overpowering relationship with the United States. He also noted that the decisions did not flow "against the preferences of Canadians as a whole. It is indicative of the general mood that neither the September nor the February decisions were controversial in Canada. They were greeted in Parliament by complete indifference."[47] Argument from absence of evidence – the dog that fails to bark – is always open to question, but with the advantage of hindsight it does appear that the Mulroney years brought a fundamental change in Canadian assessment of the precautions necessary when sharing a continent with a behemoth. The dramatic change in the world strategic picture and the growing economic integration of Canada with the United States were to have a profound effect on Canada's defence strategy, and would see the Canadian navy deployed globally.

NATO's initiative in transforming its operational structure by encouraging the formation of national task groups was important in creating the tools that were later to be employed by NATO navies, including the Canadian navy, in the Gulf and Indian ocean conflicts of the 1990s. In June 1990, seventy-one years after the evacuation of Canadian soldiers from Siberia, three Canadian warships commanded by Rear Admiral Peter Cairns paid a visit to Vladivostok. The first port visit there by western warships since 1935, the Canadian deployment played a part in encouraging the thaw in relations with the Soviet Union, and was an instance of Sir James Cable's "Expressive Force." It also served the intelligence purpose of confirming the decay of the Soviet navy.[48] In the summer of 1990 it was the Canadian navy that was to be given the lead role in the Mulroney administration's commitment to support the UN response to the Iraqi invasion of Kuwait. In 1991 the navy was to be given a role in the Balkan crisis. In 1992 it was to be sent to Somalia and in 1993 to Haiti. In 1998 it was to return to Vladivostok with two ships, *Protecteur* and *Vancouver*, and participate in relief work as part of a tour of Japan, China, Russia, Korea, and the Hawaiian Islands. In 1999 it was to take part in a UN operation following the independence of East Timor. The Canadian navy's participation in the Gulf war and the Balkan crisis, and subsequently its extended deployment to the Persian Gulf, gave it a new life, but also showed its limitations as an instrument of foreign policy. Two decades later it is fair to say that Canada's naval strategy is still a work in progress.

8

SANCTIONS ENFORCEMENT:
IRAQ

Within a year of the Bush-Gorbachev declaration ending the Cold War, the Canadian navy was committed to active operations outside the NATO area for the first time since the Korean war. The United States had sought to deter an Iraqi invasion of Kuwait, or at least to limit any incursion to the oil fields, but American credibility was undermined by the perception in Baghdad that Washington had adopted a policy of driving Saddam Hussein, the president of Iraq, from power. "From Saddam's central belief in an American conspiracy," Janice Stein writes, "it appears that most if not all else followed. His expectation that the United States sought to destroy him became a self-fulfilling prophecy."[1] Canada quickly became involved. Harald von Riekhoff writes that the Kuwait crisis differed from the Korean war, in which Canadian commitment to the United Nations was driven by "desperation based on the belief that this might be the last chance to salvage the United Nations." In contrast, the Kuwait crisis "was perceived as the first significant opportunity after the Cold War to revive the UN security role and bring it into closer alignment with the original Charter intentions."[2] Prime Minister Mulroney added his voice to those seeking to channel through the United Nations the American reaction, and when President George Bush Sr did so, Canada had a moral obligation to participate in the coalition that was formed to employ military force to prevent Iraqi forces moving into Saudi Arabia, and to expel them from Kuwait. On 2 August 1990 a sanctions regime was ordered by Security Council Resolution 661, banning all trade with Iraq and occupied Kuwait, both imports and exports, with the exception of medicines and foods required for humanitarian relief.[3] The following day the foreign ministers of the United States and the USSR, Secretary of State James Baker and Minister Eduard Shevardnadze, issued a joint declaration; Baker remarked that "that August night, a half-century after it began in mutual suspicion and ideological fervor, the Cold War breathed its last."[4]

Participation in international and multilateral security operations serves parochial Canadian interests by addressing critical situations before they can migrate to Canada's shores, and by sustaining a level of global co-operation upon which Canadian prosperity depends. It is an important part of the distant cover the Canadian Armed Forces provide to support the constabulary functions it performs in partnership with Canadian civilian agencies. When on 12 May 2008 the Department of National Defence outlined a new "Canada First Defence Strategy," it would state that "as a trading nation in a highly globalized world, Canada's prosperity and security rely on stability abroad. As the international community grapples with numerous security threats, Canada must do its part to address such challenges as they arise." It went on to say that this commitment would "require the Canadian Forces to have the necessary capabilities to make a meaningful contribution across the full spectrum of international operations, from humanitarian assistance to stabilization operations to combat." It relegated Ottawa's use of the Canadian Forces for international peace enforcement missions to a third order of priority, but in reality that does not accurately reflect the extent to which such commitments have seized centre stage. Participation in international peace-enforcement operations serves both a definitive purpose and also a purposive one vis-à-vis Canada's allies.

The refusal of successive Canadian governments to participate in American economic sanctions against the communist regime in Cuba is an indication that Canadian foreign policy could be independent even in the face of terrific pressure from Washington, and is also an indication of the importance Canadian governments have placed on the authority of the United Nations. Brian Mulroney, however, lacked the experience in international relations that had given Lester Pearson his capacity to make strategic judgments, and lacked Pierre Trudeau's experience with war and economic conflict. In the crisis of 1990, the Canadian government found that it did not have the resources to make discriminating and ethical judgments in that field of strategy. Only once during the Cold War had economic sanctions mandated by the United Nations been enforced by naval action, as a result of the unilateral declaration of independence by the racially segregated state of Southern Rhodesia, and the Canadian navy did not play any part in that operation.[5]

Baker's statement to the U.S. Senate Foreign Relations Committee, 5 December 1990, that sanctions, to be valuable, would have to "hurt Iraq so much that Saddam Hussein changes his behaviour and withdraws from Kuwait," indicates that the secretary of state was formulating his policy in the belief that economic pressure directed indiscriminately at a target state should have the power to coerce hostile governments.[6] Only the year earlier Kim Nossal had published an article in the Canadian *International Journal* showing that "sanctions are most useful as retributive punishments, and that they should be imposed in a discrete way and for definite and strictly limited period of time." Nevertheless, the Canadian government agreed to help enforce sanctions intended for "compellent punishment," and imposed by the Security Council without any time limit.[7]

Resolution 665 on 25 August authorized the use of maritime forces to monitor the sanctions, using "measures commensurate to the specific circumstances ... to halt all inward and outward maritime shipping, in order to inspect and verify their cargoes and destinations." Britain, France, Russia, and the Argentines sent ships to co-operate with the United States in the multinational force that coalesced following the request of Saudi Arabia for military assistance in resisting the invasion by Iraqi forces that American intelligence had indicated, disingenuously it appears, was to be anticipated. Twelve nations, including Canada, sent warships to join a Multinational Interception Force (MIF) to enforce the economic sanctions.[8]

It fell to the Canadian navy to manifest Canada's commitment to support the UN position in the Gulf because the Canadian Army was engaged in assistance to civil powers, occasioned by a conflict between the Iroquois Kanesetake First Nation and the province of Quebec, and the Air Force was still committed to participation in the management of European air space. Jean Morin and Richard Gimblett write that the selection of naval forces to represent Canada was also influenced by the fact that it would take over a month for them to reach the Gulf, which would delay the need to recall parliament to debate the order-in-council committing them to hostile operations. The navy deployed the modernized 280 class destroyer *Athabaskan*, with the aging steamer *Terra Nova* and the AOR *Protecteur* to Italy in August-September 1990 under the code name of "Operation Friction," with the intent that they should join the MIF in the Gulf of Oman. In order to bring the aging ships up to a safe standard for service in the dangerous waters of the Persian Gulf, they were hastily given equipment that had been ordered for the refit of *Athabaskan*'s sister *Tribal* class destroyers and for the uncompleted patrol frigates. Both *Terra Nova* and *Protecteur* had to be fitted with modern weapons, updated sonar sensors, and communication equipment. Over 90,000 person/hours were needed over a two-week period to enable the ships to sail.⁹

Commodore Ken Summers was appointed senior Canadian afloat, with Captain Duncan "Dusty" Miller his chief of staff. In a recent article, Summers wrote:

> Our dockyard, engineering personnel, and ships crews deserve full recognition for having moved heaven and earth to transform our navy virtually overnight ... The ship safety exercises to combat fires, floods, and chemical attacks, and the daily exercise program conducted as we crossed the Atlantic with a heavy emphasis on weapons control and picture compilation, prepared the force for a major validation testing off Gibraltar. Excellent surface tracking and boarding exercises set up by the UK allowed the force to hone its skills in a role that was to prove to be one of our hallmarks in the months ahead. Most importantly, however, was the free play anti-air exercise conducted against our own CF-18s from then Canadian Forces Europe, which tested our defensive capabilities to the extreme and left the force supremely confident in their capability to combat the expected air threat. Quite simply, I had never seen better AAW [Anti-Air Warfare] by our surface ships and I will always remember *Protecteur* thinking and acting like a destroyer bringing her CIWS [*Phalanx* close-in weapon system] and 3"50 gun systems to bear. I must also mention the valuable training provided after Gibraltar by the French in flying their F1 *Mirage* aircraft and its *Exocet* missile against the force to permit our operators to get used to the primary Iraqi air threat. The end result of this training was a battle group confident in their capabilities and a realization that there was no threat in the Gulf that they could not handle.¹⁰

Writing in 1992, Barbara McDougall, secretary of state for external affairs, remarked that the success of the international force mustered to deal with the Gulf crisis "demonstrated the relevance and the value, even in an environment where NATO was not directly involved, of NATO's military infrastructure and of the habits of working together."¹¹ The Canadian navy's commitment grew almost immediately when, with Cabinet approval, Summers agreed at a conference in Bahrain on 9–10 September to accept responsibility for enforcement operations in the central Persian Gulf where there was heightened danger of hostile action. Because several of the navies forming the MIF were not part of the NATO alliance, it was necessary to leave command and control on a national basis, but all were familiar with NATO or U.S. procedures; "coordination and co-operation" was as satisfactory an arrangement as it had been when the RCN was ordered to "co-operate to the fullest extent" with the RN in 1939. The U.S. Navy concentrated on providing a secure air environment for the ships of the Interception Force conducting boardings, and HMCS *Protecteur* undertook replenishment at sea operations for the assembled navies.

In their summary of Operation *Friction*, Morin and Gimblett noted the paradox that when the Canadian naval force was later joined in the Gulf by Canadian land and air units, they were not, "despite the promises of a quarter century of unification" of the services, able to work tactically together, "but each individual service was admirably prepared to combine with similar forces from allied nations."[12] More recently, Gimblett has clarified: "one of the factors that gave Summers the confidence to take that step [to deploy into the central Gulf] was the commitment of a squadron (and eventually a wing) of CF-18 Hornet fighters to fly top cover for the naval forces in the Gulf – the first expeditionary combat deployment in modern [Canadian] air force history, which was also notable as it was conducted in concert with the U.S. Navy, instead of its traditional partner, the U.S. Air Force. And then [he continued] when Summers was shifted ashore to take command of all the Canadian Forces gathering in the Middle East, his Bahrain base was the first true deployed joint headquarters ... in Canadian military history – with a sailor in charge at that."[13] The chain of command placed the Canadian task force directly under the control of the chief of defence staff.

When on 29 November the Security Council decided to adopt more forceful means to drive Iraqi forces out of Kuwait, passing Resolution 678 authorizing the use of "all necessary means," the Americans, British, and Australians promptly committed their forces to support the assault on Iraqi forces, Operation *Desert Storm*, with the Argentines co-operating so far as the limits of their air defence capabilities permitted. The Canadian Cabinet believed the Canadian public were uncertain about the speed with which the United Nations was moving from sanctions to war, and with Canadian ships not well equipped to operate in a high air-risk environment, they continued with their interceptions in the middle Gulf area. On 1 January 1991, however, it was agreed between Commodore Summers and the American battle force commander for the

Arabian [Persian] Gulf, Rear Admiral Daniel March, that they should join the U.S. Navy Combat Logistics Force in the southern Gulf supporting the four American carrier battle groups farther up the Gulf. On Summers's suggestion, this was renamed the Combined Logistics Force largely for optical reasons.

The formation consisted of thirty to thirty-three escort and supply ships serving an international fleet of eighty-six warships. With Canadian staff officers already serving in the American flagship, it was an easy step for a Canadian, Miller, to be put in command. This role reflected the experience the Canadian navy had acquired of working with the U.S. Navy, especially in connection with the NATO task of escort to the Strike Fleet logistics train. Captain Miller became the only non-American to be given responsibility for such critical work, which called for him to manage the optics in such a way that ships belonging to nations that had not committed themselves to the assault on Iraqi forces could contribute to the escort of the fleet auxiliaries. Gimblett writes in another place that "the Canadian commander had gained the cooperation of his MIF [Multinational Interception Force] associates not because it was a military alliance requirement, but through persuading them it was for the ultimate benefit of the Coalition, and that he was sensitive to the limitations on their employment." With the formation of the Combined Logistics Force, Canadian ships were almost entirely diverted from sanctions enforcement until Kuwait was liberated. Because of its equipment, and the professionalism shown by the Canadian navy, *Athabaskan* was called upon to provide escort for an American cruiser that had been mined in the upper Gulf.[14]

Initially intended, according to Sir James Cable's taxonomy, as purposive force to persuade the Iraqi government to withdraw from Kuwait, the sanctions were later extended because of the determination of successive U.S. administrations to address what it perceived to be the threat posed by Iraq to the balance of power in the region. Following the eviction of Iraqi forces from Kuwait, the sanctions were continued as a means of obliging Iraq to abandon its program for the production of chemical, biological, and nuclear weapons of mass destruction, to bring Iraq to acknowledge the territorial integrity of Kuwait defined by newly demarcated borders, and to exact reparations for the damage inflicted on Kuwait.[15] Iraq was also required to repatriate missing Kuwaiti, return stolen property, and abstain from acts of terrorism. The Security Council resolution embodying these demands, Resolution 687 of April 1991, was known familiarly as "the mother of all resolutions."[16] Restrictions on the export of food to Iraq were dropped, but controls on the sale of oil were continued.

Canadian warships returned for eight tours of duty to enforce the sanctions regime. HMCS *Huron*, a DDG-280 destroyer equipped with two *Sea King* helicopters, relieved *Athabaskan* in April 1991, and remained on duty in the Gulf into June. *Protecteur* and *Terra Nova* also returned home in April 1991, and after *Huron* departed in June no Canadian ships participated in sanctions enforcement until *Restigouche* arrived in March 1992 for a three-month tour of duty in the Red Sea enforcing sanctions off the Jordanian coast. Jordan had refused to cut its communications with Iraq. After a three-year absence and the nearly complete destruction of the Conservative party at the polls, in 1995 the new Liberal prime minister, Jean Chrétien, returned the Canadian navy to sanctions enforcement operations in the Gulf. The new patrol frigates, *Fredericton* and *Calgary*, were deployed respectively from February to April and from July to December. *Calgary* was fully integrated into U.S. Navy Task Force 50 during its tour, and because of her shallower draft was able to facilitate inshore control. *Regina* deployed to the Gulf in 1997, and *Toronto* in 1998, both serving with the U.S. fleet. *Toronto*'s deployment was a detachment from a Canadian commitment to STANAVFORLANT, a deployment that Gimblett regards as a marker of changing Canadian attitudes to NATO.[17]

✦ ✦ ✦

Considering the importance of the part the Canadian navy played in enforcing the sanctions against Iraq, it is essential to audit their effectiveness. The failure of sanctions on their own to project enough purposive force to persuade the Iraq government to withdraw from Kuwait prior to the 15 January 1991 deadline set by Security Council Resolution 678, is consistent with historical experience. Whatever contribution the naval blockade between 1914 and 1919 made to the defeat of the central powers, it was in the context of general war. Sanctions on their own were unlikely to bring a reversal of Iraqi policy once the prestige of the regime had been committed and nationalist forces unleashed by military invasion, and Secretary of State James Baker's rejection of any concession to the Iraq government effectively frustrated the principal objective. Baker, and the other coalition leaders, insisted that "partial solutions would set a very unfortunate precedent. It would set the precedent that aggression pays." On 3 January 1991 he told a reporter

HMCS *Huron* (DDH/G 281), built at Davie Shipbuilding, Lauzon, as a helicopter destroyer 1969–72, and refitted 1994 as an area defence missile destroyer. Seen here entering Gloppen Fjord, Norway, while serving in STANAVFORLANT, 31 August 1974. DND SLC74-1322

for ABC-TV that he had "been pursuing a carrot-and-stick policy here. The carrot is, if he [Saddam Hussein] withdraws completely and unconditionally from Kuwait, he doesn't get the stick."[18]

As early as the end of 1990 the director of the Central Intelligence Agency, Judge William Webster, in a speech published in the State Department's *Dispatch*, had warned against any idea that sanctions could lead to revolt in Iraq. "Services ranging from medical care to sanitation have been curtailed in Iraq. But these hardships are easier for Iraqis to endure than the combination of economic distress, high casualty rates and repeated missile and air attacks that Iraqis lived with during the eight year Iran-Iraq War. During this war incidentally, there was not a single significant public disturbance, even though casualties hit 2.3 percent of the Iraqi population."[19]

Perhaps most disturbing is the idea that the imposition of sanctions against Iraq was nothing more than a political formula to overcome a public reluctance to countenance official violence. The disjunction between means and declared ends suggested that the underlying political purpose of coalition diplomacy was to ensure that the opportunity was not lost of destroying Iraqi military potential. Sir Crispin Tickell, the British ambassador to the United Nations until mid-August 1990, specifically denied that this was the intent when he addressed the Security Council on 6 August: "economic sanctions should not be regarded as a prelude to anything else. Here I obviously refer to military action."[20] Abu Hassan, the foreign minister of Malaysia, was not convinced. Was the United Nations, he asked, "moving at this speed to make sanctions effective, or are we readying ourselves early for a situation where we will conclude that sanctions are not effective and that other measures must therefore be taken?"[21] Whatever the intent, sanctions did in fact constitute a transitional phase before resort was made to war in 1991, and again in 2003. Norman Friedman believes that the sanctions were indeed intended for political purposes: "If nothing at all had been done, it might appear to many that the West had backed off, then staged its own aggression against Iraq."[22]

Two of the goals of Resolution 687 were effected relatively quickly, and others partly fulfilled. In November 1993 Iraq agreed to the establishment of UN weapons-monitoring camera and chemical detection instruments inside Iraq. In November 1994 the Iraq government accepted the UN Boundary Demarcation Commission's findings establishing a border with Kuwait. However, Iraq resisted the demand for reparations payment to Kuwait, which had been left with its oil fields demolished and on fire. Whether that objective justified the continuation of sanctions to their full extent is an important question. Some Kuwaiti prisoners were returned, and some state property, but as of 2000 several hundred Kuwaiti were still missing, and Kuwait military equipment and private property remained in Iraqi hands. Iraq did not formally pledge to abstain from acts of terrorism.

Inspections were carried out by a United Nations Special Commission (UNSCOM), directed between 1991 and 1997 by Rolf Ekéus and from 1997 to 1999 by Richard Butler, and formed by the permanent members of the Security Council.[23] U.S. secretary of state, Madeleine Albright, described in March 1997 the success of the weapons inspectors as "stunning."[24] Following a charge that UN weapons inspectors, including Richard Butler, were working for the U.S. Central Intelligence Agency, the Iraqi government refused to permit unlimited access to defence and "Presidential" sites. This led to the inspectors being summoned home at the request of the United States government, and to U.S.

and British air strikes on Iraqi targets during 16–19 December 1998 known as Operation *Desert Fox*. U.S. president Bill Clinton indicated the objective was to degrade the ability of Iraq to use its weapons.[25] The charge that the Central Intelligence Agency was piggybacking on UNSCOM is considered to be correct, but UNSCOM was also in the debt of the CIA and other intelligence services for knowledge of where to conduct its inspections. The UN moved to protect its impartiality, and when Saddam Hussain invited the weapons inspectors to return, which they did in December 2002, they came as an agency of the United Nations, the UN Monitoring, Verification and Inspection Commission, UNMOVIC, under the direction of the former head of the International Atomic Energy Commission, Hans Blix.[26]

The concessions made in 1993 and 1994 by Iraq in permitting weapons inspectors and accepting the Kuwait border were important, but there is no clear evidence that it was the sanctions which led Saddam Hussein to admit them, or to permit their return. In the opinion of the Canadian diplomat David Malone, "there can be little doubt that only the credible threat of force by the United States opened the path to UNMOVIC's deployment in Iraq."[27] On the other hand, Yossef Bodansky, the Israeli-American director of the House of Representatives Task Force on Terrorism and Unconventional Warfare from 1988 to 2004 and the International Strategic Studies Association director of research, believes that Saddam Hussein permitted the return of UN inspectors so they could be exploited as human shields that could stop Israel responding to rocket attacks with nuclear force, and because he had used the interval to move his weapons to safe havens in Iran, Syria, and the Lebanon.[28]

In January 2003, Hans Blix reported that UNMOVIC had found no indication that Iraq possessed nuclear weapons or an active program. Peter van Walsum, chairman of the Iraq Sanctions Committee from 1 January 1999 to 31 December 2000, writes that the constraint on Iraq's money supply effected by the sanctions regime reduced the ability of the Iraq government to purchase nuclear material on the black market. The international effort, later codified by the Proliferation Security Initiative, and by Security Council Resolution 1540 of April 2004, to block the movement of prohibited materials needed for the development and delivery of weapons of mass destruction, did not depend upon the restriction of Iraqi money supply to be effective. Nevertheless, restriction of money supply did reduce the difficulty of enforcing the supply side embargo. There was more controversy about whether there continued to be a threat from Iraqi chemical and biological weapons, but none were found after the American-led invasion.[29] Following the establishment of the American-controlled interim government of occupied Iraq, the compliance of the Iraqi government with the requirement to destroy its stocks and production of weapons of mass destruction was substantiated by the International Survey Group formed by the American CIA and Defence Department under the direction of David Kay. It seems either that nothing was found connecting Iraqi compliance to the effect of sanctions, or that it did not suit American policy-makers to reveal their findings.[30] James Goldrick who commanded an Australian squadron writes that one of the measures of the success of the sanctions regime is that by the time of the American-led invasion of Iraq in 2003 the Iraqi armed forces had been seriously degraded.[31] The combination of the embargo on weapons sales to Iraq and the block of Iraqi oil exports served to degrade the Iraq military as spare parts and ammunition could not be replaced. This was not a declared purpose for the sanctions, but in the circumstances it was useful.

Perhaps the principal reason for the continuation of sanctions was President Clinton's decision that Saddam Hussein should be forcibly removed from power. In November 1997 he declared that "sanctions will be there until the end of time, or as along as [Hussein] lasts."[32] On 31 October 1998 Clinton signed the Iraq Liberation Act declaring that it was the policy of the US to "establish a program to support a transition to democracy in Iraq." Congress agreed: "It should be the policy of the United States to support efforts to remove the regime headed by Saddam Hussein from power in Iraq and to promote the emergence of a democratic government to replace that regime."[33] Regime change formed no part of the UN resolution, but the US was able to use its veto power in the Security Council to prevent any change in the sanctions mandate. Because there was no time limit set on their imposition by Resolution 687, a veto could prevent a vote to reduce or end the sanctions.

The British foreign secretary, Jack Straw, later commented: "It seemed clear that Bush had made up his mind to take military action, even if the timing was not yet decided. But the case was thin. Saddam was not threatening his neighbours, and his WMD capability was less than that of Libya, North Korea or Iran." Richard Clarke, who was appointed in 1992 by President George Bush Sr to chair the Counter-terrorism Security Group with a seat on the United States National Security Council, and was retained in his position by President Clinton, states that as early as 12 September 2001 President George W. Bush asked him to find evidence of Iraqi support for the al Qaeda terrorists, who had the day before destroyed the World Trade Center in New York, to justify American military action.[34] According to the account by Yossef Bodansky, the United States deliberately betrayed a Russian plan to overthrow Saddam Hussein by a coup d'état, and torpedoed a Russian mission by Yevgeny Primakov that might have led to Hussein accepting internal exile under international supervision, because the Bush administration wanted to take the credit, and to demonstrate its military capacity in the region.[35]

✦ ✦ ✦

The positive outcomes from the sanctions regime, such as they were, have to be seen in relation to the collateral damage they inflicted on the Iraqi population. Experience has shown that action against a nation's financial resources may be the most effective way of degrading its military abilities; no less an economist than Maynard Keynes had advised in October 1939 that "in the last war, both sides made the mistake of concentrating too much on specific goods and too little on money."[36] But targeting oil, and thereby affecting Iraqi money supply, created serious problems with respect to Iraq's civilian requirements. The Nobel Prize–winning economist Amarthya Sen has made a study of famine and emphasizes that "undernourishment, starvation and famine are influenced by the working of the entire economy and society – not just food production and agricultural activities."[37]

United Nations Secretary-General Javier Pérez de Cuéllar sent Undersecretary General Martti Ahtisaari on a fact-finding mission to Iraq and Kuwait on 10–17 March 1991 – and his report was forwarded to the president of the Security Council three days later:

> (8) It should ... be said at once that nothing that we had seen or read had quite prepared us for the particular form of devastation which has now befallen the country. The recent conflict has wrought near-apocalyptic results upon the economic infrastructure of what had been, until January 1991, a rather highly urbanized and mechanized society. Now, most means of modern life support have been destroyed or rendered tenuous. Iraq has, for some time to come, been relegated to a pre-industrial age, but with all the disabilities of post-industrial dependency on an intensive use of energy and technology ...
>
> (37) I, together with all my colleagues, am convinced that there needs to be a major mobilization and movement of resources to

deal with aspects of this deep crisis in the fields of agriculture and food, water, sanitation and health. Yet the situation raises, in acute form, other questions. For it will be difficult, if not impossible, to remedy these immediate humanitarian needs without dealing with the underlying need for energy, on an equally urgent basis.[38]

In the 1980s the oil trade constituted 60% of Iraq's GDP, and 95% of foreign currency earnings, paying for the two thirds of Iraq's food, much of which was imported. An Independent Working Group brought together to support a United Nations Independent Enquiry Committee (the Volcker Committee), assessed that, with the loss of oil revenues, employment in Iraq fell from 90% to just above 50%. Industrial production fell by half, and the Iraqi dinar which had been at par with the American dollar before the war was trading at 1,000 dinars to one American dollar in the early part of 1996. The shortage of jobs, and of imported food, led to an increase in the labour force employed on the land, from 20% to 40% between 1990 and 1996. Before the 1990 Gulf War, the average Iraqi consumed 3,200 kcal per day, well above the recognized subsistence rate. In response to the blockade, the Iraq government set up an efficient food distribution system for all except those associated with opposition groups, providing 1,600 kcal per person at a fixed price of 250 dinars, but the purchase price of free market foods needed to supplement the rations rose rapidly, and government rations fell by 1996 to 1,100 kcal. By 1993 the proportion of family income spent on food doubled, to 60%, and the UN Food and Agriculture Organization estimated that by July 1995 food costs had risen by a factor of 2,000. A family food bill rose to about twenty-five times the average income. Food supply dropped to an estimated average of 2,000 kcal per capita, a level below subsistence rates even were distribution consistent; given the hierarchy within Iraq, food supply was drastically short for the 60% of the population without connections to the government. Of the women interviewed 60% said that they suffered emotional distress, including insomnia, depression, menstrual irregularity, and inability to breastfeed.[39]

The consequence of this deprivation was inevitably a drastic decrease in life expectancy, especially amongst children. According to numbers published by the UN Population Division, infant mortality in Iraq, which had fallen from 150 per thousand in 1950–53 to 60 per thousand in 1980–85, rose dramatically to 73 per thousand in 1990–95 and to 94 per thousand in the decade beginning 1995, with under-five mortality at 124 per thousand.[40] A Child and Maternal Mortality Survey conducted in 1999 showed a rise in under-five mortality from 63 per thousand in 1989 to 108 in 1991 and 111 in 1998, with infant mortality rising from 48 per thousand in 1989 to 94 per thousand in 1991 and 101 per thousand in 1998.[41] Maternal mortality more than doubled, rising from 117 per thousand to 310 per thousand in 1994. The conclusion reached at the time by the United Nations International Children's Emergency Fund (UNICEF) Executive Director Carol Bellamy was that "if the substantial reduction in child mortality throughout Iraq during the 1980s had continued through the 1990s, there would have been half a million fewer deaths of children under-five in the country as a whole during the eight-year period 1991 to 1998."[42]

Sanctions were only one of the principal causes of the mortality. In the months immediately following *Desert Storm*, sanctions may be considered as a multiplier of the effects produced by the bombing of Iraqi infrastructure. With power stations destroyed, water and sewage systems ceased to operate. Rivers provided the only source of water, but were also carrying away sewage. The consequence was devastating water-born disease for a malnourished population, and especially for children. And hospitals lacked even basics for treating the ill because the sanctions against exports prevented payment for much-needed medicines.

The infant and under-five mortality statistics for the sanctions period were radically revised after the formation in 2004 of a UN Inter-agency Group for Child Mortality Estimates (IGME), led by UNICEF and the World Health Organization (WHO), and also including as full members the World Bank and the United Nations Population Division of the Department of Economic and Social Affairs.[43] The notes made about the decision by Dr Gareth Jones, then UNICEF Chief Strategic Information Section in New York, indicate that the IGME zero-rated the results of the 1999 Child and Maternal Mortality Survey when generating a trend-line because no parallel to the surge in mortality could be found in the more recent surveys – the Iraq Family Health Survey of 2006/07 indicating a May 1993 figure for infant mortality of only 46.2 per thousand, and 65.6 for under-fives, with a pronounced spike in Kurdistan in May 1995 of 61.1 and 86.1 respectively.[44]

The Iraqi 1999 survey could be suspect because it was conducted while the population was vulnerable to Ba'ath party pressures, but it was conducted with the support of UNICEF staff which visited all governorates during the fieldwork and also observed the training of supervisors and interviewers. Bellamy was clear that the survey's findings should not be dismissed as an effort by Iraq to mobilize opposition to UN sanctions. "In the survey completed in the south and center of Iraq, all the interviewers were female and all were medical doctors. In the survey done in the northern autonomous region, fully 80 per cent of interviewers were female – each team had at least one female interviewer – and all interviewers were trained health workers." The UNICEF information note added that the agency was "involved in all aspects of both surveys, from design to data analysis. The agency had full access to the hard copies of the interview records and the complete data sets for the surveys at all times." Its accuracy was actually assisted by the siege conditions because many of the respondents used their ration cards to establish dates for deaths. The survey reports were entered in ink to prevent them being altered.[45]

There is no reason to think the metrics gathered following the American occupation of Iraq are inherently more reliable. Not only are memories of traumatic events of a decade to a decade and a half before often frail, but perhaps insufficient allowance was made for the probability that those who had suffered most under bombs and sanctions, including those who suffered personal tragedy in the death of wife and children, were a major component of the substantial out-migration that occurred from war-ravaged Iraq. Furthermore, no attempt was made to discover the fate of those children whose mothers had themselves died. Dr Les Roberts, who conducted a survey in Iraq during that period, also questions the value of the extrapolation back to 1990 from the numbers recorded in the 2006/07 Iraq family health survey. The survival of the more robust during a period characterized by conditions of exhaustion, near famine, unsafe water supply, and debased medical services would lead to a dip in mortality figures following a return to healthy circumstances. Indeed, a dip in mortality under such circumstances might be taken as supporting evidence of an earlier spike.[46]

One of the unintended consequences of the sanctions regime was that it strengthened the control that the government of Iraq, and the Ba'ath party, was able to exert over the population. But because it could not deliver the pre-war level of prosperity, or even ensure adequate food supplies, it was no longer able to prevent the growth of petty crime and prostitution, both of which had been eradicated in pre-war Iraq. At the same time, the dependence of a sizable part of the Iraqi population on government distribution created a hand-out mentality.

To address mounting international protest at the public health impact of sanctions on ordinary Iraqis, the Security Council voted on 15 August 1991 Resolution 706 authorizing the Iraq government to sell oil for humanitarian necessities. This resolution required all humanitarian relief to be managed by UN agencies and clearly labelled as being authorized by the United Nations, and that the government of Iraq fully disclose all its financial and bullion assets. Those provisions made the offer unacceptable to the government of Iraq, which rejected the offer. It was to be another four years before the Security Council made another attempt.

On 13 April 1995 the ambassadors of the Permanent Members of the Security Council wrote a letter to the president of the council expressing their concern about the humanitarian implications of comprehensive sanctions: "while recognizing the need to maintain the effectiveness of sanctions imposed in accordance with the Charter, further collective actions in the Security Council within the context of any future sanctions regime should be directed to minimize unintended adverse side-effects of sanctions on the most vulnerable segments of targeted countries."[47] The following day, in response to a draft resolution circulated by Russia, France, and China, the Security Council voted Resolution 986 with the support of both the United States and Great Britain, to implement what became known as the Oil-for-Food Programme. When operations commenced on 10 December 1996, the Iraq government was permitted to export oil to *bona fide* oil traders, which would make payment into an escrow account until 2001 located at the Banque nationale de Paris-Paribas. The choice of banks was made by the Iraqi government, and the BNP-Paribas was controlled by Iraqi-born Nadhmi Auchi, who was to be condemned by a French court in 2003 for fraud. The Iraq government was authorized to draw from the account to pay for imports of food and other humanitarian necessities. All sales had to be approved by the 661 Committee which, because it worked by consensus, was subject to vetoes by all its members, including the United States and Great Britain. The Ba'ath regime was permitted to control the process within Iraq's borders, except in the three northern governorates of Kurdish Iraq where the authority of Baghdad was no longer respected. Relief distribution in the north was conducted by UN agencies with the agreement of Baghdad.[48]

The Oil-for-Food programme enabled the government of Iraq to sell US$64.2 billion worth of oil to 248 companies, and to purchase $34.5 billion worth of food and other humanitarian necessities from 3,614 companies.[49] These transactions made available food for 60–70% of the

Iraqi population, increasing the average daily available caloric intake from 1800 kcal in 1995 to 2800 kcal in 2000. The incidence of low birth weight babies dropped from 20% in 1995 to 12% in 2000, and the prevalence of stunted growth in children was reduced by nearly one half. In 1996, the Iraqi Ministry of Health had only been able to spend US$17 per person on medical supplies and drugs. The Oil-for-Food programme allowed it to increase expenditure to US$65 in 2000.[50] The Iraqi dinar was briefly revalued to IQD 450 to the US$, but then sank to IQD 1,850 to the US$ in early 2000. The 661 Committee, however, repeatedly blocked necessary humanitarian supplies on the grounds of possible "dual use," refusing the sale of laboratory equipment, and equipment for the repair of water and electrical systems and for health treatment, holding up the sale to Iraq of Canadian-made ambulances for over two years on the grounds that they contained communication devices.

❖ ❖ ❖

Historical study of economic warfare has suggested that food is an inefficient target for economic warfare, as direct and indirect substitution can reduce the needs for imports to a very low level.[51] Famine is only likely to overtake a substantial state as a result of its administrative failure, as happened in areas of Germany in the winters of 1916 and 1917, and in Japan in 1945. In contrast, the British government proved itself adroit in two world wars in managing the problem of consumption control and substitution. Even when famine has resulted from food control, historic precedent does not suggest that its political results will be useful. Famine alone was not enough to persuade the Japanese government in 1945 to surrender to Allied forces. Iraq lacked the domestic resources that had been available to Germany in two world wars, and, despite the efficiency of Iraqi food distribution, the weaker members of society – the children, pregnant women, the elderly – suffered extremely, and died. The historical record, however, was not entirely misleading, because the suffering did not bring about capitulation by the Iraqi government.

It was because blockade of food intended for the general public of a major state had proved to be a useless cruelty that the international community made it an illegal means of warfare. The process that began with the Declaration of Paris in 1856 was completed in 1949 by Protocol 1 Article 54 of the Geneva Convention, which made it absolutely clear that "starvation of civilians as a method of warfare is prohibited," and went on to say, "it is prohibited to attack, destroy, remove or render useless objects indispensable to the survival of the civilian population, such as food-stuffs [and] drinking water installations ... whatever the motive, whether in order to starve out civilians, to cause them to move away, or for any other motive."[52] This obligation was explicitly recognized by the United Nations. On 7 September the chairman of the committee, Marjatta Rasi, wrote to the secretary-general: "All the members of the Committee shared the view that resolution 661 (1990) must be implemented without creating conditions of starvation in Iraq and Kuwait."[53] The Aquinian "Just War" concept rules that acts of war can only be justified if they are capable of achieving the intended objective.

The huge collateral damage caused by the economic sanctions must be put in perspective with the potential of weapons of mass destruction, but more needs to be known about the role played by sanctions in Iraqi decisions to abandon its weapons program, or to move it into neighbouring countries. The use of sanctions may have been proportional to the threat, but were they capable of achieving the intended ends? And even if the death and deformity suffered by the Iraqi population was proportional to the threat posed by weapons of mass destruction, they would appear to have been excessive. It has even been argued that the death toll attributable to the sanctions regime exceeded that suffered by all the victims of weapons of mass destruction during the twentieth century.[54]

✦ ✦ ✦

The breach made in the sanctions by the Oil-for-Food programme came at a price for the strategy of the Western powers. The provisions of Resolution 986, that Iraq was to manage its own sales, and with the approval of the 661 Committee, its own purchases, gave the government of Iraq a degree of latitude that it was quick to use to reward its friends. Countries, and individuals, that participated in lobby work against the sanctions were rewarded by shipments of oil. Iraq's most important champion was Russia, and Russian companies received roughly half of Iraq's oil shipments. France was the next-largest recipient, but significantly reduced its purchases when, four years after the introduction of the Oil-for-Food programme, in the fall of 2000, Iraq began to demand supplementary payments that were not deposited in the escrow account. Sums, ultimately amounting to US$228.8 million, were paid directly into bank accounts in the Lebanon or Jordan, or to the Iraqi embassies in

Moscow and elsewhere. The rate began at $.05 per barrel of oil, and increased to $.15 and $.20, but the surcharge was abandoned in the fall of 2002 when companies refused to pay a demand for $.50, and when the 661 Committee began a policy of retroactive payment that took into account any supplementary charges. Iraq then began to offer suppliers of humanitarian goods as much as double the usual purchase price, in return for the supplier delivering substantial under-the-table kickbacks to Iraqi accounts.

The methods being employed by the Iraqi government to evade the financial terms of the sanctions became public knowledge when the U.S. Army occupied Baghdad. On 25 January 2004 the Iraqi daily newspaper, *al Mada*, published a list of individuals and organizations alleged to have received oil sales contracts via the UN's Oil-for-Food programme. This information had reportedly been found amongst some 15,000 documents in the state-owned Iraqi oil corporation. Included were the names of UN employees, notably that of Benon Sevan, who had headed the Oil-for-Food programme at the United Nations.[55] The provenance of the list remains controversial because of connections with Ahmed Chalabi, who had knowingly supplied faulty intelligence that was used to justify the invasion of Iraq.[56]

In response to the criticism directed at the United Nations' management of the Oil-for-Food programme, in April 2004 Secretary General Kofi Annan established an independent committee to investigate irregularities, headed by the former U.S. federal reserve chairman, Paul Volcker.[57] Its conclusions on managerial failure, when they were published in September 2005, were balanced, laying as much blame on the Security Council as on the UN agencies which were drawn into the work.

> The Programme was certainly the largest, most complex, and most ambitious humanitarian relief effort in the history of the United Nations Organization. In the Programme's administration, the Organization had to deal with a mixture of political, security, financial, and economic concerns. Almost every part of the United Nations family was involved, beginning with the Security Council, the Central Secretariat under the Secretary-General, and nine of the UN-related Agencies, with varying degrees of financial and operational independence ... Sadly [the successful maintenance of international pressure on Iraq while addressing the nutritional and humanitarian needs of the population] fell under an increasingly dark shadow.[58]

Acknowledging that "as the years passed, reports spread of waste, inefficiency, and corruption, even within the United Nations itself," the committee recommended a thorough overhaul of UN administrative practices. It noted that the secretary general had never been selected on the basis of managerial or personal qualifications, and was, in effect, "chief diplomatic and political agent of the United Nations." But the Volcker Committee also concluded that, "however well-conceived the Programme was in principle, the Security Council failed to define clearly the practical parameters, policies, and administrative responsibilities. Far too much initiative was left to the Iraqi regime in the Programme's design and subsequent implementation. Compounding that difficulty, the Security Council, in contrast to most past practice, retained within its own sanctions committee of national diplomats [i.e., the 661 Committee] substantial elements of operational control."

The questions surrounding the motives for the sanctions imposed on Iraq, and the motives for the criticism of the United Nations by the Bush administration, are brought into relief by the findings of the Volcker Committee's report on Iraq's manipulation of the sanctions regime. In its interim report of 3 February 2005, it noted that:

> the major source of external financial resources to the Iraqi Regime resulted from sanctions violations outside the [Oil-for-Food] Programme's framework. These illicit sales, usually referred to as "smuggling," began years before the Programme started. Exports of Iraqi oil to both Jordan and Turkey and imports from those countries generally took place within the terms of trade agreements ("protocols") negotiated with Iraq. The existence, but not necessarily the amounts, of sales and purchases under these protocols was brought to the attention of the 661 Committee and at least in the case of Jordan, it was "noted." United States law requires that assistance programs to countries in violation of United Nations sanctions be ended unless continuation is determined to be in the national interest. Such determinations were provided by successive United States administrations for both Jordan and Turkey. In the later stages of the Programme, substantial Iraqi sales of oil were made to Syria and small sales to Egypt under similar "protocols."[59]

Restrictions threatening the withdrawal of aid to any nation violating UN sanctions against Iraq were adopted by the American government in 1991, but national security waivers were issued as early as 1991; and one for Jordan signed 17 October 2002 by Deputy Secretary of State Richard Armitage shows that Jordan had been in violation of the UN sanctions against Iraq since their implementation. Turkey's illegal trades appear to go back at least to December 1998 when the Clinton Administration authorized waivers for both Turkey and Jordan. During a hearing of the U.S. Senate's Permanent Subcommittee on Investigations into Oil-for-Food programme allegations on 15 February 2005, Senator Carl Levin (D-MI) remarked: "It is clear that the whole world, including the United States, knew about Iraq's oil sales to Turkey, Jordan and Syria. In the case of the United States, we not only knew about the oil sales, we actively stopped the United Nations Iraq Sanctions Committee, known as the 661 Committee, from acting to stop those sales ... Hundreds of millions of dollars went into the pockets of Saddam Hussein as a result."[60]

In my 1991 book, *Attack on Maritime Trade*, I characterized the record of blockade, and sanctions, with a "borrowed, and transformed, aphorism to the effect that 'The businessman will always get through.'" I continued: "The motivation of those who wish to continue trading is greater than is that of those who wish to block it. Governments connive at wartime trade with the enemy, either because it is recognized that the belligerent itself must trade to live, or because business interests suborn government."[61] That caution was certainly borne out by events, although political and strategic motives were at least as corrupting. The evidence suggests that the American criticism of the United Nations for its administrative limitations, which were hardly different in kind from those revealed within the American administration by the 9/11 attacks on the United States in 2001, and the chaos that followed the destruction of New Orleans by hurricane Katrina in 2005, may have been primarily motivated by resentment at the way the United Nations had refused to rubber stamp the American rationale for invasion of Iraq in 2003.

The easy answer to the charge that the UN sanctions violated the laws of war and of humanity is that Saddam Hussein manipulated the privations of Iraqi people for his own political and strategic ends. But it is hardly a matter for remark that a despot of the calibre of Saddam Hussein should have been indifferent to the plight of the Iraqi people. What is remarkable is that the diplomatic, defence, and intelligence communities of the Security Council members instituted a strategy that was vulnerable to his manipulation. The United Nations' attempt to find a way of addressing humanitarian needs without destroying the purposive leverage the sanctions regime was intended to generate proved to be limited. It lacked experience in such a major undertaking, and the collective memory of the Security Council was inadequate to the task.

✦ ✦ ✦

The Canadian government has to take its share of responsibility for the collateral damage caused by the sanctions operations conducted against Iraq, because of the participation of the Canadian navy in their enforcement. Canada was bound to comply with the sanctions regime because it was mandated by the United Nations, but its decision to provide naval resources to extend those restrictions to Iraqi trade with other countries leaves Canada with a moral burden. A refusal to acknowledge that burden would be tantamount to an admission that Canada remains trapped in the subordinate role of implementer of strategies framed by others: it would relegate the Canadian navy to the stature of a "colonial levée." The argument expressed by a senior officer in the Canadian navy that the Iraq operations were intended to, and primarily did, serve to support a Canadian special relationship with the United States does nothing to lighten the moral load. But it is consistent with nearly a hundred years of rationale for the maintenance of a navy, and also with the criticism of Laurier's naval policy made by the Nationalists of 1911.

As a provider of some of the naval forces needed to supervise and enforce any systemic sanctions regime, Canada possesses a capacity to deny that support. Supportive suasion can be a powerful lever. The hands of Canadian diplomats seeking to persuade Security Council members to embed review dates in any sanctions order would be strengthened by the role the Canadian navy is accustomed to play in sanctions enforcement. That same leverage could also be applied to ensuring that the sanctions ordered are consistent with ethical restraints.[62]

9

SANCTIONS ENFORCEMENT:
YUGOSLAVIA AND HAITI

In the aftermath of the 1989 Defence Budget and the 1990 Kuwait crisis, the vice-chief of defence staff, Vice-Admiral Charles Thomas, proposed in April 1991 that new defence priorities should be adopted – with enhanced importance for the navy. He defended the "blue water" role of the navy: "Current events and Canadian interests as a maritime nation require that we be able to exercise influence on events and participate in events requiring combat capable forces at sea far beyond our coastal interests ... I believe that this government and future governments will use our maritime forces in potential combat environments far from Canada. I do not believe that land force combat units at the brigade group level will be similarly deployed."[1] This idea might have amounted to a realization following the end of the Cold War of the concept put forward by Lester Pearson in 1964, and taken up by Paul Hellyer, that the Canadian contribution to multi-lateral and international security should take the form of sea and air mobile forces.

In rejecting Admiral Thomas's demand, and accepting his resignation, the chief of defence staff, General John (AJGD) de Chastelain, was firm that the navy had no reason to complain. "At more than nine billion dollars, the Canadian Patrol Frigate Program (the biggest procurement plan ever undertaken in the Department of National Defence, and indeed, the Canadian Government), is about to deliver its first ship. The almost two billion dollar project to modernize our four Tribal Class destroyers is well under way. We are moving steadily ahead with plans to launch a multi-billion dollar program to outfit our fleet with new shipborne helicopters. The acquisition of these modern and effective vessels and aircraft will ensure that our navy will retain a significant blue water capability well into the next century and that Canada will be able to meet our national and alliance commitments." He admitted that the acquisition of "a modest conventional submarine replacement program" was overdue, however, and insisted that the government must be provided with "the broadest possible range of military options to ensure that the full spectrum of responses is available to meet the ever changing security challenges to Canadian interests at home and abroad."

Vice-Admiral Thomas's concern, however, was not entirely wide of the mark. The 1990s have been called the Canadian navy's second "Golden Age," with global deployments that were consistent with the intent behind the transformation of NATO's purview, but the defence budget had peaked in 1987 at $14 billion, and with the demand for a "peace dividend" it decline to less than $10 billion in 1998. Budgetary restraint was finally to lead to the withdrawal of Canadian land and air forces from Europe on 31 August 1994. But, paradoxically, standing down Canada's European garrison was to lead to Canadian forces, including the navy, being committed to intense action in the European theatre. When Prime Minister Mulroney announced in June 1991 that the Canadian garrison in Germany would be reduced, he also asserted, after a visit to the Brandenburg Gate in Berlin, that Canada would not abandon Germany. Canadian forces were to take an active part in the NATO operations that were mandated by the United Nations Security Council to deal with the violence that followed the break up of the Socialist Federal Republic of Yugoslavia. Again, the operational role for the navy was the enforcement of economic sanctions.

Richard Gimblett has pointed out that the Canadian navy's participation in the NATO operations in the Balkans occurred in the context of a diminishing Canadian participation in NATO's naval formation, STANAVFORLANT. During the decade the Canadian contribution to STANAVFORLANT was to be limited "occasionally" to a tanker, and the detachment of HMCS *Toronto* in 1998 to the Gulf was to leave a gap in the NATO formation. All the same, a Canadian officer was to command STANAVFORLANT on two occasions during the decade, both times from one of the Canadian DDG280 destroyers, and on both occasions while the formation was on operations in the Adriatic.

✦ ✦ ✦

Following the first ever meeting in January 1992 held by the Security Council at the level of heads of state and government, Secretary General Boutros Boutros-Ghali had been instructed to prepare an "analysis and recommendations on ways of strengthening and making more efficient within the framework and provisions of the Charter the capacity of the United Nations for preventive diplomacy, for peacemaking and for peace-keeping." His report was published on 17 June 1992 as *An Agenda for Peace, Preventive Diplomacy, Peacemaking and Peace-keeping*. In it Boutros Boutros-Ghali reminded that "Under Article 42 of the Charter, the Security Council has the authority to take military action to maintain or restore international peace and security. While such action should only be taken when all peaceful means have failed, the option of taking it is essential to the credibility of the United Nations as a guarantor of international security." His recommendation was that the provisions in the charter for the formation of UN forces should be implemented. This has not been done, and probably never will be. Military commanders have found the United Nations organization incompetent at directing military operations. But the *Agenda for Peace* and the disasters in Croatia and Bosnia-Herzegovina, the genocide in Rwanda in April–July 1994 when eighty thousand people were deliberately massacred, and the failure of sanctions in Haiti, did bring a harder edge to international response to violent chaos.[2]

The European Community's best efforts to manage the crisis in Yugoslavia contributed to the mounting chaos. The principle recognized by the Organization for Security and Co-operation in Europe (OSCE) in the 1974 Helsinki Final Act, and by the European Community, that historical boundaries should not be changed, and certainly not by force, could not easily be reconciled with the right of self-determination by the substantial Serbian minorities in Croatia and Bosnia-Herzegovina.[3] The German foreign minister, Hans-Dietrich Genscher, placed the highest priority on the sanctity of borders, out of concern that modification of the state boundaries in Yugoslavia would open to question all the boundaries of Europe, with incalculable consequences. The treaty defining the German-Polish border had been signed on 14 November 1990 and was still a sensitive issue. Michael Libal, at the time the head of the Southeast European Department of the German Foreign Ministry, was convinced that no one should be "allowed to question the internal Yugoslav frontiers. What was true for postwar Europe – that everything had to begin with giving peoples and governments the assurance of living within secure borders – now had to be applied to Yugoslavia." But he acknowledged that the policy had deeply troubling implications: "the quest for independence and territorial integrity of individual *republics*" failed to meet the need for "self-determination of *peoples*, which would necessarily lead to a questioning of the existing internal borders."

As divisions of a federal state, the sectarian mix could serve to strengthen the central government, but with the break-up of the federation their potential for conflict was huge.[4] Serbian, Croat, and Bosnian militias perpetrated extensive violation of the Geneva Conventions Relative to the Protection of Civilian Persons in Times of War, and to the Treatment of Prisoners of War, by forcing people to leave their homes, destroying their property, and forcing civilians to work in labour camps. Ultimately, they were guilty of mass murder to effect what became known as "ethnic cleansing," in which context there were also instances of systematic rape, which ultimately led to the births of hundreds of babies.

In a vain hope of reducing the scale of conflict, the Security Council agreed on 25 September 1991 to Resolution 713, imposing a complete embargo on all deliveries of weapons and military equipment to all parts of the former Yugoslavia. On 15 December Resolution 724 established a Sanctions Committee to monitor the arms embargo, and requested member states to report to the secretary-general on measures they took to enforce the ban. The OSCE and the European Community established Sanctions Assistance Missions to help neighbouring countries enforce the sanctions mandated by the United Nations, and to monitor them. Margaret Doxey tells us that the Yugoslavia Sanctions Committee, the 724 Committee, received "a huge volume of requests for exemptions" to the embargo: 2,000 in 1992, 18,000 in 1993 and 34,000 in 1995.[5]

With circumstances on the ground continuing to worsen, on 21 February 1992, by Resolution 743, the Security Council established a United Nations Protection Force (UNPROFOR) intended to monitor a peace that did not exist. Canada was one of the forty-one nations that eventually provided soldiers. In April 1992 an infantry company of the *Royal Canadian Regiment* from CFB Baden Soellingen were deployed to UNPROFOR, under NATO control, and ultimately the Canadian Army contributed two full battle groups. In addition, Canada contributed to re-supply, humanitarian aid, medical evacuation, and engineering support, and participated in the sanctions control. Approximately 1660 Canadian personnel saw service in UNPROFOR between the spring of 1992 and the fall of 1995, including elements of the *Royal 22e Regiment*, the *Royal Canadian Regiment*, the *Princess Patricia's Canadian Light Infantry*, armoured and engineer regiments, and military observers, and Royal Canadian Mounted Police (RCMP) officers. Major-General Lewis Wharton MacKenzie served in succession as chief of staff, commander, section Sarajavo, and deputy theatre commander. In 1995 Alex Morrison, at the time the founding president of the Pearson Peacekeeping Centre in Cornwallis, Nova Scotia, would write: "peacekeepers are not neutral. They do not stand aside, they are not indifferent. They deal with the here and the now, with that which is real. They are required to assess and to act."[6] The forces sent to stop the mayhem in the former Yugoslavia, however, were woefully inadequate for the purpose, without the equipment or authority to intervene with force against Serbian and Croatian militia terrorists.

Yugoslavia was reconstituted on 27 March 1992 into the Federal Republic of Yugoslavia (FRY) composed of Yugoslavian rump states of Serbia and Montenegro, and on 18 and 20 May 1992 the Security Council passed resolutions 753, 754, and 755, admitting the separating Yugoslavian provinces of Slovenia, Croatia, and Bosnia-Herzegovina to the United Nations as independent states.[7] On 12 August 1992 the Bosnian Serbs declared the formation of a Republika Srpska, incorporating all the areas of Bosnia with Serbian majorities, or which had had Serbian majorities prior to the persecution of the Second World War. In September the state of Montenegro declared its independence, American soldiers deploying to monitor its border with Serbia. And in an attempt to obtain control of those areas of central Bosnia-Herzegovina with a Croat population, an independent status was declared on 18 November by the Bosnian Croats, named Herzeg-Bosnia.[8] The crisis in Bosnian affairs led to President Alija Izetbegović accepting aid from the then little-known mujahideen group, al Qaeda, and arms from Iran. Richard Clarke writes that the arrival of the Islamic fundamentalists brought Clinton to commit American resources.[9]

President Slobodan Miloševic's Yugoslav government supported the actions of the Serbian militias, but the overriding consideration on the part of the European nations and the United States alike was that they did not want to be drawn into a protracted guerilla ethnic war such as Britain was still dealing with in Ireland. Hoping to find a way of putting greater pressure on Serbia without either endangering the soldiers on the ground or embarking on an all-out military campaign against the militias, on 30 May 1992, by Resolution 757, the sanctions regime against the rump of Yugoslavia was extended to a wide range of measures intended to sever economic contact with the world.

In July the North Atlantic Council agreed to provide the means to implement Resolution 757 by deploying the Standing Naval Force Mediterranean which had recently been brought into existence following the model of STANAVFORLANT. Operation *Maritime Monitor* was intended only to watch Yugoslav maritime traffic so that member states could be informed of violations of their national regulations. A new development was that, under pressure from the government of France that then still adhered to the Gaullist view that NATO was essentially an American institution, the moribund West European Union (WEU) was resurrected, and organized a squadron that served with the NATO force in the Adriatic. The WEU squadron was tasked with Operation *Sharp Vigilance* to observe traffic in the strait of Otranto. Sean Maloney writes that the partnership was not well conceived as the two forces had different logistic structures, and they reported to different international commanders. Their rules of engagement were different, but in any case the UN had not authorized the use of forceful means to implement its resolution. There was also conflict between the supreme allied commander Atlantic and the commander-in-chief of Allied Forces Southern Europe who came under the command of the supreme allied commander Europe, both American admirals and both wishing to control the operations. Initially STANAVFORMED lacked adequate resources, with the result that NATO's Defence Planning Committee temporarily replaced it for the period of 9–26 September with STANAVFORLANT. To do so, the force had to be transferred from SACLANT to SACEUR then to C-in-C South, which put it under the quasi-moribund control of the commander naval forces Southern Europe.[10]

When in September STANAVFORLANT assumed responsibility for naval activity in the Adriatic, the Canadian navy deployed the destroyer HMCS *Gatineau*, although there was concern that she was too elderly to undertake what might become a shooting war. To prepare her for her role, she was fitted with six .50 calibre machine guns, additional search lights, night vision equipment, and a rigid-hulled inflatable boat. At least one Canadian destroyer or frigate participated in the STANAVFORLANT operation throughout its duration.

On 17 November 1992 the Security Council finally agreed on Resolution 787 somewhat Delphicly granting the naval forces authority "to use such measures commensurate with the specific circumstances as may be necessary."[11] The separate NATO and WEU operations were combined on 15 June 1993, and given the name operation *Sharp Guard*. Commanded by Admiral Mario Angeli, Italian Navy, Combined Task Force 440 was composed of the Standing Naval Force Mediterranean, the Standing Naval Force Atlantic, and the WEU Contingency Maritime Force. Commodore G.R. Maddison, CF, as he then was, who took his turn in command of the Standing Naval Force Atlantic in the Adriatic in 1993–94, explains that the NATO forces were broken up and combined with WEU forces because "there were fears from the strategic and political levels that the WEU force, if operated as a complete unit, would demonstrate a lesser capability than inherent within the other two forces."[12] Supreme command was given to SACLANT. To assist this formation, the Canadian navy sailed eight ships between June 1993 and June 1996, the destroyers *Algonquin* and *Iroquois*, the new patrol frigates *Halifax*, *Toronto*, *Montreal*, *Ville de Québec*, *Calgary*, and *Fredericton* and in 1993 the AOR *Preserver*, all with embarked CH-124 *Sea King* helicopter detachments providing support. From August 1993 to May 1994, CP-140 *Aurora* Maritime Patrol aircraft joined the mission to provide surface and sub-surface surveillance patrols. Consideration was given to deploying one of Canada's submarines, HMCS *Onondaga*, but it was not sent, possibly because the optics would have been inconsistent with the role of "Peace Keeping."[13] The disarmed maritime patrol aircraft were seen in a very different light, as highly visible contributions that offset the negative diplomatic consequences of the withdrawal from German bases.

The navy of the former Yugoslavia, based on Kotor on the Montenegran coast, did not seek action with the blockading force, but nonetheless it was an important actor in the drama. It possessed four frigates, two corvettes, twelve fast-attack craft armed with *Styx* missiles, four torpedo boats, five diesel submarines, five midget submarines, and three two-man swimmer delivery craft. The base was guarded by 130-mm coastal batteries and mobile *Styx* missile batteries. The Yugoslav Air Force possessed three hundred operational aircraft. These obliged NATO forces to keep outside the twelve-mile territorial sea. Had they been determined to engage with NATO, they could have put up a hard fight, and with the advantage of local knowledge of the deeply indented coast, would certainly have inflicted heavy casualties. To deter any such threat, the U.S. Navy, the Royal Navy, and the Spanish, Italian, and French navies deployed carrier battle groups under national command in the confined waters, and during the early part of the operation British, French, Dutch, Italian, Turkish and American submarines also patrolled inshore. The Italian Air Force maintained a "supplementary" combat air patrol of eight *Tornado* aircraft. While no live-fire engagements took place, there were repeated confrontations between NATO/WEU ships and Yugoslav patrol craft, alarms when Yugoslav aircraft made threatening runs, frustrating searches for Yugoslav submarines operating close to the Montenegran coast, and illumination by Yugoslav fire-control radars.[14]

✦ ✦ ✦

During the period 22 November 1992 to 18 June 1996 about 74,000 ships were challenged by the allied force; 5,591 were inspected at sea and 1,480 were diverted and inspected in port. The only incident of enough importance to be mentioned in the AFSouth NATO fact sheet occurred on 1 May 1994 when the Yugoslav navy attempted, but failed, to prevent the seizure of a tanker, the *Lido II* registered in Malta.[15] HMCS *Iroquois* intercepted a ship laden with tanks and ammunition that was trying to evade the blockade by claiming it was carrying equipment for one of the national contributors to UNPROFOR. Late in 1995 it was possible to re-divide the Standing Naval Force Mediterranean, the Standing Naval Force Atlantic, and the WEU Contingency Maritime Force, each of which now had a full squadron staff and complement of ships.

At a time when the UN-authorized sanctions against Iraq were already known to be having a devastating effect on its civilian population, the Security Council refrained from any controls on the import of food and medicine into the Federal Republic of Yugoslavia, which in any event was relatively self-sufficient in these areas. Nevertheless, the effect of the limited-sanctions regime was to bring about siege conditions, in which the Serbian economy restructured to function without external markets or sources of supply. Statistics compiled by the U.S. State Department show that the Serbian economy contracted by 26% in 1992, and by a further 28% in 1993. Incomes fell in real terms by 50%, and industrial production fell by 22% in 1992 and 37% in 1993. Inflation in Yugoslavia rose from 122% in 1991, to 9,000% in 1992, and with Yugoslavia printing money to cover its costs, inflation reached 100-trillion % by the end of 1993. In January 1994 Belgrade introduced new currency pegged to the German Mark, and slashed government programs, which temporarily stabilized the situation, but inflation was still running at 120% at the end of 1994.[16] The restrictions on Yugoslav exports impacted on the health services because the priorities of the Milošević administration precluded spending scarce hard currency on the importation of those specialist drugs not produced domestically. The health services became dependent on international aid, and health care professionals isolated from their peers and from professional education.[17]

To minimize the strategic impact of the economic sanctions, the Belgrade government tapped criminal sources to obtain hard currency, by offering the money-laundering services of the Yugoslav central bank. Oil was smuggled into the country, notably by the collusive capture of oil barges in transit on the Danube international waterway. In an attempt to address this problem, Resolution 787 prohibited the trans-shipment of energy supplies and various commodities across the Federal Republic of Yugoslavia unless specifically authorized by the Sanctions Committee. Nothing could be done, however, about the flow of oil by pipeline under the Danube from the Slavonian oil field. Virtually all the petroleum smuggled into Serbia was appropriated by the armed forces, and civilian home heating was provided by wood and coal fires, creating a high level of air pollution. The economic conditions created by the sanctions fostered Serbian nationalism, and strengthened support for the Milošević regime. Extremist leadership had access to revenues from smuggling, but the political opposition became destitute.

In May 1993 Admiral John Anderson, now the chief of defence staff, justified the dispatch of a destroyer, HMCS *Algonquin* to take part in the Adriatic operations on the grounds that "sanctions enforcement ... is a key to moderating Serbian behaviour [and] was consistent with Canadian support for Resolution 820."[18] Certainly the sanctions had a more constructive impact on the Balkan crisis than they had on the Iraqi one. In August 1992 an international conference had assembled in London to work toward a settlement of the issues in Yugoslavia, and the co-chairmen of the Steering Committee, Cyrus Vance and Lord Owen, had held talks with the warring parties. On 4 January 1993 they promulgated a peace plan, which was accepted by the government of Bosnia and by the Croatian Serbs, but not by the Bosnian Serbs. When the last marked their refusal by the commission of further atrocities, the Security Council passed Resolution 820, of 17 April 1993, and 942, of 23 September 1994, extending the sanctions to Serb-controlled Bosnia. Owen believes that this was the event that led to President Milošević's formal disassociation with the continued resistance of Bosnian Serbs, and to his invitation to the United Nations to send a monitoring mission into Serbia, although unofficial contact and material support remained strong. Scholarly opinion is somewhat divided as to the extent to which sanctions contributed to the signing of the Vance-Owen agreement, but diplomatic opinion was more agreed.[19]

In recognition of the important change of policy in Belgrade, Resolution 943 on the same date suspended the provisions restricting air freight and freight on the Yugoslav ferry to Brindisi in Italy, and relaxed the standard for making exceptions to the sanctions. In May 1995 Britain, France, and Russia favoured ending the sanctions against the Federal

Republic of Yugoslavia, but the United States resisted on the ground that if Belgrade failed to live up to its indication that it was willing to reach a settlement, it would be difficult to re-establish sanctions at a later date.[20]

With respect to the arms embargo the picture is unclear. The application of Resolution 713 to all the Balkan states in practice had favoured the Serbian militias in Bosnia and Croatia, because they had access to the army magazines while the Total Defence Forces of the Bosnian and Croatian states could only acquire heavy weapons by taking them from their enemies. In 1993 and 1994 a group of Islamic states, with American support, obtained resolutions in the United Nations General Assembly seeking to exempt Bosnia and Croatia from the embargo, and the United States sought to obtain a modification of the Security Council resolution. Britain, France, and Russia disagreed. Unable to secure its intentions by legal means, the United States declared in November 1994 that it would no longer enforce the embargo against Bosnia, with the result that shipments with manifests for Bosnia were not intercepted by U.S. warships in the Adriatic. Cargoes were freely trans-shipped through Croatian ports, with the Croats helping themselves to what they wanted. Charles Ingrao, professor of History at Perdue University, writes that "by the beginning of 1995, there were suspicions in European capitals that US 'non-compliance' had morphed into direct, covert assistance for the Bosnian military." Admiral Leighton "Snuffy" Smith, commander-in-chief of U.S. Naval Forces Europe and Allied Forces Southern Europe, and later of the NATO Implementation Force (IFOR) in Bosnia, "silenced the indignant Europeans by pledging to resign if US assets were violating the embargo." All the same, it appears that they were. The embargo and its evasion contributed to the eventual resolution of the crisis. "By the spring of 1995, both Croatia and Bosnia had slipped enough weaponry through the holes in the arms embargo to tilt the military balance of power; the United States had even helped them forge an alliance for joint action all along their common frontier."[21]

The agreement by the breakaway Serb Krajina area of eastern Croatia to the Vance-Owen plan had led to UNPROFOR replacing the Yugoslav National Army in protecting the Croatian Serbs, but Croat forces overran the territory in 1995, and in 1998 the area was absorbed back into the Croatian state. A mass exodus of the Croatian-Serbian population was organized by the Yugoslav Army, and Croat commanders perpetrated war crimes against those who remained, to drive them out as well. Robert Frasure, the American ambassador, noted to Richard Holbrooke, the U.S. assistant secretary of state for Europe, on 17 August 1995: "Dick: We 'hired' these guys [the Croatian army] to be our junkyard dogs because we were desperate ... This is no time to get squeamish about things. This is the first time the Serb wave has been reversed. That is essential for us to get stability, so we can get out."[22]

Apart from the coercive effect of the economic sanctions on Belgrade, they also served as definitive force inhibiting the ability of Yugoslavia to continue to bear the cost of the Bosnian conflict. The economic warfare dimension may have been as important as was the diplomatic one. The naval forces deployed to enforce sanctions also served a secondary definitive purpose. Although it was not a declared objective of the NATO operations to deter the Yugoslav navy from participating in operations to resist Croatian independence, that was a secondary effect – for better or for worse.

✦ ✦ ✦

The Balkan conflict was far from over when the Canadian navy returned to Haiti because of the chaos precipitated by the election of President Jean-Bertrand Aristide in December 1990 in Haiti's first fully democratic election, and his defeat in a vote of non-confidence less than a year later, in September 1991. An attempt by him to rule without parliament was put to an end by the commander-in-chief of Haiti's armed forces, Lieutenant-General Raoul Cédras. Aristide had fled into exile, and a new president was sworn in, but Cédras continued to exercise the real power. Consistent with a "Commitment to Democracy" that members had made on 5 June at Santiago, the Organization of American States (OAS) in October instituted limited and voluntary sanctions against the junta.[23] Although supported by the General Assembly of the United Nations, and resulting in the loss of 30,000 jobs in Haiti, the sanctions proved ineffective in bringing a return to democratic government. They were not strongly supported by the United States, which was concerned by the flow of Haitian economic refugees trying to cross to Florida.

After nearly two years of internal terrorism against the political opponents of the junta, on 16 June 1993 the United Nations Security Council agreed to Resolution 841 making the OAS trade embargo mandatary, and adding prohibition on the importation into Haiti of petroleum products, arms, and ammunition, regardless of their point of origin. This quickly led to the signing on 3 July of a formal agreement at Governor's

Island between Aristide and Lieutenant-General Cédras to regularize Haiti's government. The sanctions were briefly suspended, but the agreement was not fully implemented. On 23 September 1993 the Security Council added Resolution 867 dispatching a mission to Haiti, with provision for non-combat training of Haitian police and military, but on 11 October USS *Harlan County* carrying U.S. and Canadian military personnel to Port-au-Prince was forced to make a hasty withdrawal when a hostile and armed crowd assembled on the wharf, and the 30 October 1993 deadline passed for the return of President Aristide to Haiti.

The *Harlan County* incident led to the reimposition of the oil and arms embargo, and on 16 October Security Council Resolution 875 called for members to establish a Multinational Maritime Interdiction Force to implement the blockade. This was assembled with units from France, Argentina, the Netherlands, the United Kingdom, and the United States, joined by the Canadian (AOR) *Preserver*, and the destroyers *Fraser* and *Gatineau*. Operation *Forward Action* carried out interception, inspection, and clearance of maritime trade bound for Haitian ports. By the end of the sanctions regime, 300,000 jobs had been lost in Haiti. Hal Klepak suggests that the Canadian naval commitment to Haiti was motivated as much by a wish to accommodate the United States as to support the people of the only other francophone country in the Americas.[24]

The HMCS *Fraser* (DDH 233) returning from sanctions enforcement against the Haitian government, 23 December 1993. DND HSC93-1113-2

Despite the exemption of food from the embargo, the fuel embargo and restrictions on transportation drove up food prices beyond the reach of ordinary Haitians. According to the evidence compiled by Elizabeth Gibbons, who headed the UNICEF office in Haiti during the blockade, the incidence of malnutrition amongst children rose from 27% of the population to 50% in 1994, and an increase in maternal malnutrition led to an increase in low birth-weight babies. Deaths of children between the ages of one and five rose from 56 per 1,000 in 1987 to 61 per 1,000 in 1994. The humanitarian crisis would have been more severe had not the international community mobilized to provide aid, feeding perhaps as much as 20% of the population, and providing enough medical support to prevent epidemics. As had occurred in Iraq and Yugoslavia, the sanctions regime in Haiti undermined the capacity of the political opposition, and strengthened the hands of the government that had the capacity to reward the loyal.[25]

This suffering and death did not generate sufficient purposive force to bring the junta to capitulate. It had used the period of suspension of sanctions to stockpile oil supplies and to construct a highway to the Dominican Republic to facilitate smuggling over the border. Although there was later talk of applying a doctrine of continuous voyage to imports into the Dominican Republic, this would have required an increase in the naval forces available to the United Nations, and was never implemented.

After another six months of frustrating delay, the Security Council determined to target Haitian leaders. Resolution 917 on 6 May 1994 banned all flights in and out of Haiti apart from regular commercial aviation, and denied travel to members of the Haiti junta and military. Member states were urged to freeze the assets of members of the junta and Haitian military officers, and, in the light of the systemic violence of the Haitian regime the Security Council made it clear that it required "the retirement of the Commander-in-Chief of the Haitian Armed Forces, and the resignation or departure from Haiti of the Chief of the Metropolitan Zone of Port-au-Prince, commonly known as the Chief of Police of Port-au-Prince, and the Chief of Staff of the Haitian Armed Forces; (b) Completion of the changes by retirement or departure from Haiti in the leadership of the police and military high command called for in the Governors Island Agreement." But the targeted sanctions against Haiti junta and military leaders were also ineffectual. Despairing of the hope that sanctions would bring compliance with UN demands, Resolution 940 on 31 July ordered more forceful definitive action. Determining that the crisis in Haiti continued to represent a threat to international peace and security, it authorized the formation of a multilateral force to operate under unified command and to use "all necessary means" to facilitate the return of Aristide to power. On 19 September a largely U.S. force landed on Haiti and ten days later, with Aristide back in the presidential office, the sanctions were suspended.[26] Lieutenant-General Cédras went into exile in Panama, where the United States provided him with a refuge.

✦ ✦ ✦

The severance by the Belgrade government of official political and economic relations with the Republika Srpska contained the spread of conflict, but did not serve to bring an end to the atrocities in Bosnia. The failure of sanctions on their own to bring the Haitian junta to comply with the demands of the OAS and the UN did not encourage continued reliance upon them for bringing the Bosnian Serb militias to lay down their arms. After months of escalating violence in Bosnia, on 16 June 1995 a 15,000-strong Rapid Reaction Force was authorized by Security Council Resolution 998. In a letter to the president of the Security Council, Boutros Boutros-Ghali said that the missions of the force "would in particular provide the Commander of UNPROFOR with well-armed and mobile forces with which to respond promptly to threats to United Nations personnel." He went on to say: "the three Governments have made it clear that their intention is that the reinforced UNPROFOR would continue to be a peace-keeping mission. The proposed reinforcements would not alter the fact that UNPROFOR cannot by itself end the war in Bosnia and Herzegovina. Its role is to create conditions in which progress can be made towards a peaceful settlement, to help implement agreements that are reached and to support efforts to relieve the human suffering created by the war."[27] This defensive mandate, however, was abandoned when on 25 July–1 August 1995 Ratko Mladi's militia at Srebrenica disarmed the Dutch peacekeepers, "executed" more than 7,000 Bosnian men, and threw them into mass graves. This disgrace led the North Atlantic Council to decide that further Bosnian Serb offensive action could only be deterred by a firm response and – if necessary – by the graduated use of air power. Apparently only Canada and Greece were opposed to a resort to force.

Secretary General Boutros Boutros-Ghali gave the United Nations Protection Force commander, French General Bernard Janvier, authority to initiate operations. Lightly armed UNPROFOR units were withdrawn from Serb-controlled Bosnia, to prevent them being used as hostages, and on August 30 air strikes were begun on Bosnian-Serb military targets. With the designation of Operation *Deliberate Force*, 1,026 bombs were dropped against 48 target complexes, with 338 individual aiming points. On 10 September a U.S. Navy ship fired a barrage of *Tomahawk* land attack cruise missiles to attack targets that were too well protected against the air strikes. This careful use of firepower, directed against infrastructure while minimizing collateral damage to civilians and militiamen, enabled the Bosnian army to push back the Serbian militia from some of the disputed territory, leaving the Republika Srpska in control of 49 percent of Bosnia. The successful Croatian assault into the Krajina in July contributed to the outcome as it exposed the northern flank of the Bosnian Serb position. These developments, and intense pressure from Milošević, who was himself under pressure from the economic sanctions, finally brought a capitulation by the Bosnian-Serbs. On 14 September the air strikes were suspended, and on 20 September Operation *Deliberate Force* was terminated.[28]

On 30 November 1995 the governments of Yugoslavia, Bosnia-Herzegovina, and Croatia signed an agreement brokered by Richard Holbrooke at Dayton, Ohio, by which Bosnia was partitioned by the recognition of Republika Srpska as a semi-antonymous region with its own government, but with shared governmental institutions. This fig leaf enabled the international community to preserve the form but not the substance of its ban on the movement of boundaries by force. According to Jutta Pazulla this was an entirely American effort. "The Europeans were kept informed about developments in the negotiations, but they were not consulted."[29] It was agreed that all armed forces would return to their own countries, that militia forces disengage, and that a Multinational Peace Implementation Force, IFOR, be established under the control of NATO to supervise the peace.[30] This was to be succeeded a year later by a Stabilization Force (SFOR). Canadian soldiers were deployed to serve in these commands, in 1997 increasing the overall commitment to the Balkans by deploying over 100 personnel and six CF-18 *Hornet* fighter aircraft to provided air-to-air and air-to-ground support. Their mission was completed on 15 November 1997. As part of the commitment, twelve personnel were attached to NATO's Multinational Air Movement Detachment to assist in tactical airlifts within the theatre of operation with the mission to be completed in mid-January 1998.

Even before the signing of the Dayton Accord, on 22 November 1995 the Security Council had reduced its sanctions (Resolution 1022) to a blockade of heavy weapons. On 27 February 1996 the last of the economic sanctions against the Bosnian Serbs was terminated. The ships of *Sharp Guard* continued their patrols to enforce the weapons ban until all sanctions were finally removed on 18 June 1996, following the withdrawal of Serbian militias from the zones of separation in Bosnia, and ten days after an open and monitored election. Operation *Sharp Guard* was finally terminated on 2 October 1996.[31] At time of writing in 2012, however, Bosnia continues to be kept together by European Union soldiers, and the government of Republika Srpska continues to seek a referendum to establish its independence. If that were to be permitted it is feared the Croatian population of Bosnia would also demand independence.[32] Paul Heinbecker, formerly Canada's ambassador to the United Nations, cites the American use of the veto in the Security Council in 2002 to terminate the UN mission in Bosnia-Herzegovina as an example of the irresponsibility that is sometimes associated with power. "In a bare-knuckled attempt to insulate itself from the jurisdiction of the nascent International Criminal Court ... the US held hostage the international community's multi-billion-dollar effort to ensure long-term peace in the Balkans, and ultimately vetoed the extension of the mission's mandate."[33]

✦ ✦ ✦

The conclusion of Operation *Sharp Guard* was not the end of military action by NATO in the Balkans, but it was the end of naval sanctions enforcement, and of the participation by the Canadian navy. In 1989 Miloševic had terminated the autonomous status of the Serbian province of Kosovo, which has a largely ethnically Albanian population, and as a result on 2 July 1990 the Kosovo parliament had declared independence. The issue was muted during the Bosnian conflict, and limited to a campaign of civil disobedience, but conflict intensified during the winter of 1998–99. A precipitant of the crisis was the attempt to resettle Serbian refugees from Croatia and Bosnia. Beginning in 1996, atrocities were committed by the Kosovo Liberation Army (KLA) which the government of the United States identified as a terrorist organization, and by Yugoslavia security forces. These became international news on 15 January 1999 when U.S ambassador William Walker was seen on television walking amongst the mutilated bodies of forty-five Albanians killed at Račak by Serbian Special Police. On 31 March the Security Council agreed to Resolution 1160 imposing an arms embargo on the Federal Republic of Yugoslavia, including Kosovo, but only massive military intervention could have made the embargo effective. The Yugoslav army was still one of the best equipped in Europe, and following the collapse of the Communist regime in Albania, the KLA had access to looted arsenals.

As a result of the impasse in the Security Council due to the Russian Federation's formal support for Serbia, NATO for the first time employed its status as a regional organization recognized by the United Nations to try and bring peace to the region. After a first meeting on 28 May 1998 at foreign minister level, the defence ministers met on 12 June 1998 to consider possible military options. Russian indication that it would veto any Security Council resolution imposing economic sanctions ensured that those imposed would be voluntary only. Although the United States and the European Union reimposed on Yugoslavia restrictions on financial transactions and travel, and ships continued to be visited in the Adriatic, they were not stopped if they insisted on continuing their passages to Montenegrin ports. In the absence of a formal declaration of war, NATO did not consider itself entitled to declare a blockade that would have to impose controls on "neutral" shipping. Instead, NATO turned to air power.

On 23 September the Security Council adopted Resolution 1199 demanding cessation of violence in Kosovo, and an unofficial green light was given for strong measures when Russia's foreign minister, Igor Ivanov, suggested *sotto voce* to Secretary of State Madeleine Albright that "perhaps a threat of force is needed to achieve ... a political settlement." On 13 October NATO issued an activation order for Operation *Determined Force* preparing air forces for limited air strikes and a phased air campaign against Yugoslavia. Throughout the winter, air operations were limited to interdiction of Yugoslav military flights over Kosovo, while international observers attempted to monitor a peace, but the uneasy quiet was broken by the Kosovo Liberation Army. This led to reprisals by the Serbian authorities. A conference was assembled in February 1999 at Château Rambouillet but no agreement was reached.[34] According to U.S. Naval War College professor Andrew L. Stigler, it was generally believed that a few days of demonstrative bombing would bring Milošević to concede, or at least to deter further atrocities. When continued atrocities led to the mass exodus of hundreds of thousands of

Kosovars, intense air bombardment was commenced, on 24 March 1999, against the Yugoslav army in Kosovo and eventually against infrastructure targets throughout Yugoslavia and in Belgrade. The failure of demonstrative action forced an intensification of the air effort. The USS *Theodore Roosevelt* battlegroup was diverted to the Adriatic, where she was joined by a British and a French carrier. The *Roosevelt* air wing flew over 3,000 sorties, and the British attack submarine HMS *Splendid* launched *Tomahawk* cruise missiles. Amongst the first targets were Yugoslavia's two oil refineries. The Yugoslav army proved to be well able to survive the seventy-eight days of air attacks, remaining in positions of concealment, but the bombardment of the capital eventually led to the Yugoslav government agreeing to evacuate Kosovo.[35] The dénouement was facilitated by an agreement with Russia that led to Moscow putting pressure on Belgrade, and the Security Council passing Resolution 1244 creating a "transitional administration."[36]

The Canadian Armed Forces participated in the action with eighteen CF-18s deployed to Aviano in Italy, flying a total of 678 combat sorties and delivering 532 bombs, including 361 laser-guided five-hundred and two-thousand-pound bombs, all without loss to Canadian aircrew and aircraft.[37] Paul Mitchell writes that "NATO fought under considerable constraints, which Yugoslav forces did not share. Intense political pressure was applied to minimise casualties (friendly, enemy and civilian) and attacks on civil infrastructure, and rapidly to halt ethnic cleansing. The tensions between NATO's wartime objectives were a product of the tangled negotiations that ultimately brought the alliance to the first use of force in its long history." The United States had not ratified Protocol One of the Geneva Convention prohibiting military operations that inflicted civilian casualties disproportionate to military necessity, and accordingly only treated it as "customary law" that did not affect the standards the United States regarded as appropriate.[38]

✦ ✦ ✦

The participation of the Canadian navy in the enforcement of the embargo against Yugoslavia makes it a matter of national interest to determine its effectiveness, and legality. The collateral damage inflicted on the Yugoslav people did not approach that suffered by the people of Iraq, and may not be disproportionate to the objectives of the United Nations, as enforced by NATO forces. Whether the Canadian government possessed the expertise needed to make that judgment, however, is far from certain. Clearly there is a moral requirement for the Canadian government to understand the potential of its actions, and it is in keeping with historic use of economic weapons that it should be the responsibility of the navy, or of a department of Economic Warfare were one to be created, to maintain that level of knowledge.

David Cortright and George Lopez noted that "the sanctions weakened rather than helped the progressive forces opposed to Miloševic while strengthening the hands of criminals and extremists." Nevertheless, "the desire to lift sanctions was a driving force of Serb diplomacy."[39] The report drawn up for the secretary general following a Round Table conference on the Yugoslav sanctions that was held at Copenhagen on 24 and 25 June 1996 opened with the strong statement that the sanctions against Yugoslavia and later against those parts of Bosnia and Herzegovina under Bosnian Serb control had been "remarkably effective. They modified the behaviour of the Serbian party to the conflict and may well have been the single most important reason for the Government in Belgrade changing its policies and accepting a negotiated peace agreement in Dayton ... These sanctions were – unlike the peacekeeping and humanitarian assistance operations – the only strategic instrument of the United Nations to contain the conflict and restore peace and security in the region, not involving the use of armed force."[40]

Many lessons were learned during the Bosnian strife. The Copenhagen Round Table conference attributed the degree of compliance effected by the sanctions against the fragmenting Yugoslavia to the "unique and unprecedented formula of coordinated inter-institutional, international cooperation at the regional level in support of national Governments in their endeavour to observe the mandatory measures taken by the Security Council," and the "swift implementation and strict enforcement of the mandatory measures taken by the Security Council," which was "important in reducing the risk of unnecessary deterioration of the humanitarian situation in the target State as well as limiting the special economic side effects for third countries, in particular the neighbouring countries." An important part of the Round Table's recommendations were "aimed at fine-tuning the instrument of economic sanctions and alleviating unintended human suffering by the civilian population ... The Security Council, in drafting its resolutions imposing sanctions, could make provisions to ensure that appropriate conditions are created to allow an adequate supply of humanitarian goods to reach the civilian population and to provide for exceptions on humanitarian grounds. Guidelines for the definition of these humanitarian exceptions could be incorporated in the texts of the resolutions."[41]

The United Nations Office for the Coordination of Humanitarian Affairs prepared a report: "Towards More Humane and Effective Sanctions Management: Enhancing the Capacity of the United Nations System," in which it noted that Secretary-General Boutros Boutros-Ghali in his 1995 supplement to *An Agenda for Peace* characterized sanctions as a "blunt instrument" and asked whether "suffering inflicted on vulnerable groups in the target country is a legitimate means of exerting pressure on political leaders." Similar concern was also expressed by the International Red Cross/Red Crescent, and by UNICEF. The report endorsed the recommendation of the Copenhagen Round Table conference that a "pre-assessment" should be made of the humanitarian consequences of sanctions in particular circumstances, but also noted the value of the implementation of sanctions rapidly to achieve maximum political effect before the full humanitarian impact is felt. It left the paradox of systemic sanctions unresolved: "Conventional sanctions theory holds that political change is directly proportional to economic hardship. The greater the damage caused by sanctions, the theory holds, the higher the probability of attaining the stated political objectives. This understanding fails to account for the complex and often contradictory ways in which sanctions affect the internal political dynamics of a targeted society. In many episodes, there is no direct mechanism by which hardship is translated into political change."[42]

The secondary Canadian objective of rebuilding her diplomatic position in Europe following the military withdrawal from Germany may have been promoted to some extent by her participation in Operation *Sharp Guard*, and by participation in UNPROFOR, but greater importance must be given to the fact that in the course of the decade NATO began to welcome former Warsaw Pact countries into its ranks, with Poland, Hungary, and the Czech Republic joining in 1999. The Canadian withdrawal may have been a little precipitant, but in retrospect it appears to have been the right one and one not inimical to European interests. It would be morally questionable to suggest that the sufferings of Yugoslav people during the period of the embargo could ever be justified by any diplomatic advantage gained by Canada vis-à-vis her allies.

The utility or otherwise of sanctions is fundamentally connected to their impact on public health and security. It can be argued that the sanctions imposed on the several states of the former Yugoslavia, while important in detaching Belgrade from the Bosnian Serbs, otherwise intensified the conflict; that under the stress of sanctions communities already in peril fragmented into competitors for increasingly scarce resources. Even a decade after the termination of sanctions against Serbia, in 2006, World Health Organization statistics indicate that the gross national income per capita in Serbia was only three-eighths of that in the former Yugoslavian state of Slovenia. It might have been supposed that the embargo on military supplies was a positive contribution to peace building, but in fact it was seriously protested as placing a greater burden on the legitimate forces of the Croatian and Bosnian successor states than it did on the Serbian militias, which enjoyed the backing of the Yugoslav National Army. It also appears that the weapons embargo was systematically violated by several intelligence services, including the U.S. Pentagon, which provided arms for the Bosnian Muslims when the mujahideen veterans of the Afghani resistance to the Soviet Union called in the debts owed them by the United States. The denials made at the time, that orders given to U.S Navy ships participating in *Sharp Guard* not to intercept shipping into Croatian ports extended to facilitating Croatian and Bosnian importation of arms, have not stood the test of time.[43]

It is evident that sanctions proved inadequate to stop the internal strife in Croatia and Bosnia. The crisis had also shown that the structure of traditional "peacekeeping" operations were not suitable to questions of civil war. Something more robust was required to prevent flagrant attacks against personal security, and in this instance the use of air power to disarm the Bosnian-Serb militia, and to coerce Belgrade to submit to the establishment of an interim administration in Kosovo, proved to be the decisive strategy. Despite the unprecedented use of "smart" ordnance, however, the aerial bombardments were not effected without collateral damage. Their relative effectiveness in the circumstance may be held to justify them in terms of just-war theory, but nonetheless the damage they caused cannot be ignored.

Lloyd Axworthy, as Canada's foreign minister from 1996 to September 2000, promulgated a new rationale for the existence of the Canadian Armed Forces.[44] Refocusing Canadian defence upon the concept of human security, he abandoned what Joseph Jockel and Joel Sokolsky refer to as the "shop worn" concept of national interest. A Department of Foreign Affairs concept paper in 1999 defined the Human Security policy as giving priority to "safety for people from both violent and nonviolent threats ... It is an alternative way of seeing the world, taking people as its point of reference, rather than focusing on the security of territory or governments." "With his human security concept," write Jockel and Sokolsky, Axworthy "paved the way for nothing short of rescuing Canadian defence policy from military irrelevance and strategic sterility."

This new defence philosophy requires a higher level of intellectual and political leadership to formulate policies around what Michael Ignatieff would later make a central tenet – "the lesser of evils." NATO bombing of Serbian army positions and selected targets in Belgrade was a lesser evil than the toleration of atrocities. The concept lay behind Axworthy's leadership in the Ottawa treaty process in 1999 banning the use, production, stockpiling, and transfer of anti-personnel mines. It was also to justify Canadian participation in UN operations to suppress the chaos that followed the independence of East Timor in August 1999.

In 2000, when Canada was a non-permanent member of the Security Council and occupied the revolving presidency of the Council, Foreign Minister Axworthy exercised his responsibility by organizing a meeting to discuss the concept of operations when sanctions are ordered – especially with respect to whether time limits should be embedded in resolutions ordering sanctions – and whether sanctions committees should work by majority vote. This reflected the experience of the Iraq sanctions, which lacked such a time limit and hence could not be altered or ended without the agreement of all the permanent members with veto power. It was realistic to take into account that the veto can be used as much to prevent the abandonment of flawed policies as it can prevent their adoption – and that it might be in the interest of one or more of the permanent members to extend a flawed strategy if it served its own political purposes. The preference of some of the permanent members to manage sanctions with *ad hoc* committees, rather than to establish a permanent UN organization for the purpose, is consistent with a side-agenda to maximize their individual power.

In 2005 the United Nations World Summit final communique, crafted by Axworthy and Secretary General Kofi Annan, included recognition of the responsibility of nations to protect their citizens, and of the International Community to do so if national governments failed in their obligation, although no mention was made of a possible international resort to force.[45] At the time Mitchell sounded a subdued note: "the plain reluctance of developed states to place their troops at risk in support of humanitarian missions indicates the hollowness of the values supposedly underlying their commitments to human security."[46]

Sean Maloney concludes that whatever judgment may be made about the success or failure of the naval blockade in other terms, it was unquestionably a solid demonstration of the value of NATO's policy of interoperability amongst member forces. "It would be extremely difficult for non-NATO countries to conduct this type of operation with the same high level of efficiency over such a protracted period. Forty years of combined NATO training and exercises paid off."[47] Two years after the end of the Kosovo operation, NATO was to be called upon to extend its organizational and command skills to the conduct of a land war in Asia – in Afghanistan.

10

CONSTABULARY ACTION AND INTERNATIONAL LEVERAGE: THE "TURBOT WAR"

The first of the "Three Roles" listed in the 2008 "Canada First Defence Strategy" paper is "Defending Canada": "First and foremost, the Canadian Forces must ensure the security of our citizens and help exercise Canada's sovereignty. Canadians rightly expect their military to be there for them in domestic crises. Furthermore, excellence at home requires the Forces not only to identify threats – such as over-fishing, organized crime, drug- and people-smuggling and environmental degradation – but also to possess the capacity to address them quickly and effectively."

The House of Commons Standing Committee on National Defence and Veterans Affairs in its 1990 report, "Maritime Sovereignty," suggested that "the major challenge confronting Canadian maritime policy may not be 'Soviet submarines' or the 'resupply and reinforcement of Europe,' but rather, the effective control of our coastal waters and the 200-mile economic zone. It is with a concern over our ability to exercise this control that we have undertaken our study of maritime sovereignty."[1] This focus on constabulary activity, however, obscures the place of the navy in the protection of "sovereignty." Just as the Trudeau nationalist image of defence policy was flawed by artificial distinctions between national and international defence challenges, so the Canada First concept does not make explicit that, for the constabulary role of the Canadian navy to be effective, the leverage obtained through active participation in international defence arrangements is fundamental.

The creation of the Canadian navy in 1910 had been facilitated by the resources and experience of the Fisheries Protection Service, and the navy was intended in part to support the operations of the civilian service, but not to replace it. The fisheries cruiser *Canada* was employed as the navy's first training ship, and was commissioned in the navy in 1915, but returned to civilian service in 1919. In the interwar years the government civilian service continued to grow and develop. In 1930 the Department of Marine and Fisheries, which was responsible for the management of Canadian shipping, ports, and canals, as well as the Fisheries Protection Service, became two separate departments, and in 1936 the responsibility for marine transportation shifted to the Department of Transport.

The Royal Canadian Mounted Police began to develop its own marine in the 1920s, and in 1928 it was an RCMP vessel, the *St Roch*, that completed the first transit of the Northwest Passage. In 1932 the RCMP Marine Section was formed to take over the duties of the Department of National Revenue Preventive Services. During the war its ships and personnel were transferred to the Canadian navy, but it was re-established in 1945. It was made into a division of the force in 1947 with a headquarters in Halifax, but has subsequently been broken up to service coastal districts more effectively. In January 1962, in the wake of a marine tragedy outside Vancouver in May 1959, when a Norwegian freighter, the *Ferngulf*, caught fire and the Vancouver fireboat refused to answer, the Department of Transport fleet was transferred to a new Canadian Coast Guard which was given responsibility for marine safety, including icebreaking. When the Canadian Forces were amalgamated in 1968 the Maritime commanders on the two coasts, and the Air Transport commanders at Trenton and Edmonton, were given responsibility for coordinating search and rescue. The proliferation of marine services became a focus of attention of several governmental commissions seeking greater efficiency, beginning with the Glassco Commission in 1963. The question of consolidation of marine services was looked at again in the 1970 Audette Report, the 1987 Nielsen Task Force, and the 1990 Treasury Board investigation known as the Osbaldeston Report.

Perhaps the concern was exaggerated. The Canadian navy had never been relieved of its responsibility for the security of Canadian waters. It was a duty, however, which it rarely needed to carry out. Its heavy commitments to NATO and to continental defence, the technical requirements of regulatory and safety duties, and the sparse instances of serious challenges to the constabulary authority of the Canadian marine forces in the course of the twentieth century reduced the priority the navy gave to close support of civilian services. Its job remained that of providing distant cover for the civilian services, and the Cold War had strengthened its ability to do so. The very close service relationship that developed between the Canadian navy and the U.S. Navy, in order to meet the common enemy, helped to ensure that the Americans would avoid any situation in which their navy would appear to confront that of Canada. It went further; it added the U.S. Navy to the resources Canada could look to should it be faced with any major threat to its constabulary authority or coastal security. Partnerships with the U.S. Navy and with European navies in the post–Cold War era continued to provide leverage in support of Canadian sovereign control.

That partnership between the United States and Canada dampened the dispute over the maritime boundary in the Gulf of Maine. According to Robert Hunter, who was later to serve as U.S. ambassador to NATO, in 1978 "the Canadian Navy" moved a marker in the Gulf and the U.S. Navy wanted to make an issue of it at the summit meeting of the North Atlantic Council at which he was serving as director. This, he writes, he prevented. The dispute was taken to the International Court of Justice at the Hague, which made a ruling in 1984 that largely accepted the Canadian claim, although both countries excluded ownership of Machias Seal Island from the adjudication, and its status remains unresolved.[2]

The Canadian Navy/Maritime Command possesses many assets that can contribute to regulatory action. These include not only ships capable of extended periods on station but also their onboard helicopters, shore-based fixed-wing maritime patrol aircraft, and signals intelligence. Through effective use of the transit of ships and aircraft to perform military roles, the footprint of Canadian regulatory agencies can be increased at virtually no cost. In what was to become an important development, the Canadian submarine HMCS *Ojibwa* was employed in fisheries surveillance at the junction between Canadian and American economic zones, the "Hague Line," in the Gulf of Maine 5–12 March 1993. In September 1994 HMCS *Okanagan* conducted a fisheries patrol at the Tail of the Grand Banks. According to Commander Laurence M. (Larry) Hickey who commanded *Okanagan*, similar patrols have been conducted from time to time, and have a deterrent effect on fisheries violators.[3] The use of extremely expensive naval units, and perhaps especially the use of submarines, for such purposes will always have a different significance in international politics than is the case with civilian services.

Outright defiance of Canadian constabulary authority has been sparse indeed. In December 1989 an American fishing vessel, the *Concordia*, was intercepted fishing in Canadian waters by HMCS *Saguenay*. The American vessel deliberately rammed *Saguenay*, and after making certain she had not holed her, made off. It took two hours for *Saguenay* to obtain permission to fire warning shots, which only led *Concordia* to dowse her lights. No attempt was made to board the vessel in the dangerous sea state then prevailing, and she successfully escaped into American waters, where she was seized by the U.S. Coastguard and interned.[4] In another instance, the French Navy was employed in August 1992 to enforce a French interpretation of the agreement reached under the Law of the Sea convention respecting the economic zone of the French islands of St Pierre and Miquelon. A Canadian scallop fleet was escorted outside the boundary despite the agreement between France and Canada over the shared fishery resources.[5] The Canadian navy did not become involved. Following the *Concordia* incident, the Canadian and United States governments entered into a reciprocal enforcement agreement. This made evident the mutual respect that existed between the two countries.

❖ ❖ ❖

The events of the so-called Turbot War with Spanish fishermen, which reached its climax in March and April 1995 on the Nose and Tail of the Grand Banks, can be seen as indication of the continued effectiveness of Canadian naval strategy in co-opting allied support to backstop Canadian constabulary action at sea.[6] In this melodrama, identification of a threat to fishery stocks was initially and rather belatedly reached by a civilian agency, the Department of Fisheries, supported by the reconnaissance commitment of the Canadian air force Maritime Command, and doubtless by Canadian Armed Forces signals intelligence. The initial response was made by the civilian service, under purely national authorization. On 2 April 1994 a Canadian-registered but Panamanian-flagged trawler, the *Kristina Logos*, was seized by fisheries officers, and on 10 May the Canadian fisheries minister, Brian Tobin, introduced legislation to give Canada the power to make regulations governing the conservation of fish stocks that straddle Canadian and international waters. The Coastal Fisheries Protection Act empowered fisheries officers to board and arrest foreign vessels violating conservation measures. The European Union protested that Canada had no right to regulate fishing in international waters, but on 28 July fisheries officers arrested two American draggers harvesting scallops in international waters off Newfoundland.

On 23 September 1994 the North Atlantic Fisheries Organization (NAFO) decided to set a much lower quota for the turbot fishery on the

Grand Banks, reduced by over 50 percent to 27,000 tons, but Spain and Portugal abstained from the vote. NAFO further reduced the quotas on 1 February 1995, limiting the European catch to 3,400 tons and granting Canada 16,300. This discrepancy was based on historic catch levels, but it led to an angry protest from the European Union. When on 14 February Tobin demanded that the European fishermen leave the Banks, the European Fisheries Commissioner, Emma Bonino, said NAFO's allocation was unfair and that the European boats would continue their operations. On 3 March Tobin introduced tightened regulations under the Coastal Fisheries Protection Act, banning the Spanish and Portuguese boats from the Nose and Tail of the Bank, and authorizing DFO officers to arrest them. Prime Minister Jean Chrétien telephoned the president of the European Commission, Jacques Santer, to explain the necessity for the action and suggest a sixty-day fishing moratorium while negotiations were conducted, but on 6 March the EU Foreign Affairs Council returned a strongly worded rejection.[7] On 7 March Tobin announced that Canadian Coast Guard vessels, backed by a naval destroyer, were patrolling the Nose and Tail of the Grand Banks with orders to intercept the fishermen.[8]

The threat of coast guard action was enough to persuade half the fishing vessels to leave the grounds, but about fifteen returned and on 9 March, Royal Canadian Mounted Police forcibly boarded and seized a Spanish trawler, the *Estai*. According to a later Federal Court account, "The first attempt to board the *Estai* was actively resisted by those on board, who threw the protection officers' boarding ladder into the sea and cut the *Estai*'s [trawl] warps to make the *Estai* more mobile." The Fisheries vessel *Cape Roger* gave chase, and employed a water cannon and warning shots, before the Estai's captain, Enrique Davila Gonzalez, stopped. "Boarding craft and armed boarding teams were immediately mobilized on board and along side three (3) or four (4) of the Canadian ships. Armed boarding teams, perhaps including members of the RCMP emergency response team, were prepared and proceeded to the *Estai*, under the illumination of flares. They boarded without incident."[9] The European Union immediately protested and threatened economic sanctions, and *The Times* of London noted that "Canada's unilateral action could be perceived as an act of war."

On 12 March the *Estai* was escorted to St John's, where Captain Gonzalez was charged with illegal fishing and resisting arrest. He was granted bail to appear in court on 20 April, and the trawler was released on a $500,000 bond. At a news conference on 13 March Tobin revealed that three-quarters of the *Estai*'s catch were baby fish, and when on 16 March navy divers recovered the *Estai*'s net cut loose during the confrontation with the RCMP, it was found that the mesh was 15 mm smaller than the Canadian (but not European) legal minimum of 115 mm, and that inside it was an inner net with a mesh of only 80 mm. On 21 March the Spanish naval patrol vessel *Vigia* arrived on the Banks to monitor developments, to be joined on the 30th by the *Serviola*, but on the 26th the crew of a Canadian coast guard vessel used a warp cutter to cut loose the nets of the *Pescamaro Uno*. Peter Haydon has suggested that this action was unauthorized by Cabinet, and that it indicates that the Coast Guard is unsuited for any role in gunboat diplomacy.[10] There is some diplomatic value, however, in the distinction between the routine measures undertaken by the civilian coast guard and the operational actions of the navy.

This contact phase of the encounter with European Community fishermen was the easy part. The Canadian action had indeed been virtually an act of war, although the Canadian federal court was to rule on 26 July 2005 that Canada's actions were lawful when it seized the *Estai*.[11] In the immediate aftermath of the dramatic events it was necessary to obtain a degree of legitimacy from the international community if they were to lead to any permanent solution to the problem. The diplomatic activity pursued by the Canadian government at the United Nations, where Tobin displayed the *Estai*'s net on 28 March, and at Brussels where it was necessary to deflect the threat of sanctions and obtain agreement to conservation measures, was crucial. Canadian diplomats fanned out to present Canada's case, and found very strong support in British fishing ports. As early as 17 March *The Times* had published a column headed "Canada Comes of Age," in which Bernard Levin implied that Tobin was a latter-day Sir Francis Drake confronting Spaniards reeking of stale garlic, and on 28 March it editorialized that: "Whatever the niceties of international fishing rights, it has been hard not to cheer on the Newfoundlanders in the transatlantic squabbles of the past few weeks." On 30 March it was reported that London had vetoed any possibility of economic sanctions against Canada, objecting "to the form and the style of the language used, which seemed more likely to inflame relations further at a time when we were trying to negotiate a solution," and on 31 March the British prime minister, John Major, explicitly indicated his support for Canada. Tobin remarked that it was the support for Canada's action amongst the British public which forced Major's hand. On 7 April Britain vetoed a European Union condemnation of Canada. Britain's cool attitude to the EU commissioners was shared to varying degrees by other governments, especially those of Ireland, Denmark, and Germany. Robert Hunter says he prevented the Spanish and Canadian ambassadors to NATO bringing the dispute up during an informal NATO luncheon on the grounds that problems between member nations were no concern of the alliance.[12]

Diplomacy, however, was not enough. The efforts of the Canadian government to obtain agreement to a conservation regime became bogged down, even after Spain was given a sweetener of the largest share of the turbot quota for 1995, after an offer had been made to drop the charges against the *Estai*, and after it had been agreed to repeal the national legislation under which the *Estai* had been captured. The European presidency, held by France, could not obtain a Spanish signature. A policy of toleration was extended to the continued presence of the Spanish fishing fleet in the area of the Banks; it had even done some fishing under the very close surveillance of the Canadian Coast Guard. Nonetheless, there was a riot in Madrid that underlined the problems faced by the Spanish government. In response, Canada played the naval card.

From the beginning of the encounter with the *Estai* there had been rumours that the Spanish government was prepared to send a missile-armed frigate to the Banks, and on 29 March *The Times* reported that a frigate was preparing to sail immediately to the northwest Atlantic, where the ocean patrol vessel *Serviola* would arrive the next day. A spokesman at the Defence Ministry in Madrid was reported to have said their task was "to stop the harassment, boarding and capture of the Spanish fishing boats by the Canadians" but that "they are expressly forbidden to use arms." Three days later, on 1 April, Tobin indicated at a news conference that a Canadian submarine was assisting in surveillance of the Spanish fishing fleet, and that he was in favour of the acquisition of the surplus British *Upholder* class submarines. This seems to have been part of a deception plan that capitalized on the 1993 and 1994 trial use of submarines to monitor the Gulf of Maine and Tail of the Bank fisheries. Laurence Hickey writes that "in the lead up to" the turbot crisis, "*Okanagan*, with a fisheries conservation and protection officer aboard, patrolled the Grand Banks conducting surveillance and collecting information on foreign-flagged vessels that were pushing the envelope of the groundfish moratorium. The photographs that [he] took through *Okanagan's* periscopes were published around the world."[13] By April 1995 the photographs were six months old. Not content with a public warning, the Canadian navy used the NATO Submarine Operating

Authority (SUBOPAUTH) reporting system to issue a Notice of Intention to station a submarine patrol off the Grand Banks.[14] You may be sure that Madrid was more interested in the military potential of the submarine than they were in its value as a fishery survey ship. The warning was clear, but ambiguous.

On 14 April 1995, with the fisheries negotiations stalled, Gordon Smith of the Department of Foreign Affairs warned the French and Spanish ambassadors that Canada intended to resume enforcement action. Foreign Affairs Minister André Ouellet, who Roy MacLaren, the minister for international trade, writes had been on holiday with instructions not to be disturbed, informed President Santer that a letter was required indicating acceptance of the deal.[15] HMCS *Gatineau* and *Nipigon* were ordered to the Banks to provide support for the Coast Guard, and the Spanish Navy was kept informed of their movements. The indication of intent, and obscure menace, proved adequate to the task. On Saturday afternoon, 16 April, Santer faxed Ottawa with the European Union's acceptance of the deal that, although it apparently gave Spain most of the catch, also put European Union and Canadian Fishery Inspection officers on every trawler.

✦ ✦ ✦

This is a classic example of gunboat diplomacy. The direct action taken by the Canadian Coast Guard, and the indication by the Canadian government that such action would be continued if the over-fishing problem were not addressed, imparted the necessary degree of urgency to complicated international negotiation. The deployment of the Canadian navy, as national warships representing the Canadian government and people, brought nearly a century of co-operation for collective defence into the equation. The visit to the Cornish fishing ports by Royce Frith, Canada's high commissioner to Britain, the distribution of Canadian flags, and the photographs which appeared on 12 April of them flying from the Cornish fishing boats were vital ingredients to the successful outcome of the dispute, but the naval operations linked the fisheries crisis to the Canadian naval relationship with the U.S. Navy and the historic relationship with the Royal Navy. These unquantifiable relationships were far more important than the easily assessed power of the Canadian surface, sub-surface, and air units, which amounted only to the tip of the iceberg. It is unclear whether there is a causal relationship between Tobin's indication on 1 April of Canadian interest in finally purchasing the *Upholder* submarines, and Major's indication the day before of London's support for Canada.

The Canadian "gunboats" had begun their diplomacy as far back as the 1870s, by the work of the Marine Police establishing their role in support of Canadian constabulary authority, and further developed it in the 1914–18 war when Canada's determination to support the needs of her neighbours in peace and war was demonstrated in no uncertain way. Canadian naval history throughout the rest of the century continued to express that determination. The obligation had not been earned solely by naval means; Canada's other military commitments and Canada's participation in the whole range of international collective action added to the obligation. However, in the context of maritime conflict it was the naval forces of Canada's friends that would have had to take action. This made the naval element uniquely important. In the "Turbot War," part of the debt was called in. A study I had made of the Anglo-Icelandic "Cod Wars" of the 1960s and 1970s had brought out the lesson that, although forceful action was most effective when it was operationally possible to use it in what James Cable termed definitive action to directly secure the needed end, it was also important that the action be tailored to serve the requirements of purposive force intended to persuade the opposing government to undertake the required action. The best way of achieving that purposive objective was to manage the crisis so as to involve other players with a stake in settlement.[16] Also significant in the outcome of the crisis, apparently, was the network of personal relationships that had been developed between Canadian naval officers and their counterparts in Spain, and elsewhere, through NATO exercises and training.

There was no at-sea confrontation between the Canadian navy and the galleons of Spain, amongst which could be numbered a small aircraft carrier, the *Principe de Asturias*, eight submarines and fifteen frigates, but that was the measure of Canada's successful exercise in gunboat diplomacy. Despite the general support for Spain in the European Union bureaucracy, there was no possibility of any country sending its fleet to support Spanish action, and Spain was hardly likely to act without a nod from Washington, which evidently never came. Messy as were the events of the turbot War, it is possible to agree with *The Times* that it represented a "coming of age" for Canada – in relation both to the decision of the Canadian government to draw a line in the north Atlantic and to the sophistication of the method employed. The non-event that might be termed "the battle of the Flemish Cap" should be accorded the importance it deserves. The Spanish government asked the International Court of Justice at the Hague to rule on Canada's employment of "extra-territorial force," but the Court refused to make a judgment because the Canadian government had prepared its ground carefully by making a reservation to the Court on 10 May 1994 indicating it would not accept its judgment with respect to "disputes arising out of or concerning conservation and management measures taken by Canada with respect to vessels fishing in [NAFO's] Regulatory Area ... and the enforcement of such measures."[17]

Roy MacLaren writes that the aftershocks from events at sea included the disappointing end of Canada's effort to reach a free-trade agreement with the European Community: "as my old friend from Uruguay Round days, Leon Brittan, the European commissioner for trade, affirmed during a notably chilly visit to Ottawa, EU opponents of transatlantic free trade, especially France over agriculture, lined up behind Spain and Portugal, seizing on the fish war as one more reason why free trade discussions with Canada could not possibly be contemplated."[18] Donald Barry records that "Chrétien expressed his displeasure by cancelling a scheduled meeting with Brittan, and Ouellet issued a statement defending Ottawa's actions."[19] How much the turbot episode really affected Canadian trade relations is not clear. Trade is not a charitable act, and European interest in free trade with Canada has never shown much strength. Perhaps the hope of a free trade deal with the EU had already been lost when the Canadian garrisons were withdrawn from Germany, or even earlier when Trudeau terminated Canada's direct participation in the nuclear defence of Europe. It could also be asked whether the perspective from the Department of International Trade tended to emphasize the interests of central Canada over those of the coastal fisheries. Hopefully, such events will be rare – and when they do occur it is inevitable that the outcome will not be entirely satisfactory. Barry suggests that Canada-European Union diplomacy was back on track by December 1996.

The question of the proliferation of Canadian maritime forces was again addressed by the Senate Standing Committee on National Security and Defence in 2003. This time a degree of consolidation was made, when in December the Coast Guard and Fisheries Protection Service were administratively combined within a new department of Fisheries and Oceans Canada [DFO].[20]

A report, "Breaking New Ground," released on 1 September 2005, noted that: "Compliance [to fisheries regulations] improved for a short period after the 'turbot war' of 1995, as new NAFO enforcement measures were adopted by the Contracting Parties to the NAFO Convention. However, by the end of the 1990s and the beginning of 2000, non-compliance had again increased to, and remained at, a level that Canada deemed unsatisfactory ... Concern about the scale of Illegal, Unregulated and Unreported (IUU) fishing in the NRA increased to the point that Canada augmented its enforcement regime in 2004. Three enforcement vessels now back up frequent aerial surveillance to maintain a constant presence in the area. The numbers of non-Canadian vessels fishing in the NAFO area in the first quarter of 2005 declined by 50% from the same period in 2004, apparently as a consequence of the increased enforcement."[21] Intense negotiations were also undertaken by DFO to obtain more effective agreements amongst fishery nations, and to strengthen NAFO. On 22 September 2006, a new, and possibly more effective, international regulatory regime was announced by Loyola Hearn, the minister of fisheries and oceans.[22]

11

CONTINENTAL DEFENCE AND GLOBAL POLICING

The second of the three categories described in the 2008 "Canada First" policy paper is that of "Defending North America": "Delivering excellence at home," it stated, "also helps us contribute to the defence of North America in cooperation with the United States, Canada's closest ally. Given our common defence and security requirements, it is in Canada's strategic interest to remain a reliable partner in the defence of the continent." By that date, however, the Canadian navy's commitment to "Continental Defence" had been transmogrified into the partnership with the U.S. Navy in world policing – generally in the context of multilateral operations. In February 1991 U.S. secretary of the navy Lawrence Garrett told the United States Congress that the Maritime Strategy was no longer the underlying plan for the defence of North America, and of NATO: "If our strategy for the cold war was one of containment, our new strategy should be one of stability focusing on peacetime presence and regional conflict."[1] The collapse of the Soviet Union, and virtual disappearance of the Soviet navy from the oceans, had left little of the Cold War direct naval threat to North America, but also left turmoil around the world. Distant water-policing operations, including the provision of humanitarian relief to failed states and to communities affected by natural disaster, become a regular commitment for the Canadian navy. Although the al Qaeda terrorist attacks on the World Trade Center in New York, and on the Pentagon in Washington, on 11 September 2001 led to the Canadian navy's most dramatic operational partnership with the U.S. Navy, it was only a realization of teamwork in global affairs that had begun eleven years before with the Kuwait crisis, and had included the sanctions operations against Iraq, the Federal Republic of Yugoslavia, and Haiti.

Lt (N) MacKinnon examines a Somalian patient, 1 January 1993.
DND HSC92-849-262

A Canadian naval presence having been established in the Indian ocean as a result of the United Nation's–sponsored sanctions against Iraq, it was a relatively small step to extend the Canadian naval commitment to humanitarian relief in the area. The operational measures taken for the purpose could be considered as participation in the U.S. Navy concepts *From the Sea*, and *Forward from the Sea*, which Norman Friedman says developed the idea of continuous close offshore naval support for lightly armed forces ashore.[2] Security Council Resolution 775 of 28 August 1992 urged member nations to provide Somalia with emergency relief and on 4 September HMCS *Preserver* was issued a warning order to "be prepared to sail in 12 days to support the Army off East Africa." The choice of an Auxiliary Oiler Replenishment vessel for the task was based on her ability to transport heavy stores and support the 500-man advanced infantry detachment. Her three *Sea King* helicopters were to prove invaluable for offloading supplies and men over an open beach.

They were also to be valuable for the force extraction that became necessary. In November 1992 a name was given to the Somalian relief force, Operation *Deliverance*. Two days before *Preserver*'s arrival on 5 December the Security Council passed Resolution 794 "determining that the magnitude of the human tragedy caused by the conflict in Somalia ... constitutes a threat to international peace and security," and calling on all member states "that were in a position to do so, to provide military forces and to make additional contributions, in cash or in kind."

Although the subsequent staff analysis characterized the operation as neither well planned nor well focused, and Canadian Forces had no recent experience of mounting similar littoral operations, it was carried out relatively successfully.[3] This was the first occasion in which a ship of the Canadian navy provided accommodation and tactical support for a joint task force commander and his staff, and this was Canada's first truly "joint" combat mission since the Second World War. The availability of the shipboard communications suite and accommodation enabled the Canadian contingent to establish themselves more rapidly and securely. The mission proceeded smoothly, establishing hospitals, schools, and bridges, and training the Somali police. *Preserver* also provided support for warships from Australia, India, France, Italy, Turkey, and the United States, supplying water and fuel, making available its medical facilities, and providing a communications link. The later enquiry concluded that it had been an unacceptable risk sending an AOR to anchor off a hostile and unsecured beach without an escort, but *Preserver* left the theatre safely on 6 March 1993.

The Somalia mission was to end badly, when Canadian soldiers of the *Airborne Regiment* set out food as bait and on 4 March 1993 shot dead two Somali scavengers. On 16 March a Somali teenager found nearby, Shidane Arone, was beaten to death – crying out "Canada, Canada." In the enquiry that followed, Canadian military leadership disgraced itself by attempting a cover-up. Following a further scandal over hazing rituals, the *Airborne Regiment* was abolished. On 4 May 1993 the United Nations for the first time ever assumed direct control of a military force in Somalia, which was named Operation *Continue Hope*, and its lack of resources and experience became all too evident. But none of that involved the Canadian navy.[4]

Although the Somalian experience had ended badly, it was also seen as an indication of a larger trend. Following the return of the Liberal party to power in the October 1993 election, the new minister of national defence, David Collenette, ordered a review of Canadian defence by a Special Joint Committee of the House of Commons and the Senate. After extensive public consultation with the objective of finding a basis for defence planning following the end of the Cold War, Collenette published the 1994 White Paper on Defence. Sean Maloney was told by departmental officer that the government accepted the need to continue "doing its part to ensure global security," and that it rejected the idea of "an investment in forces capable only of constabulary operations." The difficulty of understanding just what sort of future was to be expected was recognized by a new but equivocal policy indicating a determination not to "participate in every multilateral operation," but nevertheless "to remain in a position to play a meaningful role" in global security affairs. As Rear Admiral G.L Garnett had put it in his Keynote Address to the Lester B. Pearson Canadian International Peacekeeping Training Centre, 1 September 1995, "virtually all activities that can be undertaken by navies neither fully at war, nor entirely tied up along the wall, *could* be called maritime peace support operations."[5]

Budgetary limitations, however, driven in part by intelligence that the Soviet navy had largely disappeared from the seas, made a mockery of the goal. In 1998 the navy finally accepted the sweetheart deal offered by the British government for the transfer of its four decommissioned *Upholder* class submarines that had been designed as conventionally powered partners for its *Trafalgar* class nuclear attack submarines, with which they shared some capabilities. Discussion of the possible purchase of ships of this class had begun in 1985, but was discontinued when the nuclear submarine project was adopted. The Royal Navy had put the class up for sale in 1994, a year before Brian Tobin indicated Canadian interest in their acquisition, but it had taken another three years before government approval was forthcoming. Aaron Jackson suggests that the publication in 1997 by Maritime Command of a new policy paper, *Adjusting Course: A Naval Strategy for Canada*, was intended largely to support procurement of the British *Upholder* submarines. If so, it proved effective. For their service in the Canadian navy they were redesignated as the *Victoria* class.[6] They were, however, the only additional units acquired for the Canadian navy. During the delivery from Scotland in 2004 of the last of the class to be transferred to Canada, HMCS *Chicoutimi* experienced an electrical fire when water came onboard while transiting on the surface. The vessel was taken out of service awaiting refitting in the period 2010–12. *Victoria* also suffered a fire, during an extended refit at Esquimalt, when a DC feed was supplied in error and caused "catastrophic damage" to part of its electrical system. *Victoria* only emerged from dockyard hands in early 2011, when she began what was to have been six-months of technical readiness inspections and work-ups.[7]

As Sean Maloney and Douglas Bland put it in 2003: "the Liberal government set out as a major element of its 1994 defence policy to maintain the Canadian Armed Forces as a national institution that would help to support Canada's place in the world of international security affairs.

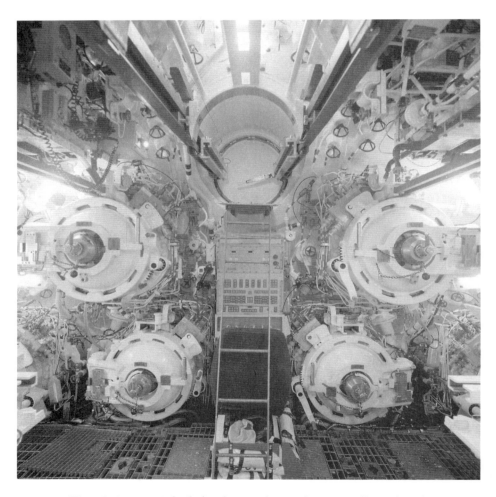

HMCS *Victoria* (SSK 876), built for the Royal Navy by Cammell Laird, Birkenhead, in 1987–91 as HMS *Unseen*, as a diesel electric partner to the *Trafalgar* class nuclear attack submarine. Transferred to the Canadian Navy in 1998 in a sweetheart deal. After extensive refitting *Victoria* commenced work-ups in early 2011. Seen here is the Torpedo Flat, 18 April 2002. DND BR816-179

Top: HMCS *Victoria* (SSK 876), Combat Control Room, 18 April 2002. DND BR816-188

Bottom: HMCS *Victoria* (SSK 876), Search Periscope, 18 April 2002. DND BR816-194

The failure, however, to adjust adequately to the practicalities of their actual policies, for instance, by doing less in international affairs as conditions changed, may have fatally damaged this policy objective."[8] To meet the stated goal, increases in personnel strength, especially for the army, were required, and investment needed in appropriate equipment for the sort of operations that the Canadian Forces were to be tasked with in the coming decade. In fact the forces' strength dropped under Jean Chrétien's leadership below the nominal 60,000 budgeted, and the government did not return it to that level until 2001 under pressure from the military and the public. As a consequence of Chrétien's pre-election posturing the EH-101 helicopter for the navy was cancelled. Not until 1998 was the Aurora Incremental Modernization Project (AIMP) initiated to upgrade LRPA aircraft and sensor electronics, and not until 2004 was it announced that Sikorsky CH-148 *Cyclone* helicopters would be acquired for the navy, a decade after the cancellation of the EH-101, and forty-one years after the acquisition for the Royal Canadian Navy of the CH-124 *Sea King* helicopter.

Despite the falling resources, the government continued to commit many of those it had to the Indian Ocean/Persian Gulf area, and the navy took another step toward transnational partnership with the U.S Navy. The integration of HMCS *Ottawa* into the USS *Abraham Lincoln* Battle Group on her arrival in late 1998 marked a milestone in the Canadian navy's relationship with the U.S. Navy. John H. Noer of the Center for Naval Analyses remarked that "the level of operational collaboration has probably not been seen since WWII." One of his colleagues asserted that "nationality was transparent. There was no discernible difference between *Ottawa* and any other ships in the Battle Group." In order to make possible the necessary degree of network capability, *Ottawa* and the ships that followed her to serve in U.S. battle groups were equipped before they sailed from Canada with the latest American command and communications equipment.

In June 1999 Jim Judd, deputy minister of national defence, and General J.M.G. Baril, chief of the defence staff, published *Strategy for 2020*, which indicated their belief that the Canadian Armed Forces should be equipped to provide Canada with "modern, task-tailored, and globally deployable combat-capable forces that can respond quickly to crises at home and abroad, in joint or combined operations. The force structure must be viable, achievable and affordable."[9] When *Regina* returned for a second tour in the Gulf from June to December 1999 it was the beginning of Operation *Augmentation*, which established a regular pattern of Canadian ships being formally incorporated into U.S. Navy/coalition formations.

+ + +

Within months of the publication of *Strategy for 2020*, the need for suitable deployable forces was demonstrated when the United Nations found it necessary to organize a force to stop the violence that broke out in East Timor following an independence vote on 30 August 1999 in the former Portuguese colony. The tiny community had been occupied by Indonesia in 1975, had suffered perhaps 100,000 deaths from civil conflict prior to the referendum, and had then been subjected to a scorched earth campaign by embittered Indonesian militia. The international community had been very reluctant to involve itself, especially because the United States had come to regard Indonesia as a key ally against Communism in Asia. The post-referendum chaos, however, was forcibly brought to the attention of world leaders by journalists. Having determined on 15 September that the situation in East Timor constituted a threat to international peace and security, the Security Council passed Resolution 1264 authorizing the formation of a multilateral force under unified command, INTERFET.[10]

The Australian government, the primary mover of the UN action, immediately offered to lead the force, which they inserted within five days. A Canadian command team was flown out to assess the situation, and Operation *Toucan* was set in motion. Again the auxiliary oiler replenishment vessel, HMCS *Protecteur*, was employed. She arrived off Dili, the capital of East Timor, on 23 October with relief supplies and stores for a company of the *Royal 22nd Regiment* that was put ashore on 28 October from HMAS *Tobruk* on the south side of Timor at Suai. *Protecteur*'s intended role as a medical centre at Dili proved not to be required, so the Canadian Joint Task Force commander, Captain Roger Girouard, was moved ashore and *Protecteur* was employed in supporting INTERFET ships and land forces, ferrying most of their fuel and fresh water from Darwin.[11] Her crew also took part in reconstruction projects that were needed. While the mission was primarily intended as one of humanitarian assistance, it also had political implications, as had the Somalian deployment. It was a demonstration not only of Canadian support for the United Nations but also of Canadian concern for events in Asia. It helped that the lead nation in the operation, Australia, was a Commonwealth partner, and integration of *Protecteur* into the Australian force made it unnecessary to provide her with a Canadian escort ship.[12]

✦ ✦ ✦

Strategy for 2020 emphasized Canada's special relationship with its principal allies in general, and with the United States in particular, and expressed the objective of "ensuring interoperable forces, doctrine and C4I (command, control, communications, computers, and intelligence)." Specifically the expressed intent was to: "1) Manage our interoperability relationship with the US and other allies to permit seamless operational integration on short notice; 2) Develop a comprehensive program to adopt new doctrine and equipment compatible with our principal allies; 3) Expand the joint and combined exercise program to include all environments and exchanges with the US." This force transformation recognized the centrality of the new concept of Network-Centric Warfare, in which enhanced information exchange made it possible for dispersed units to maximize their collective power. The Canadian fleet based on the Pacific coast was able to progress more rapidly in the direction of full interoperability with the U.S. 3rd fleet based at San Diego than was the East coast force, because it employs U.S. Navy doctrine. The Atlantic fleet employs NATO doctrine. All but one of the Canadian ships sent to work with U.S. battle groups as part of Operation *Augmentation* came from the Pacific fleet. Because of the rapid development of the technology employed, it was decided to provide new equipment for each ship being deployed to work the U.S. fleet, and to use end-of-fiscal-year "minor requirements" funds to upgrade that fitted in the ships returning from previous years' tours.

Regina was followed to the Persian Gulf in 2000 and 2001 by *Calgary* (on her second tour), *Charlottetown*, and *Winnipeg*. A Canadian press release in December 2000 remarked on the importance of the experience in ensuring interoperability with Canada's allies and particularly the United States. "It will further strengthen our Navy's relationship with the US Navy and reaffirm our commitment to peace and stability in this region."[13] Laura J. Higgins, who took part in the *Winnipeg* deployment as an observer, reported that *Winnipeg*'s commanding officer, Commander Kelly Williams, told her:

Canada's integration into the carrier battle group in the Persian Gulf means that the Battle Group Commander decides the ship's operational tasks. The US Navy Admiral develops a series of tasks and assigns them to the ship he thinks is most capable of carrying them out ... The Americans approach Gulf deployments slightly differently than Canada. According to Rear-Admiral Terrance Etnyre, Commander USS *Constellation* carrier battle group, operations in the Gulf are viewed as part and parcel of the forward deployment strategy that has characterized American foreign and defence policy objectives for the past decade. In contrast ... Canada's main objective is to contribute to the operation to implement UN-endorsed sanctions. Because of this fundamentally different approach, the American part of the battle group has a much broader task list than does the Canadian contingent.[14]

This on the face of it is a simple enough concept, but the implications of "Network-Centric" operations are comparable to those that had perturbed the early years of the Royal Canadian Navy when the strategic doctrine of global concentration of naval forces for a decisive battle had conflicted with national control of dominion forces. In a document promulgated in 2000 the vice chief of defence staff, Vice-Admiral G.L. Garnett, admitted that the trend toward interoperability "raises concern over the degree to which CF [Canadian Forces] units and Canadian political authorities can retain the ability to make autonomous decisions in future fast-paced combat situations. The trend toward integrated operations and interoperability may create an unintended interdependency if CF units become too enmeshed in Alliance controlled network systems that require automatic linkages of sensor and weapon systems for effective tactical operation."[15]

In 1997 there occurred an incident that has been used as a poster piece supposedly demonstrating the extent to which the Canadian government has lost control of its own forces. In the course of a resource dispute over salmon in British Columbia, and under pressure from environmental activists who objected to U.S. Navy nuclear-powered ships entering Canadian waters, Premier Glen Clark threatened to close the Canadian Forces Maritime Experimental Test Range at Nanoose which is used by the navy, and by the U.S. Navy, to test underwater weapons. Clark proposed to do so by not renewing the British Columbia government license permitting access to the seabed at Nanoose, and the Federal government in return commenced proceedings to expropriate the seabed. In June 1997 Dr Kenneth Calder, the assistant deputy minister (policy), prepared for the minister of national defence a briefing note which suggested that denial of access to CFMETR Nanoose would be "viewed by the US as having a direct impact on their national security interests and may lead to a US response out of proportion to the loss itself. The experience of New Zealand is an example of this type of U.S. response. It has suffered serious sanctions for denying U.S. nuclear ships access to their harbours. In addition to ceasing all defence relations, the U.S. imposed trade restrictions on New Zealand."[16] On 17 December 1999 the Canadian government announced that the agreement with the United States had been renewed for ten years.[17]

✦ ✦ ✦

At the time of the 11 September 2001 attacks the DDG280 Standard Missile armed destroyer HMCS *Iroquois* was at sea off the east coast. She immediately established a data link with North American Air Defense headquarters (NORAD), where Canadian naval officer billets had been established in the late 1990s. It was a Canadian naval officer at NORAD headquarters, Captain Mike Jellinek, who actually ordered North American air defences on alert. In the following weeks and months, measures of Continental Defence remained a high priority, but the emphasis was rapidly put on offensive measures against al Qaeda terrorist leaders anywhere in the world, characterized by President George W. Bush as a "war" on terror. The subsequent campaigns amply demonstrate that in the twenty-first century there is no neat distinction between continental defence and global commitment.

On 12 September, the day after the attacks, the Security Council passed Resolution 1373 recognizing the inherent right of self-defence available to the United States. And on 4 October NATO secretary general Lord Robertson announced that the North Atlantic Council had invoked Article 5 of the Treaty of Washington. Although the groundwork for employing NATO forces outside the "NATO area" had been done twenty years before, Article 5 had never previously been invoked by any nation. Already U.S. and British special forces were operating inside Afghanistan, establishing contact with the warlords of the "Northern Alliance" that was in a permanent state of war with the Taliban government in Kabul. On 20 September, Minister of National Defence Art Eggleton authorized the more than hundred Canadian Forces personnel serving on exchange programs in the United States and with other allied military forces to participate in any operations conducted by their host units in response to terrorist attacks.[18] On 7 October, U.S. and British aircraft began bombing targets in Kabul. That same day, Prime Minister Chrétien stated that Canada would contribute to the international force being formed, and General Ray Henault, the chief of the defence staff, issued warning orders to several Canadian units to prepare to participate in Canadian-named Operation *Apollo*, in support of the American Operation *Enduring Freedom*. Within a week of the 9/11 attacks, Vice-Admiral Ron Buck, then Canadian vice-chief of maritime forces, was authorized to commit a Canadian naval task group consisting of a destroyer (*Iroquois*), an AOR (HMCS *Preserver*), and two frigates (HMCS *Halifax* and *Charlottetown*), with a total of five embarked helicopters. *Halifax* was the first on station, being detached on 8 October from NATO's Standing Naval Force Atlantic (STANAVFORLANT) then at El Ferrol, and the other ships sailed from Halifax on 24 October.[19] Canadian Special Forces also were ordered into action, joining the fight in Afghanistan.[20]

When HMCS *Halifax* was redeployed from STANAVFORLANT to join the American coalition acting against al Qaeda, the distinctions between NATO, Continental Defence, and support for the United Nations, became moot. After making the voyage to the north Arabian Sea, *Halifax* was integrated into the USS *Carl Vinson* carrier battle group to participate in maritime interdiction operations and to perform screening duties. On 17 October the other three ships of the Canadian naval task group made their departure from Halifax to conduct a short series of exercises in Canadian waters and then make the transit to the Arabian sea, where they arrived on 20 November. They had been refitted in ten days with enhanced communications systems. *Charlottetown*, and later *Iroquois*, was incorporated into an American amphibious ready group for escort duties under a Canadian commander, Commodore Drew Robertson. Their task was to protect the American Marine Corp transports that had to be positioned close to the coast of Pakistan in order to be within helicopter ferry range of Afghanistan. On 30 October, the frigate HMCS *Vancouver* deployed from Esquimalt to San Diego, California, for integration training with the USS *John C. Stennis* carrier battle group, following which, on 12 November, *Vancouver* set sail with the battle group from San Diego for southwest Asia via Pearl Harbor. After arriving on station she was employed conducting maritime interdiction operations

(MIO) while enforcing the Iraq sanctions. On 5 December the frigate HMCS *Toronto* departed Halifax to replace HMCS *Halifax* in STANAVFORLANT, which was to be employed in the eastern Mediterranean to release U.S. Navy frigates for service in the Arabian sea.[21]

On 28 December 2001 a detachment of *Aurora* long-range maritime patrol aircraft and *Hercules* transports were deployed to forward bases, "somewhere on the Arabian peninsula." This was *Camp Mirage*, the forward logistics facility located in Dubai, United Arab Emirates. Officially a secret base, it was supplied by Dubai free of rent until the end of October 2010, when a dispute over landing rights in Canada for Emirates and Etihad airways led to Canadian Forces having to relocate rapidly, and expensively.[22]

Halifax was employed escorting supply ships through the Strait of Hormuz to the Persian Gulf oil terminals, and then in monitoring the tanker park off Fujairah in the United Arab Emirates as part of Iraq sanctions enforcement. The need to refrain from port visits to India and Pakistan during a serious confrontation with nuclear potential between those countries, the distance to the ports of the southern Gulf states, and the danger of attack by small craft while in harbour, led to Canadian ships serving record periods of time underway, at sea. Before their rotation out of the theatre, *Vancouver* and *Charlottetown* served at sea for periods of seventy-nine and seventy-five days respectively, and *Halifax* for forty-seven.[23]

The operational role of Canadian naval forces was definitive and purposive, because the overwhelming force brought into the operations area effectively ensured that the airborne invasion of Afghanistan would not be interrupted by regional naval forces. The navies of Iran and Pakistan both contain modern submarines that could have posed a real threat to the task forces, at the heart of which were aircraft carriers providing "lily pad" stages for the delivery of special forces to Afghanistan. The role of the Canadian ships was also expressive, because they demonstrated Canadian partnership with other NATO navies in the American crisis, and their participation in American-led hot-war operations showcased the professional ability of the ships and crews. Because the deterrence against adventures by Islamic Pakistan and Iran was successful, the international naval force did not attract much attention internationally, and not even very much in the United States.

But there were shadows. Richard Clarke is highly critical of the limited scale of the Bush administration's operations in Afghanistan, which gave al Qaeda leaders time to escape into Pakistan and Iran. The con-

Naval Boarding Party from HMCS *Montréal* (FFH 336) alongside MV *Golina* in the Gulf of Oman during Operation *Apollo*, 15 January 2003. DND HSO 35008 do8 Golina.

cern was that they would escape from there back to Saudi Arabia or the Sudan, and it became part of the work of Canadian warships to patrol the Gulf to intercept any who joined the passengers crossing from Iran in fast boats. Ottawa ordered that people apprehended by the Canadian navy should be transferred into the custody of the United States, but it soon became apparent that the practice made Canada an accomplice in the failure of the United States to conform to the Geneva Conventions with respect to the treatment of prisoners. Richard Gimblett reports that Commodore Eric J. Lerhe, who assumed command on the rotation of forces, was careful to assess the value of and source of intelligence before he ordered the detention of people intercepted at sea, crossing from Iran to the Arab Emirates.

American policies in the aftermath of the 9/11 crisis had characteristics that might be likened to anaphylactic shock, the natural immune system reacting so strongly that it becomes a positive danger to the body. Concern about American violation of treaties they had solemnly signed, and indeed for which generations of American statesmen had worked, had begun to cool Canadian-American relations before the end of 2001. A two-page study paper prepared by the Directorate of Strategic Analysis in the Department of National Defence predicted a significantly harder edge to American military action, a global build-up of armaments, large-scale action, and a disposition to ignore international conventions on human rights.[24] The prisoner-of-war issue became a matter of intense controversy in the House of Commons, led by backbench Liberal Member John Godfrey and New Democratic Member Svend Robinson. It contributed to the growing opinion in Canada that American foreign policy was a significant contributing factor to the terrorist attacks, an opinion shared by Clarke and by major liberal American journals.[25] There were similar expressions of concern in European capitals. When in his State of the Union speech on 30 January 2002 President George W. Bush extended his objectives to Iraq, Iran, and North Korea, which he characterized as an "axis of evil," the reaction of America's allies was distinctly cool. At the Prague summit in February 2002 one of Prime Minister Chrétien's aides was overheard referring to Bush as "a moron," an allegation that Chrétien disavowed. In April 2002 Foreign Minister Bill Graham announced that there would be a major government review of Canada's defence and foreign policy in a world dominated by the United States as a "hyperpower."[26]

✦ ✦ ✦

The problems of partnership with the United States became intense when the Bush presidency decided to use the al Qaeda attacks as justification for invading Iraq. The putative justification was Security Council Resolution 1441 of 8 November 2002, which was passed unanimously by the fifteen members and called for the compliance of Iraq with earlier UN resolutions ordering it to destroy all its nuclear, chemical, and biological weapons. But Resolution 1441 had only been passed after intense debate, following which the British ambassador to the United Nations, Sir Jeremy Greenstock, and the American ambassador, John Negroponte, made it clear that the resolution did not automatically justify a resort to war.[27] This reassurance had been echoed by the ambassadors for France, Russia, and China. In March 2003 it became evident that, in light of incomplete reports from the UN weapons inspectors in Iraq, it would be impossible to persuade a majority of the member nations of the Security Council to pass a resolution justifying an assault on Iraq by the American and British armed forces massed in Kuwait and on the

Arabian and Mediterranean seas. In consequence, the U.S. and British governments resolved to act on their own authority, evoking a right of pre-emptive self-defence. President Bush made it clear that a necessary condition for the disarmament of Iraq would be the replacement of its government.

This decision was met with dismay by the Canadian government. Early in 2002 Prime Minister Chrétien had made it clear that Canada would only involve itself in operations against Iraq if clear proof were shown that al Qaeda was using Iraq as a base. In the crisis of March 2003 the Canadian ambassador to the United Nations, Paul Heinbecker, worked hard to find a compromise formula that would see completion of the disarmament of Iraq and restore unity to the Security Council, but Chrétien and Foreign Minister Graham stated that Canada would not participate in an aggressive war to change the government of Iraq.[28]

Chrétien's public refusal to participate in a war not sanctioned by the Security Council led to a crisis in Canadian-American relations, both at the official level and in the media.[29] The prime minister was criticized publicly by the American ambassador to Canada, Paul Cellucci, for refusing to accept American leadership. The account of those days in Cellucci's memoirs goes a long way to substantiate John Holmes's observation twenty-two years earlier that American leaders suffer from an "easy assumption that right-thinking people would recognize US aims as their own."[30] The leader of the official opposition, Stephen Harper, also lashed out at Chrétien: "We should," he declared, "have been there shoulder to shoulder with our allies. Our concern is the instability of our government as an ally. We are playing again with national and global security matters."[31] Hostility to the American war in Iraq was shared by the French and German governments, amongst others, and their opposition to the deployment of American offensive forces to Turkey prevented the United States using NATO as an instrument of its Iraq policy. In Ottawa, however, the arm twisting was effective.

Despite Chrétien's public statements, following a meeting on 17 March at which Deputy Foreign Minister Gaëtan Lavertu formally advised American and British diplomats that Canada would not participate in the Iraq war, Political Director Jim Wright indicated that Canada would provide unofficial military support. "Despite public statements that the Canadian assets in the Straits of Hormuz will remain in the region exclusively to support *Enduring Freedom*, they will also be available to provide escort and will otherwise be discreetly useful to the military effort. The two ships in the Straits now are being augmented by two more enroute, and there are patrol and supply aircraft in the UAE [United Arab Emirates] which are also prepared to 'be useful.' This message," commented the U.S. deputy chief of mission in Ottawa, Stephen R. Kelly, "tracks with others we have heard. While for domestic political reasons and out of a deep-seated Canadian commitment to multilateralism the GOC [government of Canada] has decided not to join in a US coalition of the willing, they will refrain from criticism of our actions, express understanding, and focus their public comments on the real culprit, Iraq. They are also prepared to be as helpful as possible in the military margins."

The commander of Canadian naval forces in the Persian Gulf, Commodore Roger Girouard, assumed responsibility for control and liaison with as many as thirty warships, his command elevated to that of a task force, Task Force 151 (CTF151) reporting directly to the U.S. Coalition commander in Bahrain.[32] The authors of a Canadian Defence Research and Development study of Net-enabled operations, remarked that Girouard's appointment as warfare commander for the Arabian sea theatre of operations was "the first true exercise of operational-level command by a senior Canadian officer since the Second World War" and that "it could not have been accomplished as successfully or as professionally as it transpired but for the employment of networked operations." But they also acknowledge that it was not a true test of Net-centric operations as CTF151 existed specifically to manage the forces of nations that declined to be involved in the Iraq war.[33]

During the "shock and awe" bombardment of Iraq, Cellucci admitted in a speech in Toronto on 25 March 2003 that "ironically, Canadian naval vessels, aircraft and personnel ... will supply more support to this war in Iraq indirectly ... than most of those 46 countries that are fully supporting our efforts there."[34] Until the archives are opened in 2033 it cannot be known for sure that the Cabinet approved these measures. John McCallum, the minister of national defence at the time, later insisted to the CBC that he and his officials had an "extremely long and detailed meeting to make sure that [they] were not in fact committing to help the war in Iraq," but conceded that "what happens on the high seas is not something I can prove or disprove." Eugene Lang, who had been McCallum's chief of staff, confirmed that the Department had earnest internal debate about the difficulty of distinguishing between support for the U.S. actions against al Qaeda and other military operations in the Gulf supporting the invasion of Iraq. If the Canadian navy discreetly went to war in 2003 without formal approval by the government it would be consistent with the precedents set at the time of the Munich agreement and the Cuban Missile crisis, but a better reading would be that the royal prerogative was used to assuage American anger.[35] Parliament may have "decided," or at least approved of the decision to stay out of the war, but it had in fact have been deceived by the administration out of concern for Canadian-American relations.

Canadian officers who played key roles in the American assault on Iraq included a future chief of defence staff, General Walter J. Natynczyk, who was awarded by Governor General Adrienne Clarkson with a Meritorious Service Cross for his "pivotal role in the development of numerous plans and operations [which] resulted in a tremendous contribution ... to Operation *Iraqi Freedom*, and ... brought great credit to the Canadian Forces and to Canada." His service included a year in Iraq, from January 2004, where he served as the deputy director of strategy, policy and plans, and later as the deputy commanding general of the Multi-National Corps (Iraq). More threatening to Canadian democracy was the deployment of Canadian special forces, the JTF2 unit, for aggressive operations under the control of the Canadian executive in a security regimen that makes it virtually impossible for Parliament to exercise any oversight.[36]

The continued participation of Canadian soldiers and airmen in the war raises questions as to whether the independence of Canadian defence policy was entirely illusory. Operation *Apollo* was brought to a close, and the Canadian ships came home, but the question remains an important one. "As with the Cuban Missile Crisis," noted Melanie Graham, acting sub-lieutenant CF in 2004, "with an indecisive government, it is not an unreasonable possibility that professionalism, derived from a close and long-standing Canada-U.S. working naval relationship and a high degree of operational interoperability, might have led to a repeat of the breakdown in civil/military relations."[37] In 1980 John Holmes had written that "one of our reasons for joining NATO was to avoid this dilemma. Partnership with the US in continental defence is one thing, being a small part of an expedition abroad over which we could expect little control is another."[38] NATO, however, was a weak defence against the pressures to join American-led coalitions of the possibly willing. In October 2004 President Bush delivered a speech in Halifax which at once showed his satisfaction that Jean Chrétien had been replaced as prime minister by Paul Martin and gave an American perspective on partnership with Canada: "America always prefers to act with allies at our side, and we're grateful to Canada for working closely with us to confront the challenges of Iran and North Korea. Multilateral organizations can do great good in the world."[39] But the manner in which the partnership worked in the age of net-centric warfare had demonstrated the American preference for unilateralism at the technical level, somewhat muted by the "Nelsonic" brotherhood of naval officers, and unquestioning support at the national level.

✦ ✦ ✦

The momentum for interoperability continued in the following years. In 2004 Commodore Girouard followed up his tour as CTF 151 commander in the Gulf with his role as Sea Combat commander of the RIMPAC exercise involving ships of seven Pacific nations, an exercise program that has been run every second year since 1971 and is hosted by the U.S. Navy. His flagship, *Algonquin*, was able to maintain net communications with all participants, even though varying degrees of technical ability and security clearance meant that four different nets had to be maintained simultaneously. The effective use of personal networking was as important as the technological network.[40] In 2006 Commodore Nigel Greenwood, commander, Canadian Fleet Pacific, was appointed Sea Combat commander of one of the naval task forces participating in RIMPAC. The force included the carrier USS *Kitty Hawk*.

Because the acquisition for Canadian ships of the equipment needed for interoperability is dependent upon the willingness of the Americans to share their technology, and perhaps to underwrite its cost, full technical interoperability depends on the U.S. Navy's assessment that Canada is a reliable partner. Much may depend, as was argued in a 2002 paper by Dalhousie professors Dan Middlemiss and Denis Stairs, on the scale of Canadian investment: "a fully funded interoperability arrangement," they wrote, "might still leave Canadian decision-makers with at least some military options of their own because it would not deprive them of the capacity to operate independently of their larger partner."[41] Canadian participation in the American-led military Wideband Global Satellite system (WGS), which can only be guaranteed to be available for Canadian national use if Canadian servicemen are involved in all stages of its development and operation, but which is essential for bilateral interoperability, is another example of the paradox of sovereignty.[42] The Canadian navy can also arrange access to other satellites, some of which are commercial.

Paul Mitchell has spelled out the problematic "triangular relationship" inherent in Network-Centric Warfare (NCW), the fundamental importance in battlespace information management of security of data from interception or corrupting, and the political requirements of coalition strategy. "NCW aims for perfectly efficient military operations that alleviate the problems of operational choice in a confusing setting; the price is an environment of trust that permits free creative activity. Coalition strategies seek to increase political legitimacy or military resources; the price is political compromise over the plans of coalition partners. Finally, information security ultimately seeks to guard national security; the price is tight control."[43] This is the same paradox that perplexed the Canadian government and the Admiralty at the formation of the Canadian navy: the need to reconcile operational unity with political diversity; and the results are similar – if made more acute by digital technology and global communications. In order to be fully effective as a fighting force in the twenty-first century the Canadian navy and the Canadian government must earn the trust of their American partners, a requirement that inevitably jeopardizes Canadian freedom of action. At best it must generate a measure of self-censorship in the formation of national policy.

The needs of secure networking have significantly fragmenting effects on collective action, creating a spectrum hierarchy in the degree of access to information enjoyed by different national navies, or units. The effect, although probably not the intention, is to reinforce the control of the Americans, because only they have the full picture. In American-led coalitions of the willing in the digital age, ALL partner naval forces are to a greater or lesser degree relegated to the status of colonial levés. Paul Mitchell interviewed many Canadian officers who were involved in the 2003 Gulf action. Brigadier-General Angus Watt, former commander of the Canadian Joint Task Force South West Asia, remarked to him that "if you are a coalition member, you plug into the US agenda and if you don't want to follow [it], you ain't a member of the coalition. It's that simple." One, but only one, Australian ship had a terminal connected to the U.S. military SIPRNET, the Secret Internet Protocol Router Network, and that terminal was in a secure cabin staffed exclusively by U.S. personnel. Otherwise partner navies are dependent upon more or less useful downloads to lower security grades. For its part, the U.S. Navy did not have access to the COWAN network, the Coalition Wide Area Network first used during *RIMPAC* exercises in the 1990s and later replaced with Lockheed Martin's Combined Enterprise Regional Information

Exchange System CENTRIXS Global Coalition Counter-terrorism Task Force (GCTF) network, which was itself subdivided, limiting access to different partners. Timely access to information is facilitated if officers are seconded by partner navies to work in American staff positions, because personal relationships bring reassurance, but that is only possible where there is a commonality of national purpose at the political level. The adequacy of bandwidth in partner navies is a serious restriction on data networking. In that respect the Canadian navy profited from its focus on oceanic ASW and towed array sonar, which had given it an early need for satellite communications, but the demand for bandwidth continues to grow at an exponential rate. Commodores Lerhe and Robertson were both critical of network access and speed. The problems that affected NCW during the low-intensity Gulf operations in 2003 suggest that the architecture of partnership would not have served well in the event of serious escalation. Mitchell concludes in his 2006 study that "in order for computer networks to function as efficiently as possible, social networks need to be established first," but suggests that the paradox of information security may lead the U.S. armed forces in the twenty-first century increasingly to act alone.

One of the central purposes supposedly served by NATO had been the development of means to overcome differences in national systems of communications and command. For over forty years NATO navies had attached ships to the Standing Naval Force Atlantic, STANAVFORLANT, specifically for the purpose. How much the technical requirements of digital security accounts for the American move away from NATO structures, and how much that move might reflect changing political attitudes in Washington, is not clear. For Canada, the fragmenting of NATO naval command and control architecture means that efforts to increase the ability to integrate Canadian ships into U.S. Navy formations undermines the sense of partnership with European and Commonwealth navies.

✦ ✦ ✦

When at the 2002 Prague Summit it was agreed that NATO should be radically reorganized to meet its new global roles, the Supreme Allied Command Atlantic [SACLANT] was stood down. In its place were created several regional maritime commanders subordinate to the Supreme Headquarters Allied Power Europe [saceur], including the organization of the Standing Naval Forces Atlantic, Mediterranean, and Channel. The

Supreme Allied Command Europe became SAC operations with authority over all NATO operations worldwide. SACLANT became the Supreme Allied Command Transformation, responsible, in Vice-Admiral Miller's words, for "developing strategic concepts, policy and interoperability; defence planning; joint experimentation, exercises and assessment; joint education and training; future capabilities, research and technology." The Canada-US Regional Planning Group (CUSRPG) established in 1949 was finally terminated in 2003. The Canada-US Military Cooperation Committee created in 1946 by the Permanent Joint Board on Defence has lost its NATO fig leaf, and there is no NATO commander with authority over Continental North American naval defences.[44]

It appears that elements of the Canadian government decided that, in the circumstances of "global war on terror," policy independence was a luxury for better days – if not simply an illusion – and that there is no more reason to seek to stand aside from automatic participation in the naval defence of North America, and its global extension, than there is with continental air defence. In 2003 Canada and the United States agreed to form a Binational Planning Group commanded by the deputy commander of NORAD. The 2005 paper "Securing Canada's Ocean Frontiers" states without caveat that "The Canadian Forces C4ISR [C4 with Intelligence, Surveillance and Reconnaissance] operating construct requires 'network-enabled' command and control architecture to facilitate all levels of joint, interagency, and multinational integration."[45] No less important than technical means of interoperability are efforts to reconcile the legal and administrative distinctions between government agencies, including special forces, the U.S. and Canadian coast guards, and civilian police forces. The establishment on 1 February 2006 of the "Canada Command" integrated all the military formations in Canada in a form that provides a single point of contact with civilian agencies, and with the United States Northern Command, which is co-located with NORAD headquarters at Paterson Air Force base in Colorado. Completing the structure of continental partnership, the extension of NORAD to the maritime element was finally agreed to by the administration of Prime Minister Stephen Harper four months after he was sworn into office, signing an *Agreement Between the Government of Canada and the Government of the United States of America on the North American Aerospace Defense Command* on 12 May 2006.[46] In long-delayed realization of Diefenbaker's assertions, the agreement formally recognized that "this cooperation is conducted within the framework of the North Atlantic Treaty and is an important element of their contribution to the overall security of the NATO area." But these are empty words.[47] The need for formal renegotiation of the treaty every four years was terminated and replaced by undertakings to review its workings regularly. The commander of NORAD is double-hatted as commander of Northern Command, but the Canadian deputy commander of NORAD has no role either in Northern Command or in Canada Command. In the maritime element the agreement did not extend to the control of naval units and formations, meeting the continuing American refusal to share any information, let alone control, of its submarine forces with her allies. The existing Maritime Operation Centres at Halifax and Esquimalt were renamed Regional Operations Centres, and provide support for new all-agency Maritime Security Operations Centres monitoring Canada's three oceans and the Great Lakes.[48]

The 2002 NATO Prague Summit also established the Prague Capabilities Commitment, which was intended to increase the ability of NATO nations to deploy expeditionary forces rapidly and effectively. As a result, STANAVFORLANT and STANAVFORMED were stood down and replaced on 1 January 2005 with SNMG1 (Standing NATO Maritime Group 1), and SNMG2. A Canadian sailor, Commodore Denis Rouleau, was tasked by NATO in 2006 with working SNMG1 up into an operational force.[49] The Canadian government ordered the Canadian forces to prepare three new joint operational combat formations, a Special Operations Group, a Standing Contingency Task Force, and a Mission-Specific Task Force.[50] This plan was not fully implemented, as the Standing Contingency Task Force was never put together, as Pearson's musings along the same lines in 1963 had never been implemented. But the chief of defence staff in 2005–08, General Rick Hillier, did recognize a need for Canadian forces to be able to arrive in theatre with enough assets to ensure a voice for Canada in the operational strategy and tactics employed by allied and coalition formations. To do so, he made the national commitment to Afghanistan an absolute priority, and strongly discouraged any Canadian ground force commitment to the humanitarian and political crisis in the Darfur region of Sudan. Similarly, the navy's role in the Arabian sea was given priority. The level of Canadian commitment undertaken in Operation *Apollo* could not be sustained indefinitely, but a more limited Operation *Altair* had been announced in 2004, with the intention that the Canadian navy should continue to support international peace and security in the Arabian sea on a periodic basis.[51]

The prominence acquired by the chief of defence staff under Hillier contrasted with the original intent of the Hellyer policy of integration, which sought to ensure firm control by the civilian minister of national defence. Major-General Daniel Gosselin writes: "The central element of Hillier's 2005 Transformation was operational primacy, and this included placing greater emphasis on operational matters in all decision-making at NDHQ. Hillier's extensive operational experience, combined with Canada's engagement in a high-intensity, high-risk military operation in southern Afghanistan, compelled him within a year of taking over as CDS to reform military governance at NDHQ, establishing a more robust unified staff to assist him in implementing the CF transformation, in commanding the CF, and in providing advice to the government." Hillier downscaled Trudeau's 1972 "civilianization" of the Department of National Defence, enhancing military control consistent with the needs of a nation at war, and with the recommendations of the Somalia Inquiry and a 1997 DND "Report to the Prime Minister on the Leadership and Management of the Canadian Forces."[52] But he also stopped the trend that had developed in the 1990s for the three environmental chiefs, of army, navy, and air force, to take greater control of their own elements.[53] This was consistent with Bland's strongly expressed assessment published in 1995, which had called attention to deficiencies apparent in the management of Canada's part in the 1990 Gulf War.[54] All domestic responsibilities were grouped into the new Canada Command, and joint task force commanders were appointed to subordinate positions. These were double-hatted with the old element commands. Thus the commander Maritime Forces Atlantic also became the commander Joint Task Force Atlantic.[55] Michael Byers was one who viewed Hillier as having gone rogue, but if so, Hillier did so with the approval of two prime ministers, Paul Martin who appointed him, and Stephen Harper.[56]

✦ ✦ ✦

When in 2008 the Canadian navy returned to Somalian waters it sent a force of three ships, the destroyer *Iroquois*, a frigate, *Calgary*, and the AOR *Protecteur*, with a flag officer, Commodore Robert Davidson, to take command of the multi-lateral Combined Task Force CTF150 under the overall command of USNAVCENT in Bahrain. This was consistent with the May 2008 Canada First Defence Strategy paper, which states that the Canadian Forces are to maintain the capacity to "lead and/or conduct a major international operation for an extended period of time." Commodore Davidson later wrote that the navy viewed the role as important for national and also for institutional reasons: "By sending multiple ships and a Commodore and staff to act as Task Force Commander, we would draw far greater attention to the national effort, and ensure that the force was adequately resourced to deliver operational effect during our time in command. It would also be the first deliberate deployment of a Naval Task Group, showcasing the concept at a crucial time of naval capacity transition and reinvestment." It was hoped that the international naval community would recognize the competence of Canadian senior officers, and come to expect Canadians to be given command of multinational forces. "One of the principal objectives of government in assigning the mission was to demonstrate Canada's capacity to lead large international maritime operations, thus increasing Canada's reputation while allowing our perspective to influence the future course of the coalition."[57] From the navy's perspective, command of CTF 150 served to strengthen the navy-to-navy relationship with the U.S. Navy. Rear Admiral David Morse warns that "bilateral and international tasks carry the greatest consequence of error and demand the development of more sophisticated forces and skills. Of particular note is the increased emphasis ... on support to the United Nations and the re-balancing of attention between Atlantic and Pacific interests. For a task group commander, this implies a need for a range of warfare capabilities, a robust command and control structure, and an ability to manage the application of force with consideration of national and international sensitivities ... The emphasis in these operations has shifted quite dramatically from war fighting to controlled and minimal application of power, or in other words, from power to influence." This has involved major changes in training, explains Morse. "I no longer plan on the relative safety of open ocean warfare. I can rely on the assumption of the 'safe and timely arrival' of shipping to a few known choke points and I must now concentrate my efforts on a much more difficult environment. Usually the littoral area is an area congested with too many forces, it has difficult topography, hydrography and bathymetry. It has an incredibly crowded electronic spectrum and most significantly is within reach of coastal missile batteries, coastal gun forts, controlled coastal minefields, short-range gun and missile boats, coastal submarines and aircraft, and is often down-wind and in range of chemical threat. The other demand in the littoral area is the possibility of encountering evacuees or refugees and the doubtful vessels in which they travel."[58] He should have added that "influence" operations in littoral waters call for the careful selection of appropriate strategies and tactics that resonate with local and international perspectives, politically, legally, and ethically.

CTF150 was intended to deal with the ongoing concern with drug-smuggling – doubly important because it was a major source of revenue for international terrorism – and to address the horrors of people-smuggling from Somalia to Yemen. But these tasks came to take second place to the protection of shipping from piracy. Piracy around the Horn of Africa began as free-lance operations to protect Somali fisheries from foreign poachers, and grew into Somalia's only successful business, operating largely out of the semi-autonomous northeastern regions of Puntland and Somaliland, and with commercial links to interests in Kenya, Tanzania, and the United Arab Emirates. Pirates could earn as much as $30,000 per year in a country where the average income is in the order of $600, and operate far offshore. The Spanish-owned fishing trawler, *Playa de Bakio*, was seized in late June 2008 247 miles offshore. In early November the pirates, grown bolder, seized a Saudi supertanker, the *Sirus Star*. A few days later a pirate "mother ship" refused to stop for inspection by an Indian navy vessel, INS *Tabar*, reportedly opened fire on it, and was blown up by return fire.[59] The business plan of the organizations conducting the attacks depended upon the seizure of ships, crew, and cargo and their retention until an appropriate ransom was agreed to and paid.

Davidson described the importance to Canada of the anti-piracy patrols: "In a global village of international trade, all nations are dependent on the movement of goods on the waterways and through the chokepoints that make up the oceans' transportation routes ... The operations area of CTF150 comprises a region through which roughly two thirds of the world's oil moves. Although we may not rely on this source for Canadian oil, it is critical to our trading partners. Safe and unhindered navigation through this region's waters is critical to the economies of the west, including Canada, and thus our contribution to this international coalition force is not simply about altruism, or doing the right thing. Given our economic reliance on trade, worldwide maritime security is also about self-interest."[60] Davidson's argument echoes that in the Department of National Defence website quoted at the beginning of this book. It is also a central feature of a concept labelled the "1,000 ship navy," or "Global Maritime Partnership," first called for by the American chief of naval operations, Admiral Mike Mullen, in September 2005 at the International Seapower Symposium in Newport, Rhode Island.[61]

To contain the problem to international maritime trade, the United Nations Security Council, in an unprecedented modification of the concept of state sovereignty, passed on 2 June 2008 Resolution 1816 authorizing foreign naval vessels to conduct anti-piracy patrols inside Somali territorial waters for an initial period of six months, and to use "all necessary means" consistent with relevant and existing provisions of international law to protect shipping. Western navies were organized into three command structures. NATO's Operation *Ocean Shield* was conducted by SNMG1, the Standing NATO Maritime Group 1 that had replaced the Standing Naval Force Atlantic on 1 January 2005. The parallel organizations were the European Union's NAVFOR (Naval Force Somalia), which mounted Operation *Atalanta*, and the U.S.-controlled Combined Maritime Forces. In 2008 part of SNMG2 arrived to take up duties off Somalia.[62] The Chinese People's Liberation Army Navy began regular deployments to take part in the international anti-piracy patrols in December 2008, sending two destroyers or frigates and a support vessel for four-month rotations, and in July 2010 the 17,000-tonne Type 071 *Yazno* class landing platform dock *Kunlun Shan* with a platoon of marines joined the force, while the 14,000-tonne *Peace Ark* hospital ship provided medical support for coastal communities.[63] Initially the Chinese, Indian, Russian, Malaysian and Iranian navies worked independently, but in January 2010 it was reported in *Lloyd's List* that China had agreed to take on the task of coordinating international anti-piracy patrols.[64]

On 6 August 2008 the Canadian government agreed to provide escort for World Food Program ships carrying emergency relief from Mombasa in Kenya to Mogadishu in Somalia as part of the Multi-lateral CTF150 tasking. On 19 August 2008, the frigate *Ville de Québec* took her turn in the Somali operation. In April 2009, HMCS *Winnipeg* joined SNMG1 for ten weeks in the Gulf of Aden and off the Horn of Africa, and in turn *Winnipeg* was succeeded by HMCS *Fredericton*, which returned to Canada in May 2010.[65]

At time of writing, the measures taken by the international community to protect shipping have been surprisingly mild.[66] The at-sea component has amounted to patrolling the sea lanes, boarding suspicious vessels, and responding to distress calls. For that last, the embarked helicopters were especially valuable. Each national naval contribution came with its own rules of engagement formulated by its government, and the commander had to respect these in determining which ships to task. Each target posed its own difficulties. Drug smugglers could – and probably did – hide their high-value but low-volume cargoes at the bottom of holds loaded with bulk cargoes such as rice, desperately needed by the population of Somalia. Pirates could be arrested only if they were caught in the act, and if arrested, concern for universal human rights prevented them being summarily executed, as they would have been in the past. But neither could they be handed over to Somalian authorities for trial, again because of concern for their rights. No one wanted to take them back to Canada for trial, where the prisoners might claim refugee status. To meet the need, regional courts in Kenya and the Seychelles were used to prosecute captive pirates.[67] Most difficult was the interception of human smugglers taking desperate people across the Red Sea to Yemen. If intercepted, they had been known to throw their human cargo overboard. An essential component of regional security operations is the cooperation of local states, and Davidson made visits to Saudi Arabia, Yemen, Pakistan, and the United Arab Emirates. He also tried to obtain the right balance between provision of information to the public and information security for the forces involved.

The right, and obligation, of merchant ship crews to defend their ships goes back to the ancient Mediterranean Law Merchant and well into the nineteenth-century British mercantile crews knew that they would not be paid any wages until they safely delivered their ships and cargo to the port of destination.[68] The traditional response to the threat of piracy was to arm merchant ships and employ naval forces to attack pirate bases. In the present century, however, the world's mercantile marine have been reluctant to arm themselves. According to a press release by Rear Admiral Peter Hudson, the British commander of NAVFOR, Somalia, in February 2010, because of the additional costs that would be entailed, ship masters were even ignoring recommendations to zig-zag at high speed through dangerous waters and to provide passive defences in the form of barbed wire and emergency communications equipment in safe rooms. The odds against the pirates targeting any individual ship were rated at between one in 200 and one in 500, and marine insurance contracts covered the possible cost of paying ransoms to release captured ships and crews under the "sue and labour" clause, whether or not precautions were taken.[69]

Attitudes began to stiffen at the end of 2009. It was reported that shipping firms were beginning to hire teams of guards, costing from $25,000, for the passage through the Gulf of Aden, and that marine insurers were offering steep discounts on insurance for ships prepared to protect themselves.[70] At the time, the trend was strongly deprecated by national authority. On 25 January 2010 *Lloyd's List* published the warning that "the UK government strongly discourages the carriage and use of firearms onboard UK registered ships." Shipowners were advised that "neither Transec, the UK transport security body, nor the Maritime and Coastguard Agency would approve ship security plans that contain arrangements for provision of private armed guards on ships. *Lloyd's List* added that there was no requirement for shipowners to indicate whether they were in fact arming their ships.[71] Over a year later, with the incidence of piracy and armed robbery up by 20 percent, attitudes were continuing to harden. In May 2011 it was announced that the UN International Maritime Organization planned to issue guidelines on the use of armed security staff to protect ships from piracy. In June the Office of the Asia-Pacific Advisor, Maritime Forces Pacific, circulated a study recommending the establishment of a naval blockade of Somalian pirate towns, in response to the growing threat that was increasingly endangering the lives of seamen.[72] And, with the cost to world trade of piracy estimated at $7–$12 billion annually, at the end of October the British prime minister, David Cameron, indicated that Britain would soon be establishing a licensing system so that British shipping could carry armed guards in the Gulf of Aden.[73] In late November it was announced by the Baltic and International Maritime Council representing some 65 percent of the world's shipping companies that they had undertaken to develop a standard contract for members employing armed guards onboard ships to establish standards that would minimize liability.[74]

❖ ❖ ❖

Simultaneously with the Operation *Altair* deployments to the Indian ocean, the Canadian navy was engaged in relief and enforcement operations in the Caribbean. In 1992 the AOR *Protecteur* had been deployed to Florida and the Bahamas in response to the devastation caused by Hurricane Andrew, and twelve years later a destroyer and three frigates, HMCS *Athabaskan, St John's,* and *Toronto,* together with the CCGS *William Alexander* were dispatched on 6 September 2005 to aid American agencies in their response to the flooding of New Orleans by Hurricane

Katrina. In the aftermath of four hurricanes that ravaged Haiti in the summer of 2008, *St John's* was deployed to south and southwest Haiti in September as part of the Canadian Operation *Horatio* to deliver 350 metric tonnes of food and relief supplies to be distributed by the United Nations World Food Programme. Less than a year and a half later Haiti was devastated on 12 January 2010 by an earthquake measuring 7.3 on the Richter scale, and with its epicentre about 15 kilometres away and 10 kilometres beneath the Haitian capital Port-au-Prince. At least twelve aftershocks had magnitudes of between 5.0 and 5.9. HMC Ships *Athabaskan* and *Halifax* were immediately tasked as the naval component of a Canadian forces response, Operation *Hestia*, arriving on 19 January.[75] *Halifax* was ordered to the small port town of Jacmel on the Haitian south coast about 30 kilometres from Port-au-Prince, and the birth place of Canada's then governor general, Michaëlle Jean. *Athabaskan* was directed to the town on the north coast of Haiti, Leogane, about 64 kilometres southwest of Port-au-Prince. Although their capacities with respect to their equipment and to the amount of stores they could carry were far more limited for relief work than had been the case with HMCS *Preserver*, which was in refit at the time and unavailable for employment, their crews were able to contribute light engineering skills to clear roads so that relief could be distributed. They also cleared and opened the airport at Jacmel.

The evident value of the AORs for relief work, and for support of the military ashore within their limitations, reawakened the interest General Foulkes, Prime Minister Pearson, and Paul Hellyer had taken in transforming the Canadian navy into a force optimized for transport and support of Canadian expeditionary forces. The arguments for the acquisition of dedicated sea lift for Canadian ground and air forces are founded on the presumption that there will be a continuing and expanding need for Canada to respond to critical situations around the world, to deal with the consequences of natural disasters, the collapse of state organization, and deliberate conflict. With sixty percent of major cities around the world located within twenty-five miles of the sea, a capacity to operate from the sea has great appeal.[76]

In the 2005 Department of National Defence document *Securing Canada's Ocean Frontiers: Charting the Course from Leadmark*, it was stated that "while the Navy does not expect to conduct traditional amphibious operations against heavily fortified and defended beaches, the focus of future CF expeditionary operations demands a basic level of amphibious capability. In response to the challenges posed by the future security environment – particularly in failed and failing states – the CF will need the capability to rapidly deploy a high readiness joint force consisting of the appropriate mix of maritime, land, air, and special forces elements, organized under a single integrated command structure, to any region of the world where they are needed."[77] There is little or no support within the navy for the acquisition of dedicated amphibious ships capable of making contested landings, because of the scale of commitment that would be required. As noted by Lieutenant Commander Matthew F. Plaschka in 2008, the proposal "to acquire amphibious capability is beyond the resources assigned to the CF because of current requirements to replace the AORs, modernize the frigate fleet, and begin replacing the area air-defence destroyers."[78] The idea that Canada might want to acquire the ability to intervene in the affairs of other states, for whatever reason, on its own without dependence on partners is hardly credible. Much of the leverage Canada gains through the possession of military forces lies in the capacity they provide for cementing relationships with partners. In the world of gunboat diplomacy, nations are increasingly reluctant to undertake any interventionist activity without partners to lend political respectability. Any Canadian amphibious force would inevitably work as part of an international, or at the very least a multi-lateral effort. But there is recognition of the value of providing some limited space on a projected class of Joint Support Ships for military personal and vehicles, for landing craft capable of moving heavy supplies over a beach, and for command and control of landed forces. A good case could be made for ensuring that the joint support ships would be capable of large-scale and sustained work as hospital ships, to support operations ashore, and for use both in emergency relief and for medical "soft-power" diplomacy along the coasts of failed and third-world states. At the harder end of littoral operations, the upgrade being given to their *Harpoon* missile armament during the Halifax Class Modernization (HCM)/Frigate Life Extension (FELEX) mid-life overhaul will permit their use against shore targets. As part of RIMPAC 2010, a contingent of 150 "Red Devils" of Alpha Company, 1 Battalion, *Princess Patricia's Canadian Light Infantry* of Edmonton were embarked in USS *Bonhomme Richard* amphibious warfare ship, to practise extraction exercises with the U.S. Marines.[79]

✦ ✦ ✦

As a contribution to the international task in the Caribbean to detect the passage of drug smugglers seeking to carry their cargoes to the United States, the Canadian government in 2005 agreed to *Aurora* maritime patrol aircraft being deployed to the Caribbean to provide additional surveillance of the high seas.[80] In the autumn of 2009 it was HMC ships *Calgary* and *Toronto* that performed that duty, and in the early months of 2011 it is the *Victoria* class submarine HMCS *Corner Brook*.[81] It is entirely appropriate to point to these operations as fundamental not only to managing the problem of narcotics in the United States and Canada, but also to supporting the wider claims of Canadian sovereignty by co-opting American partnership. All the same, Canadian support of American drug-control operations takes place on American terms. There is no reason to think that it gives Canada any leverage for moderating the deeply flawed American drug-control strategy which, because it focuses its energy on blocking supply rather than on reducing the market through harm-control measures, might well be said to be designed to fail. The American umbrella organization, the Joint Inter-Agency Task Force South, does not even list the Canadian navy as a partner on its website.[82]

❖ ❖ ❖

The strategic and technical characteristics of the twenty-first century Canadian naval partnership with the U.S. Navy, even though it is generally expressed in multi-lateral terms, would have been rejected categorically by Canadians at the time that Wilfrid Laurier created the navy or when Mackenzie King was sorting out Canada's defence relationship with the United States. Was this the form that "manifest destiny" would take? Now that the United States was the only tiger in the jungle, would Canada slip from its back and end up inside?

Davidson, writing in 2008, gives his perspective:

> With national authority to veto any tasking and national rules of engagement for the use of force, Canada has been able to exercise the level of surety to keep this activity within the limits of national foreign policy. On the plus side for interoperability, integrating frigates into these Battle Groups has enabled the navy to align communications and cryptographic requirements, doctrine and tactics to the maximum extent possible. Shared networks improve

> the speed by which we can integrate into a US-led coalition force. Commonality of procedures and shared experience has built confidence in Canadian leadership and training.
>
> Why has this been important? It has built credibility and enabled Canada to lead combined forces. For the US, the CF is a known quantity that has proven itself on every occasion. It has built understanding at all levels in the respective militaries and fosters long term relationships at senior military and civilian levels in the respective defence departments. Trust and mutual respect on the military-to-military level has improved the Canada-US relationship at the government-to-government level. A flourishing relationship through military cooperation can set the conditions for dialogue in other areas of the mutual concern.[83]

At the navy-to-navy level there does not appear to be any dispute. Generations of Canadian political scientists have failed to establish with any degree of confidence the utility of naval co-operation on the government-to-government level outside of specifically naval files, but the history of the Turbot war, and of the muted nature of the dispute with the United States over maritime jurisdiction in the arctic, does give substance to Davidson's argument.

12

THE NAVY AND THE ARCTIC

Following the signing of the Arctic Cooperation agreement with the United States, the abandonment of the nuclear submarine project, and the formal ending of the Cold War, concern for a naval defence of Canadian interests in the arctic disappeared from the front page. The realization by the general public early in the twenty-first century that the effects of global climate change could lead to open-water transit of the Northwest Passage within decades, however, brought a returned concern for arctic sovereignty.[1] The rapid warming of the polar area stimulated a rush to define national boundaries and their implications for ownership of natural resources. In meeting this challenge, Canada continued to employ the alliancemanship it has used as a general tool of national defence.

The arctic's potential for hydrocarbon extraction, and the need for nations to define their claims within ten years of the signing of the convention on the Law of the Sea have become the main driving issues in the area. According to the U.S. Geological Survey, the arctic may contain one-quarter of the world's undiscovered energy resources, and other sources have run the proportion of the earth's remaining undiscovered reserves of hydrocarbons located north of 60°N latitude as high as 50 percent.[2] Canada ratified its signature to the Law of the Sea convention in 2003, giving it until 2013 to complete its mapping of the continental shelf north of the arctic archipelago. Russia ratified its signature in 1997, and despite the expiration of the time limit has continued aggressively working to establish its definition of national jurisdiction in the arctic.[3]

Franklyn Griffiths, in a post-retirement reassessment in 2002, made the point that the possible development of a transit route through the Canadian arctic archipelago for oil tankers, and possibly for container ships running from Asia to the European market, should be of secondary interest, for practical reasons.[4] The effect of receding summer ice in the arctic archipelago "is unpredictability rather than conditions favourable to navigation. Not only may a given shipping season include intervals during which sea-ice conditions make navigation slow and risky ... but would-be shippers will not be able to rely on use of the [Northwest] Passage from one year to the next in the coming decades. That means no assured summer-months transit and no regular use of the Passage unless shippers buy ice-strengthened vessels and Canada provides icebreaking and other support as required."[5] Should there develop a serious interest in polar navigation, the Northern Sea Route between the polar ice pack and the Siberian coast is predicted to be more practicable than the Northwest Passage, and in time the melting of polar ice fields will open the more direct route between Asia and Europe northward, over the pole.[6]

The United States has yet to ratify its signature to the Law of the Sea convention, although the U.S. Senate Foreign Relations Committee voted to do so in 2004. Delaying ratification extends the time limit on scientific assessment of arctic marine resources, and of seabed configuration. To that end, the United States is actively pursuing its survey work. Concern in the United States following the 9/11 terrorist attack, and the need this event showed for the U.S. Coastguard to increase its control of coastal waters, marginalized conflict over the legal regime in archipelagic straits.[7] In December 2005, however, it was reported in the *National Post* that an American nuclear submarine might have passed through Canadian arctic waters en route to the Arctic ocean.[8] There was no report that the Canadian government had been asked to permit the transit.

Although the United States has been the whipping boy for Canadian nationalist policies in the arctic, it is difficult to determine whether there is any substance behind the supposed "threat" from the United States, or whether it is simply a straw man that serves political interests, while stimulating Canadian defence expenditure. For Stephen Harper, wrapping himself in a frosty Canadian flag serves a political purpose. The U.S. ambassador to Canada in January 2010, David Jacobson, advised his government in a dispatch that has since been leaked to the public that Harper's rhetoric reflected his belief that "the North has never been more important to [the Conservative] Party." It might be appropriate to characterize Prime Minister Harper's naval policy in the arctic as a public relations exercise to reassure Canadians that their forces retain some purely national purpose, and are under national control. On one level the grudging respect accorded Canada's claim in the arctic archipelagic waters serves as the "canary in the coal mine" that tests the health of her defence relationships. At another, it serves the interest of the American military by strengthening that of their Canadian partner. While the rhetoric is sometimes assertive, the practice is generally co-operative. Ambassador Jacobson commented comfortably on Foreign Minister Lawrence Cannon's public statement in March and April 2009, that his "utmost priority" was "to further strengthen Canada's bilateral engagement with Arctic states. He stated that 'The United States is our premier partner in the Arctic,' that 'we have many shared interests and common purposes – in environmental stewardship, search and rescue, safety, security and sustainable resource development,' and that he was looking forward to a more enhanced level of cooperation on Arctic issues with the United States. He noted that this would include exploring 'ways to pursue a common agenda,' starting in 2013, as Canada and subsequently the United States chair the Arctic Council."[9] The Arctic Council had been established, as a Canadian initiative, in 1996.

A long-standing dispute with the Danish sovereign of Greenland over ownership of Hans Island between Ellesmere Island and Greenland had not been settled by the conclusion in 1973 of a treaty defining the division of the continental shelf. The Danish navy visited the island in 2002 and 2003 to plant the Danish flag, and in July 2005 the Canadian minister of national defence, Bill Graham, visited the island with Canadian military personnel to raise a Canadian flag. Neither country considers the Hans Island issue high on its agenda, however, and in September 2005 a joint statement was issued declaring that both countries would continue their efforts "to reach a long-term solution to the Hans Island dispute." A Danish-Canadian agreement on arctic co-operation was signed in Ottawa on 13–14 May 2010.[10] Arguably, the issue acquired what importance it enjoyed because it was seen as a demonstration to other more powerful adversaries of Canadian commitment to defend her claims. The long boundary between Canada and Danish Greenland, however, and the hydrocarbon resources that are already being mined despite concerns about potentially catastrophic pollution, suggest that relations with Denmark will be a continuing issue.

The European Union seeks to establish multinational fora for the management of arctic issues. In March 2009, EU commissioner Joe Borg stated: "The European Commission is willing to take on its responsibility for Arctic issues and to contribute to an enhanced system of governance in the Arctic in cooperation with all Arctic States, territories and stakeholders. It is in this context that the European Union has made a request to become a permanent observer at the Arctic Council."[11]

More pressing is the conflict between Canadian interests and those of Russia, which are also contested by Denmark. Of primary interest to Canada is the Russian claim to the Lomonosov Ridge, which extends north of Ellesmere Island in the direction of the central Siberian coast.[12] During the 2007 survey season, submersibles were used to plant a Russian flag on the seabed at the North Pole, and exploration continued in 2008 using unmanned submersibles.[13] In September 2009 Russian and Belarus forces conducted two arctic exercises involving over 17,000 troops and sixteen warships.[14] In preparation for a vast expansion of Russian industrial activity in the Arctic ocean, a fleet of eight floating nuclear power stations are being built.[15] The Russian government has announced that border guards, with two arctic warfare brigades and supported by naval forces, are being established to support the Russian territorial claim, which will be submitted to the United Nations in 2012.[16]

New players in the arctic are Japan, South Korea, and the People's Republic of China, which has an icebreaker fleet and maintains scientific establishments in Antarctica.[17] China also has observer status in the Arctic Council. The primary interest of these nations in the arctic is for transportation. In the shorter term this might indicate an interest in the Northwest Passage, but in the longer view a direct route from Bering Strait over the North Pole to Europe would be of greater interest.[18] In the 1980s the Japanese shipbuilding giant IHI Ishikawajima-Harima Heavy Industries Co., Ltd. showed interest in icebreaker technology, working with Wartsila of Finland.[19] China has built a fleet of nuclear submarines, which have an ability to employ this route without waiting for the effects of climate change to open the trans-polar route to surface ships. In March 2010 the Stockholm International Peace Research Institute released a study by Linda Jakobson entitled "China Prepares for an Ice-Free Arctic" and calling attention to the Chinese plan to construct a new heavy icebreaker. China, like the European Union, is seeking observer status in the Arctic Council, and Jakobson's comment is that the Chinese, while adopting a low-profile so as to avoid alarming other states, are making the point that arctic affairs, and especially arctic shipping, are matters of international interest.

✦ ✦ ✦

In a famous passage in his book *The Influence of Law on Sea Power*, the Oxford scholar Daniel O'Connell observed that "International law may be considered by some to be a simulacrum of law, but it is a phenomenon notwithstanding." Interpretation of the Law of the Sea convention is an important element in the claims made by Canada and other states.[20] Donat Pharand, in a 2007 "Final Revisit" of the Northwest Passage question, writes that Canada could not "discharge its heavy burden of proof" to substantiate a historic title to control of the arctic archipelagic waters, but that the baselines drawn around the archipelago "meet the compulsory criteria of the general direction of the coast and the close relationship between land and sea. In addition, the validity of the baselines across Lancaster Sound and Amundsen Gulf is supported by historic regional interests and [by the] needs of the Inuit." He believes the American position on Canadian control of the passage is contrary to legal norms: "In spite of the very general view that the new legal regime for 'straits used for international navigation' presupposes some *actual* use, the United States continues to maintain that *potential* use is sufficient ... The author is not aware what other counties, if any, share the view of the United States ... but it does appear to be an isolated interpretation and is completely unsupported by customary international law, which is the only law applicable to this question." Pharand's position is that "except for a couple of transits by US ships, all others have taken place after a request and prior authorization. The waters of the Passage are strictly internal waters of Canada and are not subject to the right of innocent passage for foreign ships." Internationalization of the strait would probably not substantially affect Canadian regulation of commercial shipping, but it would entitle the warships of all nations to "transit passage" as defined by the Convention on the Law of the Sea, including the submerged transit of submarines.[21]

The continuing resistance of the U.S. Navy to Canada's policy on the Northwest Passage was made explicit in January 2009 when President Obama signed a presidential directive proclaiming that the "Freedom of the seas is a top national priority." The signing had been delayed on the advice of the American embassy in Ottawa until after the Canadian general election, during which it might have been made into an election issue.[22] Asserting that "the Northwest Passage is a strait used for international navigation," it noted that the United States will "project a sovereign United States maritime presence in the arctic in support of essential United States interests."[23]

Commander James Kraska, USN, professor of international law at the U.S. Naval War College, and former oceans policy adviser to the director, Strategic Plans and Policy, U.S. Joint Chiefs of Staff, asserts in a fall 2009 article that the Northwest Passage has already been transited "nearly 70 times by surface vessels belonging to Canada, the United States, Norway, the Netherlands, Japan, the Bahamas and Liberia," and that "the deep and wide passage has been susceptible to transit for decades by submarines of the United States and the United Kingdom, and presumably, the Soviet Union and now Russia." The Canadian government had "painted itself into a corner." His opinion on the legality of Canada's mapping baselines differs fundamentally from Pharand's.[24]

At the beginning of December 2009 the House of Commons nailed its colours to the mast by passing a private member's bill renaming the Northwest Passage "Canada's Northwest Passage."[25] In early 2010, however, the Canadian government responded to Barack Obama's presidential directive with a conciliatory "Statement on Canada's Arctic Foreign Policy": "With regard to Arctic waters, Canada controls all maritime navigation in its waters. Nevertheless, disagreements exist between the United States and Canada regarding the maritime boundary in the Beaufort Sea (approximately 6,250 square nautical miles) and between Canada and Denmark over a small part of the maritime boundary in the Lincoln Sea. All disagreements are well managed, neither posing defence challenges for Canada nor diminishing Canada's ability to collaborate and cooperate with its Arctic neighbours. Canada will continue to manage these discrete boundary issues and will also, as a priority, seek to work with our neighbours to explore the possibility of resolving them in accordance with international law."[26] Ambassador Jacobson's assessment of Minister Cannon's statements, made in the Yukon and later at the Center for Strategic and International Studies in Washington, DC, was made at that time.

Consistent with the recommendation that Griffiths made in 2002, and Pharand in 2007, that the government make its regulatory regime for the arctic mandatory, in the summer of 2009 the Harper administration announced that Canada would require all ships entering Canadian waters to report their presence, and in February 2010 the government announced that on 1 July a mandatary reporting regime for large ships entering the arctic waters would replace the current voluntary ship registry system operated by the Canadian Coast Guard. Bill C-3, which came into force on 1 August 2009, an Act to amend the Arctic Waters Pollution Prevention Act, expanded the perimeter of the management regime from 100 to 200nm offshore.[27] The American government's response was that "we will be discussing the proposal with Canada" to ensure it does not violate international law.[28] The extension of the zone, and indeed the controls Canada had imposed, had already passed into customary law through their inclusion in the convention on the Law of the Sea, Article 234, which had come into force in 1994 without having been signed by the United States.

✦ ✦ ✦

Pharand warned that surveillance is not enough. If foreign navies make undeclared transits of the Northwest Passage, and no response follows detection of intruders, "those transits might indeed become prejudicial to a claim of internal waters." Pharand's long list of recommendations also included the construction of the icebreaker that had been announced by Brian Mulroney but never built, the launching of the projected Radarsat II satellite to monitor shipping, completion of the fixed sonar systems in the arctic channels, and an increase in the number of Canadian Rangers recruited in the Inuit community, on all of which fronts actions have been taken. In 2002 the Canadian Forces returned to the arctic, mounting a joint and combined operation, Operation *Narwhal*, with the participation of the RCMP, the coast guard, and Canada Customs. Rob Huebert writes: "This exercise was kept simple in order to allow the players to re-familiarize themselves with the basic skills needed to operate in the north. In fact, the Canadian Forces learned how difficult it is to provide for the necessary re-supply of any northern operations. It was also discovered that communications were more problematic than is the case in more southern locations." Two years later *Narwhal* was run again with the navy sending a major ship, HMCS *Montreal*, north for the first time since 1982, visiting Iqaluit and Pangnirtung on Baffin Island.[29] In the Speech from the Throne of October 2004, Prime Minister Paul Martin indicated that the Canadian government would be undertaking a "northern strategy" that would "protect the northern environment and Canada's sovereignty and security."[30] In March 2005 it was announced that Canada would commit $51 million to mapping in the arctic, and in April the Martin administration released an "International Policy Statement: A Role of Pride and Influence in the World," emphasizing the importance of protecting sovereignty claims.[31] In the summer of 2005 HMCS *Fredericton* was sent into Baffin Bay on a northern fisheries patrol, the RCMP ran an exercise, *Beaufort Sentinel*, in the western arctic, and the Canadian Armed Forces ran *Hudson Sentinel*, during which the coastal defence vessels HMC ships *Glace Bay* and *Shawinigan* circumnavigated the bay, making port calls to communities. The air force deployed both *Aurora* and *Hercules* aircraft, and the army exercised the Northern Rangers.

In August 2006 HMC ships *Montreal*, *Goose Bay*, and *Moncton*, a Coast Guard ship, and RCMP officers, conducted exercise *Lancaster* around Dundas Harbour, to show the flag and assert Canada's sovereignty.[32] In the summer of 2007 the Canadian navy began a series of exercises in the arctic, Operation *Nanook*, in conjunction with the coast guard. In 2007 the *Victoria* class submarine HMCS *Corner Brook* took part, and in 2008 the frigate HMCS *Toronto* and the maritime coastal defence vessel HMCS *Shawinigan* practised arctic patrol operations in Frobisher Bay with the Canadian Coast Guard Ship *Pierre Radisson*. Given the ability of the *Victoria* class of submarine to operate for protracted periods submerged, requiring only 30–60 minutes of diesel operation per day to recharge her batteries for slow-speed submerged operation, their value for operations on the edge of the ice is considerable.[33] In 2009 the RCMP joined the exercise, bringing a patrol boat down the Mackenzie river from Hay river, and into the Beaufort sea. HMC ships *Toronto* and *Corner Brook* returned to the arctic to undertake anti-submarine exercises.[34]

The project to build an icebreaker rated as *Polar 8* class according to the Canadian Arctic Shipping Pollution Protection Regulations had been formally cancelled in 1990 in favour of refurbishing Canada's largest icebreaker, the *Louis S St Laurent*, which was lengthened and given new propulsion. Confusingly, CCGS *Louis S St Laurent* is rated Polar Class 1, which is the highest arctic class recognized by the International Association of Classification Societies. Prior to its coming to power, the Conservative Party had included in its campaign platform a commitment to purchase for Canada three heavy icebreakers to patrol the north. Subsequent to its election, however, the Harper administration was persuaded that icebreakers were poor ships for naval purposes, and in July 2007 he announced a commitment to acquire for the navy six to eight ice-capable patrol vessels that would be able to operate in the arctic for most of the year. An annual armed forces operating budget for the arctic was set in 2008 at $843 million, and the cost of the patrol vessels at $3.1 billion. An arctic naval establishment was required for their support, and it was announced in the summer of 2007 that the facilities at the abandoned Nanisivik mine on Admiralty Inlet at the eastern end

CCGS *Henry Larson*, *Arctic* Class 4 Medium Icebreaker built at Versatile Pacific Shipyards, Vancouver, 1987, and HMCS *Goose Bay* (MM 707), Maritime Coast Defence Vessel, built at Halifax Shipyards Ltd. 1997–98, anchored at Pond Inlet, Nunavut, while participating in Operation *Nanook*, 21 August 2006. DND AS2006-0615a

of the Northwest Passage would be taken over and developed for the purpose. A year later, work had begun on assessment of the condition of the tank farm on the site, and mine facilities were being demolished. The deep water wharf was retained. Late in 2009 it was announced that work on the site would not be complete until 2014 or 2015, and later again the date was set as 2016.[35] In 2008 a program designated *Northern Watch* began the task of modernizing the Cold War bottom sensors in the arctic archipelago, and their base on Devon Island northwest of Baffin Island, which had fallen into disrepair. In the summer of 2009 sensors were installed in the Barrow Strait and were able to relay information for four weeks to Naval HQ in Halifax. Logistical and environmental difficulties are considerable, but it is intended to put in place a full network that can operate year-round with real-time data links. Operational control of Canadian naval forces in the arctic was divided between the Atlantic and Pacific commands, with the Change of Operational Control (CHOP) line close west of Nanisivik. That division may have had value politically but could be difficult operationally, and it is intended that the Atlantic Fleet will assume responsibility for the entire arctic archipelagic region.[36]

In June 2009 journalist sources reported that the number of ice-capable arctic patrol vessels to be ordered had been scaled back to five ships, with the planned armament of 40-mm cannon reduced to 25-mm, the same calibre deployed on the army's light-armoured vehicles, and in May 2012 it was announced that the vessels would not be completed until 2018. The full military suite to be mounted on these ships was not revealed, but will certainly include a capacity to support the use of Sikorsky CH-148 *Cyclone* helicopters, acquisition of which had been announced in July 2004 but which will not be fully operational until 2013.[37] The hulls of the patrol ships are to be constructed to a Polar 5 standard, permitting "year-round operation in thick first-year ice, which may include old ice inclusions," but they will also be suitable for off-shore patrols in more temperate waters.[38]

The Canadian government's undertaking in 2006 to construct two or more "Joint Support Ships" that would replace the aging auxiliary operational replenishment ships has an arctic dimension. The concept incorporates lessons learned from the successful use of AORs in Somalia, Haiti, Florida, and the Bahamas for relief operations and in support of forces ashore, but has extended that experience to domestic security and disaster relief needs in the Canadian arctic. If the acquisition is ever authorized, it is planned to strengthen their hulls to Polar 5 standards, permitting operations in first year ice 70–100cm thick.[39]

In the 27 February 2008 federal budget a sum of $720 million was included for the construction of a more powerful replacement for the CCGS *Louis S St Laurent*, to be named the *John G Diefenbaker*. Its role, apart from the escort of shipping, would largely be hydrographic mapping, but the concept includes suitable accommodation onboard for naval purposes, should it ever become necessary to deploy a force onboard for duty in areas of multi-year ice where the new patrol boats could not navigate.[40] Considering that Canadian relations with the United States were at an all-time low during Diefenbaker's period in office, the choice of his name for the ship is interesting. The ship, but not its name, is to be an icebreaker! The announced price tag implies, given cost inflations, that the ship, if ever built, would be more limited than the projected ASPPR Polar 8 of 1985.

Apart from the CH-148 *Cyclone* helicopters, the principal air element of the maritime team that could be put in place to monitor and manage the seaways in the arctic archipelago is provided by the *Aurora* CH-140 long-range maritime patrol aircraft based at Greenwood in Nova Scotia, and at Comox in British Columbia. The present commitment of the *Auroras* to arctic operations is limited to two "Northern Patrol" flights a year. With aging electronic systems that need updating, and given the structural limitations that prevented completion of the mid-life overhaul, the Air Force embarked on an "*Aurora* Structural Life Extension Project," or Incremental Modernization Project (AIMP). This was to have been a $1.6B project to upgrade the entire eighteen aircraft of the aging *Aurora* fleet. In September 2007 the minister of national defence, Peter MacKay, announced that AIMP would be cancelled and a replacement aircraft acquired, but this abandonment of a program after heavy expenditure had already been made caused a political furor, and in December it was announced that the project would after all be continued, but limited to ten aircraft.[41] When the *Cyclone* helicopters come into service their sophisticated signal processors will make possible extended ASW surveillance and prosecution from shipboard or land as long as there is any area of open water.

✦ ✦ ✦

The navy clearly has a role in the support of Canada's arctic policies by definitive means. But its main role to date has been expressive and purposive, to demonstrate national commitments not only to enforcement of Canadian jurisdiction but also to participation in international security. Griffiths's 1999 essay in the *International Journal* suggested that, in general but particularly in the arctic, a new spirit of internationalism was eroding politically proscriptive concepts of sovereignty. A decade later Griffiths returned to the theme with a paper for the Canadian International Council calling for a co-operative approach to arctic stewardship.[42] "The Arctic," he wrote, "is pacific in the sense that not a lot is going on as compared to other regions of the world," with the possible exception of the border between Norway and Russia." This happy state has the unfortunate by-product of minimizing any impulse toward international solutions, but Griffiths urged the value of arctic states creating a model for regional collaboration as a generator of a world stewardship culture, and urged the Canadian government to raise concerns about the arctic to the "highest political level." Canadian rhetoric is nationalistic and speaks of sovereignty, but Canadian action is predominantly co-operative and administrative. The joint mapping exercises conducted by the Canadian Coast Guard with the United States Coast Guard, and with the Royal Danish Navy, to determine boundaries between their respective countries, and between them and the Russian Republic, are the most important "naval" activity in the arctic. The 2010 Operation *Nanook* included forces from the United States and Denmark.[43] The continual participation of Canadian naval forces to collective action outside the formal NATO area is the base of the pyramid, of which the ships and aircraft designed for work in the arctic are only the tip.

Kraska urged that "both the United States and Canada have an essential national interest in developing a widely accepted and respected legal regime for the Arctic ocean and Northwest Passage before climate change alters shipping patterns." He believes that the mechanism by which an acceptable regime might be developed that meets the need to protect the waters from marine pollution should be the International Maritime Organization. The Arctic Council might provide important leverage in ensuring that the regulations protected the indigenous population of the archipelago. In November 2009 the U.S. Navy released a five-year strategic plan outlining future fleet operations in the arctic in anticipation of the region being ice-free during the summer by 2030, but also stressing international co-operation.

CONCLUSION:
THE PAST IS PROLOGUE

The metaphor of a two-edged sword aptly represents the paradox for Canada of participation in a system of collective defence as a means of avoiding national subordination. The active partnership during the first three decades of the history of the Royal Canadian Navy was with the imperial forces that had sustained Canadian independence for two hundred years. During this period lessons were learned about the compromises that were inevitable when national autonomy was confronted by the problems of collective defence, and the Second World War demonstrated convincingly that naval forces could not be improvised during the heat of battle without serious consequences, although it also demonstrated what heroism and hard work could accomplish against the odds. Following the war, with the defence organization of the Empire/Commonwealth fading away, Canada's partnership with the United States has come to replicate the degree of integration that existed within the British Empire and Commonwealth.[1] Unlike the situation that prevailed in that family of nations, however, the United States makes no show of seeking Canadian participation in the formation of a common foreign policy. Active involvement in the defence concerns of its neighbours distances Canadian policy from what was known as Finlandization during the Soviet era, but only so long as Canada can maintain control over her forces, and employ them only on operations which accord with Canadian appreciations of propriety and effectiveness. That proviso presents challenges.

Sir James Cable's taxonomy for "Gunboat Diplomacy" effectively describes the operational means by which the Canadian navy has supported Canadian foreign policy, in war as well as peace. In the two world wars "definitive force" was employed to support the ability of the Empire and Commonwealth, with its allies, to protect the shipping upon which depended every aspect of defence and ultimately counter-attack. This operational purpose rolled together the primary and secondary functions of sea power, defence against assault and defence of trade, and also served the secondary and "purposive" function of supporting recognition of Canada's autonomous character. In the inter-war period the need to reassure Washington that Canada could defend its neutrality in the event of a war between Japan and the United States was the primary operational task of the Royal Canadian Navy, one that required both an independent ability and partnership with imperial forces. The transformation of the United States into the champion of democracy, and guarantor of Canadian security, was of vital importance but even before the United States became a belligerent it was also recognized that American support came at a price, which could only be managed if Canada were able to provide significant defence of her own territory and seas. The means of meeting these challenges called for definitive acts to serve a purposive end. The postwar formation of NATO was important as a means of creating a make-weight to offset American dominance, by facilitating the ability of the United States to extend its defensive glacis well beyond Canadian territory. Canada's military contribution to the alliance throughout the Cold War served a definitive purpose vis-à-vis the Soviet threat, and a purposive one with respect to Canada's relationship with the United States. The "rust-out" of the Canadian navy following the Cuban Missile crisis and in the first years of the Pierre Trudeau administration, and the plan by the Brian Mulroney administration to construct a fleet of nuclear submarines were different approaches to the problem of managing Canada's relationship with the American super-power during a period of great danger. With the ending of the Cold War a new era dawned, and the focus of the Canadian navy's definitive operations has been increasingly directed toward global policing, but its purposive objective has continued to be that of managing the relationship with the United States.

Although the threat posed by German militarism to the Royal Navy's control of the maritime approaches to Canada was the occasion for the formation of the Royal Canadian Navy, the management of Canada's relationship with the United States has been at the heart of Canada's naval strategy. This objective has largely been served successful, but it is one that constantly challenges the independence of Canadian policy. Mackenzie King made it clear to the leaders of the Empire as long ago as 8 October 1923 that the American relationship was a matter of fundamental importance to Canadians – not without difficulties, but not unrewarding: "The United States is not ... always easy to deal with. The great diversity of occupation and cultural background in that vast area, the frequent lack of coordination among the branches of its Government, the power of unscrupulous politicians and newspapers to create a sudden stampede, must all be taken into account. But as far, at least, as Canada is concerned we have found the United States of late years an increasingly friendly and dependable neighbour. It has been our aim, the aim of all Governments, irrespective of party, in the last quarter-century, to maintain and develop that good feeling. That does not mean that we are prepared to sacrifice vital interests on the altar of American friendship, that is not the way to deal with our United States friends."[2] In 1941 he noted in his diary that he, "personally, would be strongly opposed to anything like a political union ... It is better to have two peoples and two governments on this continent understanding each other and reciprocating in their relations as an example to the world, than to have anything like continental union."[3] Thirteen years after Mackenzie King's retirement, President John F. Kennedy addressed the Canadian Houses of Parliament with the famous words: "Geography has made us neighbors. History has made us friends. Economics has made us partners. And necessity has made us allies. Those whom nature hath so joined together, let no man put asunder."[4] That last characterization might be thought to be a shade ambiguous, and the final injunction a shade threatening. It resonates with General Maurice Pope's April 1944 observation that, "to the Americans the defence of the United States is continental defence, which includes us, and nothing that I can think of will ever drive that idea out of their heads." Pope's additional observation, that Canada had to be careful to support the confidence of the United States in Canadian security, has been a dominating consideration in Canadian defence policy.[5] Kennedy went on to develop his theme: "This is a partnership, not an empire. We are bound to have differences and disappointments – and we are equally bound to bring them out into the open, to settle them where they can be settled, and to respect each other's views when they cannot be settled." President Richard Nixon echoed this thought in his 1972 address to the Canadian Parliament when he said that Canada and the United States "must realize that we are friends, not because there have been no problems between us, but because we have trusted one another enough to be candid about our problems and because our candor has nourished our co-operations."[6] These are good words, but like any marriage, the relationship between Canada and the United States is always a work in progress.

The role of the Canadian Armed Forces in this relationship was clear at the time the Royal Canadian Navy was established, and was stated by C.P. Stacey in an academic paper in November 1938: "Canada no longer arms against the United States, but the proximity of the great republic still profoundly affects her military position ... If, in a crisis, Canada is obliged to beg help from the United States, she must also accept whatever policies the United States may choose to dictate."[7] The 1994 *White Paper on Defence* was on firm ground when it stated: "First, Canada-US defence cooperation continues to serve this country's fundamental interests extremely well. Second, the Government wants the Canadian Forces to maintain the ability to work closely with their US counterparts in a variety of situations. Third, even if the Government decided to reduce significantly the level of defence cooperation with the United States, Canada would still be obliged to rely on the US for help in protecting its territory and approaches – and this assistance would then come on strictly American terms, unmitigated by the influence Canada enjoys as a result of its defence partnership with the United States and with our other NATO allies." Earlier the White Paper had also stated: "Canada should never find itself in a position where, as a consequence of past decisions, the defence of our national territory has become the responsibility of others."[8] Nor, it must be added, should the needs of bilateral defence relations be permitted to lead the Canadian government to support flawed strategies that unacceptably affect Canadian domestic and foreign policies.

There has always been a constituency within the Canadian elite willing to be led by the defence perceptions of Canada's allies. In the early twentieth century this constituency viewed as the proper policy for Ottawa the provision to the Imperial mother country of the military support requested by it. In the late twentieth century, and at the beginning of the twenty-first, that constituency has transferred its instinctive colonial attitude to the United States, and regards it as invariably appropriate policy for Canada to meet the expectations of her ally to the south. Harper's public rebuke of Chrétien for his refusal to join President George W. Bush's "coalition of the willing" is a case in point.[9] Not surprisingly, the American ambassador in Ottawa, David Wilkins, advised the State Department that the United States was "better off with [Stephen Harper] ... at the helm in Canada." He was credited with being a "strong friend of the US."[10] Harper's observation, however, was a poor representation of Canadian opinion. Frederick Monk's concern that the navy might only "be Canadian when it has to be paid for, in order to be Imperial when it is required for use" is as valid in the twenty-first century as it was at the beginning of the twentieth.

In an academic paper published in the spring of 2004, a year after the invasion of Iraq and the unofficial – and perhaps coerced – participation of Canadian ships and soldiers in its operations, Denis Stairs noted that the connection drawn by U.S. trade representative Robert Zoellick between free trade agreements and "cooperation – or better – on foreign policy and security issues ... expresses dominance, and it does not win friends (not willing friends, anyway) for the United States."[11] Later that year Michael Ignatieff, echoing Escott Reid's 1967 assessment of American unilateralist tendencies, wrote: "they are multilateral when it is to the advantage of the United States, unilateral when they can get away with it. It is a vision in which world order is guaranteed by the power and might and influence of the super power, as opposed to the spreading influence of international law."[12] The U.S. embassy's deputy head of mission Terry Breese in January 2009 characterized Ignatieff, by that date leader of the Liberal Party, as "more familiar with the United States than any other current (or even former) Canadian political leader," but the American government's preference for a Harper administration was quietly repeated in the weeks before the 2011 federal election that gave him a majority in the House of Commons.[13]

Douglas Ross warned, under the banner "Michael Ignatieff's Truncated View of Canadian-American Relations," that, because of Canada's vulnerability to the consequences for trade of any panic in Washington, "Canadians have a very large and very immediate stake in the effectiveness of American policy in waging and winning their offensive War on Terror in the Middle East and Central Asia, and in their defensive success in protecting American society from WMD attacks."[14] A recent study prepared by Edward Greenspon et al. for the Canadian International Council goes considerably further down the road of continentalism. *Open Canada: A Global Positioning Strategy for a Networked Age* urges the development of a common border agency for Canada and the United States, and a more comprehensive expansion of NORAD into maritime defence: "In the view of the GPS Panel, Canada should be applying itself to reinvigorating and expanding an institution that represents one of the most special parts of a special relationship." The retired senior diplomat Paul Heinbecker had something much less capitulatory in mind when he suggested that Canada and the United States should form "the terrorism equivalent of the Permanent Joint Board on Defence," but the panel findings appear to have been inspired [15] When Prime Minister Harper travelled to Washington in February 2011 to meet with President Obama, the two signed an agreement to enhance information sharing, and to reduce bureaucratic barriers to trade.[16]

Sensible as much of that is, the panel took a long march too far when it urged abandonment of a century of craftsmanship in Canada's defence relations: "Canada," it stated, "needs to stop crafting its international policies as a series of counterweights, in which we try to balance a policy favourable to the US with one that is multilateral – or worse, one that directly confronts the Americans."[17] This is intemperate advice. There is no doubt that for Canada splendid isolation is not an option, but there is nothing in Canadian experience to indicate that the pursuit of strategic breadth can safely be abandoned. NATO and the Commonwealth are still of importance to Canada.

With the termination of the NATO Canada-US Regional Planning Group there can no longer be any pretense that the NATO military command structure offsets American domination in North American defence. The military command structure of NATO, however, was never the most important means by which the alliance met the Canadian need for strategic breadth. Not only does NATO served Canadian needs by extending the American defensive glacis well beyond Canadian territory, but NATO continues to be important for its capacity to moderate the Hobbesian world order by means over which Canada has some influence. The civilian North Atlantic Council provides an important context for addressing issues of power and influence in a collective setting away from media pressure. The failure of Defence Minister Peter MacKay's 2010 bid to be NATO secretary general is some measure of Canada's stature in the organization, but Canadian ambassadors to NATO can still influence decisions of the Atlantic Council, in proportion to the extent of Canadian participation in NATO operations. In the paper that Ross criticized, Ignatieff had asserted that participation in multilateral peace enforcement, and in the deliberations of the North Atlantic Council, provides Canada with far more influence than comes from co-option into "coalitions of the willing" that are always *ad hoc*, and always "dominated by the coalition leader."[18] And NATO is valued in Ottawa as an international organization that provides an important forum for military diplomacy. Having extended its partnership for peace into eastern Europe prior to admitting a band of members that were formerly part of the Soviet bloc, it is now extending its partnership program into Asia.[19]

If Mackenzie King were still alive, he would certainly discover a renewed interest in the historic British connection. In 1995 Harold Klepak wrote that "only a determined effort to resuscitate those areas of Canadian-UK and Canadian-Commonwealth defence cooperation can ensure that there is a significant counterpoise to the military influence from the South." He also suggested there was a place for "a not too exaggerated effort to increase defence relations with France."[20] David Haglund argued in 2000 that "Post-Wesphalianism, soft power, and the desire to minimize burdens coupled with the zeal to preserve coalitions – all are pulling Canada back to its Atlanticist centre of strategic gravity ... Canada is certainly not ending this century as a 'European' country. It remains, however, very much an Atlanticist one."[21] The closer the embrace with the United States, he commented, the greater is the need for John Bartlet Brebner's "North-Atlantic Triangle."[22]

At a time when the U.S. Navy is shifting its focus into the Pacific to meet the new challenge from China, a closer Canadian partnership with the Royal Navy in Atlantic security does make operational as well as strategic sense. China has been methodically working toward the development of a blue-water fleet that includes nuclear-powered submarines and aircraft carriers, and has extended its influence into the Indian ocean by its participation in anti-piracy patrols, and into the Mediterranean in the context of the 2011 Libya crisis.[23] Meanwhile, the navy of the Russian Federation is beginning the process of salvaging a small but effective fleet from the wreck of the Soviet navy. Presently the Russian fleet has one aircraft carrier that has suffered repeated equipment failures and one battle cruiser in active service. Captain Fedyszyn, director of the Europe-Russia Studies Group at the U.S. Naval War College, writes that: " the navy's relative stature is growing in Russia. Ships are being built at a markedly faster pace and these ships are increasingly joining the Russian fleet, not only being sold to foreign countries ... These trends may result in a rise back into the upper crust of the World's navies." He does not foresee the regenerated fleet being used to challenge western navies, and notes that "the very likely increased Russian presence in the Arctic Ocean will have more to do with global trade and oil security than it will with bastion defense of ballistic-missile submarines." Convincing as that assessment is, however, the growth of the Russian fleet has implications for international relationships, and particularly for Canada. It presents both challenges and opportunities.[24] The by-now routine participation by Canadian naval units in American naval battle groups could be balanced by routine participation in British, and perhaps in Anglo-French, naval formations. The synergy is obvious. The massive cuts in defence spending forced upon Britain in 2010 could be an opportunity for a renewed partnership. Britain and France have signed an agreement to establish a closer naval, military, and nuclear partnership, and participation in this partnership by the bilingual Canadian navy could be an important means to provide leverage for Canadian strategic objectives.[25]

Although the Commonwealth has long ceased to be a defence organization, it is a family of nations with a common naval history as well as political institutions that to a greater or lesser degree were inherited from Britain.[26] At an Ottawa historical conference to mark the hundredth anniversary of the formation of the Canadian navy, the Australian admiral James Goldrick observed that "the efforts made over the last century to develop various national [Commonwealth] navies have brought about a shared approach and outlook – a recognizably 'naval' culture – that is distinguishable and distinctive and which has had and will continue to have important operational and perhaps even strategic consequences."[27] The Commonwealth Secretariat, formed in 1964 with a Canadian, Arnold Smith, as its first secretary general, is careful to avoid any defence role, but that does not preclude its being a valuable resource for defence planning.[28] The most egregious mistakes made over the last half-century have been a consequence of a lack of adequate local knowledge, and the Commonwealth has unparalleled resources for the development of smart policies. Trudeau's early disdain for the Commonwealth was later transformed into enthusiasm when he discovered it had grown into an effective multinational organization bringing together the wealthiest and the poorest people on the globe.[29] The linkages among Commonwealth military and naval forces exist distinct from the more formal Commonwealth Secretariat. They could be put to better use, and better linkages could be forged. As a defence organization the Commonwealth is more of a family than an alliance. Although other structures and dependencies have come to surpass it in importance, a family it remains.

Mackenzie King was engaged throughout his political life in softening the links of empire, and believed he was forging strands of partnership between Britain and the United States, but in his rejection of continental union, he also had a vision of Canada as the new centre of the Commonwealth. "Canada," he wrote in April 1941, "in time, and sooner than we expected perhaps, would become its centre."[30] In recent years Canadian interest in the Commonwealth has lapsed, but revival of its centrality in Canadian policy, and an acknowledgment of its place in Canadian defence strategy, could also revive Canada's claim to "middle power" stature. The historic Commonwealth connections, and the more recent NATO ones, should not be seen as in conflict, or as alternatives. The announcement made by Peter MacKay on 16 August 2011 that the navy is to recover its original name of Royal Canadian Navy, with the air force also returning to its Royal designator, could be symbolic of a move in the direction of strengthening Commonwealth defence partnerships.[31]

The leverage that British, Commonwealth, and NATO – and of course American – connections may give to Canadian defence policy cannot be matched elsewhere. Attention has been paid during the last decades to developing naval connections with Pacific rim countries, through participation with the U.S. Navy in RIMPAC exercises. The Canadian navy's *Westploy* is an internal commitment to deploy at least one ship to northeastern Asiatic waters on even years, and another to southeastern Asiatic waters on odd ones. James Boutilier, Maritime Forces Pacific Headquarters' special advisor on matters of defence and foreign policy and maritime security in the Asia-Pacific region, believes that 108 Canadian naval deployments were made to the western Pacific between 1960 and 1994.[32] It is always valuable to develop personal service connections through such means, relationships that might prove useful in the event of resource confrontations such as the Turbot war, or other potentially explosive situations. In October 2010 Canada was granted full voting status in the Western Pacific Naval Symposium, which is a forum for naval officers to address maritime issues of mutual concern.[33] Port visits also serve as a demonstration of Canadian interest, and a demonstration of Canadian technology. But Canada has no cultural or historical links to any Pacific rim nation, apart from the United States and the Commonwealth countries of Australia and New Zealand, on a scale that could be leveraged by means of military diplomacy. The economic benefits to Canada from its Asian trade partners have valuable strategic implications, but these do not flow from any sort of defence mutuality. If they did, that would be a matter for deep concern in Ottawa.

While strategic breadth is important, greater importance needs to be assigned to the maintenance of the highest standards in strategic staff work. The macro-scale, grand strategic, fostering of defence relationships with the United States, Commonwealth nations, and NATO allies is fundamental, but also obvious. It is at the micro-scale, where operations are planned, usually in conjunction with those allies and at least in part to support relationships with them, that the serious staff work has to be undertaken to ensure that the commitment of Canadian forces is both effective and ethical. Even if it is conceded that the maintenance of a constructive relationship with the United States is of paramount strategic importance for Canada, commitments to American led military initiatives have followed rather too closely the Mackenzie King model of abdication of responsibility for matters of overall strategy.

In 1995 Douglas Bland wrote: "whether it was the imperial needs of the British government, the defence of British interests in South Africa or Flanders, the needs of the Royal Navy, or the demands of NATO and the United Nations, Canada and many Canadian élites have always been ready to sacrifice Canadian interest to empire, international harmony, and the comfort of subordination ... James Eayrs called it 'growing up allied,' but in many important respects Canada's military profession has never grown up at all." Bland quoted John Gellner to the effect that "whenever a military effort was called for, Canada provided its full share of fine doers, but no thinkers," and quoted Adrian Preston, who wrote that "after a century of national development, and having reached a stage of political and military maturity at which she needed philosophers more urgently than technicians, Canada possessed no significant tradition of military literature, intellectualism, or scholarship." Bland is critical of the "not very glorious record" of Canada's chiefs of defence staff, deputy ministers of national defence, and the succession of ministers who knew little about defence matters and soon moved on to other portfolios.[34] Preston was writing in 1971, and Gellner in 1985. Their more sweeping criticism could be refuted by study of the articles in the *Canadian Military Journal*, and the *International Journal*. But the sorry record of Canada's role in the two Iraq wars does suggest that the wisdom of Canada's military philosophers is not always being translated into government, or alliance, policy.

Where Ignatieff and Ross share common ground is in the recognition that Canadian safety depends upon the effectiveness of policies. This is true as much for domestic security, where smart border agreements must not lead to social conflict, as it is for global intervention. Dangerous strategies, such as those that created wholesale starvation and disease in Iraq, can never make Canada safer. Participation by Canadian forces in such strategies is an act of folly. The light-hearted way in which Ottawa embarked on enforcement of sanctions against Iraq in 1990 undermines any confidence that the Canadian government could have used to good effect the leverage that the Mulroney administration's projected fleet of nuclear submarines might have given it to influence planning for aggressive strategic anti-submarine warfare into the Norwegian Sea.

At the time of the Kuwait crisis, international energy was devoted to perfecting the tactical means of implementing imperfect strategies, and to obtaining compliance. Recently Margaret Doxey has written that "national implementation is essential and for mandatory UN sanctions this means that all 192 members need to take their responsibilities seriously."[35] On the face of it, this injunction implies only that Canada needs to have the equivalent of a "war book" embodying the manner in which sanctions may be implemented according to Canadian law. However, Canada has a practical as well as a moral obligation to ensure that ethical standards are met, and to do so it needs to understand the implications of its actions, and use that understanding to influence Security Council and White House decisions. Laura Higgins has written of the sanctions enforcement operations that "the very presence of a Canadian ship in an area is a projection of Canadian values and a show of Canada's commitment to the international rule of law and stability in the region."[36] But if sanctions inflict such suffering on a civilian population that it causes hundreds of thousands of deaths and affects the health of a generation, then it casts those "Canadian values" in a poor light.

The safety of Canada depends on smart policies, resolutely carried out, in partnership with her allies. If the goal of interoperability with the U.S. Navy is not to end in the transformation of the Canadian navy into an auxiliary squadron of an Imperial American fleet, along with absorption of the rest of Canada's armed forces, Canadians need to seize a commanding height in strategic staff work. And it is fair to say that what is good for Canada is good for Canada's friends. In their strongly expressed praise of Lloyd Axworthy's refocusing of Canadian defence upon the concept of human security, Joseph Jockel and Joel Sokolsky observed in 2000 that it becomes "acceptable to be a 'partner' with a unipolar 'behemoth' when the United States uses its unmatched military might to set right wrongs committed against the innocent."[37] As Ignatieff wrote in his 2003 study *Empire Lite: Nation Building in Bosnia, Kosovo, and Afghanistan*, "Humanitarian action is not unmasked if it is shown to be the instrument of imperial power. Motives are not discredited just because they are shown to be mixed." In his commentary, Michael Morgan writes that "for an ally like Canada, the key is not to reject Washington's foreign policy automatically, or to accept it uncritically, but rather to work with the US and other allies for the sake of common interests and shared ideals."[38] Such partnership calls for judgment in Ottawa and avoidance of megaphone diplomacy on both sides of the border.

Denis Stairs warned in 2004 that one of the biggest dangers the American government faces is that "they will be blinded by their own light, and become the victims of a self-generated myopia." In consequence, "it may be worth reflecting on the possibility that Canadians serve US interests best when we tell it like we see it, and not like Americans see it. The world looks quite different, after all, when viewed from the perspective of a smaller power; a power that routinely has to put up with the international politics of give-and-take because it does not have any other choice."[39] As a former chief of defence staff responded to my comments about blind acceptance of American leadership in enforcing the Iraq sanctions: "our allies deserve better from us."[40] The capabilities needed for us to make a meaningful contribution are firstly intellectual ones, those of the economist, historian, lawyer, and philosopher of ethics, and only secondly those of ship drivers and weapons officers.

There is but too much reason to view the deeply flawed sanctions strategy employed against Iraq as instrumental in the terrorist conflict that followed hard on its heels. In November 1990, Robert Runcie, the archbishop of Canterbury, attested that "a year of sanctions would be far cheaper in every way than a very short war."[41] It is unlikely he would have made such a comment had he been better informed about the consequences of sanctions, although they were certainly multiplied by the destruction of Iraqi infrastructure in the bombing operations prior to Operation *Desert Storm*. In 1983 Trudeau had warned parliament that "the starving refugee lying in the hot dust of the Sahel can scarcely summon the strength to help himself, let alone strike out at us. If his children survive," he then added, "they will remember us, and with fury in their hearts, you can be sure."[42] Only ten years later the spiritual leader of al Quaeda, Osama bin Laden, made it clear that the Iraq sanctions had aroused just such fury.

In 1993 the British journalist Robert Fisk of the *Independent* interviewed bin Laden and reported him saying: "When sixty Jews are killed inside Palestine [by suicide bombers], all the world gathers within seven days to criticize this action, while the deaths of 600,000 Iraqi children [after UN sanctions were placed on Iraq] did not receive the same reaction. Killing those Iraqi children is a crusade against Islam. We as Muslims do not like the Iraqi regime but we think that the Iraqi people and their children are our brothers and we care about their future." In February 1998 Adil Hussein, a prominent Egyptian activist, stirred a huge crowd to fury, asking: "Can you imagine a whole nation on which these dogs have imposed starvation? They kill children, the sick, and there is no food." A Fatwa was drawn up, calling upon "Muslims around the world" by all means, including military, "to do their Islamic duty in relieving the Iraqi people from the unjust sanctions." When interviewed by Pakistani journalist Rahimullah Yusufzi following the bombing of installations near Bagdad, bin Laden said: "The American and British peoples stated widely that they support their leaders' decision to attack Iraq. This means that all individuals of these two nations, as well as the Jews in occupied Palestine, are belligerent people and every Muslim must stand against them and must kill and fight them."[43]

This author encountered a stony indifference at the United Nations to any serious scholarship on sanctions at the time they were being imposed on Iraq. That indifference, unfortunately, was also encountered in the Department of National Defence. When in May 1996 Madeleine Albright, then the U.S. ambassador to the United Nations, was asked by a reporter about the half-million children believed to have died because of the Iraq sanctions she responded: "I think that it is a very hard choice, but the price, we think, the price is worth it."[44] Only four months later, however, in September 1996 when reviewing the use of sanctions against Yugoslavia, the Copenhagen Round Table Conference "generally agreed that the instrument of sanctions is still relatively undeveloped and blunt, mainly because it has only been applied on a limited number of occasions, mostly after the end of the cold war ... Sanctions are a matter of considerable seriousness and concern and should be resorted to with utmost caution."[45] Those who have read the 1920 Royal Navy staff history of the blockade of the central powers can be forgiven for thinking that the "blunt instrument" of sanctions might have been finely honed long ago, but the Copenhagen Round Table was the beginning of a serious attempt at the United Nations to address the problem.

The British foreign secretary Robin Cook defended the air operations against Iraqi targets in the *Telegraph* on 20 February 2001, noting that by then the Security Council had removed all limits on the amount of oil that Iraq could exchange for humanitarian goods. "Why did Saddam order no medicines at all for six months at the end of last year? Is this not a cause of Iraqi suffering? Why is more than $11 billion lying unspent in the UN's oil-for-food accounts? Why is Saddam exporting food and medicine, including milk powder and asthma inhalers, to other countries while denying them to his own people?"[46] Even if Cook's facts were correct, however, by that late date the political and ethical damage had been done. In a *Naval Review* article of July 2001, Lt Cmdr D.G. Kibble qualified his statement of the obvious – that "Saddam Hussein ... is the brutal dictator responsible for this state of affairs" – with the grim truth that Saddam was making effective propaganda use of the selective nature of American and British support for UNSCR 1284 while ignoring the resolutions calling "for justice for the Palestinian Arab people."[47] The injury done to the Iraqi people by sanctions and by bombing was not the principal reason for the Islamist campaign against the United States, Britain, Spain, and around the world, but its importance in mobilizing public opinion in the Arab world should not be underrated. Ignatieff concluded his October 2001 Young Memorial lecture to the cadets at the Royal Military College of Canada, given just weeks after the destruction of the World Trade Center and attack on the Pentagon, with the words: "We have to think of ethics as our enabler and multiplier. You are in the legitimacy business – reproducing, building and strengthening the legitimacy of your society here and abroad. If you understand the role of ethics in doing that, you will be doing your job."[48]

In April 1997 Portugal's ambassador to the United Nations had begun a review process of sanctions regimes, work that was aggressively pursued by the Canadian ambassador Robert Fowler in January 1999. Several governments also hosted international efforts to resolve issues related to the use of sanctions. In 2000 the Security Council during the period of Canadian presidency formed a working group to "develop general recommendations on how to improve the effectiveness of United Nations sanctions," which finally completed its work in December 2006. At the beginning of the process, Canada's foreign minister, Lloyd Axworthy, wrote an introduction to David Cortright and George Lopez's *The Sanctions Decade* in which he indicated the awareness in Ottawa that changes had to be made: "Sanctions regimes can and must be crafted in ways that shield civilians from harm. When imposing sanctions, the Council must give the same weight to protecting civilians as it does to attaining political objectives. Otherwise, the very legitimacy – and efficacy of this tool of enforcement will be cast into doubt."[49]

The two concepts of international law and international peace were originally kept distinct in the United Nations Charter but, as Vera Gowlland-Debbas writes, they have gradually been merged by a process that is more political than judicial. "The move towards international criminal responsibility of individuals certainly serves to undermine the fiction of the black box – the monolithic state that is responsible for all acts committed within its territory – by providing a more acceptable alternative to that of holding entire populations accountable for the acts of their leaders ... The dangers of exclusion and marginalization of a greater part of humanity through coercive methods should be clear enough today."[50] An unresolved issue is whether sanctions resolutions should be open-ended or time-limited, with the United States favouring the first. Joanna Weschler believes that a pragmatic compromise has been developed by the Security Council by which time limits have been imposed on the use of sanctions for conflict management but not on those employed to address global security issues such as counterterrorism and nonproliferation.[51]

These are positive developments, but more is needed. To date, the world community does not appear to be capable of moving beyond nineteenth- and twentieth-century concepts of sanctions as punitive measures, although the focus has moved to "smart sanctions" against rogue leaders, and "persons of interest."[52] An alternative form of sanction, depending less on coercion and more on diversion of resources, and on social transformation, is described in an appendix on Pro-Active Sanctions.

The track record for Canadian attempts to divert the United States from highly dangerous and probably irrational mistakes, as Lester Pearson attempted to do during the Korean and Vietnam wars, Pierre Trudeau during the dangerous last decade of the Cold War, and Jean Chrétien prior to the American invasion of Iraq, certainly discourages. No one should be surprised when such hubris is snubbed, although similar efforts must, of course, be attempted in like circumstances in the future. Trudeau was quite right to question the safety of NATO war plans, and to opt out if they ran the risk of accidental war. His concern about the aggressive nature of American strategic ASW may have been excessive, but it was not inappropriate. Brian Mulroney's efforts to channel American response to the Kuwait crisis through the United Nations contributed to an international effort in that direction, but should not have led to Canada's blindly following the allied strategic plan.

Realistically, Canada should avoid dramatic interventions, and aim at moderating American strategy by timely participation in the planning process. "What we have needed," John Holmes has written, "is to know about US policies before they jelled and went public." There seems little alternative "to the hard diplomatic slugging involved" in discovering what the Americans have in mind.[53] Nor, it should be added, is there any alternative to Canadian effort to develop smart and proven strategies.

There is a need for the Canadian government to sustain a strong institutional consciousness of the capabilities and limitations of armed forces, and to have the courage to refuse to participate in those it sees to be based on faulty intelligence and faulty staff work. Institutional ambition should not be permitted to undermine the strategic direction of the unified Canadian Armed Forces by the chief of defence staff, or be allowed to promote insubstantial ideas of sea power. Above all, the institutions of Canadian government should understand the implications of the operations to which it commits the Canadian Armed Forces. The resources available to the government need to be strengthened, both in the Department of Foreign Affairs and in the Privy Council Office, to ensure that institutional memories are sufficient to give wisdom to policy. An attempt was made in 1984, as a consequence of Trudeau's peace initiative, to create an arm's-length "Canadian Institute for International Peace and Security" but it was soon abolished, perhaps because it was over-funded.[54] The 1921 arrangement by which Royal Navy intelligence organization for the north-western Atlantic was located in Ottawa could be the inspiration for a similar centre for strategic analysis and direction located in Canada. Fundamental to the effectiveness of Canadian strategic planning must be continuity of leadership. Not every diplomat can be given a strategist's seat and do well at the job. There is a need to return to the methods of earlier times when a Dr Sutherland, or a Dr Lindsey, could acquire experience and effectiveness in a leadership role over a matter of decades.

Perhaps the Canadian defence liaison staff at the Washington embassy should be strengthened to the point that it could hold its own in the complex world of foreign policy and defence planning in the American capital – feeding concepts and intelligence from an Ottawa centre for strategic analysis into the D.C. beltway. In 1965 Henry Kissinger wrote that the United States tries "to create a structure which physically prevents any ally (except the United States) from acting autonomously. This tends," he continued, "to turn our Allies into advisors in an American decision-making process."[55] There is no reason to think Kissinger had Canada in mind, or that Canada was welcomed as an advisor. However, Denis Healey, who was Britain's chancellor of the exchequer between 1974 and 1979, has commented that his "own experience under many

American administrations is that Washington is exceptionally open to influence by argument from outsiders whose goodwill, experience, and commonsense is accepted. The machinery for taking decisions in Washington usually involves prolonged argument between officials who favour different policies. Intelligent foreigners may often play a decisive role in such arguments."[56] Decisions about commitment of Canadian forces to bilateral, multi-lateral and international operations should be based in part on whether such commitment does or does not overcome Washington's unilateral instincts, the "not invented here" phenomenon. Strategic leadership could be leveraged by capitalizing on the Canadian navy's ability to serve as a "gateway" supporting interoperability between the U.S. Navy and the navies of wider coalitions – as Melanie Graham has suggested.[57]

✦ ✦ ✦

There are some within the Canadian navy who regard the fostering of a navy-to-navy relationship with the U.S. Navy by commitments to bilateral and international action as transformative of Canadian foreign policy. Leading from the rear, their vision is defence of the capitalist democracies behind naval barriers. This naval perspective considers the Canadian commitment of military forces to the war in Afghanistan as fundamentally mistaken, and never likely to be repeated. Possibly Mackenzie King would have agreed. On visiting the navy at Esquimalt in July 1941 he noted in his diary that his vision of the the future of Canada included: "navy on both coasts, guarding the security of this continent and helping with the air force and the army to maintain peace with the Atlantic and Pacific ocean. I am convinced, however," he added, "that the army itself will fade out in the course of time."[58] The concept of a "1,000 ship" fleet of allied navies, of a Global Maritime Partnership, greatly interests at least some Canadian naval officers. As described by Admiral Mike Mullen, USN, this concept does not interfere with the sovereign rights of states.[59] Its emphasis on the brotherhood (and no doubt sisterhood) of the sea, however, poses the danger that naval "group-think" could overwhelm national and more terrestrial perspectives.

How much influence is generated by Canada's naval effort is far from clear. Canadian diplomats have avoided linkages between files, recognizing the limitations of *quid pro quo* bargaining with "Uncle" where the administration cannot be held accountable to agreements because of the power of "the US Senate, a mindless body," as John Holmes put it, "with which one cannot deal." But Holmes recognized that linkages do influence or even determine outcomes at a personal level during negotiations.[60] Notoriously, American senators are sensitive to the track record of military partnership. Since the 1940 Ogdensburg pronouncements, Canadian naval partnership with the U.S. Navy has been an important part of Canadian-American relations.

At the end of the day, there is no sovereign formula that ensures influence for smaller states. The historical record, however, shows that there are consequences for failure of collegiality among allies. The relationship between the strategic capacity of the Canadian navy and its inventory of ships, and the air force's aircraft, is obvious. At the most fundamental level, the navy of Canada is designed for service within an alliance umbrella, and always has been. When the political leadership found that such relationships did not resonate with Canadian strategic perceptions, however, they naturally turned to thoughts of a navy that lacked the performance and reach that would make possible its being drawn into the planning of Canada's partners. Mackenzie King's preference for a small navy of small ships was later, for a while, shared by Pearson and Trudeau. The ultimate expression of this concept is a navy of coast-defence vessels, serving, as Roger Sarty says about the navy of the 1920s, as a seaward extension of harbour defences. Canada has done well out of its strategy of engagement and supportive suasion, and should continue to develop its navy with that grand strategy in mind. Canada's friends should nevertheless take note that Canada might well return to its policy of defence through minimal armament, should it ever again come to think its strategic control compromised and its strategic assessments ignored. That same lesson must be taken to heart by Canadian servicemen – lest their transnational perspective makes it appear that they are not providing Canadians with the defence force that has a potential to meet their national goals.

It is always difficult, especially in peacetime, to determine the appropriate scale of investment in a navy. But it is important to keep in mind that in April 1922 Mackenzie King wrote in his diary "No need for Navy at present" when deciding to reduce it to little more than a reserve training force.[61] Seventeen years later it was still a very limited force, and Canada found itself at war. The fleet had to be expanded from a force in 1939 of six destroyers with a seventh joining, to a peak of over 365 ships by the spring of 1945. In the circumstances it is remarkable that it did as well as it did, and the Battle of the Atlantic might well have been lost had the Canadian navy not undertaken to play such a major role, but there is no longer any disguising the fact that during the middle year of the war it was qualitatively the weakest link among the navies fighting in the Atlantic. In meeting the threat from the Soviet Union at the time of the Korean war it had once again to undertake an unacceptably large expansion, by 300 percent. Strategy is an art of the possible. It is not just about the politico-military means of employing purposive and definitive force; it is also about sustaining in the context of competing peacetime values the means to act should the necessity arise.[62]

The choice of destroyers for the Canadian fleet of the 1920s and 1930s was influenced by their utility in providing some unilateral defence against hostile cruisers, while limiting commitment to Imperial defence, but the postwar choice of destroyer escorts and a light fleet carrier was determined by the need to provide effective support to allied forces. The addition of AOR ships to the fleet, and the construction of patrol frigates continued that commitment, while the construction in the late 1990s of the *Kingston* class Maritime Coastal Defence Vessels supported the bluewater fleet through training and a capacity for coastal patrol. The acquisition first of *Argus* and then of *Aurora* long-range maritime patrol aircraft served the needs of collective defence, but also directly served those of coastal control, supported by the *Trackers* sent ashore after HMCS *Bonaventure* was scrapped. The *Victoria* class submarines also support alliance operations, both in training surface forces and as a result of their ability to participate in oceanic monitoring, but they also have a particular role in supporting Canadian sovereignty because of their covert nature. The troubled history of their modernization, and consequential delays and cost overruns, leaves serious questions about their effectiveness.[63]

As this book first reached the publisher's desk in March 2011 the Canadian Navy was once again sending a ship, HMCS *Charlottetown*, to support Canadian policy, this time to the coast of Libya where a populist revolt against the barbarous rule of Moammar Gadhafi was coming under intense military assault. The Royal Canadian Air Force sent seven CF-18 aircraft supported by tankers and two *Aurora* LRPA.[64] The bilingual Canadian forces joined British and French forces. Eight months later, with the manuscript still making a glacial pace through publication, Canadian forces are returning from Libya following the overthrow of the despot. At the same time, the Harper administration has announced that Irving Shipyards in Halifax has been selected by an administrative process to construct the next generation of naval ships, two to three joint support ships to replace the AORs, fifteen identical hulls to be armed as frigates and destroyers, and six to eight patrol vessels for the arctic.[65] In January 2012 *Charlottetown* sailed again to the Mediterranean to take part in international patrols, and continue to support the branding of Canada as a loyal ally.[66]

When Prime Minister Trudeau wondered in 1969 whether Canada's "defence policy was more to impress our friends than frighten our enemies," he was posing a false dichotomy.[67] With nearly forty years of hindsight it is possible to qualify, to a degree, Dr Robert Sutherland's 1963 assertion that, while "it would be highly advantageous to discover a strategic rationale which would impart to Canada's defence programs a wholly Canadian character ... such a rationale does not exist and one cannot be invented."[68] Holmes was certainly correct when he wrote in 1981 that "Alliancemanship is ... not enough." Alliancemanship, however, is part of the equation that constitutes what might be thought of as Canada's way of defence. Holmes also wrote that "we shall have to develop muscles, our bargaining power, our capacities to use prudently what we have to offer, and to increase where we can American dependence on us ... The art of alliancemanship is what we shall need most."[69] Sutherland himself had employed the word, writing that "no other nation ... is so much dependent upon the art and science of alliancemanship." If there is a faint echo of Admiral Tirpitz's "risk fleet theory," it is that the Canadian navy serves to establish just what are Canadian interests, and generates enough sympathy in Washington's corridors of power that careless violation of Canadian sovereignty is unlikely to be contemplated. In the relatively sunny days of 1910 the navy's existence as a symbol of sovereignty was almost enough, and in the 1920s when some in the United States viewed the British Empire as their principal enemy, Canadian military weakness had positive value for quieting the relationship with the United States, but as the United States felt the cold chill of potential existential threat in the face of a two-ocean war and the violent onset of the nuclear age, more substance was needed behind the symbol. In the second decade of the twenty-first century, with the United States slipping from its pre-eminent position in world affairs, the need for substance behind the image is of continuing importance: that substance needs to be as much intellectual as material.

APPENDIX I:
PRO-ACTIVE SANCTIONS

The most obvious weakness of punitive sanctions as a coercive force, "purposive force" in Sir James Cable's taxonomy, is that the capacity of the general public to determine the behaviour of governments is limited even in countries with representative democratic constitutions, while despotic governments may be unresponsive to the suffering of their people. The Japanese government did not surrender in 1945 because of the famine conditions produced by the American naval and air blockade, and even the atomic bombing only led to surrender because it triggered the Soviet assault on Manchoko, and because the Emperor staged a palace coup. The American action during the Suez crisis of 1956, blocking Britain's access to the International Monetary Fund and thereby undermining the stability of the British currency, is a rare example of the application of punitive sanctions leading rapidly to a reasonably satisfactory outcome. The coercion of Britain succeeded because of the strength of British democracy and liberal education. Iraq was another matter altogether. It is surprising that U.S. president George Bush Sr had any hope that the people of Iraq could compel Saddam Hussein's government to change its policies. In his 1990 report to Congress, Judge William Webster, director of the CIA, made clear his belief that economic sanctions would not lead to revolt in Iraq.[1]

For economic sanctions to have any potential for purposive force, they should be part of a creative diplomatic démarche. The psychology should be that employed by a sophisticated police force in talking a violent man out of a hostage-taking incident. The force arrayed should be massive, but a bridge must be built for surrender – consistent with Sir Julian Corbett's 1907 observation that the pressure of naval action is "tedious ... unless it be nicely coordinated with military and diplomatic pressure," and Sun Tzu's in his 600 BC *The Art of War*, that a general should build for his "opponent a golden bridge to retreat across." In the Kuwait crisis, the practice of American leaders of treating the President of Iraq, Saddam Hussein, with open contempt was not well judged for achieving the best results from efforts of coercion. At a news conference in Paris in November 1990, U.S. secretary of state James Baker said that coalition leaders were united in their conviction that there must be no partial solutions. "In no way should Saddam Hussein be rewarded or be seen to be being rewarded for his aggression."[2] If it had been possible to obtain the withdrawal of the Iraqi army from Kuwait without war, some ambiguity in the terms of withdrawal might well be considered acceptable, unless the unspoken objective was to ensure that Iraqi forces could be brought to battle and destroyed. Russia's President Gorbachev and leaders of Arab states did seek to supply Iraq with a means to extricate itself, but Hussein was overconfident that the United States would not in the end be willing to accept casualties, and, reportedly, some American officials regarded a partial Iraqi withdrawal as a "nightmare scenario" that would fracture the coalition.[3] Thirty-four years earlier, in the Suez crisis, the British government was offered a substantial carrot as well as the stick – the compromise solution suggested by Lester Pearson of inserting a United Nations Peacekeeping force.[4]

Experience shows that sanctions, as purposive force, should be designed to avoid the appearance of alien origin, and of coercion. These tainting characteristics can be used by governments to bolster the resistance to demands made by the international community, and may indeed make it dangerous for such governments to comply. In conflicts involving strong nationalist forces and a poorly educated public, international sanctions can be counter-productive. Targeted governments can exploit the nationalist instincts of their citizens to reinforce their policies, and may be prevented by those same nationalist forces from abandoning their stance. Even despotic governments depend for survival upon a balancing act between the powerful forces within society, and are far from free to develop policies that do not find approval from a consensus amongst the elite, and in the street. When the Carter administration imposed sanctions on the Soviet Union in 1979 following the invasion of Afghanistan, a Soviet trade official, V. Malkevich, wrote that "no one has yet succeeded in influencing the home or foreign policy of the USSR by means of economic blackmail, discrimination, or diktat. If it ever had any effect, moreover, it has been simply the opposite of the one counted on: tension between countries always forces each of them to harden its position."[5]

The disastrous Iraq sanctions have also demonstrated to another generation the negative consequences of international action that has any potential for creating humanitarian harm. In their wake, the United Nations Office for the Coordination of Humanitarian Affairs undertook assessments of the humanitarian implications of sanctions ordered against Sierra Leone, Afghanistan and Liberia, and in 1997 the General Assembly requested the Secretariat to make an assessment of humanitarian requirements whenever sanctions are imposed.

The international community has put some effort into devising smart "targeted sanctions" that are intended to put pressure on leaders while sparing the general population. This approach proved unproductive when employed against the Haitian junta in 1994, but has been used with some success, notably against the Sudan rebel group *Unità* between 1997 and 2002, and in response to the overthrow of legitimate government in Sierra Leone and Liberia. The problems of devising effective targeted sanctions, and finding ways of enforcing them, continue to limit their utility. Targeted leaders who control the institutions of their states have effective ways of transferring the burden of sanctions onto the general population.[6] The assessment made by David Cortright and George Lopez of the fourteen sanctions regimes imposed by the Security Council between 1990 and 2002 was that they achieved about a 36 percent success rate, and that comprehensive sanctions were more effective than targeted ones.

"The finding that comprehensive trade sanctions have been more effective than targeted or selective measures," they wrote, "poses a dilemma for the many policy-makers and analysts, ourselves included, who have expressed enthusiasm for smart sanctions."[7] The relative effectiveness of comprehensive sanctions has to be set against the humanitarian costs, but the concept of pro-active sanctions could resolve the dilemma. It is the belief of this author that a pro-active sanctions regime could exert the political force of comprehensive trade sanctions to better effect because it would minimize humanitarian concern, while putting pressure on the hostile leadership, and by doing it without triggering a nationalist response. A pro-active system, functioning in the manner of trade warfare in the eighteenth century, would employ money to halt or reverse the problem created by the target state. Trade embargos would be replaced by taxes placed on the target state's imports and exports, in its basic form set at levels designed to generated maximum revenue. The funds so raised would be employed to promote the international agenda. As was noted in the introduction, the mercantilist idea was discredited by eighteenth-century economists such as Joseph Tucker and Adam Smith as a peacetime policy, but application of the mercantilist concept to economic sanctions could minimize humanitarian concerns while retaining the political purpose.

Pro-active sanctions would depart from the concept of crime, punishment, and deterrence of crime and replace it with the concept of wardship in which governments defaulting in their duty to the international community would be deprived of a measure of control over their budgets. The Security Council would mandate a tax on all trade with the defaulting country, set at a level that would raise the maximum revenue, and mandate how that revenue was to be expended to further the objectives of the United Nations. Defaulting nations would have their tax base cut back by the tax placed on their trade by the United Nations, their credit would be damaged, and the money generated by the tax would be used by the community of nations to support programs inside or outside the defaulting country that would address the problems created by its actions or neglect. The direct action of the United Nations to address the problem would take the place of coercion. The top priorities could be given to the humanitarian and developmental needs of the target population.

Apart from the so-called sanctions decade of the 1990s, it has been difficult to obtain a consensus in the Security Council to impose punitive sanctions because they create major problems for international commerce and for the national economies based on it. And typically, enforcement of sanctions has been problematic. The protracted refusal of the British government to participate in the sanctions regime against South Africa during the international campaign against apartheid was based on the negative impact it would have on employment in Britain, as well as among the black workforce in South Africa which it was the object of the sanctions to serve.

An overriding consideration in the problem of enforcement is that the incentive for traders who wish to evade sanctions will generally be greater than that of the officials who are charged with the task of blocking it. The bureaucratic conflict between those responsible for enforcement and those in Boards of Trade responsible for maintaining a favourable balance of trade is a significant addition to the problem. Over the history of naval and administrative blockade there has been a steady improvement in the technology of enforcement, but there has never been a blockade of a major state which was impermeable. The deficiencies of wartime blockade have been more than equalled by those of peacetime sanctions, and ethical concerns are inevitably greater. As was the case with respect to the sanctions against Iraq, the national interests of the great powers continues to be a problem in the issuance of end-user certificates needed to enforce United Nations–sponsored sanctions.

The difficulty of enforcement would be minimized were a pro-active system of sanctions adopted, because trade would be deflected rather than blocked. The United Nations could order members to collect a tax on trade equal to an agreed proportion of the total value of that nation's import and export trade from and to the target state, leaving it to members to determine how the tax was applied – keeping the objectives of the United Nations in mind.

Paradoxically, the avoidance of histrionic efforts at coercion could increase the effective coercive force and at the same time smooth the way for compliance by the target government. The coercive effect would be increased not only because the target government would be subjected to less humiliation, but also because it would have less reason to hope it could outlast the will of the world community to impose the sanction. Trade is not a philanthropic activity but one of mutual benefit. Further, if the revenue gained from the punitive tax were spent in ways that were popular within the target state, the usual nationalistic resistance to sanctions could be converted into a popular movement in support of the objectives of the international community.

It may be useful to consider hypothetical examples of the manner in which pro-active sanctions could be used. One may be drawn from the history of the effort to use sanctions to change the racial policies of the Union of South Africa. India imposed a comprehensive trade ban on South Africa in 1946, in 1964 Japan banned direct investment in South Africa, and in 1973 an oil embargo was established by the Organization of Arab Oil Exporting Nations. It was only after the 1976 Soweto uprising, however, that the sanctions campaign moved into high gear, with United Nations Security Council resolution banning arms sales to the Union of South Africa, and with the collective action to stop South African participation in international sporting events. Prime Minister P.W. Botha asked for more time to resolve the problems of apartheid, but used the breathing space he was given to develop efforts at destabilizing neighbouring economies. In order to strengthen its position, to undermine the African National Congress forces operating from neighbouring states and to make life in the Union appear all the more attractive, the Union government deployed terrorist forces into Mozambique and regular military units into Angola to disrupt the economies of the "Front-Line States." In consequence, in 1985–87, individual countries established comprehensive trade bans, notably the Nordic countries and the United States, and the Commonwealth and European Community established more selective bans. Britain, however, only established a voluntary ban on investments, refusing to order comprehensive economic sanctions because of the impact they would have on the British economy.

A system of pro-active sanctions could have countered the destabilization strategy, and met Britain's economic needs. A tax collected on trade with the Union could have been used to stimulate investment in the Front-Line states, and to pay for United Nations forces combatting guerrilla attacks. Because the tax would have diverted but not interrupted world trade, it could have been continued as long as the Union of South Africa continued its racial policies. Pro-active sanctions could have stopped or even reversed the flow of people looking for work in South Africa, and supported the economic development of multi-racial states on the border of the Union. It is not improbable that the Union government would have consented to the United Nations using some of the revenue inside South Africa to promote the economic status of the black community.

In the end, the Union decided to undertake its own restructuring to eliminate apartheid, and Prime Minister de Klerk stated that a stimulus for change was the effect of conventional, prescriptive, sanctions. The literature agrees that sanctions had a significant impact on the South African economy, and that the economic effect has produced political results.[8] While it would be unscholarly to refuse to acknowledge that the incomplete embargo on trade may have been a major force for change, it is appropriate to observe that a system of sanctions which did not impact negatively on world trade might have been instituted thirty years earlier, and could have brought about the reformation of South African society somewhat earlier, and somewhat less convulsively.

An example – albeit untested – of pro-active sanctions can be found in the North American Agreement on Environmental Cooperation. In the event of one of the parties to the agreement defaulting on its responsibility to ensure that its industrial production conforms with environmental standards, a provision has been made for a "monetary enforcement assessment," or fine, which may be collected by raising tariffs to the levels of "most favoured nation." Any money so collected would be paid into a fund, and employed "to improve or enhance the environment or environmental law enforcement in the Party complained against, consistent with its law."[9] This is an agreement between partner countries, not hostile states, but one of the objectives of a pro-active sanctions structure would be to minimize interstate conflict – in part by minimizing the negative impact of sanctions on the general public.

Although it is not possible to come to any decisive judgment about how effective pro-active sanctions might have been in the three conflicts – the Iraqi, Yugoslavian, and Haitian – in which the Canadian navy played an enforcement role, it is valuable to speculate. Coercion appeals to the instincts of people of power, but the greater capacity of positive inducements to reach useful goals is well recognized. A tax on Iraqi exports would at least have funded humanitarian relief, and the revenue might have been used to fund direct incentives to the Ba'ath party. It may be pointed out that it would have had some of the same strengths and weaknesses as were seen when the Oil-for-Food Program was introduced, but the scale of the tax revenue that could have been generated should have enabled the international community to intervene in a positive way in the internal life of Iraq. It would not be inconsistent with the intent of Pro-Active Sanctions to also mandate embargos on arms sales and transfer of military technology. In the instance of Yugoslavia, a tax on trade that generated a revenue could have been used to encourage societal compromise, as ultimately took place when the European Union underwrote the Serbian opposition leader Vojislav Kostunica's campaign to encourage Serbians to come out of the cold and become "a normal part of Europe." Similarly, in Haiti the concern of the political and military leadership that democracy threatened their lifestyle could have been addressed had a revenue been available to fund developmental programs that required Haitians in teaching and managerial roles, and which could have co-opted elements of the political elite willing to make a break from the junta.

The ongoing conflict between Iran and the international community over its nuclear program, and its violations of human rights, is a context in which pro-active sanctions could prove a powerful force for positive change. The sanctions that were imposed on Iran during the Iran-Iraq War caused immense hardship within Iran, but did not bring any change in Iranian policy. A pro-active form, however, could have greater effect on a government that is concerned about the disaffection seen among its population. If funds generated by a system of pro-active sanctions were applied to such purposes as scholarships for Iranians to foreign universities, and retainers for human rights lawyers, the work of the international community could be expected to erode the support given to the Iranian regime's policy of confrontation. Over time, such erosion could be expected to bring changes to the religious leadership of the country and to the policies of the government. Had a pro-active sanctions model been deployed against Iran in 1994 when I first published my paper on the subject, an entire generation of young Iranians could have been provided with the education and professional skills to lead their nation away from international confrontation.[10] The systemic sanctions against Iranian money supply being pressed on the world community by the United States in early 2012, and agreed to by the European Community, risk the same consequences as those imposed in 1991 on Iraq. The questions asked above about changes that were made to UNICEF statistics on child mortality and published in 2011, obscuring the impact of sanctions on public health, begin to appear quite urgent.[11]

APPENDIX 2:

MILESTONES IN CANADIAN

NAVAL HISTORY[1]

1881 In July, the steam corvette *Charybdis* was given to Canada by the Royal Navy (RN) with the idea that she could be used to start training for a new naval service. She was deemed unsafe and returned to Britain in 1882.

1904 In response to calls for militia reform, Prime Minister Wilfrid Laurier presented An Act Constituting the Naval Militia of Canada to Parliament, but the concept was not adopted despite the RN dockyards in Halifax and Esquimalt being transferred to Canadian control. CGS *Canada*, a third-class cruiser, became the flagship of the Fisheries Protection Service of Canada and was used to train cadets and seamen for the future Naval Militia.

1908 Rear-Admiral Sir Charles Kingsmill, a Canadian who served in the Royal Navy, was appointed to establish a Canadian Naval Militia, based upon the Fisheries Protection Service. The first Canadian naval cadets embarked CGS *Canada*.

1909 During the British *Dreadnought* Crisis, Laurier and Kingsmill avoided being forced into commitments to Imperial defence and accepted the loan of two aging cruisers, *Niobe* and *Rainbow*, until new cruisers and destroyers could be built in Canada.

1910 Consensus for a Canadian navy quickly evaporated but Parliament passed the Naval Service Act on 4 May 1910 formally establishing the Royal Canadian Navy (RCN). *Niobe* and *Rainbow*, manned by the RN, arrived in Halifax and Esquimalt on 21 October and 7 November 1910 respectively.

1911 The Royal Naval College of Canada (RNCC) was established in Halifax as a step toward creating a national navy. Recruiting of Canadians for the navy proved to be difficult.

1912 Canadian involvement in Imperial defence was fiercely debated in Parliament. The new government, led by Prime Minister Robert Borden, cancelled contracts for new RCN ships and stopped recruiting, opting to pay for three RN battleships instead. Although this plan was quashed in the Senate, the RCN stagnated without a fleet plan.

1914 No. 1 Company Royal Naval Canadian Volunteer Reserve (RNCVR) was formed at Victoria in May 1914, under the oversight of Commander Walter Hose, Captain of *Rainbow*. At the beginning of the First World War the RCN consisted of two old cruisers, 350 people (plus 250 in the Victoria Naval Reserve) and had no mobilization or expansion plans. The submarines CC-1 and CC-2 were purchased in 1914 from the United States, and the RN sloop *Shearwater* was transferred to the RCN as their tender. The navy conducted coastal patrols on both coasts, guarding against attack by German cruisers, while politicians adamantly refused to be drawn into Imperial defence and the Allied war effort at sea. Canada's contribution was the Army Expeditionary Force.

1917 U-boats attacked shipping on the East Coast and in response coastal patrols were established under Hose. Twelve *Battle*-class trawlers were ordered for patrol and ASW duties – the first major building program for the RCN. CC-1, CC-2, and *Shearwater* were transferred to the East Coast, becoming first RN/RCN ships to use the new Panama Canal, but the submarines were not considered safe for operations in the Atlantic.

1918 RCN Air Service was established on 5 September as the first distinctive Canadian Air Force, based at Baker's Point (Dartmouth), NS, with assistance of the USN. It was disbanded soon after the war ended in November.

1919 Submarines EH-14 and EH-15 (built in Quincy, MA, rather than in Montreal where other submarines of that class were built for other navies) were given to the RCN. Admiral of the Fleet Viscount John Jellicoe was commissioned to study "Dominion" naval requirements. The Canadian naval staff proposed the creation of a 46-ship navy, over two seven-year building periods (1920–27 and 1927–34) to create a fleet of seven cruisers, 12 destroyers, 18 antisubmarine patrol craft, three submarines and three tenders, all to be manned by 8,500 officers and men. This plan was endorsed by Jellicoe but rejected by the government, causing Kingsmill to resign. He was replaced by Hose in 1921.

1920 *Niobe* and *Rainbow* were scrapped, and replaced by the RN cruiser *Aurora* and the destroyers *Patrician* and *Patriot*.

1923 Defence cuts were imposed, reflecting the postwar optimism and the era of naval arms control triggered by the Washington Agreement. *Aurora* and the submarines were paid-off, and operations were limited to training cruises with a small number of port visits in support of foreign policy. RNCC was closed and all officer training was done with the RN. The RCN was reduced to 500 officers and men. From 1923 to 1931 the RCN consisted of a destroyer and two trawlers on each coast – a force structure reminiscent of the 1904 Naval Militia. Naval Reserve Divisions were established by Hose in major cities as a way of maintaining a naval presence in Canadian cities. This initiative laid the foundations for naval mobilization in 1939.

1928 *Patrician* and *Patriot* were replaced by *Champlain* (ex-HMS *Torbay*) and *Vancouver* (ex-HMS *Toreador*).

1930 Hose presented a new fleet plan emphasizing the future role of destroyers, rather than cruisers, as the core of the Canadian fleet but the naval budget was systematically reduced from 1930 to 1935, restricting operations and maintenance even further.

1931 *Saguenay* and *Skeena*, the first major warships specifically designed and built (in Britain) for the RCN, were commissioned (22 May and 10 June respectively). They were ordered in 1929 before the financial crisis.

1934 On 1 July, Hose retired and Captain Percy Nelles became Chief of the Naval Staff (CNS), remaining until 1944.

1936 The Canadian Joint Staff recommended that over the next five years the RCN be increased to six modern destroyers and four minesweepers. This assessment was later increased to nine destroyers and eight minesweepers with the necessary infrastructure to defend the two naval ports. Subsequent estimates called for 18 destroyers to provide a full flotilla on each coast.

1937 The RCN bought two destroyers from the RN – *Fraser* (ex-HMS *Crescent*) and *St Laurent* (ex-HMS *Cygnet*) – to replace *Champlain* and *Vancouver*. Both were paid-off in November 1936.

1938 The naval budget was increased and two more destroyers, *Ottawa* (ex-HMS *Crusader*) and *Restigouche* (ex-HMS *Comet*), were bought from Britain as part of a modest re-armament program. The destroyers began training with the RN's America and West Indies Squadron. A seventh destroyer, *Assiniboine* (ex-HMS *Kempenfelt*), was purchased in October 1939 as a flotilla leader.

1939 The 1939–40 defence estimates included a further increase in the RCN's budget. To meet the long-term objective of operating eighteen destroyers and to put pay to lingering interest in cruisers, the new plan called for the RCN to buy the latest RN *Tribal*-class fleet destroyer which was able to fulfill many of the cruiser's functions. The Second World War starts in September. At that time, the RCN consisted of a dozen ships and 1,800 people. Four of the seven destroyers were stationed on the West Coast and were transferred to Halifax in the fall of 1939.

1939–45 Coastal patrols and convoys were started as soon as war was declared with the first convoy to Britain (HX-1), escorted by *Saguenay* and *St Laurent*, sailing on 16 September. In April 1940 four RCN destroyers started operating in European waters. Coastal patrol and escort requirements were then undertaken by requisitioned vessels and by six American *Town*-class destroyers (later increased to eight) provided by the U.S. Navy under the "Lend Lease" agreement. Two Canadian *Tribal*s were laid down in Britain in early 1940 and orders for two more made a year later. A further four *Tribal*s were built in Canada later. In 1940, to meet requirements for patrol vessels, escorts and mine countermeasures vessels, Canadian shipyards started to build small warships. Between August 1940 and October 1944

Canadian shipyards launched over 100 corvettes, some 60 frigates and more than 60 minesweepers. In March 1943, the Canadian Northwest Atlantic Command was set up, covering the area north of New York City and west of the 47th meridian. Rear-Admiral L.W. Murray was responsible for convoys in this area – the only Canadian officer to command a theatre of war. By the summer of 1943, Allied fortunes had improved considerably. An assault on northwest Europe in 1944 was a certainty, leaving only the defeat of Japan to be undertaken. One of the decisions of the August 1943 Quebec conference was that the RCN would operate capital ships (carriers and cruisers) and carry a greater share of the Allied naval war effort. From late 1943, the number of major warships manned by Canadians increased with the four new *Tribal*-class fleet destroyers, nine other destroyers (some to replaces war losses), two cruisers (*Uganda* – later renamed *Quebec* – and *Ontario*) and two aircraft carriers (*Nabob* and *Puncher*). The RCN also manned landing craft and fast patrol boats. By the end of the war in 1945, the RCN had expanded to a force of nearly 100,000 men and women manning and supporting ships of all types except battleships. The primary effort was in the Battle of the Atlantic, in which the navy sank or shared in sinking 33 enemy submarines at a cost of 24 warships lost and 2,024 casualties.

1945 At the end of the war, an "interim" fleet of two carriers, two cruisers and 12 fleet destroyers to be manned by 10,000 men was announced, but the RCN was never able to man all the ships. As a result, emphasis was placed on the seven *Tribal*-class destroyers and the aircraft carrier (*Warrior* initially and then *Magnificent* after March 1948); two cruisers were also maintained as training ships.

1946 Vice-Admiral G.C. Jones, who had replaced Nelles as CNS in 1944, died suddenly. Vice-Admiral Reid became the interim CNS until relieved by Vice-Admiral Harold Grant in mid-1947. Under Grant's leadership the RCN was able to regain its political support and start the process of becoming a major ASW force within NATO.

1946–47 An important piece of early Cold War planning was the creation of a North American continental defence organization. The naval part of the new security system focused on two tasks: countering any Soviet military diversionary lodgements in the Arctic; and ASW operations against Soviet submarines attempting to prevent the re-supply of Europe. At first, Canada did not have enough ships to do more than provide a token contribution. The need to carry a greater share of the collective defence burden was recognized politically, but remained unfunded until 1950. By mid-1947, the navy had changed the fleet plan and focused on building a modern ASW fleet, but it had neither the manpower nor the money to do this completely. That autumn the naval staff produced a three-part modernization program acknowledging the prevailing fiscal constraints and integrating longer-term requirements for new ships with the immediate requirement to modernize the *Tribal*-class destroyers. The "ABC" plan, as it became known, was accepted by the Minister, Brooke Claxton, who convinced Cabinet to authorize a modest re-armament that included three new *St Laurent*-class destroyer escorts.

1949 The onset of the Cold War led to the creation of the North Atlantic Treaty Organization (NATO) and the beginning of collective defence planning under a concept that would largely determine the RCN's force structure for the next forty years.

1950 The Korean War broke out in June. Three destroyers sailed for Korea in July. Maintaining the Korean commitment until 1955 required eight destroyers working in a cycle of operations, transit to and from Korea, and much-needed overhaul. During those overhauls all the destroyers were extensively modernized to re-equip them for both ASW and general-purpose operations as part of NATO. The Korean War triggered a major naval re-armament, increasing the number of *St Laurent*-class escorts under construction to 14, modernizing the destroyers *Crescent* and *Crusader* and 21 ASW frigates, and raising the manpower ceiling to provide enough people to bring the fleet up to wartime strength.

1953 NATO adopted a nuclear response strategy after the Soviet detonation of a hydrogen bomb. The RCN struggled to modernize the fleet in the face of a series of new challenges including: (1) the marriage of the modern submarine and convoy escorts; (2) NATO's growing demands for convoy escorts: (3) growing national and bilateral demands for escorts to support the new ocean surveillance system (SOSUS); and (4) the development of the ASW helicopter.

1954 *Labrador* was commissioned (8 July) and became the first naval vessel to transit the Northwest Passage, on her maiden voyage. She was transferred to the Department of Transport in 1958.

1954 Approval was given for Canada to lease three fully-manned, 'A'-class submarines and base them in Halifax for ASW training. As part of the deal, 190 Canadian officers and men were sent to England for submarine duty. This arrangement (which became the 6th Submarine Division) lasted until the early 1960s when it became obvious that the navy needed to own its own submarines.

1955 *St Laurent*, the first of the new destroyer escorts, was commissioned (29 October). Over the next 10 years she would be followed by 19 other ships of that basic design. The last two ships of the *St Laurent*-class design (*Annapolis* and *Nipigon*) were built as DDHs and commissioned in 1964.

1957 *Magnificent* was replaced by *Bonaventure* (ex-HMS *Powerful*), which had been modernized with a steam catapult, angled deck and mirror landing aid system. Armed with U.S. Navy ASW aircraft and fighters, she became the nucleus of an ASW task group assigned to NATO.

1959 Approval was given for a major fleet modernization, which saw the seven *St Laurent*-class destroyers rebuilt to carry a medium ASW helicopter (the Sea King), and the building of underway logistic support ships (*Provider* commissioned in 1963, followed by *Protecteur* and *Preserver* in 1969 and 1970). Nuclear-powered submarines were considered but were deemed too expensive and a general-purpose frigate was proposed but cancelled in 1963.

1961 *Grilse* (ex-USS *Burrfish*) was loaned to Canada to provide ASW training for the West Coast ships and aircraft. She was replaced by *Rainbow* (ex-USS *Argonaut*) in December 1968, which remained on the West Coast until paid off in 1974.

1962 *Assiniboine* was re-commissioned as the first DDH in June and began trials with Sea King ASW helicopters. The remaining six *St Laurent*-class DDHs followed at regular intervals. The Cuban Missile Crisis erupted in October. RCN and RCAF ships and aircraft conducted sustained operations against Soviet submarines in North American waters for twenty-one days.

1964 The Paul Hellyer reforms began. These included "unification" and the loss of the traditional naval identity as well as a significant reduction in the RCN's escort commitment to NATO. In December a new fleet modernization was announced that included the building of four new ASW destroyers initially known as "repeat Nipigons" but later called the DDH-280 (*Iroquois*-class) and two AORS.

1965 *Ojibwa* was commissioned (23 September), which was the first step in creating a Canadian submarine capability on the East Coast. She was followed by *Onondaga* (1966) and *Okanagan* (1967).

1966 In July Admiral William M. Landymore, Commander of Maritime Command (as the navy was called under unification) resigned in protest over the Hellyer reforms and the loss of naval identity.

1967 NATO created the Standing Naval Force Atlantic (SNFL), which became a priority function of the Canadian Navy.

1968 *Bras D'Or* was commissioned as an experimental ASW hydrofoil but the trials were abandoned in 1972 before the tactical trials were complete. *Terra Nova* was re-commissioned in May as the first of the four improved *Restigouche*-class ASW destroyers fitted with ASROC and VDS.

1969–73 The Pierre Trudeau government naval rationalization heralded the end of the Canadian aircraft carrier era (*Bonaventure* was paid-off in March 1970) and the start of the long process that eventually led to the building of the Canadian Patrol Frigates.

1977 A fleet structure of 24 destroyers was approved by Cabinet in December and authority was given to begin building the Canadian Patrol Frigates (CPFS).

1979–84 Delays in the ship replacement program meant that the aging *St Laurent*- and *Restigouche*-class destroyers had to remain in service longer than originally planned. To keep them reasonably effective they were given another modernization and life extension

(DELEX) that included a simple Link 11 automated data processing system, ADLIPS. NATO expressed concern over the general decline in fleet ASW capability. Beginning in February 1981, the three *Oberon*-class submarines were also given extensive midlife modernizations (SOUP) to upgrade their tactical ASW capabilities and were assigned to NATO as a partial offset to the decline in surface ship capability.

1981–82 Dockyard modernization was commenced. This was needed to prepare the fleet infrastructure for the CPFs and the modernized DDH-280s. Training programs were re-focused on the systems and operating concepts of the new ships. The first phase of the CPF contract (design definition) was signed (August). The early 1980s saw the beginning of a bleak period of constant defence budget cuts that delayed the CPF project and, for a while, restricted fleet operations. For financial reasons it was decided not to re-arm the four *Mackenzie*-class as general-purpose destroyers, which reduced the fleet's operational effectiveness even further. At much the same time, Soviet naval capability was increasing in both the Atlantic and Pacific with increased Soviet submarine activity off the Eastern Seaboard and along the Pacific northwest coast. Later, this led to a NATO restructuring and a political awakening in Canada over the deteriorating world situation.

1984 The *Tribal*-class upgrade and modernization program (TRUMP) was announced (January). *Algonquin*, the lead ship in the program, was taken in hand by the shipyard on 26 October 1987. The Atlantic fleet re-organized into a formal ASW task group for NATO Exercise Teamwork, setting in motion a series of actions that led to the establishment of ASW task groups on both coasts.

1985 The task group concept was further refined during NATO Exercise Ocean Safari. The official made in July 1986 and January 1987.

1987–89 The navy briefly looked at nuclear-powered submarines (SSNs) in response to political concerns over the Arctic. The SSN program would have replaced eight destroyers (Batch III of the surface ship replacement program) but when the submarines were cancelled for fiscal reasons the destroyers were not put back into the ship replacement program, capping the fleet at 16 destroyers/frigates.

1987 Approval for CPF Batch II was given. The Maritime Coastal Defence Organization as a Naval Reserve primary mission was established. Fleet re-structuring commenced with *Gatineau* transferring to the East Coast (April) and *Huron* and four *Sea King* helicopters going to the West Coast (July). The West Coast task group deployed on exercises with the USN in January 1988.

1988 *Moresby* and *Anticosti* were acquired as the beginning of a program to re-develop Canada's mine countermeasures capability. The ships would be manned primarily by members of the Naval Reserve. A plan to build 12 Maritime Coast Defence Vessels (MCDVs) in Canada was announced. *Assiniboine* was paid-off to provide people for the CPFs and because after thirty-six years it was no longer cost-effective to keep her in service. She was followed by *Saguenay* in August 1990. The remaining 14 *St Laurent*-class variants were paid-off between May 1992 and July 1998 as crews for the CPFs were needed.

1989 The Cold War ended with the tearing down of the Berlin Wall. *Annapolis* sailed for the West Coast (August) and *Terra Nova* went to the East Coast arriving in December, providing the West Coast task group with a second helicopter-capable destroyer.

1990 A task group comprising *Athabaskan*, *Terra Nova*, and *Protecteur* sailed for the Persian Gulf on 24 August after the Iraqi invasion of Kuwait for Operation *Friction* after extensive re-equipping (largely using weapons and systems being held for the CPFs) and training for a multi-threat mission with low emphasis on ASW. After some 240 days of conducting support operations, the task group left the Gulf on 12 March 1991 and returned to Halifax on 7 April. Although the situation in Kuwait had been stabilized, a UN naval force was kept in the Gulf from 1991 to 2001 to enforce UN sanctions. A Canadian destroyer or frigate was always part of this force. *Preserver* also supported UN operations in Somalia in 1992–93, in the Adriatic (Operation *Sharp Guard*) from 1993 to 1996, and in East Timor in 1999–2000.

1992 *Halifax*, the first of the 12 *City*-class frigates, began trials. The complete class was commissioned over the next four years, ending with *Ottawa* on 31 May 1996.

1998   The purchase of the four British *Upholder*-class submarines was announced. They would be extensively modernized in both Britain and Canada and put into service as the *Victoria*

2001–03   After the attack on the World Trade Center and Pentagon in September 2001, the navy embarked on *Operation Apollo*, the most intense overseas deployment since the Second World War. Initially it supported Allied Operation *Enduring Freedom* covering the invasion of Afghanistan from the sea and the removal of the Taliban. The Canadian Task Group, designated CTF 150 and 151, conducted maritime interception operations in the Arabian Sea until December 2003.

2002   The navy returned to the Arctic, taking part in 2002, 2004, 2006, and every year thereafter in Operation *Nanook,* a series of joint operations, which saw frigates and MCDVs, as well as *Corner Brook* in 2007, in the Northwest Passage and visit many isolated communities in Nunavut.

2004   At the end of Operation *Apollo*, the navy continued to support operations in the Arabian Sea through Operation *Altair*. This included deploying a single frigate with a US carrier force for six months in 2004, 2005, and 2007.

2005   The Standing NATO Maritime Group 1 (SNMG1) replaced the Standing Naval Force Atlantic (SNFL). Commodore Denis Rouleau (Canadian Navy) was the first commander of the new force.

2008   In 2008 Canada sent a task group and a Canadian commander, as CTF 150, into the Arabian [Persian] Gulf for three months. Since then Canada has maintained a frigate with SNMG1 to support Operation *Altair* and to conduct counter-piracy operations off the horn of Africa.

2010   *Athabaskan* and *Halifax* deployed to Haiti to provide humanitarian support following a devastating earthquake.

NOTES

PREFACE AND ACKNOWLEDGMENTS

1 Carl von Clausewitz (Michael Howard, Peter Paret, and Beatrice Heuser, eds.), *On War*, 28–30.
2 My work on Canada's employment of naval forces to support its independence and security began with a study that had no direct connection with Canadian policy, *Navies, Deterrence, and American Independence* (1988), which led me to write three monographs for the Canadian Department of National Defence, Directorate of Strategic Analysis: *The Enforcement of Canada's Continental Maritime Jurisdiction* (1975), *The Diplomatic Utility of Canada's Naval Forces* (1976), and *Canada's Foreign Policy Objectives and Canadian Security Arrangements in the North* (1980). These were followed up with two academic articles in the *International Journal*, "Matching Canada's Navy to her Foreign Policy and Domestic Requirements," 1983, and "Why Does Canada Want Nuclear Submarines?" 1988, and a chapter, "Canada's Security Considerations in the Arctic," in *Northern Waters: Security and Resource Issues* (Clive Archer and David Scrivener, eds.), 1986. Leaving aside for the moment my close focus on Canadian defence studies, I devoted more than a decade working on one aspect of naval strategy that has a great deal to do with Canadian naval history: *Attack on Maritime Trade* (1991), and later a document collection for the Navy Records Society: *Sea Power and the Control of Trade: Belligerent Rights from the Russian War to the Beira Patrol* (2005). From this deep field I wrote in 1994 and 1995 two monographs with particular relevance to Canadian naval policy: *Pro-Active Sanctions: A New/Old Approach to Non-violent Measures*, published by the Department of Foreign Affairs, and *Canada's Naval Strategy: Rooted in Experience*, published by the Centre for Foreign Policy Studies, Dalhousie University, as the first in their series of Maritime Security Occasional Papers. In 1997 I published a Navy Records Society volume on *The Collective Naval Defence of the Empire: 1900 to 1940*. All these precursors have contributed to the present book, but during these decades the state of scholarship on the themes addressed has progressed significantly in the fields of naval history, Canadian foreign and defence policies, and international sanctions. I hope this present book, the culmination of my study, will throw light on an important aspect of Canadian foreign and defence policy.
3 File No: 2011-31953 & 2011-31957, Mélanie Mckinnon to Nicholas Tracy, 7, 21 June 2011, Publishing and Depository Services, Crown Copyright & Licensing, 350 Albert Street, 4th Floor, Ottawa, Ontario KIA 0S5.

INTRODUCTION

1. Can., DND, Strategic Issues, *Your Navy: Your Security*, nd.
2. Ernest J. Chambers, *The Canadian Marine: A History of the Department of Marine and Fisheries*, 87; (and reprinted by Andrew C. Young, "Canada's Marine Forces, 1867–1871," in Richard H. Gimblett and Richard O. Mayne, eds., *People, Policy and Programmes*).
3. Ken Booth, *Navies and Foreign Policy*, 10.
4. Hew Strachan, "Strategy or Alibi? Obama, McChrystal and the Operational Level of War," *Survival*, vol. 52, no. 4 (Oct.–Nov. 2010): 157–82.
5. Matthew Allen, "The Changing Nature of Naval Strategy," *Naval Review*, vol. 81, no. 3 (July 1993): 235–43.
6. Sir Julian Corbett, *Some Principles of Maritime Strategy*, 20.
7. See Nicholas Tracy, *The Battle of Quiberon Bay 1759: Hawke and the Defeat of the French Invasion*, passim; and *Navies, Deterrence, and American Independence*.
8. 7 Aug. 1581. Horatio F. Brown, Rawdon Brown, and Allen B. Hinds, eds., *Calendar of State Papers and Manuscripts, relating to English affairs, existing in the archives and collections of Venice and in the other libraries of Northern Italy*, vol. 8, no. 40.
9. Nicholas Tracy, *Attack on Maritime Trade*, 54–68.
10. Sir Julian Corbett, *England in the Seven Years' War*, vol. 2, 5.
11. BL Add MSS 49008 ff. 140–3, Sir John Jellicoe to David Earl Beatty, 4 Feb. 1917 (A. Temple Patterson, ed., *The Jellicoe Papers*, 2, 142).
12. Sir Herbert W. Richmond, *Sea Power in the Modern World*, 71 2. See: NA UK, CAB 21/310, Richmond to ? Hankey, undated, 10 pages; and Geoffrey Till, "Richmond and the Faith Reaffirmed: British Naval Thinking between the Wars."
13. NA UK, ADM 116/3104 ff. 40–53, "Memorandum, 'Imperial Naval Defence,'" Oct. 1919 (Nicholas Tracy, ed., *The Collective Naval Defence of the Empire, 1900–1940*, 256).
14. William Norton Medlicott, *The Economic Blockade*, vol. 2, 631.
15. Francis Bacon, *The Essays or Counsels, Civil and Moral, of Francis Lord Verulam Viscount St. Albans*, 124.
16. Corbett, *England in the Seven Years' War*, vol. 2, 5.
17. Ibid., 206–7.
18. 2 Dec. 1772, Edmund Burke, *The Speeches of the Right Honourable Edmund Burke, in the House of Commons, and in Westminster Hall*, vol. 2, 138.
19. Quoted in Sir Francis Piggott, *The Declaration of Paris 1856*, 126; W.H. Malkin, "Blockade in Modern Conditions," *British Yearbook of International Law*, vol. 3, 1922–23: 87–98.
20. George Peabody Gooch and Harold Temperley, eds., *British Documents on the Origins of the War*, vol. 3, 402–3.
21. N.A.M. Rodger, "Queen Elizabeth and the Myth of Sea-power in English History."
22. NA UK, ADM 186/603, Lt Cmdr W.E. Arnold-Forster, *The Economic Blockade 1914–1919*, Conclusion.
23. Sir James Cable, *Gunboat Diplomacy*, 39.
24. Edward N. Luttwak, *The Political Uses of Sea Power*, 29–34.
25. Royal Navy, Directorate of Naval Staff Duties, *The Fundamentals of British Maritime Doctrine* BR1806, 87–90; and Eric Grove, "The Discovery of Doctrine, British Naval Thinking at the Close of the Twentieth century," in Geoffrey Till, *The Development of British Naval Thinking*: 182–91.

26 Kelly Williams, "Canada's Maritime Strategy: A Naval Perspective," in Robert H. Edwards and Graham Walker, eds., *Continental Security and Canada-U.S. Relations: Maritime Perspectives, Challenges and Opportunities*: 157–64.
27 Grove, "The Discovery of Doctrine."
28 Bob Davidson, "Canadian Navy, Modern Naval Diplomacy – A Practitioner's View," *Journal of Military and Strategic Studies*, vol. 11, nos. 1 and 2 (fall and winter 2008-09): 1–47.
29 Allen, "The Changing Nature of Naval Strategy."
30 Can., DHH, *Raymont Papers*, file 72/153, "Report of the Ad Hoc Committee on Defence Policy," 30 Sept. 1963, 3–7.
31 Can., House of Commons Special Committee on Defence, *Minutes of Proceedings and Evidence*, 552. See John Gellner, "Strategic Analysis in Canada," *International Journal*, vol. 33, no. 3 (1977–78): 493–505.
32 Jan Breemer, "The End of Naval Strategy: Revolutionary Change and the Future of American Naval Power," in Peter T. Haydon and Ann L. Griffiths, eds., *Maritime Security and Conflict Resolution at Sea in the Post–Cold War Era*": 135–42.
33 Can., DND, Maritime Command, *The Naval Vision: Charting the Course for Canada's Maritime Forces into the 21st Century*; and Aaron P. Jackson, *Keystone Doctrine Development in Five Commonwealth Navies: A Comparative Perspective*, Papers in Australian Maritime Affairs, 16.
34 Can., DND, *1994 White Paper on Defence*, Ottawa, 1994.
35 Henry A. Kissinger, *The Troubled Partnership*, 53.
36 Michael Byers, "Canadian Armed Forces under United States Command," *International Journal*, vol. 58, no. 1 (2002–03): 89–114.
37 Can., DND, *Leadmark: The Navy's Strategy for 2020*; and *Securing Canada's Ocean Frontiers: Charting the Course from Leadmark*, May 2005, 17–18 (emphasis mine). See Jackson, *Keystone Doctrine*, 20–5. The rather obvious characterization of the role of navies is derived from Ken Booth's 1977 *Navies and Foreign Policy*, 15.
38 Sean M. Maloney, *War with Iraq: Canada's Strategy in the Persian Gulf, 1990–2002*,. See Danford W. Middlemiss and J._. Sokolsky, *Canadian Defence: Decisions and Determinants*; Douglas Bland, *Chiefs of Defence: Government and the Unified Command of the Canadian Armed Forces*.
39 Sean O'Keefe, Secretary of the Navy, "From the Sea: Preparing the Naval Service for the 21st Century." See Nathan Miller, "The American Navy, 1922–1945," in Keith Neilson and Elizabeth Jane Errington, *Navies and Global Security*: 181–208.
40 Admiral Jay L. Johnson, U.S. Navy, Chief of Naval Operations, Foreword to O'Keefe, "From the Sea."
41 Allen, "The Changing Nature of Naval Strategy."
42 When so careful a historian as Joel Sokolsky could write in 1995, only six years before the 9/11 attacks, that "Canada will not be compelled to take part in the creation of a new fortress North America," all scholars should be warned. Joel J. Sokolsky, "The Bilateral Defence Relationship with the United States," in David B. Dewitt and David Leyton-Brown, *Canada's International Security Policy*, 198–226.

CHAPTER ONE

1 Robert Bothwell has made the point that the benevolent presence of Canada on the northern border of the United States was of inestimable value in the development of the United States. Robert Bothwell, "Has Canada Made a Difference?,"

in John English and Norman Hillmer, eds., *Making a Difference? Canada's Foreign Policy in a Changing World Order*," 1–14.

2 The Naval Defence Act of 1865 provided for the British colonies to acquire warships, and raise seamen to man them. Naval Defence Act, 1865, 8 Victoria Cap XIV. The act also allowed for Colonial warships to be made available to the Admiralty on a cost-free basis, and provided that any men raised would be deemed part of the Royal Navy Reserve.

3 The fishery concession was to run for twelve years; and a commission which sat at Halifax awarded Canada $5.5 million as compensation; but no compensation was obtained for the Fenian raids, and the Americans indicated they would not be renewing the fishery agreement.

4 William Johnston, William Rawling, Richard Gimblett, and John MacFarlane, *The Seabound Coast: The Official History of the Royal Canadian Navy, 1867–1939*, 4–9; Ernest J. Chambers, *The Canadian Marine*, 87–111; Thomas E. Appleton, *Usque ad Mare: A History of the Canadian Coast Guard and Marine Services*, 73–5; Andrew C. Young, "Canada's Marine Forces, 1867–1871"; Robert Craig Brown, *Canada's National Policy 1883–1900*, 13–41, 63–90; Graeme R. Tweedie, "The Roots of the Royal Canadian Navy: Sovereignty versus Nationalism, 1812–1910, in Michael L. Hadley, Rob Huebert, and Fred W. Crickard, *A Nation's Navy: In Quest of Canadian Naval Identity*, 91–101; Donald C. Gordon, *Dominion Partnership in Imperial Defence*, 60–71; and Thomas Richard Melville, "Canada and Sea Power: Canadian Naval Thought and Policy, 1860–1910," unpublished Phd dissertation, Duke University, 1981: 120–36. In answering a question in the British Commons on 24 July 1879, Sir Michael Hicks-Beach, then secretary of state for the colonies, said, "I believe that none of the Colonies mentioned in the Question have availed themselves of the provisions of the Colonial Naval Defence Act" (HC Deb 24 July 1879 vol. 248 c1171). This may have been technically correct, but it did not fully represent the measures being taken in Canada and in the Australian states.

5 Alice B. Stewart, "Sir John A. Macdonald and the Imperial Defence Commission of 1879," *Canadian Historical Review*, vol. 25, no. 2 (June 1954), 122. See Donald Mackenzie Schurman and John Beeler, eds., *Imperial Defence, 1868–1887*, 13.

6 Kenneth Hagan, "The Apotheosis of Mahan," in Keith Neilson and Elizabeth Jane Errington, *Navies and Global Security*, 94–5.

7 Michael Epkenhans, "Imperial Germany and the Importance of Sea Power," in N.A.M. Rodger, ed., *Naval Power in the 20th Century*, 27.

8 As Phillip Buckner put it in his 1993 presidential address to the Canadian Historical Society: "Canadian historians have locked themselves into a teleological framework which is obsessed with the evolution of Canadian autonomy and the construction of a Canadian national identity and thus downplayed the significance of the imperial experience in shaping the identity of nineteenth-century British Canadians." Phillip Buckner, "Presidential Address."

9 Danford W. Middlemiss, *Canadian Defence: Decisions and Determinants*, 11–12.

10 "If there was a war in which the naval supremacy of the Empire were to be imperilled ... I believe we should help England with all our strength." A.D. De Celles, ed., *Discours de Sir Wilfrid Laurier, 1889–1911*, 192; quoted in H. Blair Neatby, "Laurier and Imperialism," and in Ramsay Cook, Craig Brown, and Carl Berger, eds., *Imperial Relations in the Age of Laurier*, 7. See also Sir Wilfrid Laurier, *The Naval Question* and *The Canadian Navy*.

11 Clive Phillipps-Wolley, *The Canadian Naval Question*, 7.

12 Cmd 8596 /1897 Vol. LIX, *Proceedings of a Conference*, London, June and July 1897, 140–50; Douglas Cochrane, 12th Earl of Dundonald. John G. Armstrong, "The Dundonald Affair," *Canadian Defence Quarterly*, vol. 11, no. 2 (autumn 1981): 39–45 at 41.
13 Nicholas Tracy, *Attack on Maritime Trade*, 99–100; Hagan, "Apotheosis of Mahan"; Johnston et al., *Seabound Coast*, 49–59, 78–84.
14 NA UK, ADM 1/7671 ff. 277–8v, from GB Cmd 1299. Memorandum prepared for the 1902 Colonial Conference by William Waldegrave Palmer, 2nd Earl of Selborne, the First Lord of the Admiralty, 7 Aug. 1902 (Nicholas Tracy, *Collective Naval Defence of the Empire*, no. 10, 13–18).
15 Johnston et al., *Seabound Coast*, 20–1, 84, 116–17.
16 Chambers, *The Canadian Marine*, 108–11; Richard H. Gimblett, "Admiral Sir Charles E. Kingsmill: Forgotten Father," in Michael Whitby, Richard Gimblett, and Peter Haydon, *The Admirals: Canada's Senior Naval Leadership in the Twentieth Century*, 31–54; and Johnston et al., *Seabound Coast*, 85–96.
17 Richard H. Gimblett, "Reassessing the Dreadnought Crisis of 1909 and the Origins of the Royal Canadian Navy," *The Northern Mariner/Le Marin du nord*, vol. 4, no. 1 (Jan. 1994), 35–53; and see *Canadian Military Gazette*, 28 Nov. 1905; and the *Canadian Annual Review of Public Affairs*, 1905, 502.
18 NA PRO, CAB 5/1 f. 30, CID 5C, reply to CID 4C, "'Strategic Position of British Naval Bases in Western Atlantic and West Indies,' memorandum for the Committee of Imperial Defence by Battenberg," November 1903 (Tracy, *Collective*, No. 18, 27–9). In the memorandum prepared for the 1902 Colonial Conference (see above) it had been stated that British taxpayers were contributing £–/15/2 per person to the collective naval defence of the Empire and that Australians contributed £–/1/0¾. But the Admiralty numbers showed that Canadians contributed nothing at all, apart from its participation in British trade. And as to that, the Admiralty calculated that a quarter of the trade it was responsible for protecting was intercolonial trade of no direct value to the mother country.
19 GB, Parliament, *Proceedings of the Colonial Conference, 1907*, London, 1908, 130–1; and Johnston et al., *Seabound Coast*, 113.
20 Johnston et al., *Seabound Coast*, 91–107; Gordon, *Dominion Partnership*, 227–33, 239–40, 248–89 passsim; Barry Gough and Roger Sarty, "Sailors and Soldiers: The Royal Navy, the Canadian Forces, and the Defence of Atlantic Canada, 1890–1918," in Hadley, *A Nation's Navy*: 112–30; Roger Sarty, "Toward a Canadian Naval Service, 1867–1914," in Richard H. Gimblett, ed., *The Naval Service of Canada, 1910–2010: The Centennial Story*: 1–19. The lack of torpedo boats to support the fixed artillery, and destroyers for work farther off shore, was a problem.
21 Nigel D. Brodeur, "L.P. Brodeur and the Origins of the Royal Canadian Navy," in James Boutilier, ed., *RCN in Retrospect 1910–1968*, 13–32; Marc Milner, *Canada's Navy: The First Century*, 11; and Johnston et al., *Seabound Coast*, 114.
22 Several expeditions by sea to the arctic were commissioned by the Canadian government, including: two voyages in 1885 and 1886 to Hudson Bay by Lieutenant Gordon in *Alert*, a converted naval sloop on loan from the Royal Navy; that by William Wakeham in 1897 when he felt the number of foreign whaling stations already in the arctic indicated the importance of making a formal declaration of Canadian sovereignty; those by the geologist Dr Albert Peter Low in 1904 and 1906 in *Neptune*; and those by Captain Joseph-Elzéar Bernier. Gordon W. Smith, *The Transfer of Arctic Territories from Great Britain to Canada in 1880, and some related matters, as seen in official correspondence*; Mario Mimeault, "A Dundee

Ship in Canada's Arctic: SS Diana and William Wakeham's Expedition of 1897," 51–61; Tweedie, "The Roots of the Royal Canadian Navy"; Appleton, *Usque ad Mare*; and Johnston et al., *Seabound Coast*, 82–3.

23 LAC, W.L.M. King Papers, Private Diary, 27 Feb. 1908; and Johnston et al., *Seabound Coast*, 119–20. Can. House of Commons, *Journal*, 29 March 1909 and 12 Jan.–4 May 1910 passim; GB, Commons, Sessional Papers Cd. 4948/1909. See also NA UK, ADM 116/1100B ff. 99–101, Lord Grey to Earl of Crewe, 11 May 1909 (Tracy, *Collective*, no. 65, 99–101).

24 Nicholas A. Lambert, "The Opportunities of Technology: British and French Naval Strategies in the Pacific, 1905–1909." in Rodger, *Naval Power in the 20th Century*: 41–58.

25 Johnston et al., *Seabound Coast*, 137, 147.

26 Can., Commons, *Debates*, session 1909 col. 3486, 29 March 1909; Gordon, *Dominion Partnership*, 228; and Johnston et al., *Seabound Coast*, 131–9, 143–4.

27 Johnston et al., *Seabound Coast*, 151, 157.

28 In Johnston et al., *Seabound Coast*, 135. Attribution by Richard Gimblett.

29 Ibid., 163–6, 761–2.

30 NA UK, ADM116/1100C ff. 169–70, Lord Haldane, Minutes of the 109th Meeting of CID, 24 March 1911, discussing CID paper 70-C, "The International Status of the Dominions During a War in which the United Kingdom is Engaged" (Tracy, *Collective*, no. 82, 146–9).

31 Can., Commons, *Debates*, 12 Jan. 1910, vol. 1, col. 1732–1776; See Laurier, *The Naval Question*; and C.P. Stacey, *Canada and the Age of Conflict, 1867–1921*, 134–7.

32 NA UK, ADM 116/1100C f 55, W. Graham Greene, assistant secretary of the admiralty, to USS Colonies, 10 Feb. 1908 (Tracy, *Collective*, no. 53, 83–5).

33 NA UK, CAB 5/2 ff 202–5, Admiralty memorandum on "The Status of Dominion Ships of War," Aug. 1910, CID 83 C, July 1912 (Tracy, *Collective*, no. 77, 132–7).

34 GB, Commons, Cmd 8596, *Proceedings of a Conference between the Secretary of State for the Colonies and the Premiers of the Self-Governing Colonies at the Colonial Office*, London, June and July 1897, vol. LIX, 631.

35 GB, Commons, Cmd 1299, *Proceedings of a Conference between the Secretary of State for the Colonies and the Premiers of the Self-Governing Colonies*, 30 June–11 Aug. 1902, vol. LXVI, 451 (Tracy, Collective, no. 6, 4–7).

36 *Ottawa Citizen*, 24 March 1909, quoted in Johnston et al., *Seabound Coast*, 133.

37 Bethell Memorandum, 1 Nov. 1911, Churchill College, CHART21/20 f. 12a. See Nicholas Lambert, "Economy or Empire? The Fleet Unit Concept and the Quest for Collective Security in the Pacific, 1909–14," in Greg Kennedy and Keith Neilson, *Far-Flung Line: Essays on Imperial Defence in Honour of Donald Mackenzie Schurman*. In 1930 Admiral Sir Charles E. Madden warned that while "the main fleet is the basis upon which our naval strategy rests, naval requirements are not satisfied solely by its provision. The 'cover' it can provide is rarely complete, and instances have occurred in all wars of units detached by the enemy evading the main fleet and carrying out attacks of a sporadic nature on territories and trade"; NA UK, ADM 116/2746, 14 Jan. 1930, "Basis of British Naval Strategy"; see John Ferris, "The Last Decade of British Maritime Supremacy, 1919–1929," in Kennedy, *Far-Flung Lines*, 124–70.

38 Can., Commons, *Debates*, 1909–10, vol. 1, col. 1746, 12 Jan.; Sir Robert Laird Borden, *The Naval Question: Speech Delivered by Mr. R.L. Borden, M.P., 12 Jan., 1910*, [Ottawa? : s.n., 1910?]; NA UK, ADM 116/3438, 12 Jan. 1910; quoted in

NA UK, ADM 116/3438, Dudley Pound, "Admiralty Policy Vis a Vis the Dominions, Outstanding Points up to 1923," 4 May 1923 (Tracy, *Collective*, no. 191, 348–65).

39 Honoré Gervais, *Speech of Mr Honoré Gervais, M.P., on the Naval Service of Canada*, Ottawa, March 8, 1910 [Ottawa? : s.n., 1910?].

40 NA UK, CID 67-C, CAB 5/2 ff. 150–3, "Report of a Sub-Committee of the Committee of Imperial Defence assembled to formulate questions connected with Naval and Military Defence of the Empire to be discussed at the Imperial Conference," 1911, March 1911; and ADM 116/1100C f. 164, "Certified Copy of a Report of the Committee of the Privy Council of Canada," 3 March 1911 (Tracy, *Collective*, nos. 80–1: 139–49); Johnston et al., *Seabound Coast*, 172–6.

41 NA UK, ADM 1/7576, Earl of Minto to Chamberlain, 12 June 1903 (Tracy, *Collective*, No. 15, 23–4); and Johnston et al., *Seabound Coast*, 125–7.

42 Richard A. Preston, "The Military Structure of the Old Commonwealth," *International Journal*, vol. 17, no. 2 (spring 1961–62): 98–121; James Eayrs, *In Defence of Canada*, vol. 1, 167; and Richard H. Leir, "Big Ship Time; The Formative Years of RCN Officers Serving in RN Capital Ships," in Boutilier, *Retrospect*: 74–95. NA UK, ADM 116/3165 f. 11 PD 01687. Minute by V. Adm. Sir Henry F. Oliver, 2nd Sea Lord, 21 April 1922, concerning a draft of CID paper 131-C on "Washington Conference in its Effect on Empire Naval Policy and Co-operation" (Tracy, *Collective*, no. 182: 311–12).

43 C.P. Stacey, *Arms, Men and Government*, 324–6.

44 Anon., "The Future of the Royal Canadian Navy," *Naval Review*, 1915, 369.

45 BL Add. MS 49005: 3–32 and 49057, John Jellicoe, "Report on the Mission to Canada"; and Canada, House of Commons, Sessional Papers 1920, no. 61, "Report of Admiral of the Fleet Viscount Jellicoe of Scapa G.C.B., O.M., G.C.V.O. on Naval Mission to the Dominion of Canada, Nov.–Dec. 1919," Ottawa: Thomas Mulvey, 1920. BL Add. MS 49048: 1–13; "Report on the Naval Mission to Australia," covering letter from Admiral Jellicoe to Sir Ronald Munro-Ferguson, GG Australia, 12 Aug. 1919; and Jellicoe to the Duke of Devonshire, GG Canada, 31 Dec. 1919, both abstracted in A. Temple Patterson, *The Jellicoe Papers*, vol. 2, 320, 374–8.

46 NA UK, ADM 116/1100C ff. 264–7, *Imperial Conference 1911*, "Memorandum of Conferences Between the British Admiralty and Representatives of the Dominions of Canada and Australia," Confidential, June 1911 (Tracy, *Collective*, no. 85, 153–9); Can., *Statutes of Canada*, 1910, 9–10 Edward VII, vols. 1–2, chap. 43, "An Act respecting the Naval Service of Canada," assented to 4 May 1910, Clause 23; Great Britain, House of Commons, Cd. 4948 *Correspondence, Proceedings and Papers re: Imperial Conference, 1911*: 25–6, answer to an enquiry from Canada, 5 Feb. 1910. See Nigel Brodeur, "L.P. Brodeur and the Origins of the Royal Canadian Navy," in Boutilier, *Retrospect*; and Johnston et al., *Seabound Coast*, 176–82.

47 Can., Commons, *Debates*, 1910–11, col. 612, 1 Dec. 1910 and J.S. Ewart, *Kingdom Papers*, Ottawa: no imprint, 1912, Nos. 6, 9, 11, 15. See Frederick Debartzch Monk, *Discours de M.F.D. Monk, M.P., sur la défense navale du Canada*.

48 Béatrice Richard, "Henri Bourassa and Conscription: Traitor or Saviour?" *Canadian Military Journal*, vol. 7, no. 4 (winter 2006–07).

49 There is an analogy between the constitutional relationship Canada had with the British Empire at the turn of the century, and the federal structure of Canada. Several provinces have their own articulated positions on policies with international implications, such as immigration, but nonetheless accept the necessity of Cana-

da's having a single defence and foreign policy. The analogy can be developed further because provincial attorneys general have direct access to the governor general, as commander in chief of the Canadian Armed Forces, if they need military support for the civil power. The sovereignty movement in Quebec is analogous to that in Canada at the turn of the century, and the attempt to counter it by increasing provincial influence on the formation of federal policies has some resemblance to the similar efforts to create truly Imperial institutions.

50 Can., Commons, *Debates*, 1900, col. 1846; and GB, Commons, Cmd 1299, *Proceedings of a Conference* (Tracy, *Collective*, no. 6, 4–7). See Richard A. Preston, *Canada and "Imperial Defense": A study of the origins of the British Commonwealth's defense organization, 1867–1919*, 344–50.

51 Kim Richard Nossal, currently Sir Edward Peacock Professor of International Relations at Queen's University, "Defending the 'Realm': The Canadian Strategic Culture Revisited," *International Journal*, vol. 59, no. 2 (2004): 503–20.

52 Borden to Harcourt, 16 May 1912, Bodlean Library, Harcourt Mss, f. 21 dep. 462. See Lambert, "Economy or Empire?" in Kennedy, *Far-Flung Lines*; *Canadian Annual Review*, Toronto: Annual Review Pub. Co., 1909: 153, Borden, speech in Toronto 29 October 1909; NA UK, ADM 116/3381, Borden to Churchill, 28 Aug. 1912, and GB, Commons, Cmd 6513,1912, Vol. LIII: 445, "Naval Defence: Memorandum on Naval Defence Requirements," prepared by the Admiralty for the Government of Canada, Dec. 1912 (Tracy, *Collective*, nos. 91, 107: 165, 178–80); Can., Commons, *Debates*, 5 Dec. 1912, 1912–13, cols. 675–94.

53 GB, Commons, 1902, Cmd 1299, Vol. LXVI, 451, *Proceedings of a Conference*, 30 June–11 Aug. 1902 (Tracy, *Collective*, no. 6, 4–7); Herbert Henry Asquith, later Lord Asquith, GB, Commons, Cmd 5745, 71; Ewart, *Kingdom Papers*, vol. 2, no. 15, 151–6; Johnston, *Seabound*, 183–210; and Michael Hadley and Roger Sarty, *Tin Pots and Pirate Ships: Canadian Naval Forces and German Sea Raiders, 1880-1914*, 53–64.

54 NA UK, ADM 116/3485, Memorandum, marked "A", on Canadian attitudes to the British Empire, by Lionel George Curtis, sent to Masterman Smith, private secretary to the 1st Lord, 9 Jan. 1914 (Tracy, *Collective*, no. 130, 224). See James Eayrs, "The Round Table Movement in Canada," in Cook et al., *Imperial Relations in the Age of Laurier*: 61–80.

55 NA UK, CID 101-C, CAB 5/3 f. 63, "Representation of the Dominions on the Committee of Imperial Defence," Note by the secretary, Capt. M.P.A. Hankey, Secret, 4 April 1913; A. Gordon Dewey, *The Dominions and Diplomacy: The Canadian Contribution*, vol. 1, 287–94.

56 NA UK, ADM 116/3485, Robert L. Borden to Winston S. Churchill, 1st Lord, Ottawa, 25 June 1913 (Tracy, *Collective*, no. 123, 204–7); and see Anon., *Comments on the Senate's rejection of the Naval Aid Bill*; Eugene (Alfred) Forsey, *Freedom and Order*, 130.

57 Charles Perry Stacey. NA UK, ADM 1/7671 ff. 277–8v *(from GB Cmd 1299)* Memorandum prepared for the 1902 Colonial Conference by Lord Selborne, the First Lord of the Admiralty, 7 Aug. 1902 (Tracy, *Collective*, no. 10 13–18); Robert Laird Borden, "Canada and the Navy," Liberal Party of Canada, no. 31, Halifax, Oct. 1909: 11; quoted in Dewey, *Dominions and Diplomacy*, vol. 1, 225; and NA UK, ADM 116/3381, R.L. Borden to W.S. Churchill, 3 and 5 Oct. 1912, and reply, 4 Nov. (Tracy, *Collective*, nos. 94–5, 101, 168–9, 174).

58 William Scott Chalmers (writing as B.X.), "Canada and the Navy," 100. Note also Chalmers, *The Life and Letters of David, Earl Beatty*, London: Hodder and

Stoughton, 1951; *Full Cycle: A Biography of Admiral Sir Bertram Home Ramsay*, Hodder and Stoughton, 1952. (For attribution see John Hattendorf and James Goldrick, *Mahan Is Not Enough*, 342.)
59 Stacey, *Age of Conflict*, 158–61.
60 Brian Tennyson and Roger Sarty, *Guardian of the Gulf: Sydney, Cape Breton, and the Atlantic Wars*, 113–88.
61 Hadley, *Tin Pots*, chapters 10–11; William Johnston, "The Royal Canadian Navy and the First World War," in Gimblett, *Centennial Story*, 23–40.
62 Bernard Ransom, "A Nursery of Fighting Seamen? The Newfoundland Royal Naval Reserve, 1901–1920," in Hadley, *A Nation's Navy*, 239–55; Roger Sarty, "Canada and Submarine Warfare 1909–1950"; Sarty, "Canadian Anti-submarine Forces and Operations During the First World War"; and Sarty, "Canadian Naval Policy 1867–1939." See also Hadley, *Tin Pots*, passim.
63 Phillip Wigley characterized the "persistent acknowledgment of their autonomy" as "irritating, and before long utterly perverse." Phillip Wigley, *Canada and the Transition to Commonwealth: British-Canadian Relations 1917–26*, 21–44.
64 On 4 January 1916 Borden drafted an angry letter to the acting Canadian high commissioner, George Halsey Perley: "It can hardly be expected that we shall put 400,000 or 500,000 men in the field and willingly accept the position of having no more voice and receiving no more consideration than if we were toy automata. Any person cherishing such an expectation harbours an unfortunate and even dangerous delusion. Is this war being waged by the United Kingdom alone or is it a war waged by the whole Empire?" On reflection, he wired Perley and told him to take no action. Can., DEA, *Documents on Canadian External Relations*, Ottawa: DEA, vol. 1, 96; and see: LAC, MG 27 II-D12 (R3895-0-3-E), George Halsey Perley fonds, vol. 5, File 1, 127, A–B, Sir Robert Borden to Perley, 4 Jan. 1916.
65 Stephen Wentworth Roskill, "The U-boat Campaign of 1917 and Third Ypres," RUSI *Journal*, vol. 104, no. 616 (Nov. 1959), 440–2.

CHAPTER TWO
1 James Eayrs, *In Defence of Canada*, vol. 1, 1–12; NA UK, CAB 32/2, 415–30, Arthur Meighen, Stenographic notes of the 26th meeting of representatives of UK, the Dominions, and India, 19 July 1921.
2 Robert Craig Brown, "Sir Robert Borden and Canada's War Aims," in Barry Hunt and Adrian Preston, eds., *War Aims and Strategic Policy in the Great War*, 55–66.
3 Carlton Savage, *Policy of the United States Toward Maritime Commerce in War*, vol. 2, 8; and Daniel M. Smith, *Robert Lansing and American Neutrality 1914–1917*, 27–8.
4 Stephen Wentworth Roskill, *Naval Policy Between the Wars: The Period of Anglo-American Antagonism, 1919–1929*, vol. 1, 81.
5 William Johnston, William Rawling, Richard Gimblett, and John MacFarlane, *The Seabound Coast: The Official History of the Royal Canadian Navy, 1867–1939*, 733–7, 744–5; and see Arthur S. Link, *Wilson Campaigns for Progressivism and Peace 1916 1917*, vol. 3, 296ff., 340ff., 411–16; Karl E. Birnbaum, *Peace Moves and U-boat Warfare: A Study of Imperial Germany's Policy towards the United States, April 18, 1916–January 9, 1917*, 315–39; Z.A.B. Zeman, *A Diplomatic History of the First World War*, 183–206; Edward Henry Buehrig, *Woodrow Wilson and the Balance of Power*, 135 8, 189; and Nils Ørvik, *The Decline of Neutrality, 1914–1941*, 73 88; Nicholas Tracy, *Attack on Maritime Trade*, 153–74.
6 Mary Halloran, "Canada and the Origins of the Post-War Commitment," in Mar-

garet O. MacMillan and David S. Sorenson, *Canada and* NATO: *Uneasy Past, Uncertain Future*, 1–14; Norman Hillmer, "O.D. Skelton, and the North American Mind," *International Journal*, vol. 60, no. 1 (2004–05): 93–110, at 102.

7 C.P. Stacey, *Mackenzie King and the Atlantic Triangle*, 29–45, 64.
8 LAC, Mackenzie King Diary, 27 Nov. 1919: 339 (3252).
9 NA UK, ADM 116/3104 ff. 40–53 (also in ADM 167/56 ff. 545–55), Admiralty memorandum "Co-operation of the Dominions and Colonies in a System of Imperial Naval Defence," Oct. 1919 (Tracy, *Collective*, no. 160, 251–62). See Admiralty memorandum "Co-operation of the Dominions and Colonies in a System of Imperial Naval Defence," Aug. 1920, CID 129-C, pub. Feb. 1921, CAB 5/3 ff. 269–72.
10 NA UK, CAB 21/187, (UK, Cmd 1474), "Naval Defence of the Empire: Imperial Naval Policy," abstracted in summary of proceedings of the 1921 Imperial Conference (Tracy, *Collective*, no. 179, 303–4).
11 NA UK, ADM 116/3438, Dudley Pound, "Admiralty Policy Vis à Vis the Dominions: Outstanding Points up to 1923," 4 May 1923 (Tracy, *Collective*, no. 191, 349–65).
12 LAC, *Mackenzie King Diary*, 11 Sept. 1923: 207–8 (3883–4); See NA UK, ADM 116/3149, Duke of Devonshire, secretary of state for the colonies, to the five Dominions, draft, 27 March 1923 (Tracy, *Collective*, no. 190, 347).
13 LAC, Mackenzie King Papers, Imperial Conference, 8 Oct. 1923, Stenographic Notes of the Fourth Meeting, ff. C62621-38 (J.L. Granatstein, *Canadian Foreign Policy: Historical Readings*, 16, and C.P. Stacey, *Historical Documents of Canada: Vol. 5, The Arts of War and Peace, 1914–1945*, 435–43; Lovell C. Clark, ed., *Documents on Canadian External Relations*, Vol. 3, 252). See Johnston et al., *Seabound Coast*, 793–4.
14 NA UK, CAB 21/315, Feakes to Wilson, 29 Nov. 1927 (Tracy, *Collective*, no. 231, 435).
15 NA UK, CAB 104/17, Sir William Clark to Sir Edward Harding, PUSS Dominion Affairs, 24 July 1929 (Tracy, *Collective*, no. 237, 440); and Norman Hillmer, "Defence and Ideology: The Anglo-Canadian Military 'Alliance' in the 1930s," *International Journal*, vol. 33, no. 3 (summer 1977–78), 585–612.
16 Can., DND, Directorate of History, File 112.3S 2009 (D23), Maurice Pope, "Memorandum on a Canadian Organization for the Higher Direction of National Defence: 8 March 1937," quoted in Douglas Bland, *Canada's National Defence*. Vol. 2, *Defence Organization*, 1–20.
17 Brian McKercher, "Between Two Giants: Canada, the Coolidge Conference, and Anglo-American Relations in 1927," *Anglo-American Relations in the 1920's: The Struggle for Supremacy*, 96–7.
18 John Erskine Read, "Problems of an External Affairs Legal Adviser, 1928–1946," *International Journal*, vol. 22, no. 3 (summer 1967): 376–94.
19 Oskar Douglas Skelton.
20 LAC, Department of External Affairs fonds, RG 25, A4, vol. 3419, file 1-1926/22: 17, O.D. Skelton, "The Locarno Treaties," 1 Jan. 1926, quoted in Norman Hillmer, "O.D. Skelton, and the North American Mind," 102.
21 Christopher M. Bell, "Thinking the Unthinkable: British and American Naval Strategies for an Anglo-American War, 1918–1931," *The International History Review*, vol. 19, no. 4 (Nov. 1997): 789–808.
22 LAC, Mackenzie King Papers, Imperial Conference, 1923, Stenographic Notes of the Fourth Meeting, ff. C62621-38 (Granatstein, *Historical Readings*, 16; and Stacey, *Historical Documents*, no. 173, 435–43).

23 Hillmer, "Defence and Ideology."
24 NA UK, CID 213-C, ADM 116-2247 ff. 121-5, "Empire Naval Policy and Co-operation," Memorandum by the Naval Staff for the Committee of Imperial Defence, Feb. 1924 (Tracy, *Collective*, no. 196, 376-3). See Johnston et al., *Seabound Coast*, 795-6, 852.
25 NA UK, ADM 116/3485, Lewis Harcourt, ss Colonies, to Winston S. Churchill, 1st Lord, 14 July 1914, and 116/1815 ff. 5-6, "Proposed visit of Lord Jellicoe to the Dominions and India to Advise on Naval Matters," Admiralty memorandum for War Cabinet by Sir Eric Geddes, 1st Lord 17 Dec. 1918 (Tracy, *Collective*, nos, 132, 149: 224-5, 241-2); and see Johnston et al., *Seabound Coast*: 208, 735-9.
26 NA UK, ADM 116/3438, "Admiralty Policy Vis-à-Vis the Dominions" by Captain Dudley Pound, director of plans, 4 May 1923 (Tracy, *Collective*, no. 191, 348-64). "In his report to the Canadian Government, Lord Jellicoe stated that Canada had two courses of action open, either to provide a squadron for her own safety consisting of three Light Cruisers, 10 Torpedo Craft and 8 Submarines, or, alternatively, to provide herself with a much larger Fleet and thereby assist in Empire Naval Defence. Halifax & Esquimalt to be developed as Light Cruiser bases. A site to be found for a future Capital ship base on the West Coast." Johnston et al., *Seabound Coast*, 755.
27 BL Add. MS 49005: 3-32 and 49057, Jellicoe, "Report on the Mission to Canada," 13 para. 12.
28 Johnston et al., *Seabound Coast*: 748-9.
29 The "National Liberal and Conservative party" was in office 10 July 1920-9 Dec. 1921. Johnston et al., *Seabound Coast,* 740-1; C.P. Stacey, *Canada and the Age of Conflict, 1867-1921*, 324-5; and Barry D. Hunt, "The Road to Washington: Canada and Empire Naval Defence, 1918-1921," in James Boutilier, ed., *RCN in Retrospect*: 44-61.
30 Sarty, "Canada and Submarine Warfare."
31 Ibid., 30, 44-6.
32 Imperial Conference and Stanley Baldwin, *Summary of Proceedings: Imperial Conference, 1926*, 28-30. Johnston et al., *Seabound Coast*, 940.
33 NA UK, CID 194-C, ADM 116/3415, "Empire Naval Policy and Co-operation," 1923, App. 3, Canada, 18 July 1923. See Roskill, *Naval Policy*, vol. 1, 282, 294-5, 409, 465; Johnston et al., *Seabound Coast*: 858, 860, 887; and Kenneth Hansen, "The 'Destroyer Myth' in Canadian Naval History," *Canadian Naval Review*, vol. 2, no. 3 (fall 2006): 5-9.
34 Roger Sarty and Kenneth Gough, "Sailors and Soldiers: The Royal Navy, the Canadian Forces, and the Defence of Atlantic Canada, 1890-1918"; Roger Sarty, "The Origins of Canada's Second World War Maritime Forces, 1918-1940"; and Johnston et al., *Seabound Coast*, 859-60.
35 William Scott Chalmers, "Canada and the Navy," and Anon., "The Future of the Royal Canadian Navy," *Naval Review*, 1913, 100 and 1915, 369. Chalmers's pseudonym was "BX." See John B. Hattendorf and James Goldrick, *Mahan Is Not Enough*, Appendix.
36 Richard Gimblett, "A Century of Canadian Maritime Force Development: A Reinterpretive History," in Edward L. Tummers, *Maritime Security in the Twenty-first Century*, 17; Hugh Francis Pullen, "The Royal Canadian Navy between the Wars, 1922-39," in Boutilier, *Retrospect*: 62-73.
37 LAC, *Mackenzie King Diary*, 22 April 1922, and see 29 April: 176, 186 (3712, 3716). The Royal Navy Reserve in Newfoundland had been abolished in 1921.

Bernard Ransom, "A Nursery of Fighting Seamen?"; Johnston et al., *Seabound Coast*, 786.
38 NA UK, CID 176-C, Memorandum by the Naval Staff, 28 July 1922, CAB 5/4 ff. 171-3v, "The Washington Conference and its Effect upon Empire Naval Policy and Co-operation." See Johnston et al., *Seabound Coast*, 788, 792-3.
39 NA UK, ADM 116/3415: 4 NA, "Naval Expenditure, GB (& Ireland to 1920-21) and the Dominions," Admiralty Statistics Department, 12 March 1923 (Tracy, *Collective*, no. 189, 337-46).
40 NA UK, CID 145-C, CAB 5/4 ff. 95-6: "Reserves of Oil Fuel," Memorandum by Lord Lee of Fareham, 1st Lord, 21 June 1921, "The Admiralty have recommended that the Dominions should be urged to look upon the provision of oil fuel reserves as one of their principal naval commitments for some years to come, for on the mobility of the main fleet rests the guarantee for their safety" (Tracy, *Collective*, no. 175, 290-5); and NA UK, ADM 116/3415: 23-4 and E32, "Empire Naval Policy: Brief Summary of the Recommendations by the Admiralty," 11 July 1921 (Tracy, *Collective*, no. 177, 298-9).
41 Johnston et al., *Seabound Coast*, 972.
42 Ibid., 741.
43 James Goldrick, "From Fleets to Navies: The Evolution of Dominion Fleets into the Independent Navies of the Commonwealth."
44 William Glover, "The RCN: Royal Colonial or Royal Canadian Navy?" in Michael Hadley, Rob Huebert, and Fred W. Crickard, *A Nation's Navy: In Quest of Canadian Naval Identity*: 71-90. The Royal Naval College of Canada was destroyed by the 1917 Halifax explosion, before moving briefly to Kingston and then re-opening at Esquimalt.
45 NA UK, ADM 116/3165 f. 11, Minute by V. Adm. Sir Henry F. Oliver, 2nd Sea Lord, concerning a draft of CID paper 131-C, 21 April 1922, referring to Charles Colquhoun Ballantyne's suggestion (Tracy, *Collective*, no. 182, 311-12).
46 Richard A. Preston, "The Military Structure of the Old Commonwealth," *International Journal*, vol. 17, no. 2, (spring 1961-62): 98-121; and Richard H. Leir, "Big Ship Time: The Formative Years of RCN Officers Serving in RN Capital Ships," in Boutilier, *Retrospect*: 74-95.
47 Sarty, "Canadian Naval Policy," 50-1, citing RCN Annual Report, 31 March 1929, 5-11; Johnston et al., *Seabound Coast*, 163-6, 761-71.
48 NA UK, ADM 116/2247 ff. 10-3, 121-5, 161-4, "Imperial Conference, 1923. Proposed methods for obtaining naval staff co-ordination between the British and Dominion navies," minutes by L.H. Haggan, DTSD, 31 July 1923, and Dudley Pound, 7 Sept. 1923; "Empire Naval Policy and Co-operation," memorandum by the Naval Staff for CID, Feb. 1924; and Memorandum of 7 April 1926 (Tracy, *Collective*, nos. 194, 196, 213: 309-74, 376-8, 406-9).
49 NA UK, CAB 4/15, ff. 170-83, Imperial Conference, 1926, Extracts from the Stenographic Notes of the 12th meeting, 15 Nov. 1926 (Tracy, *Collective*, no. 217, 414-20).
50 NA UK, ADM 116/2567 ff. 4-7, 82v, 89, 93, 112-13, 144, "Canadian Government Naval Policy," Admiralty minutes and internal letters, April to Aug. 1927, V. Adm. Sir Frederick Field, DCNS to Commodore Hose, Canadian Director of the Naval Service, 12 Aug., and Telegram from SS External Affairs, W.L. Mackenzie King, to SS for Dominion Affairs, L.C.M.S. Amery, 9 Nov. (Tracy, *Collective*, nos. 220-9, 423-32). Johnston et al., *Seabound Coast*, 887-8, 905-6, 942.
51 LAC, *Mackenzie King Diary*, 14 Oct. 1924: 321-2 (4055-6).

52 NA UK, CAB 21/307, Belligerent Rights at Sea and the Relations Between the United States and Great Britain, 16 and 26 Oct. 1927.
53 Brian McKercher, "Between Two Giants": 99–110. Hose was promoted to Commodore 14 Aug. 1923.
54 Herbert C. Hoover, *The Memoirs of Herbert Hoover*, vol. 2, 342. See also ADM 116/2686, Esme Howard to Austen Chamberlain, 9 May 1929; and passim. Brian McKercher, *Transition of Power: Britain's Loss of Global Pre-eminence to the United States, 1930–1945*, 32–62.
55 Sir Arthur D. Fanshawe, "Freedom of the Seas," *Naval Review*, 1929-2, 382.
56 James P. Baxter, 3rd, "Some British Opinions as to Neutral Rights, 1861 to 1865," *Naval Review*, 1930-1, 73–96.
57 LAC, *Mackenzie King Diary*, 19 Oct. 1929: 472 (5510). See Johnston et al., *Seabound Coast*, 856.
58 John Ferris, "The Last Decade of British Maritime Supremacy, 1919–1929," in Kennedy, *Far-Flung Lines*: 124–170. See Johnston et al., *Seabound Coast*, 851–2.
59 Richard Bedford Bennett.
60 Eayrs, *In Defence*, vol. 1, 278; see Serge Durflinger, "In Whose Interests? The Royal Canadian Navy and Naval Diplomacy in El Salvador, 1932," in Ann L. Griffiths, Peter T. Haydon, and Richard H. Gimblett, *Canadian Gunboat Diplomacy: The Canadian Navy and Foreign Policy*: 27–44; Johnston et al., *Seabound Coast*, 907–15.
61 Johnston et al., *Seabound Coast*, 856–9. "Treasury Board Meeting," synopsis by Commodore Hose, CNS, 23 June 1933, quoted in Eayrs, *In Defence*, vol. 1, 270–87.
62 Roosevelt's mouthpiece was Norman H. Davis, the American diplomat and delegate to the 1932 Geneva Disarmament Conference.
63 NA UK, ADM 116/4080, Admiralty minutes, authors unknown (April or May 1935?) and 9 May; minute by J.S. Barnes, 19 June; Commodore Percy Nelles, Canadian CNS, to V. Adm. Sir Charles J.C. Little, DCNS, 27 June; and F.L.C. Floud, high commissioner to Canada, to Sir Edward Harding, PUSS for Dominion Affairs, 23 July 1935 (Tracy, *Collective*, nos. 283–5, 511–14).
64 Galen Roger Perras, *Franklin Roosevelt and the Origins of the Canadian-American Security Alliance, 1933–1945*, 7–32.
65 LAC, MG 27, vol. 32, file X-53, Percy Nelles, "Canadian Naval Policy in Regard to Her Western Seaboard," 24 Sept. 1936; Johnston et al., *Seabound Coast*, 944–6.
66 Pope, "Memorandum on ... the Higher Direction of National Defence: 8 March 1937," 8.
67 LAC, MG 27, III B-5 vol 30, file X-18, "Joint Staff Committee Plan for the Maintenance of Canadian Neutrality in the Event of War between the United States and Japan," 20 Jan. 1938. It was anticipated that there might be: "attempts on the part of Japan to make use of remote harbours or other territorial waters as refuelling or repair bases or as places of refuge for submarines, armed merchantmen and cruisers, the two latter categories being probably equipped with aircraft. The unlawful entry into Canadian jurisdiction of Japanese battleships and aircraft carriers is not anticipated ... The naval plan recommended contemplates in co-operation with the Air Force, a continuous patrol of the territorial waters adjacent to the British Columbian coast by all vessels of the Royal Canadian Navy assisted by such additional auxiliary craft as may be required, and as are available."
68 LAC, *Mackenzie King Diary*, 24 Oct. 1938, 869 (804).
69 Writing in 1995, Harald von Riekhoff characterized the attitude of the Canadian

governments during the League period as "profoundly ambivalent." Von Riekhoff, "Canada and Collective Security." In 1925 Senator Dandurand became the first British Commonwealth statesman elected president of the Assembly.

70 Lester B. Pearson, *Mike: The Memoirs of the Right Honourable Lester B. Pearson*, vol. 1, 92–102; and John A. Munro, "The Riddell Affair Reconsidered," 366–75.
71 LAC, *Mackenzie King Diary*, 28 Sept. 1936, 448 (363) and 3 May 1938, 368 (330). George Howard Ferguson had been Conservative premier of Ontario.
72 Peter Gellman, "Lester B. Pearson, Collective Security, and the World Order Tradition of Canadian Foreign Policy," 68–101.
73 LAC RG 25, vol. 755, DND, "The Naval Service of Canada: A Resume of its Necessity, Resources and Requirements," Aug. 1936, 238; Johnston et al., *Seabound Coast*, 940–2, 946–50.
74 NA UK, ADM 116/4080, Interview between Mr Mackenzie, M [National] Defence, Canada, and 1st Sea Lord, 6 Aug. 1936; Message to First Sea Lord from NSHQ Ottawa, 4 Sept.; Minute by A.S. Le Maitre for Head Military Branch of Admiralty Secretariat [under V. Adm. William M. James], 4 Sept.; and Message to Naval Ottawa, from head of Military Branch Admiralty, 4 Sept. 1936 (Tracy, *Collective*, nos. 303, 308–9, 536–7, 543–4). Eayrs, *In Defence*, vol. 2, 134–54.
75 Johnston et al., *Seabound Coast*, 971.
76 NA UK, ADM 116/4144, R. Adm. Percy Nelles, Canadian CNS, to Admiral of the Fleet Lord Chatfield, 1st Sea Lord, 16 June 1938 (Tracy, *Collective*, no. 342, 593–4); Malcolm MacLeod, "The Royal Canadian Navy, 1918–39," *The Mariner's Mirror*, vol. 56, 1970, 169–86.
77 LAC, *Mackenzie King Diary*, 15 Dec. 1939, 1283 (1315). Holland was killed in action 24 May 1941 when HMS *Hood* blew up while engaging *Bismarck*.
78 Sarty, "Origins."
79 Norman McLeod Rogers. LAC, *Mackenzie King Diary*, 15 Sept. 1939, 1003–8 (1035–40); see Can., Commons, *Debates*, 13 May 1939, 4: 4016–17.
80 GB, Statute of Westminster 1931 c.4 22 and 23 Geo 5, 11 Dec. 1931, "And whereas it is mete and proper to set out by way of preamble to this Act that, inasmuch as the Crown is the symbol of the free association of the members of the British Commonwealth of Nations, and as they are united by a common allegiance to the Crown."
81 Hillmer, "Defence and Ideology."
82 NA UK, CAB 53/3 ff. 273–6, Chiefs of Staff subcommittee of CID, 22 Oct. 1930; see Stacey, *Arms, Men and Government*, 93–4.
83 Escott Meredith Reid, "Canada and the Threat of War: A Discussion of Mr Mackenzie King's Foreign Policy," 242–53.
84 NA UK, CAB 21/670, Hankey to Harding, 9 May 1938, (Jack Granatstein, *Canada's War*, 3); NA UK, CAB 104/18 and 19, S.H. Phillips (Admiralty) to USS Dominions, 16 May 1938; Note on a discussion at the War Book Sub-Committee Meeting on 18th May, 1938, on the desirability of amending the War Book to meet the case where one or more of the dominions may delay their entry into the war, or remain neutral; Hankey to Harding, 20 May 1938 (Tracy, *Collective*, nos. 337–8, 584–5); and Eayrs, *In Defence*, vol. 2, 81–91.
85 NA UK, CAB 104/18, Harding to Sir Francis Floud, and Floud to Harding (Dominions Office), Secret, 14, 21 June 1938 (Tracy, *Collective*, nos. 341, 343: 593–5).
86 NA UK, ADM 116/3802 ff 14, 16–17, 21, 77, 134–8, Telegrams from the UK acting high commissioner in Canada to the secretary of the admiralty, 29, 30 Sept. 1938; letter from O.D. Skelton USS External Affairs, to Stephen Holmes, acting

high commissioner, 30 Sept. 1938, confirming the substance of these telegrams; and S.L. Holmes, principal officer, Dominions Office, to Commander (E) H. Dixon, attached to Admiral Sir Charles Little, 2nd Sea Lord, 18 Oct. 1938 (Tracy, *Collective*, nos. 349, 351, 359: 597–9, 610–2).
87 NA UK, ADM 116/3802 f. 147, C-in-C America and West Indies to First Sea Lord, 14 Oct. 1938 (Tracy, *Collective*, no. 353, 600–1).
88 NA UK, CAB 104/18 and 19, Unattributed paper, Nov. 1938; William Elliot to "Secretary," Secret, 21 Jan. 1939; and S.H. Phillips to USS Dominions, 1 Feb. 1939, passim. (Tracy, *Collective*, nos. 360, 368: 612–13, 627–9).
89 Perras, *Roosevelt and the Origins*, 33–63.

CHAPTER THREE

1 NA UK, FO 371/22969/C5262/15/18, Hankinson to Harvey, 30 March 1939; and LAC, DEA Records Vol 54 file 319-2, "Canada and the Polish War. A Personal Note" 25 Aug. 1939. Both quoted in J.L. Granatstein and Robert Bothwell, "'A Self-Evident National Duty': Canadian Foreign Policy, 1935–1939," *Journal of Imperial and Commonwealth History*, vol. 3, no. 2 (Jan. 1975): 212–33; See J.L. Granatstein, *Canada's War*, 6.
2 Can., Commons, *Debates*, 8 Sept. 1939: 8–41.
3 LAC, External Affairs Records, vol. 54, file 265, Pearson to Skelton, 9 June 1939, Granatstein and Bothwell, "'A Self-Evident National Duty.'"
4 The Hon. Clarence Decatur Howe was minister of munitions and supply between 9 April 1940 and 31 Dec. 1945.
5 J.H.W. Knox, "An Engineer's Outline of RCN History: Part 1," in James Boutilier, ed., *RCN in Retrospect*: 96–116; W.A.B. Douglas, Roger Sarty, and Michael Whitby, *No Higher Purpose: The Official Operational History of the Royal Canadian Navy in the Second World War, 1939–1943*, vol. 2, pt. 1, 77–9.
6 W.A.B. Douglas, *The Creation of a National Air Force: The Official History of the Royal Canadian Air Force*, 2: 376, 394.
7 LAC, *Mackenzie King Diary*, 19 Oct., 4 and 19 Nov. 1940: 1019, 1048, 1088. 194: 970, 1011).
8 Adrian W. Preston, "Canada and the Higher Direction of the Second World War 1939–1945," 28–44; and James Eayrs, *In Defence of Canada*, vol. 2: 154–59.
9 Pearson, *Mike*, vol. 1, 170; see C.P. Stacey, *Arms, Men and Government*, 141–2.
10 LAC, *Mackenzie King Diary*, 3 Jan. 1931: 4 (5933). Churchill was in the political wilderness at the time on account of opposition to Indian independence.
11 LAC, *Mackenzie King Diary*, 10 June 1939: 663 (679).
12 Ibid., 27 Jan. 1940: 95 (94).
13 Stacey, *Arms, Men and Government*, 2, 138–9, 145–56, 180–1; Robert Rhodes James, ed., *Winston Churchill: His Complete Speeches, 1897–1963*, vol. 6, 6565; J.W. Pickersgill and D.F. Forster, *Mackenzie King Record*, 1: 528:9; LAC, *Mackenzie King Diary*, 24 July 1943: 706–10 (567–71); and W.A.B. Douglas, Roger Sarty, Michael Whitby, *A Blue Water Navy: The Official Operational History of the Royal Canadian Navy in the Second World War, 1943–1945*, Vol. 2 pt. 2, 167.
14 LAC, *Mackenzie King Diary*, 24 May 1940: 584 (520).
15 Ibid., 20 July 1943: 697 (558).
16 LAC, RG 24 vol. 3842 NSS 1017-10-23, CNS to Minister (Ian Alistair Mackenzie), 12 Sept. 1939.
17 Stacey, *Arms, Men and Government*, 308–10; Douglas et al., *No Higher Purpose*, 56–7.

18 LAC, RG 2 A-5-b Cabinet War Committee, MF C11789, 10, 17, 23 May 1940; Stacey, *Arms, Men and Government*, 321.
19 Douglas et al., *No Higher Purpose*, 130, 151-8.
20 LAC, RG 2 A-5-b vol. 5669 No. 67, (R165-94-7-E): 2-3, *Minutes*, Cabinet War Committee, "Defence of Canada," 26 Feb. 1941; and Hansen, "The 'Destroyer Myth' in Canadian Naval History," *Canadian Naval Review*, vol. 2, no. 1 (spring 2006), 34.
21 LAC, RG 2 A-5-b, MF C11789, Cabinet War Committee, 24 June 1941; Stacey, *Arms, Men and Government*, 311.
22 Douglas, *No Higher Purpose*, 183-9; Roger Sarty, "Canada's Emergence as a Naval Power, 1910-1950," Conference paper, 3 Feb. 2002; Bernard Ransom, "Canada's 'Newfyjohn' Tenancy: The Royal Canadian Navy in St John's, 1941-1945," *Acadiensis* 23 (spring 1994), 45-71; Tucker, *The Naval Service of Canada: Its Official History*, vol. 2, 189- 97.
23 Stacey, *Arms, Men and Government*, 313-14.
24 Douglas, *No Higher Purpose*. 207-35, 488-90.
25 Ibid., 389-93.
26 Ibid., 303-17, 481-2.
27 LAC, *Mackenzie King Diary*, 10 Feb. 1943: 112 (109).
28 Douglas et al., *No Higher Purpose*, 549-50.
29 Marc Milner, "Rear-Admiral Leonard Warren Murray: Canada's Most Important Operational Commander," in Whitby, *Admirals: Canada's Senior Naval Leadership in the Twentieth Century*, 109.
30 Douglas et al., *No Higher Purpose*, 579-81; Richard O. Mayne, *Betrayed: Scandal, Politics, and Canadian Naval Leadership*, 92-100.
31 Douglas et al., *No Higher Purpose*, 553-4, 576-8.
32 Secretary of state for external affairs to dominions secretary, telegram 3, 9 Jan. 1943, in John F. Hilliker, ed., *Documents on Canadian External Relations*, vol. 9, 359.
33 Stacey, *Arms, Men and Government*, 307-14; W.G.D. Lund, "The Royal Canadian Navy's Quest for Autonomy in the North West Atlantic 1941-43," in Boutilier, *Retrospect*: 138-157; Mark Milner, *North Atlantic Run*, 58-61, 229-33; Douglas, *Blue Water Navy*, 29, 61-5, 491-2, 504, 579-98, 621-30; Roger Sarty, "Canada and Submarine Warfare 1909-1950"; Catherine E. Allan, "A Minute Bletchley Park: Building a Canadian Naval Operational Intelligence Centre, 1939-1943," in Hadley, *A Nation's Navy*: 157-72.
34 Mayne, *Betrayed*, 41-67, 208-18.
35 Stacey, *Arms, Men and Government*, 315-18; meeting of the author with Sir Peter Gretton 1972; Mayne, *Betrayed*, 25-8, 67-92.
36 Douglas, *Blue Water Navy*: 39-50, 175-84; Ken Macpherson and Marc Milner, *Corvettes of the Royal Canadian Navy 1939-1945*, 89-126; Richard O. Mayne, "Vice-Admiral George C. Jones: The Political Career of a Naval Officer," in Whitby, *Admirals*: 125-55; Mayne, *Betrayed*, 120-79.
37 Doug M. McLean, "Muddling Through: Canadian Anti-submarine Doctrine and Practice, 1942-1945," in Hadley, *A Nation's Navy*: 173-89 at 176; Douglas et al., *No Higher Purpose*, 504, 525-6, 531; and *Blue Water Navy*, 381-3; Mark Milner, "The Implication of Technological Backwardness: The Royal Canadian Navy 1939-45," *Canadian Defence Quarterly*, vol. 19 no. 3, Dec. 1989: 46-52; and David Zimmerman, *The Great Naval Battle of Ottawa*, 25 and passim.
38 Douglas, *Blue Water Navy*, 33-4; Nicholas Tracy, *Convoy ONS 5*, unpublished, 1971.

39 Richard H. Gimblett, "Command in the Canadian Navy: An Historical Survey," *The Northern Mariner/Le marin du nord*, 14, no. 4, Oct. 2004: 41–60.
40 Peter Padfield, *Dönitz: The Last Führer*, 250. See also Keith W. Bird, *German Naval History: A Guide to the Literature*, 578 80.
41 Admiralty, *Fuehrer Conferences on Naval Affairs*, vol. 2, 46. See Carl Dönitz (R.H. Stevens, trans.), *Memoirs: Ten Years and Twenty Days*, 406 8.
42 NA PRO, ADM 199/327: 382–3, Horton to Fraser, 31 May 1944; See Andrew Lambert, "Seizing the Initiative: The Arctic Convoys 1944–45," in Nicholas Rodger, *Naval Power in the 20th Century*: 151–62.
43 Douglas, *Blue Water Navy*, 185–203.
44 Ibid., 231–2, 407–8.
45 Douglas et al., *No Higher Purpose*, 337–8.
46 William Glover, "Royal Colonial or Royal Canadian Navy?"
47 Shawn Cafferky, *Uncharted Waters: A History of the Canadian Helicopter-Carrying Destroyer*, 42.
48 Stacey, *Arms, Men and Government*: 183–4, 319–23; Douglas, *Blue Water Navy*, 168–73, 452, 511–19; LAC, *Mackenzie King Diary*, 10 and 27 Nov., 16 Dec. 1943: 1255, 1333, 1388 (994, 1055, 1109), 9 and 11 Oct. 1944: 1000, 1004 (958, 962); See Documents on Canadian External Relations, "Memorandum from Chiefs of Staff Committee to Cabinet Defence Committee," Ottawa, 10 Oct. 1946.
49 Douglas Charles Abbott.
50 LAC, *Mackenzie King Diary*, 13 Sept. 1944, and see 11 Oct.: 841, 1004 (824, 962).
51 Douglas, *Blue Water Navy*, 546–56; Michael Hennessy, "Canada's Pacific Carriers: A Study of Manipulation and Neglect, 1944–1950," in Griffiths, Haydon, and Gimblett, *Canadian Gunboat Diplomacy*: 45–76.
52 McLean, "Muddling Through."
53 Gimblett, "Command in the Canadian Navy."
54 James Goldrick, "Strangers in Their Own Seas? A Comparison of the Australian and Canadian Naval Experience, 1910–1982," in Rob Hadley and Fred Crickard, *A Nation's Navy*: 325–30; and "From Fleets to Navies." See Whitby, *Admirals*: 69–176.
55 Lambert, "The Opportunities of Technology"; and Tracy, *Collective*: 558.
56 LAC, *Mackenzie King Diary*, 5 Jan. 1944: 10 (9).
57 Can., Commons, *Debates*, 1910–11 col. 612, 1 Dec. 1910, and J.S. Ewart, *Kingdom Papers*, Ottawa: no imprint, 1912, Nos. 6, 9, 11, 15. See Frederick Debartzch Monk, *Discours de M.F.D. Monk, M.P., sur la défense navale du Canada*, Ottawa, jeudi, 3 février 1910, Ottawa : [s.n.], 1910.

CHAPTER FOUR

1 LAC, MG 30, E159, vol. 2, file 5: Defence and Foreign Affairs, Report, "A Programme of Immediate Canadian Action drawn up by a Group of Twenty Canadians Meeting at the Chateau Laurier, Ottawa, July 17–18, 1940," 1–12. RG 2 A-5-b, MF C11789, Cabinet War Committee, 14 June 1940.
2 David Beatty, "The 'Canadian Corollary' to the Monroe Doctrine and the Ogdensburg Agreement of 1940," *The Northern Mariner/Le marin du nord*, vol. 1, no. 1 (1991): 3–22.
3 LAC, RG 2 A-5-b, MF C11789, Cabinet War Committee, 7 Nov. 1940.
4 William Douglas, Roger Sarty, and Michael Whitby, *No Higher Purpose: The Official Operational History of the Royal Canadian Navy in the Second World War, 1939–1943*, vol. 2, pt. 1, 418–20.

5 James Eayrs, *In Defence of Canada*, vol. 3, 321.
6 W.A.B. Douglas, "Conflict and Innovation in the Royal Canadian Navy, 1939–1945," in Gerald Jordan, ed., *Naval Warfare in the Twentieth Century 1900–1945, Essays in Honour of Arthur Marder*: 210–32.
7 Can., DEA, *Report of the Advisory Committee on Post-Hostilities Problems*, "Postwar Canadian Defence Relationship with the United States: General Considerations"; Eayrs, *In Defence*, vol. 3, 375–80.
8 LAC, *Mackenzie King Diary*, 10 Aug. 1945: 808 (760).
9 Jack Granatstein, *Ottawa Men*, 125–33; and Lester B. Pearson, *Mike: The Memoirs of the Rt. Hon. Lester B. Pearson*, vol. 1, 284.
10 J.W. Pickersgill, *Mackenzie King Record*, vol. 3, 219.
11 Can., DEA, *Statements and Speeches*, no. 47/2, 13 Jan. 1947: 3–11; Louis St Laurent, "The Foundation of Canadian Policy in World Affairs," inaugurating the Gray Foundation Lectureship at the University of Toronto.
12 Winston Churchill's "Iron Curtain" speech at Westminster College in Fulton, Missouri, on 5 March 1946, quoted in John Gellner, *Canada in NATO*, 3–5. Use of Article 52 in the Charter authorizing regional bodies would have been subject to Security Council veto. See Escott Reid, "Canada and the Creation of the North Atlantic Alliance, 1948–1949," in Michael Fry, ed., *Freedom and Change: Essays in Honour of Lester B. Pearson*: 106–35.
13 Isabel Campbell, "Canadian Insights into NATO Maritime Strategy, 1949–69: The Role of National and Service Interests," Proceedings ... *From Empire to In(ter)dependence*.
14 Escott Reid, "The United States and the Soviet Union: A Study of the Possibility of War and some of the Implication for Canadian Policy," 30 Aug. 1947, in *Documents on Canadian External Relations*, vol. 13: 367–82.
15 John Holmes, *The Shaping of Peace: Canada and the Search for World Order 1943–57*, vol. 1, 105–24, 154–6; vol. 4, 76; and Mary Halloran, "Canada and the Origins of the Post-War Commitment," in Margaret MacMillan and David Sorenson, *Canada and NATO: Uneasy Past, Uncertain Future*.
16 Pearson, *Mike*, vol. 2, 32–3.
17 Escott Reid, "Canada and the Creation"; *Time of Fear and Hope: The Making of the North Atlantic Treaty 1947–1949*: 126–32; and see John Holmes, *Life with Uncle: The Canadian-American Relationship*, 35.
18 David G. Haglund and Stéphane Roussel, "Escott Reid, the North Atlantic Treaty, and Canadian Strategic Culture," in Greg Donaghy and Stéphan Roussel, *Escott Reid: Diplomat and Scholar*: 44–66, at 49 and 52; LAC, RG25, Accession 90-91/008 vol. 26, Escott Reid, "Paper on Canadian Policy in NATO," 28 April 1951. Reid preferred federation of western Europe and North America, but that was well in advance of his colleagues, let alone of international realities. It was important, he wrote in 1951, that an alliance take a form that would lead "the Free World to become increasingly subject to some sort of common constitutional structure."
19 The U.S. State Department took the position "that the Canadian economy should be treated as nearly as possible like our own in peacetime as well as in war." Mackenzie King decided that the Canadian public would not accept so complete an abandonment of the Imperial relationship. The freezing of Imperial Preference Tarrifs in the negotiations that led to the General Agreement on Tarrifs and Trade was as much as the public would accept. NARA, State Department Records, 842.20, Defense/4-2745, W.L. Batt to Edward Browning and Robert Turner, 27 April

1945, quoted in Robert Bothwell, *Alliance and Illusion, Canada and the World, 1941–1984*, 33, and see 33–40, 47.
20 On 17 March the Cabinet listened on the radio to President Truman's address to a joint session of Congress calling for a return to conscription, and the British signed on to the Brussels Treaty creating the Western European Union (WEU) the same day. Congress finally agreed to the Marshall Plan.
21 David Bercuson, Claxton's biographer, remarks on the inconsistency of Claxton's position in the light of his conviction that it was weakness during the Ethiopian and Munich crises that had made the last war unavoidable. David Bercuson, *True Patriot, The Life of Brooke Claxton, 1898–1960*, 193–9.
22 LAC, *Mackenzie King Diary*, 17 March, 30 June, 1948: 283–92, 631–7 (281–90, 628–634).
23 Can., Commons, *Debates*, 29 April 1948, vol. 4 col. 3449–50. Reid, *Time of Fear and Hope*: 99–112. St Laurent's speech was useful in persuading a reluctant United States Senate to agree to a formal treaty. USA, Department of State, Publications 3497, "The Signing of the North Atlantic treaty," June 1949: 3. See Sokolsky, "The Bilateral Defence Relationship," in David B. Dewitt and David Leyton-Brown, *Canada's International Security Policy*,
24 See von Riekhoff, "Canada and Collective Security"; and Escott Reid, "The Birth of the North Atlantic Alliance," *International Journal*, vol. 32, no. 3 (1966–67): 426–40. An easily revoked unilateral American guarantee would have been less stabilizing, and less supported by Americans. In June 1948 Reid wrote to Hume Wrong in Washington: "if you scratch almost any American long enough, you will find an isolationist. They suffer, and you can hardly blame them, from a homesickness for isolation." See Reid, "Canada and the Creation"; and *Time of Fear and Hope*, 108–9. See Tom Keating and Larry Pratt, *Canada, NATO and the Bomb: The Western Alliance in Crisis*, 20–3.
25 Eayrs, *In Defence*, vol. 4, 140–3; Sean Michael Maloney, *Securing Command of the Sea: NATO Naval Planning 1948–1954*; and NATO Information Service, *NATO Facts and Figures*, 218–21.
26 Haglund and Roussel, "Escott Reid, the North Atlantic Treaty, and Canadian Strategic Culture," 54–5; and Maloney, *Securing Command of the Sea*, 97–8, 104, 151.
27 Peter T. Haydon, "Sailors, Admirals, and Politicians: The Search for Identity after the War"; and Maloney, *Securing Command of the Sea*, 123–37, 15–22.
28 Sean Michael Maloney, "Parry and Thrust: Canadian Maritime Forces and the Defence of North America, 1954–62," *The Northern Mariner/Le marin du nord*, vol. 18, no. 1 (Jan. 2008), 39–54, at 40.
29 Eayrs, *In Defence*, vol. 3, 319, 321, 344–9.
30 Mackenzie King thought "a great mistake had been made in selecting Reid of the Navy for his post. I don't think he is any good at all. He looks like a man who has been doing a great deal of drinking and eating and one who has not to much in the way of Intellectual power or wisdom." LAC, *Mackenzie King Diary*, 13 Nov. 1946: 1099 (1029).
31 Douglas, *No Higher Purpose*, 51, 66; Wilfred G.D. Lund, "Vice-Admiral Howard Emmerson Reid and Vice-Admiral Harold Taylor Wood Grant: Forging the New 'Canadian' Navy," and Marc Milner, "Rear-Admiral Leonard Warren Murray: Canada's Most Important Operational Commander," in Michael Whitby, *The Admirals*, 112, 157–86.

32 Maloney, *Securing Command of the Sea*, 54; Dwight N. Mason, "Continental Security: A View From the USA," in Robert Edwards and Graham Walker, eds., *Continental Security*: 41–50; and John Orr,"Some Policy Aspects of Canadian Involvement in Strategic ASW, 1945–1968," Richard Gimblett, *People, Policy and Programmes*: 183–203. The Military Cooperation Committee continued to act as a direct link between national military staffs, but shed its civilian diplomatic component.

33 Can., Foreign Affairs, *Documents on Canadian External Relations*, vol. 12, chap. 11, Relations with the United States, Part III, Defence, Section C, Defence Planning, Memorandum from Secretary, Cabinet Defence Committee, Cabinet, 21 Oct. 1946, Ottawa, Permanent Joint Board on Defence, 35th Recommendation (Revised), 973.

34 Can., 12 Feb. 1947. See David Bercuson, "Continental Defense and Arctic Sovereignty, 1945–50," in Keith Neilson and Ronald G. Haycock, eds., *The Cold War and Defense*, 153–70; and William R. Willoughby, "Canadian-American Defense Co-operation," *Journal of Politics*, vol. 13, no. 4 (Nov. 1951), 682–3.

35 *Documents on Canadian External Relations*, vol. 13, 866, Mackenzie King Fonds, J1, vol. 422, Claxton to King, 7 Jan. 1947. See also Heeney Papers, vol. 1, File "Clerk of the Privy Council, 1947–1949," Claxton to Heeney plus attachments, 17 Feb. 1947; noted in Bercuson, *True Patriot: The Life of Brooke Claxton*, 165.

36 LAC, RG 24, Vol. 8084, File 1,272-10-14, "Canada-US Basic Security Plan, Joint Planning Committee, Sub-Committee on Protection of Sea Communications"; and Naval Member PJBD files, "Implementation of Canada-US Basic Security Plan," file no. TS 11272-11, 26 Aug. 1947; quoted in Haydon, "Sailors, Admirals, and Politicians."

37 LAC, *Mackenzie King Diary*, 12 Dec. 1946: 1191 (1117).

38 Peter T. Haydon and Paul T. Mitchell, "Canada-US Naval Cooperation in the 21st Century," in Fred W. Crickard, Paul T. Mitchell, and Katherine Orr, eds., *Multinational Naval Cooperation and Foreign Policy into the 21st Century*; cf. LAC, RG 24-B-1 (R112-41-5-E), Joint Staff and Chiefs of Staff Committee: *Minutes of Chiefs of Staff Committee*, meeting No. 417, 2 March 1948, para. 4.

39 James Goldrick, "Strangers in Their Own Seas? A Comparison of the Australian and Canadian Naval Experience, 1910–1982," in Michael L. Hadley, Rob Huebert, and Fred Crickard, *A Nation's Navy*: 325–30; and Glover, "Royal Colonial or Royal Canadian Navy?" in Hadley, Huebert, and Crickard, *A Nation's Navy*: 71–90.

40 Norman Friedman, *Network-Centric Warfare: How Navies Learned to Fight Smarter in Three World Wars*, 65–9 and passim.

41 As H.P. Willmott points out, "The fleet that raided Tokyo bay in February 1945 contained only four ships that had not been built subsequent to the Japanese attack on Pearl Harbour." Willmott, *The Last Century of Sea Power*, vol. 2: *From Washington to Tokyo, 1922–1945*, 373.

42 Britain's expenditure on military or military-related expenditures during the Second World War reached 80% of GNP, compared to the American maximum of 30%. At the end of the war Britain's national debt stood at about 250% of her Gross Domestic Product. J.L. Granatstein, "How Britain's Weakness Forced Canada into the Arms of the United States," 1988 Joanne Goodman Lecture; Philip Pugh, *The Cost of Seapower*, 9–20; and H. Duncan Hall, *North American Supply*, 489–92; Philip Thornton, "Britain pays off final instalment of US loan – after 61 years," *The Independent*, 29 Dec. 2006.

43 Part VI(5)a of the Act provides that when Canadian and allied forces are formally declared to be "acting in combination any officer of the other force appointed, by agreement between Her Majesty in right of Canada and the government of the country to which that force belongs, to command the combined force, or any part thereof, shall be treated and shall have over members of the Canadian Forces the like powers of command, punishment and arrest." *Revised Statutes of Canada, 1985*, VIII, ch. V2.

44 "The Canadian Forces Exchange Program," Can., DND, *Backgrounder*, Sept. 1990.

45 Dave Freeman - LCdr (ret'd), "The CANADA Badge: Forging a Canadian Identity," CFB Esquimalt Naval & Military Museum.

46 Lund, "Reid and Grant," 176.

47 In 1950 Grant, by then a vice-admiral, defended the need for the Canadian Navy to retain its carrier aviation on the grounds that without that capacity the navy would inevitably find itself incorporated into British or American task forces under the command of British or American admirals. LAC, Minutes of special meeting of the COS Committee, 31 Jan. 1950. See Jan Drent, "'A Good, Workable Little Fleet': Canadian Naval Policy, 1945–1950," in Hadley, *A Nation's Navy*: 205–20.

48 Marc Milner, "More Royal than Canadian? The Royal Canadian Navy's Search for Identity, 1910–68," in Phillip Buckner, *Canada and the End of Empire*: 272–84.

49 "Until recently, Canadian Naval officers have received their first five years' training in the Royal Navy ... During this time they have had superimposed upon them a type of life and a style of leadership not only foreign to themselves and their own social background but also to the social background of the men whom they command. There is no form of artificial superiority which Canadians resent more than the variety imported from another land." Canada: DND (Naval Service), "Report of Certain Incidents that Occurred onboard HMC Ships *Athabaskan*, *Crescent*, and *Magnificent* ..." Rear-Admiral E.R. Mainguy, RCN, Chairman, Ottawa, Oct., 1949; and see Richard Gimblett, "Too Many Chiefs and Not Enough Seamen: The Lower-Deck Complement of a Postwar Royal Canadian Navy Destroyer – The Case of HMCS *Crescent*, March 1949," *Northern Mariner/Le marin du nord*, vol. 9, no. 3 (July 1999), 1–22.

50 Wilfred Lund comments that "the commission relied heavily on USN printed sources for information and guidance on personnel administration and leadership. These reflected the norms of North American society – a style of officer-man relationships that Mainguy embraced. The RCN was already inclining itself towards the USN model." Wilfred G.D. Lund, "Vice-Admiral E. Rollo Mainguy: Sailors' Admiral," in Whitby, *Admirals*, 195. See also David Zimmerman, "The Social Background of the Wartime Navy: Some Statistical Data," in Hadley, *A Nation's Navy*: 256–79.

51 "The inadequacy of the sum of his education [is] usually most apparent among those Officers holding very high rank or filling appointments which require them to consider subjects beyond the confines of strictly naval life ... I do not think that this absence of a more liberal education gives him a proper sense of broad social responsibility, nor does it prepare him to deal with problems beyond the scope of his technical Naval duties." Mayne, *Betrayed*, 40.

52 Nicholas Rodger, "Training or Education: A Naval Dilemma over Three Centuries," in N.A.M. Rodger, ed., *Essays in Naval History, from Medieval to Modern*, no. 17.

53 Gimblett's view is that too much has been made of a supposed cultural gulf between Canada's regular force officers and those coming from the reserve, both during and following the war. He disputes the "stereotype that the RCN officers were somewhat indifferent to the plight of their ratings (ostensibly because the officers had trained in the class-riddled RN system)." He acknowledges, however, the very different war experiences of the escort forces and the more classical naval experiences of the larger ships, commanded by regular force officers serving with the Home Fleet, or in the Channel. Richard H. Gimblett, "What the Mainguy Report Never Told Us: The Tradition of 'Mutiny' in the Royal Canadian Navy Before 1949," *Canadian Military Journal,* summer 2000: 85–92; and "Command in the Canadian Navy: An Historical Survey," *The Northern Mariner/Le marin du nord,* vol. 14, no. 4 (Oct. 2004).

54 Haydon, "Sailors, Admirals, and Politicians"; and Isabel Campbell, "A Brave New World, 1945–60," in Richard Gimblett, *Centennial Story:* 123–37.

55 Shawn Cafferky, *Uncharted Waters: A History of the Canadian Helicopter-Carrying Destroyer,* 68–82.

56 Joel Sokolsky, "The US, Canada and the Cold War in the North Atlantic: The Early Years," paper presented to the Canadian Political Science Association, May 1981: 30–1, and quoted in Sharon Hobson, *The Composition of Canada's Naval Fleet, 1946–85,* 19.

57 Maloney, *Securing Command of the Sea,* 93, 207; Owen J. Cote, *The Third Battle: Innovation in the US Navy's Silent Cold War Struggle with Soviet Submarines,* on line resource: 16; *Documents on Canadian External Relations,* vol. 13, chap. 5, "Canada and a Bipolar World" DEA/50028-B-40, "Political Appreciation of the Prospects of Soviet Aggression against North America," Memorandum from Head, Second Political Division to Under-Secretary of State for External Affairs, Ottawa, Feb. 13, 1947; "Strategic Appreciation," Report by Joint Intelligence Committee, (f) Navy, Ottawa, March 15, 1947; and Norman Polmar and Kenneth J. Moore, *Cold War Submarines: the Design and Construction of US and Soviet Submarines,* 22–31.

58 John Orr, "Some Policy Aspects of Canadian Involvement in Strategic ASW," in Gimblett and Mayne, eds., *People;* Edward C. Whitman, "SOSUS, The 'Secret Weapon' of Undersea Surveillance," *Undersea Warfare, The Official Magazine of the US Submarine Force,* vol. 7, no. 2 (winter 2005). The British shallow-water LOFAR system was called CORSAIR.

59 Lund, "Reid and Grant."

60 Michael A. Hennessy, "The Rise and Fall of a Canadian Maritime Policy, 1939–1965: A Study of Industry, Navalism and the State," 228–9.

61 Norman Friedman, *Network-Centric Warfare: How Navies Learned to Fight Smarter in Three World Wars,* 70–1.

62 Peter T. Haydon, "When Military Plans and Policies Conflict: The Case of Canada's General Purpose Frigate Program," *The McNaughton Papers,* Nov. 1991, 14. In 1943 Captain Frank Llewellyn Houghton was senior Canadian naval officer, London.

63 Can., DND, *Canada's Defence: Information on Canada's Defence Achievements and Organization,* 1947; and S. Mathwin Davis, "Naval Procurement, 1950–1965," in David G. Haglund, ed., *Canada's Defence Industrial Base: The Political Economy of Preparedness and Procurement,* 97–117.

64 Reid, "Canada and the Creation"; S. Mathwin Davis, "The 'St. Laurent' Decision: Genesis of a Canadian Fleet," in W.A.B. Douglas, ed., *The RCN in Transition,*

1910–1985: 187–208; J.H.W. Knox, "An Engineer's Outline of RCN History: Part II," in James Boutilier, ed., *RCN in Retrospect, 1910–1968*: 317–33; and Sharon Hobson, *The Composition of Canada's Naval Fleet, 1946–85*.
65 Bothwell, *Alliance and Illusion*, 94.
66 Lund, "Rollo Mainguy: Sailors' Admiral," 200.
67 Hennessy, "The Rise and Fall of a Canadian Maritime Policy," 220.
68 LAC, *Mackenzie King Diary*, 9 Jan. 1947: 33 (32).
69 Cafferky, *Uncharted Waters*, 227–8.
70 Haydon, "When Military Plans," 20; LAC, RG 24, vol. 11, 129, file: Acts 11279-11: A(ii), *Minutes of the 11th Senior Officers' Conference*, 12–14 May 1954; and D.H. Tate, *Grumman CS2F/CP-121 Tracker Royal Canadian Navy*, Canada Aviation Museum, n.d.
71 Arnold Danford Patrick Heeney. Campbell, "Canadian Insights"; and A.D.P. Heeney to Secretary of State for External Affairs, 3 Oct. 1952, in LAC, RG 24, 1983–84/167, box 424, file 1640-21-14, vol. 1. Emphasis in original.
72 LAC, RG 24 B-1 (R112-41-5-E) vol. 21814, file 10, Joint Staff and Chiefs of Staff Committee: *Minutes of Chiefs of Staff Committee*, meeting No. 417, 2 March 1948, para. 4.
73 John Foster Dulles, address 12 Jan. 1954, *Department of State Bulletin*, vol. 30, 25 Jan. 1954: 107–10.
74 M.C. 48 (FINAL) 22 Nov. 1954, *North Atlantic Military Committee Decision on M.C. 48, A Report by the Military Committee on the Most Effective Pattern of NATO Military Strength for the Next Few Years*, CONCLUSIONS: Para. 32. As a result of its recent study of the impact of new weapons on a war involving NATO, the Military Committee has reached the following conclusions: (a.) Superiority in atomic weapons and the capability to deliver them will be the most important factor in a major war in the foreseeable future. (b.) Surprise will be a major factor in any future war involving NATO, and the degree of surprise attained by the enemy could greatly influence the outcome of the war. The ability of NATO to withstand and react to the first blow will depend on the extent of the resistance of our populations to such action and the state of preparedness of our forces at the time of the enemy's surprise attack. (c.) Should war occur, it will most likely consist of two phases: – a relatively short initial phase of intensive atomic exchange; – a subsequent phase involving operations of indeterminable length and of lesser intensity. The ultimate victory, however, would probably have been determined by the outcome of the initial phase. (d.) Should war occur, the best defense against atomic attack lies in the ability of the Allied nations to reduce the threat at source by immediate and intensive atomic counter-attack. Para. 33. In face of the threat of such a war, the primary aim of NATO, must more than ever before, be to prevent war.
75 Operation CANAVHED 1–49. Richard Gimblett, "HMCS *Crescent* and the Chinese Civil War," in Ann Griffiths, Peter Haydon and Richard Gimblett, *Canadian Gunboat Diplomacy*, 79.
76 UNSC Resolutions 82–5, and Can. Commons, *Debates*, "Situation in Korea – Canada's Part in Collective Action under United Nations," 30 June 1950: 4459–61. See Christopher D. O'Sullivan, *The United Nations: A Concise History*, 24–7; Robert Bothwell, *Canada and the United States: The Politics of Partnership*, 46; and Harald von Riekhoff, "Canada and Collective Security," in David B. Dewitt and David Leyton-Brown, *Canada's International Security Policy*.
77 Bothwell, *Alliance and Illusion*: 83–8; Edelgard Mahant and Graeme S. Mount, *Invisible and Inaudible in Washington: American Policies toward Canada*, 34–9.

78 See above, p. 7.
79 Douglas S. Thomas, "The Canadian Maritime Contribution to Peace-Support Operations," in Griffiths, *Canadian Gunboat Diplomacy*: 184–8; Thor Thorgrimsson and E.C. Russell, *Canadian Naval Operations in Korean Waters, 1950–1955*, 3; and Haydon, "Sailors, Admirals, and Politicians."
80 Dean Acheson, *Present at the Creation: My Years in the State Department*, 481.
81 Extract from Cabinet Conclusions, Ottawa, 9 Dec. 1950, *Documents on Canadian External Relations*, vol. 16, 1950, chap. 2, "Korean Conflict," part 6, no. 186.
82 Resolution 377, 3 Nov. 1950: "*Resolves* that if the Security Council, because of lack of unanimity of the permanent members, fails to exercise its primary responsibility for the maintenance of international peace and security in any case where there appears to be a threat to the peace, breach of the peace, or act of aggression, the General Assembly shall consider the matter immediately with a view to making appropriate recommendations to Members for collective measures ..." The history of the "Uniting for Peace" formula is not long. To date it has only been used ten times to summon "Emergency Special Sessions." The tenth session on the Israeli-Palestinian conflict that convened in 1997 for the first time extended beyond a single sitting and was still in session a decade later. Soviet intransigence was not the only problem.
83 Holmes, *Life with Uncle*, 26.
84 Lester Pearson, "The Role of the United Nations in a Two-Power World," 31 March 1951, and "Canadian Foreign Policy in a Two-Power World," 10 April 1951, Can., DEA *Statements and Speeches*, 51/13 and 14; Bothwell, *Canada and the United States*, 51–5, and *Alliance and Illusion*, 99–101; John W. Holmes, "Unquiet Diplomat: Lester B. Pearson," *International Journal*, vol. 62, 2006–07: 291–310; von Riekhoff, "Canada and Collective Security."
85 Peter Gellman, "Lester B. Pearson, Collective Security, and the World Order Tradition of Canadian Foreign Policy," *International Journal*, vol. 44, no. 1, 1988–89: 68–101.
86 Henry A. Kissinger, *The Troubled Partnership*, 53.
87 DHH, *The Raymont Papers*, file no. 73/1223 (403), Memorandum from Dr R.J. Sutherland to Minister of National Defence, 31 May 1963, covering a paper "The General Purpose Frigate," 4.
88 David J. Bercuson, "Canada, NATO, and Rearmament, 1950–1954: Why Canada Made a Difference (But Not for Very Long)," in John English and Norman Hillmer, eds., *Making a Difference?*: 103–24.
89 Leolyn Dana Wilgress. LAC, MG 32 Box 5 (R3306-0-1-E), Claxton Papers, vol. 126, file "US Defence Policy, 1954," Wilgress to USSEA, 25 Feb. 1954.
90 L.B. Pearson, "A New Look at the 'New Look,'" 15 March 1954, Ottawa, DEA, *Statements and Speeches*, 54/16: 7; See Tom Keating and Larry Pratt, *Canada, NATO and the Bomb: The Western Alliance in Crisis*, 66.
91 Eayrs, *In Defence*, vol. 4, 253, 379–82. That alarmist perspective was not shared by Wilgress, who had questioned "whether the 'new look' implies such a fundamental change."
92 Minutes of the 423rd Naval Board Meeting, 9 Nov. 1954, DHist 1000-100/2, quoted in Cafferky, *Uncharted Waters*, 133.
93 Haydon, "When Military Plans," 21, and Sean Maloney, "Parry and Thrust: Canadian Maritime Forces and the Defence of North America, 1954–62," *The Northern Mariner/le marin du nord*, vol. 18, no. 1, Jan. 2008, 45.

94 Jon B. McLin, *Canada's Changing Defence Policy, 1957–1963: The Problems of a Middle Power in Alliance*, 120–1. Norman Polmar and Kenneth J. Moore write that the Soviet Navy's reaction to the thermo-nuclear age was to downgrade, or abandon, planning for a tactical campaign against mercantile shipping. But they date the realization of the changing strategic objectives a decade later, with the coming into service of the Soviet Navy's torpedo-armed *Victor* class and submerged-launched short-range SS-N-7 cruise missile–armed *Charlie* class SSNs from 1967. Norman Polmar and Kenneth Moore, *Cold War Submarines: The Design and Construction of US and Soviet Submarines*: 159–64, 172.
95 Polmar and Moore, *Cold War Submarines*, 35–107.
96 Maloney, "Parry and Thrust," 53–4.
97 Orr, "Some Policy Aspects"; see also R.J. Sutherland, "Canada's Long-Term Strategic Situation," *International Journal*, vol. 17, no. 3 (summer 1962), 199–223.
98 Haydon, "When Military Plans," 26.
99 Maloney, "Parry and Thrust," 44; DHH, NBM (17 Nov. 55), memo VCNS to CNS, "Final Screening Committee."

CHAPTER FIVE
1 By the London Declaration of 26 April 1949 the British Commonwealth had been transformed into the Commonwealth of Nations, a provision that enabled India to remain in the Commonwealth after becoming a republic, and recognized the independence of indigenous monarchs.
2 Anthony Eden had been made a knight of the Garter in 1954.
3 Can., Commons, *Debates*, 1956 (Special Session), 22–3.
4 L.B. Pearson, "Forty Years On: Reflections on Our Foreign Policy," *International Journal*, vol. 22, no. 3, 1966–67: 357–63
5 Granatstein added that the role Pearson performed of reconciling Washington with London and Paris "would never happen again." J.L. Granatstein, "Canada and Peacekeeping: Image and Reality," *Canadian Forum*, Aug. 1974: 14–19. See John Holmes, "Unquiet Diplomat: Lester B. Pearson," *International Journal*, vol. 62, 2006–07. See also Robert Bothwell, *Alliance and Illusion: Canada and the World, 1945–1984*, 133.
6 LAC, RG 2 A-5-a (R165-93-5-F), Privy Council Records, RG 2/1892, Cabinet Conclusions, 9 May 1957.
7 J.L. Granatstein, "Peacekeeping: Did Canada Make a Difference? And What Difference did Peacekeeping Make to Canada?" in John English and Norman Hillmer, eds., *Making a Difference?* 231.
8 Bothwell, *Alliance and Illusion*, 140–1. Diefenbaker's rhetorical flourishes about empire trade preferential tariffs, the diversion of Canadian trade to Britain, and a possible Commonwealth economic conference collapsed when Britain offered a free-trade deal he hastily but secretly refused. It was too evident that British markets could not replace Canadian sales to the United States. Having called Diefenbaker's bluff, London began the process that was to lead to Britain's joining the Common Market or European Economic Community/Union in 1973.
9 John Hilliker and Greg Donaghy, "Canadian Relations with the United Kingdom at the End of Empire, 1956–73," and José E. Igartua, "'Ready, Aye, Ready' No More? Canada, Britain, and the Suez Crisis in the Canadian Press," both in Phillip Buckner, *Canada and the End of Empire*; Diane B. Kunz, *The Economic Diplo-*

macy of the Suez Crisis, passim; Knowlton Nash, *Kennedy and Diefenbaker: Fear and Loathing across the Undefended Border*, 174–5.

10 Nash, *Kennedy and Diefenbaker*, 51–2; Ron Purver, "The Arctic in Canadian Security Policy, 1945 to the Present," in David Devitt and David Leyton-Brown, *Canada's International Security Policy*: 81–110.

11 Owen Connor Struan Robertson.

12 Donat Pharand, "The Arctic Waters and the Northwest Passage: A Final Revisit," *Ocean Development & International Law*, vol. 38, no. 1/2, Jan–June 2007: 3–69.

13 John Holmes, *Life with Uncle: The Canadian-American Relationship:* , 49.

14 Jan Drent, "'A Good, Workable Little Fleet': Canadian Naval Policy, 1945–1950," in Michael Hadley, Rob Huebert, and Fred Crickard, *A Nation's Navy*: 205–20; Michael Whitby, "Showing the Flag across the North: HMCS *Labrador* and the 1954 Transit of the Northwest Passage," *Canadian Naval Review*, vol. 2, no. 1 (spring 2006): 21–4; and Norman Polmar and Kenneth Moore, *Cold War Submarines: The Design and Construction of US and Soviet Submarines*, 21.

15 Canada, Treaties, E101015-CTS 1958 No. 9, *Agreement between the Government of Canada and the Government of the United States of America Concerning the Organization and Operation of the North American Air Defence Command* (NORAD), the Ambassador of Canada to the United States of America to the Secretary of State of the United States of America, 12 May 1958.

16 Joseph T. Jockel, *No Boundaries Upstairs*, 91–117; Jon McLin, *Canada's Changing Defence Policy, 1957–1963*: 52–7; and C.A. Cannizzo, " NORAD-NATO Linkages," *Canadian Defence Quarterly*, vol. 19, no. 5 (April 1990): 21–7.

17 Holmes, *Life with Uncle*, 52.

18 Shawn Cafferky, *Uncharted Waters: A History of the Canadian Helicopter-Carrying Destroyer*, 136, 168, 195–6, 234, 264–6 and passim; DHH, 1000-100/2, Minutes of the 584th Meeting of the Naval Board, 14 and 16 Jan. 1959.

19 Isabel Campbell, "A Transformation in Thinking: The RCN's Naval Warfare Study Group of 1956," in Richard Gimblett and Richard Mayne, eds., *People, Policy and Programmes*: 165–81; Isabel Campbell "A Brave New World, 1945–60" and "Canadian Insights," referencing: DHH, 2002/17, File 118, Capt. Charles "SACLANT'S EDP 1-60" to ACNS (P), VCNS and CNS; Cafferky, *Uncharted Waters*, 233; and Polmar, *Cold War Submarines*, 22.

20 LAC, RG 24 83-84/167, vol. 89, file 1270–78, vol. 3, "Nuclear Weapons for ASW," Sea/Air Warfare Committee, 5 Jan 1956. Sean Maloney, "Parry and Thrust: Canadian Maritime Forces and the Defence of North America, 1954–62," *The Northern Mariner/le marin du nord*, vol. 18, no. 1, Jan. 2008, 45, 48.

21 "Since NATO would be unable to prevent the rapid overrunning of Europe unless NATO immediately employed nuclear weapons both strategically and tactically," it stated, "we must be prepared to take the initiative in their use." MC 14/2 (Revised) (Final Decision) 23 May 1957, "A Report by the Military Committee to the North Atlantic Council on Overall Strategic Concept for the Defense of the North Atlantic Treaty Organization Area," Reference: C-M(56)138 (Final), Section 2 para. 13/c.

22 David Bercuson, *True Patriot: The Life of Brooke Claxton, 1898–1960*, 243. In 1977 John Gellner employed the example of the Canadian acquisition of CF-104 Starfighters for low-level tactical nuclear delivery, stationed unprotected on permanent air stations in Germany, as evidence that the Canadian defence leadership was more than willing to follow the flawed strategic plans of Canada's allies, especially when the institutional ambitions of one of the services could be gratified

by doing so. John Gellner, "Strategic Analysis in Canada," *International Journal*, vol. 33, no. 3, 1977–78.
23 NA UK, CAB 5/2 ff. 202–5, Admiralty Memorandum on "The Status of Dominion Ships of War," Aug. 1910, CID 83 C, July 1912.
24 Maloney, "Parry and Thrust," 50.
25 Peter Haydon and Paul Mitchell, "Canada-US Naval Cooperation in the 21st Century," in Fred Crickard, Paul Mitchell and Katherine Orr, eds., *Multinational Naval Cooperation and Foreign Policy into the 21st Century*.
26 Michael Whitby, "Vice-Admiral Harry G. DeWolf: Pragmatic Navalist," in Michael Whitby, Richard Gimblett, and Peter Haydon, *The Admirals: Canada's Senior Naval Leadership in the Twentieth Century*: 213–46.
27 Michael A. Hennessy, "The RCN and the Postwar Naval Revolution, 1955–1964," in Gimblett, *People*: 143–64.
28 Not the more capable ship design by the same name, which was abandoned as too expensive.
29 Whitby, "Harry G. DeWolf": 213–46; and Julie Ferguson, *Through a Canadian Periscope: The Story of the Canadian Submarine Service*, 244–7.
30 Ken Reynolds, "'One Stop Shopping': Replenishment at Sea and the Royal Canadian Navy," in Gimblett, *People*: 229–50; Peter Haydon, "When Military Plans and Policies Conflict: The Case of Canada's General Purpose Frigate Program," *The McNaughton Papers*, 39; DHH, Navy Board, *Minutes*, No. 642-1, 17–18 Jan. 1961; Naval Staff Working Paper, File No. NSTS 1650-36 (Staff), 25 Jan. 1962, "RCN Future Requirements Planning Guide for the Period 1962–1972"; and Jason Delaney, "The One Class of Vessel that is Impossible to Build in ~~Australia~~ Canada," *Proceedings ... From Empire to In(ter)dependence*.
31 Hennessy, "The Rise and Fall of a Canadian Maritime Policy, 1939–1965: A Study of Industry, Navalism and the State," 376.
32 Ibid., 374–5; [LAC RG 24-B-1 (R112-41-5-E)] D/Hist, Chiefs of Staff Committee, Minutes 692, 18 May 1961.
33 Bothwell, *Alliance and Illusion*, 164–5.
34 William Tompson, *Khrushchev: A Political Life*, 248.
35 See: Henry Maximilian Pachter, *Collision Course: The Cuban Missile Crisis and Coexistence*. See also Neil H. Alford, *Modern Economic Warfare (Law and the Naval Participant)*, especially, "Analysis of the Quarantine": 269–83. The blockade was confined to "offensive equipment under shipment to Cuba." Quincy Wright demolished the special pleading that was used in Washington to justify the quarantine. In particular, he dismissed the claim that it was an instance of Pacific Blockade. "The episode," he concluded, "has not improved the reputation of the United States as a champion of international law." Wright, "The Cuban Quarantine," *American Journal of International Law*, 57 (1963), 547.
36 Carlo Christol and Charles Davis, "Maritime Quarantine: The Naval Interdiction of Offensive Weapons and Associated Materiel to Cuba, 1962," *The American Yearbook of International Law*, vol. 57 (1963), 528.
37 Jeffrey G. Barlow, "The Cuban Missile Crisis," in Bruce Elleman and Sarah Paine, eds., *Naval Blockades and Seapower: Strategies and Counter-Strategies, 1805–2005*, 157–68.
38 After the dust had settled the United States attempted to extend its naval control to Cuban trade, but the international community firmly resisted. In February 1963 Edward Heath, answering a question in the British House of Commons, said: "We have made clear throughout that Her Majesty's Government do not approve of

any restriction on freedom of navigation in times of peace." Nicholas Tracy, ed., *Sea Power and the Control of Trade: Belligerent Rights from the Russian War to the Beira Patrol,* 531.

39 Peter Haydon, *The 1962 Cuban Missile Crisis: Canadian Involvement Reconsidered,* 67–87, and "Vice-Admiral Herbert S. Rayner: The Last Chief of the Canadian Naval Staff," in Whitby, *Admirals:* 247–74; and Richard Oliver Mayne, "Years of Crisis: The Canadian Navy in the 1960s," in Richard Gimblett, *The Centennial Story,* 145. See also Polmar, *Cold War Submarines,* 203–4, and Jan Drent, "Confrontation in the Sargasso Sea: Soviet Submarines During the Cuban Missile Crisis," *The Northern Mariner/Le marin du nord,* vol. 13, no. 3 (July 2003): 1–19.

40 And much later, when in 2003 the second Bush administration published faulty intelligence at the United Nations when seeking world approval for its intended invasion of Iraq.

41 Nash, *Kennedy and Diefenbaker,* 191–3, 205–6.

42 NARA RG 59, box 213, folder Canada, U.S. State Department General Records of the Policy Planning Staff, quoted in Edelgard Mahant and Graeme Mount, eds, *Invisible and Inaudible in Washington: American Policies toward Canada,* 46; Escott Reid, "The Birth of the North Atlantic Alliance," *International Journal,* vol. 22, no. 3 (summer 1967); see above, p. 118.

43 Polmar, *Cold War Submarines,* 111; Robert Michael Gates, *From the Shadows: The Ultimate Insider's Story of Five Presidents and How They Won the Cold War,* 40.

44 The valiant effort of Sir Harold MacMillan's Conservatives to retain a post-Imperial military role, including the maintenance of 68,000 military in counter-insurgency operations in Malaya, was brought to an end by his Labour successor. Sir Harold Wilson, and his defence minister, Denis Healy, pulled the plug in 1968 on commitments that Britain could not afford. British military strength was cut from 700,000 men to 375,000, and it was ordered that British fleets and bases "east of Suez," apart from the small one at Hong Kong, be withdrawn by 1971. See Richard Hill, "British naval thinking in the nuclear age," in Till, *British Naval Thinking:* 160–81.

45 Bothwell, *Canada and the United States,* 85. In November 1962 American secretary of defence, Robert MacNamara, sought to put an end to the independent British nuclear deterrent which was to have been mounted on the *Skybolt* air-launched ballistic missile being developed in the United States. The cancellation of *Skybolt* created pandemonium in the British House of Commons, and Prime Minister Harold Macmillan persuaded President Kennedy that the 1958 US–UK Mutual Defence Agreement necessitated co-operation in sustaining the British deterrent.

46 Quoted in Canadian Institute for International Affairs, *Canada in World Affairs,* vol. 12, 131; Nash, *Kennedy and Diefenbaker,* 222–4.

47 Diefenbaker was well aware that the public was influenced by service opinion, and believed the airmen were Kennedy's stooges. The U.S. State department weighed in with an unprecedented press release confirming that the Canadian government had indeed made commitments that included the acceptance of nuclear weapons under two-key control. Knowlton Nash has graphically described the breakdown of civility in the cabinet over Diefenbaker's determination to call an election on an anti-American platform, and Harkness's resignation. With the government obviously in disarray, it was defeated by a vote of non-confidence on the govern-

ment's defence policy, in which the Liberals were joined by the Social Credit and New Democratic Parties. During the election campaign air force officers continued to press the importance of nuclear weapons. Edelgard Mahant and Graeme Mount believe that McGeorge Bundy who wrote the State Department press release "effectively torpedoed the minority Diefenbaker government," but Pearson later told Kennedy that it had cost him fifty seats. The Liberals were returned to power in April 1963 four seats short of a majority.

48 Maloney, "Parry and Thrust," 53.
49 J.L. Granatstein, "The American Influence on the Canadian Military, 1939–1963," in Barry D. Hunt and Ron G. Haycock, eds., *Canada's Defence: Perspectives on Policy in the Twentieth Century*, 129–39; Bothwell, *Canada and the United States*, 85–7; Nash, *Kennedy and Diefenbaker*, 222–72; U.S., State Department, *Bulletin*, no. 48, Feb. 1963, 243–4, pub. in McLin, *Canada's Changing Defence Policy*: 235–6; and Mahant, *Invisible and Inaudible in Washington*, 49.
50 Can., *Royal Canadian Navy Year End Roundup*, 1963; press release by director of naval information, 27 Dec. 1963.
51 Haydon, "When Military Plans," 49–50; DHH, *The Raymont Papers*, file no. 73/1223 (403), Memorandum from Dr R.J. Sutherland to Minister of National Defence, 31 May 1963, covering a paper "The General Purpose Frigate."
52 DHH, *The Raymont Papers*, file 72/153, "Report of the Ad Hoc Committee on Defence Policy," 30 Sept. 1963, 3–7; See Douglas Bland and Sean Maloney, *Campaigns for International Security: Canada's Defence Policy at the Turn of the Century*, 76–7.
53 Robert J. Sutherland, "Canada's Long Term Strategic Situation," *International Journal*, vol. 17, no. 3 (summer 1962): 199–223.
54 LAC MG 32 Box 33, vol. 1, file 42 [1961], Paul T. Hellyer, "A Role for Canada in Collective Defence."
55 LAC, MG 31-E87 (R5497-505-9-E), vol. 7, file 10, Cabinet, Secret Notes for Minutes, 20 Jan. and 9 Feb. 1965. See Bothwell, *Alliance and Illusion*, 209, 223–7.
56 John Holmes, "Canada and the Vietnam War," in J.L. Granatstein and R.D. Cuff, eds., *War and Society in North America*: 184–99. See Holmes, "Unquiet Diplomat"; Peter Stursberg, *Lester Pearson and the American Dilemma*, 216–24; Lester B. Pearson, "Canada, the United States, and Vietnam," in Norman Hillmer, ed., *Partners Nevertheless, Canadian-American Relations in the Twentieth Century*, 121; Mahant, *Invisible and Inaudible in Washington*, 49–60; and Gordon Stewart, "'An Objective of US Foreign Policy since the Founding of the Republic': The United States and the End of Empire in Canada," in Phillip Buckner, *Canada and the End of Empire*: 94–116.
57 NSF, Country file: Canada, v, Box 166, item 125, ix, LBJ, *quoted in* Mahant, *Invisible and Inaudible in Washington*, 45.
58 McLin, *Canada's Changing Defence Policy*, 207–12.
59 James Solomon, *Multilateral Force: America's Nuclear Solution for NATO (1960–1965)*, 124; Bothwell, *Alliance and Illusion*, 247.
60 Lieutenant Jason M. Delaney, "Submarine Procurement and the *Victoria*-class Acquisition from an Historical Perspective: Having Submarines is the Point!" *Canadian Naval Review*, vol. 4, no. 2 (summer 2009): 22–7. As an RCN university training cadet I saw the first of the Canadian O boats on the slip at Chatham inside a shed that had served the Nelsonic navy.
61 Hennessy, "The Rise and Fall of a Canadian Maritime Policy," 379–84; private communication with the author, 28 Oct. 2011, by Norman Friedman, who was

at the Hudson Institute in 1973–84, working for the Defense Department, and in-house consultant to the secretary of the navy 1985–94.
62 Mayne, "Years of Crisis"; and Michael A. Hennessy, "Fleet Replacement and the Crisis of Identity," in Hadley et al., *A Nation's Navy*: 131–53.
63 Paul Hellyer, *Damn the Torpedoes: My Fight to Unify Canada's Armed Forces*, 234–7. President Linden Johnson explored the possibility that Canada might send naval forces to participate in an international force to keep open the gulf of Aqaba when Nasser evicted the UN post monitoring the Scharm el Sheike, but Pearson did not agree to do so. Two days later, on 27 May 1967, Nasser, complaining that Canada was pro-Israel, expelled the Canadians in the United Nations monitoring force. Douglas S. Thomas, "The Canadian Maritime Contribution to Peace-Support Operations," in Ann Griffiths, Peter Haydon, and Richard Gimblett, *Canadian Gunboat Diplomacy*, 188; Bothwell, *Alliance and Illusion*, 265–7.
64 Bothwell, *Alliance and Illusion*, 268.
65 Private communication from Norman Friedman, 28 Oct. 2011.
66 Douglas Bland, *Chiefs of Defence: Government and the Unified Command of the Canadian Armed Forces*, 31–62; Haydon, "When Military Plans," 8.
67 Hellyer, *Damn the Torpedoes*: 32–44.
68 LAC, *Mackenzie King Diary*, 7 Oct. 1942: 926 (846).
69 Maurice Pope, "Memorandum on a Canadian Organization for the Higher Direction of National Defence: 8 March 1937." William Johnston, P. Rawling, Richard Gimblett, and John MacFarlane, *The Seabound Coast: The Official History of the Royal Canadian Navy, 1867–1939*, 861.
70 LAC MG 32, box 33 (R1278-0-4-E), Hellyer Papers, vol. 82, file 8 (81–8), 17–19: General Charles Foulkes, "The Case for One Service," July 1961; and see Robert H. Caldwell, "Rear-Admiral William M. Landymore: The Silent Service Speaks Out," in Whitby, *Admirals*: 275–305.
71 Hellyer, *Damn the Torpedoes*, 60–2, 122–5, 152–91.
72 Richard Gimblett, "What the Mainguy Report Never Told Us;" and Richard O. Mayne, "Protesters or Traitors? Investigating Cases of Crew Sabotage in the Royal Canadian Navy: 1942–45," *Canadian Military Journal*, summer 2000: 85–92 and vol. 6, no. 1 (spring 2005).
73 Can., Bill C-90, "An Act to Amend the National Defence Act," 1 Aug. 1964; Bill C-243, "Canadian Forces Reorganization Act," 1966. Wilfred Lund, "Integration and Unification of the Canadian Forces," CFB Esquimalt Naval & Military Museum, n.d. In 1969 the Canadian brigade in Germany was also redeployed out of the British Army on the Rhine and joined the Canadian Air Force at Lahr in southern Germany, where it was operationally linked with American forces.
74 Richard Gimblett, "Command in the Canadian Navy: An Historical Survey," *The Northern Mariner/Le marin du nord*, vol. 14, no 4, Oct. 2004.
75 Joel Sokolsky, "Canada and the Cold War at Sea, 1945–68," in Douglas, *The RCN in Transition*: 218–220; and Tony German, *The Sea is at Our Gates: The History of the Canadian Navy*, 280–92.
76 Note by Rear Admiral Robert W. Timbrell, in Whitby, *Admirals*, 321–26.
77 Douglas Bland, *Canada's National Defence*, vol. 2, 93–157, at 97.
78 Stephen W. Roskill, *The War at Sea*, vol. 1, 419.
79 Bland, *Chiefs of Defence*, 64–7.
80 Hellyer, *Damn the Torpedoes*, 236.
81 The Naval Reserve Headquarters was moved in 1983 to Quebec City where a new Canadian Forces Fleet School is located. In 1985–86 three new Naval Reserve Di-

visions were opened in Quebec province. In May 1992 the minister of national defence, M. Marcel Masse, signed a memorandum of understanding increasing liaison positions between the Canadian forces and those of the Republic of France from twelve to twenty-three, in the hope that increasing exchange postings would help to make a career in the Canadian armed services more attractive for francophones. Serge Bernier, "HMCS Ottawa III: The Navy's First French-Language Unit, 1968–1973," in Hadley et al., *A Nation's Navy*: 310–24; Michelle Daviluy, "Communicating among Linguistic Communities onboard a Canadian Navy Ship"; and Can., DND, *Backgrounders*: "Official Languages in the DND and the Canadian Forces," Nov. 1987; "Franco-Canadian Military Cooperation Committee," May 1992; and "Women in the Canadian Forces," Feb. 1990. See also LAC, MG 26-G (R10811-0-X-F), Laurier Papers, 92017, Laurier to W. Gregory, 11 Nov. 1904, quoted in Blair Neatby, "Laurier and Imperialism," and in Ramsay Cook, Craig Brown, and Carl Berger, *Imperial Relations in the Age of Laurier*, 1.

82 German, *The Sea is at Our Gates*, 315–16. See also: Michael Young, "STANAVFORLANT in 1970: The First Canadian Command," *Canadian Naval Review*, vol. 1, no. 3 (fall 2005): 14–19.

83 Tom Keating and Larry Pratt, *Canada, NATO and the Bomb: The Western Alliance in Crisis*, 32–3; and conversations by the author with Canadian and Norwegian officers in 1977.

CHAPTER SIX

1 J.H.A. Watson, Assistant Under-Secretary of State, Foreign Affairs (UK) and Mr K. Schutz, Secretary of State Foreign Affairs (Germany), NATO, Report of Sub-Group I: "East-West Relations," 14 Dec. 1967. See also, John Gellner, *Canada in NATO*, 90–2.

2 Robert Gates, *From the Shadows: The Ultimate Insider's Story of Five Presidents and How They Won the Cold War*, 49.

3 LAC, MG 31-E87 (R5497-501-1-E), Can., Cabinet Minutes 27, 29, 30 March 1969. See: Bothwell, *Canada and the United States: The Politics of Partnership*, 101.

4 Can., DEA, *Statements and Speeches*, No. 69/7 and 8, Trudeau, 3 and 12 April 1969. Abstracted in Gellner, *Canada in NATO*, 100–4.

5 Writing in 1974, Jack Granatstein dated the refocusing of Canadian defence strategy from the evacuation of Canadian peacekeepers from Egypt prior to the 1967 Six Day war, but twenty-one years later Paul Buteux concluded that "the 1969 review of Canadian security policy marked a watershed in Canadian alliance policy, and thereafter NATO was never as important again." Douglas Bland and Sean Maloney write that Trudeau "took direct control of the defence and foreign policy reviews and formed small, elite teams close to his office to prepare papers and policy recommendations to guide the government's decisions." Committee reports repeatedly expressed conservative views that Trudeau rejected. In June 1970 the results of his redrafted foreign policy review, or reviews, were published as six booklets entitled *Foreign Policy for Canadians*. Canada, Department of External Affairs, *Foreign Policy for Canadians*, Ottawa: Information Canada, 1970; J.L. Granatstein, "Canada and Peacekeeping: Image and Reality"; Paul Buteux, "NATO and the Evolution of Canadian Defence and Foreign Policy," in David Devitt and David Layton-Brown, *Canada's International Security Policy*, 163; and Douglas Bland, *Campaigns for International Security: Canada's Defence Policy at the Turn of the Century*, 195. See J.L. Granatstein and Robert Bothwell, *Pirouette: Pierre Trudeau and Canadian Foreign Policy*, 236–44; and Michel Fortmann and Martin

Larose, "Emerging Strategic Counterculture: Pierre Elliott Trudeau, Canadian Intellectuals and the Revision of Liberal Defence Policy concerning NATO (1968–69)," *International Journal*, vol. 59, no. 3 (2002): 537–56.
6 John Holmes, "Canada and the Vietnam War," in J.L. Granatstein and R.D. Cuff, eds, *War and Society in North America*: 184–99.
7 NARA, RG 59 Box 1527, 1967-69, DEF 4 CAN-US, State Department to US Embassy, 9 June 1967. Robert Bothwell, *Alliance and Illusion: Canada and the World, 1945–1984*, 277.
8 This was partly accomplished by accelerate promotions, leading to the situation in the mid-1970s when in the Canadian forces as a whole there were 4.5 officers for every enlisted man, and 106 admirals and generals.
9 Michael Hennessy, "Fleet Replacement and the Crisis of Identity"; and Stuart Soward, "Canadian Naval Aviation, 1915–69," in James Boutilier, RCN *in Retrospect 1910–1968*: 270–85.
10 Tony German, *The Sea is at Our Gates*, 298–301; Pat Barnhouse, "Of Hydrofoils and Things," *Canadian Naval Review*, vol. 2, no. 1 (spring 2006), 32–3.
11 The 1960 Glassco Commission expressed concern at the extent to which the minister of national defence was dependent upon the chiefs of staff for advice, and in June 1971, following Trudeau's replacement in September 1970 of Léo Cadieux as defence minister with Donald Macdonald, a Management Review Group was established. Its "real aim," Douglas Bland says, "was to reorder the structure of the defence establishment and to take the decision making process out of the hands of the CDS," the chief of defence staff. Bland quotes General Dextraze as saying that his acceptance of this structure was "the worst decision of my period as CDS." The succession of seven ministers between 1970 and 1973 did nothing to ensure strong political control of the Department of National Defence. Civilian and military positions in the Department of National Defence became frozen. It was found during the highly charged crisis at Oka in the late summer of 1990, when the Quebec attorney general called for military aid to civil authority, that central direction by the CDS was essential. Douglas Bland, *Chiefs of Defence: Government and the Unified Command of the Canadian Armed Forces*, 96–9, 107–9; Bland, *Campaigns for International Security*, 37–8; Bland, *Canada's National Defence*, vol. 2, "Defence Organization,":159–65; Bothwell, *Canada and the United States*, 89; German, *The Sea is at Our Gates*, 301–6; Peter T. Haydon, "When Military Plans and Policies Conflict: The Case of Canada's General Purpose Frigate Program," *McNaughton Papers*, 7.
12 Can., "Report of the Sub-Committee on National Defence of the Standing Senate Committee on Foreign Affairs: Canada's Maritime Defence," 35–6, 113; Dan W. Middlemiss, "Economic Considerations in the Development of the Canadian Navy since 1945," in W.A.B. Douglas, ed., *The RCN in Transition, 1910–1985*, 279.
13 In announcing the reduction on 3 April Trudeau indicated that his reason was the stability that had been achieved by European nations since 1948, and their greater economic capacity to meet the cost of their own defence. In his subsequent longer speech on 12 April he added that "NATO had developed too much into a military alliance and not enough into a political alliance, not enough into an alliance which is interested not only in keeping the balance of deterrence of tactical power in Europe but into an alliance which is interested in arms control and de-escalation." In 1972 the *Bomarc* air defence missiles in eastern Canada were also dismantled, but USAF detachments continued to store *Genie* nuclear air defence missiles at Bagotville, Quebec, and Comox, British Columbia, until the RCAF *Voodoo* fighter

squadron there was stood down in 1984. None of this was popular with Canada's NATO allies, or satisfied Canadian anti-nuclear activists. Bothwell, *Alliance and Illusion*, 285–90; Costas Melakopides, *Pragmatic Idealism: Canadian Foreign Policy, 1945–1995*, 90; Peter Stursberg, *Lester Pearson and the American Dilemma*, 298–318; Tom Keating and Larry Pratt, *Canada, NATO and the Bomb*, 34; and Matthew Trudgen, "Do We Want 'Buckets of Instant Sunshine'? Canada and Nuclear Weapons 1945–1984," *Canadian Military Journal*, vol. 10, no. 1. See Can., Commons, SCEAND, Statement by Cadieux, 3 March 1970, 16: 8, "Probably the most important and far-reaching of our decisions was our rejection of any suggestion of Canada adopting a non-aligned or neutral role in world affairs;" Can., DND, *Defence in the 70s,*; and Can., Senate, Special Committee on National Defence, *Canada's Territorial Air Defence*, Jan. 1985, 1/13–96.

14 U.S. Department of State, Foreign Relations. 1969–1976, vol. E-1, *Documents on Global Issues, 1969–1972*.
15 John Holmes, *Life with Uncle: The Canadian-American Relationship*, 70.
16 Maxwell Cohen, "The Arctic and the National Interest," *International Journal*, vol. 26, no. 1 (1970–71): 52–81; Colin S. Gray, *Canadian Defence Priorities: A Question of Relevance*, 136–53; and John Kirton and Don Munton, "The Manhattan Voyages and their Aftermath," in Franklyn Griffiths, ed., *Politics of the Northwest Passage*: 67–97.
17 Bland, *Chiefs of Defence*: 232–3, 236.
18 Canada, Department of External Affairs, *Foreign Policy for Canadians*, 6.
19 Alex Morrison, "Canada and Peacekeeping: A Time for Reanalysis?" in Devitt, *Canada's International Security Policy*: 198–226.
20 During the brief return to power of the Conservative party under Joe Clark between 4 June 1979 and 2 March 1980, Clark's minister of national defence, Allan McKinnon, created a "Task Force on Review of Unification of the Canadian Forces" chaired by G.M. Fyffe, but its conclusion that the three services should be treated as distinct entities was not implemented before Clark's defeat in the House. A casualty in this enhanced independence of the Navy, Air Force, and Army was the office of chief of defence staff. Douglas Bland, *Canada's National Defence*, vol. 2: 249–56.
21 Gates, *From the Shadows*, 36, 39.
22 Can., PMO, transcript of prime minister's press conference, Moscow, 20 May 1971, no. 20, 31 May 1971, quoted in J.L. Granatstein and Robert Bothwell, *Pirouette: Pierre Trudeau and Canadian Foreign Policy*, 195; See David Farr, "Prime Minister Trudeau's Opening to the Soviet Union, 1971," in Joseph Black and Norman Hillmer, eds., *Nearly Neighbours: Canada and the Soviet Union, from Cold War to Détente and Beyond*: 102–118; and Robert Ford, *Our Man in Moscow: A Diplomat's Reflections on the Soviet Union*, 119.
23 Robert Bothwell characterizes Treasury Secretary John Connally's threatened abrogation of the Autopact as "an uncharacteristic American lapse into cowboy diplomacy." It was concern about such dangers that led Mitchell Sharp in a 1972 paper, "Canada-US Relations: Options for the Future," to call for diversification of Canadian trade by expanding Canadian economic relations with Europe and Japan – an objective it referred to as "The Third Option." Scholarly perspectives on Canadian-American relations during the Trudeau years are inconsistent. Robert Bothwell concludes that "Pierre Trudeau's relations with Richard Nixon were not as good as he thought," but that they were ' better than most Canadians believed, then and later ... Like the Democratic Johnson administration before it, Nixon's

Republicans refused to let the war stand in the way of maintaining good relations." Edelgard Mahant and Graeme Mount, however, believe that for much of the 1960s and 1970s Canada hardly figured in American policy considerations. Mahant, *Invisible and Inaudible in Washington: American Policies toward Canada*, 70–6. For their parts, Tom Keating and Larry Pratt believe the threat of American punitive economic measures was important it bringing Trudeau to reconsider the value of European connections. Keating and Pratt, *Canada, NATO and the Bomb*, 35.

24 *New York Times*, quoted in Dale C. Thomson and Roger F. Swanson, *Canadian Foreign Policy: Options and Perspectives*, 73.
25 Can., Commons, *Debates*, 14 April 1972, 1328–9.
26 Bothwell, *Canada and the United States*: 127; quoting Kissinger to Brent Scowcroft, 3 Dec. 1974; and *Alliance and Illusion*, 314; and Henry Kissinger, *White House Years*, 383.
27 Trudeau's visit to Cuba in 1976 was bitterly resented in Washington, and occurred at a time when Cuban soldiers were deployed in Angola and the Horn of Africa in support of world revolution, but Canada was also taking an active role in implementing "Basket 3" of the Final Act of the Conference on Security and Cooperation in Europe agreed to between the Soviet Block and the West in July and August 1975. Ford had taken a great political risk in going to Helsinki, but Basket 3 commitments to human rights created the opportunity for activists in the Eastern block to start the process that ultimately brought the collapse of the Soviet system. Ford ensured that Canada was invited to participate when the G-5 group of industrialized nations was expanded to the G-7, and Trudeau was invited in February 1977 to address a joint session of the American Congress, a first for Canada. Granatstein, "Canada and Peacekeeping: Image and Reality"; and Bothwell, *Alliance and Illusion*, 327–31, 343.
28 The United Nations General Assembly did not finally agree to a ban until 10 September 1996, and it has not yet entered into force because India, North Korea, and Pakistan have not yet signed it. Geoffrey Pearson, "Trudeau and Foreign Policy," *Peace Magazine*, Jan.–March 2001, 7.
29 NATO, Defence Planning Committee, *Final Communiqué*, 13–14 May 1980.
30 *Bulletin of the Atomic Scientists*, William M. Arkin, "A Global Role for NATO," Jan. 1986, 4.
31 Polmar, *Cold War Submarines*, 195.
32 See above, p. 157, and Ron Purver, "The Control of Strategic Anti-submarine Warfare," *International Journal*, vol. 38, no. 3 (1982–83): 409–31.
33 George Lindsey, "Canadian Maritime Strategy: Should the Emphasis be Changed?" DRAE Report No. 5. Canada, DND, July 1969.
34 George Lindsey in G.M. Dillon's "Canadian Naval Policy since World War II: A Decision-making Analysis," Halifax: Dalhousie, Centre for Foreign Policy Studies, Occasional Paper, Oct. 1972. See Albert Legault and George Lindsey, *The Dynamics of the Nuclear Balance*, 96–123.
35 Middlemiss, *Canadian Defence Decisions and Determinants*, 39–40.
36 Quoted in Larry Stewart, *Canada's European Force: 1971–1980, A Defence Policy in Transition*, 105; See Colin S. Gray, "Is the Canadian Military Relevant?" Background paper prepared for the Fall Seminar of the Canadian Institute of Strategic Studies, 23 Oct. 1976. Gray was director of the Centre for Strategic Studies at the University of Reading and Senior Associate to the National Institute for Public Policy.

37 Gray, *Canadian Defence Priorities*, 90–1.
38 Gellner, "Strategic Analysis in Canada," *International Journal*, vol. 33, no. 3 (1977–78): 493–505.
39 Polmar, *Cold War Submarines*, 183–8.
40 Norman Friedman, *Seapower as Strategy, Navies and National Interests*, 201; and private communication, 31 Oct. 2011.
41 Can., "Report of the Sub-Committee on National Defence of the Standing Senate Committee on Foreign Affairs: Canada's Maritime Defence," 40.
42 "The attempt by the government of Pierre Trudeau to assert Canada's strategic independence was in fact premised on the ability of Canada to 'free-ride' on the collective good of security provided by the Atlantic Alliance. What Ottawa soon discovered was that those providing the collective good were prepared to exact a price from Canada in other ways." Buteux, "NATO and the Evolution of Canadian Defence and Foreign Policy," 163.
43 Communications made to the author in 1977 when interviewing German leaders.
44 Stewart, *Canada's European Force*, 37-86; Bland, *Chiefs of Defence*, 136–8, 235; Harald von Riekhoff, "The Impact of Prime Minister Trudeau on Foreign Policy," *International Journal*, vol. 33, no. 2 (spring 1978): 267–86; *Halifax Chronicle-Herald*, 28 May 1975.
45 Can., House of Commons, *Minutes of Proceedings and Evidence of the Standing Committee ...* 30th Parl. 1st Session, no. 33, 23 March 1976, 5–6.
46 Stewart, *Canada's European Force*, 115.
47 Buteux, "NATO and the Evolution of Canadian Defence and Foreign Policy;" and Keating and Pratt, *Canada, NATO and the Bomb*, 42.
48 John Halstead, foreword to Joseph T. Jockel and Joel J. Sokolsky, *Canada and Collective Security: Odd Man Out*, viii.
49 Stewart, *Canada's European Force*, 102–7.
50 Barnett Danson, speech to the Conference of Defence Associations 13 Jan., and Admiral Falls at the Canada Club 13 Feb. 1977, quoted in Stewart, *Canada's European Force*, 112, 118; and see 79–85. See Rob B. Byers, "Defence and Foreign Policy in the 1970s: The Demise of the Trudeau Doctrine," *International Journal*, vol. 33, no. 2 (1978–79): 312–38; Martin Shadwick, "Aurora Renaissance," *Canadian Military Journal*, vol. 8, no. 4 (winter 2007–08): 102–4; and Gray, *Canadian Defence Priorities*, 134–5. See also: Intervention by Dan Mainguy at the Corbett Richmond Conference at the United States Naval War College, Newport, 27–29 Sept. 1992. Apparently my own reports, "The Enforcement of Canada's Continental Maritime Jurisdiction," ORAE Report No. R44, Ottawa, DND, 1975; and "The Diplomatic Utility of Canada's Naval Forces," no. R60, 1976, were employed in making the case. The angry rejection of the first by Vice-Admiral Douglas Boyle, who was commander Maritime Command, led to its coming to the attention of Vice-Admiral Robert Falls, and to the second study being commissioned. Vice-Admiral J. Andrew Fulton, in a note in Michael Whitby, Richard Gimblett, and Peter Haydon *The Admirals*, 333, suggests that Trudeau's conversion may have had something to do with an invitation he had extended to Trudeau's family to visit several ships of the fleet. See also Peter Haydon, "Choosing The Right Fleet Mix: Lessons from the Canadian Patrol Frigate Selection Process," *Canadian Military Journal*, vol. 9, no. 1 (2008).
51 Richard Gimblett, "Command in the Canadian Navy" and Kenneth Hansen, "How We Really Got Here," *Canadian Naval Review*, vol. 2, no. 1 (spring 2006), 34. Norman Friedman writes: "Whatever people said, I doubt that anyone imag-

ined HALIFAXes operating hundreds of miles apart; they'd have been wiped out" (28 Oct. 2011).

52 Julie Ferguson, *Through a Canadian Periscope: The Story of the Canadian Submarine Service*, 287; Peter Haydon, "The Evolution of the Canadian Naval Task Group," in Griffiths, *Canadian Gunboat Diplomacy*, 119.

53 In October 1970, four months after the publication of *Foreign Policy for Canadians*, the kidnapping of the British trade commissioner in Montreal, James Cross, the kidnapping and murder of the Quebec minister of labour, Pierre Laporte, and Trudeau's declaration of the War Measures Act to containing the danger put national unity issues on the front page.

54 Lieutenant B. Fenton, "Foreign Policy and Naval Forces: A Canadian Perspective," in Fred W. Crickard, ed., *Maritime Security Working Papers*, 73.

55 Joseph T. Jockel and Joel J. Sokolsky "Canada and NATO," *International Journal*, vol. 64, no. 2 (spring 2009) "NATO at 60": 311–15; Can., DEA, Statements and Speeches 83/8, 9 May 1983, "Canada's Position on Testing Cruise Missiles and Disarmament: An Open Letter to All Canadians."

56 The focus was still on European defence, but Hayward had developed plans for aggressive action against Soviet naval forces based in eastern Siberia, exploiting the leverage provided by Soviet concern for any possible Chinese participation. His objective was at once to prevent Soviet naval forces in the Pacific acting against American interests and allies in that theatre, but also to prevent the transfer of Soviet assets to reinforce the Northern Fleet. In the Mediterranean, Vice-Admiral William N. Small revised war plans that had provided for withdrawal of carriers into the western basin until Soviet units were eliminated, instead planning to send them eastward to provide air support along the southern flank of NATO.

57 U.S.A., Senate, Committee on Armed Forces, Subcommittee on Sea Power and Force Projection, Hearings on Department of Defense Authorization for Appropriations for Fiscal Year 1985, 14 March 1984. Writing in a supplement to the United States Naval Institute's *Proceedings* two years later, Admiral Watkins made his views more explicit: "The Soviets place great weight on the nuclear correlation of forces, even during the time before nuclear weapons have been used. Maritime forces can influence that correlation, both by destroying Soviet ballistic missile submarines and by improving our own nuclear posture." James D. Watkins, "The Maritime Strategy," supplement to United States Naval Institute *Proceedings*, no. 112, Jan. 1986: 2–17.

58 Interview with John Lehman, "Lehman Seeks Superiority," *International Defense Review*, no. 5 (1982), 547–8; and Steven Miller, "The United States: Strategic Interests," in Clive Archer and David Scrivener, *Northern Waters, Security and Resource Issues*: 115–24; See also Geoffrey Till, "Strategy in the Far North," idem, 69–84.

59 Watkins, "The Maritime Strategy," Jan. 1986: 2–17.

60 Employing high technology sensors, communications systems, and accurate long-range conventional weapons systems, new tactical systems were believed to enable carrier battle groups to fight their way into the Norwegian and Barents seas and the northwest Pacific – to tie up Soviet forces in defence of the homeland so that they could not be used offensively, and to threaten the ability of the Soviet Union to reserve its submarine-based ballistic missile systems, its SSBN forces, for "post exchange bargaining." Increasingly Soviet naval ships were being armed with anti-submarine weapons to defend their SSBNs against American and British attack submarines that might enter defensive "bastions" in the Barents and Kara seas

close to the Kola Peninsula directly across the permanent polar ice cap from Canadian territory, and in the Sea of Okhotsk. Rosenberg added that the U.S. Navy was not really prepared to fight a conventional global war against the Soviet Union, which it calculated would require a fleet of twenty-four attack aircraft carriers when it only had about thirteen, and more than its hundred nuclear attack submarines, but that it adopted the aggressive stance nonetheless. David Alan Rosenberg, "American Naval Strategy in the Era of the Third World War: An Inquiry into the Structure and Process of General War at Sea, 1945–90," in Nicholas Rodger, ed., *Naval Power in the 20th Century*: 242–54; and David F. Winkler, *Cold War at Sea: High-Seas Confrontation between the United States and the Soviet Union*, 142.

61 Friedman, *Seapower as Strategy*, 202–6; and private communication, 31 Oct. 2011.
62 W. Harriet Critchley, "Polar Deployment of Soviet Submarines," *International Journal*, vol. 39, no. 3 (1984): 828–65.
63 Laurence Hickey, "Our Submarine Service: Cross-Connect Open to the Allied System," Proceedings ... *From Empire to In(ter)dependence*; and Michael Whitby, "'Doin' the Biz': Canadian Submarine Patrol Operations Against Soviet SSBNs, 1983–87," in Bernd Horne, ed., *Fortune Favours the Brave: Tales of Courage and Tenacity in Canadian Military History*.
64 Melakopides, *Pragmatic Idealism*: 221–2. Michael Howard, the life president of the International Institute for Strategic Studies, wrote in 1991 that "all strategy is in principle teleological; military operations should be planned to achieve the political object for which the war is fought. But it is a principle honored more often in the breach than in the observance. Normally the priorities are reversed. In spite of himself the strategist finds that his plans are being shaped by immediate military and political necessities, which cumulatively shape the object of war." Michael Howard, "British Grand Strategy in World War 1," in Paul Kennedy, ed., *Grand Strategies in War and Peace*, 31.
65 Robert Gates writes in his memoirs that "an enfeebled Soviet leadership, presiding over a country confronting serious economic and social problems, knew they could not compete." An alarmist Canadian perspective was that the American interest in ballistic missile defences betrayed a tendency to abandon mutual nuclear deterrence, returning to 1950s thinking about nuclear war fighting. Vice-President George Bush Sr, Reagan's secretary of state George Shultz, and former U.S. secretary of defense James R. Schlesinger, who had served under Nixon and Ford, were careful to restate that deterrence was the only safe strategy, but not everyone was convinced. Keating and Pratt, *Canada, NATO and the Bomb*, 55–9.
66 David Winkler, *Cold War at Sea*, 147–8.
67 Gates, *From the Shadows*, 258–73; John Clearwater, *Just Dummies: Cruise Missile Testing in Canada*, 3–63.
68 RyaN (Raketno-Yadernoe Napadenie), meaning Nuclear Missile Attack.
69 Theodore Hesburgh, "Religious, Scientific Leaders on Arms Race," *Bulletin of the Atomic Scientists*, April 1985: 49–50.
70 Can., Commons, *Debates*, 15 June 1981, North-South Relations, Vol. 10: 10592–5.
71 Pierre Elliott Trudeau, "A Peace Initiative from Canada," speech at the University of Guelph, 27 Oct. 1983, *Bulletin of the Atomic Scientists*, Jan. 1984: 15–19; See Harald von Riekhoff and John Sigler, "The Trudeau Peace Initiative: The Politics of Reversing the Arms Race," in Brian W. Tomlin and Maureen Malot, eds., *Canada Among Nations, 1984: A Time of Transition*: 50–69.

72 Michael Pearson, Gregor Mackinnon, and Christoper Sapardanis, "'The World is Entitled to Ask Questions': The Trudeau Peace Initiative Reconsidered," *International Journal*, vol. 41, no. 4 (1985–86): 129–58.
73 Can., Commons, *Debates*, 9 Feb. 1984: 1215–17.
74 Bothwell, *Alliance and Illusion*, 385–6.

CHAPTER SEVEN

1 Robert Bothwell, *Alliance and Illusion: Canada and the World, 1945–1984*, 395.
2 Canada remained active in multilateral and international fora. As Costas Melakopides writes, "Mulroney's Ottawa conducted copious opinion polls which established beyond doubt that the idealist impulse of Canadians remained entrenched. It therefore follows that the Mulroney governments would have been highly unwise (if not masochistic) to change Canada's forty-year-long prestigious, effective, highly popular and widely respected internationalism." Melakopides, *Pragmatic Idealism: Canadian Foreign Policy, 1945–1995*, 228.
3 Ken Booth, "Naval Strategy and the Spread of Psycho-Legal Boundaries at Sea," *International Journal*, vol. 38, no. 3 (1982–83): 373–96.
4 David Winkler, *Cold War at Sea: High-Seas Confrontation between the United States and the Soviet Union*, 146.
5 Douglas Bland, *Chiefs of Defence: Government and the Unified Command of the Canadian Armed Forces*, 245–52. In work I undertook for the Directorate of Strategic Analysis, DND, in 1977 I pointed out that the shorter air route between the Canadian base at Frobisher Bay and northern Norway could have been used to facilitate a politico-military strategy that would reduce the windows of opportunity for Soviet occupation of northern Norway without provoking Soviet anger. Norway had, and has, a policy against permanent foreign bases on its soil.
6 Two years later Kim Nossal remarked that the decision "was a singularly out-of-character step for the Canadian state" because of the lack of any obvious clients for that class of ship, and lack of serious interest by the industry for commitment of so large an investment in only one yard. Kim Richard Nossal, "Polar Icebreakers: The Politics of Inertia," in Franklyn Griffiths, *Politics of the Northwest Passage*, 238.
7 Can., Commons, *Debates*, 5 Dec. 1986: 1823.
8 Can., Commons, SCEAND, *Minutes of Proceedings and Evidence*, 33rd Parliament, 2nd session, no. 1, 2 Dec. 1986, 35.
9 Ibid., 1st session, no. 52, 6 Dec. 1985, 12–13.
10 Ibid., no. 50, 28 Nov. 1985, 38.
11 Harriet Critchley, "Polar Deployment of Soviet Submarines," *International Journal*, vol. 39, no. 3, 1984.
12 Canada-U.S. Test and Evaluation Program Agreement, 1983. See James Lee, "Cruise Missile Testing in Canada: The Post-Cold War Debate," Ottawa: Library of Parliament, Research Branch, Political and Social Affairs Division, 27 May 1983, revised 14 April 1993, 19.
13 SCEAND, 1st session, no. 50, 28 Nov. 1985, 39; and see *Minutes*, and no. 33, evidence of Brigadier-General Carl Bertrand (director general, Military Plans and Operations, DND) 3 Oct. 1985, 21. *The Military Balance 1985–86*, London: International Institute for Strategic Studies 1985, 24; and George Gruca, *The Sea-Launched Cruise Missile as a Weapon System: Characteristics, Operation and Capabilities*.
14 See evidence presented by Franklyn Griffiths in Canada, Special Joint Committee

of the Senate and of the House of Commons on Canada's International Relations, *Minutes of Proceedings and Evidence*, no. 49, 13 March 1986, 12.

15 Can., DND, *Challenge and Commitment: A Defence Policy for Canada*, 1987, 52; Rob B. Byers, "The 1987 Defence White Paper: An Analysis," Autumn 1987; Rob Huebert, "The Politics of Arctic Security: In Search of a Canadian Arctic Maritime Security Policy," in Ann Griffiths, ed., *Canadian Gunboat Diplomacy: The Canadian Navy and Foreign Policy*, 293.

16 Jason Delaney, "The One Class of Vessel that is Impossible to Build in ~~Australia~~ Canada."

17 Can., Commons, SCEAND, *Minutes of Proceedings and Evidence*, 33rd Parliament, 1st session, no. 52, 6 Dec. 1985, 12–13.

18 Laurence Hickey, "Our Submarine Service: Cross-Connect Open to the Allied System"; Whitby, "'Doin' the Biz': Canadian Submarine Patrol Operations Against Soviet SSBNs, 1983–87"; and Polmar, *Cold War Submarines: The Design and Construction of US and Soviet Submarines*, 159–61.

19 Phil Webster, "Arctic Sovereignty, Submarine Operations and Water Space Management," *Canadian Naval Review*, vol. 3, no. 3 (fall 2007): 14–16.

20 USA, Senate, Subcommittee on Seapower and Force Projection, Hearings, 14 March 1984.

21 Can., Commons, *Debates*, 5 Dec. 1986: 1823.

22 See: Can., DND, *Defence Policy Initiatives Questions and Answers* (Supplemental Information to the White Paper), 1987; Nathaniel French Caldwell, *Arctic Leverage*: 58–66; and Hickey, "Our Submarine Service."

23 Rear Admiral John Anderson, "Canadian Perspective on Arctic Security Issues," 17 March 1988, 22–23. See: Huebert, "The Politics of Arctic Security": 291–311.

24 Can., Commons, Standing Committee on National Defence, *Minutes of Proceedings and Evidence*, no. 10, 14 April 1988, 10: 12–13.

25 Crickard testimony to SCEAND, 28 Nov. 1985, 41.

26 "Nuclear Submarines to Enable Canada to Fight Modern War, Minister Says," *Globe and Mail*, 18 June 1987. And see: Can., Commons, *Debates*, 9 June 1988: 16282.

27 In 1998 it was admitted that plans to install an operational system had been abandoned because of cost and limited effectiveness: a parliamentary statement acknowledged that "all proposals received to date have been extremely expensive and have offered only limited undersea surveillance capability." It lamely asserted that it was the intention to "continue our efforts to find a realistic and affordable solution." Can., "Government of Canada Response to the Report of the Standing Committee on Foreign Affairs and International Trade 'Canada and the Circumpolar World: Meeting the Challenges of Cooperation into the Twenty-first Century,'" May 1998: 29; see Derek Blackburn, "Maritime Defence Policy: A New Democrat's Perspective," in William J. Yost, *In Defence of Canada's Oceans*: 21–8.

28 Private conversation with a very senior Canadian defence official. Adam Lajeunesse, "Sovereignty, Security and the Canadian Nuclear Submarine Program," *Canadian Military Journal*, vol. 8, no. 4 (winter 2007–08).

29 Can., House of Commons, *Debates*, 33rd Parl. 2nd Sess., 6 April 1987: 4965. See Christopher Kirkey, "Smoothing Troubled Waters: The 1988 Canada-United States Arctic Co-operation Agreement," *International Journal*, vol. 50, no. 2, 1994–95: 401–26.

30 *Agreement between the Government of Canada and the Government of the United States of America on Arctic Cooperation*, Ottawa, 11 Jan. 1988.

31 Frank B. Kelso, II, "Defence of the Atlantic," *Canadian Defence Quarterly*, vol. 19, no. 4 (1990): 13–17.
32 Douglas Bland, "Continuity in Canadian Naval Policy, 1961–1987," *Canadian Defence Quarterly*, vol. 18, no. 5 (1989): 29–32.
33 Delaney, "The One Class of Vessel"; and Rob Huebert, "Canadian Arctic Maritime Security: The Return to Canada's Third Ocean," *Canadian Military Journal*, vol. 8, no. 2 (summer 2007).
34 Sean Maloney, "Maple Leaf Over the Caribbean: Gunboat Diplomacy Canadian Style," in Ann Griffiths, Peter Haydon, and Richard Gimblett, *Canadian Gunboat Diplomacy* ; and Douglas S. Thomas, "The Canadian Maritime Contribution to Peace-Support Operations," in Griffiths, Haydon, and Gimblett, *Canadian Gunboat Diplomacy*, 151, 189–98.
35 Bland, *Chiefs of Defence*, 191–8.
36 Gina Combden, "Old Flag Flies Again."
37 Tony German, *The Sea is at Our Gates: The History of the Canadian Navy*, 308–9.
38 Peter Haydon, "The Evolution of the Canadian Naval Task Group, in Griffiths, Haydon, and Gimblett, *Canadian Gunboat Diplomacy*": 95–129, and "From Uncertainty to Maturity, 1968–89," in Richard Gimblett, ed., *The Naval Service of Canada, 1910–2010: The Centennial Story*: 163–79.
39 Frank Langdon and Douglas Ross, "Towards a Canadian Maritime Strategy in the North Pacific Region," *International Journal*, vol. 42, no. 3 (1986–87): 848–9.
40 *Canadian Security, A Force Structure Model for the 21st Century*, June 1994: 20–1.
41 Canada, DND, *Backgrounder*, May 1989, "Re-allocation of Maritime Resources," and Can., DND, Maritime Command, *The Naval Vision: Charting the Course for Canada's Maritime Forces into the 21st Century*, 21.
42 Denis Healey, *Labour and a World Society*, 3.
43 William M. Arkin, formerly of U.S. Army Intelligence, director of the Arms Race and Nuclear Weapons Research Project at the Institute for Policy Studies in Washington, D.C., "A Global Role for NATO," *Bulletin of the Atomic Scientists*, Jan. 1986, 4.
44 The U.S. Senate would only agree to the reflagging of Kuwaiti tankers as American merchant ships if Britain and France participated in an international naval force – which they eventually did, and were joined by Belgium, Netherlands, and Italian warships. The refusal of those nations to form a combined command structure, which might have been moderated by the North Atlantic Council, has been characterized as creeping unilateralism, but the reality is subtler. The Royal Navy could not directly support the reflagged Kuwaiti ships because Britain's interpretation of the law of naval warfare did not allow that neutral merchant ships were immune to search and seizure by belligerents, even if they were escorted by naval forces. In effect, Britain was less interested in this war than in a possible future one in which she as a belligerent might wish to employ traditional belligerent rights. British warships "coordinated their passages" through the war zone with those of British merchant ships to provide some defence and deterrence against violent attack. Given the difference in American and British rules of engagement, and their different political policies, it is not surprising that American demands for NATO co-operation in the defence of Persian Gulf merchant shipping were ineffectual. France flatly rejected a Kuwaiti request in June 1987 that it join the United States in convoying

tankers. Nicholas Tracy, *Attack on Maritime Trade*, 228; Tom Keating, *Canada, NATO and the Bomb: The Western Alliance*, 206–7; and Anthony H. Cordesman, *The Gulf and the West: Strategic Relations and Military Realities*, 349–50.
45 Whitby, "'Doin' the Biz,'" 323.
46 Winkler, *Cold War at Sea*: 159–60, 210.
47 Kim Richard Nossal, "Succumbing to the Dumbell, Canadian Perspectives on NATO in the 1990s," in *Canada and NATO: The Forgotten Ally?* 27.
48 Harold A. Skaarup, *Out of Darkness – Light: A History of Canadian Military Intelligence*, 176.

CHAPTER EIGHT

1 The triggering circumstances for the Iraqi invasion were Iraq's impoverishment due to the cost of the Iran-Iraq war between 1980 and 1988, and over-production by the Organization of the Petroleum Exporting Countries (OPEC) that depressed the price of crude oil between January and June 1990 from $20.50 to $13. Iraq's foreign minister Tariq Aziz laid the blame for OPEC's over-production on Kuwait, and said that servicing Iraq's debt of $80 billion while paying the cost of food imports could not be done with oil at that price. Iraqi forces invaded Kuwait to stop what Bagdad believed was Kuwaiti slant-drilling into Iraq's Rumaila oil field, to assert an irredentist claim to Kuwait as a lost province of Iraq, and to seize Kuwaiti financial reserves. Janice Stein's analysis is that Hussein made significant tactical mistakes. He occupied all the sheikdom so as to provide the United States with no place to insert forces, but he was not careful to reassure King Fahd, whose reluctance to admit foreign soldiers into Saudi Arabia was only with difficulty overcome by Washington. Janice Gross Stein, "Deterrence and Compellence in the Gulf, 1990–91: A Failed or Impossible Task?" *International Security*, vol. 17 (fall 1992): 147–79. Milton Viorst, "Report from Baghdad," *The New Yorker*, 24 Sept. 1990: 89–97, at 90.
2 Harald von Riekhoff, "Canada and Collective Security," in David B. Dewitt and David Leyton–Brown, *Canada's International Security Policy*.
3 UNSC Resolution 666 on 13 September limited the distribution of food to UN-approved agencies, which did not in fact have access to Iraq. Resolution 670 extended the controls to the airways, and resolution 678 of 29 Nov. 1990 made it clear that "all necessary means" might be employed to enforce the sanctions.
4 David M. Malone, *The International Struggle Over Iraq: Politics in the UN Security Council 1980–2005*, 61. On 21 Dec. 1991 all the Soviet republics except Georgia signed a protocol at Alma-Ata ending the Soviet Union and establishing the Commonwealth of Independent States.
5 The Royal Navy blockaded the port of Beira in Mozambique from which a pipeline ran to Rhodesia, sustaining a deployment in the Mozambique Channel for nearly ten years between December 1965 and June 1975. Between March 1966 and June 1971 a British air reconnaissance squadron was also based at Majunga in the Malagasy Republic. The futility of this effort was suggested by the fact that the Rhodesian government was able to import oil through Lorenzo Marques via the South African railway system, accessing the pipeline while avoiding the port of Beira, and by truck from South Africa. The blockade was sustained largely for demonstrative purposes, and to provide political cover for the continued presence of British warships in the Indian Ocean following the signing in September 1965 by India of a naval arms agreement with the Soviet Union, the establishment by

the Soviet Navy in 1968 of an Indian Ocean squadron, and its use to establish a Soviet naval and missile base at Berbera on the Red Sea coast of Somalia where Siad Barre seized power in 1969. The economic sanctions later mounted against the Union of South Africa were not implemented by naval forces. Nicholas Tracy, *Attack on Maritime Trade*, 222, 243; and, *Sea Power and the Control of Trade*, nos. 87–8: 531–3; Richard A. Mobley, "The Beira Patrol: Britain's Broken Blockade against Rhodesia," in Bruce A. Elleman and Sarah C.M. Paine, eds., *Naval Blockades and Seapower: Strategies and Counter-Strategies, 1805–2005*: 181–8; Alexey D. Muraviev, *The Russian Pacific Fleet from the Crimean War to Perestroika*: 36–40; conversation with Admiral Sir Edward Ashmore, First Sea Lord, 12 Nov. 1975.

6 Secretary Baker, "America's Strategy in the Persian Gulf Crisis," Statement before the Senate Foreign Relations Committee, Washington, DC, Dec. 5, 1990, U.S. Department of State, Dispatch, Bureau of Public Affairs, vol. 1, no. 15, 10 Dec. 1990: 307–8.

7 Kim Richard Nossal, "Knowing When to Fold: Western Sanctions against the USSR 1980–1983," *International Journal*, vol. 44, no. 3 (1988–89): 698–724.

8 Jean H. Morin and Richard Gimblett, *Operation Friction, 1990-1991*, 13–30.

9 Ibid., 24, 28, 38–44, 268–9; Duncan Miller, *The Persian Excursion: The Canadian Navy in the Gulf War*, 20–1.

10 Ken Summers, "The Canadian Navy in the 1990–91 Gulf War: Some Personal Observations," in Richard Gimblett and Richard Mayne, *People, Policy and Programmes*: 113–20.

11 Barbara McDougall, "Canada, NATO, and the North Atlantic Cooperation Council," in *Canada and NATO: The Forgotten Ally?* Special Report 1992, 5.

12 Morin, *Operation Friction*, 160.

13 Richard H. Gimblett, "The Transformation Era, 1990 to the Present," in Richard Gimblett, ed., *The Naval Service of Canada, 1910–2010: The Centennial Story*: 185–219.

14 Richard H. Gimblett, "MIF or MNF? The Dilemma of the 'Lesser' Navies in the Gulf War Coalition," in Michael Hadley, Rob Huebert, and Fred Crickard, *A Nation's Navy: In Quest of Canadian Naval Identity*: 190–204. Gimblett lists the ships deployed to the MIF and MNF and that took part in the CLF; Morin, *Operation Friction*, 19–23; Miller, *The Persian Excursion*; Allan English, Richard Gimblett, and Howard Coombs, *Beware of Putting the Cart Before the Horse: Networ-Enabled Operations as a Canadian Approach to Transformation*, 49; Fred Crickard and Gregory L. Witol, "The Political Uses of Medium Power Navies," in Ann Griffiths, Peter Haydon, and Richard Gimblett, *Canadian Gunboat Diplomacy*, 258.

15 Central Intelligence Agency "Comprehensive Report of the Special Advisor to the DCI on Iraq's WMD," 30 September 2004, chap. 5, Iraq's Chemical Warfare Program. During the 1970s and 1980s weapons of mass destruction had been under extensive development in Iraq, with support from companies in France, Italy, Britain, the United States, Russia, and elsewhere; chemical weapons had been used in action against Iranian forces between 1983 and 1988; extensive provision had to be made against their possible use against American coalition forces in 1991; and they may have been used later in 1991 to suppress the Shia revolt in southern Iraq that followed the liberation of Kuwait.

16 UNSC Resolution 687, 3 April 1991. See David Malone, *The International Struggle Over Iraq*, 74–5.

17 Richard Gimblett, "The Transformation Era, 1990 to the Present," in *The Naval Service of Canada, 1910–2010: The Centennial Story*.
18 Secretary Baker's answers at a news conference, New York City, U.S. Department of State, *Dispatch*, 1/12, 19 Nov. 1990, 273; *Dispatch*, 2/1, 17 Jan. 1991.
19 U.S., Department of State, *Dispatch*, 2/3 (21 Jan. 1991), 37.
20 UNSCVR, Provisional, 6 Aug. 1990 S/PV 2933 – discussion of document S/21441.
21 UNSCVR, Provisional, 25 September 1990, S/PV 2943.
22 Norman Friedman, *Seapower as Strategy: Navies and National Interests*, 190. Stein is at pains to deny that American leadership had a hidden agendum to ensure that the coalition army organized under Washington's leadership was not denied an opportunity to put an effective end to Saddam Hussein's capacity to dominate the Gulf, but her argument is not entirely convincing. Stein, "Deterrence and Compellence in the Gulf"; Viorst, "Report from Baghdad."
23 Although the intention had been that the Iraqi government would be pressured by the sanctions into revealing the details of their weapons programs, and the inspectors would only need to corroborate their admissions, in fact they had to do the initial investigations in a climate of obstruction. Nevertheless, they discovered documentary evidence of the biological and chemical weapons' programs, and their work was greatly assisted by defections, especially that in August 1995 of General Hussein Kamel Hassan, Saddam Hussein's son-in-law who had been responsible for all Iraqi weapons programs. Unable to continue its denials, Iraq adopted a new policy of "openness," and disclosed large quantities of hidden evidence, especially at a "chicken farm" at al-Hakam. After extensive questioning of the head of production, Rihab Rashid Taha, a disposal site was uncovered with 157 bombs and 16 missile warheads loaded with botulin toxin, and 50 bombs and five missile warheads loaded with anthrax. UNSCOM destroyed al-Hakam in 1996.
24 Madeleine K. Albright, "Preserving Principle and Safeguarding Stability: United States Policy Toward Iraq," 26 March 1997.
25 Text of President Clinton's speech, "They are designed to degrade Saddam's capacity to develop and deliver weapons of mass destruction, and to degrade his ability to threaten his neighbors." http://www.cnn.com/ALLPOLITICS/stories/1998/12/16/transcripts/clinton.html
26 UNSC Resolutions 1284, 17 Dec. 1999, and 1441, Nov. 8, 2002. On 17 Dec. 1999 the United States and Great Britain put to the Security Council a resolution, number 1284, which offered Iraq a bargain of reduced sanctions in return for greater co-operation, but it passed with the abstentions of the remaining three Permanent Members – and seeing the Security Council divided, the Iraq government refused to comply. UNVOVIC was not admitted to Iraq until 8 Nov. 2002 after the Security Council passed Resolution 1441, and after years of air operations over Iraq, and the threat of further military action by the United States.
27 Malone, *The International Struggle Over Iraq*, 165–8, 282.
28 Yossef Bodansky, *The Secret History of the Iraq War*, 99, 494–501.
29 Wesley Wark, review of Hans Blix, "Disarming Iraq," *International Journal*, vol. 60, no. 1 (2004–05): 282–5.
30 See Frank L. Jones, "Rolling the Dice of War: Military Necessity and Nation Building," *International Journal*, vol. 61, no. 4, 2005–06: 945–58. In the autumn of 2004 the Iraq Survey Group, chaired by Charles Duelfer, issued a report confirming that Saddam Hussein had not reactivated the program to develop weapons of mass destruction after the Gulf War of 1991. But the report also supported the view that Hussein's aim was to rid himself of the sanctions, after which he would

have a free hand to develop nuclear weapons; "several of us on the committee assumed that he was quietly waiting for the sanctions to crumble, after which he could use Iraq's huge oil revenue to purchase all the plutonium or highly enriched uranium he needed to reactivate his nuclear weapons program." Private communication to Peter van Walsum, 16 April 2007, 10:49:47.

31 James Goldrick, "Maritime Sanctions Enforcement against Iraq, 1990–03," in Elleman and Paine, eds., *Naval Blockades and Seapower*, 201–13, 296–8; and "The Maritime Element in the 1990–91 Gulf Crisis: Drawing on the Dividends of Half a Century of Multinational Naval Operations," in Bruce A. Elleman and S.C.M. Paine, *Naval Coalition Warfare: From the Napoleonic War to Operation Iraqi Freedom*: 158–68.

32 David Cortright and George A. Lopez, *The Sanctions Decade: Assessing UN Strategies in the 1990s*, 56.

33 Congress of the United States, Iraq Liberation Act of 1998, 150(2) Thomas H.R. 4655; passed 360/38 in the House of Representatives and unanimously in the Senate. In the absence of a mandate from the United Nations for regime change, one that was not likely to be granted, the United States found it would have no support from its friends. In testimony before the British House of Commons enquiry into the Iraq war, Sir William Patey, who at the time had been head of Middle East policy at the British Foreign and Commonwealth Office, said that the British government had rejected the idea of imposing a regime change on Bagdad "as having no basis in law." "Regime change had 'no basis in law,'" *Defence Management*, 25 Nov. 2009.

34 Richard A. Clarke, *Against All Enemies: Inside America's War on Terror – What Really Happened*, 30–3, 244–7, 272–3. See also Michael Byers, "War, Law, and Geopolitical Change: The Lessons of History," in *International Journal*, vol. 61, vol. 1 (2005–06): 201–13. A leaked memorandum giving an overview of a secret meeting of United Kingdom Labour government, defence and intelligence leaders on 23 July 2002, eight months before the war, contains a note attributed to Sir Richard Dearlove, who was the head of the British foreign intelligence service, MI6, and had just returned from Washington: "C [i.e., Dearlove] reported on his recent talks in Washington. There was a perceptible shift in attitude. Military action was now seen as inevitable. Bush wanted to remove Saddam, through military action, justified by the conjunction of terrorism and WMD [Weapons of Mass Destruction]. But the intelligence and facts were being fixed around the policy. The NSC [National Security Council] had no patience with the UN route, and no enthusiasm for publishing material on the Iraqi regime's record. There was little discussion in Washington of the aftermath after military action." *The Sunday Times*, 1 May 2005. This was taken as meaning that U.S. intelligence on Iraqi weapons of mass destruction prior to the war was deliberately falsified, rather than simply mistaken.

35 Yossef Bodansky, *The Secret History of the Iraq War*, 149–50, 154, 508–14.

36 NA UK, FO 837/5, J.M. Keynes to Sir Frederick Leith Ross, 10 Oct. 1939.

37 Amarthya Sen, *Development as Freedom*, 160.

38 UNSC, S/22366, 20 March 1991, paras 8, 37, "Report to the Secretary-General on Humanitarian Needs in Kuwait and Iraq in the Immediate Post-Crisis Environment by a Mission to the Area Led by Mr Martti Ahtisaari, Under Secretary-General for Administration and Management, 10–17 March 1991."

39 UN, Independent Enquiry Committee into the Oil-for-Food Programme [the Volcker Committee], Report of an Independent Working Group, *Impact of the Oil-*

for-Food Programme on the Iraqi People, 7/9/2005: 5–33. See also Editorial: "Starvation in Iraq," *The Lancet*, 11 Sept. 1991, vol. 338, no. 8776: 1179; Alberto Archerio et al., "The Effect of the Gulf War on Infant and Child Mortality in Iraq," *New England Journal of Medicine*, 23 Sept.1992, vol. 327: 931–6.

40 UNPD, World Mortality Report, 2007, Iraq, 142.
41 UN Inter-agency Child Mortality Estimates, Iraq. See Mohamed, M. Ali, and Iqbal H. Shah, "Sanctions and childhood mortality in Iraq," *The Lancet*, vol. 355, no. 9218, 27 May 2000: 1851–7, doi:10.1016/S0140-6736(00)02289-3.
42 UNICEF, *Information Newsline*, "Iraq surveys show 'humanitarian emergency,'" Wednesday, 12 Aug. 1999. See also UNICEF, *Child and Maternal Mortality Survey, 1999, Preliminary Report*, work undertaken under the direction of Mr Mohammed Ali of the London School of Hygiene and Tropical Medicine, jointly for UNICEF and the government of Iraq Ministry of Health, Preventive Health Department and Statistical Department. Information supplied by Edilberto Loaiza, Senior Programme Officer, Strategic Information Section, DPP, 3 UN Plaza, New York, NY 10017.
43 Its mandate is to share data on child mortality, harmonize estimates within the UN system, improve methods for child mortality estimation, report on progress toward the Millennium Development Goals and enhance country capacity to produce timely and properly assessed estimates of child mortality. The revision is based on the information from latest surveys including Living Conditions Survey 2003, MICS 2006 and Iraq Family Health Survey 2006. Estimates referring to the 1990s generated before 2007 are primarily based on the data from Child and Maternal Mortality Survey 1999, which has higher mortality level than data from all other surveys. The Child and Maternal Mortality Survey 1999 has been excluded in the estimation process since 2007, when more recent surveys became available indicating a lower level of child mortality for 1990s. http://www.childinfo.org/files/Child_Mortality_Report_2011.pdf
44 Iraq, Family Health Survey 2006/07, Table 25: Indirect childhood mortality (per 1000 live births). The following is from Dr Gareth Jones's notes to explain the rationality of the changes in the estimates: "The cmn91 (Infant and Child Mortality and Nutrition Survey 1991), cmm99 (Child and Maternal Mortality Survey 1999) and, to a certain extent, the cen97 (Census 1997) data point to a high child mortality. The more recent surveys lcsa03, mics06 and ifhs06 point to a considerably lower mortality. Members of the Iraq child mortality review group have noted that the cen97 data are problematic, particularly due to the impact of the non-response on children surviving, which also results in large and difficult to support mortality differences between governorates. The argument against the cmm99 data are that no such rise can be found in any of the three more recent surveys, lcs03 (Living Conditions Survey 2003), mics06 (MICS 2006) and ifhs06 (Iraq Family Health Survey 2006). While there has been a considerable movement of people out of Iraq since 1999, such movements would still not cause such a large peak in the cmm99 data to disappear – which is what the three more recent surveys report.

There is a suggestion from mics06 of a peak in U5MR around 1990, and ifhs06 data also appear to be pointing to a higher level of mortality in the early 1990s. Nevertheless, neither survey suggests anything even approaching the level of cmm99 in the 1990s. This lack of evidence of a substantially raised mortality level after 1990 from lcs03, mics06 and ifhs06 forces the conclusion that either the cmm99 survey reflects the reality and lcs03, mics06 and ifhs06 do not, or cmm99 does not reflect reality and the other three sources do. In the face of this situation, the conclusion of the review group is to give zero weights for cmn91 and cmm99, as well as cen97. In addition, chs89d data are clearly much lower than other sources, and as a result have been given zero weights." Private communication from Dr Danzhen You, statistics and monitoring specialist, Division of Policy and Practice, UNICEF, New York. A total of 23,015 women were interviewed for the 1999 mortality survey and 14,675 women were interviewed for the 2006–07 Iraq family health survey.

45 UNICEF, *Information Newsline*, "Iraq surveys show 'humanitarian emergency,'" Wed. 12 Aug. 1999; Iraq, *Child and Maternal Mortality Survey, Preliminary Report*, 1999, 6, 12.

46 Dr Les Roberts writes that "the assumption that demographers can make 5 year assumptions or year to year assumptions and collect data 5, 10 or 20 years back makes complete sense to me in Sweden and Canada, and makes no sense to me in volatile Iraq. Low mortality in the last year of sanctions (2002) has nothing to do with what was happening in 1995 or 1999. In fact, I have seen a couple of times where high mortality and hardship can lead to exceedingly low mortality in the years afterwards (see Bull. WHO, Kasongo Study on Measles ~1985, in Goma the year after the genocide the CMR was very very low and the birth rate very high, 8 or 9% I believe)." Communication from Dr Les Roberts, Columbia University, 6 Jan. 2012. See: www.childmortality.org, at Iraq.

47 UNSC, S/1995/300, 13 April 1995, *Permanent Members of the Security Council to the President of the Council*.

48 Malone, *The International Struggle Over Iraq*, 117, 95.

49 UN, Independent Enquiry Committee into the Oil-for-Food Programme [the Volcker Committee], *Manipulation of the Oil-for-Food Programme by the Iraq Government*, 1.

50 Ibid., Report of an Independent Working Group, "Impact of the Oil-for-Food Program on the Iraqi People – Report Summary," 7 Sept. 2005. UN Charter 24(2) stipulates that the Security Council must discharge its duties "in accordance with the Purpose and Principles of the United Nations." See also Mohamed M. Ali and Iqbal H. Shah, "Sanctions and Childhood Mortality in Iraq."

51 Mancur Olson Jr, *The Economics of Wartime Shortage*, passim.

52 Tracy, *Sea Power and the Control of Trade*, 416–17.

53 During the debate in the Security Council on 25 Aug. 1990 discussing Resolution 665 authorizing the use of force against Iraq, Alarcón de Quesada, the ambassador for Cuba, declared that "no action or decision adopted or to be adopted by this Council can give it the political, legal or moral authority to undertake any kind of action that is in itself inhuman." UNSCVR, Provisional, 25 Aug. 1990, S/PV 2938 discussion of draft resolution S/21640 (resolution 665). Three days later, at a meeting of the 661 committee, he attempted to persuade his fellow ambassadors that the term "humanitarian circumstances" should be interpreted not only as applying to a need to avert imminent death, but also "where withholding food could have long-term effect – on the growth or mental development of children for example." Mr Richardson, the British ambassador, objected: "If the Security Council had intended to exempt foodstuffs systematically," it would not have included the proviso "in humanitarian circumstances." UN, S/AC 25/S2.4, Provisional Summary Record of the 4th Meeting of the 661 Committee, 28 Aug. 1990.

54 John and Karl Mueller, "Sanctions of Mass Destruction," *Foreign Affairs*, vol. 78, no. 3 (May–June 1999): 43–53. A Brown University study published in June 2011 estimated that the wars and counter-terrorist operations since the 9/11 attacks have

caused the deaths of 225,000 people, with a further 365,000 wounded, and cost USD $4.4 trillion. "The Costs of War Since 2001: Iraq, Afghanistan, and Pakistan," June 2011.
55 Suspended from his position on 7 Feb. 2005, he resigned from the United Nations on 7 Aug. 2005 and returned to his native Cyprus where he is safe from the threat of extradition to the United States.
56 *Daily Telegraph*, 19 Feb. 2004, Jack Fairweather in Baghdad and Anton La Guardia, "Chalabi stands by faulty intelligence that toppled Saddam's regime."
57 Also on the committee: Justice Richard Goldstone of South Africa, who previously served as the chief prosecutor of the United Nations International Criminal Tribunals for the former Yugoslavia and Rwanda, and Mark Pieth of Switzerland, a professor of Criminal Law and Criminology at the University of Basel with expertise in money-laundering. The committee was given unrestricted access to national documents, and UN personnel were instructed to co-operate fully.
58 UN, Independent Enquiry Committee [the Volcker Committee], *Management of the United Nations Oil-for-Food Programme*, vol. 1, Preface: 7–10.
59 UN, Independent Enquiry, interim report "Oil-for-Food vs Smuggling," 3 Feb. 2005. http://www.oilforfoodfacts.org/smuggling.aspx
60 See also Malone, *The International Struggle Over Iraq*: 120–40.
61 Tracy, *Attack on Maritime Trade*, 238.
62 Margaret Doxey, *United Nations Sanctions: Trends and Problems*, 39, 46–8, 51–2. See also Peter Augustus, "Naval Boarding Party Operations," *Canadian Naval Review*, vol. 3, no. 4 (winter 2008): 26–7.

CHAPTER NINE

1 Can., DND, News Release, 26 April 1991, letter from V. Adm. Thomas to Gen. De Chastelain, 24 April 1991, and reply 25 April; see Douglas Bland, *Chiefs of Defence:Government and the Unified Command of the Canadian Armed Forces*: 271–2.
2 United Nations, A/47/277 - S/24111, Boutros Boutros-Ghali, "An Agenda for Peace, Preventive diplomacy, Peacemaking and Peace-keeping," Report of the Secretary-General pursuant to the statement adopted by the Summit Meeting of the Security Council on 31 Jan. 1992.
3 Conference on Security and Co-operation in Europe, *Final Act*, Helsinki, 1 Aug. 1975, 1(3) Inviolability of frontiers: "The participating States regard as inviolable all one another's frontiers as well as the frontiers of all States in Europe and therefore they will refrain now and in the future from assaulting these frontiers. Accordingly, they will also refrain from any demand for, or act of, seizure and usurpation of part or all of the territory of any participating State." (8) Equal rights and self-determination of peoples: "The participating States will respect the equal rights of peoples and their right to self-determination, acting at all times in conformity with the purposes and principles of the Charter of the United Nations and with the relevant norms of international law, including those relating to territorial integrity of States."
4 Michael Libal, *Limits of Persuasion: Germany and the Yugoslav Crisis, 1991–1992*, 9–10, 38–9, 78–9, 108–12, 132–5; Dennis P. Hupchick and Harold E. Cox, *The Palgrave Concise Historical Atlas of the Balkans*, Maps 33–6, 44–5, 48–50.
5 Margaret Doxey, *United Nations Sanctions: Trends and Problems*, 23.
6 Morrison, "Canada and Peacekeeping: A Time for Reanalysis?" in David Devitt and David Leyton-Brown, *Canada's International Security Policy*.

7 It was the declarations of independence in June 1991 by the Yugoslav states of Slovenia and Croatia that had made the conflict urgent. The Yugoslav National Army moved immediately to secure the Slovenian border and airports, and fighting broke out between it and the Slovenian Total Defence Force militia. Chancellor Helmut Kohl's speech on 1 July made it clear that the fighting had moved German policy toward supporting the states in their bid for democratization and independence. On 23 December Germany extended recognition of Slovenia and Croatia as independent states, despite the strong opposition to that move by the United States. The rest of the European Community followed with their recognitions on 15 Jan. 1992. Libal, *Limits of Persuasion*: 77–87.
8 *New York Times*, 11 Dec. 1999, "Franjo Tudjman, Ex-Communist General Who Led Croatia's Secession, Is Dead at 77." The territory had been incorporated as parts of Croatia in 1941 when as a protectorate of Germany and Italy it recovered its medieval independence during the Second World War. It is believed that Tudjman and Miloševic met several times during 1991 to discuss the partition of Bosnia.
9 Clarke, *Against All Enemies: Inside America's War on Terror – What Really Happened*, 138–40.
10 Sean Michael Maloney, *The Hindrance of Military Operations Ashore: Canadian Participation in Operation Sharp Guard, 1993–1996*, 3–11, 52–3.
11 This authority was reaffirmed by UNSC Resolution 820 of 17 April 1993.
12 Vice-Admiral G.R. Maddison, "Operations in the Adriatic," *Canadian Naval Review*, vol. 2, no. 1 (spring 2006), 25–7.
13 Can., DND, Memo to CDS, "HMCS *Onondaga: Operation Sharp Guard*," 10 Aug. 1993, referred to in Maloney, *The Hindrance of Military Operations Ashore*, 31.
14 Maloney, *The Hindrance of Military Operations Ashore*, passim.
15 Regional Headquarters Allied Forces Southern Europe, AFSOUTH Fact sheets, updated: 18 Aug. 2003.
16 U.S.A. Department of State, "UN Sanctions against Belgrade: Lessons Learned for Future Regimes," Interagency Task Force on Serbian Sanctions, Washington, D.C., June 1996: 1–3.
17 Richard Garfield, "Economic sanctions on Yugoslavia," *The Lancet*, 18 Aug. 2001, vol. 358, Issue 9281, 580.
18 ATI DND (25 May 1993), memo to MND, "Sanctions Against the Federal Republic of Yugoslavia: Deployment of HMCS *Algonquin* to the Adriatic;" quoted in Maloney, *The Hindrance of Military Operations Ashore*, 23.
19 David Owen, *Balkan Odyssey*, 125.
20 Richard Holbrooke, *To End a War*, 88.
21 Charles Ingrao, "Western Intervention in Bosnia: Operation *Deliberate Force*," in Bruce A. Elleman and S.C.M. Paine, eds., *Naval Coalition Warfare: From the Napoleonic War to Operation Iraqi Freedom*, 175–7.
22 Quoted in Holbrooke, *To End a War*, 73.
23 OAS, AG/RES. 1080 (XXI-O/91) *Representative Democracy*, Resolution adopted at the fifth plenary session, held on 5 June 1991.
24 Harold P. Klepak, "Cuba and Haiti, Test Cases for Canada, but Tests of What?" *International Journal*, vol. 61, no. 3 (2005–06): 677–98.
25 Elizabeth Gibbons, *Sanctions in Haiti: Human Rights and Democracy Under Assault*, 9–46, 72.
26 Laura J. Higgins, *Canadian Naval Operations in the 1990's: Selected Case Studies*, 127–35; Doxey, *United Nations Sanctions*, 22.

27 UN S/1995/470, Secretary General to President of Security Council, 9 June 1995.
28 NATO, AFSOUTH Fact Sheet: *Significant Events*; Charles Ingrao, "Western Intervention in Bosnia": 177–81.
29 Jutta Pazulla, "The Long, Difficult Road to Dayton: Peace Efforts in Bosnia-Herzegovina," *International Journal*, vol. 60, no. 1, 2004–5: 255–72.
30 Summary of the Dayton Peace Agreement on Bosnia-Herzegovina, Released by the Department of State 30 Nov. 1995. http://www.pbs.org/newshour/bb/bosnia/dayton_peace.html
31 NATO, AFSOUTH Fact Sheet: *Operation Sharp Guard.*
32 Mark Lowen, "Bosnia Nears Political Crisis Point," BBC *News*, 23 Feb. 2010, 14:31:54 GMT.
33 Paul Heinbecker, *Getting Back in the Game: A Foreign Policy Playbook for Canada*, 250.
34 U.S. Department of State, *Rambouillet Agreement, Interim Agreement for Peace and Self-Government in Kosovo*, n.d. (ca March 1999). Failure may have occurred because the proposed terms were heavily prejudiced against Belgrade – applying a formula similar to that establishing a devolved Scottish parliament in 1997 while retaining the full representation of Scotland at Westminster. Miron Rezun's observation is that the talks were intended to fail so that the Serbs could be taught again to respect NATO air power. Rezun, *Europe's Nightmare: The Struggle for Kosovo*, 53.
35 NATO, AFSOUTH Fact Sheet: *Significant Events;* Andrew L. Stigler, "Coalition warfare over Kosovo," in Bruce A. Elleman and Sarah C.M. Paine, eds, *Naval Coalition Warfare: From the Napoleonic War to Operation Iraqi Freedom*, 182–92.
36 David Harland, "Kosovo and the UN," *Survival*, IISS, vol. 52, no. 5 (Oct.–Nov. 2010): 75–98.
37 According to an account by Lieutenant-Colonel David L. Bashow and others, "the Serb Integrated Air Defence System proved to be both robust and redundant. The opposing fireworks of enemy AAA [Anti-Aircraft Artillery] ground fire and SA3 and SA6 surface-to-air missile launches accompanied virtually all missions flown into Kosovo and Serbia ... While possessing only two percent of the combat aircraft involved in the campaign, Canadian aircraft flew in nearly ten percent of the Battlefield Air Interdiction (BAI) missions, arguably amongst the highest risk and most significant missions of the war." The campaign was prolonged because "NATO did not follow its own doctrine in terms of the decisive application of air power, that is, overwhelming use of force as opposed to carefully meted-out penny-size packages designed to progressively test Serbian resolve." Lieutenant-Colonel David L. Bashow et al., "Mission Ready: Canada's Role in the Kosovo Air Campaign," *Canadian Military Journal*, spring 2000: 55–61.
38 Paul T. Mitchell, *Network-Centric Warfare: Coalition Operations in the Age of US Military Primacy*, 23.
39 David Cortright and George A. Lopez, *The Sanctions Decade: Assessing UN Strategies in the 1990*, 67–8, 76.
40 United Nations Security Council, S/1996/776, 24 Sept. 1996, "Report of the Copenhagen Round Table on United Nations Sanctions in the Case of the former Yugoslavia, held at Copenhagen on 24 and 25 June 1996," paragraphs 1 and 2.
41 Ibid., paragraphs 78, 80, 82, 95.
42 Larry Minear, *Towards More Humane and Effective Sanctions Management: Enhancing the Capacity of the United Nations System* (1998): United Nations, A/50/60, Boutros Boutros-Ghali, *Supplement to an Agenda for Peace*, 3 Jan. 1995;

Peter Walker, "Sanctions: A Blunt Weapon," Red Cross, Red Crescent, no. 3, 1995; Eric Hoskins, "A Study of UNICEF's Perspective on Sanctions," consultant's report, Jan. 1997.

43 Richard J. Aldrich, "America Used Islamists to Arm the Bosnian Muslims: The Srebrenica Report Reveals the Pentagon's Role in a Dirty War," *Guardian*, 22 April 2002; Maloney, *The Hindrance of Miiitary Operations Ashore*, 52–3; Cortright and Lopez, *The Sanctions Decade*, 65. Yossef Bodansky also shows evidence to support a thesis that the Clinton administration was prepared to accept an Islamist revolution in Egypt as the price for Muslim co-operation in Bosnia and Croatia: *Bin Laden, the Man Who Feclared War on America*: 212–27.

44 Lloyd Axworthy, "Canada and Human Security: The Need for Leadership," *International Journal*, vol. 52, no. 2 (1996–97): 183–96.

45 United Nations General Assembly, *2005 World Summit Outcome*, Para. 138–9; S/PRST/2003/27, 15 Dec. 2003 (S/PRST/2010/25), Annex, *Protection of Civilians in Armed Conflict*, Aide Mémoire: For the consideration of issues pertaining to the protection of civilians in armed conflict; *New York Times*, 11 March 2012, Letter, Gareth Evans, Melbourne, "In Defense of 'R2P.'" Gareth Evans is a former foreign minister of Australia, co-chair of the New York–based Global Center for the Responsibility to Protect, and author of "The Responsibility to Protect: Ending Mass Atrocity Crimes Once and For All."

46 Canada, Department of Foreign Affairs and International Trade, *Human Security: Safety for People in a Changing World*, Ottawa: DFAIT, April 1999: 5; Joseph Jockel and Joel Sokolsky, "Lloyd Axworthy's Legacy: Human Security and the Rescue of Canadian Defence Policy," *International Journal*, vol. 56, no. 1 (2000–01): 1–18; Mitchell, *Network-Centric Warfare*, 22. UN Resolution 1973 in March 2011, which authorized and triggered the international effort to stop Colonel Gaddafi of Libya committing genocide against the Libyan population that sought his ouster suggests that in some circumstances at any rate the new order is superseding the old.

47 Maloney, *The Hindrance of Military Operations Ashore*, 54–5.

CHAPTER TEN

1 Can., Commons, SCNDVA, *Maritime Sovereignty*, November 1990, 2.
2 Robert E. Hunter, "Managing the North Atlantic Alliance," in Ann-Sofie Dahl and Norman Hillmer, *Activism and (Non) Alignment*, 4; International Court of Justice, "Case Concerning Delimitation of the Maritime Boundary in the Gulf of Maine Area," Judgment of 12 October 1984.
3 Laurence M. Hickey, "The Submarine as a Tool of Maritime Enforcement," *Integrated Coastal Zone Management* (spring 2000): 118–22. The two operations were code-named *Ambuscade* and *Grouse*. See Whitby, "'Doin' the Biz': Canadian Submarine Patrol Operations against Soviet SSBNs, 1983–87," in Bernd Horne, ed., *Fortune Favours the Brave*, 323. The Hague line is so called because the demarcation was effected by a judgment of 12 Oct. 1984 at the World Court.
4 Can., Commons, SCNDVA, *Maritime Sovereignty*, 53–54.
5 James D. Kiras, "Maritime Command, National Missions, and Naval Identity," in Michael Hadley, Rob Huebert, and Fred Crickard, *A Nation's Navy*: 339–50.
6 See *Globe and Mail*, Toronto, 10, 14–6, 22, 27, 29 March 1995; 1, 7, 17 April; and *The Times of London*, 11, 15–17, 27–31 March; 7, 12, 15, 17 April. See also Peter Davies, "The EC/Canadian Fisheries Dispute in the Northwest Atlantic," *International and Comparative Law Quarterly*, vol. 44, no. 4 (Oct. 1995): 927–38;

and Jennifer L. Bailey, "Hot Fish and (Bargaining) Chips," *Journal of Peace Research*, vol. 33 (Aug. 1996): 257–62.
7 Europe, no. 6434, 6/7 March 1995; *European Report*, no. 2022, 8 March 1995. See Donald Barry, "The Canada-European Union Turbot War: Internal Politics and Transatlantic Bargaining," *International Journal*, vol. 53, no. 2 (1997–98): 253–84.
8 Tobin's critics have accused him of stirring up a hornets' nest and courting nationalist reactions from the Canadian public, to support a bid to succeed Chrétien as prime minister.
9 Can., Federal Court Judgment, 26 July 2005, Docket T-1602-95, Jose Pereira E. Hijos, S.A. and Enrique Davila Gonzalez (Plaintiffs) and The Attorney General of Canada.
10 Peter T. Haydon, *Canadian Naval Future: A Necessary Long-Term Planning Framework*, Nov. 2004, 13.
11 The *Estai*'s owners were awarded demurrage costs, but in all other respects the action was dismissed with each party paying its own legal costs.
12 Hunter, "Managing the North Atlantic Alliance," 4.
13 Hickey, "The Submarine as a Tool of Maritime Enforcement," 118; and "Gob Smacked," *Maclean's*, "Maclean's Readers Respond," 8 Nov. 2004.
14 Captain Phil Webster, "Arctic Sovereignty, Submarine Operations and Water Space Management," *Canadian Naval Review*, vol. 3, no. 3 (fall 2007): 14–16.
15 Roy MacLaren, *The Fundamental Things Apply*, 205.
16 See Nicholas Tracy, *The Enforcement of Canada's Continental Maritime Jurisdiction*; *The Diplomatic Utility of Canada's Naval Forces*; *Canada's Naval Strategy, Rooted in Experience*, Maritime Security Occasional Paper No. 1, 1995; and letter of 3 April 1995 to the Rt. Hon. Jean Chrétien.
17 International Court of Justice, 4 Dec. 1998, Press Release 1998/41, *Case concerning Fisheries Jurisdiction (Spain v. Canada)*: Court declares that it has no jurisdiction to adjudicate upon the dispute. Denis Stairs has pointed out the hypocrisy of the reservation in the context of Canadian claims to value the rule of law. Denis Stairs, "Myths, Morals, and Reality in Canadian Foreign Policy," *International Journal*, vol. 58, no. 2 (2002–03): 239–56, at 249.
18 MacLaren, *Fundamental Things Apply*, 205.
19 Barry, "The Canada-European Union Turbot War."
20 The Coast Guard remained a civilian service, and in an editorial published in the *Toronto Star* in October 2003, Senator Colin Kenny, chairman of the Committee, expressed concern that "the Canadian navy is not defending our coasts – other than assisting with surveillance – and that the navy has no jurisdiction over interior waters, such as the Great Lakes. The navy prefers to do its defending on waters far away. We learned that, despite its name, the Canadian Coast Guard does not guard Canada's coasts. Nor does it guard our interior waters." G.D. MacDonald, "A Better Fit: The Canadian Coast Guard under National Defence: Safety, Security and Sovereignty Enhanced," Canadian Forces College, 2004; and Senator Colin Kenny, "A Porous Coastal Defence," *Toronto Star*, 29 Oct. 2003, 1.
21 Can., DFO, "Breaking New Ground: An Action Plan for Rebuilding the Grand Banks Fisheries," Report of the Advisory Panel on the Sustainable Management of Straddling Fish Stocks in the Northwest Atlantic, 1 Sept. 2005.
22 Can., DFO, "Canada Achieves Major Reforms at Historic Meeting of the Northwest Atlantic Fisheries Organization," 22 Sept. 2006.

CHAPTER ELEVEN

1 U.S.A., House of Representatives Committee on Armed Services, Hearings on National Defense Authorization, 102nd Congress, 1st Series, 1991, Department of the Navy, Lawrence Garrett, *Fiscal Years 1992–93 Report to Congress*, 21 Feb. 1991: 7 (p. 312).
2 Norman Friedman, *Seapower as Strategy: Navies and National Interests*, 219–25.
3 Can., DND, "Report of the Somalia Commission of Inquiry," and Lt Cmdr Matthew F. Plaschka, "The Proposed Amphibious Ship Purchase: A Strategic Misstep," in Ann Griffiths and Kenneth Hansen, eds., *Marines: Is an Amphibious Capability Relevant for Canada?* 93.
4 Laura Higgins, *Canadian Naval Operations in the 1990's: Selected Case Studies*, 49–56.
5 G.L Garnett, "The Future of Maritime Peacekeeping," in Fred Crickard, *Maritime Security Working Papers*, no. 3, 3.
6 Can., DND, Maritime Command, *Adjusting Course: A Naval Strategy for Canada*; Aaron Jackson, *Keystone Doctrine Development in Five Commonwealth Navies: A Comparative Perspective*, 19; Jason Delaney, "Submarine Procurement and the *Victoria*-class Acquisition," 22–7; Julie Ferguson, *Deeply Canadian: New Submarines for a New Millennium*, 187–8.
7 CBC News, "Navy technicians blew submarine's electrical system: report," 14 May 2006; *Saanich News*, 19 April 2011, "HMCS Victoria returns to sea." Norman Friedman reports that the *Victoria* class was the first in the world to be equipped with a full remote control periscope and the first to have it fully integrated into the Command Data System, *The Naval Institute Guide to World Naval Weapon Systems*, 689.
8 Douglas Bland, *Campaigns for International Security*, 117, 122–38; Can., DND, *White Paper on Defence*, Ottawa, 1994, 31.
9 Deputy Minister Jim Judd, and General J.M.G. Baril, chief of the defence staff, *Shaping the Future of Canadian Defence: A Strategy for 2020*, Can., DND, June 1999.
10 Major Thomas Rippon, Commodore Roger Girouard, and Eliot Lowery, "Leadership for a Sustainable Culture of Peace: The UN Mission in East Timor," *Canadian Military Journal*, vol. 5, no. 3 (autumn 2004).
11 Comment to author by Commander Steve Thompson, who was *Protecteur*'s executive officer at the time, 12 Oct. 2011.
12 Higgins, *Canadian Naval Operations in the 1990's*, 49–56.
13 Can., DND, "Canada's contribution to the Arabian Gulf continues," 7 Dec. 2000. See Maloney, *War with Iraq: Canada's Strategy in the Persian Gulf, 1990–2002*, 48–54; and John H. Noer, "The Roles of Navies in the 21st Century," in Ann Griffiths, Peter Haydon, and Richard Gimblett, *Canadian Gunboat Diplomacy: The Canadian Navy and Foreign Policy*, 341–2; and Can., DND, *Backgrounder*, "Canadian Navy Ships Integrated into US Naval Forces for Operations in the Persian Gulf (Arabian Gulf)" nd.

YEAR	SHIP	MONTHS	U.S. NAVAL FORCES
1997	HMCS *Regina*	Feb.–Aug.	U.S. Surface Task Group
1998	HMCS *Ottawa*	June–Dec.	USS Araham Lincoln Carrier Battle Group
1999	HMCS *Regina*	June–Dec.	USS Constellation Carrier Battle Group

2000	HMCS *Calgary*	June–Nov.	U.S. Surface Task Group
2001	HMCS *Charlottetown*	Jan.–July	USS Harry S. Truman Carrier Battle Group
2001	HMCS *Winnipeg*	March–Sept.	USS Constellation Carrier Battle Group

14 Higgins, *Canadian Naval Operations in the 1990's*, 68–9.
15 Vice-Admiral G.L. Garnett, *Strategic Capability Planning for the Canadian Forces*, Can., DND, 2000, 8.
16 Briefing Note for the Minister of National Defence, Canadian Forces Maritime Experimental and Test Ranges, ADM Policy, National Defence, 12 June 1997, quoted in John Clearwater, *Just Dummies: Cruise Missile Testing in Canada*, 200–1.
17 Fred R. Fowlow, "Nanoose Bay – Let's Get The Facts Straight," *Starshell*, vol. 7, no. 7 (summer issue); "Canada and US renew agreement on shared use of Nanoose Bay Test Ranges," National Defence and the Canadian Forces, NR-99.276 –Dec. 17, 1999; John Clearwater, "Naval nuclear weapons at CFMETR Nanoose, 1965–2001," The ACTivist Magazine, 29 July 2004.
18 Can., DND News Item, BG-01.035a, 10 Dec. 2001.
19 Richard Gimblett, *Operation Apollo: The Golden Age of the Canadian Navy in the War against Terrorism*, 16.
20 With the continued support of Anglo-American air and special forces, the Northern Alliance captured Kabul on 13 November, and on 20 December the Security Council agreed to Resolution 1386 authorizing for six months the dispatch of an international security force to Afghanistan.
21 Can., DND News Item, BG-01.035a, 10 Dec. 2001; Robert J. Schneller, "Operation Enduring Freedom, Coalition Warfare from the Sea and on the Sea," in Bruce Elleman and Sarah C.M. Paine, eds., *Naval Coalition Warfare: From the Napoleonic War to Operation Iraqi Freedom*: 193–207.
22 Jane Taber, "Ottawa Will Spend $300-million to Close Camp Mirage," *Globe and Mail*, Toronto, 4 Nov. 2010, 8:15PM EDT.
23 The 1990 deployment had been labelled "Operation Friction," and subsequent deployments had each been given their own name, "Flag," "Barrier," "Deliverance," "Promenade," "Tranquillity," "Prevention," "Determination," "Mercator," and "Augmentation."
24 Can., DND, Directorate of Strategic Analysis, Policy Planning Division, Policy Group, Elizabeth Speed, et. al., "Strategic Assessment 2001," Ottawa, Sept. 2001.
25 See Stanley Hoffmann, "On the War," *New York Review of Books*, vol. 48, no. 17 (1 Nov. 2001): 4–6. At the news conference on 26 May 2006, President George W. Bush went so far as to admit that the abuse of prisoners under interrogation at Abu Ghraib prison in Iraq was a major mistake for which the United States was paying a heavy price, and the extra-legal detention of prisoners at a detention facility established at Guantanamo Bay in Cuba continued to be one of the few points of real disagreement amongst the Anglo-American allies. The refusal of the Harper administration to intervene in the military trial of the Canadian child soldier Omar Khadr for murder in 2010 marks it as the only western nation to do so. CBC "Omar Khadr sentenced to symbolic 40 years," 31 Oct. 2010. The prisoner of war issue resurfaced in 2010, when the governments in Ottawa and London came under intense criticism for permitting the transfer of prisoners taken in Afghanistan to cruel treatment by the Afghan secret police. The speaker of the Canadian House, Peter Milliken, made a historic ruling on 27 April 2010 that a

government refusal to release to parliament unredacted documents relating to the charges would constitute contempt of parliament. After nearly two months of negotiations it was agreed that a sworn committee of members of Parliament would have access to the files and that a panel of experts would determine what and how they should be released to the House and to the public "without compromising national security." That formula will protect "cabinet confidentiality," and will also protect the foreign sources of information. It will not, however, enable the public to gauge the conduct of the government. CBC News, "Milliken OK's Afghan records deal," 17 June 2010.

26 The expression was attributed to François Ducros: see "Canadian official called Bush 'a moron,'" *CBC News*, 12:54 PM ET, 26 Nov. 2002: *Globe and Mail*, Toronto, 15 April 2002: 1. Subsequently, the review was downgraded to an invitation to the Canadian public to express its views at "town hall" meetings and in letters to the minister.

27 "In the Matter of the Potential Use of Armed Force by the UK against Iraq and in the matter of reliance for that use of force on United Nations Security Council Resolution 1441," http://www.cnduk.org/briefing/opinion.htm. See: Michael Byers, "War, Law, and Geopolitical Change: The Lessons of History," *International Journal*, vol. 61, no. 1 (2005–06): 201–3.

28 See 03Ottawa49, Michael Gallagher to Secretary Rumsfeld, Ottawa, 2003 01 09 13:13; and 03Ottawa747, Deputy Chief of Mission Stephen R. Kelly [to State Department], 2003 03 17 23:54, *Wikileaks*.

29 "Canada won't join military action against Iraq without another UNSC resolution," 03Ottawa773, Deputy Chief of Mission Stephen R. Kelly [to State Department], 2003-03-19 15:24, *Wikileaks*. See also "Canada-Iraq: What Now? 03Ottawa917, Ambassador Paul Cellucci [to Secretary of State], 2003-03-28 22:31, *Wikileaks*

30 John Holmes, *Life with Uncle: The Canadian-American Relationship*, 26, and Paul Cellucci, *Unquiet Diplomacy*, 131–46.

31 Canadian Press Newswire, 11 April 2003.

32 Richard Gimblett, "The Transformation Era: 1990 to the Present"; David B. Crist, "The Formation of a Coalition of the Willing and Operation *Iraqi Freedom*," in Elleman and Paine, eds., *Naval Coalition Warfare*: 209–18.

33 Allan English, *Beware of Putting the Cart Before the Horse: Network Enabled Operations as a Canadian Approach to Transformation*.

34 Paul Cellucci, Speech, Economic Club of Toronto, 25 March, 2003. See also Tim Harper, "US Ambassador Paul Cellucci," *International Journal*, vol. 58, no. 4 (2002–03): 711–20.

35 CBC, 16 May 2011, Greg Weston, "Canada offered to aid Iraq invasion: WikiLeaks."

36 Private archives, correspondence of the author with Honourable John McCallum, minister of defence, Aug.–Oct. 2002, concerning the employment of Canadian special forces and the duty to report to parliament; CBC, 15 July 2005, "JTF2: Canada's Super-Secret Commandos"; 18 Jan. 2011, "JTF2 command 'encouraged' war crimes, soldier alleges"; 30 April 2008, "Ex-commando arrested day before JTF2 tell-all hits bookstores." In 2006 the Canadian Special Operations Forces Command was stood up. In 2010 questions began to be asked about the extent to which Canadian Special Forces had been incorporated into an American command structure that interfered with Canadian rules of engagement and obstructed Canadian servicemen from passing their concerns up the chain to any Canadian authority.

37 Melanie Graham, "Interoperability and Integration: Blessing or Curse?" Robert Edwards and Graham Walker, eds., *Continental Security: Maritime Perspectives, Challenges and Opportunitie*: 61–73.
38 Holmes, *Life with Uncle*, 99.
39 Dan Arsenault and Barry Dorey, "Bush in Halifax: Thousands March in Peaceful Opposition," *Halifax Herald*, 2 Dec. 2004. George W. Bush, "Remarks on US and Canada Relations and the War on Terrorism," delivered 1 Dec. 2004, Halifax, Nova Scotia, Canada, *American Rhetoric, On-Line Speech Bank*.
40 English, *Beware of Putting the Cart*; Joe Sharpe and Allan English, "Network Enabled Operations: The Experiences of Senior Canadian Commanders." Defence Research and Development Canada – Toronto, report CR 2006-112, 31 March 2006: 29–34.
41 Danford Middlemiss and Denis Stairs, "The Canadian Forces and the Doctrine of Interoperability: The Issues," *Policy Matters*, vol. 3, no. 7 (June 2002).
42 "Canada invests in US satellite system," *Vancouver Sun*, 27 Oct. 2011.
43 Paul Mitchell and Peter Haydon, *Network-Centric Warfare: Coalition Operations in the Age of US Military Primacy*, 72.
44 Duncan Miller, "Editorial: NATO Transformation: Good for NATO, Good for Canada?" *Canadian Naval Review*, vol. 2, no. 1 (spring 2006): 2–5; Sean Maloney, "'To secure the command of the sea': NATO command organization and naval planning for the cold war at sea, 1945–1954," Master's thesis, University of New Brunswick, 1992, 144; and communication from Commander Steve Thompson, 12 Oct. 2011. See Can., DEA, *Documents on Canadian External Relations*, vol. 15, 396, chap. 4, North Atlantic Security, "Implementation of the North Atlantic Treaty."
45 Can., DND, *Charting the Course from Leadmark*, 35.
46 Dwight N. Mason, "Canadian–American North American Defence Alliance in 2005," *International Journal*, vol. 60, no. 2 (2004–05): 385–96.
47 Agreement Between the Government of Canada and the Government of the United States of America on the North American Aerospace Defense Command, signed 12 May 2006 by Gordon O'Connor, minister of national defence, for the Government of Canada, and by David H. Wilkins, the U.S. ambassador to Canada.
48 Patrick Lennox, "Interoperability: The New Frontier," *Canadian Naval Review*, vol. 3, no. 3 (autumn 2007), 103.
49 Gimblett, "The Transformation Era"; and see David Morse, "Standing Naval Force Atlantic (SNFL) 1999–2000," *Canadian Naval Review*, vol. 2, no. 1 (spring 2006): 27–30.
50 Can., DND, *Canada's International Policy Statement, A Role of Pride and Influence in the World*, Ottawa, 2005: 13.
51 Stephen Thorne, "Movers & Shakers: Rick Hillier," *International Journal*, vol. 60, no. 3 (2004–05): 824–30.
52 Can., DND, Douglas Young, "Report to the Prime Minister on the Leadership and Management of the Canadian Forces," 25 March 1997.
53 Major-General Daniel Gosselin has noted in a recent article that "because Canada was not expected to engage independently in overseas military commitments, the CF never fully developed the command organizational structure necessary to ensure coordination with government policy, to provide strategic guidance and direction from a central defence authority, and to nationally command the deployed forces ... [General] Hillier's vision ... was to change this 'colonial' mindset and to establish a higher command organization that could think in strategic terms for

Canada, and would be suited to the particular needs of the CF." Daniel Gosselin, "Hellyer's Ghosts: Unification of the Canadian Forces Is 40 Years Old," *Canadian Military Journal*, vol. 9, nos. 2, 3 (nd). See also Bland, *Campaigns for International Security*, 141–51.

54 Douglas Bland, *Chiefs of Defence: Government and the Unified Command of the Canadian Armed Forces*, 122–4.
55 Gosselin, "Hellyer's Ghosts."
56 Michael Byers, "Is Hillier out of line?" *TheStar.com*, 20 Feb. 2007. Chiefs of defence staff are appointed by the governor in council and retain their position so long as they retain the confidence of the prime minister, although the CDS normally reports through the minister of national defence.
57 Bob Davidson, "Modern Naval Diplomacy – A Practitioner's View," *Journal of Military and Strategic Studies*, vol. 11, nos. 1 and 2 (fall and winter 2008–09): 5, 35. Note by Steve Thompson, 12 Oct. 2011.
58 David Morse, "The Canadian Naval Task Group," in Griffiths, *Canadian Gunboat Diplomacy*, 284–6, 288.
59 BBC *News*, 19 Nov. 2008, "India 'sinks Somali pirate ship.'"
60 Davidson, "Modern Naval Diplomacy," 11–12.
61 Dr Stanley Weeks, "The 100-ship Navy Global Maritime Partnership Initiative," Synot Lecture, in Andrew Forbes and Michelle Lovi, eds., *Australian Maritime Issues 2006*: 27–36; and the November 2005 issue of the U.S. Naval Institute *Proceedings*.
62 Devrm Yayiali, "Turkish Bulk Carrier Hijacked off Somalia," *Bosphorus Naval News*, 30 Oct. 2008.
63 "China's Three-Point Naval Strategy," *Strategic Comments*, International Institute for Strategic Studies, vol. 16, comment 37, 15 Oct. 2010; Leah Aberitt, "Chinese Hospital Ships and Soft Power," *Semaphore*, Issue 03, April 2011, Sea Power Centre, Australia.
64 *Lloyd's List*, David Osler, 29 Jan. 2010, "China to co-ordinate patrols off Somalia – Beijing commits to permanent deployment in transit corridor"; Doug Thomas, "Warship Developments: The Chinese Navy," *Canadian Naval Review*, vol. 5, no. 1 (spring 2009): 38–9. See Stuart Palliser, *Salt Water Thieves: Policy Reforms to Address Somali Piracy*.
65 "Canadian navy frigate deploys on 6-month counter terrorism mission," *Canadian Press*, 26 Oct. 2009.
66 MARPAC's *In Focus*, 30 July 2008, Christian Bedford, "Piracy in Somalia: Why solutions can't be found at sea"; Can., DND, *News Release*, CEFCOM NR 08.030, 19 Aug. 2008, "HMCS Ville de Québec starts World Food Programme escort mission."
67 *Cable News Network*, 27 July 2010, "Seychelles convicts 11 Somali pirates."
68 Jean Sutton, *Lords of the East: The East India Company and Its Ships*, 88–92.
69 *Strategy Page*, 3 Feb. 2010, "Pirates Feast on Gamblers"; BBC *News*, 05 Feb. 2010 "Nato troops free ship off Somalia after pirate attack."
70 *Newser*, 5 Jan. 2010 [*Wall Street Journal*], Rob Quinn, "Ships Take Up Arms Against Pirates – Maritime tradition fades amid rise in attacks."
71 *Lloyd's List*, 25 Jan. 2010, Richard Meade, "UK government seeks to deter use of armed guards onboard."
72 *In Focus*, "Tightening the Noose: Time for a New Approach against Somali Pirates?" Office of the Asia-Pacific Advisor, Maritime Forces Pacific, 17 June 2011.
73 *Reuters: Africa*, "EU faces warship shortage for Somali piracy mission," 23 Nov.

2011, 6:39 GMT; *Defensemanagement.com*, "Merchant ships 'can use armed guards,'" 31 Oct. 2011.
74 *defenceWeb*, "Shippers mull armed guard ramifications," 23 Nov. 2011 14:26; *Defense News*, 6 Dec. 2011, UK ships' armed guards rules set.
75 Task Group commander was Captain Art McDonald, with Commanders Peter Crain and Josée Kurtz commanding *Athabaskan* and *Halifax*. Virginia Beaton, "International Stories: Naval task group assists in Haiti relief effort," Canadian Navy website, ca 19 Jan. 2010.
76 Milan N. Vego, *Naval Strategy and Operations in Narrow Seas*, 184; Lt Cmdr Jon Allsopp, *Beyond JSS: Analyzing Canada's Amphibious Requirement*, Canadian Forces College, CSC 33, Master of Defence Studies research paper.
77 Can., DND, *Charting the Course from Leadmark*, 26.
78 Lt Cmdr Matthew F. Plaschka, "The Proposed Amphibious Ship Purchase: A Strategic Misstep," in Griffiths and Hansen, eds., *Marines: Is an Amphibious Capability Relevant for Canada?*, 81.
79 Can., DND, Canadian Armed Forces Website, Mary Ellen Green, "Canadian commodore takes top sea job at multinational exercise."
80 Ambassador David Wilkins to Secretary of State, Ref. 05Ottawa3105, 17 Oct. 2005 22:07, *Wikileaks*.
81 09Ottawa840, Ambassador David Jacobson to Secretary of State, 2009 11 03 20:36, *Wikileaks*; Slt Jonathan Douglas, "From the Arctic to the Caribbean," and "HMCS *Corner Brook* Returns from Caribbean," in *Canadian Navy*, News and Events, autumn 2009, and 4 Jan. 2001–; Stockwell Day, "Canadian navy plays a part in big Caribbean drug bust," BCLocalNews.Com, 27 Feb. 2011.
82 http://www.jiatfs.southcom.mil/index.aspx
83 Davidson, "Modern Naval Diplomacy – A Practitioner's View," 9–10.

CHAPTER TWELVE

1 Matthew Carnaghan and Allison Goody, *Canadian Arctic Sovereignty*, Parliamentary Information and Research Service: Political and Social Affairs Division, 26 January 2006; Arctic Council and the International Arctic Science Committee, *Impacts of a Warming Arctic: Arctic Climate Impact Assessment*, Cambridge University Press, Cambridge, 2004; Office of Naval Research, Naval Ice Center, Oceanographer of the Navy, and the Arctic Research Commission, "Naval Operations in an Ice-Free Arctic," Symposium, April 2001; Institute of the North, US Arctic Research Commission, and International Arctic Science Committee, Arctic Marine Transport Workshop, 2004: 5; Kristin Bartenstein, "Flag-Planting: What Legal Framework Governs the Division of the Arctic Continental Shelf," *International Journal*, vol. 65, no. 1 (winter 2009–10): 187–207.
2 Paul Reynolds, "The Arctic's New Gold Rush," BBC *News*, 25 Oct. 2005.
3 UN, Chronological lists of ratifications of, accessions and successions to the Convention and the related Agreements as at 4 May 2009.
4 Professor emeritus of political science and George Ignatieff Chair Emeritus of Peace and Conflict Studies at the University of Toronto.
5 Franklyn Griffiths, "The Shipping News, Canada's Arctic Sovereignty not on Thinning Ice," *International Journal*, vol. 58, no. 2, 2002–03: 257–82.
6 See Jack L. Granatstein, "Does the Northwest Passage still matter? The shrinking Arctic icecap may soon ease Canada's sovereignty problem," *Globe and Mail*, 12 Jan. 2008.

7 Andrea Charron, "The Northwest Passage: Is Canada's Sovereignty Floating Away?" *International Journal*, vol. 60, no. 3 (summer 2005), 847.
8 Chris Wattie, "US Sub May Have Toured Canadian Arctic Zone," *National Post*, 19 Dec. 2005: A1.
9 Ambassador David Jacobson to Secretary of State, Para. 8, Comment: "Canada places great import on its Arctic partnership with the United States and at this juncture the Conservatives in particular see special value in enhancing that partnership. Not only is that partnership materially significant for Canada, which benefits greatly from American resources invested in Arctic science and in defence infrastructure, but also Canada has much to gain from leveraging the stature and standing of the United States. Amongst the Arctic coastal states (and perhaps amongst all countries) Canada and the United States typically have the most closely aligned policy interests and generally share a common viewpoint on international law and common objectives in multilateral fora (such as the Arctic Council). From Canada's point of view, if the two countries can find bilateral common-ground on Arctic issues, the chance for Canadian success is much greater than going it alone against the interests of other countries or groups of countries." Ref: 10Ottawa29, 21 Jan. 2010, 16:52, *Wikileaks*; CBC, 12 May 2011, "WikiLeaks: US dismisses Harper's Arctic talk." See also: Ambassador David Wilkins to Secretary of State, 06Ottawa1904, 19 June 2006, *Wikileaks*.
10 Can., DFAIT, "Canada and Denmark Issue Statement on Hans Island," 19 Sept. 2005; "Canada and Denmark Sign Arctic Cooperation Arrangement," 14 May 2010.
11 EU commissioner Borg, "Opportunities and responsibilities in the Arctic Region: The European Union's perspective," 11 March 2009, SP09-018EN.
12 "Russia races for Arctic Resources," *Christian Science Monitor*, 31 July 2007.
13 *Reuters*, 8 Aug. 2007.
14 "Large strategic exercise in Russia," *Barents Observer*, 28 Sept. 2009.
15 BBC, Richard Galpin, "Nuclear Power at Heart of Russia's Arctic Ambition," 21 Sept. 2010.
16 "Russia's new Arctic force to focus on border protection," *RIA Novosti*, 30 March 2009; "Russia Launches Arctic expedition, beefs up military presence," *Montreal Gazette*, 6 July 2011; "Russia to build up submarine task force along Northern Sea Route," *RIA Novosti*, 10 Nov. 2011, 3:23.
17 "First Antarctic voyage for South Korean icebreaker," Kris Molle, PCO [Polar Conservation Organisation], 13 Jan. 2010, 02:41 PM; "Araon," Kopri [Korean Polar Research Institute]; "Chinese ice breaker back to Zhongshan Station on Antarctica with supplies," *People's Daily Online*, 24 Feb. 2008, 11:25; "China Sets Sail for the Arctic," Agence France-Presse (AFP) 29 June 2010.
18 Randy Boswell, "China moves to become major Arctic player," Canwest News Service, *Vancouver Sun*, 1 March 2010. Linda Jakobson is director of the SIPRI Programme on China and Global Security.
19 Franklyn Griffiths, "Where Vision and Illusion Meet," in Franklyn Griffiths, ed., *Politics of the Northwest Passage*: 19.
20 Daniel Patrick O'Connell, *The Influence of Law on Sea Power*, 3.
21 Donat Pharand, "The Arctic Waters and the Northwest Passage: A Final Revisit," *Ocean Development & International Law*, vol. 38, no. 1/2, Jan.–June 2007: 3–69. Pharand lists four main reasons for concluding that the Canadian claim to historic rights over the archipelagic waters could not be supported: "First, neither the British nor Canadian explorers ever took possession of any part of the Arctic waters,

especially not those of the Northwest Passage. Second, the first official claim that the waters of the Canadian Archipelago were historic internal waters was made only in 1973. Third, as soon as Canada delineated its claim of historic waters, by providing for straight baselines around the Archipelago, the United States and EC Member States sent notes of protest. Fourth, Canada has not succeeded in subjecting all foreign ships to prior authorization to enter the Northwest Passage, in particular U.S. ships. The United States agreed in 1988 that it would request prior authorization for its icebreakers, but on the express understanding that it would not affect its refusal to recognize Canada's claim. In addition, the 1988 agreement does not affect the rights of passage of commercial vessels or government ships (warships) other than icebreakers."

22 Ambassador David Wilkins to Secretary of State, Ref: 08Ottawa1198, 12 Aug. 2008, *Wikileaks*; and see BBC, 12 May 2011, Meirion Jones and Susan Watts, "Secret US embassy cables released by Wikileaks show nations are racing to 'carve up' Arctic resources – oil, gas, and even rubies – as the ice retreats."

23 USA, National Security Presidential Directive and Homeland Security Presidential Directive, "Arctic Region Policy," 9 January 2009; CBC (*Canadian Press*), "Bush signs new Arctic policy, outlining US intentions in the North," 12 Jan. 2009, 11:00 PM ET.

24 Commander James Kraska, "A Way Out for Arctic Diplomacy," *Canadian Naval Review*, vol. 5, no. 3 (fall 2009): 17–22.

25 *Vancouver Sun*, 3 Dec. 2009.

26 Can., "Statement on Canada's Arctic Foreign Policy: Exercising Sovereignty and Promoting Canada's Northern Strategy Abroad," ca. 2010. See also *Canada's Northern Strategy: Our North, Our Heritage, Our Future*, minister of Indian affairs and northern development and federal interlocutor for Métis and non-status Indians, Ottawa, 2009. *Strategic Comments*, International Institute for Strategic Studies, "Diplomatic shifts in the warming Arctic," vol. 16, comment 50, Dec. 2010.

27 Toronto *Globe and Mail*, "Ottawa to keep tabs on large ships in northern waters," 26 Feb. 2010; Can., Department of Transport, no. H 110/09, "Legislation to protect Canada's arctic waters comes into force," 6 Aug. 2009. See Griffiths, "Shipping News."

28 *Canwest News Service*, 28 Aug. 2008.

29 Huebert, "Canadian Arctic Maritime Security: The Return to Canada's Third Ocean," *Canadian Military Journal*, vol. 8, no. 2 (summer 2007).

30 Can., Governor General, *Speech from the Throne*, 5 Oct. 2004.

31 Pierre Pettigrew, Canadian minister of foreign affairs, speech at the Northern Strategy Consultations, Round Table on Reinforcing Sovereignty, Security and Circumpolar Cooperation, "Canada's Leadership in the Circumpolar World," 22 March 2005.

32 Bob Weber, " Forces' Arctic patrol more than just an exercise," Canadian Press, Dundas Harbour, Nunavut, *Globe and Mail*, posted 21 Aug. 2006, 5:26 PM EDT

33 Peter T. Haydon, "The Chicoutimi Accident: Lessons Learned and Not Learned," *Canadian Military Journal*, vol. 6, no. 3 (autumn 2005). The fuel-cell project was intended for a possible retrofit of this class, but was abandoned when in 2000 the cost of retrofitting one of the *Victoria* class with a full air independent propulsion system, supported by the necessary ice strengthening, the enhanced life support systems, and the improved sensors and communications needed for under-ice operations, was estimated to be in excess of $300M. Dalhousie University, Centre

for Foreign Policy Studies, October 2007, "Backgrounder: Victoria Class Submarines, Northern Operations & Air Independent Propulson." On 17 June 2009 *Channel News Asia* announced that the navy of the Republic of Singapore had launched in Sweden its first *Archer* class submarine after a four-year refit that gave it an Air Independent Propulsion system. J. David Perkins, "Submarines and the Canadian Navy Today: One Man's View," and Michael Craven, "Comment of the Perkins and Webster Articles," *Canadian Naval Review*, vol. 3, no. 3 (autumn 2007): 22–5 and no. 4 (winter 2008): 28–9. The First Canadian Submarine Squadron was stood down in 1996 after thirty years of service, because of concerns about discipline that had surfaced with the court martial of Lieutenant-Commander D.C. Marsaw, and the *Victoria* class submarines were incorporated into a new formation, the Fifth Maritime Operations Group. Laurence Hickey, "Our Submarine Service: Cross-Connect Open to the Allied System," *Integrated Coastal Zone Management* (spring 2000): 118–22.

34 Canadian Armed Forces: "Operation Nanook wraps up in the Eastern Arctic"; CBC, "Mackenzie River patrol asserts Canada's Arctic presence," 29 July 2009; Canada, "Canada planning anti-sub exercises in the Arctic," Canada.com, 7 Aug. 2009; *Halifax Chronicle Herald*, "MacKay: Warmer Arctic, new challenges," 8 Aug. 2009; *Times Colonist*, "PM vows more military resources to safeguard the North," 19 Aug. 2009; *Ottawa Citizen*, "DND plans to test model of proposed Arctic patrol vessels," 19 Aug. 2009.

35 *Canadian American Strategic Review* (CASR), "Canada Announces Deepwater Port at Nanisivik on Baffin Island & Army Base at Resolute: Key Points on North-West Passage," Aug. 2007; CBC, "Preliminary work underway on High Arctic naval port," 5 Aug. 2008; *Northern News Services*, , "Navy fuel depot construction to begin in 2011," 7 Sept. 2009; *Ottawa Citizen*, 26 Nov. 2009, "Building of Canadian Forces Arctic Naval Facility Faces Delays"; CTV News (*Canadian Press*), "Arctic naval facility years from completion," 29 May 2011.

36 Can., DND, *Charting the Course from Leadmark*, 10; *CBC News*, "Arctic surveillance research moves ahead," 3 Nov. 2009; *Ottawa Citizen*, "Building of Canadian Forces Arctic Naval Facility Faces Delays," 26 Nov. 2009; information supplied by Captain Joe Sipos, 12 Oct. 2011.

37 CTV, 17 June 2009, "Navy waters down plans for Arctic patrol ships." On taking up his duties as chief of naval staff on 24 June 2009, Vice-Admiral Dean McFadden iterated his commitment to the planned construction of the Arctic patrol vessels, and the planned Joint Support Ship (JSS), *Globe and Mail*, 24 June 2009; Sharon Hobson, "Plain Talk: The Process of (Not) Acquiring Maritime Helicopters," *Canadian Naval Review*, vol. 4, no. 4 (winter 2009): 39–40; Canada: *Postmedia News*, 8 May 2012, "Armed Arctic vessels face delay in latest procurement setback."

38 Kim Richard Nossal, "Polar Icebreakers: The Politics of Inertia," in Franklyn Griffiths, *Politics of the Northwest Passage*; and Transport Canada, Zone/Date System Map and Dates of Entry Table, Shipping Safety Control Zones.

39 This commitment was renewed on 14 July 2010, with the number of ships stipulated as two, with an option for a third. Canada, DND, *Backgrounder*, "Canada Begins Joint Support Ships Procurement for the Canadian Forces," 14 July 2010. See Doug Thomas, "Responding to Disaster," *Canadian Naval Review*, vol. 1, no. 3 (autumn 2005): 31–2.

40 Chris Windeyer, "Feds to replace old icebreaker," *Nunatsiaq News*, 29 Feb. 2008; Doug Thomas, "Warship "Developments: Arctic/Offshore Patrol Ships," and "Canadian Naval Arctic Patrol Vessels," *Canadian Naval Review*, vol. 3, no. 3,

(fall 2007): 36–7 (and winter 2009). Thomas questions the need to design new ships that will not be ready for service until 2013–17.
41 CASR, Canadian Forces Aircraft, Lockheed Martin CP-140 Aurora.
42 Franklyn Griffiths, "The Northwest Passage in Transit," *International Journal*, vol. 54, no. 2, 1998–99: 189–202; "Towards a Canadian Arctic Strategy," *Canadian International Council*, 2009.
43 CBC, "Arctic seabed mapping renewed," 29 July 2009; "Military's Arctic exercise to include US, Denmark," 18 Aug. 2010; "Arctic sovereignty 'non-negotiable': Harper," 20 Aug. 2010; Bridget Hunter, "Joint U.S.-Canadian Mission Surveys Outer Edge of North America: Scientists collaborate in exploring continent's extended continental shelf," *America. Gov.*, 15 Sept. 2009; "US navy plots Arctic push," *Ottawa Citizen*, 28 Nov. 2009.

CONCLUSION

1 In March 2010 Captain Stephen W. Jordan, USN, naval attaché, USDAO, Ottawa, said to John Hattendorf, Ernest J. King professor of Maritime History at the U.S. Naval War College, that the roots of the relationship between the Canadian and U.S. navies lie "in the day-to-day maritime operations in NATO, where we have a history of sailing together side by side for over 60 years with the NATO Standing Maritime Forces – interoperability between our navies is not a new idea. This has evolved into a relationship where Canadian warships regularly operate as an equal partner in a USN Battle Group – a compliment and honor we afford no other nation (not even the UK)"; quoted in John B. Hattendorf, "Commonwealth Navies as Seen by the United States Navy, 1910–2010," Proceedings ... *From Empire to In(ter)dependence*.
2 LAC, Mackenzie King Papers, Imperial Conference, 1923, Stenographic Notes of the Fourth Meeting, ff. C62621-38 (J.L. Granatstein, *Canadian Foreign Policy: Historical Readings*, 16; and C.P. Stacey, *Historical Documents of Canada*, no. 173: 435–43). See also R. MacGregor Dawson, *William Lyon Mackenzie King: A Political Biography, 1874–1923*, 464.
3 LAC, *Mackenzie King Diary*, 23 April 1941: 366 (344).
4 U.S. Embassy, Ottawa, Canada Website, Selected Presidential Quotes on Canada, President Kennedy, Address before the Canadian Parliament, 17 May 1961.
5 Eayrs, *In Defence of Canada*, vol. 3, 321.
6 See above, page 163.
7 C.P. Stacey, "Canadian Defence Policy," *Canadian Journal of Economics and Political Science*, vol. 4, no. 4 (Nov. 1938): 490–504.
8 Canada, DND, *White Paper on Defence*, 1994.
9 Matthew Allen, "The Changing Nature of Naval Strategy," *Naval Review*, vol. 81, no. 3 (July 1993): 235–43. Canadian Press Newswire, 11 April 2003. See above, page 269.
10 CBC, Amber Hildebrandt, "Liberals feared too close ties with the US: WikiLeaks." 16 May 2011. See also: 07Ottawa819, Ambassador David Wilkins to Secretary of State, 5 July 2007 18:12, *Wikileaks*. Prior to the May 2011 general election that gave Harper a surprise majority of the House of Commons the American consul general in Halifax, Anton K. Smith, made a speaking tour in which he expressed strong support for him. Ignatieff may have been the best prime minister Canada never had, but Harper can say, with Boris Pasternak's General Yevgraf Zhivago, "I didn't think he was a better man. Besides, I've executed better men than me with a small pistol."

11 Dr Denis Stairs and Dr Danford Middlemiss, "Continental Security: The Issue and Challenges," in Robert Edwards and Graham Walker, eds., *Continental Security and Canada-U.S. Relations: Maritime Perspectives, Challenges and Opportunities*: 34–40.
12 Michael Ignatieff, "Canada in the Age of Terror: Multilateralism Meets a Moment of Truth," in Graham F. Walker, *Independence in an Age of Empire: Assessing Unilateralism and Multilateralism*, Halifax: 31–40.
13 CBC, Hildebrandt, "Liberals feared too close ties," 16 May 2011. See also 09Ottawa68, Deputy Head of Mission Terry Breese to Secretary of State, 23 Jan. 2009, 19:54, *Wikileaks*.
14 Douglas Ross, "Michael Ignatieff's Truncated View of Canadian-American Relations," in Graham Walker, *Independence in an Age of Empire*: 345–55.
15 Paul Heinbecker, *Getting Back in the Game: A Foreign Policy Playbook for Canada*, 245.
16 "Border talks 'not about sovereignty': Harper," CBC *News*, 4 Feb. 2011; "Harper and Obama eye sweeping change in border security," *Globe and Mail*, 4 Feb. 2011; Steven Chase, "Canada negotiating perimeter security deal with US," *Globe and Mail*, 8 Dec. 2010.
17 Edward Greenspon et al., *Open Canada: A Global Positioning Strategy for a Networked Age*, 88. See also Dwayne Lovegrove, "Sutherland in the 21st Century: Invariants in Canada's Policy Agenda Since 9/11," *Canadian Military Journal*, vol. 10, no. 2 (summer 2010).
18 Ignatieff, "Canada in the Age of Terror."
19 *Strategic Comments*, "NATO: more consensus, but challenges remain."
20 Harold P. Klepak, "Changing Realities and Perceptions of Military Threat," in David Dewitt and David Leyton-Brown, *Canada's International Security Policy*.
21 David G. Haglund, *The North Atlantic Triangle Revisited: Canadian Grand Strategy at Century's End*, 105.
22 Ref. to John Bartlet Brebner, *North Atlantic Triangle: The Interplay of Canada, the United States, and Great Britain*.
23 Beginning in March 2010 China's carefully tended benign image began to change following an announcement that it would regard the contested and resource rich waters of the South China Sea as an area "of vital national interest." The People's Liberation Army Navy began to patrol the area aggressively, and Beijing vigorously protested when the Japanese Maritime Self-Defence Force arrested a Chinese fishing vessel close to the Japanese-administered but contested Senkaku Islands. The protest was backed up with a temporary embargo on the export of rare earths used in electronics manufacture. India is becoming concerned by Chinese diplomatic and military activity on the Indian Himalayan frontier and at sea. India is planning to deploy an aircraft carrier into the Bay of Bengal, and is warily watching Chinese support for the development of ports in Myanmar and Pakistan. Complaints about the artificial depression of the value of the Chinese currency have met with scant consideration. James Boutilier, "The Canadian Navy and the new Naval Environment in Asia," *International Journal*, vol. 58, no. 1, 2002–03: 181–200; Christian Bedford, "The View from the West: Asia's Race for Carriers," and Eric Lerhe, "The *Impeccable* Affair: China's New Twist to the Law of the Sea Convention," *Canadian Naval Review*, vol. 5, no. 1 (spring 2009), 30–1, 33–5; "Chinese navy's new strategy in action," "China's Three-Point Naval Strategy," "India and China eye each other warily," "Lost in translation: China's opaque defence white paper," and "Behind recent gunboat diplomacy in the South

China Sea," *Strategic Comments*, vol. 16, comments 16, 37, and 47, 6 May, 15 Oct., and Dec. 2010; vol. 17, comment 17 and 28–April and Aug. 2011; Matt Linfoot, "China's Re-Emergent Sea Power," Gregory P. Gilbert and Michelle Jellett, eds., *Australian Maritime Issues 2009, SPC-A Annual*, Papers in Australian Maritime Affairs, no. 32, Australia: Sea Power Centre, 2009: 189–92; BBC News, 8 June 2011, "China aircraft carrier confirmed by general"; Christian Le Mière, "The Return of Gunboat Diplomacy," Sarah Raine, "Bejing's South China Sea Debate," *Survival*, vol. 53, no. 5 (Oct.–Nov. 2011): 53–67, and 69–87.

24 In February 2008 a Russian battlegroup completed the first deployment into the Atlantic and Mediterranean in fifteen years. In October 2008 a smaller naval task group from the Northern Fleet crossed the Atlantic to visit Venezuela, then South Africa, before participating in an exercise with the Indian Navy. Future naval development in Russia is unclear. Reports in 2008 indicated an intention to develop six aircraft carrier battle groups. Russian shipyards were reportedly working at a pace that compared to the Soviet era, although aircraft carrier construction would require either the development of a new yard or a defence deal with the Ukraine. In December 2010, however, Defence Minister Anatoly Serdyukov confirmed suspicions that the plans to construct aircraft carriers were abandoned because of lack of funds. Instead, Russia has signed a contract with France for four *Mistral* class LHD (Landing Helicopter Dock) ships capable of conducting complex littoral operations. The first two will be built in France. "Will Russia create the World's Second Largest Surface Navy?," "Russia could order Aircraft Carriers from Ukraine," "Russian Warships Head to Mediterranean," "Russian Naval Task Force Starts Venezuelan Visit," RIA *Novosti*, 13 Nov. 2007, 24 Sept., 1 Oct., 25 Nov. 2008; "Russia halts aircraft carriers building," *United Press International*, 10 Dec. 2010; "Russian navy's regeneration plans," *Strategic Comments*, vol. 17, comment 8 (Feb. 2011).

25 This could take the form of maritime air support by the Canadian Air Force Maritime Command 14 Wing (Greenwood) for the British SSBN force following the elimination of British *Nimrod III* LRPA squadron, and of escort for the new British carriers due to come into service in 2020. Richard Norton-Taylor, "New Era Dawns for Anglo-French Defence," *The Guardian*, 28 Oct. 2010: 4; "Cameron and Sarkozy hail UK-France defence treaties," BBC *News*, 2 Nov. 2010 17:06 ET; "The ambitious UK-France defence accord," and "Anglo-French defence: 'Entente frugale plus,'" *Strategic Comments*, vol. 16, comment 41 (Nov. 2010), and vol. 17, comment 47 (Dec. 2011).

26 The Commonwealth lost its designation as "British" in 1949.

27 James Goldrick, "From Fleets to Navies." See Nicholas Tracy, *The Collective Naval Defence of the Empire: 1900–1940*, passim.

28 W. David McIntyre, "Canada and the Creation of the Commonwealth Secretariat, 1965," *International Journal*, vol. 53, no. 4, 1997–98: 753–77; Margaret Doxey, "Evolution and Adaptation in the Modern Commonwealth," *International Journal*, vol. 45, no. 4 (1989–90): 889–912.

29 Harald von Riekhoff, "The Impact of Prime Minister Trudeau on Foreign Policy"; Margaret Doxey, "Canada and the Commonwealth," in John English, *Making a Difference?*: 34.

30 LAC, *Mackenzie King Diary*, 23 April 1941: 366 (344).

31 CBC *News*, Meagan Fitzpatrick, "Mackay confirms 'royal' renaming of military," 16 Aug. 2011, 8:55 AM ET. Probably, however, it is a piece of political theatre intended to distract from the administration's agreement to an American participa-

tion in Canadian border control, and American access to confidential Canadian files. In 2010, in recognition of the hundredth anniversary of the formation of the Royal Canadian Navy, officers' rank insignia were restored to the original "British" form with an "executive curl" on the gold rings.

32 Boutilier, "The Canadian Navy and the New Naval Environment in Asia."
33 Canada, DND Press Release, 26 Oct. 2010, and *People's Daily*, 27 Oct. 2010.
34 Douglas Bland, *Chiefs of Defence: Government and the Unified Command of the Canadian Armed Forces*: 1–30; John Gellner, "The Defence of Canada: Requirements, Capabilities, and the National Will," in *Behind the Headlines*, vol. 42, no. 3, 1985: 1; Adrien Preston, "The Profession of Arms in Postwar Canada," in *World Politics* 23 (Jan. 1971), 197.
35 Margaret Doxey, *United Nations Sanctions: Trends and Problems*, 50–1.
36 Laura Higgins, *Canadian Naval Operations in the 1990's: Selected Case Studies*, 72.
37 Joseph Jockel and Joel Sokolsky, "Lloyd Axworthy's Legacy: Human Security and the Rescue of Canadian Defence Policy," *International Journal*, vol. 56, no. 1 (2000–01): 1–18.
38 Michael Ignatieff, *Empire Lite: Nation Building in Bosnia, Kosovo, Afghanistan*, 11, 18–21; Michael Cotey Morgan, "Michael Ignatieff: Idealism and the Challenge of the 'Lesser Evil'" *International Journal*, vol. 61, no. 4 (2005–06): 971–88.
39 Stairs and Middlemiss, "Continental Security: The Issue and Challenges."
40 Private conversation, 2008.
41 Statement by the Archbishop of Canterbury: 15 Nov. 1990. Noted by F.M. Malbon, "The Just War in the Modern World" (First published in Seaford House Papers 1991 and reprinted by permission of the Royal College of Defence Studies), *Naval Review*, vol. 80, no. 4 (Oct. 1992): 287–99.
42 Can., Commons, *Debates*, North-South Relations, 15 June 1981, vol. 10: 10592–5.
43 Robert Fisk, *The Great War for Civilisation: The Conquest of the Middle East*, 25; also Bodansky, *Bin Laden: The Man Who Declared War on America*: 191, 219, 221, 369; and see D.G. Kibble "February's Bombing of Baghdad: Reviewing British and American Policy on Iraq," *Naval Review*, vol. 89, no. 3 (July 2001): 222–6.
44 CBS, *60 Minutes*, May 1996, Lesley Stahl and Madeleine Albright.
45 UNSC, S/1996/776, 24 Sept. 1996, "Report of the Copenhagen Round Table," paragraphs 69, 70.
46 Robin Cook, "Why it is in the interest of the Iraqi people to bomb Saddam," *The Telegraph*, 20 Feb. 2001, 12:00AM GMT.
47 Kibble "February's Bombing of Baghdad."
48 Michael Ignatieff, "Ethics and the New War," *Canadian Military Journal*, winter 2001–2: 5–10.
49 Lloyd Axworthy, foreword to George Lopez and David Cortright, *The Sanctions Decade*, ix.
50 Vera Gowlland-Debbas, "Security Council Change: The Pressure of Emerging International Public Policy UN Sanctions," *International Journal*, vol. 65, no. 1 (winter 2009–10): 119–42.
51 Joanna Weschler, "Evolution of Security Council Innovations in Sanctions," *International Journal*, vol. 65, no. 1 (winter 2009–10): 31–44.
52 The arbitrary capacity of Security Council permanent members to put anyone's

name on a UN watch list that prevents them holding employment or accessing their bank accounts, and to keep it there, is an abuse that deeply affects people's lives. See the case of Abousfian Abdelrazik. "Montreal man on watch list rallies supporters," *Canadian Press*, 12 Dec. 2010.
53 John Holmes, *Life with Uncle: The Canadian-American Relationshi*, 57.
54 Geoffrey Pearson, "Trudeau and Foreign Policy," *Peace Magazine*, Jan.–March 2001, 7.
55 Henry Kissinger, *The Troubled Partnership*, 53.
56 Denis Healey, *Labour and a World Society*, 6.
57 Melanie Graham, "Interoperability and Integration: Blessing or Curse?" in Edwards, *Continental Security*: 61–73.
58 LAC, *Mackenzie King Diary*, 1 July 1941: 581 (541).
59 See above, p. 280.
60 Holmes, *Life with Uncle*, 65, 70.
61 LAC *Mackenzie King Diary*, 22 April 1922: 176 (3712).
62 In April HMCS *Victoria* completed its major refit and entered a period of work-ups. The original British armament of *Spearfish* torpedoes not suiting Canadian objectives, the class is being refitted to fire American-made upgraded Mark 48 torpedoes, but not until March 2012 was one of the class, *Victoria*, able to make a test fire of its main ordnance. As the remaining submarines return to service, they will be the main support of Canadian foreign policy in the coming decade. During the *Halifax*-Class Modernization (HCM)/Frigate Life Extension (FELEX) program, the American *Harpoon* missiles are to be ungraded to permit land attack roles, and the *Sea Sparrow* missile will be upgraded. The command-and-control system to be developed for retrofitting, on the other hand, is a joint project involving Lockheed Martin Canada and Saab Electronics System of Sweden. The navy expressed an intention to explore the possibility of developing with the Royal Navy a joint project for the ship to eventually replace the *Halifax* class frigates and the *Iroquois* DDG-280s, but domestic political pressures put an end to that concept. It was reported in January 2010 that the Canadian Navy intends to move away from the use of American equipment during the mid-life refit to the patrol frigate force. The reasons given were that "American weapon and defence technology exports fall under the rules of the International Traffic in Arms Regulations (ITAR), which the US strictly enforces. ITAR provisions frequently delay the delivery of military equipment to Canada and closely govern what Canada can and cannot do with the equipment. Additionally, agreements with the US have occasionally been problematic due to broader national security concerns in Washington; in 2006, U.S. government officials tried unsuccessfully to bar Canadians who were born in certain countries or who possess dual citizenship from working on U.S. technology. The request, which violated Canadian law, was denied. Consequently, Ottawa intends to use technology that is not regulated by the ITAR." The expressed intention is that, where possible, equipment will be imported from other sources, or developed in Canada. Particularly interesting is the prospect outlined by the minister of national defence, Peter MacKay, of Canada's acquiring logistical support bases in as many as seven different locations around the world to facilitate Canadian participation in international military efforts. The economics appear to be obvious, as experience has shown how wasteful it is to operate without a hub, or to establish and tear down one for each mission, but the calculations depend upon an assessment of the probability of continuing to despatch forces globally for peace support and humanitarian missions. It is also necessary

to take into account the strategic implications of relying upon foreign governments to permit use of the facilities without imposing constraints. Were the Commonwealth revived to any extent as a defence organization it could provide the same sort of access to bases and resources as is available in NATO countries, without the sunk costs of permanent Canadian facilities around the world. *Defence Industry Daily*, "Victoria Class Submarine Fleet Creating Canadian Controversies," 31 Oct. 2011 16:02 ED"; *Saanich News*, "HMCS *Victoria* returns to sea," 19 April 2011"; Canada, DND, *Backgrounder*, "Halifax-Class Modernization and Life Extension," BG – 10.028 – 1 Oct. 2010; Andrew Chuter, "U.K., Canada Discuss Joint Frigate Development," *Defense News*, 1 Feb. 2011; *Times Colonist*, 24 Jan. 2010: "Canadian Navy to modernize ships without US equipment," 24 Jan. 2010"; Lieutenant Colonel Roy C. Bascot, USAF, "Global Movements and Operational Support Hub Concept: Global Reach for the Canadian Forces, "*Canadian Air Force Journal*, vol. 2, no. 3 (summer 2009): 9–17; and CBC *News*, "Sub HMCS Victoria fires 1st torpedoes in test Navy hopes submarine will be fully operational this summer" 16 March 2012, 4:03 p.m. ET.

63 On 17 March the Security Council agreed to French and British demands, also called for by the Arab League and belatedly supported by the United States, that the international community act to protect Libyan citizens from the violent measures being taken by Gadhafi to restore his control over the country. Security Council Resolution 1973 authorized "Member States that have notified the Secretary-General, acting nationally or through regional organizations or arrangements, and acting in cooperation with the Secretary-General, to take all necessary measures, notwithstanding paragraph 9 of resolution 1970 (2011), to protect civilians and civilian populated areas under threat of attack in the Libyan Arab Jamahiriya, including Benghazi, while excluding a foreign occupation force of any form on any part of Libyan territory." A no-fly zone was imposed on Libya, and HMCS *Charlottetown* participated in an international naval cordon to enforce an embargo on arms sales to the Libyan government and to prevent the naval forces of Libya being employed against the rebels. In March it was announced that seven CF-18s and two Canadian *Aurora* aircraft would join the coalition forces, which would pass into NATO command arrangements, and on 25 March it was announced that Lt.-Gen. Charles Bouchard, CF, would be assuming overall command: "Operation *Mobile*," DND CEFCOM Home, International Operations; "PM pledges $5M for Libya aid," CBC *News*, 2 March 2011; "CF-18 jets to help enforce Libya no-fly zone," CBC *News*, 17 March 2011; "Libya: direct military hits, unclear political targets," *Strategic Comments*, vol. 17, comment 12, March 2011; and CBC, "Who's contributing what to the Libya offensive," and "Canadian to command NATO's Libya mission," CBC *News* and the *Canadian Press*, 22 and 25 March 2011. Perversely, however, the government carefully avoided invoking the UN commitment to protect the nationals of failed states which had been crafted in 2005 by Foreign Minister Lloyd Axworthy and Secretary General Koffi Annan.

64 Reuters: "Canada selects shipyards to modernize Navy," 19 Oct. 2011. CBC, "Shipbuilding deals will stabilize industry, Harper says," 12 Jan. 2012 8:54 AM AT. The process was not entirely apolitical. Harper remarked that Peter MacKay, minister and also MP for Central Nova, was convinced Halifax would win the contract if political pressures from central Canada could be deflected.

65 CBC *News*, "HMCS Charlottetown sails for Mediterranean, Halifax ship joining NATO anti-terrorism patrol," 8 Jan. 2012

66 See above, p. 157; Can., DEA, *Statements and Speeches, 69/9.*

67 See above, p. 157; Directorate of History, file no. 73/1223(403), Memorandum from Dr R.J. Sutherland to Minister of National Defence, 31 May 1963, covering a paper "The General Purpose Frigate"; file 72/153, "Report of the Ad Hoc Committee on Defence Policy," 30 Sept. 1963, 6-7.
68 Holmes, *Life with Uncle*, 85, 102.

APPENDIX ONE

1 Judge William Webster, director of the Central Intelligence Agency, "Report for the 101st Congress," 7 Dec. 1990 5:40 EST.
2 U.S. Department of State, *Dispatch*, 1/12, 19 Nov. 1990: 273.
3 Sir Julian S. Corbett, *England in the Seven Years' War*: 5-6; Sun Tzu, *The Art of War*, 600 BC; Janice Stein, "Deterrence and Compellence in the Gulf"; R.W. Apple Jr, "US 'Nightmare Scenario': Being Finessed by Iraq," *New York Times*, 19 Dec. 1990, A16.
4 See Diane B. Kunz, *The Economic Diplomacy of the Suez Crisis*, passim; Peter Wright, *Spy Catcher: The Candid Autobiography of a Senior Intelligence Officer*, 85; and Robin Renwick, *Economic Sanctions*: 61-4.
5 V. Malkevich, *East-West Economic Cooperation and Technological Exchange*, 14, as quoted by Peggy L. Falkenheim, "Post-Afghanistan Sanctions," 105.
6 Margaret Doxey, *United Nations Sanctions*:,24-38, 50-1; UN Doc. A/51/242 (1997); Norrin M. Ripsman, "Challenge of Targeting Economic Sanctions, The Review Essay," *International Journal*, vol. 57, no. 4 (2001-02): 647-51.
7 David Cortright and George A. Lopez, *Smart Sanctions: Targeting Economic Statecraft*: 8-9.
8 See, for instance, Bronwen Manby, "South Africa: The Impact of Sanctions," *Journal of International Affairs*, vol. 46, no. 1 (summer 1992), 193; Joseph Hanlon, "Successes and Future Prospects of Sanctions Against South Africa," Discussion Paper No. 2; and "Quarterly Report, November 1992."
9 *North American Agreement on Environmental Co-operation between the Government of Canada, the Government of the United Mexican States, and the Government of the United States of America*, Final Draft, 13 Sept. 1993, Articles 34 and 36, Annexes 34 and 36 A/B. See also Keith H. Christie, *Stacking the Deck: Compliance and Dispute Settlement in International Environmental Agreements*.
10 Nicholas Tracy, "Pro-Active Sanctions: A New/Old Approach to Non-violent Measures," Canada, Department of Foreign Affairs and International Trade, Staff Paper, 1994; and *McNaughton Papers*, Canadian Institute for Strategic Studies, 1994. DFA Policy Paper, ISBN 0919769888, 30 pp.
11 BBC, "EU Iran sanctions: Ministers adopt Iran oil imports ban," 23 Jan. 2012.

APPENDIX TWO

1 "Milestones in Canadian Naval History" originally appeared in the centennial issue of *Canadian Naval Review*, vol. 6, no. 1 (spring 2010). It was a collaborative effort, written by Richard Gimblett, Peter Haydon, Danford Middlemiss, Marc Milner, and Doug Thomas. Reproduced with permission from the board.

BIBLIOGRAPHY

BODLEIAN LIBRARY, OXFORD, UK.
Harcourt MS, f. 21 dep. 462, Robert Borden to Lewis Harcourt, 16 May 1912

BRITISH LIBRARY, ST PANCRAS, LONDON, UK
Add. MS 49055-57   Report on the Mission to Canada.
Add. MS 49048   Jellicoe Papers.

CHURCHILL COLLEGE, CAMBRIDGE
CHART21/20 f. 12a, Memorandum by R Adm Alexander Bethell, 1 Nov. 1909.

LIBRARY AND ARCHIVES CANADA, OTTAWA, CANADA
MG 26 G (R10811-0-X-F), Laurier Papers, c2017, Laurier to W. Gregory, 11 Nov. 1904.
MG 27 II-D12 (R3895-0-3-E), George Halsey Perley fonds, vol. 5, file 1, 127. A-B, Sir Robert Borden to Perley. 4 Jan. 1916.
MG 27 III B-5 vol 30, file X-18, "Joint Staff Committee Plan for the Maintenance of Canadian Neutrality in the Event of War between the United States and Japan." 20 Jan. 1938.
MG 27 III B-5 vol. 32, file X-53, Percy Nelles, "Canadian Naval Policy in Regard to Her Western Seaboard." 24 Sept. 1936.
MG 30 E159, vol. 2, file 5, Defence and Foreign Affairs, Report "A Programme of Immediate Canadian Action drawn up by a Group of Twenty Canadians Meeting at the Chateau Laurier, Ottawa, July 17–18, 1940," 1–12.
MG 31 E87 (R5497-501-1-E), Canada, Cabinet Minutes, 27, 29, 30 March 1969.
MG 31 E87 (R5497-505-9-E), vol. 7, file 10, Canada, Cabinet, Secret Notes for Minutes, 20 Jan. and 9 Feb. 1965.
MG 32 Box 5 (R3306-0-1-E), Claxton Papers, vol. 126, file "US Defence Policy, 1954." Wilgress to USSEA, 25 Feb. 1954
MG 32 Box 33 *Hellyer Papers* vol. 1, file 42 [1961], Paul T. Hellyer, "A Role for Canada in Collective Defence [1961]."
MG 32 Box 33 *Hellyer Papers* (R1278-0-4-E), vol. 82, file 8, General Charles Foulkes, "The Case for One Service," July 1961.
RG 2 A-5-a (R165-93-5-F) Privy Council Records, RG 2/1892, Cabinet Conclusions, 9 May 1957.

RG 2 A-5-b, MF C11789, C4877, C4654, C4874 (Index C4873), Cabinet War Committee, 1939–1945.
RG 24 Vol. 3842 NSS 1017-10-23, CNS to Minister, 12 Sept. 1939.
RG 24 Vol. 8084, File 1272-10-14, "Canada-US Basic Security Plan, Joint Planning Committee, Sub-Committee on Protection of Sea Communications."
RG 24 B-1 (R112-41-5-E), Joint Staff and Chiefs of Staff Committee.
RG 24 Vol. 21, 814, 1948, file 10, Minutes of Chiefs of Staff Committee, meeting No. 417, 2 March 1948.
RG 24 Sub-Committee on Protection of Sea Communications: Royal Canadian Navy third central registry system (R112-616-8-E).
RG 24 G-17-6 (R112-720-3-E) BAN 2003-01101-3, box 1, and BAN 2004-00336-7, Boxes 1-3, Canadian Contingent United Nations Iraq-Kuwait Observation Mission 1991–93. DND fonds (R112-0-2-E).
RG 24 (Acc 1983-84/167) vol. 11, 129, File ACTS 11,279-11 p. A(ii), *Minutes of the 11th Senior Officers' Conference*, 12–14 May 1954.
RG 24 (Acc 1983-84/167), box 89, vol. 3, file 1270-78, "Nuclear Weapon's for ASW," Sea/Air Warfare Committee, 5 Jan. 1956.
RG 24 (Acc 1983-84/167), box 424, vol. 1, file 1640-21-14, A.D.P. Heeney to Secretary of State for External Affairs, 3 Oct. 1952 (also in declassified photocopies held at DHH).
RG 25 (Acc 1990-91/008), vol. 26, Escott Reid, *Paper on Canadian Policy in* NATO, 28 April 1951.
RG 25 Vol. 755, DND, "The Naval Service of Canada: A Resume of its Necessity, Resources and Requirements," Aug. 1936.
RG 25 A4, vol. 3419, file 1-1926/22, 17, O.D. Skelton, "The Locarno treaties," 1 Jan. 1926.

DIRECTORATE OF HISTORY AND HERITAGE:
NATIONAL DEFENCE AND THE CANADIAN FORCES
The Raymont Papers
- "Report of the Ad Hoc Committee on Defence Policy." File 72/153, 30 Sept. 1963.
- Memorandum from Dr R.J. Sutherland to Minister of National Defence, covering a paper "The General Purpose Frigate." File no. 73/1223 (403). 31 May 1963.
- Capt. Charles "SACLANT'S EDP 1-60" to ACNS (P), VCNS and CNS. File 118, 2002/17.
Navy Board Minutes: 17 Nov. 1955 (memo VCNS to CNS, "Final Screening Committee,"); No. 642-1, 17–18 Jan. 1961.
Naval Staff Working Paper. "RCN Future Requirements Planning Guide for the Period 1962–1972." File no. NSTS 1650-36 (Staff), 25 Jan. 1962.

NATIONAL ARCHIVES AND RECORDS ADMINISTRATION,
COLLEGE PARK, MARYLAND, U.S.A.
RG 59 Box 1527, 1967-69, DEF 4 CAN-US, State Department to US Embassy, 9 June 1967.

NATIONAL ARCHIVES, UNITED KINGDOM (KEW)
ADM1/7671 Admiralty In-letters and papers: 1900–1909.
ADM 116/ Admiralty: Record Office: Cases
- 1100B Imperial Conference on the Defence of the Empire, 1909.

BIBLIOGRAPHY 409

–1100C Colonial Ships of War: Status of, 1909–1912.
–1815 Admiral Jellicoe's visit to Colonies - Naval Defence of British Empire, 1918–1920.
–2247 Empire Naval Policy: Imperial Conference 1923, 1923–1926.
–2567 Canadian Government Naval Policy, 1927–1928.
–2686 U.S.A. and British Naval policy, 1929.
–3104 Co-operation with the armed forces of Dominion and Colonies; requirements of Imperial Defence and comments on naval aspects, 1919.
–3165 Washington conference and its Effect on Empire Naval Policy and co-operation considered by committee of Imperial Defence, 1922–1923.
–3381 First Lord of the Admiralty: miscellaneous papers, 1911–1914.
–3415 Imperial Conference 1923: British Naval policy with regard to Dominions, Ireland and India,1923.
–3438 Imperial Conference: Admiralty policy with regard to Domionion Navies, 1923.
–3485 Canadian naval policy, 1912–1914.
–3802 Establishment of Naval Control Service in Dominions in event of war, 1938–1939.
–4080 Sale to Canada of C Class Destroyers: possible construction of sloops, 1934–1940.
–4144 Transfer of HM Destroyers to Royal Canadian Navy, 1937–1940.
ADM 167/56 Admiralty Board Minutes,1929.
ADM 186/11 Handbook for Boarding Officers.
ADM 186/603 Lt Cmdr W.E. Arnold-Forster, *The Economic Blockade 1914–1919*, Admiralty Staff History, 1920.
CAB 4/15 Committee of Imperial Defence: Miscellaneous Memoranda (B Series), Nos. 701–750, 22 June–17 Dec. 1926.
CAB 5/2 Committee of Imperial Defence: Colonial Defence Memoranda (C Series), Nos. 41–89, 29 May 1906–13 June 1911.
CAB 5/3 Committee of Imperial Defence: Colonial Defence Memoranda (C Series).
CAB 5/4 Committee of Imperial Defence: Colonial Defence Memoranda (C Series), Nos. 131–80, 5 Aug. 1920–23 Oct. 1922.
CAB 21/ Cabinet Office:
  –187 Naval defence to the Empire: Imperial naval policy, 1921.
  –307 Belligerent Rights: The Freedom of the Seas: British Policy, 1928.
  –310 Belligerent Rights: The Freedom of the Seas, 1928.
  –315 Imperial Defence, General principles affecting the overseas Dominions and Colonies, 1928.
  –328 Belligerent Rights, 1930.
  –670 Supply of war materials from industrial establishments in the Dominions, 1938.
CAB 32/2 Imperial Conferences, Stenographic Notes of Meetings: E.1–E.34, 20 June–5 Aug. 1921.
CAB 53/3 Committee of Imperial Defence: Chiefs of Staff Committee: Minutes of Meetings nos. 76–100, 14 Jan. 1929–19 May 1931.
CAB 104/17 Imperial Defence: Dominions and Imperial Defence Policy, 1929–1931.
CAB 104/18 Imperial Defence: Dominions and Imperial Defence Policy, 1938.
FO 837/5 Ministry of Economic Warfare and Successors: Records, Economic Warfare: Policy, 1939.

UNITED STATES, DEPARTMENT OF STATE

03Ottawa49, Chargé d'Affaires Michael Gallagher to Secretary Rumsfeld, 2003-01-09 13:13, *Wikileaks*.

03Ottawa747, Deputy Chief of Mission Stephen R. Kelly [to State Department], 2003-03-17 23:54, *Wikileaks*.

03Ottawa773, Deputy Chief of Mission Stephen R. Kelly [to State Department], 2003-03-19 15:24, *Wikileaks*.

03Ottawa917, Ambassador Paul Cellucci [to Secretary of State], 2003-03-28 22:31, *Wikileaks*.

05Ottawa3105, Ambassador David Wilkins to Secretary of State, 2005-10-17 22:07, *Wikileaks*.

06Ottawa1904, Ambassador David Wilkins to Secretary of State, 2006-06-19, *Wikileaks*.

07Ottawa819, Ambassador David Wilkins to Secretary of State, 2007-05-07 18:12, *Wikileaks*.

08Ottawa1198, Ambassador David Wilkins to Secretary of State, 2008-09-12, *Wikileaks*.

08Ottawa1258, Ambassador David Wilkins to Secretary of State, 2008-09-22 18:59, *Wikileaks*.

09Ottawa68, Deputy Head of Mission Terry Breese to Secretary of State, 2009-23-01 19:54, *Wikileaks*.

09Ottawa840, Ambassador David Jacobson to Secretary of State, 2009-11-03 20:36, *Wikileaks*.

10Ottawa29, Ambassador David Jacobson to Secretary of State, 2010-01-21 16:52, *Wikileaks*.

OFFICIAL SOURCES, PUBLISHED DOCUMENTS, AND REFERENCE WORKS

Admiralty [from Captured Tambach archives]. *Fuehrer Conferences on Naval Affairs*, 2 vols. London, Aug. 1947.

Albright, Madeleine K. "Preserving Principle and Safeguarding Stability: United States Policy Toward Iraq," speech at Georgetown University, Washington D.C., 26 March 1997.

Bird, Keith W. *German Naval History: A Guide to the Literature*. New York: Garland, 1985.

Blanchette, Arthur E., ed. *Canadian Foreign Policy, 1955–65: Selected Speeches and Documents* Toronto: McClelland & Stewart, 1980.

– *Canadian Foreign Policy, 1966–76: Selected Speeches and Documents*. Ottawa: The Carleton Library 118, 1980.

– *Canadian Foreign Policy, 1972–92: Selected Speeches and Documents*. Ottawa: Carleton University Press, 1994.

Brown, Horatio F., Rawdon Brown, and Allen B Hinds, eds. *Calendar of state papers and manuscripts, relating to English affairs, existing in the archives and collections of Venice and in the other libraries of Northern Italy*. Great Britain: Public Record Office, 1864.

Canada. Agreements. *Agreement between the government of Canada and the Government of the United States of America on Arctic Cooperation*. Ottawa, 11 Jan. 1988. http://www.lexum.org/ca_us/en/cts.1988.29.en.html

– *North American Agreement on Environmental Cooperation between the Government of Canada: The Government of the United Mexican States, and the*

Government of the United States of America. Final Draft, 13 Sept. 1993, Articles 34 and 36, Annexes 34 and 36 A/B.
- "Government of Canada Response to the Report of the Standing Committee on Foreign Affairs and International Trade: 'Canada and the Circumpolar World: Meeting the Challenges of Cooperation into the Twenty-first Century.'" Ottawa, Government of Canada, May 1998.
- *Statement on Canada's Arctic Foreign Policy: Exercising Sovereignty and Promoting Canada's Northern Strategy Abroad*, 2010.

Canada. Department of External Affairs. *Report of the Advisory Committee on Post-Hostilities Problems*. "Post-war Canadian Defence Relationship with the United States: General Considerations." Ottawa: DEA, 23 Jan. 1945.
- Permanent Joint Board on Defense. 35th Recommendation (Revised). *Documents on Canadian External Relations*, vol. 12, chap. 11, p. 973, Relations with the United States, Part III, Defence, Section C, Defence Planning. Memorandum from Secretary, Cabinet Defence Committee, Cabinet, 21 Oct. 1946.
- *Statements and Speeches*, no. 47/2, Louis St Laurent, "The Foundation of Canadian Policy in World Affairs," inaugurating the Gray Foundation Lectureship at the University of Toronto. 13 Jan. 1947: 3–11.
- *Statements and Speeches*, no. 51/13, Lester Pearson, "The Role of the United Nations in a Two-Power World," 31 March 1951.
- *Statements and Speeches*, no. 51/14, Lester Pearson, "Canadian Foreign Policy in a Two-Power World," 10 April 1951.
- *Statements and Speeches*, no. 54/16 p. 7, L.B. Pearson, "A New Look at the 'New Look,'" 15 March 1954.
- *Statements and Speeches*, nos. 55/8 and 10, Lester Pearson, 14 and 24 March 1955.
- *Statements and Speeches* no. 69/7. Pierre Elliott Trudeau. "A Defence Policy for Canada," 3 April 1969.
- *Statements and Speeches* no. 69/8. Pierre Elliott Trudeau. "Speech to the Alberta Liberal Association," 12 April 1969.
- *Statements and Speeches* 83/8. Department of External Affairs. "Canada's position on testing cruise missiles and disarmament: An open letter to all Canadians," 9 May 1983.
- "Government of Canada Response to the Report of the Standing Committee on Foreign Affairs and International Trade 'Canada and the Circumpolar World: Meeting the Challenges of Cooperation into the Twenty-first Century.'" Ottawa, Government of Canada, May 1998.
- *Statement on Canada's Arctic Foreign Policy: Exercising Sovereignty and Promoting Canada's Northern Strategy Abroad*, 2010.
- *Documents on Canadian External Relations*. Ottawa: DEA, 1967–.
- *Foreign Policy for Canadians*. Ottawa: Information Canada, 1970.

Canada, Department of Fisheries and Oceans. A.W. May (Chair), Dawn A. Russell, Derrick H. Rowe. "Breaking New Ground: An Action Plan for Rebuilding the Grand Banks Fisheries," Report of the Advisory Panel on the Sustainable Management of Straddling Fish Stocks in the Northwest Atlantic, 1 Sept. 2005.
- "Canada Achieves Major Reforms at Historic Meeting of the Northwest Atlantic Fisheries Organization," 22 Sept. 2006.

Canada, Department of Foreign Affairs and International Trade (DFAIT). *Human Security: Safety for People in a Changing World*. Ottawa: DFAIT, April 1999.
- "Canada and Denmark Issue Statement on Hans Island," 19 Sept. 2005.

- Pierre Pettigrew, Canadian Minister of Foreign Affairs. Speech at the Northern Strategy Consultations, Round Table on Reinforcing Sovereignty, Security and Circumpolar Cooperation, "Canada's Leadership in the Circumpolar World," 22 March 2005. http://www.international.gc.ca/circumpolar/sec06_speeches_003-en.asp.
Canada, Department of National Defence. *The Canadian Navy list for ... Department of National Defence.* Ottawa: F.A. Acland, Printer, 1929–39.
- *Canada's Defence: Information on Canada's Defence Achievements and Organization.* Ottawa: King's Printer, 1947.
- (Naval Service). "Report of Certain Incidents that Occurred onboard HMC Ships *Athabaskan, Crescent,* and *Magnificent* ..." Rear-Admiral E.R. Mainguy, RCN, Chairman, Ottawa, Oct. 1949.
- *Defence in the 70s.* Ottawa: Information Canada, 1971.
- *Challenge and Commitment: A Defence Policy for Canada.* Ottawa: Department of Supply and Services, 1987: 52.
- *Defence Policy Initiatives Questions and Answers* (Supplemental Information to the White Paper). Ottawa: Supply and Services, 1987.
- *Backgrounder,* Nov. 1987, "Official Languages in the DND and the Canadian Forces."
- *Backgrounder,* May 1989, "Re-allocation of Maritime Resources."
- *Backgrounder,* Feb. 1990, "Women in the Canadian Forces."
- *Backgrounder,* Sept. 1990, "The Canadian Forces Exchange Program."
- *News Release,* 26 April 1991, letter from V. Adm. Thomas to Gen. De Chastelain, 24 April 1991.
- *Backgrounder,* May 1992, "Franco-Canadian Military Cooperation Committee."
- *The Naval Vision: Charting the Course for Canada's Maritime Forces into the 21st Century.* Ottawa: DND, May 1994.
- *White Paper on Defence.* Ottawa, 1994.
- *Briefing Note for Arctic Subsurface Surveillance System [Canada] ... Source-Route,* 25 May 1994;
- *Adjusting Course: A Naval Strategy for Canada.* Maritime Command, Canada Communications Group. Ottawa, 1997.
- Douglas Young. "Report to the Prime Minister on the Leadership and Management of the Canadian Forces," 25 March 1997.
- Deputy Minister Jim Judd, and General J.M.G. Baril, Chief of the Defence Staff. *Shaping the Future of Canadian Defence: A Strategy for 2020,* June 1999.
- "Canada and US renew agreement on shared use of Nanoose Bay Test Ranges," NR-99.276, 17 Dec. 1999.
- Canadian Armed Forces Web Site, "Canada's contribution to the Arabian Gulf continues," 7 Dec. 2000.
- File MCU2000 0548, 8 Dec 2000, Secret: Canadian Eyes Only, Briefing Note for the Minister, "Putin may raise this during his visit to Canada."
- Vice Chief of the Defence Staff, *Strategic Capability Planning for the Canadian Forces,* 2000.
- *Leadmark: The Navy's Strategy for 2020,* 18 June 2001.
- Directorate of Strategic Analysis, Policy Planning Division, Policy Group, Elizabeth Speed, et al. "Strategic Assessment 2001." Ottawa, Sept. 2001.
- News Item, BG-01.035a, 10 Dec. 2001.
- *Securing Canada's Ocean Frontiers: Charting the Course from Leadmark,* May 2005.

- *Canada's International Policy Statement: A Role of Pride and Influence in the World.* Ottawa, 2005.
- *News Release* CEFCOM NR 08.030. "HMCS *Ville de Québec* starts World Food Programme escort mission," 19 Aug. 2008.
- Canadian Armed Forces Web Site, ca 15 Jan. 2010, Virginia Beaton. "International Stories: Naval task group assists in Haiti relief effort."
- "Canada and Denmark Sign Arctic Cooperation Arrangement," 14 May 2010.
- *Backgrounder*, 14 July 2010, "Canada Begins Joint Support Ships Procurement for the Canadian Forces."
- *Backgrounder*, 1 Oct. 2010, BG-10.028. 'Halifax-Class Modernization and Life Extension."
- Strategic Issues: *Your Navy: Your Security*, nd.
- Canadian Navy Ships Integrated into US Naval Forces for Operations in the Persian Gulf, nd.
- Canadian Armed Forces Web Site, "Operation Nanook wraps up in the Eastern Arctic," nd. http://www.navy.forces.gc.ca/cms_operations/operations_e.asp?category=12&id=674.
- Canadian Armed Forces Web Site, Mary Ellen Green. "Canadian commodore takes top sea job at multinational exercise," Canadian Navy, Operations and Exercises, nd. http://www.navy.forces.gc.ca/cms/4/4-a_eng.asp?id=669.
- Press Release. "Canada Awarded Full Member Status in the Western Pacific Naval Symposium," 26 Oct. 2010.
- Office of the Asia-Pacific Advisor, Maritime Forces Pacific. "Tightening the Noose: Time for a New Approach against Somali Pirates?" *In Focus*, 17 June 2011.
- "Operation *Mobile*," CEFCOM Home, International Operations.
- Directorate of History. Maurice Pope. "Memorandum on a Canadian Organization for the Higher Direction of National Defence: 8 March 1937," file 112.3S 2009 (D23); reprinted in Douglas Bland, *Canada's National Defence*, vol. 2, "Defence Organization." Kingston: Queen's University, 1998: 1–20.

Canada, Department of Transport. No. H 110/09. "Legislation to protect Canada's arctic waters comes into force," 6 Aug. 2009
- Zone/Date System Map and Dates of Entry Table, Shipping Safety Control Zones.

Canada, Federal Court Judgment, 2005-07-26, Docket T-1602-95, Jose Pereira E. Hijos, S.A. and Enrique Davila Gonzalez (Plaintiffs) and the Attorney General of Canada.

Canada, Governor General: *Speech from the Throne*, 5 Oct. 2004.

Canada, House of Commons. *Debates*, sessions 1900 (col. 1846); 1909 (col. 3486, 29 March); 1910 (vol. 1, cols. 1732–76 12 Jan.); 1909–10 (vol. 1, col. 612, 1 Dec. 1910; col. 1746E); 1912 (pp. 657–94, 5 Dec.; 1939 (IV: 4016–17, 13 May); 1950 (4459–61 "Situation in Korea: Canada's Part in Collective Action under United Nations," 30 June); 1972 (Address by President Richard Nixon), 14 April, 1328–9; 1984 (Trudeau's Peace Mission, 9 Feb., 1215–17; 1986 (5 Dec., 1823); 1988 (9 June, 16282).
- *Journal*, 1909–10.
- Sessional Papers 1920 no. 61. "Report of Admiral of the Fleet Viscount Jellicoe of Scapa G.C.B., O.M., G.C.V.O. on Naval Mission to the Dominion of Canada, Nov.–Dec. 1919." Ottawa: Thomas Mulvey, 1920.
- Special Committee on Defence. *Minutes of Proceedings and Evidence*. No. 16, 24 Oct. 1963.

- Standing Committee on External Affairs and National Defence, Statement by Prime Minister Trudeau, 3 March 1970.
- *Minutes of Proceedings and Evidence of the Standing Committee on External Affairs and National Defence.* 30th Parl. 1st Sess., no. 33, 23 March 1976: 5–6.
- Standing Committee on External Affairs and National Defence. *Minutes*, 33rd Parl. 1st Sess., no. 33, evidence of Brigadier-General Carl Bertrand (director general, Military Plans and Operations, DND), 3 Oct. 1985: 21.
- Standing Committee on External Affairs and National Defence. *Minutes of Proceedings and Evidence.* 33rd Parl. 1st Sess., no. 52, 6 Dec. 1985.
- Special Joint Committee of the Senate and of the House of Commons on Canada's International Relations. *Minutes of Proceedings and Evidence*, no. 49, 13 March 1986, 12.
- Standing Committee on National Defence. *Minutes of Proceedings and Evidence*, 33rd Parl., 2nd Session, no. 1, 2 Dec. 1986, 35.
- Standing Committee on National Defence. *Minutes of Proceedings and Evidence*, no. 10 (14 April 1988), 10: 12–13.
- Standing Committee on National Defence and Veterans Affairs. *Maritime Sovereignty*, Nov. 1990.

Canada, Minister of Indian Affairs and Northern Development and Federal Interlocutor for Métis and Non-Status Indians. *Canada's Northern Strategy: Our North, Our Heritage, Our Future.* Ottawa, 2009.

Canada, Navy. *Canadian Naval Force and Royal Canadian Navy, 1910–1914.* Ottawa: Queen's Printer, 1955.

Canada. Permanent Joint Board on Defence, 35th recommendation, 12 Feb. 1947.

Canada. Prime Minister's Office. Transcript of Prime Minister's Press Conference, Moscow, 20 May 1971, no. 20, 31 May 1971.

Canada. Privy Council Office, Cabinet Minutes 27, 29, 30 March 1969.

Canada. *Revised Statutes of Canada.* Ottawa: Queen's Printer, 1985.

Canada. *Royal Canadian Navy Year End Roundup*, 1963.

Canada, Senate. Special Committee on National Defence, *Canada's Territorial Air Defence.* Ottawa: Minister of Supply and Services, Jan. 1985, 1/13-96A.

- Special Joint Committee of the Senate and of the House of Commons on Canada's International Relations. *Minutes of Proceedings and Evidence*, no. 49, 13 March 1986: 12.

Canada, Treaties. E101015–CTS 1958 no. 9. *Agreement between the Government of Canada and the Government of the United States of America Concerning the Organization and Operation of the North American Air Defence Command* (NORAD), Ambassador of Canada to the United States of America to Secretary of State of the United States of America, 12 May 1958.

- E105060. *Agreement between the Government of Canada and the Government of the United States of America on the North American Aerospace Defense Command*, 28 April 2006.

Canadian Institute for International Affairs. *Canada in World Affairs, 1961–1963*, vol. 12. Toronto: Oxford University Press, 1968.

Clark, Lovell C., ed. *Documents on Canadian External Relations*, vol. 3, 1919–1925. Ottawa: Department of External Affairs, 1970.

De Celles, A.D., ed. *Discours de Sir Wilfrid Laurier, 1889–1911.* Montreal, 1920.

Eayrs, James. *The Commonwealth and Suez: A Documentary Survey.* London: Oxford University Press, 1964.

European Union. No. 6434, 6/7 March 1995.
European Report. No. 2022, 8 March 1995.
EU Commissioner Borg. "Opportunities and responsibilities in the Arctic Region: the European Union's perspective," 11/3/2009, SP09-018EN.
Gooch, George Peabody and Harold Temperley, eds. *British Documents on the Origins of the War.* London: HMSO, 1932.
Great Britain, House of Commons. Naval Defence Act, 1865, 8 Victoria Cap XIV.
– Sessional Papers: Cmd 8596 /1897 vol. LIX, *Proceedings of a Conference between the Secretary of State for the Colonies and the Premiers of the Self-Governing Colonies at the Colonial Office.* London, June and July 1897.
–Cmd 1299/1902 vol. LXVI, *Proceedings of a Conference between the Secretary of State for the Colonies and the Premiers of the Self-Governing Colonies,* 30 June–11 Aug. 1902.
–Cmd 3404, 3406, 3523, 3524, *Proceedings of the Colonial Conference, 1907,* London: HMSO, 1907.
–Cmd 2009, *Imperial Economic Conference (1923),* Record of Proceedings and Documents, London: HMSO, 1924.
–Cmd 4948 Imperial Conference, "Naval and Military Defence of the Empire, 1909," vol. LIX for 1909, 335.
–Cmd 5745, *Minutes of proceedings of the Imperial Conference,* 1911. (Papers laid before the conference are printed separately in Cd.5746-1 and Cd.5746-2), July 1911. London: HMSO, 1911.
–Cmd 6513,1912, vol. LIII: 445, "Naval Defence. Memorandum on Naval Defence Requirements"; prepared by the Admiralty for the Government of Canada, Dec. 1912.
Great Britain, Statutes. Statute of Westminster 1931 c.4 22 and 23 Geo 5, 11 Dec. 1931.
Hilliker, John F., ed. *Documents on Canadian External Relations.* vol. 9, 1942–1943. Ottawa: Department of External Affairs, 1980.
Hinds, Allen B. *Calendar of State Papers ... Venice.* See Brown, Horatio F. and Rawdon, eds., 1864.
International Court of Justice. Judgment, "Case Concerning Delimitation of the Maritime Boundary in the Gulf of Maine Area," 12 Oct. 1984.
– Press Release 1998/41. *Case concerning Fisheries Jurisdiction (Spain v. Canada);* Court declares that it has no jurisdiction to adjudicate upon the dispute. 4 Dec. 1998,
Imperial Conference and Stanley Baldwin. *Summary of Proceedings: Imperial Conference, 1926.* London: F.A. Acland, 1926.
Iraq, Child and Maternal Mortality Survey, Preliminary Report, 1999.
– Iraq Family Health Survey 2006/7, s.v. Table 25: Indirect childhood mortality (per 1000 live births).
North Atlantic Treaty Organization. M.C. 48 (FINAL) 22 Nov. 1954, "North Atlantic Military Committee Decision on M.C. 48": A Report by the Military Committee on the Most Effective Pattern of NATO Military Strength for the Next Few Years.
– MC 14/2 (Revised) (Final Decision) 23 May 1957, "A Report by the Military Committee to the North Atlantic Council on Overall Strategic Concept for the Defense of the North Atlantic Treaty Organization Area," Reference: C-M (56) 138 (Final), Section 2 para. 13/c.

- Report of Sub-Group I: "East-West Relations," 14 Dec. 1967, J.H.A.Watson, Assistant Under-Secretary of State, Foreign Affairs (UK) and Mr K. Schutz, Secretary of State Foreign Affairs (Germany).
- NATO Information Service. *NATO Facts and Figures*. Brussels: NATO, 1976.
- Defence Planning Committee, *Final Communiqué*, 13–14 May 1980.
- Regional Headquarters Allied Forces Southern Europe: AFSOUTH Fact sheets. Updated: 18 Aug. 2003, http://www.afsouth.nato.int/operations/sharpguard/SharpGuardFactSheet.htm.
- Regional Headquarters Allied Forces Southern Europe: AFSOUTH Fact Sheet: *Significant Events*. http://www.afsouth.nato.int/archives/chronology.htm.

Organization of American States: AG/RES. 1080 (XXI-O/91). *Representative Democracy*, Resolution adopted at the fifth plenary session, held on June 5, 1991.

Pickersgill, J.W. and D.F. Forster. *Mackenzie King Record*, 4 vols. Toronto: University of Toronto Press, 1960–70.

Royal Navy, Directorate of Naval Staff Duties. *The Fundamentals of British Maritime Doctrine*. BR1806, HMSO, 1996.

Stacey, Charles Perry, *Historical Documents of Canada: vol. 5. The Arts of War and Peace, 1914–1945*. Toronto: Macmillan of Canada, 1972.

Temperley, Harold, ed. *British Documents*, see Gooch, George Peabody.

Tracy, Nicholas, ed. *The Collective Naval Defence of the Empire, 1900–1940*. Navy Records Society No. 160. Basingstoke, Hampshire: Ashgate, 1997.
- ed. *Sea Power and the Control of Trade: Belligerent Rights from the Russian War to the Beira Patrol*, Navy Records Society, Aldershot: Ashgate, 2005.

United Nations: Chronological lists of ratifications, accessions and successions to the Convention and the related Agreements as at 4 May 2009.
- Independent Enquiry Committee into the Oil-for-Food Programme [the Volcker Committee]. Interim report "Oil-for-Food vs Smuggling," 3 Feb. 2005. http://www.oilforfoodfacts.org/smuggling.aspx
- Report of an Independent Working Group, "Impact of the Oil-for-Food Programme on the Iraqi People," 7 Sept. 2005. http://iic-offp.org/documents/Sept05/WG_Impact.pdf
- *Manipulation of the Oil-for-Food Programme by the Iraq Government*: 1. http://www.iic-offp.org/
- *Management of the United Nations Oil-for-Food Programme*, vol. 1, preface: 7–10. http://www.iic-offp.org/documents/Sept05/Mgmt_V1.pdf

United Nations Children's Fund (UNICEF). *Child and Maternal Mortality Survey, 1999, Preliminary Report*; work undertaken under the direction of Mr Mohammed Ali of the London School of Hygiene and Tropical Medicine, jointly for UNICEF and the government of Iraq Ministry of Health, Preventive Health Department and Statistical Department. http://www.childinfo.org/iraq.htm Information supplied by Edilberto Loaiza, Senior Programme Officer, Strategic Information Section, DPP 3 UN Plaza, New York, New York 10017.
- *Child Mortality Estimates*.

United Nations General Assembly, Resolution 377, "Uniting for Peace," 3 Nov. 1950.
- 2005 World Summit Outcome, Paras. 138–9.

United Nations Security Council, Security Council Resolutions:
  –Resolution 82: Complaint of aggression upon the Republic of Korea, 25 June 1950.
  –Resolution 83: Complaint of aggression upon the Republic of Korea, 27 June 1950.

–Resolution 84: Complaint of aggression upon the Republic of Korea, 7 July 1950.
–Resolution 85: Complaint of aggression upon the Republic of Korea, 31 July 1950.
–Resolution 118: Complaint by France and the United Kingdom against Egypt, 26 July 1956.
–Resolution 661: Iraq-Kuwait, 2 Aug. 1990.
–Resolution 665: Iraq-Kuwait, 25 Aug. 1990.
–Resolution 666: Iraq-Kuwait, 13 Sept. 1990.
–Resolution 670: Iraq-Kuwait, 25 Sept.1990.
–Resolution 678: Iraq-Kuwait, 29 Nov. 1990.
–Resolution 687: Iraq-Kuwait, 3 April 1991.
–Resolution 706: Iraq-Kuwait, 15 Aug.1991.
–Resolution 713: Socialist Federal Rep. of Yugoslavia, 25 Sept. 1991.
–Resolution 724: Socialist Federal Rep. of Yugoslavia, 15 Dec.1991.
–Resolution 743: Socialist Federal Rep. of Yugoslavia, 21 Feb.1992.
–Resolution 753: New member: Croatia, 18 May 1992.
–Resolution 754: New member: Slovenia, 20 May 1992.
–Resolution 755: New member: Bosnia and Herzegovina, 20 May 1992.
–Resolution 757: Bosnia and Herzegovina, 30 May 1992.
–Resolution 775: Somalia, 28 Aug. 1992.
–Resolution 794: Somalia, Nov. 1992.
–Resolution 787: Bosnia and Herzegovina, 17 Nov. 1992.
–Resolution 820: Bosnia and Herzegovina, 17 April 1993.
–Resolution 841: Haiti, 16 June 1993.
–Resolution 867: Haiti, 23 Sept. 1993.
–Resolution 875: Haiti, 16 Oct. 1993.
–Resolution 917: on sanctions for restoration of democracy and return of the legitimately elected President to Haiti, 6 May 1994.
–Resolution 940: on authorization to form a multinational force under unified command and control to restore the legitimately elected President and authorities of the Government of Haiti and extension of the mandate of the UN Mission in Haiti, 31 July 1994.
–Resolution 942: on reinforcement and extension of measures imposed by the Security Council resolutions with regard to those areas of Bosnia and Herzegovina under the control of Bosnian Serb forces, to assist the parties to give effect to the proposed territorial settlement in ... 23 Sept. 1994.
–Resolution 943: on the closure of the border between the Federal Republic of Yugoslavia and Bosnia and Herzegovina with respect to all goods except foodstuffs, medical supplies and clothing for essential humanitarian needs, 23 Sept. 1994.
–Resolution 986: on authorization to permit the import of petroleum and petroleum products originating in Iraq, as a temporary measure to provide for humanitarian needs of the Iraqi people, 14 April 1995.
–Resolution 998: on establishment of a rapid-reaction force within the UN Protection Force, 16 June 1995.
–Resolution 1022: on suspension of measures imposed by or reaffirmed in Security Council resolutions related to the situation in the former Yugoslavia, 22 Nov. 1995.
–Resolution 1160: on the letters from the United Kingdom (s/1998/223) and the United States (s/1998/272), 31 March 1998.

–Resolution 1199: on the situation in Kosovo (FRY), 23 Sept. 1998.
–Resolution 1244: on the situation relating Kosovo, 10 June 1999.
–Resolution 1264: on the Protection of civilians in armed conflict, 15 Sept. 1999.
–Resolution 1284: on the situation between Iraq and Kuwait, 17 Dec. 1999.
–Resolution 1368: Threats to international peace and security caused by terrorist acts, 12 Sept. 2001.
–Resolution 1373: Threats to international peace and security caused by terrorist acts, 12 Sept. 2001.
–Resolution 1386: on the situation in Afghanistan, 20 Dec. 2001.
–Resolution 1441: The situation between Iraq and Kuwait, 8 Nov. 2002.
–Resolution 1540: Non-proliferation of weapons of mass destruction, 28 April 2004.
–Resolution 1816: The situation in Somalia, 2 June 2008.
–Resolution 1973: The situation in Libya, March 2011.
United Nations Security Council, Security Council Verbatim Reports:
–Provisional, 6 Aug. 1990 S/PV 2933: discussion of document S/21441.
–Provisional, 25 Aug., 1990, S/PV 2938: discussion of draft resolution S/21640 (resolution 665).
–Provisional Summary Record of the 4th Meeting of the 661 Committee, 28 Aug. 1990. S/AC 25/S2.4.
–Provisional Rules of Procedure, 25 Sept. 1990, S/PV.2943
–S/22366, 20 March 1991, "Report to the Secretary-General on Humanitarian Needs in Kuwait and Iraq in the Immediate Post-Crisis Environment by a Mission to the Area Led by Mr Martti Ahtisaari, Under-Secretary General for Administration and Management, 10–17 March 1991."
–A/47/277–S/24111, Boutros Boutros-Ghali, "An Agenda for Peace, Preventive diplomacy, peacemaking and peace-keeping," Report of the Secretary-General pursuant to the statement adopted by the Summit Meeting of the Security Council on 31 Jan. 1992.
–A/50/60, Boutros Boutros-Ghali, *Supplement to An Agenda for Peace*, Jan. 3, 1995.
–S/1995/200 Annex 1, Letter Dated 13 April 1995, Addressed to the President of the Security Council.
–S/1995/300, *Permanent Members of the Security Council to the President of the Council*, 13 April 1995.
–S/1995/470, Secretary General to President of Security Council, 9 June 1995.
–S/1996/776, 24 Sept. 1996, Report of the Copenhagen round Table on United Nations Sanctions in the Case of the former Yugoslavia, held at Copenhagen on 24 and 25 June 1996.
–Hoskins, Eric, "A Study of UNICEF's Perspective on Sanctions," consultant's report, Jan. 1997.
United Nations, Population Division, 2005. *World Mortality Report*, 2005, s.v. Iraq: 214–15.
United States, Central Intelligence Agency, Judge William Webster, Director. Report for the 101st Congress, 7 Dec. 1990 5:40 EST.
– Comprehensive Report of the Special Advisor to the DCI on Iraq's WMD, 30 Sept. 2004, chap. 5, "Iraq's Chemical Warfare Program."
United States, Department of State, Publications 3497, "The Signing of the North Atlantic treaty," June 1949.

- *Bulletin*, Bureau of Public Affairs, 30 (25 Jan. 1954). John Foster Dulles. Address, 12 Jan. 1954, 107–10.
- *Bulletin*, Bureau of Public Affairs, 48 (Feb. 1963) Press Release on US and Canadian Negotiations Regarding Nuclear Weapons, 243–4.
- *Dispatch*, Bureau of Public Affairs, 1/12, 19 Nov. 1990, 273.
- *Dispatch*, Bureau of Public Affairs, 1/15, 10 Dec. 1990.
- *Dispatch*, Bureau of Public Affairs, 2/3, 21 Jan. 1991, 37.
- *Summary of the Dayton Peace Agreement on Bosnia-Herzegovina*, Nov. 30, 1995. http://www.pbs.org/newshour/bb/bosnia/dayton_peace.html
- Interagency Task Force on Serbian Sanctions. *UN Sanctions against Belgrade: Lessons Learned for Future Regimes*. Washington, D.C., June 1996,
- *Rambouillet Agreement: Interim Agreement for Peace and Self-Government in Kosovo*, nd., ca March 1999.

United States, Department of State, Foreign Relations, 1969–1976, vol. E-1. *Documents on Global Issues, 1969–72*.

United States Embassy in Canada, Website. *Selected Presidential Quotes on Canada*, nd.

United States, House of Representatives Committee on Armed Services. *Hearings on National Defense Authorization*, 102nd Congress, 1st Series, 1991, Department of the Navy: Lawrence Garrett, *Fiscal Years 1992–93 Report to Congress*, 21 Feb. 1991: 7, 312

United States, National Security Presidential Directive and Homeland Security Presidential Directive. "Arctic Region Policy," 9 Jan. 2009.

United States Navy. Sean O'Keefe, Secretary of the Navy. "From the Sea: Preparing the Naval Service for the 21st Century," Sept. 1992.

- Letter from Director, International Agreements, USN to Commander Legaarden, 2 June 1994, ser 03B2/4U006835.
- Office of Naval Research, Naval Ice Center, Oceanographer of the Navy, and the Arctic Research Commission, "Naval Operations in an Ice-Free Arctic," Symposium, April 2001.

United States Permanent Joint Board on Defence, 35th recommendation, 1946.

United States Senate, Committee on Armed Forces, Subcommittee on Sea Power and Force Projection, *Hearings on Department of Defense Authorization for Appropriations for Fiscal Year 1985*, 14 March 1984.

JOURNALISTIC SOURCES

Agence France-Presse (AFP). "China Sets Sail for the Arctic," 29 June 2010.

America.Gov. Bridget Hunter. "Joint U.S.-Canadian Mission Surveys Outer Edge of North America: Scientists collaborate in exploring continent's extended continental shelf," 15 Sept. 2009.

Barents Observer. "Large strategic exercise in Russia," 28 Sept. 2009.

BCLocalNews.Com. Stockwell Day. "Canadian navy plays a part in big Caribbean drug bust," 27 Feb. 2011.

Bosphorus Naval News. Devrm Yayiali. "Turkish Bulk Carrier Hijacked off Somalia," 30 Oct. 2008.

British Broadcasting Corporation, BBC *News*. Paul Reynolds. "The Arctic's New Gold Rush," 25 Oct. 2005.

- "India 'sinks Somali pirate ship,'" 19 Nov. 2008.
- "Nato troops free ship off Somalia after pirate attack," 5 Feb. 2010.

- Mark Lowen, "Bosnia nears political crisis point," 23 Feb. 2010.
- Richard Galpin. "Nuclear Power at Heart of Russia's Arctic Ambition," 21 Sept. 2010.
- "Cameron and Sarkozy hail UK-France defence treaties," 2 Nov. 2010 17:06 ET.
- Meirion Jones and Susan Watts, "Secret US embassy cables released by Wikileaks show nations are racing to 'carve up' Arctic resources – oil, gas and even rubies – as the ice retreats," 12 May 2011.
- "Piracy: IMO guidelines on armed guards on ships," 21 May 2011.
- "China aircraft carrier confirmed by general," 8 June 2011.
- "EU Iran sanctions: Ministers adopt Iran oil imports ban," 23 Jan. 2012.

Bulletin of the Atomic Scientists. Pierre Elliott Trudeau. "A Peace Initiative from Canada." Speech at the University of Guelph, 27 Oct. 1983, Jan. 1984: 15–19.
- William M. Arkin. "A Global Role for NATO," Jan. 1986: 4.

Cable News Network. "Seychelles convicts 11 Somali pirates," 27 July 2010.

Canada: *Postmedia News*, 8 May 2012, "Armed Arctic vessels face delay in latest procurement setback."

Canada.com. "Canada planning anti-sub exercises in the Arctic," 7 Aug. 2009.

Canadian American Strategic Review (CASR). "Canada Announces Deepwater Port at Nanisivik on Baffin Island & Army Base at Resolute – Key Points on North-West Passage," Aug. 2007.

Canadian Annual Review. Toronto: Annual Review Publishing Co., 1909.

Canadian Annual Review of Public Affairs. Toronto: University of Toronto Press, 1905.

Canadian Broadcasting Corporation (CBC). "Spies, Lies and Secret Weapons: The History of the Shkval Torpedo and Canada," *Fifth Estate*, ca 2002.
- "Canadian official called Bush 'a moron,'" 26 Nov. 2002.
- "JTF2: Canada's Super-Secret Commandos," 15 July 2005.
- "Navy technicians blew submarine's electrical system: report," 14 May 2006.
- "Ex-commando arrested day before JTF2 tell-all hits bookstores," 30 April 2008.
- "Preliminary work underway on High Arctic naval port," 5 Aug. 2008.
- (*Canadian Press*). "Bush signs new Arctic policy, outlining US intentions in the North," 12 Jan. 2009, 11:00 PM ET.
- "Arctic seabed mapping renewed," 29 July 2009.
- "Mackenzie River patrol asserts Canada's Arctic presence," 29 July 2009.
- "Arctic surveillance research moves ahead," 3 Nov. 2009.
- "Military's Arctic exercise to include US, Denmark," 18 Aug. 2010.
- "Arctic sovereignty 'non-negotiable': Harper," 20 Aug. 2010.
- "Omar Khadr sentenced to symbolic 40 years," 31 Oct. 2010.
- "JTF2 command "encouraged' war crimes, soldier alleges," 18 Jan. 2011.
- "Border talks 'not about sovereignty': Harper," 4 Feb. 2011.
- "PM pledges $5M for Libya aid," 2 March 2011.
- "CF-18 jets to help enforce Libya no-fly zone," 17 March 2011.
- "Who's contributing what to the Libya offensive," 22 March 2011.
- (*Canadian Press*). "Canadian to command NATO's Libya mission," 25 March 2011.
- "WikiLeaks: US dismisses Harper's Arctic talk," 12 May 2011.
- Greg Weston. "Canada offered to aid Iraq invasion: WikiLeaks," 16 May 2011.
- "Canada considering international bases: MacKay," 2 June 2011.

- Meagan Fitzpatrick. "Mackay confirms 'royal' renaming of military," 16 Aug. 2011.
- "HMCS Charlottetown sails for Mediterranean, Halifax ship joining NATO anti-terrorism patrol," 8 Jan. 2012.
- "Shipbuilding deals will stabilize industry, Harper says," 12 Jan. 2012 8:54 AM AT.

Canadian Military Gazette, 28 Nov. 1905.

Canadian Navy. News and Events. Slt Jonathan Douglas. "From the Arctic to the Caribbean," autumn 2009.
- "HMCS *Corner Brook* Returns from Caribbean," 4 Jan. 2001.

Canadian Press. "Canadian navy frigate deploys on 6-month counter terrorism mission," 26 Oct. 2009.
- "Montreal man on watch list rallies supporters," 12 Dec. 2010.

Canwest News Service. 28 Aug. 2008.

CBS. *60 Minutes*. Lesley Stahl and Madeleine Albright, May 1996.

Channel News Asia. 17 June 2009.

Christian Science Monitor. "Russia races for Arctic Resources," 31 July 2007.

CTV *News*. "Navy waters down plans for Arctic patrol ships." 17 June 2009.
- (*Canadian Press*) "Arctic naval facility years from completion," 29 May 2011.

Defensemanagement.com. "Merchant ships 'can use armed guards,'" 31 Oct. 2011.

Defense News. Andrew Chuter. "U.K., Canada Discuss Joint Frigate Development," 1 Feb. 2011.
- "UK ships' armed guards rules set," 6 Dec. 2011.

defenceWeb. "Shippers mull armed guard ramifications," 23 Nov. 2011 14:26.

Globe and Mail. "Nuclear Submarines to Enable Canada to Fight Modern War, Minister Says," 18 June 1987.
- 10, 14–16, 22, 27, 29 March; 1, 7, 17 April 1995; 15 April 2002.
- (*Canadian Press*) Bob Weber. "Forces' Arctic patrol more than just an exercise." Dundas Harbour, Nunavut, 21 Aug. 2006.
- J.L. Granatstein. "Does the Northwest Passage still matter? The shrinking Arctic icecap may soon ease Canada's sovereignty problem," 12 Jan. 2008.
- "Ottawa to keep tabs on large ships in northern waters," 26 Feb. 2010.
- Jane Taber. "Ottawa will spend $300-million to close Camp Mirage," 4 Nov. 2010.
- Steven Chase. "Canada negotiating perimeter security deal with US," 8 Dec. 2010.
- John Ibbitson and Steven Chase. "Harper and Obama eye sweeping change in border security," 4 Feb. 2011.

The Guardian. Richard J. Aldrich. "America Used Islamists to Arm the Bosnian Muslims: The Srebrenica Report Reveals the Pentagon's Role in a Dirty War"; 22 April 2002.
- Richard Norton-Taylor, "New Era Dawns for Anglo-French Defence," 28 Oct. 2010.

Halifax Chronicle-Herald. "Detection System in Arctic Revealed," 21 Aug. 1985.
- "MacKay: Warmer Arctic, new challenges," 8 Aug. 2009.

Indian Express. "No go-ahead from Ministry, so Navy opts out of US exercise," 29 Sept. 2009.

International Defense Review. "Lehman Seeks Superiority," no. 5 (1982): 547–8.

Khaleej Times, 10 Sept. 2007.

Kopri [Korean Polar Research Institute], "Araon," nd.
The Lancet. Editorial. "Starvation in Iraq," 11/9/91, vol. 338, issue 877: 1179.
– Richard Garfield. "Economic sanctions on Yugoslavia," 18 June 2001, vol. 358, issue 9281: 580.
Lloyd's List. Richard Meade. "UK government seeks to deter use of armed guards onboard," 25 Jan. 2010.
– David Osler. "China to co-ordinate patrols off Somalia – Beijing commits to permanent deployment in transit corridor," 29 Jan. 2010.
MARPAC's *In Focus.* "Piracy in Somalia: Why Solutions can't be found at sea," 30 July 2008.
– "HMCS Ville de Québec starts World Food Programme escort mission," 19 Aug. 2008.
Military Balance 1985–86. London: International Institute for Strategic Studies, 1985.
Montreal Gazette. "Russia Launches Arctic expedition, beefs up military presence," 6 July 2011.
National Post, Toronto. Chris Wattie. "US Sub May Have Toured Canadian Arctic Zone," 19 Dec. 2005: A1.
Naval Review. Anon. "The Future of the Royal Canadian Navy," 1915, 369.
– Anon. "The Royal Canadian Naval College," 1942: 157–8.
– B.X. [attributed to William Scott Chalmers]. "Canada and the Navy," 1913.
Navy News Service 6 Oct. 92 (NavNews 048/92). Sean O'Keefe, secretary of the navy, "From the Sea: Preparing the Naval Service for the 21st Century," Sept. 1992.
New England Journal of Medicine. Alberto Archerio et al. "The Effect of the Gulf War on Infant and Child Mortality in Iraq," 23 Sept. 1992, vol. 327: 931–6.
Newser (Wall Street Journal). Rob Quinn. "Ships Take Up Arms Against Pirates – Maritime tradition fades amid rise in attacks," 5 Jan. 2010.
New York Review of Books. Charles Simic. "Witness to Horror," vol. 57, no. 2 (11 Feb. 2010), 7.
New York Times. R.W. Apple Jr. "US 'Nightmare Scenario': Being Finessed by Iraq," 19 Dec. 1990. A16.
– "Franjo Tudjman, Ex-Communist General Who Led Croatia's Secession, Is Dead at 77," 11 Dec. 1999.
Northern News Services. "Navy fuel depot construction to begin in 2011," 7 Sept. 2009.
Nunatsiaq News. Chris Windeyer "Feds to replace old icebreaker," 29 Feb. 2008.
Ottawa Citizen. "DND plans to test model of proposed Arctic patrol vessels," 19 Aug. 2009.
– "Navy fuel depot construction to begin in 2011," 26 Nov. 2009.
– "Building of Canadian Forces Arctic Naval Facility Faces Delays," 28 Nov. 2009.
PCO [Polar Conservation Organisation]. Kris Molle. "First Antarctic voyage for South Korean icebreaker," Jan 13, 2010, 02:41 PM.
People's Daily Online. "Chinese ice breaker back to Zhongshan Station on Antarctica with supplies," 24 Feb. 2008, 11:25.
– "Canada upgraded to full member in western pacific naval symposium," 27 Oct. 2010.
Reuters. "Canada selects shipyards to modernize Navy," 19 Oct. 2011.

BIBLIOGRAPHY   423

– "EU faces warship shortage for Somali piracy mission," 23 Nov. 2011, 6:39am GMT.
RIA *Novosti*, "Will Russia create the World's Second Largest Surface Navy?" 13 Nov. 2007.
– "Russia could order Aircraft Carriers from Ukraine," 24 Sept. 2008.
– "Russian Warships Head to Mediterranean," 1 Oct. 2008.
– "Russian Naval Task Force Starts Venezuelan Visit," 25 Nov. 2008.
– "Russia's new Arctic force to focus on border protection," 30 March 2009.
– "Russia to build up submarine task force along Northern Sea Route," 10 Nov. 2011.
Saanich News. "HMCS Victoria returns to sea," 19 April 2011.
Strategic Comments. International Institute for Strategic Studies:
  –"Chinese navy's new strategy in action," vol. 16, comment 16, 6 May 2010.
  –"China's Three-Point Naval Strategy," vol. 16, comment 37, 15 Oct. 2010.
  –"The ambitious UK-France defence accord," vol. 16, comment 41, Nov. 2010.
  –"NATO: more consensus, but challenges remain," vol. 16, comment 45, Nov. 2010.
  –"India and China eye each other warily," vol. 16, comment 47, Dec. 2010.
  –"Diplomatic shifts in the warming Arctic," vol. 16, comment 50, Dec. 2010.
  –"Russian navy's regeneration plans," vol. 17, comment 8, Feb. 2011.
  –"Libya: direct military hits, unclear political targets," vol. 17, comment 12, March 2011.
  –"Lost in translation: China's opaque defence white paper," vol. 17, comment 17, April 2011.
  –"Behind recent gunboat diplomacy in the South China Sea," vol. 17, comment 28, Aug. 2011.
  –"Anglo-French defence: 'Entente Frugale plus,'" vol. 17, comment 47, Dec. 2011.
Strategy Page. "Pirates Feast on Gamblers," 3 Feb. 2010.
Sunday Times. 1 May 2005.
The Independent. Philip Thornton. "Britain pays off final instalment of US loan – after 61 years," 29 Dec. 2006.
The Star.com. Michael Byers. "Is Hillier out of line?" 20 Feb. 2007.
The Telegraph. Robin Cook. "Why it is in the interest of the Iraqi people to bomb Saddam," 20 Feb. 2001, 12:00AM GMT.
–Jack Fairweather in Baghdad and Anton La Guardia. "Chalabi stands by faulty intelligence that toppled Saddam's regime," 19 Feb. 2004.
Times of London, 11, 15–17, 27–31 March; 7, 12, 15, and 17 April, 1995.
Times Colonist. "PM vows more military resources to safeguard the North," 19 Aug. 2009.
– "Canadian Navy to modernize ships without US equipment," 24 Jan. 2010.
Toronto Star. Senator Colin Kenny. "A Porous Coastal Defence," 29 Oct. 2003, 1
Trident. Gina Combden. "Old Flag Flies Again," 8 May 1991.
UNICEF, *Information Newsline.* "Iraq surveys show 'humanitarian emergency,'" Wed. 12 Aug. 1999.
United Press International. "Russia halts aircraft carriers building," 10 Dec. 2010.
Vancouver Sun. Randy Boswell. "China moves to become major Arctic player," 1 March 2010.
– "Agreement clears way for Canadian military presence in Kuwait," 12 July 2011.
– "Canada invests in US satellite system," 27 Oct. 2011.

PUBLISHED ANALYTIC WORKS

Aberitt, Leah. "Chinese Hospital Ships and Soft Power." *Semaphore*, issue 03 (April 2011). Canberra: Sea Power Centre.

Agarwal, Gyan P. *New Horizons of Globalization: India and Canada*. New Delhi: Deep & Deep, 2007.

Alford, Jonathan. "Some Reflections on Technology and Seapower." *International Journal*, vol. 38, no. 3 (1982–83): 397–408.

Alford, Neil H. *Modern Economic Warfare (Law and the Naval Participant)*. Washington: United States Naval War College, 1967.

Ali, Mohamed, M. and Iqbal H. Shah, "Sanctions and Childhood Mortality in Iraq." *The Lancet*, vol. 355, issue 9218 (27 May 2000): 1851–7: doi:10.1016/s0140-6736(00)02289-3.

Allan, Catherine E. "A Minute Bletchley Park: Building a Canadian Naval Operational Intelligence Centre, 1939–1943." In Michael Hadley, Rob Huebert, and Fred Crickard, *A Nation's Navy*: 157–72.

Allen, Matthew. "The Changing Nature of Naval Strategy." *Naval Review*, vol. 81, no. 3 (July 1993): 235–43.

Allsopp, Jon. *Beyond JSS: Analyzing Canada's Amphibious Requirement*. Master of Defence Studies research paper, Canadian Forces College, CSC 33,.

Anon. *Canada and the Navy: Answers to important questions: On what grounds did Parliament decide upon a Canadian naval Service : What were the view of Hon. Geo E. Foster who introduced the resolution?* Ottawa: Central Information Office of the Canadian Liberal Party, 1913.

– *Canada and the navy: the memorandum prepared by the Board of Admiralty on the general naval situation ... what it discloses*. Ottawa: Central Information Office of the Canadian Liberal Party, 1913.

– *Comments on the Senate's rejection of the Naval Aid Bill*. [Ottawa?: s.n., 1913?]

Appleton, Thomas E. *Usque ad Mare: A History of the Canadian Coast Guard and Marine Services*. Ottawa: Department of Transport, 1968 (1969).

Archer, Clive, and David Scrivener. *Northern Waters: Security and Resource Issues*. London: Croom Helm, 1986.

Arctic Council and the International Arctic Science Committee. *Impacts of a Warming Arctic: Arctic Climate Impact Assessment*. Cambridge: Cambridge University Press, 2004.

Armstrong, John G. "The Dundonald Affair." *Canadian Defence Quarterly*, vol. 11, no. 2 (autumn 1981): 39–45.

Arnold-Forster, W.E. *The Economic Blockade 1914–1919*. Admiralty Staff History. 1920.

Augustus, Peter. "Naval Boarding Party Operations." *Canadian Naval Review*, vol. 3, no. 4 (winter 2008): 26–7.

Axworthy, Lloyd. "Canada and Human Security: The Need for Leadership." *International Journal*, vol. 52, no. 2 (1996–97): 183–96.

Bacon, Francis. "Of the True Greatness of Kingdoms and Estates." In *The Essays or Counsels, Civil and Moral, of Francis Lord Verulam Viscount St Albans*. Mount Vernon, New York: Peter Pauper Press, nd.

Bailey, Jennifer L. "Hot Fish and (Bargaining) Chips." *Journal of Peace Research*, vol. 33 (Aug. 1996): 257–62.

Baldwin, Stanley. *Summary of Proceedings: Imperial Conference, 1926*. London: F.A. Acland, 1926.

Barnhouse, Pat. "Of Hydrofoils and Things." *Canadian Naval Review*, vol. 2, no. 1 (spring 2006): 32–3.
Barry, Donald. "The Canada-European Union Turbot War: Internal Politics and Transatlantic Bargaining." *International Journal*, vol. 53, no. 2 (1997–98): 253–84.
Bartenstein, Kristin. "Flag-Planting: What Legal Framework Governs the Division of the Arctic Continental Shelf." *International Journal*, vol. 65, no. 1 (winter 2009–10): 187–207.
Bascot, Roy C., USAF, "Global Movements and Operational Support Hub Concept: GlobalReach for the Canadian Forces." *Canadian Air Force Journal*, vol. 2, no. 3 (summer 2009): 9–17.
Bashow, David L. et al., "Mission Ready: Canada's Role in the Kosovo Air Campaign." *Canadian Military Journal*, spring 2000: 55–61.
Baxter, 3rd, James P. "Some British Opinions as to Neutral Rights, 1861 to 1865." *Naval Review*, vol. 18, no 1 (1930–31): 73–96.
Beaton, Leonard. "Imperial Defence without the Empire." *International Journal*, vol. 23, no. 4 (1967–68): 531–40.
Beatty, David. "The 'Canadian Corollary' to the Monroe Doctrine and the Ogdensburg Agreement of 1940." *The Northern Mariner*, vol. 1, no. 1 (1991): 3–22.
Bedford, Christian. "The View from the West: Asia's Race for Carriers." *Canadian Naval Review*, vol. 5 no. 1 (spring 2009): 33–5.
Behrens, C.B.A. *Merchant Shipping and the Demands of War*. London: HMSO, 1955.
Bell, Christopher M. "Thinking the Unthinkable: British and American Naval Strategies for an Anglo-American War, 1918–1931." *International History Review*, vol. 19, no. 4 (Nov. 1997): 789–808.
Bercuson, David Jay. "Continental Defense and Arctic Sovereignty, 1945–50." In Keith Neilson and Ronald G. Haycock, eds. *The Cold War and Defense*: 153–70.
– "Canada, NATO, and Rearmament, 1950–1954: Why Canada Made a Difference (But Not for Very Long)." In John English and Norman Hillmer, eds., *Making a Difference?*: 103–24.
– *True Patriot: The Life of Brooke Claxton, 1898–1960*. Toronto: University of Toronto Press, 1993.
Berger, Carl, ed. *Imperial Relations in the Age of Laurier*. See Cook, Ramsay.
Berger, Thomas R. et al., *The Arctic Choices for Peace and Security*. West Vancouver: Gordon Soules Book Publishers, 1989.
Berghahn, V.R. *Germany and the Approach of War in 1914*. London: Macmillan, 1973.
Bernier, Serge. "HMCS Ottawa III: The Navy's First French-Language Unit, 1968–1973." In Michael Hadley, Rob Huebert, and Fred Crickard, *A Nation's Navy*: 310–24.
– and John MacFarlane, eds. *Canada, 1900–1950: Un pays prend sa place/A Country Comes of Age*. Ottawa: Organization for the History of Canada, 2003: 111–26.
Bidwell, Shelford. *Fire-power*. See: Graham, Dominic.
Birnbaum, Karl E. *Peace Moves and U-boat Warfare: A Study of Imperial Germany's Policy towards the United States, April 18, 1916–Jan. 9, 1917*. Hamden, Connecticut: Archon Books, 1970.

Black, Joseph Laurence, and Norman Hillmer. *Nearly Neighbours: Canada and the Soviet Union, from Cold War to Détente and Beyond.* Kingston: Frye Publishers, 1989.

Blackburn, Derek. "Maritime Defence Policy: A New Democrat's Perspective." In William J. Yost, *In Defence of Canada's Oceans*: 21–8.

Blanchette, Arthur E, ed. *Canadian Foreign Policy, 1955–65: Selected Speeches and Documents.* Toronto: McClelland & Stewart, 1980.

– *Canadian Foreign Policy, 1966–76: Selected Speeches and Documents.* Ottawa: The Carleton Library 118, 1980.

– *Canadian Foreign Policy, 1972–92: Selected Speeches and Documents.* Ottawa: Carleton University Press, 1994.

Bland, Douglas. "Continuity in Canadian Naval Policy, 1961–1987." *Canadian Defence Quarterly*, vol. 18, no. 5, 1989: 29–32.

– *Chiefs of Defence: Government and the Unified Command of the Canadian Armed Forces.* Toronto: CISS, 1995.

– ed. *Canada's National Defence.* 2 vols., *Defence Policy* and *Defence Organization.* Kingston, Ontario: Queen's University, School of Policy Studies, 1997–98.

– and Sean Maloney. *Campaigns for International Security: Canada's Defence Policy at the Turn of the Century.* Montreal and Kingston: McGill-Queen's University Press, 2004.

Bodansky, Yossef. *Bin Laden: The Man Who Declared War on America.* Forum, c. 1999, 2001.

– *The Secret History of the Iraq War.* New York: Regan Books (HarperCollins), 2004.

Booth, Ken. *Navies and Foreign Policy.* London: Croom Helm, 1977.

– "Naval Strategy and the Spread of Psycho-Legal Boundaries at Sea." *International Journal*, vol. 38 no. 3 (1982–83): 373–96.

Borden, Robert Laird. "Canada and the Navy." Halifax: Liberal Party of Canada, no. 31, Oct. 1909.

– "The Naval Question": Speech delivered by Mr R.L. Borden, M.P., 12 Jan. 1910 [Ottawa? : s.n., 1910?].

Bothwell, Robert. *Pirouette: Pierre Trudeau and Canadian Foreign Policy.* See Granatstein, J.L.

– *Canada and the United States: The Politics of Partnership.* Toronto: University of Toronto Press, 1992.

– "Has Canada Made a Difference? The Case of Canada and the United States." In John English and Norman Hillmer, eds., *Making a Difference?*: 1–14.

– "The Cold War and the Curate's Egg: When Did Canada's Cold War Really Begin? Later Than You Might Think." *International Journal*, vol. 53, no. 3 (1997–98): 407–18.

– *Alliance and Illusion: Canada and the World, 1945–1984.* Vancouver: University of British Columbia Press, 2007.

Boulden, Jane, and Andrea Charron. "Evaluating UN Sanctions: New Ground, New Dilemmas, and Unintended Consequences." *International Journal*, vol. 65, no. 1 (winter 2009–10): 1–12.

Boutilier, James, ed. *RCN in Retrospect, 1910–1968.* Vancouver: University of British Columbia Press, 1982.

– "The Canadian Navy and the New Naval Environment in Asia." *International Journal*, vol. 58, no. 1 (2002–03): 181–200.

Brebner, John Bartlet. *North Atlantic Triangle: The Interplay of Canada, the United*

States, and Great Britain. Toronto and New Haven: Ryerson and Yale University Press, 1945.
Breemer, Jan. "The End of Naval Strategy: Revolutionary Change and the Future of American Naval Power." In Peter T. Haydon and Ann L. Griffiths, eds., *Maritime Security and Conflict Resolution at Sea in the Post-Cold War Era*: 135–42.
Brown, Robert Craig. *Canada's National Policy 1883–1900.* Princeton, New Jersey: Princeton University Press, 1964.
– "Sir Robert Borden and Canada's War Aims." In Barry Hunt and Adrian Preston, eds., *War Aims and Strategic Policy in the Great War*: 55–66.
– ed. *Imperial Relations in the Age of Laurier.* See Cook, Ramsay.
Buckner, Phillip. "Presidential Address: Whatever Happened to the British Empire?" Canadian Historical Association, 1993.
– *Canada and the End of Empire.* Vancouver: University of British Columbia Press, 2004.
Buehrig, Edward Henry. *Woodrow Wilson and the Balance of Power.* Gloucester, Massachusetts: P. Smith, 1968.
Burke, Edmund. *The Speeches of the Right Honourable Edmund Burke, in the House of Commons, and in Westminster Hall.* 4 vols. London: Longman & Co.; J. Ridgway, 1816.
Bush, George W. "Remarks on US and Canada Relations and the War on Terrorism." 1 Dec. 2004, Halifax, Nova Scotia. *American Rhetoric, On-Line Speech Bank.*
Bush, James T. "Maritime Strategy and Nuclear-Free Zones." In Thomas R. Berger et al., *The Arctic Choices for Peace and Security*: 227–36.
Buteux, Paul. "Nato and the Evolution of Canadian Defence and Foreign Policy." In David B. Devitt and David Leyton-Brown, *Canada's International Security Policy*: 163.
Byers, Michael. "Canadian Armed Forces under United States Command." *International Journal*, vol. 58, no. 1 (2002–03): 89–114.
– "War, Law, and Geopolitical Change: The Lessons of History." *International Journal*, vol. 61, no. 1 (2005–06): 201–13.
Byers, Rob B. "Defence and Foreign Policy in the 1970s: The Demise of the Trudeau Doctrine." *International Journal*, vol. 33, no. 2 (1978–79): 312–38.
– "The 1987 Defence White Paper: An Analysis." Halifax: Centre for Foreign Policy Analysis, Dalhousie University, autumn 1987.
Cable, Sir James. *Gunboat Diplomacy.* London: Chatto and Windus, 1971.
Cafferky, Shawn. *Uncharted Waters: A History of the Canadian Helicopter-Carrying Destroyer.* Halifax: Centre for Foreign Policy Studies, Dalhousie University, 2005.
Caldwell, Nathaniel French. *Arctic Leverage.* New York: Praeger, 1990.
Caldwell, Robert H. "Rear-Admiral William M. Landymore: The Silent Service Speaks Out." In Michael Whitby, Richard Gimblett, and Peter Haydon, *The Admirals*: 275–305.
Campbell, Isabel, "A Transformation in Thinking: The RCN's Naval Warfare Study Group of 1956." In Richard Gimblett and Richard Mayne, eds., *People, Policy and Programmes*: 165–81.
– "A Brave New World, 1945–60." In Richard H. Gimblett, ed., *The Naval Service of Canada, 1910–2010: The Centennial Story*: 123–37.
– "Canadian Insights into NATO Maritime Strategy, 1949-69: The Role of National and Service Interests." Proceedings of the Canadian Navy Centennial /

Ninth Maritime Command (MARCOM) History Conference, *From Empire to In(ter)dependence: The Canadian Navy and the Commonwealth Experience, 1910–2010*. Ottawa: Canadian Naval Heritage Press, May 2010.

Cannizzo, CA, "NORAD-NATO Linkages," *Canadian Defence Quarterly*, vol. 19, no. 5 (April 1990): 21–7.

Carnaghan, Matthew, and Allison Goody. *Canadian Arctic Sovereignty*. Parliamentary Information and Research Service: Political and Social Affairs Division, 26 Jan. 2006.

Cellucci, Paul. Speech, Economic Club of Toronto, 25 March 2003.

– *Unquiet Diplomacy*. Toronto: Key Porter, 2005.

Chalmers, William Scott [writing as BX]. "Canada and the Navy." *Naval Review* 1913, 100.

Chambers, Ernest J. *The Canadian Marine: A History of the Department of Marine and Fisheries*. Toronto: Canadian Marine and Fisheries History, 1905.

Charron, Andrea. "The Northwest Passage: Is Canada's Sovereignty Floating Away?" *International Journal*, vol. 60, no. 3 (summer 2005): 831–48.

– and Jane Boulden. "Evaluating UN Sanctions: New Ground, New Dilemmas, and Unintended Consequences." *International Journal*, vol. 65, no. 1 (winter 2009–10): 1–12.

Christie, Keith H. *Stacking the Deck: Compliance and Dispute Settlement in International Environmental Agreements*. Canada, Department of Foreign Affairs and International Trade, Policy Staff Paper No. 93/15, Dec. 1993.

Christol, Carlo Q. and Charles R. Davis. "Maritime Quarantine: The Naval Interdiction of Offensive Weapons and Associated Materiel to Cuba, 1962." *The American Yearbook of International Law*, vol. 57 (1963): 525–45.

Churchill, Winston (Robert Rhodes James, ed.). *Winston Churchill: His Complete Speeches, 1897–1963*, 8 vols. London, Chelsea House Publishers, 1974.

Clark, Lovell C., ed. *Documents on Canadian External Relations*, vol. 3, 1919–28. Ottawa: Department of External Affairs, 1970.

Clarke, Richard A. *Against All Enemies: Inside America's War on Terror – What Really Happened*. New York: Free Press, 3 Oct. 2004.

Clausewitz, Carl von (Michael Howard, Peter Paret, Beatrice Heuser, eds.). *On War*. London: Oxford University Press, 2007.

Clearwater, John. "Naval nuclear weapons at CFMETR Nanoose, 1965–2001." *The ACTivist Magazine*, 29 July 2004.

– *Just Dummies: Cruise Missile Testing in Canada*. Calgary: University of Calgary Press, 2006.

Cohen, Maxwell. "The Arctic and the National Interest." *International Journal*, vol. 26, no. 1 (1970–71): 52–81.

Conference of Defence Associations. *Canadian Security: A Force Structure Model for the 21st Century*. Ottawa, June 1994: 20–1.

Cook, Ramsay, Craig Brown, and Carl Berger, eds. *Imperial Relations in the Age of Laurier*. Toronto: University of Toronto Press, Canadian Historical Readings, 1969.

Coombs, Howard. *Beware of Putting the Cart Before the Horse*. See: English, Allan.

Corbett, Sir Julian. *England in the Seven Years' War*, 2 vols. London: Longmans, Green and Co., 1907 [1918].

– *Some Principles of Maritime Strategy*. London: Longmans, Green & Co., 1911.

Cordesman, Anthony H. *The Gulf and the West: Strategic Relations and Military Realities*. Boulder, Colorado: Westview, 1988.
Cortright, David, and George A. Lopez. *The Sanctions Decade: Assessing UN Strategies in the 1990s*, Boulder and London: Lynne Rienner, 2000.
– *Smart Sanctions: Targeting Economic Statecraft*. Lanham, Maryland: Rowman & Littlefield Publishers, 2002.
Cote, Owen J. *The Third Battle: Innovation in the US Navy's Silent Cold War Struggle with Soviet Submarines*. http://www.navy.mil/navydata/cno/n87/history/cold-war-asw.html
Cox, Harold E. *The Palgrave Concise Historical Atlas of the Balkans*. See: Hupchick, Dennis P.
Craven, Michael. "Comment of the Perkins and Webster Articles," *Canadian Naval Review*, vol. 3 no. 4 (winter 2008): 28–9.
Crickard, Fred W. ed. "Maritime Security Working Papers, No. 3." Halifax: Centre for Foreign Policy Studies, Dalhousie University, May 1996.
– *A Nation's Navy*. See: Hadley, Michael L.
–and Gregory L. Witol. "The Political Uses of Medium Power Navies." In Ann Griffiths, Peter Haydon, and Richard Gimblett, *Canadian Gunboat Diplomacy*: 258.
– and Paul T. Mitchell and Katherine Orr, eds. *Multinational Naval Cooperation and Foreign Policy into the 21st Century*. Aldershot: Ashgate, 1998.
Crist, David B. "The Formation of a Coalition of the Willing and Operation *Iraqi Freedom*," In Bruce Elleman and Sarah Paine, eds., *Naval Coalition Warfare*: 209–18.
Critchley, W, Harriet. "Polar Deployment of Soviet Submarines." *International Journal*, vol. 39, no. 3 (1984): 828–65.
– "Defence and Policing in Arctic Canada." In Franklyn Griffiths, *Politics of the Northwest Passage*: 200–15.
Dalhousie University, Centre for Foreign Policy Studies, Oct. 2007, *Backgrounder: Victoria Class Submarines, Northern Operations & Air Independent Propulson*.
Davidson, Bob. "Canadian Navy, Modern Naval Diplomacy – A Practitioner's View." *Journal of Military and Strategic Studies*, vol. 11, issues 1 and 2 (autumn and winter 2008–09): 1–47.
Davies, Peter G.G. "The EC/Canadian Fisheries Dispute in the Northwest Atlantic." *International and Comparative Law Quarterly*, vol. 44, no. 4 (Oct. 1995): 927–38.
Daviluy, Michelle. "Communicating among linguistic communities onboard a Canadian Navy Ship," http://www.ualberta.ca/~mdaveluy/Daveluy_APLA.pdf
Davis, Charles R. "Maritime Quarantine." See: Christol, Q.
Davis, S. Mathwin. "It Has All Happened Before: The RCN, Nuclear Propulsion and Submarines – 1958–68." *Canadian Defence Quarterly*, vol. 17, no. 2 (Oct. 1987): 34–40.
– "The 'St Laurent' Decision: Genesis of a Canadian Fleet." In W.A.B. Douglas, ed., *The RCN in Transition, 1910–1985*: 187–208.
– "Naval Procurement, 1950–1965." In David G. Haglund, ed., *Canada's Defence Industrial Base*: 97–117.
Delaney, Jason M. "Submarine Procurement and the *Victoria*-class Acquisition from an Historical Perspective: Having Submarines is the Point!" *Canadian Naval Review*, vol. 4, no. 2 (summer 2009): 22–7.

– "The One Class of Vessel that is Impossible to Build in ~~Australia~~ Canada," Proceedings of the Canadian Navy Centennial / Ninth Maritime Command (MARCOM) History Conference, *From Empire to In(ter)dependence: The Canadian Navy and the Commonwealth Experience, 1910-2010*. Ottawa: Canadian Naval Heritage Press, May 2010.
Dewey, A. Gordon. *The Dominions and Diplomacy: The Canadian Contribution*, vol. 1. London: Longmans, 1929.
Dewitt, David B. and David Leyton-Brown. *Canada's International Security Policy*. Scarborough, Ontario: Prentice Hall, 1995.
Dillon, G.M. "Canadian Naval Policy since World War II: A Decision-making Analysis." Occasional Paper. Halifax: Centre for Foreign Policy Studies, Dalhousie University, Oct. 1972.
Dobell, Peter C. and Robert Willmot. "John Holmes," *International Journal*, vol. 33, no. 1 (1977–78): 104–14.
Donaghy, Greg. "Canadian Relations with the United Kingdom at the End of Empire." See: Hilliker, John.
– and Stéphan Roussel. *Escott Reid: Diplomat and Scholar*. Montreal and Kingston: McGill-Queen's University Press, 2004.
Dönitz, Carl (R.H. Stevens, trans). *Memoirs: Ten Years and Twenty Days*. Westport, Connecticut: Greenwood Press, 1976.
Douglas, William Alexander Binny. "Conflict and Innovation in the Royal Canadian Navy, 1939–1945." In Gerald Jordan, ed., *Naval Warfare in the Twentieth Century 1900–1945: Essays in Honour of Arthur Marder*: 210–32.
– *The Creation of a National Air Force: The Official History of the Royal Canadian Air Force*. Toronto: University of Toronto Press. 1986.
– *The RCN in Transition, 1910–1985*. Vancouver: University of British Columbia Press, 1988.
– with Roger Sarty, and Michael Whitby. *No Higher Purpose: The Official Operational History of the Royal Canadian Navy in the Second World War, 1939–1943*, vol. 2, pt. 1. St Catharines, Ontario: Vanwell Publishing, 2002.
– with Roger Sarty, Michael Whitby, Robert H. Caldwell, William Johnston, and William G. P. Rawling, *A Blue Water Navy: The Official Operational History of the Royal Canadian Navy in the Second World War, 1943–1945*, vol. 2, pt. 2. St Catharines, Ontario: Vanwell Publishing, 2007.
Doxey, Margaret P. "Evolution and Adaptation in the Modern Commonwealth." *International Journal*, vol. 45, no. 4 (1989–90): 889–912.
– "Canada and the Commonwealth." In John English and Norman Hillmer, eds., *Making a Difference?*: 34.
– *International Sanctions in Contemporary Perspective*. London: MacMillan, 1996.
– "Sanctions through the Looking Glass: The Spectrum of Goals and Achievements." *International Journal*, vol. 55, no. 2 (1999–2000): 207–23.
– *United Nations Sanctions: Trends and Problems*. Halifax: Centre for Foreign Policy Studies, Dalhousie University, 2007.
Drent, Jan. "'A Good, Workable Little Fleet': Canadian Naval Policy, 1945–1950." In Michael Hadley, Rob Huebert, and Fred Crickard, *A Nation's Navy*: 205–20.
– "Confrontation in the Sargasso Sea: Soviet Submarines During the Cuban Missile Crisis." *The Northern Mariner/Le Marin du nord*, vol. 13, no. 3 (July 2003): 1–19.
Durflinger, Serge. "In Whose Interests? The Royal Canadian Navy and Naval

Diplomacy in El Salvador, 1932." In Ann Griffiths, Peter Haydon, and Richard Gimblett, *Canadian Gunboat Diplomacy*: 27–44.

Eayrs, James. *The Commonwealth and Suez: A Documentary Survey*. London: Oxford University Press, 1964.

– *In Defence of Canada* 5 vols: Vol. 1, *From the Great War to the Great Depression*, 1964; Vol. 2, *Appeasement and Rearmament*, 1964-65; Vol. 3, *Peacemaking and Deterrence*, 1972; Vol. 4, *Growing Up Allied*, 1980; Vol. 5, *Indochina: Roots of Complicity*. Toronto: University of Toronto Press, 1964–1983.

– "The Round Table Movement in Canada.' In Ramsay Cook, Craig Brown, and Carl Berger, eds., *Imperial Relations in the Age of Laurier*: 61–80.

Edwards, Robert H, and Graham Walker, eds. *Continental Security and Canada-U.S. Relations: Maritime Perspectives, Challenges and Opportunities*. Halifax: Centre for Foreign Policy Studies, Dalhousie University, May 2004.

Eisenhower Study Group. "The Costs of War Since 2001: Iraq, Afghanistan, and Pakistan." Providence, Rhode Island: Eisenhower Research Project, Thomas J. Watson Jr. Institute for International Studies (Brown University), June 2011.

Elleman, Bruce A, and Sarah C.M. Paine, eds. *Naval Blockades and Seapower: Strategies and Counter-Strategies, 1805–2005*. London and New York: Routledge, 2006.

– *Naval Coalition Warfare: From the Napoleonic War to Operation Iraqi Freedom*. London and New York, Routledge, 2008.

Elliott, Kimberly Ann. *Economic Sanctions Reconsidered*. See Hufbauer, Gary Clyde.

English, Allan, with Richard Gimblett and Howard Coombs. *Beware of Putting the Cart Before the Horse: Network Enabled Operations as a Canadian Approach to Transformation*. Canada: Defence Research and Development Canada, 19 July 2005.

English, John and Norman Hillmer, eds. *Making a Difference? Canada's Foreign Policy in a Changing World Order*. Toronto: Lester Publishing, 1992.

Epkenhans, Michael. "Imperial Germany and the Importance of Sea Power." In N.A.M. Rodger, *Naval Power in the 20th Century*: 27.

Errington, Elizabeth Jane. *Navies and Global Security*. See, Neilson, Keith.

Ewart, J.S. *Kingdom Papers*. Ottawa: no imprint, 1912.

Fakash, Mahmud A. "The Prospects of Islamic Fundamentalism in the Post–Gulf War Period," *International Journal*, vol. 49, no. 3 (1993–94): 613–34.

Falkenheim, Peggy L. "Post–Afghanistan Sanctions." In David Leyton–Brown, ed., *The Utility of International Economic Sanctions*: 105.

Fanshawe, Sir Arthur D. "Freedom of the Seas," *Naval Review*, vol. 2, 1929: 382.

Farr, David. "Prime Minister Trudeau's Opening to the Soviet Union, 1971." In Joseph Laurence Black and Norman Hillmer, *Nearly Neighbours*: 102–18.

Fedyszyn, Thomas R., "Renaissance of the Russian Navy?" *U.S. Naval Institute Proceedings*, vol. 138/3/1, 309: 31–5.

Fenton, Bruce. "Foreign Policy and Naval Forces: A Canadian Perspective." In Fred Crickard, ed., *Maritime Security Working Papers*: 73–9.

Ferguson, Julie H. *Through a Canadian Periscope: The Story of the Canadian Submarine Service*, Toronto: Dundurn Press, 1995.

– *Deeply Canadian: New Submarines for a New Millennium*. Port Moody: Beacon Publishing, 2000.

Ferris, John. "The Last Decade of British Maritime Supremacy, 1919–1929." In Greg Kennedy and Keith Neilson, *Far-Flung Lines*: 124–70.

Fisk, Robert. *The Great War for Civilisation: The Conquest of the Middle East.* Fourth Estate, 2005.

Forbes, Andrew, ed. *Australia's Response to Piracy: A Legal Perspective.* Papers in Australian Maritime Affairs No. 31. Canberra: Sea Power Centre, 2011.

– and Michelle Lovi, eds. *Australian Maritime Issues 2006.* Canberra: Sea Power Centre, 2007.

Ford, Robert A.D. *Our Man in Moscow: A Diplomat's Reflections on the Soviet Union.* Toronto: University of Toronto Press, 1989.

Forsey, Eugene Alfred. *Freedom and Order.* The Carleton Library No. 73. Toronto: McClelland & Stewart Ltd., 1974.

Forster, D.F. *Mackenzie King Record, 1960–1970.* See: Pickersgill, J.W.

Fortmann, Michel, and Martin Larose. "Emerging Strategic Counterculture: Pierre Elliott Trudeau, Canadian Intellectuals and the Revision of Liberal Defence Policy concerning NATO (1968–1969)." *International Journal,* vol. 59, no. 3 (2002): 537–56.

Fowlow, Fred R. "Nanoose Bay – Let's Get The Facts Straight." *Starshell,* vol. 7, no. 7 (summer 1999).

Freeman, Dave. "The CANADA Badge: Forging a Canadian Identity." CFB Esquimalt Naval & Military Museum.

Friedman, Norman. *Seapower as Strategy: Navies and National Interests.* Annapolis, Maryland: Naval Institute Press, 2001.

– *The Naval Institute Guide to World Naval Weapon Systems,* 5th ed. Annapolis, Maryland: Naval Institute Press, 2006.

– *Network-Centric Warfare: How Navies Learned to Fight Smarter in Three World Wars.* Annapolis Maryland: Naval Institute Press, 2009.

– "The Commonwealth Approach to Atlantic Warfare, 1945–55." Proceedings of the Canadian Navy Centennial / Ninth Maritime Command (MARCOM) History Conference, *From Empire to In(ter)dependence: The Canadian Navy and the Commonwealth Experience, 1910–2010.* Ottawa: Canadian Naval Heritage Press, May 2010.

Fry, Michael. ed. *Freedom and Change: Essays in Honour of Lester B. Pearson.* Toronto: McClelland & Stewart, 1975.

Fulton, J. Andrew. Note in Michael Whitby, Richard Gimblett, and Peter Haydon, *The Admirals*: 333.

Garnett, G.L. "The Future of Maritime Peacekeeping." In Fred Crickard, ed., *Maritime Security – Working Papers,* No. 3 (3 May 1996).

Gates, Robert Michael. *From the Shadows: The Ultimate Insider's Story of Five Presidents and How They Won the Cold War.* New York: Simon & Schuster, 1996 (2007).

Gellman, Peter. "Lester B. Pearson, Collective Security, and the World Order Tradition of Canadian Foreign Policy." *International Journal,* vol. 44, no. 1 (1988–89): 68–101.

Gellner, John. *Canada in NATO.* Toronto: Ryerson Press, 1970.

– "Strategic Analysis in Canada." *International Journal,* vol. 33, no. 3 (1977–78): 493–505.

– "The Defence of Canada: Requirements, Capabilities, and the National Will." *Behind the Headlines,* vol. 42, no. 3, 1985: 1.

German, Tony. *The Sea is at Our Gates: The History of the Canadian Navy.* Toronto: McClelland & Stewart, 1990.

Gervais, Honoré. Speech of Mr Honoré Gervais, M.P., on the naval service of Canada. Ottawa, Tuesday, March 8, 1910 [Ottawa?: s.n., 1910?].

Gibbons, Elizabeth. *Sanctions in Haiti: Human Rights and Democracy Under Assault*. Centre for Strategic and International Studies, Washington Papers 177. Westport Connecticut: Praeger, 1999.

Gimblett, Richard Howard. "Reassessing the Dreadnought Crisis of 1909 and the Origins of the Royal Canadian Navy." *The Northern Mariner/Le Marin du nord*, vol. 4, no. 1 (Jan. 1994): 35–53.

– "MIF or MNF? The Dilemma of the 'Lesser' Navies in the Gulf War Coalition." In Michael Hadley, Rob Huebert, and Fred Crickard, *A Nation's Navy*: 190–204.

– *Operation Friction*. See: Morin, Jean H.

– ed., *Canadian Gunboat Diplomacy*. See: Griffiths, Ann L.

– "HMCS Crescent and the Chinese Civil War." In Ann Griffiths, Peter Haydon, and Richard Gimblett. *Canadian Gunboat Diplomacy*: 77–94.

– "Too Many Chiefs and Not Enough Seamen: The Lower-Deck Complement of a Postwar Royal Canadian Navy Destroyer: The Case of HMCS Crescent, March 1949," *Northern Mariner/Le Marin du nord*, vol. 9, no. 3 (1999): 1–22.

– "A Century of Canadian Maritime Force Development: A Re-interpretive History." In Edward L. Tummers, *Maritime Security in the Twenty-first Century*: 17.

– "What the Mainguy Report Never Told Us: The Tradition of 'Mutiny' in the Royal Canadian Navy Before 1949." *Canadian Military Journal*, summer 2000: 85–92.

– *Operation Apollo: The Golden Age of the Canadian Navy in the War against Terrorism*. Ottawa: Magic Light Publishing, 2004.

– "Command in the Canadian Navy: An Historical Survey." *The Northern Mariner/Le Marin du nord*, vol. 14, no. 4 (Oct. 2004), 41–60.

– *Beware of Putting the Cart Before the Horse*. See: English, Allan.

– *The Admirals: Canada's Senior Naval Leadership in the Twentieth Century*. See: Whitby, Michael.

– "Admiral Sir Charles E. Kingsmill: Forgotten Father." In Michael Whitby, Richard Gimblett, and Peter Haydon, *The Admirals*: 31–54.

– and Richard O. Mayne, eds. *People, Policy and Programmes: Proceedings of the 7th Maritime Command (MARCOM) Historical Conference (2005)*. Ottawa: Canadian Naval Heritage Press, 2008.

– ed., *The Naval Service of Canada, 1910–2010: The Centennial Story*. Toronto: Dundurn Press, 2009.

– "The Transformation Era: 1990 to the Present." In Richard Gimblett, ed., *The Naval Service of Canada, 1910–2010: The Centennial Story*: 185–219.

– *The Seabound Coast: The Official History of the Royal Canadian Navy*. See under Johnston, William.

Girouard, Roger. "Leadership for a Sustainable Culture of Peace." See: Rippon, Major Thomas.

Glazebrook, George Parkin de Twenebroker. *A History of Canadian External Relations*. Toronto: Oxford University Press, 1950.

Glover, William. "The RCN: Royal Colonial or Royal Canadian Navy?" In Michael Hadley, Rob Huebert, and Fred Crickard, *A Nation's Navy*: 71–90.

Goldrick, James, ed. *Mahan Is Not Enough*. See: Hattendorf, John.

– "Strangers in Their Own Seas? A Comparison of the Australian and Canadian

Naval Experience, 1910–1982." In Michael Hadley, Rob Huebert, and Fred Crickard, *A Nation's Navy*: 325–30.
- "Maritime Sanctions Enforcement against Iraq, 1990–2003." In Bruce Elleman and Sarah Paine, eds., *Naval Blockades and Seapower*: 201–13, 296–98.
- "The Maritime Element in the 1990–91 Gulf Crisis: Drawing on the Dividends of Half a Century of Multinational Naval Operations." In Bruce Elleman and Sarah Paine, eds., *Naval Coalition Warfare*: 158–68.
- "From Fleets to Navies: The Evolution of Dominion Fleets into the Independent Navies of the Commonwealth." Proceedings of the Canadian Navy Centennial / Ninth Maritime Command (MARCOM) History Conference, *From Empire to In(ter)dependence: The Canadian Navy and the Commonwealth Experience, 1910–2010*. Ottawa: Canadian Naval Heritage Press, May 2010.
Goody, Allison. *Canadian Arctic Sovereignty*. See: Carnaghan, Matthew.
Gordon, Donald C. *Dominion Partnership in Imperial Defence*. Baltimore: Johns Hopkins University Press, 1965.
Gosselin, Daniel, and Craig Stone. "From Minister Hellyer to General Hillier: Understanding the Fundamental Differences Between the Unification of the Canadian Forces and its Present Transformation." *Canadian Military Journal*, vol. 6, no. 4 (winter 2005–06): 9.
- "Hellyer's Ghosts: Unification of the Canadian Forces Is 40 Years Old," *Canadian Military Journal*, vol. 9, nos. 2, and 3, nd.
Gough, Barry. "Sea Power and Canada: The Long View of History." *Canadian Defence Quarterly*, vol. 20, issue 3 (Dec. 1990): 41–9.
- and Roger Sarty. "Sailors and Soldiers: The Royal Navy, the Canadian Forces, and the Defence of Atlantic Canada, 1890–1918." In Michael Hadley, Rob Huebert, and Fred Crickard, *A Nation's Navy*: 112–30.
Gowlland-Debbas, Vera. "Security Council Change: The Pressure of Emerging International Public Policy UN Sanctions." *International Journal*, vol. 65, no. 1 (winter 2009–10): 119–42.
Graham, Dominic, and Shelford Bidwell. *Fire-power: British Army Weapons and Theories of War, 1904–1945*. London: George Allen & Unwin, 1982.
Graham, Melanie. "Interoperability and Integration: Blessing or Curse?" In Robert H. Edwards and Graham Walker, eds., *Continental Security and Canada-U.S. Relations*: 61–73.
Granatstein, J.L. "Canada and Peacekeeping: Image and Reality." *Canadian Forum*, Aug. 1974: 14–19.
- *Canada's War: The Politics of the Mackenzie King Government, 1939–1945*. Toronto, Oxford University Press, 1975.
- *Canadian Foreign Policy: Historical Readings*. Toronto: Copp Clark Pitman, 1986.
- *How Britain's Weakness Forced Canada into the Arms of the United States*. 1988 Joanne Goodman Lecture. Toronto: University of Toronto Press, 1989.
- and R.D. Cuff, eds. *War and Society in North America*. Toronto: Nelson, 1971.
- and Robert Bothwell. "'A Self-Evident National Duty': Canadian Foreign Policy, 1935–1939." *Journal of Imperial and Commonwealth History*, vol. 3, no. 2 (Jan. 1975).
- *Ottawa Men: The Civil Service Mandarins, 1935–1957*. Toronto: Oxford University Press, 1982.
- and Robert Bothwell. *Pirouette: Pierre Trudeau and Canadian Foreign Policy*. Toronto: University of Toronto Press, 1990.
- "Peacekeeping: Did Canada Make a Difference? And What Difference Did

Peacekeeping Make to Canada?" In John English and Norman Hillmer, eds., *Making a Difference?*: 231.
- "The American Influence on the Canadian Military, 1939–1963." In Barry Hunt and Ron Haycock, eds. *Canada's Defence: Perspectives on Policy in the Twentieth Century*: 129–39.

Gray, Colin S. *Canadian Defence Priorities: A Question of Relevance*. Toronto: Clarke Irwin, 1972.
- *Canada's Maritime Forces*. Wellesley Paper No. 1. Canadian Institute of International Affairs, Jan. 1973.
- *The Leverage of Sea Power: The Strategic Advantage of Navies in War*. New York: Free Press, 1992.
- "Sea Power for Containment: The US Navy in the Cold War." In Keith Neilson and Elizabeth Jane Errington, *Navies and Global Security*: 181–208.

Grebler, Leo, and Wilhelm Winkler. *The Cost of the World War to Germany and to Austria Hungary*. New Haven, USA: Yale University Press, 1940.

Greenspon, Edward et al. *Open Canada: A Global Positioning Strategy for a Networked Age*. Toronto: Canadian International Council, 2010.

Griffin, Watson, "A Canadian Navy." *North American Review*, vol. 190, no. 649 (Dec. 1909): 765–72.

Griffiths, Ann L., Peter T. Haydon, and Richard H. Gimblett. *Canadian Gunboat Diplomacy: The Canadian Navy and Foreign Policy*. Halifax: Centre for Foreign Policy Studies, Dalhousie University, 1998.
- , ed. *Maritime Security and Conflict Resolution at Sea*. See: Haydon, Peter T.
- and Kenneth P. Hansen, eds. *Marines: Is an Amphibious Capability Relevant for Canada?* Maritime Security Occasional Paper No. 15. Halifax: Centre for Foreign Policy Studies, Dalhousie University, 2008.

Griffiths, Franklyn, ed. *Politics of the Northwest Passage*. Montreal and Kingston: McGill-Queen's University Press, 1987.
- "Where Vision and Illusion Meet." In Franklyn Griffiths, ed., *Politics of the Northwest Passage*, 1987.
- "The Northwest Passage in Transit." *International Journal*, vol. 54, no. 2 (1998–99): 189–202.
- "The Shipping News: Canada's Arctic Sovereignty not on Thinning Ice." *International Journal*, vol. 58, no. 2 (2002–03): 257–82.
- "Towards a Canadian Arctic Strategy." *Canadian International Council*, 2009.

Grove, Eric. "The Discovery of Doctrine: British Naval Thinking at the Close of the Twentieth Century." In Geoffrey Till, *The Development of British Naval Thinking*: 182–91.

Gruca, George. *The Sea-Launched Cruise Missile as a Weapon System: Characteristics, Operation and Capabilities*. ORAE project report PR396. Ottawa: DND, Oct. 1986.

Hadley, Michael L., and Roger Sarty. *Tin Pots and Pirate Ships: Canadian Naval Forces and German Sea Raiders, 1880–1914*. Montreal and Kingston: McGill-Queen's University Press, 1991.
- , Rob Huebert, and Fred W. Crickard. *A Nation's Navy: In Quest of Canadian Naval Identity*. Montreal and Kingston: McGill–Queen's University Press, 1996.

Hagan, Kenneth. "The Apotheosis of Mahan: American Naval Strategy, 1889–1922." In Keith Neilson, *Navies and Global Security*: 94–5.

Haglund, David G., ed. *Canada's Defence Industrial Base: The Political Economy of Preparedness and Procurement*. Kingston: Frye, 1988.

- *The North Atlantic Triangle Revisited: Canadian Grand Strategy at Century's End*. Toronto: Irwin, 2000.
- and Stéphane Roussel. "Escott Reid, the North Atlantic Treaty, and Canadian Strategic Culture." In Greg Donaghy and Stéphan Roussel, *Escott Reid: Diplomat and Scholar*: 44–66.

Haight, Ian Ellis. "Canadians Overseas: The Organization, Administration and Logistics of Canadian Troop Convoys during the Second World War." Master's thesis. University of New Brunswick. Dept. of History, 2008.

Hall, H. Duncan. *North American Supply*. London: HMSO, 1955.

Halloran, Mary. "Canada and the Origins of the Post-War Commitment." In Margaret O. MacMillan and David S. Sorenson, *Canada and NATO: Uneasy Past, Uncertain Future*: 1–14.

Halstead, John. Foreword to Joseph T. Jockel and Joel J. Sokolsky, *Canada and Collective Security*.

Hanlon, Joseph. "Successes and Future Prospects of Sanctions Against South Africa." Discussion Paper No. 2. London: London School of Economics, Centre for the Study of the South African Economy and International Finance, 1990.
- "Quarterly Report, Nov. 1992." London: London School of Economics, Centre for the Study of the South African Economy and International Finance, 1992.

Hansen, Kenneth P. "How We Really Got Here." *Canadian Naval Review*, vol. 2, no. 1 (spring 2006): 34.
- "The 'Destroyer Myth' in Canadian Naval History" *Canadian Naval Review*, vol. 2, no. 3 (autumn 2006): 5–9.
- , ed. *Marines: Is an Amphibious Capability Relevant for Canada?* See Griffiths, Ann L.

Hardach, Gerd. *The First World War*. London: Allen Lane, 1977.

Harland, David. "Kosovo and the UN." *Survival*, IISS, vol. 52, no. 5 (Oct.–Nov. 2010): 75–98.

Harper, Tim. "US Ambassador Paul Cellucci." *International Journal*, vol. 58, no. 4 (2002–03): 711–20.

Hattendorf, John, and James Goldrick. *Mahan Is Not Enough: The Proceedings of a Conference on the Works of Sir Julian Corbett and Admiral Sir Herbert Richmond*. Newport, Rhode Island: Naval War College Press, 1993.
- "Commonwealth Navies as Seen by the United States Navy, 1910–2010," Proceedings of the Canadian Navy Centennial / Ninth Maritime Command (MARCOM) History Conference, *From Empire to In(ter)dependence: The Canadian Navy and the Commonwealth Experience, 1910–2010*. Ottawa: Canadian Naval Heritage Press, May 2010.

Haycock, Ron G., ed. *Canada's Defence: Perspectives on Policy in the Twentieth Century*. See: Hunt, Barry D.

Haydon, Peter T. "When Military Plans and Policies Conflict: The Case of Canada's General Purpose Frigate Program." The McNaughton Papers, The Canadian Institute of Strategic Studies, Nov. 1991: 24–38.
- "Sailors, Admirals, and Politicians: The Search for Identity after the War." Halifax: Maritime Command Historical Conference, 8–9 Oct. 1993.
- *The 1962 Cuban Missile Crisis: Canadian Involvement Reconsidered*. Toronto: Canadian Institute of Strategic Studies, 1993.
- and Ann L. Griffiths, eds. *Maritime Security and Conflict Resolution at Sea in the Post–Cold War Era*. Proceedings of the June 1993 Colloquium held by the Centre for Foreign Policy Studies. Halifax: Dalhousie University, 1993.

– , ed. *Canadian Gunboat Diplomacy.* See: Griffiths, Ann L.
– "The Evolution of the Canadian Naval Task Group." In Ann Griffiths, Peter Haydon, and Richard Gimblett, *Canadian Gunboat Diplomacy*: 95–129.
– and Paul T. Mitchell, "Canada-US Naval Cooperation in the 21st Century." In Fred W. Crickard, Paul T. Mitchell, and Katherine Orr, eds. *Multinational Naval Cooperation and Foreign Policy into the 21st Century.*
– "Canadian Naval Future: A Necessary Long-Term Planning Framework." Institute for Research in Public Policy Working Paper Series, no. 2004-12 (Nov. 2004): 13.
– "The Chicoutimi Accident: Lessons Learned and Not Learned," *Canadian Military Journal*, vol. 6, no. 3 (autumn 2005).
– *The Admirals: Canada's Senior Naval Leadership in the Twentieth Century.* See: Whitby, Michael.
– "Vice-Admiral Herbert S. Rayner: The Last Chief of the Canadian Naval Staff." In Michael Whitby, Richard Gimblett, and Peter Haydon, *The Admirals*: 247–74.
– "Choosing The Right Fleet Mix: Lessons From the Canadian Patrol Frigate Selection Process." *Canadian Military Journal*, vol. 9, no. 1 (2008),
– "From Uncertainty to Maturity, 1968–89." In Richard H. Gimblett, ed., *The Naval Service of Canada, 1910–2010: The Centennial Story*: 163–79.
– "A Tale of Two Navies: Building the Canada–US Cold War Naval Relationship," Proceedings of the Canadian Navy Centennial / Ninth Maritime Command (MARCOM) History Conference, *From Empire to In(ter)dependence: The Canadian Navy and the Commonwealth Experience, 1910–2010.* Ottawa: Canadian Naval Heritage Press, May 2010.

Healey, Denis. *Labour and a World Society.* London: Fabian Tract 501, Jan. 1985.

Heckscher, Eli F. (M. Shapiro trans.). *Mercantilism*, 2 vols. London: George Allen & Unwin; New York: Macmillan, 1955 [1956].

Heinbecker, Paul. *Getting Back in the Game: A Foreign Policy Playbook for Canada.* Toronto: Key Porter, 2010.

Hellyer, Paul. *Damn the Torpedoes: My Fight to Unify Canada's Armed Forces.* Toronto: McClelland & Stewart, 1990.

Hennessy, Michael A. "The Rise and Fall of a Canadian Maritime Policy, 1939–1965: A Study of Industry, Navalism and the State." PhD dissertation. University of New Brunswick, 1995.
– "Fleet Replacement and the Crisis of Identity." In Michael Hadley, Rob Huebert, and Fred Crickard, *A Nation's Navy*: 131–53.
– "Canada's Pacific Carriers: A Study of Manipulation and Neglect, 1944–1950." In Ann Griffiths, Peter Haydon, and Richard Gimblett, *Canadian Gunboat Diplomacy*: 45–76.
– "The RCN and the Postwar Naval Revolution, 1955–1964." In Richard Gimblett and Richard Mayne, eds., *People, Policy and Programmes*: 143–64.

Hesburgh, Theodore. "Religious, Scientific Leaders on Arms Race." *Bulletin of the Atomic Scientists*, April 1985: 49–50.

Hickey, Laurence. "The Submarine as a Tool of Maritime Enforcement." *Integrated Coastal Zone Management* (spring 2000): 118–22.
– "Our Submarine Service: Cross-Connect Open to the Allied System." Proceedings of the Canadian Navy Centennial / Ninth Maritime Command (MARCOM) History Conference, *From Empire to In(ter)dependence: The Canadian Navy and the Commonwealth Experience, 1910–2010.* Ottawa: Canadian Naval Heritage Press, May 2010.

Higgins, Laura J. *Canadian Naval Operations in the 1990's: Selected Case Studies*. Occasional Paper No. 12. Halifax: Centre for Foreign Policy Studies, Dalhousie University, 2002.
Hill, Richard. "British Naval Thinking in the Nuclear Age." In Geoffrey Till, *The Development of British Naval Thinking*: 160–81.
Hilliker, John, and Greg Donaghy. "Canadian Relations with the United Kingdom at the End of Empire, 1956–73." In Phillip Buckner, *Canada and the End of Empire*: 25–46.
Hillmer, Norman. "Defence and Ideology: The Anglo–Canadian Military 'Alliance' in the 1930s." *International Journal*, vol. 33, no. 3 (1977–78): 585–612.
– , ed. *Partners Nevertheless: Canadian-American Relations in the Twentieth Century*. Toronto: Copp Clark Pitman, 1989.
– and Joseph Laurence Black. *Nearly Neighbours: Canada and the Soviet Union, from Cold War to Détente and Beyond*. Kingston: Frye, 1989.
– ed. *Making a Difference?* See English, John.
– "O.D. Skelton and the North American Mind." *International Journal*, vol. 60, no. 1 (2004–05): 93–110.
Hobson, Sharon. *The Composition of Canada's Naval Fleet, 1946–85*. Halifax: Centre for Foreign Policy Studies, Dalhousie University, 1986.
– "Plain Talk: the Process of (Not) Acquiring Maritime Helicopters." *Canadian Naval Review*, vol. 4, no. 4 (winter 2009): 39–40.
Hoffmann, Stanley. "On the War," *New York Review of Books*, vol. 48, no. 17 (1 Nov. 2001): 4–6.
Holbrooke, Richard. *To End a War*. New York: Random House, 1998.
Holmes, John Wendell, "Canada and the Vietnam War." In J.L. Granatstein and R.D. Cuff, eds., *War and Society in North America*: 184–99.
– *The Shaping of Peace: Canada and the Search for World Order, 1943–57*. Toronto: University of Toronto Press, 1979.
– *Life with Uncle: The Canadian-American Relationship*. Toronto: University of Toronto Press, 1981.
– "Unquiet Diplomat: Lester B. Pearson." *International Journal*, vol. 62 (2006–07): 291–310.
Hoover, Herbert C. *The Memoirs of Herbert Hoover*. New York: Hollis and Carter, 1951–52.
Hore, Peter, ed. "The Genesis of Naval Thinking since the End of the Cold War." Maritime Strategic Studies Institute Paper no. 2. London: HMSO, March 1999.
Horne, Bernd, ed. *Fortune Favours the Brave: Tales of Courage and Tenacity in Canadian Military History*. Toronto: Dundurn, 2009.
Howard, Michael. "British Grand Strategy in World War I." In Paul Kennedy, ed., *Grand Strategies in War and Peace*: 31.
Huebert, Rob. *A Nation's Navy*. See: Hadley, Michael L.
– "The Politics of Arctic Security: In Search of a Canadian Arctic Maritime Security Policy." In Ann Griffiths, Peter Haydon, and Richard Gimblett, *Canadian Gunboat Diplomacy*: 293.
– "Canadian Arctic Maritime Security: The Return to Canada's Third Ocean." *Canadian Military Journal*, vol. 8, no. 2 (summer 2007).
Hufbauer, Gary Clyde, Jeffrey J. Schott, Kimberly Ann Elliott, and Barbara Oegg. *Economic Sanctions Reconsidered*. Washington: Peterson Institute for International Economics, Nov. 2007.

Hugo, Victor. *Toilers of the Sea*. London and New York: George Routledge and Sons, 1888.
Hunt, Barry D. "The Road to Washington Canada and Empire Naval Defence, 1918–1921." In James Boutilier, ed., *RCN in Retrospect*: 44–61.
– "British Policy on the Issue of Belligerent and Neutral Rights, 1919–1939." In Craig L. Symonds, ed., *New Aspects of Naval History: Selected Papers Presented at the Fourth Naval History Symposium, United States Naval Academy, 25–26 Oct. 1979*. Annapolis, Maryland: 1981.
– *Sailor-Scholar*. Waterloo, Ontario: Wilfrid Laurier University Press, 1982.
– and Ron G. Haycock, eds. *Canada's Defence: Perspectives on Policy in the Twentieth Century*. Toronto: Copp Clark, 1993.
Hunter, Robert E. "Managing the North Atlantic Alliance." In Ann-Sofie Dahl and Norman Hillmer, *Activism and (Non) Alignment*: 4.
Hupchick, Dennis P., and Harold E. Cox. *The Palgrave Concise Historical Atlas of the Balkans*. New York: Palgrave, 2001.
Igartua, José E. "'Ready, Aye, Ready' No More? Canada, Britain, and the Suez Crisis in the Canadian Press." In Phillip Buckner, *Canada and the End of Empire*, 2004.
Ignatieff, Michael. "Ethics and the New War." *Canadian Military Journal*, winter 2001–02: 5–10.
– *Empire Lite: Nation Building in Bosnia, Kosovo, and Afghanistan*. London: Vintage, 2003.
– "Canada in the Age of Terror: Multilateralism Meets a Moment of Truth." In Graham F. Walker, *Independence in an Age of Empire: Assessing Unilateralism and Multilateralism*: 31–40.
Ingrao, Charles. "Western Intervention in Bosnia: Operation *Deliberate Force*." In Bruce Elleman and Sarah Paine, eds., *Naval Coalition Warfare*: 175–7.
Institute of the North, US Arctic Research Commission, and International Arctic Science Committee, Arctic Marine Transport Workshop, 2004.
Jackson, Aaron P. *Keystone Doctrine Development in Five Commonwealth Navies: A Comparative Perspective*. Papers in Australian Maritime Affairs, No. 33. Canberra: Sea Power Centre, 2010.
Jellicoe, John Rushworth, Earl. "Report of Admiral of the Fleet, Viscount Jellicoe of Scapa … on Naval Mission to the Dominion of Canada, Nov.–Dec., 1919." Ottawa : Department of the Naval Service, [1919?]; Canada, House of Commons, Sessional Papers, No. 61. Ottawa: Thomas Mulvey, 1920.
Jockel, Joseph T. *No Boundaries Upstairs*. Vancouver: University of British Columbia Press, 1987.
– and Joel J. Sokolsky. *Canada and Collective Security: Odd Man Out*. Washington Papers No. 121. New York: Praeger, 1986.
– and Joel J. Sokolsky. "Lloyd Axworthy's Legacy: Human Security and the Rescue of Canadian Defence Policy." *International Journal*, vol. 56, no. 1 (2000–01): 1–18.
– and Joel J. Sokolsky. "Canada and NATO." *International Journal*, vol. 64, no. 2 (spring 2009).
Johnson, James Turner. *Just War: Tradition and the Restraint of War*. Princeton, New Jersey: Princeton University Press, 1981.
Johnston, William. "The Royal Canadian Navy and the First World War." In Richard H. Gimblett, ed., *The Naval Service of Canada, 1910–2010: The Centennial Story*: 23–40.

– with William G.P. Rawling, Richard H. Gimblett, and John MacFarlane. *The Seabound Coast: The Official History of the Royal Canadian Navy, 1867–1939*. Toronto: Dundurn Press, 2010.

Jones, Frank L. "Rolling the Dice of War: Military Necessity and Nation Building." *International Journal*, vol. 61, no. 4 (2005–06): 945–58.

Jordan, Gerald, ed. *Naval Warfare in the Twentieth Century 1900–1945: Essays in Honour of Arthur Marder*. London: Croom Helm, 1977.

Kealy, J.D.F., and E.C. Russell. *A History of Canadian Naval Aviation, 1918–1962*. Ottawa: Queen's Printer, 1967.

Keating, Tom, and Larry Pratt. *Canada, NATO and the Bomb: The Western Alliance in Crisis*. Edmonton: Hurtig, 1988.

Keenleyside, Hugh L. "The Canada-United States Permanent Joint Board on Defence, 1940–1945." *International Journal*, vol. 16, no. 1 (winter 1960/61): 50–77.

Kelso, Frank B. II, "Defence of the Atlantic." *Canadian Defence Quarterly*, vol. 19, no. 4 (1990): 13–17.

Kennedy, Greg, and Keith Neilson. *Far-Flung Lines: Essays on Imperial Defence in Honour of Donald Mackenzie Schurman*. London: Frank Cass, 1996.

Kennedy, Paul, ed. *Grand Strategies in War and Peace*. New Haven: Yale University Press, 1991.

Kibble, D.G. "The Attack on the USS Cole." *Naval Review*, vol. 89, no. 1 (Jan. 2001): 19–22.

– "February's Bombing of Baghdad: Reviewing British and American Policy on Iraq." *Naval Review*, vol. 89, no. 3 (July 2001): 222–6.

Kirkey, Christopher. "Smoothing Troubled Waters: The 1988 Canada-United States Arctic Co–operation Agreement." *International Journal*, vol. 50, no. 2 (1994–95): 401–26.

Kirton, John, and Don Munton. "The Manhattan Voyages and their Aftermath." In Franklyn Griffiths, *Politics of the Northwest Passage*: 67–97.

Kissinger, Henry A. *The Troubled Partnership*. New York: McGraw-Hill, 1965.

– *The White House Years*. Boston: Little, Brown, 1979.

Klepak, Harold P. "Changing Realities and Perceptions of Military Threat." In David B. Dewitt and David Leyton–Brown, *Canada's International Security Policy*, 1995.

– "Cuba and Haiti: Test Cases for Canada, but Tests of What?" *International Journal*, vol. 61, no. 3 (2005–06): 677–98.

Knox, J.H.W. "An Engineer's Outline of RCN History: Part 1." In James Boutilier, ed., *RCN in Retrospect*: 317–33.

Kraska, James. "A Way Out for Arctic Diplomacy." *Canadian Naval Review*, vol. 5, no. 3 (autumn 2009): 17–22.

Kunz, Diane B. *The Economic Diplomacy of the Suez Crisis*. Chapel Hill, University of North Carolina Press, 1991.

Lagasse, Philippe. "Nils Ørvik's Defence against Help." *International Journal*, vol. 65, no. 2 (spring 2010): 451–62.

Lajeunesse, Adam. "Sovereignty, Security and the Canadian Nuclear Submarine Program." *Canadian Military Journal*, vol. 8, no. 4 (winter 2007–08).

Lambert, Andrew. "The Royal Navy, 1856–1914: Deterrence and the Strategy of World Power." In Keith Neilson and Elizabeth Jane Errington, *Navies and Global Defense*: 69–92.

- "Seizing the Initiative: The Arctic Convoys 1944–45." In Nicholas Rodger, ed., *Naval Power in the 20th Century*.
Lambert, Nicholas A. "Economy or Empire? The Fleet Unit Concept and the Quest for Collective Security in the Pacific, 1909–14." In Greg Kennedy and Keith Neilson, *Far-Flung Lines*: 44–83.
- "The Opportunities of Technology: British and French Naval Strategies in the Pacific, 1905–1909." In Nicholas Rodger, ed., *Naval Power in the 20th Century*: 41–58.
Langdon, Frank, and Douglas Ross. "Towards a Canadian Maritime Strategy in the North Pacific Region." *International Journal*, vol. 42, no. 3 (1986–87): 848–9.
Larose, Martin. "Emerging Strategic Counterculture." See: Fortmann, Michel.
Laurier, Sir Wilfrid. *The Naval Question: Speech by Sir Wilfrid Laurier* [Ottawa?: s.n., 1910?].
- *The Canadian Navy: Speech by Sir Wilfrid Laurier in reply to amendments of Mr R.L. Borden and Mr Monk, Nov. 29th, 1910* [Ottawa? : s.n., 1910?].
Lee, James. "Cruise Missile Testing in Canada: The Post–Cold War Debate." Ottawa: Library of Parliament, Research Branch, Political and Social Affairs Division, 27 May 1983, revised 14 April 1993.
Legault, Albert, and George Lindsey. *The Dynamics of the Nuclear Balance*. Ithaca: Cornell University Press, 1974.
Leir, Richard H. "Big Ship Time: The Formative Years of RCN Officers Serving in RN Capital Ships." In James Boutilier, *Retrospect*: 74–95.
Le Mière, Christian. "The Return of Gunboat Diplomacy." *Survival*, vol. 53, no. 5 (Oct.–Nov. 2011): 53–67.
Lennox, Patrick. "Interoperability: The New Frontier." *Canadian Naval Review*, vol. 3, no. 3 (fall 2007): 103.
Lerhe, Eric. "The *Impeccable* Affair: China's New Twist to the Law of the Sea Convention." *Canadian Naval Review*, vol. 5, no. 1 (spring 2009): 30–1.
Leyton-Brown, David. *Canada's International Security Policy*. See: Dewitt, David B.
Libal, Michael. *Limits of Persuasion: Germany and the Yugoslav Crisis, 1991–1992*. Westport, Connecticut and London: Praeger, 1997.
Liberal-Conservative Party. *The farce and the cost of Liberal naval policy compared with the practical, economical and effective policy of the Borden government* [issued by the Federal Press Agency, Ottawa ... Central Publication and Distribution Office for the Liberal-Conservative Party of Canada], [Ottawa?: s.n.], 1913.
- *Give credit to whom credit is due: Sir Robert Borden thrice predicted with startling truth the coming of a naval emergency* [Ottawa : Federal Press Agency], 1914.
- *Imperial naval defence: the record of the Liberal Party*. Ottawa: Federal Press Agency, 1915.
Lindsey, George, *Canadian Maritime Strategy: Should the Emphasis be Changed?* DRAE Report No. 5. Canada, DND, July 1969.
- Appendix, in G.M. Dillon "Canadian Naval Policy since World War II: A Decision-making Analysis." Occasional Paper. Halifax: Centre for Foreign Policy Studies, Dalhousie University, Oct. 1972.
- *The Dynamics of the Nuclear Balance*. See: Legault, Albert.
Linfoot, Matt. "China's Re-Emergent Sea Power." In Gregory P. Gilbert and Michelle Jellett, eds., *Australian Maritime Issues 2009*, SPC-A Annual, Papers

in Australian Maritime Affairs, No. 32. Canberra: Sea Power Centre, 2009: 189–92.
Link, Arthur S. *Wilson Campaigns for Progressivism and Peace 1916 1917*. 4 vols. Princeton, New Jersey: Princeton University Press, 1965.
Longstaff, F.V. *Esquimalt Naval Base: A History of its Work and its Defences*. Victoria: Victoria Book and Stationery Company, 1941.
Lopez, George A. *The Sanctions Decade*. See: Cortright, David.
– *Smart Sanctions*. See: Cortright, David.
Lovegrove, Dwayne. "Sutherland in the 21st Century: Invariants in Canada's Policy Agenda Since 9/11." *Canadian Military Journal*, vol. 10, no. 3 (summer 2010).
Lovi, Michelle, ed. *Australian Maritime Issues 2006*. See: Forbes, Andrew.
Lowery, Eliot. "Leadership for a Sustainable Culture of Peace." See: Rippon, Major Thomas.
Lund, Wilfred G.D. "The Royal Canadian Navy's Quest for Autonomy in the North West Atlantic, 1941–43." In James Boutilier, ed., RCN *in Retrospect*: 138–57.
– "Integration and Unification of the Canadian Forces." CFB Esquimalt Naval & Military Museum, nd.
– "Vice-Admiral Howard Emmerson Reid and Vice-Admiral Harold Taylor Wood Grant: Forging the New 'Canadian' Navy." In Michael Whitby, Richard Gimblett, and Peter Haydon, *The Admirals*: 157–86.
– "Vice-Admiral E. Rollo Mainguy: Sailors' Admiral." In Michael Whitby, Richard Gimblett, and Peter Haydon, *The Admirals*: 187–212.
Luttwak, Edward N. *The Political Uses of Sea Power*. Baltimore: Johns Hopkins University Press, 1974.
MacDonald, G.D. "A Better Fit: The Canadian Coast Guard under National Defence – Safety, Security and Sovereignty Enhanced." Toronto: Canadian Forces College, 2004.
MacFarlane, John. *The Seabound Coast: The Official History of the Royal Canadian Navy*. See: Johnston, William.
– *Canada, 1900–1950: Un pays prend sa place/A Country Comes of Age*. See Bernier, Serge.
MacGregor Dawson, R. *William Lyon Mackenzie King: A Political Biography, 1874–1923*. Toronto: University of Toronto Press, 1958.
MacInnis, A. "Sovereignty Through Sonar?" *Canada's Navy Annual*, 1991–92: 48.
Mackenzie, Kenneth S. "C.C. Ballantyne and the Canadian Government Merchant Marine, 1917–1921." *The Northern Mariner/Le Marin du nord*, vol. 2, no. 1 (Jan. 1992): 1–13.
Mackinnon, Gregor. "'The World is Entitled to Ask Questions': The Trudeau Peace Initiative Reconsidered." See: Pearson, Michael.
MacLaren, Roy. *The Fundamental Things Apply*. Montreal and Kingston: McGill-Queen's University Press, 2011.
MacLeod, Malcolm. "The Royal Canadian Navy, 1918–39." *The Mariner's Mirror*, vol. 56, 1970: 169–86.
MacMillan, Margaret O, and David S. Sorenson. *Canada and* NATO: *Uneasy Past, Uncertain Future*. Waterloo: University of Waterloo Press, 1990. Maddison, G.R. "Operations in the Adriatic." *Canadian Naval Review*, vol. 2, no. 1 (spring 2006): 25–7.
Mahant, Edelgard, and Graeme S. Mount. *Invisible and Inaudible in Washington:*

American Policies toward Canada. Vancouver: University of British Columbia Press, 1999.

Malkin, W.H. "Blockade in Modern Conditions." *British Yearbook of International Law* 3 (1922-23): 87-98.

Malone, David M. *The International Struggle Over Iraq: Politics in the UN Security Council, 1980-2005.* Toronto: Oxford University Press, 2006.

Maloney, Sean Michael. "'To Secure the Command of the Sea': NATO Command Organization and Naval Planning for the Cold War at Sea, 1945-1954." Master's thesis, University of New Brunswick, 1992.

– *Securing Command of the Sea: NATO Naval Planning 1948-1954.*" Annapolis, Maryland: Naval Institute Press, 1995.

– "Maple Leaf Over the Caribbean: Gunboat Diplomacy Canadian Style." In Ann Griffiths, Peter Haydon, and Richard Gimblett. *Canadian Gunboat Diplomacy.*

– *The Hindrance of Military Operations Ashore: Canadian Participation in Operation Sharp Guard, 1993-1996.* Halifax: Centre for Foreign Policy Studies, Dalhousie University, 2000.

– *War with Iraq: Canada's Strategy in the Persian Gulf, 1990-2002.* Kingston: Centre for International Relations, Queen's University, 2002.

– *Campaigns for International Security: Canada's Defence Policy at the Turn of the Century.* See Bland, Douglas.

– "Parry and Thrust: Canadian Maritime Forces and the Defence of North America, 1954-62." *The Northern Mariner/Le Marin du nord,* vol. 18, no. 1 (Jan. 2008): 39-54.

Malot, Maureen, ed. *Canada Among Nations, 1984,* See: Tomlin, Brian W.

Manby, Bronwen. "South Africa: The Impact of Sanctions." *Journal of International Affairs,* vol. 46, no. 1 (summer 1992): 193.

March, William A. "A Canadian Departure: The Evolution of HMCS Royal Roads, 1942-1948." In Michael Hadley, Rob Huebert, and Fred Crickard, *A Nation's Navy:* 297-309.

Mason, Dwight N. "Continental Security: A View From the U.S.A." In Robert Edwards and Graham Walker, eds., *Continental Security and Canada-U.S. Relations:* 41-50.

– "Canadian–American North American Defence Alliance in 2005." *International Journal,* vol. 60, no. 2 (2004-05): 385-96.

May, A.W., Dawn A. Russell, and Derrick E. Rowe. "Breaking New Ground: An Action Plan for Rebuilding the Grand Banks Fisheries." Report of the Advisory Panel on the Sustainable Management of Straddling Fish Stocks in the Northwest Atlantic. Fisheries and Oceans Canada, 1 Sept. 2005.

Mayne, John W. *Operational Research in the Canadian Armed Forces during the Second World War.* 2 vols. Operational Research and Analysis Establishment, ORAE Report no. R68. Ottawa: DND, 1978.

Mayne, Richard Oliver. "Protesters or Traitors? Investigating Cases of Crew Sabotage in the Royal Canadian Navy: 1942-45." *Canadian Military Journal,* vol. 6, no 1 (spring 2005).

– "Vice-Admiral George C. Jones: The Political Career of a Naval Officer." In Michael Whitby, Richard Gimblett, and Peter Haydon, *The Admirals:* 125-55.

– *Betrayed: Scandal, Politics, and Canadian Naval Leadership.* Vancouver: University of British Columbia Press, 2006.

– and Richard H. Gimblett, eds. *People, Policy and Programmes:* Proceedings of

the 7th Maritime Command (MARCOM) Historical Conference (2005), *From Empire to In(ter)dependence: The Canadian Navy and the Commonwealth Experience, 1910–2010*. Ottawa: Canadian Naval Heritage Press, 2008.
- "Years of Crisis: The Canadian Navy in the 1960s." In Richard H. Gimblett, ed. *The Naval Service of Canada, 1910–2010: The Centennial Story*: 141–59.

McDougall, Barbara. "Canada, NATO, and the North Atlantic Cooperation Council." In *Canada and NATO: The Forgotten Ally?* Special Report 1992, Institute for Foreign Policy Analysis, Inc., Cambridge, etc.: Brassey's (U.S.), 1992.

McIntyre, W. David. "Canada and the Creation of the Commonwealth Secretariat, 1965." *International Journal*, vol. 53, no. 4 (1997–98): 753–77.

McLean, Doug M. "Muddling Through: Canadian Anti-submarine Doctrine and Practice, 1942–1945." In Michael Hadley, Rob Huebert, and Fred Crickard, *A Nation's Navy*: 173–89.

McLin, Jon B. *Canada's Changing Defence Policy, 1957–1963: The Problems of a Middle Power in Alliance*. Baltimore: Johns Hopkins Press, 1967.

McKercher, Brian. *Anglo-American Relations in the 1920s: The Struggle for Supremacy*. Edmonton: University of Alberta Press, 1990.
- *Transition of Power: Britain's Loss of Global Pre-eminence to the United States, 1930–1945*. Cambridge: Cambridge University Press, 1999.

McRae, D.M. "Arctic Waters and Canadian Sovereignty." *International Journal*, vol. 38, no. 3 (1982–83): 476–92.

Medlicott, William Norton. *The Economic Blockade*. 2 vols. London: HMSO and Longmans, Green and Co., 1952–59.

Melakopides, Costas. *Pragmatic Idealism: Canadian Foreign Policy, 1945–1995*. Montreal and Kingston: McGill-Queen's University Press, 1998.

Melville, Thomas Richard. "Canada and Sea Power: Canadian Naval Thought and Policy, 1860–1910." Unpublished PhD dissertation: Duke University, 1981.

Middlemiss, Danford W. and Joel J. Sokolsky. *Canadian Defence: Decisions and Determinants*. Toronto: Harcourt, Brace and Jovanovich, 1989.
- and Denis Stairs. "The Canadian Forces and the Doctrine of Interoperability: The Issues." *Policy Matters*, vol 3, no. 7 (June 2002). http://www.irpp.org/pm/archive/pmvol3no7.pdf.

Miller, Duncan ("Dusty"). *The Persian Excursion: The Canadian Navy in the Gulf War*. Toronto: Canadian Peacekeeping Press, 1995.
- "Editorial: NATO Transformation: Good for NATO, Good for Canada?" *Canadian Naval Review*, vol. 2, no. 1 (spring 2006): 2–5.

Miller, Nathan. "The American Navy, 1922–1945." In Keith Neilson and Elizabeth Jane Errington, *Navies and Global Security*.

Miller, Steven. "The United States: Strategic Interests." In Clive Archer and David Scrivener, *Northern Waters: Security and Resource Issues*: 115–24.

Milner, Marc. *North Atlantic Run: The Royal Canadian Navy and the Battle for the Convoys*. Toronto: University of Toronto Press, 1985.
- "The Implication of Technological Backwardness: The Royal Canadian Navy 1939–45." *Canadian Defence Quarterly*, vol. 19, no. 3 (Dec. 1989).
- *Corvettes of the Royal Canadian Navy 1939–1945*. St Catharines, Ontario: Vanwell Publishing, 1993.
- *Canada's Navy: The First Century*. Toronto: University of Toronto Press, 1999.
- "More Royal than Canadian? The Royal Canadian Navy's Search for Identity, 1910–68." In Phillip Buckner, *Canada and the End of Empire*: 272–84.

- "Rear-Admiral Leonard Warren Murray: Canada's Most Important Operational Commander." In Michael Whitby, Richard Gimblett, and Peter Haydon, *The Admirals*: 97–124.
Mimeault, Mario. "A Dundee Ship in Canada's Arctic: SS Diana and William Wakeham's Expedition of 1897." *The Northern Mariner/Le Marin du nord*, vol. 8, no. 3 (July 1998): 51–61.
Minear, Larry. *Towards More Humane and Effective Sanctions Management: Enhancing the Capacity of the United Nations System*. Institute for International Studies (Brown University). Providence, Rhode Island: Thomas J. Watson Jr Institute for International Studies, 1998.
Mitchell, Paul T., and Peter T. Haydon. "Canada-US Naval Cooperation in the 21st Century." In Fred Crickard, Paul Mitchell, and Katherine Orr, eds., *Multinational Naval Cooperation and Foreign Policy into the 21st Century*, 1998.
- *Network-Centric Warfare: Coalition Operations in the Age of US Military Primacy*. Adelphi Paper 385, Abingdon, Oxfordshire: Routledge, 2006.
Mobley, Richard A. "The Beira Patrol: Britain's Broken Blockade against Rhodesia." In Bruce Elleman and Sarah Paine, eds., *Naval Blockades and Seapower*: 181–8.
Monk, Frederick Debartzch. *Discours de M. F.D. Monk, M.P., sur la défense navale du Canada, Ottawa, jeudi, 3 février 1910*. Ottawa: [s.n.], 1910.
Moore, Kenneth J. *Cold War Submarines*. See: Polmar, Norman.
Morgan, Michael Cotey. "Michael Ignatieff: Idealism and the Challenge of the 'Lesser Evil.'" *International Journal*, vol. 61, no. 4 (2005–06): 971–88.
Morin, Jean H. and Richard Gimblett. *Operation Friction, 1990–1991*. Toronto: Dundurn Press, 1997.
Morrison, Alex. "Canada and Peacekeeping: A Time for Reanalysis?" In David B. Devitt and David Leyton-Brown, *Canada's International Security Policy*: 198–226.
Morse, David. "The Canadian Naval Task Group." In Ann Griffiths, Peter Haydon, and Richard Gimblett, *Canadian Gunboat Diplomacy*, 1998.
- "Standing Naval Force Atlantic (SNFL) 1999–2000." *Canadian Naval Review*, vol. 2, no. 1 (spring 2006): 27–30.
Mount, Graeme S. *Invisible and Inaudible in Washington*. See: Mahant, Edelgard.
Mueller, John and Karl Mueller. "Sanctions of Mass Destruction." *Foreign Affairs*, vol. 78, no. 3 (May–June 1999): 43–53.
Munro, John A. "The Riddell Affair Reconsidered." Ottawa: DEA, 1969: 366–75.
Munton, Don, and John Kirton. "The Manhattan Voyages and their Aftermath." In Franklyn Griffiths, *Politics of the Northwest Passage*: 67–97.
Muraviev, Alexey D. *The Russian Pacific Fleet from the Crimean War to Perestroika*. Canberra: Sea Power Centre, 2007.
Nash, Knowlton. *Kennedy and Diefenbaker: Fear and Loathing across the Undefended Border*. Toronto: McClelland & Stewart, 1990.
Neatby, H. Blair. "Laurier and Imperialism." In Ramsay Cook, Craig Brown, and Carl Berger, eds., *Imperial Relations in the Age of Laurier*: 1–9.
Neilson, Keith, and Elizabeth Jane Errington. *Navies and Global Security*. Westport, Connecticut, and London: Praeger, 1995.
- *Far-Flung Lines: Essays on Imperial Defence in Honour of Donald Mackenzie Schurman*. See Kennedy, Greg.
Neustadt, Richard E. *Report to JFK: The Skybolt Crisis in Perspective*. Ithaca and London: Cornell University Press, 1999.

Nevins, Allan. *Hamilton Fish: The Inner History of the Grant Administration.* New York: F. Ungar, 1957.
Nixon, Edgar B., ed. *Franklin D. Roosevelt and Foreign Affairs.* Vol. 2: March 1934–Aug. 1935, Cambridge: Belknap Press of Harvard University Press, 1969.
Noer, John H. "The Roles of Navies in the 21st Century." In Ann Griffiths, Peter Haydon, and Richard Gimblett, *Canadian Gunboat Diplomacy*: 341–42.
Nossal, Kim Richard. "Polar Icebreakers: The Politics of Inertia." In Franklyn Griffiths, *Politics of the Northwest Passage.*
– "Knowing When to Fold: Western Sanctions against the USSR 1980–1983." *International Journal*, vol. 44, no. 3 (1988–89): 698–724.
– "The Imperial Congress: The Separation of Powers and Canadian-American Relations." *International Journal*, vol. 44, no. 4 (1988–89): 863–83.
– "Succumbing to the Dumbell: Canadian Perspectives on NATO in the 1990s." In *Canada and NATO: The Forgotten Ally?* Special Report 1992, Institute for Foreign Policy Analysis, Inc. Cambridge, etc.: Brassey's (US), 1992: 17–32.
– "Defending the 'Realm,' The Canadian Strategic Culture Revisited." *International Journal*, vol. 59, no. 2 (2004): 503–20.
O'Connell, Daniel Patrick. *The Influence of Law on Sea Power.* Manchester: Manchester University Press, 1975.
Oegg, Barbara. *Economic Sanctions Reconsidered.* See: Hufbauer, Gary Clyde.
O'Keefe, Sean, secretary of the navy. "From the Sea: Preparing the Naval Service for the 21st Century." Sept. 1992. Navy News Service 6 Oct. 92 (NavNews 048/92).
Olson, Mancur, Jr. *The Economics of Wartime Shortage.* Durham, North Carolina: Duke University Press, 1963.
Orr, John. "Some Policy Aspects of Canadian Involvement in Strategic ASW, 1945–1968." In Richard Gimblett and Richard Mayne, eds., *People, Policy and Programmes*: 183–203.
Orr, Katherine, Fred W. Crickard, and Paul T. Mitchell, eds. *Multinational Naval Cooperation and Foreign Policy into the 21st Century.* Aldershot: Ashgate, 1998.
Ørvik, Nils. *The Decline of Neutrality, 1914–1941: With Special Reference to the United States and the Northern Neutrals.* London: F. Cass, 1971.
– "Semi-neutrality and Canada's Security." *International Journal*, vol. 29, no. 2 (1973–74): 186–215.
O'Sullivan, Christopher D. *The United Nations: A Concise History.* Malabar, Florida: Krieger, 2005.
O'Sullivan, Meghan L. *Shrewd Sanctions: Statecraft and State Sponsors of Terrorism.* Washington: Brookings Institution, 2003.
Owen, David. *Balkan Odyssey.* New York: Harcourt, Brace and Co, 1995.
Pachter, Henry Maximilian. *Collision Course: The Cuban Missile Crisis and Coexistence.* London, Dunmow: Pall Mall Press, 1964.
Padfield, Peter. *Dönitz: The Last Führer.* London: Gollancz, 1984.
Paine, Sarah C.M., ed. *Naval Blockades and Seapower.* See: Elleman, Bruce A.
Pazulla, Jutta. "The Long, Difficult Road to Dayton: Peace Efforts in Bosnia–Herzegovina." *International Journal*, vol. 60, no. 1 (2004–05): 255–72.
Palliser, Stuart J. *Salt Water Thieves: Policy Reforms to Address Somali Piracy.* Halifax: Centre for Foreign Policy Studies, Dalhousie University, 2010.
Pearson, Geoffrey. "Trudeau and Foreign Policy." *Peace Magazine*, Jan.–Mar. 2001: 7.

Pearson, Lester B. "Forty Years On: Reflections on Our Foreign Policy." *International Journal*, vol. 22, no. 3 (1966–67): 357–63.
- *Mike: The Memoirs of the Right Honourable Lester B. Pearson.* Toronto: University of Toronto Press, 1972–73.
- "Canada, the United States, and Vietnam." In Norman Hillmer, ed., *Partners Nevertheless, Canadian–American Relations in the Twentieth Century*: 121.
Pearson, Michael, Gregor Mackinnon, and Christoper Sapardanis. "'The World Is Entitled to Ask Questions': The Trudeau Peace Initiative Reconsidered." *International Journal*, vol. 41, no. 1 (1985–86): 129–58.
Perkins, J. David. "Submarines and the Canadian Navy Today: One Man's View." *Canadian Naval Review*, vol. 3, no. 3 (autumn 2007): 22–5.
Perras, Galen Roger. *Franklin Roosevelt and the Origins of the Canadian-American Security Alliance, 1933–1945: Necessary, but Not Necessary Enough.* Westport, Connecticut: Praeger, 1998.
Pharand, Donat. "The Arctic Waters and the Northwest Passage: A Final Revisit." *Ocean Development & International Law*. vol. 38, issue 1/2 (Jan.–June 2007): 3–69.
Phillipps-Wolley, Clive. *The Canadian Naval Question, Addresses Delivered by ...* Toronto: William Briggs, 1911.
Pickersgill, J.W., and D.F. Forster. *Mackenzie King Record.* 4 vols. Toronto: University of Toronto Press, 1960–70.
Piggott, Sir Francis. *The Declaration of Paris, 1856.* London: University of London Press, 1919.
Plaschka, Matthew F. "The Proposed Amphibious Ship Purchase: A Strategic Misstep." In Ann Griffiths and Kenneth Hansen, eds., *Marines: Is an Amphibious Capability Relevant for Canada?*.
Polmar, Norman, and Kenneth J. Moore. *Cold War Submarines: The Design and Construction of US and Soviet Submarines.* Dulles, Virginia: Brassey's/ Potomac Books Inc, 2004.
Pope, Maurice. "Memorandum on a Canadian Organization for the Higher Direction of National Defence: 8 March 1937." See: Canada, DND, Directorate of History: Maurice Pope, File 112.3S 2009 (D23). Reprinted in Douglas Bland, *Canada's National Defence*, vol. 2, "Defence Organization": 1–20.
Pratt, Larry. *Canada, NATO and the Bomb.* See: Keating, Tom.
Preston, Adrian W. "Canada and the Higher Direction of the Second World War 1939–1945." *Journal of the Royal United Services Institute*, vol. 110, no. 637 (Feb. 1965): 28–44.
- "The Profession of Arms in Postwar Canada." *World Politics*, vol. 23 (Jan. 1971): 197.
Preston, Richard A. "The Military Structure of the Old Commonwealth." *International Journal*, vol. 17, no. 2 (spring 1962): 98–121.
- *Canada and "Imperial Defense": A Study of the Origins of the British Commonwealth's Defense Organization, 1867–1919.* Duke University Commonwealth Studies Center. Publication Number 29. Durham, North Carolina: Duke University Press, 1967.
Pugh, Philip. *The Cost of Seapower.* London, Conway Maritime Press, 1988.
Pullen, Hugh Francis. "The Royal Canadian Navy between the Wars, 1922–39." In James Boutilier, *RCN in Retrospect*: 62–73.
Pullen, Tom C. "Convoy O.N. 127 & the Loss of HMCS *Ottawa*, 13 Sept. 1942:

A Personal Reminiscence." *The Northern Mariner/Le Marin du nord*, vol. 2, no. 2 (April 1992): 1–27.

Purver, Ron. "The Control of Strategic Anti-submarine Warfare." *International Journal*, vol. 38, no. 3 (1982–83): 409–31.

– "The Arctic in Canadian Security Policy, 1945 to the Present." In David B. Devitt and David Leyton–Brown, *Canada's International Security Policy*, 1995: 81–110.

Raine, Sarah. "Bejing's South China Sea Debate." *Survival*, vol. 53, no. 5 (Oct.–Nov. 2011): 69–87.

Ransom, Bernard. "Canada's 'Newfyjohn' Tenancy: The Royal Canadian Navy in St. John's, 1941–1945." *Acadiensis* 23, spring 1994.

– "A Nursery of Fighting Seamen? The Newfoundland Royal Naval Reserve, 1901–1920." In Michael Hadley, Rob Huebert, and Fred Crickard, *A Nation's Navy*: 239–55.

Rawling, William G.P. *The Seabound Coast: The Official History of the Royal Canadian Navy*. See: Johnston, William.

Read, John Erskine. "Problems of an External Affairs Legal Adviser, 1928–1946." *International Journal*, vol. 22, no. 3 (summer 1967): 376–94.

Reid, Escott. "Canada and the Threat of War: A Discussion of Mr. Mackenzie King's Foreign Policy." *University of Toronto Quarterly*, vol. 6 (Jan. 1937).

– "The Birth of the North Atlantic Alliance." *International Journal*, vol. 32, no. 3 (summer 1967): 426–40.

– "Canada and the Creation of the North Atlantic Alliance, 1948–1949." In Michael Fry, ed., *Freedom and Change: Essays in Honour of Lester B. Pearson*: 106–35.

– *Time of Fear and Hope: The Making of the North Atlantic Treaty 1947–1949*. Toronto: McClelland & Stewart, 1977.

Renwick, Robin. *Economic Sanctions*. Cambridge Massachusetts: Center for International Affairs, Harvard University, 1981.

Reynolds, Ken. "'One Stop Shopping': Replenishment at Sea and the Royal Canadian Navy." In Richard Gimblett and Richard Mayne, eds., *People, Policy and Programmes*: 229–250.

Rezun, Miron. *Europe's Nightmare: The Struggle for Kosovo*. Westport, Connecticut: Praeger, 2001.

Rhodes, Benjamin D. "The Image of Britain in the United States, 1919–1929: A Contentious Relative and Rival." In Brian McKercher, ed., *Anglo-American Relations in the 1920's: The Struggle for Supremacy*: 187–208.

Richard, Béatrice. "Henri Bourassa and Conscription: Traitor or Saviour?" *Canadian Military Journal*, vol. 7, no. 4 (winter 2006–07).

Richmond, Sir Herbert, *Imperial Defence and Capture at Sea in War*. London: Hutchinson & Co. 1932.

– *Sea Power in the Modern World*. London: Reynal & Hitchcock, 1934.

– *The Navy as an Instrument of Policy*. Cambridge: Cambridge University Press, 1953.

Riddell, Walter Alexander. *Documents on Canadian Foreign Policy, 1917–1939*. Toronto: Oxford University Press, 1962.

Riekhoff, Harald von. "The Impact of Prime Minister Trudeau on Foreign Policy." *International Journal* vol. 33, no. 2 (spring 1978): 267–86.

– and John Sigler. "The Trudeau Peace Initiative: The Politics of Reversing the

Arms Race." In Brian W. Tomlin and Maureen Malot, eds., *Canada Among Nations, 1984: A Time of Transition*: 50–69.
- "Canada and Collective Security." In David B. Dewitt and David Leyton-Brown, *Canada's International Security Policy*.

Ries, John C. "NATO Reorganization: A Critique and Analysis." *Western Political Quarterly*, vol.18, no. 1 (March 1965): 64–72.

Rippon, Thomas, Roger Girouard, and Eliot Lowery. "Leadership for a Sustainable Culture of Peace: The UN Mission in East Timor." *Canadian Military Journal*, vol. 5, no 3 (autumn 2004).

Ripsman, Norrin M. "The Challenge of Targeting Economic Sanctions." *International Journal*, vol. 57, no. 4 (autumn 2002): 647–51.

Rodger, Nicholas A.M. "Queen Elizabeth and the myth of sea–power in English History." *Transactions of the Royal Historical Society*, vol. 14 (6th series). Cambridge, 2004: 153–74.
- ed., *Naval Power in the 20th Century*. London: Palgrave Macmillan, and Annapolis Maryland: Naval Institute Press, 1996.
- and Randolph Cock, eds. *Essays in Naval History, from Medieval to Modern*. Aldershot: Ashgate, 2009.

Rosenberg, David Alan. "American Naval Strategy in the Era of the Third World War: An Inquiry into the Structure and Process of General War at Sea, 1945–90." In Nicholas Rodger, *Naval Power in the 20th Century*: 242–54.

Roskill, Stephen Wentworth. *The War at Sea* (3 vols.), vol.1. London: HMSO, 1954.
- "The U-boat Campaign of 1917 and Third Ypres." *RUSI Journal*, vol. 104, no. 616 (Nov. 1959): 440–2.
- *The Strategy of Sea Power: Its Development and Application: Based on the Lees-Knowles Lectures ... 1961*. London: Collins, 1962.
- *Naval Policy Between the Wars: The Period of Anglo-American Antagonism, 1919–1929*. London: Collins, 1968.
- *Naval Policy Between the Wars: The Period of Reluctant Rearmament, 1930–1939*. London: Collins, 1976.

Ross, Douglas. "Towards a Canadian Maritime Strategy in the North Pacific Region." See: Langdon, Frank.
- "Michael Ignatieff's Truncated View of Canadian-American Relations." In Graham Walker, ed., *Independence in an Age of Empire*: 345–55.

Roussel, Stéphan, and Greg Donaghy. *Escott Reid: Diplomat and Scholar*. Montreal and Kingston: McGill-Queen's University Press, 2004.

Rowe, Derrick H. *Breaking New Ground*. See: May, A.W.

Russell, Dawn A. *Breaking New Ground*. See: May, A.W.

Russell, E.C. *Canadian Naval Operations in Korean Waters*. See: Thorgrimsson, Thor.
- *A History of Canadian Naval Aviation, 1918–1962*. See: Kealy, J.D.F.

Sapardanis, Christoper. "'The World is Entitled to Ask Questions': The Trudeau Peace Initiative Reconsidered." See: Pearson, Michael.

Sarty, Roger. "Canada and Submarine Warfare, 1909–1950." Canadian Anti-submarine Forces and Operations During the First World War." Paper read at the Service Historique de la Marine, 1988. Ottawa: DND, Directorate of History, nd.
- *Tin Pots and Pirate Ships*. See: Hadley, Michael.
- "The Origins of Canada's Second World War Maritime Forces, 1918–1940." Paper presented to a Colloquium, "Maritime Forces in Global Strategy As We

Approach the 21st Century." Halifax: Centre for Foreign Policy Studies, Dalhousie University, 24–26 June 1994.
- "Canadian Naval Policy 1867–1939." Draft chapter for William Johnson et al. *The Official History of the Royal Canadian Navy*: 20–36.
- and Barry Gough "Sailors and Soldiers: The Royal Navy, the Canadian Forces, and the Defence of Atlantic Canada, 1890–1918." In Michael Hadley, Rob Huebert, and Fred Crickard, *A Nation's Navy*: 112–30.
- and Brian Tennyson. *Guardian of the Gulf: Sydney, Cape Breton, and the Atlantic Wars*. Toronto: University of Toronto Press, 2000.
- "Canada's Emergence as a Naval Power, 1910–1950." Conference paper, 3 Feb. 2002. In Bernier and MacFarlane, eds. *Canada, 1900–1950: Un pays prend sa place/A Country Comes of Age*: 111–26.
- *No Higher Purpose*. See: Douglas, W.A.B.
- *A Blue Water Navy*. See: Douglas, W.A.B.
- "Toward a Canadian Naval Service, 1867–1914." In Richard H. Gimblett, ed., *The Naval Service of Canada, 1910–2010: The Centennial Story*: 1–19.
Savage, Carlton. *Policy of the United States Toward Maritime Commerce in War*. Washington: Department of State, 1934.
Schneller, Robert J. "Operation Enduring Freedom: Coalition Warfare from the Sea and on the Sea." In Bruce A. Elleman and Sarah C.M. Paine, eds., *Naval Coalition Warfare*: 193–207.
Schott, Jeffrey J. *Economic Sanctions Reconsidered*. See: Hufbauer, Gary Clyde.
Schurman, Donald Mackenzie, and John Beeler, eds. *Imperial Defence, 1868–1887*. London: Frank Cass, 1999.
Schuyler, Robert Livingston. *The Fall of the Old Colonial System: A Study in British Free Trade*. London: Oxford University Press, 1945.
Scrivener, David. *Northern Waters: Security and Resource Issues*, See Archer, Clive.
Sen, Amartya. *Development as Freedom*. New York: Alfred A. Knopf, 1999.
Shadwick, Martin. "Aurora Renaissance." *Canadian Military Journal*, vol. 8, no. 4 (winter 2007–08): 102–04.
Shah, Iqbal H. "Sanctions and Childhood Mortality in Iraq." See: Ali, Mohamed M.
Sigler, John, "The Trudeau Peace Initiative." See: Riekhoff, Harald von.
Simic, Charles "Witness to Horror." *New York Review of Books*, vol. 57, no. 2 (11 Feb. 2010): 7.
Skaarup, Harold A. *Out of Darkness–Light: A History of Canadian Military Intelligence*. 3 vols. iUniverse, 2005.
Smith, Daniel M. *Robert Lansing and American Neutrality 1914–1917*. New York: Da Capo Press, 1972.
Smith, Gordon W. *The Transfer of Arctic Territories from Great Britain to Canada in 1880, and some related matters, as seen in official correspondence*. St Jean, Quebec: Department of History, Collège Militaire Royal, 1961.
Sokolsky, Joel J. "The US, Canada and the Cold War in the North Atlantic: The Early Years." Paper presented to the Canadian Political Science Association, May 1981: 30–1.
- *Canada and Collective Security*. see: Jockel, Joseph T.
- "Canada and the Cold War at Sea, 1945–68." In W.A.B. Douglas, ed., *The RCN in Transition*: 209–32.
- *Canadian Defence: Decisions and Determinants*. See: Middlemiss, Danford W.
- "The Bilateral Defence Relationship with the United States." In David Dewitt and David Leyton-Brown, *Canada's International Security Policy*: 177–8.

- "Lloyd Axworthy's Legacy: Human Security and the Rescue of Canadian Defence Policy." See: Jockel, Joseph T.
- and Joseph T. Jockel. "Canada and NATO." *International Journal*, vol. 64, no. 2 (spring 2009).
Solomon, James. *Multilateral Force: America's Nuclear Solution for NATO (1960–1965)*. Annapolis Maryland: United States Naval Academy, 1999.
Soward, Stuart. "Canadian Naval Aviation, 1915–69." In James Boutilier, ed., *RCN in Retrospect*: 270–85.
Stacey, Charles Perry. "Canadian Defence Policy." *Canadian Journal of Economics and Political Science*, vol. 4, no. 4 (Nov. 1938): 490–504.
- "The Canadian–American Permanent Joint Board on Defence, 1940–1945." *International Journal*, vol. 9, no. 2 (1954): 105–24.
- *Six Years of War: The Army in Canada, Britain and the Pacific*. (The Official History of the Canadian Army in the Second World War, vol. 1). Ottawa: Canadian DND, 1955.
- *Arms, Men and Governments: The War Policies of Canada, 1939–1945*. Canada: DND, 1970.
- *Mackenzie King and the Atlantic Triangle*, Toronto: Macmillan, 1976.
- *Canada and the Age of Conflict: A History of Canadian External Policies. Vol. 1, 1867–1921*. Toronto: Macmillan, 1977.
Stairs, Denis. "The Canadian Forces and the Doctrine of Interoperability: The Issues." See: Middlemiss, Danford W.
- "Myths, Morals, and Reality in Canadian Foreign Policy." *International Journal*, vol. 58, no. 2 (2002–03): 239–56.
- and Danford Middlemiss. "Continental Security: The Issue and Challenges." In Robert H. Edwards and Graham Walker, eds., *Continental Security and Canada-U.S. Relations*: 34–40.
Stein, Janice Gross. "Deterrence and Compellence in the Gulf, 1990–91: A Failed or Impossible Task?" *International Security*, vol. 17 (autumn 1992): 147–79.
Stevenson, William. *A Man Called Intrepid: The Secret War*. New York: Lyons Press, 1976 (2000).
Stewart, Alice B. "Sir John A. MacDonald and the Imperial Defence Commission of 1879." *Canadian Historical Review*, vol. 25, no. 2 (June 1954): 122.
Stewart, Gordon T. "'An Objective of US Foreign Policy since the Founding of the Republic': The United States and the End of Empire in Canada." In Phillip Buckner, *Canada and the End of Empire*: 94–116.
Stewart, Larry R. *Canada's European Force: 1971–1980: A Defence Policy in Transition*. National Security Series, 5/80, Kingston, Ontario: Centre for International Relations, Queen's University, 1980.
Stigler, Andrew L. "Coalition Warfare over Kosovo." In Bruce Elleman and Sarah Paine, eds., *Naval Coalition Warfare*: 182–92.
Stone, Craig. "From Minister Hellyer to General Hillier." See: Gosselin, Daniel.
Strachan, Hew. "Strategy or Alibi? Obama, McChrystal and the Operational Level of War." *Survival*, vol. 52, no. 5 (Oct.–Nov. 2010): 157–82.
Stursberg, Peter. *Lester Pearson and the American Dilemma*. Toronto: Doubleday, 1980.
Summers, Ken. "The Canadian Navy in the 1990–91 Gulf War: Some Personal Observations." In Richard Gimblett and Richard Mayne, eds., *People, Policy and Programmes*: 113–20.
Sun Tzu. *The Art of War*, 600 BC (New York: Dover Publications, 2002).

Sutherland, Robert J. "Canada's Long Term-Strategic Situation." *International Journal*, vol. 17, no. 3 (summer 1962): 199–223.
Sutton, Jean. *Lords of the East: The East India Company and its Ships*. London: Conway Maritime Press, 1981.
Swanson, Roger F. and Dale C. Thomson. *Canadian Foreign Policy: Options and Perspectives*. Toronto: McGraw-Hill Ryerson, 1971.
Symonds, Craig L., ed. *New Aspects of Naval History: Selected Papers Presented at the Fourth Naval History Symposium, United States Naval Academy, 25–26 Oct. 1979*, Annapolis, Maryland, 1981.
Tate, D.H. *Grumman CS2F/CP–121 Tracker Royal Canadian Navy*. Canada Aviation Museum, n.d.
Temple Patterson, A., ed. *The Jellicoe Papers* (2 vols.) London: Navy Records Society, 1966–68.
Tennyson, Brian, and Roger Sarty. *Guardian of the Gulf: Sydney, Cape Breton, and the Atlantic Wars*. Toronto: University of Toronto Press, 2000.
Thomas, Douglas S. "The Canadian Maritime Contribution to Peace-Support Operations." In Ann Griffiths, Peter Haydon, and Richard Gimblett, *Canadian Gunboat Diplomacy*: 184–8.
– "Responding to Disaster." *Canadian Naval Review*, vol. 1, no. 3 (autumn 2005): 31–2.
– "Warship "Developments: Arctic/Offshore Patrol Ships." *Canadian Naval Review*, vol. 3, no. 3 (autumn 2007): 36–7.
– "Warship Developments: The Chinese Navy." *Canadian Naval Review*, vol. 5, no. 1 (spring 2009: 38–9.
– "Canadian Naval Arctic Patrol Vessels." *Canadian Naval Review*, winter 2009.
Thomson, Dale C., and Roger F. Swanson. *Canadian Foreign Policy: Options and Perspectives*, Toronto: McGraw-Hill Ryerson, 1971.
Thorgrimsson, Thor, and E.C. Russell. *Canadian Naval Operations in Korean Waters, 1950–1955*. Ottawa: Queen's Printer, 1965.
Thorne, Stephen. "Movers & Shakers: Rick Hillier." *International Journal*, vol. 60, no. 3 (2004–05): 824–30.
Till, Geoffrey. "Strategy in the Far North." In Clive Archer and David Scrivener, *Northern Waters: Security and Resource Issues*: 69–84.
– "The Soviet Navy, the North Atlantic, and Canada." In Margaret MacMillan and David Sorenson, *Canada and NATO: Uneasy Past, Uncertain Future*: 85–100.
– "Richmond and the Faith Reaffirmed: British Naval Thinking between the Wars." In Geoffrey Till, *The Development of British Naval Thinking*: 103–33.
– *The Development of British Naval Thinking: Essays in Memory of Bryan Ranft*. Abingdon, Oxfordshire: Routledge, 2006.
– "A Commonwealth Naval Strategy in the 21st Century?" Proceedings of the Canadian Navy Centennial / Ninth Maritime Command (MARCOM) History Conference, *From Empire to In(ter)dependence: The Canadian Navy and the Commonwealth Experience, 1910–2010*. Ottawa: Canadian Naval Heritage Press, May 2010.
Tomlin, Brian W., and Maureen Malot, eds. *Canada Among Nations, 1984: A Time of Transition*. Toronto: James Lorimer, 1985.
Tompson, William J. *Khrushchev: A Political Life*. New York: St Martin's Press, 1995.
Tracy, Nicholas. "The Enforcement of Canada's Continental Maritime Jurisdiction." ORAE Report No. R44. Ottawa, DND, 1975.

- "The Diplomatic Utility of Canada's Naval Forces." ORAE Report No. R60. Ottawa, DND, 1976.
- "Canada's Foreign Policy Objectives and Canadian Security Arrangements in the North," ORAE Extra Mural Paper No 8. Ottawa: DND, 1980.
- "Matching Canada's Navy to her Foreign Policy and Domestic Requirements." *International Journal*, vol. 38, no. 3 (summer 1983): 459–75.
- "Why does Canada want Nuclear Submarines?" *International Journal*, vol. 43, no. 3 (1987–88): 499–518.
- "Canada's Security Considerations in the Arctic." In Clive Archer and David Scrivener, *Northern Waters: Security and Resource Issues*: 146–54.
- *Navies, Deterrence, and American Independence*. Vancouver: University of British Columbia Press, 1988.
- *Attack on Maritime Trade*. Basingstoke: Macmillan, and Toronto: University of Toronto Press, 1991.
- *Canada's Naval Strategy: Rooted in Experience*. Maritime Security Occasional Paper No 1. Halifax: Centre for Foreign Policy Studies, Dalhousie University, 1995.
- *The Collective Naval Defence of the Empire: 1900–1940*. Vol. 136. Navy Records Society. Aldershot, England: Ashgate, 1997.
- *Sea Power and the Control of Trade: Belligerent Rights from the Russian War to the Beira Patrol*. Navy Records Society, Aldershot, England: Ashgate, 2005.
- *The Battle of Quiberon Bay, 1759: Hawke and the Defeat of the French Invasion*. Barnsley, South Yorkshire: Pen & Sword Maritime, 30 May 2010.

Trudgen, Matthew. "Do We Want 'Buckets of Instant Sunshine'? Canada and Nuclear Weapons 1945–1984." *Canadian Military Journal*, vol. 10, no. 1.

Tucker, Gilbert. *A History of the Royal Canadian Navy*. Ottawa: King's Printer, 1951.
- *The Naval Service of Canada: Its Official History*. 2 vols. Vol. 2: *Activities on Shore During the Second World War*. Ottawa: King's Printer, 1952.

Tummers, Edward L. *Maritime Security in the Twenty-first Century*. Maritime Security Occasional Paper No. 11. Halifax: Centre for Foreign Policy Studies, Dalhousie University, 2000.

Tweedie, Graeme R. "The Roots of the Royal Canadian Navy: Sovereignty versus Nationalism, 1812–1910." In Michael L. Hadley, Rob Huebert, and Fred W. Crickard, *A Nation's Navy*: 91–101.

Vego, Milan N. *Naval Strategy and Operations in Narrow Seas*. London: Frank Cass, 1999.

Vine, David. *Island of Shame: The Secret History of the US Military Base on Diego Garcia*. Princeton, New Jersey; Princeton University Press, 2009.

Viorst, Milton. "Report from Baghdad." *The New Yorker*, 24 Sept. 1990: 89–97.

Walker, Graham, ed. *Continental Security and Canada-U.S. Relations*. See: Edwards, Robert H.
- ed. *Independence in an Age of Empire: Assessing Unilateralism and Multilateralism*. Halifax: Centre for Foreign Policy Studies, Dalhousie University, 2004.

Walker, Peter. "Sanctions: A Blunt Weapon." *Red Cross, Red Crescent*, no 3, 1995.

Wark, Wesley. Review of Hans Blix, "Disarming Iraq." *International Journal*, vol. 60, no. 1 (2004–05): 282–5.

Watkins, James D. "The Maritime Strategy." Supplement to United States Naval Institute *Proceedings*, 112 (Jan. 1986): 2–17.

Webster, Phil. "Arctic Sovereignty, Submarine Operations and Water Space Management." *Canadian Naval Review*, vol. 3, no. 3 (fall 2007): 14–16.

Weeks, Stanley. "The 100-ship Navy Global Maritime Partnership Initiative." Synot Lecture. In Andrew Forbes and Michelle Lovi, eds., *Australian Maritime Issues 2006*: 27–36.

Weschler, Joanna. "Evolution of Security Council Innovations in Sanctions." *International Journal*, vol. 65, no. 1 (winter 2009–10): 31–44.

Whitby, Michael. *A Blue Water Navy* and *No Higher Purpose*. See: Douglas, W.A.B.

– with Richard Gimblett, and Peter Haydon. *The Admirals: Canada's Senior Naval Leadership in the Twentieth Century*. Toronto: Dundurn Press, 2006.

– "Vice-Admiral Harry G. DeWolf: Pragmatic Navalist." In Michael Whitby, Richard Gimblett, and Peter Haydon, *The Admirals*: 213–46.

– "Showing the Flag across the North: HMCS *Labrador* and the 1954 Transit of the Northwest Passage." *Canadian Naval Review*, vol. 2, no. 1 (spring 2006): 21–4.

– "The Long Reach: The RCN and the Korean War." *Naval Review*, vol. 1 no. 4 (winter 2006): 19–23.

– "'Doin' the Biz': Canadian Submarine Patrol Operations Against Soviet SSBNs, 1983–87." In Bernd Horne, ed., *Fortune Favours the Brave*.

Whitman, Edward C. "SOSUS, The 'Secret Weapon' of Undersea Surveillance." *Undersea Warfare, The Official Magazine of the US Submarine Force*, vol. 7, no. 2 (winter 2005).

Wigley, Phillip. *Canada and the Transition to Commonwealth: British-Canadian Relations, 1917–26*. Cambridge: Cambridge University Press, 1977.

Wilkinson, John W. *Canada and naval defence: Canada's attitude both before and since the war with regard to naval defence: letters by J.W. Wilkinson, late RNAV, together with other correspondence and newspaper reports*. Toronto, 1918.

Williams, Kelly. "Canada's Maritime Strategy: A Naval Perspective." In Robert Edwards and Graham Walker, eds., *Continental Security and Canada-U.S. Relations*: 157–64.

Willmot, Robert. "John Holmes." See: Dobell, Peter C.

Willmott, H.P. *The Last Century of Sea Power*. Vol. 2, *From Washington to Tokyo, 1922–1945*. Bloomington: University of Indiana Press, 2010.

Willoughby, William R. "Canadian–American Defense Co-operation." *Journal of Politics*, vol. 13, no. 4 (Nov. 1951): 682–3.

Winkler, David F. *Cold War at Sea: High-Seas Confrontation between the United States and the Soviet Union*. Annapolis, Maryland: Naval Institute Press, 2000.

Winkler, Wilhelm. *The Cost of the World War*. See: Grebler, Leo.

Wright, Peter. *Spy Catcher: The Candid Autobiography of a Senior Intelligence Officer*. New York: Viking, 1987.

Wright, Quincy. "The Cuban Quarantine." *American Journal of International Law*, vol. 57 (1963): 546–66.

Wright, Steven M. *The United States and Persian Gulf Security: The Foundations of the War on Terror*. Ithaca, New York: Garnet & Ithaca Press, 2007.

Yost, William J. *In Defence of Canada's Oceans*. Conference of Defence Associations Institute, 1988.

Young, Andrew C. "Canada's Marine Forces, 1867–1871." In Richard Gimblett and Richard Mayne, eds., *People, Policy and Programmes*: 77–96.

Young, Michael. "STANAVFORLANT in 1970: The First Canadian Command." *Canadian Naval Review*, vol. 1, no 3 (autumn 2005): 14–19.

Zeman, Z.A.B. *A Diplomatic History of the First World War*. London: Weidenfeld and Nicolson, 1971.
Zimmerman, David. *The Great Naval Battle of Ottawa*. Toronto: University of Toronto Press, 1989.
– "The Social Background of the Wartime Navy: Some Statistical Data." In Michael Hadley, Rob Huebert, and Fred Crickard, *A Nation's Navy*: 256–79.

INDEX

GENERAL

10th Cruiser Squadron, 37
1st (Commonwealth) Division (Korea), 117
3rd Fleet, 262
509th Airborne Infantry Combat Team, 165
9/11 Crisis, 14, 218, 263–4, 267, 288

Abbott, Douglas, 87
Acheson, Dean, 100, 117–19
Act to amend the Arctic Waters Pollution Prevention Act: Bill C-3, 292
Advisory Committee on Post-Hostilities Planning, 86, 95
African National Congress, 323
Ahtisaari, Martti, 209
Air Command, 162
Air Defence Command, 162
Air Transport Command, 162
Airborne Regiment, 256
al Mada, 216
Alabama claims, 8, 18.
Albert Einstein Peace Prize, 178
Albright, Madeleine, 206, 236, 311
Allard, Gen Jean-Victor, 154
American Revolutionary War, 4, 7
Anderson, John, 181
Anderson, R Adm John, 188, 228
Andrews, Gen Frank Maxwell, 55
Andropov, Yuri, 178
Angeli, Adm Mario, 225
Anglo-American Staff Conversation, 94

Anglo-Icelandic "Cod Wars," 251
Anglo-Japanese Alliance, 39, 46
Anglo-Japanese War, 51
Annan, Kofi, 216, 241
Aquinas, St Thomas, 10, 215
Arctic Council, 289–90, 298
Arctic Shipping Pollution Prevention Regulations, 180, 294–6
Arctic Waters Pollution Prevention Act, 161, 180–1, 292
Aristide, Jean-Bertrand, 230–1
Armitage, Richard, 218
Arnold-Forster, Lt Cmdr W.E., 10
Arone, Shidane, 256
Ashton, M-Gen E.C., 56
Asia-Pacific Advisor, Maritime Forces Pacific, 282
Asquith, Herbert, 34
Atlantic Coast Command, 72, 78
Atlantic Convoy Conference (1943), 78
Atlantic Fleet, 73
Attlee, Clement, 118
Auchi, Nadhmi, 213
Audette, Cmdr Louis, 105, 244; Audette Report (1970), 244
Aurora Incremental Modernization Project, 260
Australian Defence College, 48
Axworthy, Lloyd, 240–1, 309, 312; Axworthy Concept of Sanctions Operations, 241

Baker, James, 198, 204, 320
Balkan Crisis, 197, 221, 228–30, 234–41

Ballantyne, Charles Colquhoun
  (C.C.), 48
Ballard Technologies Inc., 192
Ballistic Missile Submarine, SSBN, 16,
  132, 141, 166–7, 174–5, 181–6,
  196
Baltic and International Maritime
  Council, 282
Banque nationale de Paris-Paribas,
  213
Baril, Gen J.M.G., 260
baselines, 180, 291–2
Battenberg, Prince Louis of, 22–3
Beatty, Perrin, 183, 189
Beatty, Vice-Adm. Sir David, 6, 35, 94
Bellamy, Carol, 211–12
belligerent Rights, 7, 9, 50–1
Bennett, Richard Bedford (R.B.), 54–5
Benson, Adm William S., 39
Bernier, Capt Joseph-Elzéar, 24
Bethell, R Adm Alexander, 29
bin Laden, Osama, 310–11
Blix, Hans, 207
blockade, 4–6, 9–11, 22, 37–9, 51,
  98, 108, 138, 204, 210, 214, 218,
  227, 231–2, 235–6, 242, 282, 311,
  319, 322
Boating Magazine, 79
Bonar Law, Andrew, 37
Bonino, Emma, 247
Borden, Sir Robert, 29, 32–40, 44, 68,
  195, 328
Borg, Joe, 289
Botha, Pieter Willem, 323
Bourassa, Henri, 32, 90, 142, 160
Bourbon, 7
Boutilier, James, 307
Boutros-Ghali, Boutros, 221–2, 233,
  239; *An Agenda for Peace* (1992),
  222, 239
Breese, Terry, 303
Brezhnev, Leonid, 141, 176–8
Bristol, R Adm A. LeR. 73
British Admiralty Technical Mission,
  65
British Empire, 19–20, 23–48, 55–7,
  60, 104, 132, 299–301, 306–8, 318
Brittan, Leon, 252
Brock, R Adm Jeffrey V., 136–7, 151,
  191

Brodeur, Louis-Philippe, 23
Brodeur, V-Adm Nigel D., 181
Brown, George, 3
Buck, V-Adm Ron, 265
Bulletin of the Atomic Scientists, 195
Bundy, McGeorge, 140
Bureau, Jacques, 47
Burke, Adm Arleigh, 15–16
Bush, George, 156, 196–8, 208, 319
Bush, George W., 20, 156, 208–9,
  217, 264–5, 268–71, 302
Butler, Richard, 206

Cabinet War Committee, 71–2, 86–7,
  93–4
Cadieux, Léo, 160
Cairns, V-Adm Peter, 197
Calder, Kenneth, 264
Cameron, David, 282
Cammell Laird Shipyard, Birkenhead,
  258
Camp Mirage, 266
Campbell, Isabel, 110
Campney, Ralph, 128
Canada: Bill C-243, 152
Canada Club, 118
Canada Command, 275–7
Canada Customs, 293
Canada-United States: Binational
  Planning Group (2003), 275; Basic
  Security Plan, 101–03, 132; Defence
  Plan, 101; Military Cooperation
  Committee (1946), 100, 275
Canadian Military Journal, 308
Canadian Air-Sea Transportable
  Brigade, 155
Canadian Coast Guard, 113–14, 180,
  244, 247–52, 292–4, 298
Canadian Defence Plan No. 2 (1936),
  55
Canadian Defence Quarterly, 191
Canadian Forces Europe, 201, 221
Canadian Forces Headquarters, 158
Canadian High Commission, 37
Canadian Institute for International
  Peace and Security, 314
Canadian Institute of International Af-
  fairs, 61
Canadian International Council, 297,
  303

INDEX

459

Canadian Joint Staff Mission in London, 86
Canadian Joint Task Force South West Asia, 273
Canadian Naval Mission Overseas, 80, 86
Canadian North-West Atlantic Command, 78, 95, 100; *see also* North Atlantic Treaty Organization
Canadian Rangers, 293
Canadian Task Force 151, 270, 277–80, 337
CANCOM, 194, 278
Cannon, Lawrence, 289, 292
Carter, Jimmy, 164, 180, 320
Castro, Fidel, 137–8, 147
Cédras, Lt-Gen Raoul, 230–1
Cellucci, Paul, 269–70
Center for Naval Analyses, 260
Center for Strategic and International Studies, 292
Central Intelligence Agency, 156, 176, 205–7
central powers, 5–6, 9–10, 38, 204
Chalabi, Ahmed, 216
Chamberlain, Austin, 50
Chamberlain, Joseph, 33
Chamberlain, Neville, 56–7
Chanak crisis, 40, 98, 126
Chastelain, Gen John de, 192, 220
Château Laurier, 92
Château Rambouillet (1999), 236
Chief of Defence Staff, 150–2, 192
Chiefs of Staff Committee, 124, 136, 149–50
Chiefs of Staff Sea/Air Warfare Committee, 131
Child and Maternal Mortality Survey (1999), 211
Chinese People's Liberation Army Navy, 280
Chrétien, Jean, 13, 204, 247, 252, 260, 265, 268–71, 302, 313
Churchill, Winston S., 25, 29, 33–4, 68–72, 76–8, 85–7, 90, 97, 100, 110, 113.
Civil War, 4–9, 18
Clarendon, George Villiers, 4th Earl, 8
Clark, Glen, 263
Clark, Joe, 181, 187–8

Clarke, Richard, 208, 224, 266–8
Clarkson, Adrienne, 271
Claxton, Brooke, 92, 98–9, 102, 110, 332
Clinton, Bill, 207–8, 218, 224
Coalition Wide Area Network, 273
Coastal Fisheries Protection Act (1994), 246–7
Coates, Robert, 180
Cold War, 4–6, 9–13, 16, 105–8, 121, 126–99, 220, 244–5, 254, 257, 287, 295, 311–13, 331–2, 336
Collenette, David, 256–7
Colonial Conference: (1897) 21, 28; (1902) 22, 28, 33; (1907): 23–4
Combined Enterprise Regional Information Exchange System, 273–4
Combined Logistics Force, 203
Combined Maritime Forces (Somalia), 280
Committee of Imperial Defence, 22–3, 28–30, 33, 37, 42, 49, 50, 61, 94, 132; *Memorandum on Empire Naval Policy and Co-operation* (1923), 49
Committee of Twenty, 92–3
Common Border Agency, 303
Commonwealth, 41, 50, 54, 57, 60, 68, 92, 95, 98, 101, 114, 117, 125–6, 141, 176, 262, 274, 299, 304–7, 324
Commonwealth Prime Ministers Conference (1940), 69; 1962, 128
Confederate States, 6
Confederation, 3, 8, 13, 18
Conference of Defence Associations, 170, 195
Connolly, John J., 79–80
Conservative Party, 204, 288, 294
Continental Defence, 93–5, 100–3, 107, 124–5, 129–30, 137, 157, 244, 254–86, 301
Continental Shelf, 3, 287–9
Convoy: ONS-154, 76–7; ONS-5, 81
Cook, Robin, 311
Corbett, Sir Julian, 4, 7; *England in the Seven Years' War*, 4, 7; *Some Principles of Naval Strategy*, 4
Cortright and Lopez, *The Sanctions Decade*, 312

Counter-terrorism Security Group, 208
Craig, Gen Malin, 56
Crerar, Col Harry D.G., 55
Crickard, R Adm Fred W, 182, 186–8
Crowe, Sir Eyre, 8
Cruise Missile Testing, 173–5, 182
Cuban Missile Crisis (1962), 21, 124–33, 137–41, 147, 151–5, 172, 199, 271, 300, 333
Cunningham, Adm Andrew, 142–53

Dalhousie Univeristy, 12–13, 272
Dandurand, Raoul, 57
Danson, Barnett, 169–70
Davidson, R Adm Bob, 12, 277–81, 285–6
Davie Shipbuilding, Lauzon, 205
Dayton Accord (1995), 234–5
de Cuéllar, Javier Pérez, 209
de Gaulle, Charles, 140, 146, 154
de Klerk, Frederik Willem, 324
Declaraton of Paris, 8–9, 214
Defence Budget, 33, 47–9, 54–5, 59–60, 66, 85, 107–9, 120, 136–9, 147–8, 157–8, 168–9, 181, 191, 220–1, 257, 260, 294–6, 322, 329–30, 335
Defence Council, 47, 192
Defence Management Committee, 192
Defence Planning Committee, 225
Defence Research Board, 108, 166
Department of External Affairs, 42, 58, 61, 89, 93–4, 97–100, 115–16, 122, 169, 180–2, 186, 190; *Foreign Policy for Canadians* (1970), 162–3
Department of Fisheries, 161
Department of Fisheries and Oceans Canada, 252
Department of Foreign Affairs, 14, 240, 250, 314; *International Policy Statement: A Role of Pride and Influence in the World* (2005), 293; *Statement on Canada's Arctic Foreign Policy* (2010), 292
Department of Marine and Fisheries, Fisheries Protection Service, 19–26, 30, 161, 243–6, 252–3
Department of National Defence, 13–14, 70, 120, 143–4, 150, 166, 169, 181–2, 192, 199, 220, 243, 264, 268, 277–9, 283, 311 (*see also* Minister of, and National Defence Headquarters); Ad Hoc Committee on Defence Policy (1963), *see* Sutherland, 144; Ad Hoc Committee on Naval Objectives (1961), *see* Brock, 136; *Appreciation of the Defence Problems Confronting Canada*, Crerar (1936), 55; *Canada First Defence Strategy* (2008), 199, 243, 277; *Challenge and Commitment* (1987), 183, 191, 194; *Defence Policy Review*, 13; *Defence Structure Review* (1974–75), 166; *Defence White Paper* (1971), 161; Management Review Group (1971), 166; *Memorandum on ... The Higher Direction of National Defence* (1937), Pope, 42, 56; Naval Warfare Study Group (1956), 131; *Report to the Prime Minister* (1997), 277; *The Naval Vision* (1994), 13; *Securing Canada's Ocean Frontier* (2005), 14, 275, 283; Somalia Enquiry (1993), 256, 277; *Strategy for 2020*, *see* Baril, 260–2; *The Case for One Service* (1961), *see* Foulkes, 150; *White Paper on Defence*: (1964), 151; (1994), 13–14, 145, 151–2, 257, 302
Department of National Revenue Preventive Services, 244
Department of Transport, 244
Desbarats, Georges, 39, 150
détente, 143, 156, 162–3, 169, 176–7
Devonshire, Victor Cavendish, 9th Duke of, 41
DeWolf, Adm Harry G., 76
Dextraze, Gen Jacques, 161, 168
Diefenbaker, John George, 128–9, 132–4, 137–42, 157, 163, 188, 275, 296
Directorate of Plans, 88
Directorate of Strategic Analysis, 106, 268
Directorate of Strategic Policy Planning, 166
Dispatch (U.S. State Department), 205
Distant Early Warning (DEW) line, 113–14, 180

INDEX 461

Dockyard, 22–3, 43, 71, 75, 184, 201, 258, 327, 335
Dönitz, Grand Adm Karl, 73, 81–2
Drake, Sir Francis, 248
dreadnought, 24, 29, 33, 327
Drew, George, 115
Dubček, Alexander, 156
Dulles, John Foster, 113, 129
Dundonald, Gen Douglas Cochrane, Earl of, 21
Duvalier, Papa Doc, 143
Dyer, R Adm Kenneth L., 139, 142, 153–4

Eastern Air Command, 59, 66, 78
Economic zone, 3, 161, 179, 243–6
Eden, Sir Anthony, 58, 126–7
Eggleton, Art, 264
Eisenhower, Dwight D., 113, 126, 129
Ekéus, Rolf, 206
Elizabeth, Queen Consort, 65
Emirates Airways, 266
Empire Club (Toronto), 118
Ethiopian/Abyssinian Crisis, 57–9
Etihad Airways, 206
Etnyre, R Adm Terrance, 263
European Commission, 247, 252, 289
European Fisheries Commission, 247
European Union, 235–6, 246–51, 280, 289–90, 325
exercises: *Able Archer* (1972), 176; *Mainbrace* (1952), 110; *Mariner* (1953), 110; *Norploy*, 161, 191; *Slamex* (1964), 147; RIMPAC, 272–3, 284, 307

Falls, Adm Robert H., 161, 170
Fanshawe, Adm of the Flt Sir Arthur D., 51
Fenian, 18
Ferguson, Howard, 58
Ferranti, 108
Finlandization, 299
First Canadian Division, 71
Fisheries Protection Service, 19, 22–3, 26, 243–4, 252, 327
Fisheries, 3, 245, 249–53, 279, 293, 327
Fishery, 246
Fisk, Robert, 310

Fitz, Capt H.C., 76
Floud, Sir Francis, 61–2
Ford, Gerald, 164
Foster, George E., 25
Foulkes, Gen Charles, 100, 123, 150–2, 283
Fowler, Robert, 312
Frasure, Robert, 229
Free Trade, 25, 98, 145, 179, 252, 303
Freedom of Navigation, 180
Freedom of the Seas, 9, 39, 51, 291
Frith, Royce, 250
Front de la Libération du Québec, 171

Gadhafi, Moammar, 317
Garnett, R Adm G.L., 257, 263
Garrett, Lawrence, 254
Gates, Robert M., 156
General Staff, 35, 54, 93, 100, 150
Geneva Convention, 214, 223, 237, 267
Geneva Disarmament Conference (1927), 49–50
Genscher, Hans-Dietrich, 222
George VI, King, 65
German navy, 20
Germany, 6, 22, 37, 54, 60–2, 65, 68, 73, 82–4, 91
Gervais, Honoré, 30
Gibbons, Elizabeth, 232
Girouard, R Adm Roger, 261, 270–2
Glassco Commission, 150, 244
Global Coalition Counter-terrorism Task Force network, 274
Global Maritime Partnership (1,000 ship navy), 279–80, 315
Godfrey, John, 268
Gonzalez, Capt Enrique Davila, 247
Gorbachev, Mikhail, 175–8, 196–8, 320
Gorshkov, Adm of the Flt Sergey Georgiyevich, 141
Goschen, George, 28
Gosselin, M-Gen Daniel, 277
Graham, Bill, 268–9, 289
Graham, George Perry, 47
Grant, R Adm Harold T.W., 104, 107, 331
Great White Fleet, 24

Greenspon: *Open Canada*, 303
Greenstock, Sir Jeremy, 268
Greenwood, R-Adm Nigel S., 272
Gretton, V-Adm Sir Peter, 79, 81
Grey, Albert Henry George Grey, 4th Earl, 24
Grey, Sir Edward, 34
Grove and Codner, *Fundamentals of British Maritime Doctrine*, 12
Guelph, University of, 177
Guerre de course, 8, 9

Haggard, V-Adm Sir Vernon H.S., 54
Haig, Gen Alexander, 165
Halifax Class Modernization / Frigate Life Extension, 284
Halifax Shipyards, 135, 295
Halstead, John, 169
Hamilton, Alvin, 128
Hankey, Sir Maurice, 61
Hans Island dispute, 289
Harcourt, Lewis, 33
Harding, Sir Edward, 61
Harding, Warren G., 39
Hardwicke, Philip Yorke, Lord Chancellor, 7
Harkness, Douglas, 138
Harland & Wolff Shipyards, Belfast, 111–12, 133
Harmel, Pierre, 156, 165, 169
Harper, Stephen, 269, 275–7, 288, 292–4, 302–3, 317
Harvard University, 188
Hassan, Abu, 206
Hayward, Adm Thomas, 174
Healey, Denis, 195, 314
Hearn, Loyola, 253
Heeney, Arnold, 110, 122
Heinbecker, Paul, 235, 269, 303
Heldyard, Lt Gen Reginald, 62
Hellyer, Paul, 144–56, 162, 220, 227, 283, 334; "Address on the Canadian Forces Reorganization Act," 152; *Damn the Torpedoes*, 148
Helsinki Final Act (1974), 222
Henault, Gen Ray, 265
Hickey, Cmds Laurence M., 245, 249
Hillier, Gen Rick, 276–7
Hill-Norton, Adm of the Flt Sir Peter, 170

Hitler, Adolph, 58, 65, 82
Holbrooke, Richard, 229, 234
Holland, Adm Lancelot, 59
Hoover, Herbert, 51
Horton, Adm Sir Max, 76, 82
Hose, Adm Walter, 35, 38, 47, 49, 55, 150, 328–9
Houghton, R Adm Frank, 108
House of Commons, 13, 24–25, 33–4, 60, 65–7, 94, 115, 126, 138, 152, 160, 177–8, 181, 186–7, 190, 243, 257, 268, 292, 303; Special Committee on Defence (1963), 13; Special Joint Committee ... on Canada's International Relations (1986), 181, *see also* Canada, Senate, Standing Committees on External Affairs and National Defence, 153, 169, 181–2, 188, 243, 252; Standing Committee on National Defence and Veterans Affairs, 243; *Maritime Sovereignty* (1990), 243
House of Lords, 8
Hudson, Adm Peter, 281
Human Security Policy (1999), 157, 240–1, 309
Hunter, Robert, 245, 249
Hurricane Katrina (2005), 218
Hussein, Adil, 311
Hussein, Saddam, 198–200, 205–9, 218, 311–12, 319–20
Hutchinson, Bruce, 92

Icebreaker, 113–14, 160, 180, 190, 290, 293–4
Ignatieff, Michael, *Empire Lite: Nation Building in Bosnia, Kosovo, and Afghanistan* (2003), 309
IHI Ishikawajima-Harima Heavy Industries Co., Ltd., 290
Imperial Conference: (1909) on Defence, 25–6, 29, 34, 99; (1911), 33; (1921), 40; (1923), 41–6; (1926), 42, 46–8; (1937), 61
Imperial Defence Commission (1879) (Carnarvon), 19
Imperial Federalism, 32, 34
Incident at Sea (1988), 196
Incidents at Sea Agreement (1972), 176

Independent, The (Britain), 310
Independent Enquiry Committee (Volcker Committee), 210
Ingersoll, Capt Royal E., 56
Inskip, Sir Thomas, 64
Intelligence, 22–3, 29–31, 42–4, 47, 70–4, 77–8, 107, 156, 167, 175–7, 186–7, 197, 200, 205–7, 216–18, 240, 245–6, 257, 262, 267, 275, 314
Inter-agency Group for Child Mortality Estimates, 211
Intermediate-Range Nuclear Forces reduction treaty, 165, 176
International Association of Classification Societies, 294
International Journal, 200, 297, 308
International Seapower Symposium (2005), 280
Inuit, 291–3
Iran-Contra (1985), 195
Iran-Iraq War, 9, 196
Iraq Ba'ath party, 211
Iraq Family Health Survey (2006/07), 211
Iraq Liberation Act (1998), 208
Iraq Ministry of Health, 214
Iraq Sanctions, 197–219, 227–8, 232, 237, 241, 254–5, 266, 308–12, 319–25
Iraq Sanctions Committee, 207
Iraq War, 104, 153, 208, 218, 267–72, 303, 308, 312, 320
Iroquois Kanesetake First Nation, 200
Irving Shipbuilding, 317
Ivanov, Igor, 236
Izetbegovi, Alija, 224

Jackobson, Linda, 290
Jacobson, David, 288–9, 292
Janvier, Gen Bernard, 233
Japan: Imperial Japanese Navy, 36; Japanese War, 56, 59, 73, 84–91, 214, 300, 319, 331
Jean, Michaëlle, 283
Jellicoe, Adm. Sir John, 6, 31, 40, 44, 89, 104, 193, 329
Jellinek, Capt Mike, 264
Jenson, Lt L.B., 87
Johnson, Adm Jay L., 16

Johnson, Lyndon B., 144–5
Joint Chiefs of Staff, 129, 292
Joint Headquarters, 131, 202
Joint Inter-Agency Task Force South, 285
Joint Staff Committee, 47
Joint Support Ships, 284, 296, 317
Joint Task Force Atlantic, 277
Joint War Plans Committee, 103
Jones, Adm George C., 66–7, 80, 86–9, 101, 331
Jones, Gareth, UNICEF, 211
JTF2, 271
Judd, Jim, 260
Jutland, 6, 35

KAL-007, 176
Kauffmann, Henrik, 96
Kay, David, 208
Keenleyside, Hugh L., 92–3
Kelly, Stephen R., 270
Kelso, Adm Frank B., 191
Kemal Atatürk, 40
Kennedy, Edward, 187
Kennedy, John F., 134, 138–41, 144, 301
Keynes, Maynard, 209
Khrushchev, Nikita, 137–8, 141
Kibble, Lt Cmdr D.G., 312
King, Adm Ernest J., 73, 78, 94–95
Kingsmill, Adm Charles E., 24, 39, 44, 47, 327–9
Kissinger, Henry, 14–15, 119, 164, 314
Kohl, Helmut, 164
Korean War, 9, 11, 83, 106, 109, 113–21, 125, 198, 313, 317, 332
Kosovo Crisis, 235–7, 240–2, 309
Kostunica, Vojislav, 325
Kraska, Cmdr James, 292
Kuwait Sanctions, 196–209, 215, 320, 336
Kuznetzov, Adm Nikolai G., 141

Lancaster Exercise (2006), 294
Landymore, R Adm William, 152–3
Lang, Eugene, 270
Lansing, Robert, 38
Laurier, Sir Wilfrid, 20–33, 44, 219, 285, 327

Lavertu, Gaëtan, 269
Law of the Sea Convention, 102, 179, 187, 190, 246, 287–8, 291–3
Law of the State Border (1982), 180
Lay, Adm Horatio Nelson, 78, 86, 102
Leadmark (2001), 14
League of Nations, 5, 38, 42–3, 57–8, 61, 99, 126
Leahy, Adm Daniel, 56
Lehman, John, 174
Lerhe, Com Eric J., 267, 274
Libal, Michael, 222
Liberal Party, 3, 30–4, 40, 54, 67, 128, 141–2, 156, 179, 204, 256–8, 268, 303, 319
Libya raid (1986), 195
Lie, Trygve, 117
Lindsey, George, 166, 314; *Canadian Maritime Strategy: Should the Emphasis be Changed?*, 166
Lloyd George, David, 37–40, 69
Lloyd's List, 280–2
London Naval Conference (1930), 51, 53–4
London, 10, 22, 33–4, 37–42, 51, 54–8, 61, 64–5, 70, 77–80, 86, 98, 115–17, 122–3, 126–7, 132, 138, 165, 228, 247–8, 251
Long, Walter, 37
Louis XIV, King, 7
Louis XVI, King, 7
Lovett, Robert, 96
Lower, Arthur R.M., 92
Luns, Joseph, 170
Lynch, Charles, 142

MacArthur, Gen Douglas, 117
MacBrien, M-Gen Sir James, 150
Macdonald, Angus L., 65–7, 72, 76, 79–80, 86–7, 105
MacDonald, Ramsay, 51
Macdonald, Sir John A, 19–21
MacKay, Peter, 297, 304, 307
MacKay, Robert Alexander, 94
Mackenzie King, William Lyon, 24, 40–3, 47–51, 55–78, 84–90, 93–102, 112, 117, 130, 150, 285, 300–1, 305–8, 315–16
Mackenzie, Ian, 59–60

MacKenzie, M-Gen Lewis Wharton, 223
MacLaren, Roy, 250–2
MacLean, Cmdr Andrew Dyas, 79
MacMillan, Harold, 138, 141
Maddison, V-Adm Paul A., 225
Mahan, Adm Alfred Thayer, 19, 28; *Influence of Sea Power upon History*, 19
Mainguy, R Adm Dan, 193
Mainguy, R Adm Rollo, 105–6, 109
Major, John, 248
Malik, Jacob, 115
Malkevich, V., 320
Manchoko, 319
Manifest Destiny, 285
Manigat, Leslie-François, 192
Manley, Michael, 172
Manson, Gen Paul, 183
March, R Adm Daniel, 203
Marine Industries, Sorel, 114
Marine Insurance, 281
Marine Police, 19
Maritime Air Group, 162, 170, 195
Maritime Coastal Defence Organization, 326
Maritime Command, 131, 151–4, 162, 192, 244–6, 257, 274, 334, *see also* Royal Canadian Navy; *Adjusting Course: A Naval Strategy for Canada* (1997), 257
Maritime Security Operations Centres, 276
Martin, Paul, 271, 277, 293
Martin, R Adm Michael, 158
Massachusetts Institute of Technology, 174
Massive Retaliation, 15, 113, 123, 137, 145
Matchpoint, 68
MC14/2, 131
MC48, 114, 123
McCallum, John, 270
McDougall, Barbara, 201
McGrigor, Adm of the Flt Sir Rhoderick Robert, 123
McKenna, Reginald, 25, 193
McNamara, Robert, 152
McNaughton, M-Gen Andy, 54–5
Mediterranean Law Merchant, 281

INDEX

465

Meighen, Arthur, 39–40
mercantalist trade war, 5, 6
Meritorious Service Cross, 271
Meyrick, V-Adm Sir Sidney, 62
Military Committee, 170
Militia Council, 47
Miller, Air Marshal Frank, 142
Miller, V-Adm Duncan (Dusty), 201–3
Miller, V-Adm Michael H., 275
Milner, Viscount Alfred, 34
Milner's Kindergarten, 34
Milošević, Slobodan, 224, 227–8, 234–8
Minister of National Defence, 47–9, 59, 70, 98, 102, 128, 134, 138, 144, 150, 160, 168, 180, 256, 264, 270, 277, 289, 297
Minister of National Defence for Naval Service, 65, 105
Minto, Sir Gilbert J.M.K. Elliot, 4th Earl, 30
Mission Specific Task Force, 276
Mladi, Ratko, 233
Monk, Frederick Debartzch, 32, 90–1, 302
Monroe, James, 5; Doctrine, 5, 21, 25
Morrison, Alex, 223
Morse, R-Adm David, 278
Mountbatten, Louis, 1st Earl Mountbatten of Burma, 151
Mujahideen, 165, 224
Mullen, Adm Mike, 280, 315
Mulroney, Brian, 178
Multi-National Corps (Iraq), 271
Munich Crisis, 57, 62, 65, 139, 271
Murray, Adm Leonard W, 71–2, 75–8, 89, 95, 331

Napoleon, Emperor Bonaparte, 5–7
Nassau (1962), 141–2
Nasser, Gamel Abdel, 126–7, 147
National Defence Act (1950), 150
National Defence Headquarters, 192
National Energy Program, 176
National Post, 288
National Research Council, 166
National Security Council, 208
Nationalist Party, 32, 219
Natynczyk, Gen Walter J., 271
Naval Aid Bill (1912), 33–4

Naval Board of Canada, 72, 105, 122, 146, 192
Naval Brigade, 18
Naval Discipline Act (1866), 30
Naval Force Somalia, 280
Naval Intelligence and Plans Division, 47
Naval Militia, 18
Naval Review, 4, 31, 35, 46, 51, 312.
Naval Service Act (1910), 25–6, 327; (1944), 30
Naval Service of Canada (Royal Canadian Navy), 25–6, 59
Naval Services Headquarters, 62, 73, 76
Naval Staff, 48–9, 55, 60, 70, 80, 86, 89, 101, 104, 108–9, 124, 134–6
Naval Tactical Data System, 108, 136
Navy League of Canada, 20–1
Navy List, 48
Negroponte, John, 268
Nelles, Adm Percy, 55–6, 59, 70, 76, 80, 85–7, 95, 101, 329–31
Network-Centric, 188, 251, 260–3, 270–5, 285, 295, 303
New Democratic Party, 268
New Look strategy, 113, 122, 125, 154
New York Times, 163
Newfoundland Command, 72, 78
Newfoundland Escort Force, 71–4, 76, 78
Nielsen Task Force (1987), 244
Nielsen, Erik, 180, 183, 244
Nixon, Richard, 163–4, 301
Noble, Adm Sir Percy, 86
Noer, John H., 260
Norstad, Gen Louis, 142
North American Aerospace Defense Command. *See* North American Air Defence Command
North American Agreement on Environmental Cooperation, 324
North American Air Defence Command, 129–32, 157, 264, 275–6, 303
North Atlantic Fisheries Organization, 246
North Atlantic Treaty Organization (NATO), 14, 16, 43, 60, 92, 98–103,

107, 110, 113–16, 119–25, 129–33, 137–47, 151–77, 180–2, 186–8, 193, 196–98, 201–4, 218, 221–30, 234–9, 241–5, 249–51, 254, 262–6, 269–71, 274–6, 280, 298–304, 307–8, 313, 331–7; Allied Forces Southern Europe, 225, 229; Canada-United States Regional Planning Group, 100, 275, 304; Commander Barrier Forces Atlantic, 133; Commander in Chief Western Approaches, 72, 82; Commander North Anti-Submarine Defence Force Atlantic, 133; Multinational Air Movement Detachment, 234; North Atlantic Council, 99–100, 134, 165, 169, 224, 233, 245, 264, 304; North Atlantic Regional Planning Group, 107; Northern Command, 188; Prague Summit (2002), 268, 274–6; Rapid Deployment Force, 165; Rapid Reaction Force (1995), 233; Standing NATO Maritime Group, 276, 280, 337; Standing Naval Force Atlantic, 154–5, 172, 193, 204–5, 221, 224–5, 265–6, 274–6; Standing Naval Force Mditarranean, 225, 276; Strike Fleet Atlantic, 192, 203; Submarine Allied Command Atlantic, 188; Submarine Operating Authorities, 186–7, 250; Supreme Allied Command Operations, 275; Supreme Command Transformation, 275; Supreme Commander Atlantic, 100, 131–3, 137, 151, 165, 191–3, 225–6, 274–5; Supreme Commander Europe, 142, 165, 225, 274
Northern Region Headquarters, 161
Northern Sea Route, 288
Northern Watch (2008), 295
North-West Mounted Police, 24

Obama, Barack, 156
O'Connell, D.P., 291; *The Influence of Law on Sea Power*, 291
Octagon Conference (1944), 86–7
Ogdensburg Agreement, 93–4, 316
Oil-for-Food Program, 213–18
Operations: *Altair*, 276, 282, 337; *Apollo*, 265–7, 271, 276, 337; *Atalanta* (2008), 280; *Augmentation*, 261–2; *Beaufort Sentinel* (2005), 293; *Continue Hope*, 256; *Deliberate Force* (1995), 234; *Deliverance* (1992), 256; *Desert Fox*, 207; *Desert Storm*, 149, 202, 211, 310; *Determined Force* (1998), 236; *Enduring Freedom*, 265, 269, 337; *Forward Action*, 231; *Freedom of Navigation*, 180; *Friction*, 149, 200–2, 336; *Frostbite*, 96, 110; *Goodwood III*, 86; *Hestia* (2010), 283; *Horatio* (2008), 283; *Hudson Sentinel* (2005), 294; *Iraqi Freedom*, 271; *Maritime Monitor* (1992), 224; *Nanook*, 294–5, 298, 337; *Narwhal*, 293; *Neptune*, 83; *Ocean Shield* (2005), 280; *RyaN* (1983), 177; *Sharp Guard* (1992–96), 225, 235, 239–40; *Sharp Vigilance* (1992), 225; *Torch*, 69, 74–5; *Toucan*, 149, 261
Operational Surveillance Patrols, 173–5, 184
Organization for Security and Co-operation in Europe, 222–3
Organization of American States, 230
Organization of Arab Oil Exporting Nations, 323
Osbaldeston Report (1990), 244
Ottawa, 10, 26, 40, 44, 47, 50–1, 56, 61, 64–70, 77–9, 89, 92, 95–8, 102, 108, 113, 117–19, 122–5, 128–32, 138–9, 142, 151, 154, 163, 167, 170, 186, 190, 194, 199, 241, 250–2, 267–70, 289–91, 302–14
Ottawa Citizen, 29
Ottawa Process (1999), 241
Ottley, R Adm Sir Charles Langdale, 23
Ouellet, André, 250–2
Owen, David Baron Owen, 228–9

Pacific Fleet, 73, 88, 272
Pacific Headquarters, 307
Pan-American Union, 62
Paris Peace Conference, 39
Passchendaele, 37
Paterson Air Force base, 275
Peacekeeping, 112, 127, 147, 162–4, 172, 176, 222–4, 233, 238–40, 257

Pearkes, Gen George R., 134
Pearson Peacekeeping Centre, 223, 263
Pearson, Lester, 58, 65–7, 89, 97–100, 110, 115–19, 122, 126–7, 142–5, 152–4, 157, 162, 178, 199, 220, 223, 257, 283, 313, 316, 320
Pentagon, 129, 240, 254, 312, 337
Perdue University, 229
Permanent Joint Board on Defence, 94, 100–3, 107, 157, 275, 303
Pharand, Donat, 128–9, 291–3
Phillipps-Wolley, Clive, 20
Pickersgill, Jack, 92
Pine Tree line, 113
Pirates, 9, 279–81
Pitt, William, 7
Polson's shipyard, 22
Pope, Col Maurice, 42, 95, 101
Pound, Adm Dudley, 41, 85
Préfontaine, Hon J. Raymond, 22–3
Primakov, Yevgeny, 209
Princess Patricia's Canadian Light Infantry, 223, 284
Priuli, Lorenzo, 5
Privy Council Office, 89, 314
Progressive Conservative Party, 179
Provincial Marine, 18

Q-ships, 87
Quadrant Conference (1943), 69–70, 85, 90, 137
Queen's University, 57

Radar II Satellite, 293
Ralston, James, 47, 54
Ramsay, Adm Bertram, 35
Rasi, Marjatta, 215
Rayner, V-Adm H.S., 236–7, 151–2
Read, John Erskine, 42
Reagan, Ronald, 20, 164, 174–80, 190
Reid, Escott, 61, 64, 97–8, 140
Reid, R Adm Howard Emerson (Rastus), 101, 331
Richardson, James, 168–9
Richmond, Adm Sir Herbert, 6, 51
Riddell, Dr Walter A, 58
Robertson, Adm Drew, 265, 274
Robertson, George, Baron, 264
Robertson, Norman, 86, 96, 129–30

Robinson, Svend, 268
Rogers, Norman, 60, 65, 68
Roosevelt, Franklin D., 55–7, 62, 68–72, 87, 90, 93–7
Roosevelt, Theodore, 21, 24
Rouleau, V-Adm Denis, 276, 337
Round Table Review, 34, 40
Royal 22e Regiment, 223
Royal Air Force, 98
Royal Canadian Air Force, 47, 59, 98, 105, 110, 113, 149, 152, 317
Royal Canadian Mounted Police, 223, 244, 247–8, 293–4
Royal Canadian Naval Air Service, 36, 44
Royal Canadian Navy, 26, 151, 307 and passim; *see also* Naval Service of Canada *and* Maritime Command
Royal Canadian Navy Volunteer Reserve, 36, 47, 79, 89, 105
Royal Canadian Regiment, 223
Royal Danish Navy, 298
Royal Naval College of Canada, 26, 36, 48, 328
Royal Naval Reserve, 22, 36
Royal Navy, 4–5, 12, 17–36, 43–51, 59, 62, 65, 70–4, 79, 82–4, 87–9, 101–6, 109–12, 115–16, 133, 146, 153, 226, 250, 257–8, 300, 305, 308, 311, 314, 327
Royal Navy Canadian Volunteer Reserve, 328
Royal Roads, 105
Rule of War (1756), 7
Runcie, Robert, 310
Rush-Bagot treaty (1817), 42
Rusk, Dean, 150

Saint John Shipbuilding, 149, 172
Sanctions, 5–6, 9–11, 57, 92, 97, 104, 115–19, 125–7, 140–2, 145, 162–4, 176, 187, 198–9, 202, 206, 209, 210–39, 248, 256, 261, 268, 278, 283, 290, 311–12, 320–4
Santer, Jacques, 247, 250
Schmidt, Helmut, 168
Scott, F.F., 92
Seattle-Tacoma Shipbuilding, 87
Secret Internet Protocol Router Network, 273

Selborne, William Waldegrave Palmer, 2nd Earl of, 22
Senate, 34, 57, 158–9, 168, 186, 252, 257, 328; Special Joint Committee ... on Canada's International Relations (1986), 181; *see also* Canada, House of Commons; Subcommittee on Canada's Maritime Defence (1983), 158, 168
Serbian Special Police, 236
Sevan, Benon, 216
Seven Years' War, 4, 8
Shevardnadze, Eduard, 198
Signals Corps, 113
Simpson, Cmdr G.W.G., 79
Single Integrated Operational Plan, 15
Six-Day war, 133, 172
Skelton, Oscar Douglas (O.D.), 42, 55–7, 63–4, 69, 94
Smith, Adam, 322
Smith, Adm Leighton (Snuffy), 229
Smith, Arnold, 306
Smith, Gordon, 250
Somalian crisis (1992), 149, 197, 255–6, 261, 277–81, 296, 336
SOSUS Sound Location System, 107, 124, 128, 131–2, 148, 189, 332
South African Sanctions, 322–4
South African war, 32
Soviet Union, 9, 15–16, 85, 97, 101, 118, 129, 138, 141, 146, 156, 163, 172, 175–8, 182–3, 197, 240, 254, 292, 317, 320
Soweto, 323
Spaak, Paul-Henri, 129
Spanish-American war, 22
Special Forces, 265–6, 271, 275, 284; *see also* JTF2
Special Operations Group, 276
Special Service Brigade (Korea), 117
St Laurent, Louis, 96–8, 115, 122, 126–8
Standing Contingency Task Force (projected), 276
Stockholm International Peace Research Institute, 290
Strange, Lt Cmdr William, 79–80
Strategic Anti-Submarine operations, 16, 21, 110, 120, 123–4, 131–6, 143, 148, 151, 154, 166–8, 170, 174, 187–9, 274, 297, 313, 328, 331–6
Strategic Defence Initiative (1983), 176
Straw, Jack, 208
Submarine Operational Update Program, 171, 175, 195, 335
Suez Crisis, 100, 131–3, 137, 151, 165, 191–3, 225–6, 274–5
Summers, R-Adm Kenneth J., 201–3
Sun Tzu, *The Art of War*, 319
Survival (journal), 4
Sutherland Brown, Lt Col James (Buster), 42

Taliban, 264, 337
Tarr, Edgar J., 92
Task Force: 50, 151, 204, 270
Technical Liaison Group, 80
Telegraph, The (London), 311
Temple University, Philadelphia, 145
Thatcher, Margaret, 164
Thomas, V-Adm Charles, 220–1
Tickell, Sir Crispin, 206
Timbrell, R Adm Robert, 152
Times, The (London), 247–51
Tirpitz, Grand Adm Alfred von, 20, 318
Tobin, Brian, 246–50, 257
Todd, Lt Cmdr George Frederick, 85, 95
Tracy, N., *Attack on Maritime Trade*, 218
Training, 19, 22–3, 26, 30, 47–8, 60, 66–71, 74–7, 80–2, 101–6, 110–11, 146, 154, 162, 193–5, 201, 211, 231, 242–3, 151, 256–7, 265, 275, 278, 286, 315–17, 327–33
Transec, 282
Treaty of Ghent (1814), 5
Treaty of Washington (1871), 19; (1949), 99, 264
Trent affair, 18
Tribal Class Update and Modernization Project, 194–5, 335
Trudeau, Pierre, 142, 154–78, 182, 199, 243, 252, 277, 300, 306, 310, 313–18, 334
Truman, Harry S., 96–7, 100, 115–19
Tucker, Joseph, 322
Turbot War, 243–53, 286, 307
Turner, John, 179

INDEX 469

Tweedsmouth, Edward Marjoribanks, 2nd Baron, 23

United Nations: Emergency Force, 127, 147; Food and Agriculture Organization, 210; General Assembly, 118, 127–30, 321: Resolution 377, 118; International Children's Emergency Fund, 211; International Control Commission (Vietnam), 145; International Control Commission and Supervision (Vietnam), 164, 171; International Court of Justice at the Hague, 245, 252; International Criminal Court, 235; International Institute for Strategic Studies, 4; International Maritime Organization, 282, 298; International Monetary Fund, 127, 319; Interfet (1999), 261; Monitoring, Verification and Inspection Commission, 207; Multinational Interception Force (1990), 200, 203; Multinational Maritime Interdiction Force (1993), 231; Multinational Peace Implementation Force (1995), 229, 234; Multinational Peace Implementation Force (1995), 234; Office for the Coordination of Humanitarian Affairs, 239 (*Towards More Humane and Effective Sanctions Management*, 1998), 239; Population Division, 210–11; Proliferation Security Initiative, 207; Protection Force (1992), 223–7, 233–4; Round Table Conference (Yugoslav Sanctions), 238–39, 311; Secretary General, 117, 209, 215–17, 221–3, 233, 238–41; Security Council, 5, 9, 115, 118, 126–7, 198–209, 213, 216–38, 241, 255–6, 261, 264, 268–9, 280, 309–13, 321–3; Security Council Resolutions: 118, 126; 661, 198; 665, 200; 678, 202–4; 687, 203, 206–8; 706, 213; 986, 213–15; 713, 223, 229; 724, 223; 743, 224; 757, 224; 775, 255; 787, 225, 228; 794, 256; 820, 228; 841, 230; 867, 231; 875, 231; 917, 232; 940, 232; 943, 228; 998, 233; 1022, 235; 1160, 236; 1199, 236; 1244, 237; 1264, 261; 1373, 264; 1441, 268; 1540, 207; 1816, 280; Special Commission (1991), 206; Stabilization Force (1996), 234; Uniting for Peace, 118, 127; World Bank, 211; World Food Programme, 283; World Health Organization, 240; World Summit (2005), 241

United States: Congress, 15, 55, 118, 144, 208, 254, 319; Department of Defence, 190; Geological Survey, 287; House Armed Services Committee, 165; House Task Force on Terrorism and Unconventional Warfare, 207; Secretary of Defence, 152; Senate, 115, 174, 181, 187, 199, 218, 288, 315–16; Foreign Relations Committee, 288; Subcommittee on Sea Power and Force Projection, 174; State Department, 117, 145, 157, 160, 180, 190, 205, 227, 302

U.S. Air Force, 113: Strategic Air Command, 12, 16, 122, 166, 173–5, 183, 189, 196, 254

U.S. Navy, 13–21, 24, 38, 65, 72–6, 88, 95–6, 100–8, 124, 128, 138–9, 144–8, 158–60, 168, 173, 187, 190–1, 195–6, 202–4, 226, 234, 244–5, 250, 254–5, 260–3, 266, 272–4, 278, 285, 291–2, 298, 305–9, 315–16, 330; *Forward . . . From the Sea* (1994), 16, 255; *From the Sea* (1992), 16, 255; *Maritime Strategy*, 12, 16, 122, 166, 173–5, 183, 189, 196, 254; Naval Forces in Europe, 165, 229; Naval War College, 174, 236; Navy Act (1890), 19

U.S. Northern Command, 275–6

U.S./G.B. Anglo-American military staff conversations (1941), 71

U.S./G.B. Destroyers for Bases Exchange, 124, 132

u-boat, 9, 71–84, 101, 328

uniform, 104, 152–3, 179, 192

Union Caucus, 44

Unità, 321

University of Toronto, 35, 96

US-UK Mutual Defence Agreement, 190

Vance, Cyrus, 228–9
Vergennes, Charles Gravier, chevalier de, 38
Versailles peace treaty, 38
Versatile Pacific Shipyards, 295
Vickers Barrow, 59
Vickers Shipbuilding, 83
Vickers-Armstrong, 9, 127, 142–6, 171
Vietnam War, 9, 127, 142–6, 171
Visiting Forces Act, 103
Volcker, Paul, 216–17; Committee, 217

Walker, William, 235
Walsum, Peter van, 207
War of 1812, 4, 18
War on Drugs, 285
War Plan Red, 43
Warsaw Pact, 165, 239
Wartsila, 290
Washington Naval Conference (1921–22), 39–40, 47
Washington Press Club, 23, 54, 57, 62–3, 70–1, 330
Washington, 19, 39–40, 47, 54–6, 68, 76, 93–9, 102, 115–19, 122–9, 132, 140–2, 145–6, 157, 163–4, 174–5, 194–9, 251, 254, 264, 274, 292, 300, 303–4, 309, 314–15, 318, 329; see also Treaty of
Watkins, Adm James D., 174, 187
Watt, B-Gen Angus, 273
Webster, Judge William, 205, 219
West European Union, 225
Western Pacific Naval Symposium, 307
Westploy, 307
White Ensign, 30, 151–3
White House, 55, 62, 309
Wilgress, Dana, 122
Wilkins, David, 302
William II, Kaiser, 20
Williams, Capt Kelly, 12, 262
Williamsburg summit (1983), 177
Wilson, Woodrow, 9
Woodward, Stanley, 117
World Trade Center, 14, 209, 254, 312, 337
World War I (First World War), 6, 9, 11, 38, 49, 60, 70, 90, 328

World War II (Second World War), 6, 14, 30, 64–99, 300, 330, 337
Wright, Jim, 269
Wrong, Hume, 89, 96

Young Memorial Lecture (2001), 312
Yugoslavia Sanctions Committee, 223
Yusufi, Rahimullah, 311

Zoellick, Robert, 303
Zumwalt, Adm Elmo, 168

DEFENCE SCHOLARS

Allen, Matthew, 4, 13, 16
Arkin, William M., 195

Bacon, Sir Francis, 6–7, 12, 116
Barry, Donald, 252
Baxter, James P. III, 51
Beatty, David
Bell, Alexander Graham, 50
Bell, Christopher, 43
Bercuson, David, 121, 131
Bland, Douglas, 152, 161, 191, 258, 277, 308
Bodansky, Yossef, 207–9
Booth, Ken, 3, 179
Bothwell, Robert, 109, 115, 147, 164, 179
Brebner, John Bartlet, 305
Breemer, Jan, 13
Buteux, Paul, 169
Byers, Michael, 14, 277
Byers, Rob, 170–1

Cable, Sir James, 11–12, 37, 115, 197, 203, 251, 299, 319
Cafferky, Shawn, 107
Caldwell, Robert, 151
Chalmers, Lt William Scott, 35, 46
Codner, Cmdr Mike, 12
Corbett, Sir Julian, 4, 6–8, 28, 319
Cortright, David, 238, 312, 321
Critchley, Harriet, 182
Curtis, Lionel, 34

Delaney, Jason, 183

INDEX

471

Doxey, Margaret, 223, 309

Eayrs, James, 308

Ferguson, Julie, 136
Ferris, John, 51
Friedman, Norman, 103, 146–8, 168, 175, 206, 225

Gellman, Peter, 58, 117–19
Gellner, John, 13, 167, 308
German, Tony, 154
Gimblett, Richard, 26, 81, 89, 106, 151, 200–4, 221, 267
Glover, Bill, 84, 106
Goldrick, Adm James, RAN, 48, 89, 103–6, 208, 306
Gowlland-Debbas, Vera, 312
Graham, Melanie, 271, 315
Granatstein, Jack, (J.L.), 64, 127–8
Gray, Colin S, 167
Greenspon, Edward, 303
Griffiths, Franklyn, 287, 297
Grove, Eric, 12

Haglund, David, 97, 305
Hansen, Cmdr Kenneth, 72
Haydon, Peter, 102, 108, 123–4, 132, 137, 143, 148, 193, 248
Hennessy, Michael, 108–9, 134, 137, 146
Higgins, Laura J., 262, 309
Hillmer, Norman, 40, 60
Holmes, John, 118, 128–30, 145, 157, 161, 271, 313–18
Huebert, Rob, 293

Ignatieff, Michael, 241, 302–4, 308–9, 312
Ingrao, Charles, 229

Jackson, Aaron, 13
Jockel, Joseph T., 173, 240–1, 309

Kirkey, Christopher, 190
Klepak, Hal, 231, 304–5

Langdon, Frank, 194
Levin, Bernard, 248

Lindsey, George, 166, 314
Lopez, George, 238, 312, 321
Lund, Wilfred, 104, 108–9
Luttwak, Edward, 11

Mackinnon, Gregor, 178
Mahan, Adm Alfred Thayer, 19, 28
Malone, David, 207
Maloney, Sean, 15, 123, 225, 242, 257–8
Mayne, Richard, 79–80, 139
McLean, Doug, 80, 88
McLin, Jon, 123, 146
Medlicott, W.N., 6
Melakopides, Costas, 162
Middlemiss, Dan, 272
Miller, Steven, 174
Milner, Marc, 75–6, 101
Mitchell, Paul, 102, 132, 160, 237, 241, 273–4
Morgan, Michael, 309
Morin, Jean, 200–2

Nash, Knowlton, 140, 160
Nossal, Kim Richard, 32, 196, 200

O'Connell, Daniel, 291

Pazulla, Jutta, 234
Pearson, Michael, 178
Perras, Galen, 55
Plaschka, Matthew F., 284
Preston, Adrian, 308
Purver, Ron, 166

Richmond, Adm Sir Herbert, 6, 51
Rickhoff, Harald von,
Roberts, Les, 212
Rodger, Nicholas, 9, 105
Rosenburg, David, 174
Ross, Douglas, 194, 303–4
Roussel, Stéphane, 97

Sapardanis, Christopher, 178
Sarty, Roger, 316
Sen, Amarthya, 209
Sigler, John, 177
Sokolsky Joel J., 173, 240–1, 309
Solomon, James, 146

Stacey, Col C.P., 35, 40, 69, 73, 302
Stairs, Denis, 272, 303, 310
Stein, Janice, 198
Stigler, Andrew L., 236
Strachan, Hew, 4
Sutherland, Dr Robert J., 13, 120, 143–4, 148, 154, 166, 314, 318

Weschler, Joanna, 313
Whitby, Michael, 115, 134, 186

GAZETTEER

Adriatic, 221, 224–5, 228–9, 236–7, 336
Admiralty Inlet, 294
Afghanistan, 165, 242, 264–6, 276–7, 309, 315, 320–1, 337
Alaska, 21, 24, 113, 180
Albania, 236
Amundsen Gulf, 291
Angola, 323
Arctic, 24, 77, 82–3, 86, 96, 110–13, 116, 128–9, 136, 160–3, 167, 173–5, 179–83, 186–92, 286
Argentia, 72, 97, 128, 133, 142
Argentina, 200–2
Australia, 22–5, 30–5, 40–3, 46–8, 85, 89–90, 103–5, 115, 132, 202, 208, 256, 261–2, 273, 306–7
Aviano, 237

Baden Soellingen, 223
Baffin Bay, 182
Baffin Island, 293
Baghdad, 198, 213, 216
Bahamas, 107, 147, 282, 292, 296
Bahrain, 277
Baker's Point, 328
Baltic, 8, 107, 167, 282
Barents Sea, 181
Barrow Strait, 161, 295
Beaufort Sea, 182, 292
Beirut, 176
Belgrade, 227–30, 233, 237–41
Bering Strait, 182
Berlin, 98, 108, 137, 196, 221, 336
Bermuda, 22, 36, 44, 62, 71

Bosnia-Herzegovina, 222–4, 228–30, 233–5, 238–40, 309
Brest, 13
Brindisi, 228
British Columbia, 25, 46, 55–6, 59, 84–5, 194–5, 263, 297
Burma, 87–90

Caribbean, 57, 63, 70, 84, 95, 282, 285
Churchill, 110
Colorado, 275
Comox, 49, 195, 297
Cornwallis, 224
Croatia, 222–4, 228–30, 234–5, 240
Cuba, 21, 124–33, 137–41, 147, 151–5, 172, 199, 271, 300, 333
Cyprus, 145, 172
Czechoslovakia (Czech Republic), 58, 62, 97, 156, 239

Danube, 228
Darfur, 276
Dartmouth, 36
Darwin, 261
Dayton, 234–5
Denmark, 7, 96, 155, 172, 192, 249, 289–92, 298
Devon Island, 295
Dili, 261
Dubai, 266
Dundas Harbour, 294

East Timor, 149, 197, 241, 261, 336
Edmonton, 244
Egypt, 126–7, 217, 311
El Ferrol, 265
El Salvador, 54, 57
Ellesmere Island, 289
Esquimalt, 23, 26, 35, 43–7, 51, 105, 115, 143, 257, 265, 276, 315, 327

Federated Malay States, 33
Finland, 290
Flanders, 5, 37, 308
Flemish Cap, 251
France, 5–7, 20, 65, 68–70, 74, 92, 127, 130, 146, 187, 190, 200, 213–15, 225, 228–31, 246, 249, 252, 256, 268, 305–6

Fujairah, 266

Gloppen Fjord, Norway, 205
Governor's Island, 230-1
Grand Banks, 7, 37, 161, 245-50
Great Lakes, 18, 22, 42, 276
Greenland, 96, 113, 133, 180-4, 289
Greenland-Iceland-United Kingdom gap, 133, 174, 182
Greenwood, 195, 297
Grenada, 176
Guam, 21
Guelph, 24, 177
Gulf of Aden, 280-2
Gulf of Maine, 245, 249
Gulf of Oman, 200, 267
Gulf of St. Lawrence, 36, 74, 78-80, 120
Gulf of Tonkin, 144

Haiphong, 9, 164
Haiti, 10, 143, 192, 197, 222, 230-3, 254, 283, 296, 321, 325, 337
Halifax, 18, 22-3, 26-7, 36, 43-7, 51, 62, 66, 71-3, 78, 85, 101, 133-5, 143, 151, 170-2, 175, 185-7, 192-4, 226, 244, 265-6, 271, 276, 295, 317, 327-30, 333, 336-7
Hanoi, 164
Hans Island, 289
Hawaii, 21, 197
Hay river, 294
Helsinki, 222
Herschell Island, 113
Herzeg-Bosnia, 224
Hong Kong, 84, 88
Horn of Africa, 279
Hudson Bay, 110, 128, 294
Hungary, 239

Iceland, 251
Iceland-Faroes gap, 133
Île Royale, 7
India, 44, 47, 87-90, 165, 197, 255-6, 260, 266, 279-82, 305, 323
Iqaluit, 293
Iraq, 10, 21, 197-219, 227-8, 232, 237, 241, 254-5, 266
Ireland, 249

Israel, 126-7, 147, 207
Italy, 54, 57-60, 176, 200, 228, 237, 256

Jacmel, 283
Jacques Cartier, 32
Jamaica, 22, 172
Japan, 25, 36, 39, 46, 51, 54-6, 59-61, 73, 84-91, 109, 158, 176, 197, 290-2, 323
Jordan, 204, 215-18

Kabul, 264-5
Kara Sea, 181
Kashmir, 127
Kenya, 279-81
Kola Peninsula, 181
Korea, 21, 176, 197, 208, 268, 272, 290
Kosovo, 235-7, 240-2, 309
Kotor, 226
Kurdistan, 211-13
Kuwait, 196-209, 215, 220, 254, 268, 309, 313

Labrador, 175, 182
Lachine Rapids, 23
Lancaster Sound, 291, 294
Lebanon, 215
Leogane, 283
Liberia, 321
Libya, 195, 208, 305, 317
Lincoln Sea, 292
Liverpool, 72
Lomonosov Ridge, 290
London. *See* General Index
Louisbourg, 4

Machias Seal Island, 245
Mackenzie river, 294
Madrid, 249
Malaysia, 206, 280
Malta, 196
Melville Island, 24
Mexico, 179
Milford Haven, 133
Mogadishu, 280
Mombasa, 280
Montenegro, 224

Montreal, 23, 30, 59
Moscow, 178, 216, 237
Mozambique, 323

Nanisivik, 294–6
Nanoose, 263–4
Naples, 165
Netherlands, 7, 133, 231, 292
New Brunswick, 8, 18, 71
New Orleans, 218
New Zealand, 23–5, 33, 40, 264
Newfoundland, 22, 36, 71–4, 77–9, 93
Newport, 280
Northwest Passage, 113–14, 128, 160–1, 183, 187, 287–95, 333, 337
Norwegian Sea, 82, 90, 132, 135, 155, 167–9, 174, 180–3, 189, 244, 309
Nova Scotia, 8, 34–6, 65, 73, 93–4, 104, 124, 195, 224, 297
Nunavut, 295, 337

Ontario, 21–4, 57, 135
Ottawa. *See* General Index

Palestine, 127, 310–11
Pearl Harbor, 73, 84, 265
People's Republic of China, 117–19, 163, 197, 213, 268, 280, 290, 305
Persian/Arabian Gulf, 149, 196–7, 200–4, 210, 260–3, 266–7, 270, 336–7
Philippines, 21
Poland, 64, 154, 239
Pond Inlet, 295
Port-au-Prince, 231–2, 283
Portugal, 247, 252, 312
Prince of Wales Strait, 161
Prince Rupert, 49
Puget Sound, 194
Puntland, 279

Quebec, 4, 8, 32, 40, 46, 55, 59, 69–70, 85–90, 98, 137, 154, 159, 171, 184, 200, 331
Quincy, 328

Raćak, 236
Rangoon, 87, 90

Red Sea, 204, 281
Republica Srpska, 224, 234
Reykjavik, 178
Rhode Island, 280
Rhodesia, 9, 199
Russia, 19–20, 67, 77, 163, 168, 173–5, 181, 197, 200, 209, 213–15, 228–9, 236–7, 268, 280, 287, 290–2, 297–8, 305, 320
Rwanda, 222

Saint John, 19, 71, 149, 172
Saint-Jacques, 30
San Cristóbal, 128
San Diego, 262
Santiago, 230
Saudi Arabia, 200, 267, 281
Sea of Okhotsk, 182
Serb Krajina, 229, 234
Serbia, 222–4, 227–9, 234–41, 325
Seychelles, 280
Shanghai, 87–90
Shelburne, 124
Siberia, 197, 288
Sierra Leone, 321
Singapore, 147
Skagerrak, 9, 149, 197, 255–6, 261, 277–82, 296, 336
Slavonia, 224, 228
Somalia, 149, 197, 255–6, 261, 277–81, 296, 336
Somaliland, 279
South Africa, 32
Soviet Union, 9, 15–16, 85, 97, 101, 118, 129, 138–41, 146, 156, 163, 172, 175–8, 182–3, 197, 240, 254, 292, 317, 320
Spain, 5–7, 247–52, 312
Srebrenica, 233
St John's, 37
St Lucia, 16, 120, 171–3, 183–6, 309
St Margaret's Bay, 43
St Pierre and Miquelon, 246
Strait of Hormuz, 266, 269
Suai, 261
Subic Bay, 90, 112, 125–8, 141, 154, 179, 319–20
Sudan, 276
Sydney, 36, 73
Syria, 217

Tanzania, 279
Toronto, 20, 35, 96, 108, 118, 270
Trenton, 244
Trinidad, 25
Tsushima, 138–40, 145, 217–18, 256, 269
Turkey, 179, 187, 190, 246, 287–8, 291–3

United Arab Emirates, 266, 270, 279

Vancouver, 21, 24, 171, 192, 244, 295
Vatican, 177
Venezuela, 5, 21
Venice, 7
Victoria, 20, 56, 328
Vladivostok, 197

Washington. *See* General Index
West Indies, 14, 254, 312, 337
Winnipeg, 112

Yellowknife, 161
Yemen, 280
Yugoslavia, Federal Republic of, 224, 229
Yugoslavia, Socialist Federal Republic of, 221
Yukon, 292

SHIPS AND AIRCRAFT

Australia: *Tobruk*, 261

Canada: *Arctic*, 24; *Annapolis*, 134, 147, 333, 336; *Anticosti*, 336; *Argus* CP107, 110, 158, 161, 317; *Assiniboine* (1939), 66, 330, 333, 336; *Athabaskan*, 192, 200, 203–4, 282–3, 33–7; *Athabaskan* (1948), 115–17, 336; *Aurora*, 44–5, 50, 329; *Aurora* CP-140, 158, 170–71, 184–6, 195, 226, 260, 266, 285, 294, 297, 317; *Banshee* F2H, 110, 134, 137; *Bonaventure*, 110, 133–4, 137–9, 143, 148, 158–60, 317, 333–4; *Bras d'Or*, 158–9; *Calgary*, 204, 226, 262, 277, 285; *Canada*, 22, 243; *Cape Roger*, 247; *Cayuga*, 115; CC1, 36, 328; CC2, 36, 328; CH/EH14, 36, 328; CH/EH15, 36, 328; *Champlain*, 50, 55, 329–30; *Charlottetown*, 262, 265–6, 317–18; *Chebogue*, 75; *Cherybdis*, 19, 327; *Chicoutimi*, 257; *Concordia*, 245–6; *Corner Brook*, 294; *Coromorant*, 191; *Crescent*, 114; *Crusader*, 332; *Cyclone* CH-148, 260; *EH-101* (projected), 260; *Fort Erie*, 111; *Fraser*, 172, 231, 330; *Fraser* (1937), 59, 330; *Fredericton*, 204, 226, 280, 293; *Gatineau*, 147, 225, 231, 250, 336; *Goose Bay*, 294–5; *Grilse*, 146; *Halifax*, 265–6, 283–4, 336–7; *Henry Larson* CCGS, 295; *Hornet* CF18, 201–2; *Huron* (1943), 83; *Huron*, 204–5, 336; *Iroquois*, 194, 226–7, 264–5, 277, 334; *John G Diefenbaker* (projected), 296; *Kootenay*, 171; *Kristina Logos*, 246; *Labrador*, 113–14, 333; *Louis S St Laurent* CCGS, 294–6; *Mackenzie*, 136, 158, 223, 335; *Mackenzie* (projected) class, 132; *Magnificent*, 110–12, 127, 136, 331, 333; *Margaree* (1940), 67; *Micmac*, 85; *Moncton* CCGS, 294; *Montreal*, 226, 267, 293–4, 328; *Moresby*, 336; *Neptune*, 24; *Niobe*, 26–7, 36, 327–9; *Nipigon*, 134; *Oberon*, 146–7, 171–3, 184, 191, 335; *Ojibwa*, 147, 175, 186; *Okanagan*, 175, 245, 249, 334; *Onondaga*, 184–6, 226, 334; *Ontario*, 109–11, 151, 331; *Ottawa*, 260; *Patrician*, 44–5, 49–50, 329; *Patriot*, 44–5, 49–50, 329; *Peterborough*, 66; *Pierre Radisson* CCGS, 294; *Preserver*, 148, 161, 192–3, 226, 231, 255–6, 265, 283, 333, 336; *Prestonian*, 110–11, 132, 136; *Prince David*, 84, 87; *Prince Henry*, 84, 87; *Prince Robert*, 84, 88; *Protecteur*, 148–9, 161, 193, 197, 200–4, 261–2, 277, 282, 333, 336; *Provider*, 136, 147–8, 219, 33; *Quebec*, 109–10; *Quest*, 191; *Rainbow* (1910), 26, 35–6, 327–9; *Rainbow*, 146, 333; *Regina*, 204, 260–2; *Restigouche* (1938), 66, 330; *Res-*

tigouche, 110, 134–6, 147, 158, 204, 334; *Saguenay* (1931), 53–4, 59, 329–30; *Saguenay*, 135, 245, 336; *Saskatchewan*, 143; *Sea King* CH-124, 134–6, 147–8, 204, 226, 255, 260, 333, 336; *Shawinigan*, 294; *Shearwater*, 328; *Sioux* (1944), 115–17, 121; *Skeena* (1928), 53–4, 59, 329; *Skeena*, 192–3; *St Laurent* (1937), 59, 330; *St Laurent*, 108, 131–5, 146–7, 294, 332–6; *St John's*, 283; *St Roch*, 244; *Tench*, 146; *Terra Nova*, 171, 200, 204, 334–6; *Toronto*, 204, 221, 266, 270, 282, 285, 294; *Tracker* CS2F, 110, 134, 317; *Uganda/Quebec*, 88, 109–10, 331; *Upholder/Victoria*, 249–59, 285, 294, 317, 337; *Vancouver* (1928), 50, 54–5; *Vancouver*, 197, 265–6, 329–30; *Victoria*, 257–9, 285, 294, 317, 337; *Vigilant*, 22; *Ville de Québec*, 226, 280; *Warrior*, 110; *William Alexander* CCGS, 282; *Winnipeg*, 262, 280
China: *Kunlun Shan*, 280; *Peace Ark*, 280; *Yazno*, 280

France: *Mirage F1*, 201

Germany: *Admiral Scheer*, 71; *Bismarck*, 59; *Leipzig*, 36; *Nürnberg*, 36; *Scharnhorst*, 83; *Tirpitz*, 86–7; *U-53*, 36; *U-774*, 81
Great Britain: *Comet*, 330; *Crescent*, 330; *Crusader*, 330; *Cygnet*, 330; *Dreadnought*, 190; *Good Hope*, 36; *Hood*, 59; *Jervis Bay*, 71; *Lion*, 35; *Nabob*, 86–7, 331; *Powerful*, 333; *Prince of Wales*, 59; *Puncher*, 86, 331; *Splendid*, 237; *Torbay*, 329; *Toreador*, 329; *Trafalgar*, 257

India: *Tabur*, 279

Malta: *Lido II*, 227

Norway: *Ferngulf*, 244

Saudi Arabia: *Sirus Star*, 279
Soviet Union: *Badger* TU16, 135; *Charlie*, 148; *Delta*, 175, 182–5; *Hotel*, 124, 132; *November*, 131; *Papa*, 148; *Typhoon*, 165, 182; *Victor III*, 184; *Whiskey*, 107; *Yankee*, 132, 175, 182; *Zulu*, 107, 123
Spain: *Estai*, 247–9; *Pescamaro Uno*, 248; *Playa de Bakio*, 279; *Principe de Asturias*, 251; *Serviola*, 248; *Vigia*, 248

United States: *Abraham Lincoln*, 260; *Argonaut*, 333; *Barbel*, 137; *Bonhomme Richard*, 284; *Burrfish*, 333; *Carl Vinson*, 265; *Constellation*, 263; *George Washington*, 124; *Harlan County*, 231; *Indiana*, 19; *John C. Stennis*, 265; *Kitty Hawk*, 272; *Manhattan*, 160, 180; *Massachusetts*, 19; *Midway*, 96, 110; *Nautilus*, 110, 131; *Oregon*, 19; *Polar Sea* USCG, 180; *Seadragon*, 128–9; *Skate*, 128; *Theodore Roosevelt*, 237; *Town* (class), 330; *Trident*, 194